T0332571

New Technologies for Digital Crime and Forensics:

Devices, Applications, and Software

Chang-Tsun Li
University of Warwick, UK

Anthony T.S. Ho
University of Surrey, UK

Senior Editorial Director:	Kristin Klinger
Director of Book Publications:	Julia Mosemann
Editorial Director:	Lindsay Johnston
Acquisitions Editor:	Erika Carter
Development Editor:	Mike Killian
Production Coordinator:	Jamie Snavely
Typesetters:	Keith Glazewski & Natalie Pronio
Cover Design:	Nick Newcomer

Published in the United States of America by
Information Science Reference (an imprint of IGI Global)
701 E. Chocolate Avenue
Hershey PA 17033
Tel: 717-533-8845
Fax: 717-533-8661
E-mail: cust@igi-global.com
Web site: http://www.igi-global.com

Library of Congress Cataloging-in-Publication Data

New technologies for digital crime and forensics : devices, applications, and
software / Chang-Tsun Li and Anthony T.S. Ho, editors.
       p. cm.
  Includes bibliographical references and index.
  Summary: "This book provides theories, methods, and studies on digital crime
prevention and investigation, which are useful to a broad range of researchers
and communities"--Provided by publisher.
  ISBN 978-1-60960-515-5 (hardcover) -- ISBN 978-1-60960-516-2 (ebook) 1.
Criminal investigation--Technological innovations. I. Li, Chang-Tsun. II. Ho,
Anthony T.S., 1958-
  HV8073.N468 2011
  363.25'968--dc22
                              2011000066

British Cataloguing in Publication Data
A Cataloguing in Publication record for this book is available from the British Library.

All work contributed to this book is new, previously-unpublished material. The views expressed in this book are those of the authors, but not necessarily of the publisher.

Table of Contents

Section 3
Content Protection through the Use of Extrinsic Data

Section 4
Application of Pattern Recognition and Signal Processing Techniques to Digital Forensics

Detailed Table of Contents

Section 1
Digital Evidence

Chapter 1

    Simson L. Garfinkel, Naval Postgraduate School & Harvard University, USA

This article presents improvements in the Advanced Forensics Format Library version 3 that provide for digital signatures and other cryptographic protections for digital evidence, allowing an investigator to establish a reliable chain-of-custody for electronic evidence from the crime scene to the court room. No other system for handling and storing electronic evidence currently provides such capabilities. This article discusses implementation details, user level commands, and the AFFLIB programmer's API.

Chapter 2

    Jill Slay, University of South Australia, Australia
    Matthew Simon, University of South Australia, Australia

With the tremendous growth in popularity and bandwidth of the Internet, VoIP technology has emerged that allows phone calls to be routed over Internet infrastructure rather than the traditional Public Switched Telephone Network (PSTN) infrastructure. The issues faced by law enforcement authorities concerning VoIP are very different from that of traditional telephony. Wiretapping is not applicable to VoIP calls and packet capturing is negated by encryption. This article discusses experimental work carried out to explore methods by which electronic evidence may be collected from systems where VoIP conversations play an important role in suspected criminal activity or communications. It also considers the privacy issues associated with the growing use of VoIP.

Antonio Savoldi, University of Brescia, Italy

Paolo Gubian, University of Brescia, Italy

Most enterprises rely on the continuity of service guaranteed by means of a computer system infra-structure, which can often be based on the Windows operating system family. For such a category of systems, which might be referred to as mission-critical for the relevance of the service supplied, it is indeed fundamental to be able to define which approach could be better to apply when a digital investi-gation needs to be performed. This is the very goal of this paper: the definition of a forensically sound methodology which can be used to collect the full state of the machine being investigated by avoiding service interruptions. It will be pointed out why the entire volatile memory dump, with the necessary extension which is nowadays missing, is required with the purpose of being able to gather much more evidential data, by illustrating also, at the same time, the limitation and disadvantages of current state of-the-art approaches in performing the collection phase.

Chris K. Ridder, Stanford University, USA

Computer forensic software is used by lawyers and law enforcement to collect and preserve data in a "forensic image" so that it can be analyzed without changing the original media, and to preserve the chain of custody of the evidence. To the extent there are vulnerabilities in this software, an attacker may be able to hide or alter the data available to a forensic analyst, causing courts to render judgments based on inaccurate or incomplete evidence. There are a number of legal doctrines designed to ensure that evidence presented to courts is authentic, accurate and reliable, but thus far courts have not applied them with the possibility of security weaknesses in forensic software in mind. This article examines how courts may react to such claims, and recommends strategies that attorneys and courts can use to ensure that electronic evidence presented in court is both admissible and fair to litigants.

Section 2
Combating Internet-Based Crime

Tobius Eggendorfer, Universität der Bundeswehr München, Germany

Unsolicited commercial email has become a major threat for email communication. Although the de-gree of sophistication of spam filters has increased over time, such filters still produce high rates of false positives and false negatives, thereby reducing the reliability of email and introducing communication risks on their own. Due to more and more complex filtering methods implemented, the hardware re-quirements for mail servers are increasing to avoid the risk of denial of service situations. Therefore, some authors point out that mail filtering has reached its limits and ask for more preventive solutions to fight spam. One way to prevent email abuse would be to significantly increase the risk of a spammer being sued for damage compensation or, if legislation permits, for criminal offence. This approach believes in an assessment of risk and expected revenue by the offender. But by hiding their real identity, spammers are very successful in evading prosecution. This paper discusses several methods to identify spammers and analyses under which circumstances those methods might be valid evidence in court.

Chapter 6
Chengcui Zhang, University of Alabama at Birmingham, USA
Xin Chen, University of Alabama at Birmingham, USA
Wei-Bang Chen, University of Alabama at Birmingham, USA
Lin Yang, University of Alabama at Birmingham, USA
Gary Warner, University of Alabama at Birmingham, USA

In this article, we propose a spam image clustering approach that uses data mining techniques to study the image attachments of spam emails with the goal to help the investigation of spam clusters or phishing groups. Spam images are first modeled based on their visual features. In particular, the foreground text layout, foreground picture illustrations and background textures are analyzed. After the visual features are extracted from spam images, we use an unsupervised clustering algorithm to group visually similar spam images into clusters. The clustering results are evaluated by visual validation since there is no prior knowledge as to the actual sources of spam images. Our initial results show that the proposed approach is effective in identifying the visual similarity between spam images and thus can provide important indications of the common source of spam images.

Chapter 7
Svein Yngvar Willassen, Norwegian University of Science and Technology, Norway

Timestamps play an important role in digital investigations, since they are necessary for the correlation of evidence from different sources. Use of timestamps as evidence can be questionable due to the reference to a clock with unknown adjustment. This work addresses this problem by taking a hypothesis based approach to timestamp investigation. Historical clock settings can be formulated as a clock hypothesis. This hypothesis can be tested for consistency with timestamp evidence by constructing a model of actions affecting timestamps in the investigated system. Acceptance of a clock hypothesis with timestamp evidence can justify the hypothesis, and thereby establish when events occurred in civil time. The results can be used to correlate timestamp evidence from different sources, including identifying correct originators during network trace.

Chapter 8
Dennis K. Nilsson, Chalmers University of Technology, Sweden
Ulf E. Larson, Chalmers University of Technology, Sweden

The introduction of a wireless gateway as an entry point to the automobile in-vehicle network reduces the effort of performing diagnostics and firmware updates considerably. Unfortunately, the same gateway also allows cyber attacks to target the unprotected network which currently lacks proper means for detecting and investigating security-related events. In this article, we discuss how to perform a digital forensic investigation of an in-vehicle network. An analysis of the current features of the network is performed, and an attacker model is developed. Based on the attacker model and a set of generally accepted forensic investigation principles, we derive a list of requirements for detection, data collection, and event reconstruction. We then use the Integrated Digital Investigation Process proposed by Carrier and Spafford (2004) as a template to illustrate how our derived requirements affect an investigation. For each phase of the process, we show the benefits of meeting the requirements and the implications of not complying with them.

Chapter 9

Jan Sablatnig, Technische Universität Berlin, Germany
Fritz Lehmann-Grube, Technische Universität Berlin, Germany
Sven Grottke, University of Stuttgart, Germany
Sabine Cikic, Technische Universität Berlin, Germany

Virtual environments and online games are becoming a major market force. At the same time, the virtual property contained in these environments is being traded for real money and thus attains a real value. Although the legal issues involved with this virtual property have not yet been decided, they will have to be soon. It is foreseeable that the next generation of very large virtual worlds will carry the possibility of multiple truths existing at the same time. Under such circumstances, it will be impossible to physically protect virtual property. In order to protect virtual property, virtual environment systems will therefore have to conform to certain requirements. We analyze what these requirements are in order to either prevent cheating or at least prove a digital offence has transpired. Along with greater security, this will also simplify end user support, which is one of the major cost factors for online games.

Section 3
Content Protection through the Use of Extrinsic Data

Chapter 10

Andrew D. Ker, Oxford University Computing Laboratory, UK

A fundamental question of the steganography problem is to determine the amount of data which can be hidden undetectably. Its answer is of direct importance to the embedder, but also aids a forensic investigator in bounding the size of payload which might be communicated. Recent results on the information theory of steganography suggest that the detectability of payload in an individual object is proportional to the square of the number of changes caused by the embedding. Here, we follow up the implications when a payload is to be spread amongst multiple cover objects, and give asymptotic results about the maximum secure payload. Two embedding scenarios are distinguished: embedding in a fixed finite batch of covers, and continuous embedding in an infinite stream. The steganographic capacity, as a function of the number of objects, is sublinear and strictly asymptotically lower in the second case. This work consolidates and extends our previous results on batch and sequential steganographic capacity.

Chapter 11

Hongxia Jin, IBM Almaden Research Center, USA

This article discusses a forensic technology that is used to defend against piracy for secure multimedia content distribution. In particular we are interested in anonymous rebroadcasting type of attack where the attackers redistribute the per-content encrypting key or decrypted plain content. Traitor tracing technology can be used to defend against this attack by identifying the original users (called traitors) involved in the rebroadcasting piracy. While traitor tracing has been a long standing cryptographic problem that has attracted extensive research, existing academia researches have overlooked many practical concerns in a real world setting. We have overcome many practical concerns in order to bring a theoretical traitor tracing solution to practice. The main focus of this article is on designing efficient forensic analysis algorithms under various practical considerations that were missing from existing work. The efficiency of our forensic analysis algorithms is the enabling factor that ultimately made the first time large scale commercialization of a traitor tracing technology in the context of new industry standard on content protection for next generation high-definition DVDs.

Chapter 12

Chang-Tsun Li, University of Warwick, UK
Yue Li, University of Warwick, UK
Chia-Hung Wei, Ching Yun University, Taiwan

Picture archiving and communication systems (PACS) are typical information systems, which may be undermined by unauthorized users who have illegal access to the systems. This article proposes a role-based access control framework comprising two main components – a content-based steganographic module and a reversible watermarking module, to protect mammograms on PACSs. Within this frame-work, the content-based steganographic module is to hide patients textual information into mammo-grams without changing the important details of the pictorial contents and to verify the authenticity and integrity of the mammograms. The reversible watermarking module, capable of masking the contents of mammograms, is for preventing unauthorized users from viewing the contents of the mammograms. The scheme is compatible with mammogram transmission and storage on PACSs. Our experiments have demonstrated that the content-based steganographic method and reversible watermarking tech-nique can effectively protect mammograms at PACS.

Chapter 13

Gaurav Gupta, Macquarie University, Australia
Josef Pieprzyk, Macquarie University, Australia

There has been significant research in the field of database watermarking recently. However, there has not been sufficient attention given to the requirement of providing reversibility (the ability to revert back to original relation from watermarked relation) and blindness (not needing the original relation for detection purpose) at the same time. This model has several disadvantages over reversible and blind watermarking (requiring only the watermarked relation and secret key from which the watermark is detected and the original relation is restored) including the inability to identify the rightful owner in case of successful secondary watermarking, the inability to revert the relation to the original data set (required in high precision industries) and the requirement to store the unmarked relation at a secure secondary storage. To overcome these problems, we propose a watermarking scheme that is reversible as well as blind. We utilize difference expansion on integers to achieve reversibility. The major advantages provided by our scheme are reversibility to a high quality original data set, rightful owner identification, resistance against secondary watermarking attacks, and no need to store the original database at a secure secondary storage. We have implemented our scheme and results show the success rate is limited to 11% even when 48% tuples are modified.

Chapter 14

Chang-Tsun Li, University of Warwick, UK
Yue Li, University of Warwick, UK

In this work we propose a Repetitive Index Modulation (RIM) based digital watermarking scheme for authentication and integrity verification of medical images. Exploiting the fact that many types of medical images have significant background areas and medically meaningful Regions Of Interest (ROI), which represent the actual contents of the images, the scheme uses the contents of the ROI to create a content-dependent watermark and embeds the watermark in the background areas. Therefore when any pixel of the ROI is attacked, the watermark embedded in the background areas will be different from the watermark calculated according to the attacked contents, thus raising alarm that the image in question is inauthentic. Because the creation of the watermark is content-dependent and the watermark is only embedded in the background areas, the proposed scheme can actually protect the content/ROI without distorting it.

Section 4
Application of Pattern Recognition and Signal Processing Techniques to Digital Forensics

Chapter 15

Matthew J. Sorell, University of Adelaide, Australia

This chapter investigates an unexpected phenomenon observed in a recent digital photograph, in which the logo of a non-sponsoring sports company appears on the jersey of a famous football player in just one of a sequence of images. After eliminating deliberate image tampering as a cause, a hypothetical sequence of circumstances is proposed, concerning the lighting, dominant colours, infrared sensitivity, optical pre-processing, image enhancement and JPEG compression. The hypotheses are tested using a digital SLR camera. The investigation is of interest in a forensic context, firstly as a possible explanation in case such a photograph is observed, and secondly to be able to confirm or refute claims of such artifacts put forward claiming that a hypothetical image is not really what it claims to be.

The choice of Quantization Table in a JPEG image has previously been shown to be an effective discriminator of digital image cameras by manufacturer and model series. When a photograph is recompressed for transmission or storage, however, the image undergoes a secondary stage of quantization. It is possible, however, to identify primary quantization artifacts in the image coefficients, provided that certain image and quantization conditions are met. This paper explores the conditions under which primary quantization coefficients can be identified, and hence can be used image source identification. Forensic applications include matching a small range of potential source cameras to an image.

#### Chapter 17

In this article, a new dynamic structural statistical model based online signature verification algorithm is proposed, in which a method for statistical modeling the signature's characteristic points is presented. Dynamic time warping is utilized to match two signature sequences so that correspondent characteristic point pair can be extracted from the matching result. Variations of a characteristic point are described by a multi-variable statistical probability distribution. Three methods for estimating the statistical distribution parameters are investigated. With this dynamic structural statistical model, a discriminant function can be derived to judges a signature to be genuine or forgery at the criterion of minimum potential risk. The proposed method takes advantage of both structure matching and statistical analysis. Tested in two signature databases, the proposed algorithm got much better signature verification performance than other results.

#### Chapter 18

Retrieval based approach has recently emerged as an attractive option for image copy detection. The Content Based Copy Detection (CBCD) can be treated as a restricted case of near duplicate image detection. Near duplicate images can be: (i) perceptually identical images (e.g. allowing for change in color balance, change in brightness, compression artifacts, contrast adjustment, rotation, cropping, filtering, scaling etc.), (ii) images of the same 3D scene (from different viewpoints). As we are searching for copies which are altered versions of the original image, the images with slight viewpoint variations of the same scene should not be retrieved. In this chapter, we focus on image matching strategy based on local invariant features that will assist in the detection of forged (copy-paste forgery) images. So far, no specific robust homography estimation method exists for this application. The state of the art methodologies tend to generate many false positives. In this chapter, we have introduced a novel strategy for pattern matching of key point distributions for copy detection. Typical experiments conducted on real case images demonstrate the success in near duplicate image retrieval for the application of digital image forensics. Efficiency of the proposed method is corroborated by comparison, with contemporary methods.

Chapter 19
    Samaan Poursoltan, University of Adelaide, Australia
    Matthew J. Sorell, University of Adelaide, Australia

The review of video captured by fixed surveillance cameras is a time consuming, tedious, expensive and potentially unreliable human process, but of very high evidentiary value. Two key challenges stand out in such a task; ensuring that all motion events are captured for analysis, and demonstrating that all motion events have been captured so that the evidence survives being challenged in court. In previous work (Zhao, Poursoltanmohammadi & Sorell, 2008), it was demonstrated that tracking the average brightness of video frames or frame segment provided a more robust metric of motion than other commonly hypothesized motion measures. This paper extends that work in three ways; by setting automatic localized motion detection thresholds, by maintaining a frame-by-frame single parameter normalized motion metric, and by locating regions of motion events within the footage. A tracking filter approach is used for localized motion analysis, which adapts to localized background motion or noise within each image segment. When motion is detected, location and size estimates are reported to provide some objective description of the motion event.

Chapter 20
    Emanuele Maiorana, Università degli Studi Roma TRE, Italy
    Patrizio Campisi, Università degli Studi Roma TRE, Italy
    Alessandro Neri, Università degli Studi Roma TRE, Italy

With the widespread diffusion of biometrics-based recognition systems, there is an increasing awareness of the risks associated with the use of biometric data. Significant efforts are therefore being dedicated to the design of algorithms and architectures able to secure the biometric characteristics, and to guarantee the necessary privacy to their owners. In this work we discuss a protected on-line signature-based biometric recognition system, where the considered biometrics are secured by applying a set of non-invertible transformations, thus generating modified templates from which retrieving the original information is computationally as hard as random guessing it. The advantages of using a protection method based on non-invertible transforms are exploited by presenting three different strategies for the matching of the transformed templates, and by proposing a multi-biometrics approach based on score-level fusion to improve the performances of the considered system. The reported experimental results, evaluated on the public MCYT signature database, show that the achievable recognition rates are only slightly affected by the proposed protection scheme, which is able to guarantee the desired security and renewability for the considered biometrics.

Preface

The last few decades have witnessed the unprecedented development and convergence of information and communication technology (ICT), computational hardware and multimedia techniques. At the personal level, these techniques have revolutionized the ways we exchange information, learn, work, interact with others and go about our daily life. At the organisational level, these techniques have enabled a wide spectrum of services through e-commerce, e-business and e-governance. This wave of ICT revolution has undoubtedly brought about enormous opportunities for the world economy and exciting possibilities for every sector of the modern societies. Willingly or reluctantly, directly or indirectly, we are all now immersed in some ways in the cyberspace, full of 'e-opportunities' and 'e-possibilities', and permeated with data and information. However, this type of close and strong interweaving also poses concerns and threats. When exploited with malign or intentions, the same technologies provide means for doing harms at colossal scale. These concerns create anxiety and uncertainty about the reality of the information and business we deal with, the security the information infrastructures we are relying on today and our privacy. Due to the rise of digital crime and the pressing need for methods of combating these forms of criminal activities, there is an increasing awareness of the importance of digital forensics and investigation. As a result, the last decade has also seen the emergence of the new interdisciplinary research field of digital forensics and investigation, which aims at pooling expertise in various areas to combat the abuses of the ICT facilities and computer technologies.

The primary objective of this book is to provide a media for advancing research and the development of theory and practice of digital crime prevention and forensics. This book embraces a broad range of digital crime and forensics disciplines that use electronic devices and software for crime prevention and investigation, and addresses legal issues. It encompasses a wide variety of aspects of the related subject areas and provides a scientifically and scholarly sound treatment of state-of-the-art techniques to students, researchers, academics, personnel of law enforcement and IT/multimedia practitioners, who are interested or involved in the study, research, use, design and development of techniques related to digital forensics and investigation. This book is divided into four main sections according to the thematic areas covered by the contributed chapters.

- Section 1. Digital Evidence
- Section 2. Combating Internet-Based Crime
- Section 3. Content Protection through the Use of Extrinsic Data
- Section 4. Applications of Pattern Recognition and Signal Processing Techniques to Digital Forensics

However, it should be noted that these four sections are closely related, e. g., Chapter 6 of Section 2 fits in Section 4 quite well because of its use of pattern recognition and image processing techniques. Such a division is only meant to provide a structural organisation of the book to smooth the flow of thoughts and to aid the readability, rather than proposing taxonomy of the study of digital forensics.

Section 1: Digital Evidence

Maintaining the chain-of-custody for evidence is of paramount importance in civil and criminal legal cases. To ensure the admissibility of evidence, technical measures, including hardware and software, applied in the digital forensic investigation procedures are required to assure not only that evidence is not tampered with or manipulated due to their application, but that malicious attacks aiming at hiding or manipulating evidence are effectively detected. To serve these purposes, like physical world forensic investigation, digital forensic investigation has to follow three main steps:

1) *Event preservation* which entails, for example, the need for a bit-by-bit duplication of the volatile memory or file systems;
2) *Evidence search* which aims at collecting forensic information such as making timelines of system and file activities, device fingerprint (e.g., sensor pattern noise of digital cameras), keywords, contraband media, telecommunication data, steganography;
3) *Event Reconstruction* which is about interpreting the collected information /evidence in order to establish what have happened and who has involved in what.

To address the need for maintaining the chain-of-custody for evidence, the first section of this book covers four chapters concerning with technical and legal issues surrounding the chain-of-custody for evidence. In Chapter 1 - *Providing Cryptographic Security and Evidentiary Chain-of-Custody with the Advanced Forensic Format, Library, and Tools*, Simson Garfinkel proposes a method for assuring the integrity of digital evidence collected from data storage media based on novel public key cryptography. Garfinkel points out two potential problems the current practice of manually recording hash codes and including them in investigative reports has, i.e., 1) it is difficult to perform automated processing and validation because the hash codes are recorded in a free-format report narrative, and 2) If the disk image becomes damaged, the hash code will only indicate that it no longer matches, but does not allow the damage to be detected or corrected. He also discusses the vulnerabilities of the commonly used hashing algorithm MD5 and presents his recent work for addressing these problems. In addition to its capability of assuring the integrity of digital evidence, his method can also allow for digital documentation of evidential transfer, reconstruction of damaged evidence, recovery of partial evidence when reconstructing damaged evidence is infeasible, encryption with both symmetrical and asymmetrical cryptosystems.

With the emergence of VoIP technology as one of the important form for telecommunications, Chapter 2 - *Voice Over IP: Privacy and Forensic Implications*, presented by Jill Slay and Matthew Simon provides the authors' insight into the issues of *VoIP and Security*, such as denial of service, exploitations of server and protocol vulnerability, call surveillance and hijacking, identity theft, tampering of audio streams, and VoIP and crime, such as the possibilities available to criminals and terrorists to communicate through the decentralised systems that use strong encryption algorithms and require no verification of users' details. The authors also conduct experiments on the use of several techniques in the process of recovering VoIP evidence in an *after the event* Win XP to Win XP communication scenario and report their findings surrounding the issues of privacy, telecommunication interceptions and digital evidence preservation. They also advise as to whether the VoIP technology should be used in restricted environments from a technical point of view.

Most enterprises conducting e-business and e-commerce rely on mission-critical computer systems to guarantee continuity of their service even when the system is under attack or forensic investigation. In Chapter 3 - *Volatile Memory Collection and Analysis for Windows Mission-Critical Computer Systems*, Antonio Savoldi and Paolo Gubian propose a *live forensic* technology for collecting the full state of mission-critical systems under investigation without interrupting services. Savoldi and Gubian start with the review of the state-of-the-art techniques related to data collection from the volatile memory with three factors considered, namely *fidelity*, *atomicity* and *integrity*. Fidelity refers to the capability of collecting admissible bit-by-bit content of the volatile memory. Atomicity refers to the capability of collecting a snapshot of the volatile memory without altering it. Integrity is about preventing malicious tampering of memory snapshot, e. g., subversive actions conducted by kernel root kits. The authors then present a method for virtual memory space reconstruction and a possible way of collecting the page file on Windows-based mission-critical systems.

While the previous three chapters are contributed by computer scientists, Chapter 4 - *Evidentiary Implications of Potential Security Weaknesses in Forensic Software*, on the other hand, contributed by Chris Ridder from a law practitioner's perspective, is concerned with the vulnerabilities that could be exploited by an attacker to hide, add or change data without being detected so as to prevent forensic software from collecting admissible evidence or mislead investigators and courts. He discuss a number of legal doctrines designed to ensure that the chain-of-custody of the evidence presented to the courts of law is preserved, but thus far the courts law have not enforced them due to the concerns over the possibility of security weaknesses in forensic software. He also studies how the courts of law may react to such claims, and recommends approaches that attorneys and courts can adopt to ensure that digital evidence presented in court is both fair to litigants and admissible.

Section 2: Combating Internet-Based Crime

Computer networks are one of the main avenues for various forms of malicious activities and cybercrime. Section 2 of this book focuses on some forms of these malicious activities, aiming at providing insight into their characteristics, how they work and how to detect or prevent them. For most, if not all, email users, unsolicited email spam constitutes the majority of the messages they received in their inbox, mainly for advertising purpose. These inundating adverts do represent a significant waste of resources, including the abuse of systems and the time the recipients spend on deleting them and avoiding over looking non-spam emails. However, the number of fraudulent emails intended for collecting recipient identities or credit card details (i.e., phishing schemes) is on the rise and the consequences of their success is far greater than the advertising email spam can incur. To address these issues surrounding email spam, in Chapter 5 - *Methods to Identify Spammers*, Tobias Eggendorfer discusses how spammers work, including email addresses acquisition through address traders, spam delivery (e. g., the use of botnets, which are responsible for the delivery of over 80% of email spam), and the operation of anonymous online shops and payment mechanism. Although spam filtering has provided some degree of relief, it has also given rise to a range of problems, such as high rates of false positives (i.e., mistaking authentic emails as spam) and false negatives (i. e., mistaking spam emails as authentic), increased system overheads and risk of security breaches. With these problems in mind, Eggendorfer proposes some alternatives for tracking spammers, including email analysis, observing botnets, surveillance of purchases, partner shops, payment process and server owners and methods for indentifying address traders through email address identification and distributed tar pit networks.

In order to help with the identification of spam clusters and phishing groups, in Chapter 6 - *Spam Image Clustering for Identifying Common Sources of Unsolicited Emails*, Chengcui Zhang et al. propose a spam image clustering method based on data mining techniques to analyse the image attachments of spam emails. This chapter is of particular interest because, unlike most spam filers which rely on textual analysis, it presents a new pictorial content based approach which is rarely attempted. Given a large set of emails with attached images, they first model attached images based on their visual features, such as foreground text layout, foreground picture illustration and background texture analysis. An unsupervised clustering algorithm is then applied to cluster the emails into groups according to the similarity of the images' visual features. Since there is no *a priori* knowledge about the actual sources of the spam emails, visual validation is conducted to evaluate the clustering results. Different feature matching techniques such as Scale Invariant Feature Transform (SIFT) similarity metrics, are applied to measure the feature similarity of different visual features extracted from the images.

In many digital investigations, attributing events to specific people or sources is crucial and, in a networked environment, attribution depends much on the identification of which computers were using what IP-addresses at what points in time. If the IP-addresses are dynamically assigned, the originating computers can only be identified if logs of the usage of the addresses can be acquired, and the points in time of the relevant events can be accurately established. However, the use of timestamps (records of specific moments in time) as evidence may not be admissible in a networked environment due to the inconsistent settings of clocks at various nodes. In Chapter 7 - *A Model Based Approach to Timestamp Evidence Interpretation*, Svein Willassen addresses this challenge by formulating historical clock settings as a clock hypothesis and tests the hypothesis for consistency with timestamp evidence by modelling actions affecting timestamps in the system under investigation. Acceptance of a clock hypothesis with timestamp evidence can help establish when events occurred in civil time and can be used to correlate timestamp evidence from various sources, including detecting correct originators.

The introduction of a wireless gateway to the automobile in-vehicle networks enables remote diagnostics and firmware updates, thus reducing costs considerably. Unfortunately, insufficiently protected wireless gateways are not immune from cyber attacks and proper means for detecting and investigating security-related events are yet to be developed. In Chapter 8 - *Conducting Forensic Investigations of Cyber Attacks on Automobile In-Vehicle Networks*, Dennis Nilsson and Ulf Larson carry out an analysis of the current features of in-vehicle networks and develop an attacker model to help devising countermeasures. Based on their attacker model and informed by a set of commonly practised forensic investigation principles, they also derive a set of requirements for event detection, forensic data collection and event reconstruction. They then use the Integrated Digital Investigation Process (IDIP) proposed by Carrier and Spafford in 2004 as a template to illustrate the impact of the adoption of the derived requirements on digital investigations.

The emergence of online games as an avenue for providing entertainment and a vehicle for generating revenue has pave the way for trading and exchange of virtual properties to become another type of cyber financial activity. Virtual properties can attain their physical value and be traded for physical currency. However, disputes among the players are also foreseeable and measures for resolving them are necessary, but not in place yet. Chapter 9 - *Dealing with Multiple Truths in Online Virtual Worlds*, Jan Sablatnig et al analyse the system requirements needed to prevent or resolve the problem of simultaneous existence of multiple truths and cheating. They start the chapter with a discussion on the real value of virtual property and the future of the online game in a virtual environment, including object complexity and scalability of the number of players. They then discuss the potential forms of fraud and cheating. They also studied ways for simplifying end user support in order to reduce the cost of running online games.

Section 3: Content Protection through the Use of Extrinsic Data

This section is concerned with multimedia content protection and authentication through cryptography and the embedding of extrinsic data. Cryptography is a mature scientific discipline and has a long application history in protecting digital content. Content protection through the use of extrinsic data, a relatively younger discipline, is about protecting the value of digital content or verifying the integrity and authenticity by embedding secret data in the host media and matching the hidden secret data against the original version at a later stage. Digital watermarking is a typical example of content protection and authentication based on extrinsic data and has been an active research area in the past 15 years. This set of digital watermarking techniques have found their applications in *copyright protection*, such as ownership identification, transaction tracking/traitor tracing and copy control, which is of great interest to the multimedia and movie industry, and *content integrity verification and authentication*, which is of high interest to the security sector, medical community, legal systems, etc. To ensure the security of these content protection schemes, the sophistication of countermeasures and attack models have to be in the mind of the developers of the protection schemes.

The greater the amount of extrinsic data (i.e., payload or capacity) is embedded, the better in the covert communication applications (i.e., steganography). High payload also strengthens security of digital watermarking schemes. However, hiding extrinsic data in host media inflict distortion, making imperceptibility an issue for the scheme designers to contend with. Results stemmed from recent research on information theory of steganography indicate that the detect ability of payload in a stego-object (a piece of media carrying hidden messages) is proportional to the square of the number of changes made during the embedding process. In Chapter 10 - *Locally Square Distortion and Batch Steganographic Capacity*, Andrew Ker investigates the implication when a payload is to be spread amongst multiple cover objects, and give asymptotic estimations about the maximum secure payload. Kerr studied two embedding scenarios, namely *embedding in a fixed finite batch of covers* and *continuous embedding in an infinite stream* and observed that the steganographic capacity, as a function of the number of objects, is sub-linear and strictly asymptotically lower in the second scenario.

Broadcast encryption is widely used for protecting the content of recordable and pre-recordable media. The encryption of the *media key* is stored in the header of media and used to encrypt the content stored after the header. The media key is repeatedly encrypted using all the chosen *device keys* to form a Media Key Block (MKB), which is then sent along with the content when the content is distributed. Proposed in Chapter 11 - *Efficient Forensic Analysis for Anonymous Attack in Secure Content Distribution*, due to Hongxia Jin, is a forensic technology aiming at preventing piracy and tracing traitors in the context of secure multimedia content distribution, with a specific focus on defending against anonymous attack where the attacker can rebroadcast the per-content encryption key or decrypted plain content. Jin also discusses the lack of some practical considerations in existing systems and points out four requirements that need to be implemented in the design of the future systems.

Picture archiving and communication systems (PACS) are typical information systems, which may be undermined by unauthorized users who have illegal access to the systems. In Chapter 12 - *Protection of Digital Mammograms on PACSs Using Data Hiding Techniques*, Li et al. propose a role-based access control framework comprising two main components – a content-based steganographic module, called *Repetitive Index Modulation* (RIM), and a reversible watermarking module, to protect mammograms on PACSs. Within this framework, the content-based steganographic module is to hide patients' textual information into mammograms without having to change the important details of the pictorial contents and to verify the authenticity and integrity of the mammograms. The reversible watermarking module, capable of masking the contents of mammograms, is for preventing unauthorized users from viewing the contents of the mammograms. The scheme is compatible with mammogram transmission and storage on PACSs.

Digital watermarking schemes introduce extrinsic data into the host media, which distort the fidelity of the content of the host media. In some applications where even incidental distortion is not acceptable, reversibility (i.e, the capability of the scheme's being able to restore the original version of the watermarked media after verification or authentication) is desirable. Moreover, many watermarking schemes also require the availability of original version of the host media at the verification stage, thus reducing the scheme applicability in various scenarios, e.g., multimedia database applications. Chapter 13 - *Reversible and Blind Database Watermarking Using Difference Expansion*, presented by Gaurav Gupta and Josef Pieprzyk, aims at addressing these two issues so as to provide a reversible and oblivious (also called blind) method for multimedia database watermarking. By incorporating the popular *Difference Expansion* technique in their scheme, the scheme provides reversibility to high quality media, effective identification of rightful owner, resistance against secondary watermarking attacks, and does not require a duplicated secure database of the original media for verification purpose.

In Chapter 14 - *Medical Images Authentication through Repetitive Index Modulation Based Watermarking*, Li and Li proposed a RIM-based digital watermarking scheme for authentication and integrity verification of medical images. By exploiting the fact that many types of medical images have significant background areas and medically meaningful Regions of Interest (ROI), which represent the actual contents of the images, the authors separate the ROIs from the background and scramble a little amount of information extracted from the contents of the ROI under the control a secret key to create a content-dependent watermark. The watermark is then embedded in the background areas, using the same Repetitive Index Modulation (RIM) scheme proposed in Chapter XII. On the verification side, the same operations are performed under the control of the same key as the one used in the embedding side to create the original watermark. This newly calculated watermark is compared against the watermark embedded in the background area. If both versions are the same, the received image is deemed authentic. Otherwise it is not trustworthy. By doing so, when any pixel of the ROI is attacked, the watermark embedded in the background areas will be different from the watermark calculated according to the attacked contents, thus raising alarm to alert that the image in question is inauthentic. Because the creation of the watermark is content-dependent and the watermark is only embedded in the background areas, the proposed scheme can actually protect the content/ROI without distorting it.

Section 4: Applications of Pattern Recognition and Signal Processing Techniques to Digital Forensics

Pattern recognition and digital signal processing techniques have been in use by expert witnesses in forensic investigations for decades. Section 4 of this book deals with methods that harness these two sets of techniques for biometric applications and multimedia forensics. Identity authentication is of paramount importance in many aspects of our everyday life and business. While traditional authentication measures, such as PINs and passwords, may be forgotten, stolen or cracked, biometrics provides authentication mechanisms based on unique human physiological and behavioural characteristics that cannot be easily duplicated or forged.

When audio, image and video are presented in the court of law as evidence, their authenticity became an immediate concern and expert witnesses have to be called in for assistance. The following four chapters focus on the use of signal processing techniques in aiding digital forensic investigations. Matthew Sorell presented an interesting case in Chapter 15 - *Unexpected Artifacts in a Digital Photograph* surrounding the appearance of an unexpected logo of a non-sponsoring sports company on the jersey of a famous footballer in just one of a sequence of images of tournament. With deliberate video tampering as a cause eliminated, Sorell proposes a hypothetical sequence of circumstances, concerning optical pre-processing, infrared sensitivity, colour filtering and micro lens, exposure and lighting conditions, image acquisition, processing and enhancement and JPEG compression. The hypotheses are tested using a digital SLR camera. The investigation is of interest in a forensic context as a possible explanation as to why such a phenomenon has occurred.

Quantisation tables in a JPEG images have previously been shown to be an effective discriminator of the manufacturers and model series of digital cameras. There have been reports on using quantisation tables as device model signature for identifying source digital cameras. However, JPEG compressed images may be further compressed for making better use of transmission bandwidth or storage space. The secondary quantization during the further compression process will undoubtedly erase or damage the signature of the initial quantization, making source device identification based on JPEG compression difficult, if not impossible. Matthew Sorell points out in Chapter 16 - *Conditions for Effective Detection and Identification of Primary Quantisation of Re-Quantized JPEG Images*, that it is possible to identify initial quantisation artefacts in the image coefficients, provided that certain image and quantisation conditions are met. This chapter studies the conditions under which primary quantisation coefficients can be detected, and hence can be used image source identification. Forensic applications include matching a small range of potential source cameras to an image.

Although signature verification is an ancient authentication technique, which has been practised for centuries, because of the simplicity in acquiring signatures and the cost-effectiveness in verification, it is still in intensive use today, even in a networked environment. The main challenges of signature verification lie in detecting forgeries while accepting certain degree of variations in the authentic signatures of the same person and in the inadequacy of training samples. Both problems may lead to high rates of false positives and false negatives. To address these problems, Yan Chen, Xiaoqing Ding and Patrick Wang propose a dynamic structural statistic model based online signature verification algorithm in Chapter 17 - *Dynamic Structural Statistical Model Based Online Signature Verification*. Dynamic time warping is adopted to match two signature sequences in order to extract a correspondent characteristic point pair from the matching result. A multi-variable statistical probability distribution is then employed to describe the variations of a characteristic point. Three methods, namely point dependent distribution model, point independent distribution model and point cluster distribution model, for estimating the statistical distribution parameters are evaluated. With this dynamic structural statistical methodology and based on the criterion of minimum potential risk, a discriminate function is derived to decide as to whether a signature in question is genuine or not.

Chapter 18 - *Efficient Image Matching Using Local Invariant Features for Copy Detection*, is concerned with the retrieval based approach, which has recently emerged as an attractive option for image copy detection. The Content Based Copy Detection (CBCD) can be treated as a restricted case of near duplicate image detection. Near duplicate images can be: (1) perceptually identical images (e.g. allowing for change in color balance, change in brightness, compression artifacts, contrast adjustment, rotation, cropping, filtering, scaling etc.), (ii) images of the same 3D scene (from different viewpoints). In this chapter, H.R. Chennamma et al., focus on image matching strategy based on local invariant features that will assist in the detection of forged (copy-paste forgery) images. They also introduce a novel strategy for pattern matching of key point distributions for copy detection. Typical experiments conducted on real case images demonstrate the success in near duplicate image retrieval for the application of digital image forensics. Efficiency of the proposed method is corroborated by comparison, with contemporary methods.

The manual review of videos captured by surveillance cameras is an inefficient and error-prone process, but of significant forensic value. In Chapter 19 - *Reliable Motion Detection, Location and Audit in Surveillance Video*, the authors, Samaan Poursoltan and Matthew Sorell discuss two key challenges often encountered in such a tedious video review task: 1) ensuring that all motion events are detected for analysis and 2) demonstrating that all motion events have been detected so that the evidence survives challenges in the court of law. The authors have demonstrated in one of their previous works that tracking the average brightness of video frames can provide a more robust measurement of motion than other commonly hypothesised motion metrics. This chapter extends that work by setting automatic localised motion detection thresholds, maintaining a frame-by-frame single parameter normalised motion metrics, and locating regions of motion events within the footage. A tracking filter approach is utilised to analyse localised motion, which adapts to localised background motion or noise within each image segment. After motion detection, location and size are estimated and used to describe motion events.

As identity theft is a big concern and the number of unique physiological and behavioral characteristics for each person is limited (e.g., each person has one face, two eyes, ten fingerprints, one signing style, etc.), re-issuing biometric traits for identifying the same person can be problematic. To resolve this non-reissuable problem and to thwart identity theft, researches on cancellable biometrics is gaining more momentum. Cancellable biometrics is the technique that utilizes non-invertible transformation functions to operate on the same original biometric sample in order to generate multiple variants/templates to represent the same person. The idea of this approach is to issue a transform template for authentication and verification purpose, and should the template is stolen or copied, the stolen or copied template is revoked with no fear of having the original sample obtained by the attacker through inverse transformation. The non-invertibility is to make it computationally infeasible to obtain the original sample from the stolen transformed template. Since the features of transformed variants of the same original template are similar in the feature space, a new transformed template can be issued after the stolen one is revoked / cancelled from the system. Contributed by Emanuele Maiorana, Patrizio Campisiand Alessandro Neri, Chapter 20 - *Cancellable Biometrics for On-Line Signature Recognition* is concerned with the renewability of a protected online signature based on this idea. They use a Dynamic Time warping (DTW) strategy to compare the transformed templates and carry out several experiments on the public MCYT signature database to evaluate their methodology.

The afore-mentioned six chapters provide technical treatment of various forensics aspects that require the use of pattern recognition and signal processing techniques. However, techniques alone should not be expected to provide resolutions to all legal cases. The reader is referred to the J. Tibbitts and Y. Lu's work entitled *Forensic Applications of Signal Processing*, IEEE Signal Processing Magazine, March 2009, for detailed discussions on issues such as scientific interpretation of reasonable doubt, lack of understanding of scientific principles, lack understanding of signal processing, and in particular, lack of understanding of speech and image processing.

Chang-Tsun Li
University of Warwick, UK

Anthony T. S. Ho
University of Surrey, UK

Section 1
Digital Evidence

Chapter 1

Providing Cryptographic Security and Evidentiary Chain-of-Custody with the Advanced Forensic Format, Library, and Tools[1]

Simson L. Garfinkel
Naval Postgraduate School & Harvard University, USA

ABSTRACT

This article presents improvements in the Advanced Forensics Format Library version 3 that provide for digital signatures and other cryptographic protections for digital evidence, allowing an investigator to establish a reliable chain-of-custody for electronic evidence from the crime scene to the court room. No other system for handling and storing electronic evidence currently provides such capabilities. This article discusses implementation details, user level commands, and the AFFLIB programmer's API.

INTRODUCTION

Chain-of-custody for evidence from the crime scene to the court room is a bedrock principle of both civil and criminal law. Without a clear and unambiguous chain-of-custody there is no way

to be sure that an object presented to the court is the same object that was collected at the scene of the crime. Even evidence presented to technical experts needs to have chain-of-custody: without it, there is no way to assure that the expert's testimony pertains to evidence from the actual case that is under consideration.

DOI: 10.4018/978-1-60960-515-5.ch001

A paper notebook found at a crime scene can be put into an evidence bag, tagged, and locked away in an evidence locker. Each time the evidence is accessed or moved to another location this fact will be noted. In this manner the prosecution can show that the evidence has not been tampered; in the rare cases where tampering takes place, it can be detected.

But unlike records written with pen and paper, digital files can be modified without leaving a trace of the original message. This is one of the great challenges of digital forensics—establishing that a particular arrangement of bits on a digital storage medium is the result of on specific computational history (*e.g.,* deleting a file) and not of another (*e.g.,* using a hex editor to write raw sectors onto the disk drive that are indicative of a deleted file) [Carrier, 2006].

Of course, hard drives, USB memory sticks, and cell phones are tagged and bagged. But at some point, the information on these devices needs to be copied onto another computer system for analysis. In a modern forensic laboratory these files might be placed on a high-capacity server or a Storage Area Network (SAN) to allow for flexible use and simultaneous access by multiple examiners. Such environments require highly reliable technical measures to provide assurances that evidence is kept intact and unmodified.

Although computer forensics practitioners understand the importance of chain-of-custody, today's tools for preserving this chain are poor. Programs such as EnCase[Keightley, 2003] and dcfldd[Harbour, 2006] will compute an MD5 or SHA-1 cryptographic hash of a disk when it is copied by an investigator into an *image file*. Later, when the image file is provided to a forensic analyst, the analyst can compare the hash of the image received with the hash of the original to determine if the file has been modified. If the hashes match, the assumption is that the file is unchanged from the original.

This article introduces an improved method for assuring the integrity of digital evidence that is based on public key cryptography. In addition to providing improved integrity, the method presented also allows for:

- digital documentation of evidentiary transfer from one agent to another;
- reconstruction of evidence that has been inadvertently damaged during transfer;
- forensically sound methods for recovering partial evidence in cases where so much digital evidence has been damaged that reconstruction is no longer possible;
- encryption with both symmetric and public key cryptography, so that evidence that is acquired in a hostile environment can be safely transferred back to a secure facility.

These new methods have been implemented in the Advanced Forensic Format Library (AF-FLIB) Version 3[Garfinkel, 2008]. AFFLIB is an open source software package written in the C/C++ programming language that allows for the imaging, manipulation, storage and use of digital evidence. The software is available free of charge for incorporation into both open source and proprietary forensic applications.

BACKGROUND AND PRIOR WORK

Disks and Disk Images

Computer hard drives, optical drives, and solid state drives are mass storage devices that organize the information they store as a series of numbered, fix-sized *sectors*. Traditionally hard drives employ a sector size of 512 bytes and CDROM drives used 2048-byte sectors, although a standard for 4096-byte sectors is currently under development [Fonseca, 2007].

A *disk image file*, or more generally an *image file*, is a file that contains a sector-for-sector copy of the contents of a mass storage device. Image files are intended to be perfect copies of the disk's contents. Image files are produced with programs called *imagers*.[2]

Although the discussion to this point has focused on disk image files, in practice any data carrying device can be imaged. Once a device is imaged, the forensic investigator works with the image, rather than the original device, in order to preserve the device's integrity: most computer forensic tools can directly read and process disk image files.

Image files are particularly important when it is necessary to record the state of a device that must then be returned to service—for example, in the event of a network attack. In these cases, the image file may be the only tangible evidence of the crime that has taken place after the system has been restored to operation.

Imaging also provides a simple and operating system independent means for backing up a hard drive: the drive is simply imaged into a file or onto another drive. To restore the backup, the image is *restored* on the original drive. The image can also be restored on another drive of similar size, a process sometimes called *cloning*.

Disk image files can be stored in different formats. The most basic format is the *raw* format in which the bytes in the image file have a one-for-one correspondence to the bytes on the physical device (*e.g.,* bytes 0–511 in the file represent the first 512-byte sector, bytes 512–1023 represent the second 512-byte sector, and so on). The advantage of the raw format is that it is easy to understand and easy to implement; the disadvantage is that raw files consume as much storage space as the device being imaged: imaging a newly purchased 80GB hard drive will produce an 80GB raw file, even though each one of the drive's 160 million 512-byte disk sectors is filled with ASCII NULLs.

Disk Image Formats

There are two important shortcomings that forensic examiners experience when working with raw disk images: the images are unwieldy, and they do not capture important information such as the time that the disk was imaged, who performed the imaging, or even the device sector size. Because of these shortcomings, developers have created a number of disk image formats, each with its own intended purpose.

One of the most widely used file formats today is the EnCase Evidence File Format. This format is based on the ASR Data Expert Witness Compression Format [ASR, 2002]. Disk images are stored as a series of files, each file not exceeding 2GB ($2-1=2147483647$ bytes). The first file contains a "Case Info" header, a table containing a 32-bit CRC and the offset of each "blocks" in the disk image (the default block size is 64 sectors), and a footer containing an MD5 hash for the entire physical disk. Also contained in the header are the date and time of acquisition, an examiner's name, notes on the acquisition, and an optional password; the header concludes with its own CRC. Images that require more than 2GB of storage are split into multiple files and given file names such as FILE.E01, FILE.E02, *etc.* Disk images can be split into files smaller than 2GB for storage to archival CDROM. The EnCase/Expert Witness file format can be read by a number of commercial programs and by the Open Source Libewf[Kloet et al., 2008].

Other forensic file formats include a proprietary format used by AccessData's Forensic Toolkit (FTK), the file format used by Safeback[NTI Forensics Source, 2008], and the file format used by ILook Investigator[US Treasury, 2008]. A detailed survey of forensic file formats appears in [Garfinkel et al., 2006].

In almost all cases it is faster to perform a forensic investigation with a an uncompressed raw file than it is to work with a compressed file. This is because modern forensic programs frequently need to skip from one part of a disk image to another: when a compressed format is used, parts of the disk image are constantly being read off the disk, decompressed, and then discarded. Using an uncompressed format avoids the decompression step, which is computationally intensive.

Assuring Integrity with Hash Functions

Forensic practitioners today largely rely on the MD5[Rivest, 1992] and SHA-1[Computer Systems Laboratory and Technology, 1993] cryptographic hash functions to assure the integrity of images that they acquire.

A cryptographic hash is a one-way function which takes an arbitrary amount of input and produces an output of a fixed size. (Cryptographers will sometimes call the input a *pre-image* and refer to the hash value as the *residue*.) To be considered strong, a cryptographic hash function should have these properties:

- **Preimage resistance**: Given any hash, it should be computationally infeasible to find a specific preimage that produces the residue.
- **Second preimage resistance**: Given a message $m311$, it should be computationally infeasible to find a message $m2$ that has the same hash.
- **Collision resistance**: It should be computationally infeasible to find *any* two messages $m1$ and $m2$ that have the same hash. [Friedl, 2005, Boneh, 2001]

The MD5 algorithm produces a 128-bit cryptographic hash; this hash is typically written as 32 hexadecimal digits. The SHA-1 algorithm produces a 160-bit hash which is typically written as 40 digits.

Today it is common practice for computer forensic investigators to record the MD5 or SHA-1 of a disk when it is imaged. The hash is computed by the acquisition tool as the data is read from disk being imaged and displayed on the computer's screen; the investigator records this number in the investigative report.

For example, in the case of US v. Zacarias Moussaoui, when the contents of Moussaoui's laptop were duplicated by the FBI with Safeback, a program was used to compute the MD5 of both the laptop's drive and the copy made by the FBI. A copy of the laptop's drive was then provided to Mr. Moussaoui's defense team. The MD5 of this copy was computed and compared with the MD5 of the original laptop's drive. According to court filings:

"The significance of this point is two-fold. First, there can be no question that the defense has the exact same copy of the original that the Government has, so they can conduct any further investigation on their copy that they wish. Second, the results of the MD5 program as to these two laptops further demonstrate the reliability of the Safeback program."[Novak, 2002]

There are several advantages to the current practice of manually recording hash codes and incorporating them into investigative reports:

- The practice is easy to understand.
- The practice is in general use.
- The practice is easy to explain in court.
- The hash codes are easily recorded in an investigative report which the investigator is presumably already keeping for other purposes.
- The same procedures which assure for integrity of the investigative report will similarly assure for the integrity of the hash codes.

But today's practice has potential problems as well:

- Because the hash codes are recorded in what is essentially a free-format report narrative, it is difficult to apply automated processing and validation.

- If the disk image becomes corrupted, the hash code will only report that it no longer matches: it does not allow the error to be isolated or corrected.

MD5 Vulnerabilities

In recent years a number of vulnerabilities have been found in the MD5 hashing algorithm, culminating with the discovery of MD5 collisions [Wang et al., 2004]. For this reason MD5 is no longer considered by computer scientists to be a good choice for security-critical applications. Although as of this writing no SHA-1 collisions have been publicly announced, many researchers feel that it is only a matter of time [Schneier, 2004]. Increasingly security software uses the SHA-256 algorithm, which produces a 256-bit hash, and NIST has started an effort to develop a new hash standard [NIST, 2007].

There are at least two reasons that the discovery of MD5 collisions was not as catastrophic for computer security in practice as they might otherwise have been:

- First, although it is possible to generate MD5 collisions, it still takes a considerable amount of computer power and expertise to do so.
- A second and perhaps more important reason is that modern security engineering practice is to use a plug-in architecture for cryptographic algorithms. To be "pluggable" formats must store version numbers, algorithm names and key lengths in data that transmitted or stored. The practical result of this engineering practice is that most programs that employ hash functions can work with a wide range of algorithm. Software that relies on cryptographic hashes can then validate using any or all of

these algorithms, dramatically reducing the chances that an attack will be successful.

Piecewise Hashing

In addition to computing a hash of the entire disk image, some tools will compute a hash for individual sections or "pieces" of the image. For example, dcfldd [Harbour, 2006] can compute a hash for each block and store the hashes in a separate file. This approach of separately hashing each piece of the file is called *piecewise hashing*.

Piecewise hashing is an important advance for digital forensics. Whereas a single hash code for an image can establish that an image has not been modified, if the file is modified the piecewise hashes can be used to help determine the location and extent of the alternation. Changing a single bit from a 0 to a 1 will change the hash for the entire image, but it will only change one of the piecewise hashes. In such a case, the remaining pieces would still have evidentiary value. Even if a file is truncated—for example, an 80GB file cut into a 20GB file—the piecewise hashes will allow the remaining evidence to be used, as long as it is otherwise unaltered.

Digital Signatures for Data Integrity

Digital signatures were invented by Diffie and Hellman for the purpose of securing mail sent over digital networks such as the Internet[Diffie and Hellman, 1976]. Digital signatures in the form of digital certificates have been applied for the purpose of certifying cryptographic keys[Kohnfelder, 1978], and now provide authentication for the vast majority of encrypted communications on the Internet through their incorporation into the SSL and TLS protocols[Dierks and Allen, 1999]. Digital signatures have also been widely applied to code signing in the Windows and Macintosh operating systems, as well as signing Linux software updates. But prior to the work presented in this article, digital signatures have not been applied to imaging of digital media for forensic purposes.

Modern digital signatures are implemented as functional compositions of cryptographic hash functions and public key cryptography. In practice a document that is to be signed is hashed with a function such as SHA-1. The hash is then encrypted using an asymmetric encryption algorithm such as RSA[Rivest et al., 1977].

Asymmetric encryption algorithms have the property that data encrypted with an *encryption key* can only be decrypted with a matching *decryption key*. In practice one key is kept confidential (the *private key*) while the other key is disclosed (the *public key*). When used for digital signatures, the private key is used to sign the signature while the public key is used to validate to signature.

Verifying a digital signature accomplishes two purposes: it verifies that the digital document has not been modified, and it verifies that a particular private key was used to create the signature. Verification is typically performed in three steps. First, the document's hash function is computed for a second time. Next, the signature is decrypted with the signer's public key. Finally, the computed hash is compared with the decrypted hash: if they match, the signature verifies.

Hash Functions Alone are not Digital Signatures

It is important for forensic practitioners to understand that what gives the digital signature its security is the use of a private key to mathematically sign the cryptographic hash: a cryptographic hash by itself is not a digital signature.

This is an important distinction, because the terms "digital signature" and "forensic signature" are frequently—and incorrectly—used by forensics practitioners in reference to a simple cryptographic hash (see [Haggerty and Taylor, 2007, ICS, 2008]). A hash value by itself is not a signature, because it is not based on any secret information: anyone in possession of the data can generate the hash; thus, having the hash is not proof that a specific person or system had posession of the data.

True digital signatures are important for establishing chain-of-custody because of their *non-repudiability* properties. If the signer's private key has not been compromised and if the signature is valid, then the private key was used to create the signature[3]. One can easily imagine a future in which digital evidence is routinely signed using trusted hardware such as a US Department of Defense Common Access Card[US Department of Defense, 2008]. Such a signature provides not such an assurance that the evidence has not been tampered—it provides an electronic proof that a specific person (or, at least, a specific CAC) was used to sign the evidence *when* it was acquired. Other information such as GPS coordinates or a secure timestamp[Adams et al., 2001] could be included in the signature as well.

AFF AND AFFLIB 3

The Advanced Forensic Format (AFF) is a format for storing digital evidence and associated metadata. Similar to the Expert Witness Format, AFF stores digital information as a series of blocks, range in size from 512 bytes to 4GB, which can be optionally compressed and stored in one or more disk files. Unlike Expert Witness, AFF is an extensible format which can store any kind of arbitrary data or metadata. To this end, AFF can be thought of as two parts: a container file format, similar to the ZIP file format, and a schema for mapping digital evidence to specific name/value pairs. A detailed description of the disk representation for the AFF format has been previously published[Garfinkel et al., 2006].

AFFLIB*TM* is an implementation of AFF written in a portable C++ that can be called from either C or C++. Rather than forcing the programmer

Figure 1. AFF Design Goals, from [Garfinkel et al., 2006]

- Ability to store:
  - disk images with or without compression.
  - disk images of any size.
  - metadata within disk images or separately.
  - images in a single file of any size or split among multiple files.
  - Arbitrary metadata in the form of user-defined name/value pairs.
- Extensibility.
- Simple design.
- Multi-platform, open source implementation.
- Freedom from any intellectual property restrictions.
- Provisions for internal self-consistency checking, so that part of an image could be recovered even if other parts of the image were rendered corrupt or otherwise lost.
- Provisions for certifying the authenticity of evidence files both with traditional hash functions like MD5 and SHA-1 and with advanced digital signatures based on X.509(v)3 certificates.

to understand segments, data segments, compression and so on, AFFLIB implements a simple abstraction that makes the AFF image file appear as two resources: a simple name/value database that can be accessed with traditional put and get semantics; and a stream that can be accessed using af_open(), af_read(), and af_seek() function calls. If af_open() is used to open a non-AFF file, the library defaults to a pass-through mode of operation, allowing AFF-aware programs to work equally well with raw files. In this manner, it is easy to modify existing forensics software to work with AFF yet retain compatibility with raw files.

AFF Design

Specific goals for AFF are presented in [Garfinkel et al., 2006] and repeated in Figure 1. AFF accomplishes these goals by partitioning the format into two layers: a **data storage layer**, which specifies how the named AFF segments are stored in an actual file, and a **data schema layer**, which defines how the information stored in the named segments is to be interpreted.

AFF Data Storage Layer

The AFF data storage layer stores any number of name/value pairs within a single AFF object. AFF calls these name/value pairs *segments*. The segment name consists of a Unicode string between 1 and 64 characters long; the value consists of a 32-bit unsigned integer and a sequence of between 0 and 2−1 bytes. As discussed below in Section 3.3, different names are used to store different kinds of data and metadata.

When AFF is used to store disk images, the pagesize segment stores the size of each section of the disk image, the name page0 is used to store the first section, page1 is used to store the second, and so on. As the name implies, these sections of the disk image are called *pages*. By default AFF uses pages that are 16MB (2) bytes in length, although this can be changed on a file-by-file basis when the image file is created.

AFFLIB Version 3 was released in the fall of 2007 and has been steadily improved since. AFFLIB 3 includes supports for five different data storage layers:

- **AFF: A disk image in a single file.** The AFF file format stores AFF segments in a single file that consists of a file header, one or more AFF segments, and a file footer. The format is designed to allow easy parsing and validation of AFF files and easy data recovery in the event of media failure.

Unlike the Expert Witness format, the AFF format store an entire disk image and associated metadata in a single file. This is designed to aid processing and ease-of-use in environments that work with dozens or even thousands of drives simultaneously. As a result, we could not use an existing archive format such as ZIP or JAR because neither supported files larger than 4GB due to the use of 32-bit offsets within the file directory. Likewise, we couldn't use compressed tar files because they do not provide for random access. In retrospect we could have used the ZIP64 format, but at the time we did not have an implementation of ZIP64 that was both clean and Open Source.

When an application asks AFFLIB to open an AFF file with the af_open() call, AFFLIB scans the entire file, noting the offset of each segment, and builds an in-memory table of contents with this information. Offsets stored within each segment allows the file to be read quickly, without necessitating the reading of each byte in the file. Although it would be possible to store the table of contents at the end of the file, the way the ZIP file format does, we decided to force a trip through the segment headers within the file as a way of quickly verifying the file's integrity. Offsets stored within the file allow reading only the segment headers, rather than forcing a read of the entire file contents. In practice this process takes between 10 and 30 seconds on a modern desktop system for image files of devices ranging from 10GB to 200GB. Modern operating systems cache disk sectors, so once a file is opened, subsequent file openings are nearly instantaneous as long as these sectors remain in the host operating system's cache.

- **AFD: Multiple AFF files in a single directory.** Despite the fact that the AFF file format supports files larger than 4GB, some file systems (*e.g.,* MSDOS) do not support files larger than 2GB. On these systems AFFLIB supports an alternative storage mode called AFD, in which multiple AFF files are stored in a single directory. When a directory ending in the exten-

sion.afd is passed to AFFLIB's af_open() routine, AFFLIB scans the directory for.aff files and builds a single table of contents for all of the files. The maximum size of each AFF file within the AFD directory can be specified as an option.

- **AFM: Raw files with AFF annotations.** A single AFF file can be used to store metadata or other annotations (for example, digital signatures) for a disk image that is stored in one or more raw files. In this case the file is given an AFM extension.

For example, if a disk image is stored in three files, file.000, file.001 and file.002, annotations can be stored in a file called file.afm. Opening the file.afm file with AFFLIB causes the library to automatically locate and reference the data in the raw files when the forensic application attempts to read file data.

- **RAW and Split-Raw: Support for raw files.** The AFFLIB library can also directly open raw or split-raw files if their file names are passed to the af_open() call.
- **S3: Storing on Amazon's Simple Storage Service.** For supporting grid computing applications using Amazon's EC2, AFFLIB has the ability to directly store disk images inside Amazon's Simple Storage Service[Amazon, 2008].
- **Libewf: Legacy support for EnCase.** Finally, LIBAFF can directly read disk images created in the Guidance Software EnCase file format using libewf[Kloet et al., 2008].

The AFFLIB af_open() determines which storage layer implementation to use based on the string *pathname* argument that it is provided. For example, an attempt to open or create a file which has an extension of.aff results in an AFF file being opened or created; opening a directory with a.afd

Table 1. Some of the segment names used in the AFFLIB 3 schema

Device Characteristics:	
pagesize	The size of each AFF page, in bytes
imagesize	The number of bytes in the image
sectorsize	The size of each sector, in bytes
devicesectors	The number of sectors on the device.
Metadata:	
case_num	Case number; for compatibility with EnCase.
image_gid	A randomly generated 128-bit number used to uniquely identify each acquired image.
Image characteristics:	
pagesize	Size (in bytes) of each uncompressed AFF data page is stored in segment "flag" field.
parity0	The parity page; an XOR of all existing pages
imaging_commandline	The complete command used to create the image.
imaging_date	The date and time when the imaging was started.
imaging_notes	Notes made by the forensic examiner when the imaging was started.
imaging_device	The device that was used as the source of the image.
blanksectors	The number of sectors that are completely blank
AFF segments that are repeated for each page %d:	
page%d	The named sector for each page of the disk image; %d is replaced with the page number, from 0 to *devicesectors*, *pagesizesectors*.
page%d_md5	The segment for the MD5 hash of the page
page%d_sha1	The segment for the SHA-1 hash of the page
page%d_sha256	The segment for the SHA256 hash of the page
Bad Sector Management:	
badsectors	The number of sectors in the image which could not be read due to a hardware failure

extension results in the directory being treated as a collection of AFF files; calling af_open() with a path that has an an extension of.afd and the O_CREAT flag results in a directory being created. S3 files are specified with a URI in the form s3://bucketname/prefix. Split-raw files are automatically detected when a file is opened with a.000 extension and a file is present with the same basename and a.001 extension. EnCase files are specified with the standard.E01 extension.

AFF Schema

The AFF schema defines specific segment names, their purposes, and the interpretation of the 32-bit flag and variable-length data areas. A list of the segments that have been defined as of AFFLIB v3.0.6 appears in Table 1. Because of the open nature of AFF, applications are able to create their own named segment and store that information in the AFF file.

Some of the more important AFF segments appear in Table 1.

Additional segment types used for integrity and privacy will be discussed later in this article.

AFFLIB Streams Layer

In order to facilitate the integration of AFF into existing and new forensic software, AFFLIB implements a *streams layer* which provides a

Table 2. The AFF streams layer

AFFLIB POSIX-like functions	
af_open	Opens an AFF/AFD/AFM/Encase/S3/raw/split raw file
af_reopen	Opens an existing file handle for reading or writing using the AFFLIB system
af_popen	Opens a process for reading or writing using the AFFLIB system
af_read	Read bytes from the file
af_seek	Seek to a different position in the disk image file
af_tell	Reports the current position in the disk image file
af_eof	Reports if the file pointer is at the end of the file
af_write	Write bytes to the file (used when imaging, not when performing forensic analysis)
af_close	Closes an AFF file
Nonstandard extensions:	
af_is_badsector	Reports if the specified sector is bad
af_set_error_reporter	Establishes a callback function for alerting the operator that is called when AFF encounters an error
af_set_cachesize	Sets the size of the AFF page cache
af_vstat	Returns status information about the AFF implementation and the opened file
af_stats	Returns statistics about an AFF file
af_set_option	Sets an implementation option

standard POSIX-like streams abstraction through a standard set of interfaces (Table 2).

Transparent Integration with AFUSE

Although support for AFF is relatively easy to add to an existing program by replacing calls to open(), read() and with seek() with af_open(), af_read(), and af_seek(), occasionally it is not possible or desired to make source code modification to forensic tools.

To accommodate these problems AFFLIB includes a user-level program called affuse. Implemented on top of the Filesystem in Usespace (FUSE)[Szeredi, 2008], affuse allows a compressed AFF file to appear as a raw file in the computer's own file system. FUSE takes care of automatically decompressing pages as necessary and caching the uncompressed pages with all available memory.

For example, if the user has an AFF file called evidence.aff, this can be made to appear as a raw file in the same file system with these commands:

```
# ls -l evidence.aff
-rw-r--r-- 1 simsong 555   409039930
Mar 23  2006 evidence.aff
# affuse evidence.aff evidenceraw
# ls -ld evidence*
-rw-r--r-- 1 simsong  555   409039930
Mar 23  2006 evidence.aff
drwxr-xr-x 2 root    root         0
Dec 31  1969 evidence.raw
# ls -l evidence.raw
total 0
-r--r--r-- 1 root root 2111864832 Dec
31  1969 evidence.aff.raw
```

Notice that the current FUSE implementation reports that the raw file occupies 0 blocks and has a time stamp of the Unix Epoc. A future version of affuse will make all of the named segments inside the AFF file visible in their own named files.

With affuse, any Linux forensics tool can access not only AFF files, but also EnCase files and files stored on S3. Windows can be run on the same workstation using VMWare Player[VMWare, 2008]. VMWare Player can be configured to allow the Windows operating system (and therefore Windows applications) to view the host computer's file system; with affuse, that file system can include the contents of an AFF evidence file.

AFFLIB 3 INTEGRITY FEATURES

AFFLIB 3 includes four important mechanisms for assuring the integrity.

1. Picewise hashing of image pages
2. Digital signatures of pages and all metadata
3. Parity pages
4. Chain-of-custody segments

The extensible design of the AFF storage system, allowed each of these features to be added to the original AFF specification[Garfinkel et al., 2006] without the need to make changes to the underlying AFF Data Storage Layer.

Piecewise Hashing of Data Pages

AFF files store image data in special "page" segments which are typically 16MB in size. As each page segment is written, AFFLIB can automatically compute the page's MD5, SHA-1, and/or SHA256 hash and write an associated segment containing the hash value. The name of the hash page is simply the page name followed by the string _md5, _sha1 or _sha256. Each hash may be individually enabled or disabled at runtime. For example, when SHA-1 piecewise hashing is enabled and the page page3 is written, AFFLIB computes that page's SHA-1 and writes it into a segment named page3_sha1.

These piecewise hashes are used as a data integrity checks, similar to the way that the Expert Witness/EnCase format uses a CRC32. Even the MD5 is dramatically more secure than the CRC32. Nevertheless, these hashes are not intended to provide cryptographic protection for evidence:

for that purpose AFF uses digital signatures, described below.

Digital Signatures

Digital signatures represent a significant improvement for evidence integrity over today's standard practice of recording the MD5 or SHA-1 of an imaged disk in an investigator's notebook:

- Unlike a hash code written into an investigator's report, digital signatures are mathematical structures created for the purpose of assuring the integrity of data: their suitability for this purpose have been considered for decades and is widely understood.
- By using standard digital signatures, it is possible to integrate digital electronic evidence with existing software that already understands how to process digital certificates.
- Unlike a hash code, which simply protects the image data, AFF digital signatures protect the entire disk image, and all of the associated metadata.
- The private key used to sign the signature can be tied to a specific device or investigator, allowing the signature to be used for non-reputability in addition to integrity.
- But the most important reason is that the use of digital signatures will permit the migration to imaging based on trusted hardware which can then help to assure the chain-of-custody of evidence from the system being imaged to the courtroom.

AFF computes digital signatures for both metadata and data. When computing signatures on metadata, the segment name, 32-bit argument, and metadata value is signed. In the case of digital signatures computed on image data ("pages"), the signatures are calculated on the uncompressed data. As a result, it is possible to acquire and digitally sign a disk image and then later compress the image without compromising the integrity of the digital signatures. Calculating the signature on the uncompressed data further assures that the compression algorithm does not modify the data between compression and decompression: if the data were modified, the signature would not validate.

AFFLIB uses OpenSSL to generate and verify all digital signatures; signatures are stored in PKCS#7[Laboratories, 1993] format. Signatures that are stored directly in segments are stored as raw PKCS #7 objects, while signatures stored inside or adjacent to XML blocks are stored as Base64-encoded PKCS #7 objects.

AFF digital signatures complement the existing AFF integrity measures. Because the signature is stored in its own metadata segment, the signature does not change the content of the acquired disk image. And because AFM files can be used to annotate raw images, AFF signatures can be applied to raw image files without modifying the data itself. This is similar to PGP's ability to create "detached signatures,"[Zimmermann, 1995] although it is more powerful because PGP's facility can only detect that an alteration has taken place, whereas AFF's signature facility can report which page has been modified.

Notice that AFF signatures are independent of the underlying storage system. The signatures can be stored in one file and the data in another file (as in an AFM file), or in multiple AFF files (as in an AFD directory). They can even be stored in the S3 network-based object storage system.

Signing AFF Segments

AFFLIB 3 allows each AFF segment to be individually signed. The signatures for these segments are stored in their own segments which are included as part of the AFF file.

The data in an AFF segment consists of three parts: the segment name, the 32-bit flag, and the segment bytestream. Because the name and the flag determine how the contents of the bytestream

are interpreted, all three must be included in the computation of the signature.

AFFLIB 3 actually supports two signature modes, both of which include these three data elements. Both sign a hash of the segment data; the difference is how the hash is computed:

- **Signature Mode 0.** The hash is computed from the segment name, a NULL byte, the segment argument (as a 32-bit number in network byte order), and the segment data.
- **Signature Mode 1.** This mode is reserved for AFF data pages. The signature is computed by calculating the hash of the segment name, five NULL bytes, and the uncompressed page data.[4] In this manner, the signature is computed over the original data, rather than data that has been compressed or otherwise processed.

As indicated above, the signatures are written into segments themselves, with the segment name being *name*/sha256 where *name* is the original segment name sha256 is the hash algorithm used for computing the signature. This format allows easy migration to signatures based on SHA512, should the need arise, or NIST's future signature algorithm. Indeed, the AFF signature format allows a single AFF file to be simultaneously signed with multiple schemes.

The observant reader will note that since AFF signatures are themselves stored in segments, it is possible that signatures themselves can be signed. While this is certainly a true observation, it is not a useful one, since the integrity of a signature is assured when the signature is validated.

Signing AFF Files with X.509 Certificates

Signatures can be written with either self-signed certificates or with X.509[ITU, 2005] certificates that are issued as part of an organization's PKI. AFFLIB 3 uses the pluggable "EVP" signature support in the OpenSSL library[OpenSSL, 2008] to compute signatures; this library includes full support for both RSA and DSA X.509 certificates with 1024, 2048 or larger keys.

The easiest way to get a private key and a corresponding X.509 certificate is to make a self-signed certificate using the openssl command:

```
$ openssl req -x509 -newkey rsa:1024
-keyout sign.key -out sign.key -nodes
Generating a 1024 bit RSA private key
....................++++++
.....................++++++
writing new private key to 'sign.key'
-----
You are about to be asked to enter
information that will be
incorporated
into your certificate request.
What you are about to enter is what
is called a Distinguished Name or
a DN.
There are quite a few fields but you
can leave some blank
For some fields there will be a de-
fault value,
If you enter '.', the field will be
left blank.
-----
Country Name (2 letter code) [AU]:US
State or Province Name (full name)
[Some-State]:California
Locality Name (eg, city) []:Monterey
Organization Name (eg, company) [In-
ternet Widgits Pty Ltd]:Naval
Postgraduate School
Organizational Unit Name (eg, sec-
tion) []:Department of Computer
Science
Common Name (eg, YOUR name) []:Simson
L. Garfinkel
Email Address []:slgarfin@nps.edu
$
```

When this command is run the user is asked a number of questions; OpenSSL uses the responses to these questions to build the CN field of the X.509 signing certificate and certificate request.

The contents of the certificate can be viewed with the openssl x509 -text command, as shown in Figure 2.

Certification of X.509 Certificates

As an alternative to creating a self-signed certificate, the practitioner can can create an RSA private/public key pair, create a certificate request (CSR), send the CSR to a certificate authority, and use the certificate that the authority returns. This procedure is the same procedure that the practitioner would use to obtain an X.509 key for email or running a secure web server[Housley and Polk, 2001, Adams and Lloyd, 2002].

Security for X.509 Private Keys

The openssl command presented in Section 4.2.2 places both the RSA private key, the public key, and the self-signed certificate into the same file. If the private key is stored without encryption, then the key file must be protected if non-repudiation is to be assured. Typically the contents of this file will be protected with the computer's operating system using the same mechanisms that are used to protect the computer's device drivers, operating system, and the afflib tools themselves: if these tools are secure, then so is the file containing the private key, and if these tools can be compromised, putting a passphrase on the private key adds little additional protection.

In some situations it is advantageous to have the private key stored separately from the operating system—for example, in a cryptographic device such as a smart card (*e.g.,* the Department of Defense Common Access Card[US Department of Defense, 2008]) or a USB token. Although OpenSSL has support for these devices, we have not implemented this functionality at the AFFLIB

Figure 2. The OpenSSL command can be used to decode the contents of a certificate

```
$ openssl x509 -text -in sign.key -noout
Certificate:
    Data:
        Version: 3 (0x2)
        Serial Number:
            a3:e1:ef:44:63:04:74:00
        Signature Algorithm: sha1WithRSAEncryption
        Issuer: C=US, ST=California, L=Monterey, O=Naval Postgraduate School,
            OU=Department of Computer Science,
            CN=Simson L. Garfinkel/emailAddress=slgarfin@nps.edu
        Validity
            Not Before: May 17 01:40:13 2008 GMT
            Not After : Jun 16 01:40:13 2008 GMT
        Subject: C=US, ST=California, L=Monterey, O=Naval Postgraduate School,
            OU=Department of Computer Science,
            CN=Simson L. Garfinkel/emailAddress=slgarfin@nps.edu
        Subject Public Key Info:
            Public Key Algorithm: rsaEncryption
            RSA Public Key: (1024 bit)
                Modulus (1024 bit):
                    00:be:4e:10:cc:e4:ae:76:c2:d1:7c:72:c7:74:32:
                    f3:43:04:51:ed:ba:ed:a4:26:4d:46:b8:98:6c:bc:
                    28:10:13:7c:7d:20:a7:69:c7:9d:f1:66:4c:d3:b1:
                    12:48:fc:07:2d:87:83:f3:e4:0c:c8:64:b2:38:6a:
                    4a:18:39:bf:3f:08:ba:37:e1:69:3f:57:0c:06:8a:
                    c6:95:9d:f5:4a:62:fd:4d:04:49:f1:f7:23:b0:e3:
                    e4:ad:41:a1:4a:64:78:d2:fb:16:3d:22:2f:e1:59:
                    0d:47:07:85:1a:e7:aa:fa:3b:61:fe:0f:56:21:48:
                    c3:e1:49:c5:ad:32:08:4d:57
                Exponent: 65537 (0x10001)
        X509v3 extensions:
            X509v3 Subject Key Identifier:
                AE:A6:63:40:52:BF:08:1D:E1:D3:A5:85:75:16:D8:BD:76:71:1E:BB
            X509v3 Authority Key Identifier:
                keyid:AE:A6:63:40:52:BF:08:1D:E1:D3:A5:85:75:16:D8:BD:76:71:1E:BB
                DirName:/C=US/ST=California/L=Monterey/O=Naval
                Postgraduate School/OU=Department of Computer Science/CN=Simson
                L. Garfinkel/emailAddress=slgarfin@nps.edu
                serial:A3:E1:EF:44:63:04:74:00

            X509v3 Basic Constraints:
                CA:TRUE
    Signature Algorithm: sha1WithRSAEncryption
        34:6d:22:50:28:72:3b:e5:4d:fd:99:3f:79:6a:37:e0:75:45:
        fb:df:a5:c8:29:a5:4d:62:3f:58:8a:a6:1a:48:86:83:c7:03:
        d7:59:84:b9:5:67:2b:2b:7a:8a:13:72:ec:82:d0:9a:56:b3:
        fd:a5:8a:7f:c1:68:6a:db:ea:d2:1f:41:b9:ab:23:16:f1:59:
        ca:91:3d:cb:fc:58:08:01:ab:4b:7b:15:c5:c5:7a:fc:a9:e8:
        ea:09:fc:8d:4f:1b:68:a7:e5:34:19:9d:ed:73:46:e5:95:87:
        3e:e2:65:58:0f:a2:66:d3:a5:6f:62:47:78:e8:65:34:30:b4:
        49:9d
```

level due to our limited development resources. A future version of AFFLIB can support this functionality if it is required by AFF users.

Bill of Materials and Chain-of-Custody

AFFLIB 3 introduces a special XML structure that contains a list of every AFF segment in the file, a signature for each segment, a set of "notes," and a public key. This structure is called an "AFF Bill Of Materials" (AFFBOM). An example of the XML structure appears in Figure 3.

When an AFF image is created with aimage, afconvert, copied with afcopy, or signed with afsign, an AFFBOM is created and signed with the private key belonging to the person who did

Figure 3. The AFF Bill of Materials (AFFBOM) with signature at end.

```
<affbom version="1">
<! –Date XML was written:–>
<date type="ISO 01">19980708T13:33:11</date>
<! –Base64 encoding of certificate used to sign CCB–>
<program>afcopy</program>
<signingcertificate>
YXNkYXNkZgphZHN…
…s39fjasl3JSFCmYK
</signingcertificate>
<notes>
Human-readable notes from the examiner
</notes>
<! –What follows is an array of elements, one for each AFF segment.–>
<affsegments>
<segmenthash segname='myname1' mode='0' alg='sha256'>
base64 encoding of the hash of the named segment
</segmenthash>
…<! –multiple segmenthash segments will be present–>
</affsegments>
</affbom>
7zzW9WJO7RPuTH4G291b6YSW5SUQacD7UGJTiwpA+NgPm6/RRoJwSQcud6RxwkkL
thQrN0poqv8T8U7p8cSiuphrL29oBY9J4okjv1xXTdLoHoaf5Ft6kt+QqeSX4bOB
...
```

the acquisition. This is stored in a special segment called affbom0.

Of course an individual AFFBOM segment can be removed from an AFF file; indeed, all of the signatures can be removed as well. This is not a shortcoming specific to the AFF signature scheme: any digital signature scheme suffers from the shortcoming that signatures can be stripped and the content can be changed by an adversary. Signatures can be stripped from signed code, producing code that is unsigned. Signatures can be removed from S/MIME signed email messages, producing conventional, unsigned email message. There is, in principle, no way to tell the difference between an object that has had its signature removed from one that was never signed in the first place. The only way to know that a signature has been removed is through the use of policy—for example, a protocol that prohibits an organization from releasing an unsigned data object. But even then, there is no way to tell the difference between a genuine data object that was released and later had its signature stripped, and a fraudulent data object that was never signed in the first place.

AFF Bill of Materials

When an AFF file is created or copied, an AFF Bill of Materials can be added. This block is an XML data structure that includes the date that it was signed, the certificate used to create the signature, notes, and an array of elements that represent each segment in the AFF file. An example of the schema appears in Figure 3.

The segment is called a *bill of materials* because it is literally a parts list of all the segments that make up the specific AFF file. Since AFF files are segmented and segments can be added or removed at will, the need exists for a single structure that lists all of the segments that need to be present for a file to be complete. Without the AFFBOM segments could be added, removed, or changed without detection.

The AFFBOM contains XML elements for the date that the signature was created, the program that created the signature, human-readable notes, and an XML array containing a cryptographic hash of each AFF segment in the AFF file. Hashes can be computed in mode 0 or mode 1, as discussed in Section 4.2.1. At the end of the XML structure is stored a Base64-encoded digital signature of the structure.

What makes it possible to detect change is not just the fact that there is an AFFBOM, but the fact that it is digitally signed. Provided that the private key is guarded and that the signature process is trusted, a relying party can be assured that the specific set of segments with the specific hashes existed in the AFF file at the time the signature was created.

The XML block is signed using the OpenSSL signature routines; the resulting signature is placed at the end of the XML block as a base-64 coded PKCS #7 object. Although the W3C XML-Signature Recommendation[Bartel et al., 2002] might have been a better choice, we were unable to find a suitable implementation, and the complexity of the specification is such that we did not wish to attempt writing it ourself. (The W3C reference implementation contains more than 130 C source files and requires two additional open source packages for proper operation.) Our implementation has the advantage of being small, easy to validate, and implemented. It would not be difficult to migrate to XML-Signature if such functionality is required, however.

Providing a Chain of Custody

Each time a signed AFF file is copied with afcopy, a new AFFBOM can be created which includes a new AFFBOM that covers all of the original segments and all of the previous AFFBOMs. In this manner the sequence of signed bill-of-materials becomes a custody chain, showing who has copied the image and verifying that no evidentuary segments have been added, deleted, or modified. These AFFBOMs are stored in segments named affbom1, affbom2, *etc.,* where the number is incremented for each copy generation.

The AFFLIB source code contains a demonstration script called test_signing.sh that creates an evidence file and three X.509 certificates: one for Mr. Agent, one for Ms. Analyst, and one for

Dr. Librarian, all officials in the fictional town of Remote, CA. The evidence file rawevidence.iso is converted into a file evidence.aff with afconvert and then signed with afsign using this command:

```
$ afsign -s agent.pem evidence.aff
The signature can be verified using
the afverify command:
$ afverify evidence.aff
```

Notice that the afverify command does not need the user to specify a certificate to use for verification, because the signing certificate is embedded in the evidence.aff file. When the program runs it displays the certificate that was used for verification, so that the investigator can verify that the file is still signed with the correct certificate.

Mr. Agent transfers the evidence to Ms. Analyst. This is done with the afcopy command:

```
$ afcopy -n -s analyst.pem evidence.
aff evidence2.aff
Enter notes. Terminate input with a
'.' on a line by itself:
This copy was made by the analyst.
.
Thank you.
Copying evidence.aff --> evidence2.
aff
evidence2.aff: 20017252 bytes trans-
fered in 10.07 seconds. xfer rate:
1.99 MBytes/sec
```

Notice that the file is automatically signed because a public/private keypair is provided in the file analyst.pem. The -n option tells afcopy to take a note from standard input.

Of course, an AFF file can still be copied without using the afcopy command. In this case the file will be copied without a new XMLBOM segment being added.

Figure 4. afverify applied to file evidence2.aff created as part of the AFFLIB test routines

```
Filename: evidence2.aff
# Segments signed and Verified:      11
# Segments unsigned:                  0
# Segments with corrupted signatures: 0

SIGNING CERTIFICATE :
    Subject: C=US, ST=California, L=Remote, O=Country Govt., OU=Sherif Dept,
        CN=Mr. Agent, emailAddress=agent@investiations.com
    Issuer: C=US, ST=California, L=Remote, O=Country Govt., OU=Sherif Dept,
        CN=Mr. Agent, emailAddress=agent@investiations.com


Number of custody chains: 2
--------------------
Signed Bill of Material #1:

SIGNING CERTIFICATE :
    Subject: C=US, ST=California, L=Remote, O=Country Govt., OU=Sherif Dept,
        CN=Mr. Agent, emailAddress=agent@investiations.com
    Issuer: C=US, ST=California, L=Remote, O=Country Govt., OU=Sherif Dept,
        CN=Mr. Agent, emailAddress=agent@investiations.com

Date: 2008-04-26T11:06:06
Notes:

--------------------
Signed Bill of Material #2:

SIGNING CERTIFICATE :
    Subject: C=US, ST=California, L=Remote, O=State Police, OU=Forensics,
        CN=Ms. Analyst, emailAddress=analyst@investiations.com
    Issuer: C=US, ST=California, L=Remote, O=State Police, OU=Forensics,
        CN=Ms. Analyst, emailAddress=analyst@investiations.com

Date: 2008-04-26T11:06:21
Notes:
This copy was made by the analyst.

--------------------

EVIDENCE FILE VERIFIES.
```

Verification

Verification is done with the AFFLIB program afverify. This program opens the requested AFF file and scans for the affbom*n* segments. For each segment the program then verifies the signature on the XML block, then opens each AFF segment and verifies that segment's cryptographic hash. (Segment hashes are cached after they are computed for efficiency.)

The afverify program can report:

- Missing segments that were signed but are now missing.
- Extra segments that were not signed but have been added to the file.

- AFF segments whose signature no longer verify.
- AFF segments that were modified at one point during the conveyance of evidence. These will appear as segments that do not verify for older AFFBOMs but to verify for later AFFBOMs. In this manner it is possible to determine when the segment was modified.

Figure 4 shows afverify applied to the file evidence2.aff created in the previous section.

AFF Parity Pages

To allow for the recovery of data after corruption or data loss, AFFLIB 3 introduces the concept of

AFF Parity Pages. Similar to parity drives used in a hard drive storage array, the AFF parity page is written for each disk image file at the conclusion of disk imaging; each byte of the parity page is computed by taking the XOR of the corresponding byte of all the other disk pages in the AFF file. Thus, the contents of any other page can be reconstructed simply by taking the XOR of all the remaining pages and the parity page.

AFF parity pages work with piecewise hashes and digital signatures to provide enhanced data recovery. If the hash or digital signature indicates that a page has been corrupted, that page can be erased and then reconstructed using all of the other AFF pages and the parity page. Once reconstruction is complete, the signature or page hash (which are stored in a different location) can be used to determine if the reconstruction is correct.

Parity pages are automatically created when an image is signed with the afsign utility. They can also be created by the aimage disk imaging utility, which was previously part of AFFLIB but is now its own standalone distribution.

Because they are the same size as the data pages, parity pages are not limited to correcting a single error. Indeed, the combination of parity pages and per-page hashes and/or signatures allows a wide number data corruption events to be not only detected but corrected, including:

- One or more bytes changed within a single page.
- One of more bytes changed across multiple pages, provided that bytes with the same offset are not modified on different pages.

Finally, overlapping ranges of bytes on multiple pages that are damaged can be reconstructed using a brute force operation. In these cases multiple "trail reconstructions" must be attempted, with each reconstructed tested by computing the pages' hash and seeing if the hash matches the hash that was previously calculated. Essentially, this approach uses a brute force search for the correct data: once the correct set of bytes is found, the signatures validates. In practice such an approach would only work if the overlap region in each page is confined to 4 bytes or less; beyond that, the computational overhead is simply too great. If entire sectors are corrupt or missing, reconstruction will not be successful. (Such a reconstruction is not currently implemented by the afverify command, but may be in a future version.)

Signed Raw Files

AFF's AFM format allows a disk image to be stored in an uncompressed raw file (eg file.iso) and the associated metadata to be stored in a.afm file. The AFM format can also handle raw data stored as a series of split raw files (eg file.001, file.002, *etc.*).

Beacuse AFF tools operate on named segments that are independent of the underlying storage container, the AFM format allows any ISO-file to be signed using the afsign command. The afsign program will automatically detect if it is signing a raw file and will create a.afm file to hold the signature. When filename.iso is signed, the afsign create a new file called filename.afm which contains the signatures, the signed bill of materials, and other metadata:

```
$ ls -l myfile.iso
-rw-r--r--  1 simsong  simsong
63107908 Apr 26 11:30 myfile.iso
$./afsign -s agent.pem myfile.iso
Signing segments...
Calculating BOM for page0...
Calculating BOM for page1...
Calculating BOM for page2...
Calculating BOM for page3...
$ ls -l myfile*
-rw-------  1 simsong  simsong
16785481 Apr 26 11:30 myfile.afm
-rw-r--r--  1 simsong  simsong
63107908 Apr 26 11:30 myfile.iso
$
```

Figure 5. Demonstration of file corruption and recovery using afrecover

```
$ dd if=/dev/random of=myfile.iso count=1 skip=1 conv=notrunc
$ afverify myfile.afm
Filename: myfile.afm
# Segments signed and Verified:        13
# Segments unsigned:                     0
# Segments with corrupted signatures: 1

SIGNING CERTIFICATE :
    Subject: C=US, ST=California, L=Remote, O=Country Govt., OU=Sherif Dept,
            CN=Mr. Agent, emailAddress=agent@investiations.com
     Issuer: C=US, ST=California, L=Remote, O=Country Govt., OU=Sherif Dept,
            CN=Mr. Agent, emailAddress=agent@investiations.com

Bad signature segments:
page0

Number of custody chains: 1
--------------------
Signed Bill of Material #1:

SIGNING CERTIFICATE :
    Subject: C=US, ST=California, L=Remote, O=Country Govt., OU=Sherif Dept,
            CN=Mr. Agent, emailAddress=agent@investiations.com
     Issuer: C=US, ST=California, L=Remote, O=Country Govt., OU=Sherif Dept,
            CN=Mr. Agent, emailAddress=agent@investiations.com

Date: 2008-04-26T11:35:18
Notes:


--------------------

EVIDENCE FILE DOES NOT VERIFY; EVIDENTUARY VALUE MAY BE COMPROMISED.
$ afrecover myfile.afm
myfile.afm has a bad signature
Attempting to repair page0
Page page0 successfully repaired
$
```

Although it is also possible to sign ISO files using existing tools such as PGP with detached signatures, afsign has several advantages:

- afsign will sign every 16 megabytes chunk of the ISO file. In this way, if the file is corrupted, it is possible to pinpoint what data is invalid and what data is still good.
- Unlike PGP, afsign allows the addition of notes and other metadata when a signature is written.
- afsign utilizes X.509 certificates, allowing easy integration into existing PKI-based systems.
- Because afsign also computes a parity page, it is possible to repair a damaged raw file using afrecover (as discussed in Section 4.4).

Figure 5 illustrates recovery of a corrupted file. First the file is corrupted with a block of random data. Next the file is checked with afverify. Finally the file is recovered using afrecover (Figure 5).

AFFLIB 3 ENCRYPTION FEATURES

AFFLIB 3 introduces the ability to encrypt AFF evidence files with the AES-256 algorithm[NIST, 2001].

Each segment of each AFF file may be optionally encrypted with a unique, randomly generated 256 bit AES *session key*. This key can then itself be encrypted using a passphrase provided by the user or encrypted with an X.509 public key. Because of this two-step process, the passphrase or public key used to encrypt an AFF file can be changed in just a few seconds without having to decrypt and re-encrypt the entire disk image.

Whereas some other forensic programs provide the ability to put a "password" on an evidence file, those passwords can be disregarded by non-conformant programs. (For example, GetData claims that it's MountImage Pro program can "open EnCase password protected image files without the password."[GetData Software, 2008] Libewf allows the user to ignore the passphrase for EnCase images when the images are opened.) AFFLIB 3 uses true encryption: if you do not know the correct decryption key, the only way to access the evidence is to brute-force the encryption passphrase or the X.509 private key.

AFF Encryption Schema

Similar to the design of AFF Signatures, AFF Encryption is layered on top of the basic AFF functionality that stores name/value pairs.

Three encryption layers are implemented:

1. **AFF Base Encryption**, which provides encryption of the AFF segment contents, but not the segment names or the segment flags. All of the segments in an AFF file are encrypted with a the same randomly generated *affkey*.
2. **AFF Passphrase Encryption**, a scheme for storing the AFF file's affkey in an AFF segment that is itself encrypted with a passphrase.
3. **AFF Public Key Encryption**, which stores the AFF file's *affkey* in an AFF segment that is encrypted with an X.509 public key.

AFF Base Encryption

Encrypted AFF segments are stored in segments where name is generated by taking the name of the unencrypted segment and appending a slash followed by the encryption algorithm and keysize. For example, whereas the first 16MB of a disk image are typically stored in a segment named page0, in an encrypted AFF file the page is named page0/aes256.

As discussed above, a single AFF session key is used to encrypt all of the AFF segments in a given file. In AFFLIB 3 this key is randomly generated and is not accessible to the user.

Encryption is implemented as modifications to the af_update_seg and af_get_seg functions inside the lib/afflib.cpp source file:

- When a program linked with AFFLIB attempts to store a segment, AFFLIB checks to see if an encryption key has been set; if one has, the segment's content is encrypted and the segment is stored at the modified name (*e.g.*, page0/aes256 instead of page0).
- When a program linked with AFFLIB attempts to fetch a segment and the segment does not exist, AFFLIB checks to see if an encryption key is set. If one is, AFFLIB attempts to fetch the segment with the modified name. If the segment can be fetched, AFFLIB attempts to decrypt the segment with the key that has been set. If decryption is successful the data is returned to the caller.

By implementing encryption at this layer, we provide for data to be encrypted after it is compressed by the AFFLIB page system. This is the preferred approach, as data cannot be compressed after it is encrypted.

If a key is set, then pages that are written are automatically encrypted, then written to the data store.

If an unencrypted page is updated and encryption is enabled, the encrypted page is first written, then the unencrypted page is deleted. The delete operation involves overwriting the unencrypted segment with NULLs inside the AFF file. Multiple overwrites are not implemented, as they are not required to preserve data privacy on modern hardware[NIST, 2006].

It is an error to change the affkey encryption key once it has been set.

Encryption Modes and Blocking

Encryption is performed with Cipher Block Chaining mode. The initialization vector is the name of the sector padded with NULLs. Every segment in an AFF file has a different segment name, thus a different IV. (IVs do not need to be kept secret to ensure privacy; the sole purpose of the IV is to assure that different pages with the same data nevertheless have different encryptions.)

Block ciphers such as AES require that all buffers be padded to the block size; with AES the block size is 16 bytes. For performance AFF does not add padding if the page is already a multiple of the block size. If the size of the vector is not a multiple of the AES block size, two values are computed:

$$\textbf{extra} = \textbf{len}(\textit{mod}\,\textbf{blocksize}) \qquad (1)$$

$$\textbf{pad} = 16-\textbf{extra} \qquad (2)$$

The buffer is padded by **pad** bytes; the buffer is now a multiple of the AES block size. The buffer is encrypted. Finally, **extra** pad bytes are appended. Although the buffer is expanded, it is now possible to recover the original length of the buffer when the segment is read and decrypted.

To decrypt the buffer and recover the original length, the values **extra** and **pad** are computed once again. The **extra** pad bytes are removed, the buffer is decrypted, and last **pad** bytes are removed. The length of the resulting buffer is set to be the length of the encrypted buffer minus the AES block size, and the decrypted data buffer is returned. In this way, the length does not need to be explicitly coded. This scheme is the same as the one employed by PKCS #7 ([Laboratories, 1993]; in keeping with PKCS #7, the pad byte is

hex 01 if one pad byte is required, hex 02 02 if two bytes are required, and so on.

The integrity of decrypted page data can be checked by comparing the MD5 of the decrypted page$n$/aes256 segment with the decrypted contents of the page$n$_md5/aes256 segment using the afverify command, or by verifying the AFF signatures if they are present.

Design Limitations

There are a number of limitations that arise from the way that AFFLIB 3 implements encryption. In this section we will briefly discuss the limitations and explain why we think they are inconsequential:

- **AFF Encryption only encrypts the bytestream of segments; the segment name and 32-bit flag are unencrypted.**

AFF encryption is created for the specific purpose of encrypting data and metadata that are acquired from disk images. For this reason, we concluded that there was no reason to attempt to obscure the segment names or 32-bit flags with cryptography, because these do not hold information that needs to be kept confidential.

- **A single AFF file may contain information that is both encrypted and not encrypted.**

Because encryption is performed on a persegment basis, it is possible to have segments that are both encrypted and unencrypted. We see this ability as an advantage, as it allows files that are unencrypted to be encrypted in place without the need to allocate double the disk space. Should the encryption process be interrupted (for example, by a power failure), the process can continue where it left off at some later point.

- **The *affkey* cannot be changed once it is set for a specific file.**

bytes	purpose
0–3	The version number, stored in network byte order.
4–67	The affkey, encrypted with AES in Electronic Codebook (ECB) mode using SHA-256 of the passphrase as the encryption key.
68–131	The SHA-256 of the affkey (for verification purposes).

We believe that the added complexity to support multiple *affkeys* within a single file would not be worth the complexity. In part this is because the key is not intended to be used by the user: it is really just a session key that is used by the passphrase or the public key encryption system. Should the *affkey* be compromised, every segment would need to be reencrypted. The easiest way to do this would be to copy one encrypted AFF file to another file using the afcopy command.

AFF Passphrase Encryption

Most investigators would prefer to work with a simple passphrase than with a 256-bit encryption key that needs to be specially maintained, so AFFLIB 3 provides this ability as well.

AFF Passphrase Encryption builds upon the Base Encryption. When a passphrase is entered AFFLIB uses the SHA256 algorithm to change the passphrase into a 256-bit hash. But instead of using this has as an encryption key directly, the hash is used to encrypt the randomly generated *affkey*. The encrypted session key is then stored in the affkey-aes256 segment.

This scheme could easily be modified to support multiple passphrases on each file, storing them in segments such as affkey-aes256_0, affkey-aes256_1, *etc.*, although there have been no requests for such functionality.

The contents of the affkey_aes256 segment is a 68 byte structure:

With this scheme the passphrase can be changed without requiring the entire disk image to be reencrypted—all that needs to be done is that the affkey-aes256 segment is read, decrypted using the old passphrase, and and re-encrypted with the new passphrase. (If a disk image does need to be re-encryped—for example, if the *affkey* is compromised—this can be easily done by copying the file with the afcopy command from one AFF file to another.)

A further advantage of this scheme is that the passphrase is not cached in memory.

AFF Public Key Encryption

AFF's public key encryption facilities allow a disk image to be encrypted when it is created with a public key; to use the disk image at a later time requires the corresponding private key. This might be useful if an image is to be acquired in the field: once the image is acquired, it would be cryptographically protected so that it could not be deciphered even if the machine (or person) doing the encryption was later intercepted.

In practice, the disk image's public key is specified when the file is created. At this point a random *affkey* is created, encrypted with the public key, and cached in memory. As long as the file remains open it can be read and written. But when the file is closed the in-memory copy of the *affkey* is erased. Thus, once the file is closed, access to the data for either reading or writing requires the corresponding private key.

Public key encryption is implemented by taking the affkey and encrypting it using the OpenSSL "envelope" provisions. This involves creating a random session key and initialization vector, encrypting the affkey with the session key using a block cipher, and then encrypting the session key with the public key that will be used for sealing. The resulting encrypted session key, encrypted affkey, and initialization vector are all stored it in a segment called affkey-evp*n* where *n* starts at 0 and increases. Padding is according to PKCS #1[Laboratories, 2002]. In this manner the same affkey is never encrypted twice with two different RSA public keys.

For encrypting, the public key used for sealing can be specified in one of two ways:

- In a file whose name is provided on the command line, using the "-C" option ("C" for Certificate).
- The filename referenced by the environment variable AFFLIB_ENCRYPTING_ PUBLIC_KEYFILE

For decrypting, the private key used for unsealing can be specified in one of two ways:

- In a file whose name is provided on the command line, using the "-K" option ("K" for Key).
- The environment variable AFFLIB_ DECRYPTING_PRIVATE_KEY.

Although AFFLIB does not currently support the entering of a passphrase to decrypt private keys that protected with a passphrase or for using a smart card or cryptographic token, these capabilities can be added to a future release if requested by users. OpenSSL already has support for these capabilities; all that is required is passing this capability through to the AFFLIB API).

Integrating Encryption with Existing Tools

Specifying a Passphrase as Part of a Filename

AFFLIB understands Uniform Resource Identifier[Berners-Lee et al., 2005] (URI) syntax, and URIs have provisions for specifying passwords. Thus, it is relatively straightforward to integrate passphrase-protected AFF files with existing command-line forensic tools by simply specifying the passphrase as part of the filename.

URIs such as http://www.afflib.org/download/ afflib.tar.gz consists of *scheme* (*e.g.,* http), an *authority* (www.afflib.org), a path (download/ afflib.tar.gz), a query and a fragment (not shown

here). Although the *authority* is typically just a hostname, the full syntax for the authority is:

```
authority = [ userinfo "@" ] host [
":" port]
```

Userinfo was traditionally represented as username:password. Although this syntax is deprecated in the current version of RFC3986, to avoid for the possible leakage of confidential information, we have chosen to use it to provide forensic workers with an easy means of specifying passwords on the command line.

A file can be encrypted using AFF afcopy command like this:

```
$ afcopy myfile.iso
file://:password@/myfile.aff
```

The resulting file can only be accessed if the passphrase is used:

```
$ afcat myfile.aff\verb|wc
afcat: This file has 5 encrypted seg-
ments.
afcat: No unencrypted pages could be
found.
        0        0        0
$ afcat file://:password@/myfile.aff
| wc
 5481881 5980668 63107908
5.4.2  Specifying a passphrase in an
environment variable
```

As an alternative to specifying the passphrase on the command line, AFFLIB 3 allows passphrases to be specified in the AFFLIB_PASSPHRASE environment variable:

```
$ export AFFLIB_PASSPHRASE=password
$ afcat myfile.aff | wc
 5481881 5980668 63107908
$
```

Table 3.

AFF Base Encryption	
af_set_aes_key	Sets the *affkey* that will be used for the currently open AFF file. Returns an error if the key is already set.
af_cannot_decrypt	Returns true if there are encrypted pages present that cannot be decrypted with the currently specified *affkey*.
af_has_encrypted_segments	Returns true if the currently open AFF file has encrypted segments.
af_is_encrypted_segment	Returns true if *segname* is encrypted.
AFF Passphrase Encryption	
af_establish_aes_passphrase	If no key has been set, creates a random *affkey*, encrypts the key with the *passphrase* and stores the segment in the AFF file. Returns an error if a key has already been set.
af_change_aes_passphrase	Changes the passphrase for an AFF file from *oldphrase* to *newphrase*. Returns an error if *oldphrase* is not the correct phrase.
af_use_aes_passphrase	Tests to see if *passphrase* is in fact the correct passphrase for the currently opened AFF file. If it is, the passphrase will be used. An error is returned otherwise.
AFF Public Key Signatures	
af_set_sign_files	Opens the files containing a private key and certificate. The cryptographic information they contain are thereafter used to sign all segments that are updated.
af_sign_seg	Asks AFF to sign a specified segment.
af_sign_all_unsigned_segments	Asks AFF to sign all of the unsigned segments.
af_is_signed_segment	Returns TRUE if there is a signature segment for the segment *segname*.
AFF Public Key Encryption(Sealing)	
af_set_seal_certificates	Creates an *affkey*, encrypts the key with each of the provided X.509 certificates, and stores each encrypted *affkey* in its own segment
af_set_unseal_keybuffer	Specifies a string buffer containing an unencrypted RSA key in PEM format.

Using Encryption with Affuse

Finally, an encrypted image can be mounted using affuse; the decryption is done in the user-level affuse program, so that operating system (and application program) are able to directly process unencrypted, uncompressed data:

```
# affuse file://:password@/myfile.aff
mnt
# ls -l mnt
total 0
-r--r--r-- 1 root root 67108864 Dec
31  1969 myfile.aff.raw
```

Notice that this command must be executed as root. Also note that modification time of the raw file is incorrectly set to the Unix epoch in the current implementation.

SIGNATURE AND ENCRYPTION API

Table 3 describes the API for the AFF encryption layer.

CONCLUSION

This article introduces the provisions for cryptographic security, integrity, and chain-of-custody that have been incorporated in Version 3 of the Advance Forensic Format Library (AFFLIB). These provisions build upon the AFF format introduced by Garfinkel *et. al* in 2006[Garfinkel et al., 2006], allowing transparent access to evidence files that are digital signed or encrypted.

Compared with other approaches and alternatives, AFF Signatures and Encryption offers the following advantages:

- The scheme was simple to implement and test.
- AFFLIB offers real encryption of evidentiary data, not a simple "password" as is present in other systems.
- Raw files can be signed without the need to modify the original data.
- Unencrypted evidence files can be encrypted in-place.

Because of design decisions, AFFLIB encryption does have a few disadvantages. Specifically:

- Segment names and the 32-bit argument stored with AFF segments are digitally signed but they are not encrypted. Since segment names and the 32-bit argument never hold evidentiary data or metadata, this lack of encryption is not considered to be significant.
- Each AFF file is encrypted with its own key; the only way to change the key is to copy the data from one encrypted file to another. However, the passphrase used to encrypt a file can be changed instantly.
- AFFLIB caches the encryption key in memory in the AF structure, allowing the key to be stolen by hostile software. This shortcoming can overcome through the use of trusted operating systems or cryptographic tokens.

Future Work

We continue to make improvements in AFF and aimage. More information about AFF, including the source code for AFFLIB 3, can be found at http://www.afflib.org/.

ACKNOWLEDGMENT

Brian Carrier and Peter Wayner both provided useful feedback on the initial design of the AFF system. Jesse D. Kornblum provided usefulf eedback on the design of the cryptographic layer. Chris Beeson and Bryant Ling at the FBI's Silicon Valley Regional Computer Forensics Laboratory provided useful feedback on the requirements of cryptography for law enforcement. Basis Technology Corp. provided substantial funding for initial work on AFF. Additional funds for AFF development were provided by the Naval Postgraduate School's Research Initiation Program.

The author would also like to thank the anonymous reviewers: your comments were very helpful in improving this manuscript.

AFF and AFFLIB are trademarks of Simson L. Garfinkel and Basis Technology, Inc.

REFERENCES

Adams, C., Cain, P., Pinkas, D., and Zuccherato, R. (2001). Internet x.509 public key infrastructure time-stamp protocol (tsp).

Adams, C. and Lloyd, S. (2002). *Understanding PKI: Concepts, Standards, and Deployment Considerations*. Addison-Wesley Professional, 2 edition.

Amazon (2008). Amazon simple storage service (amazon s3). Amazon Web services. http://aws.amazon.com/s3.

ASR. (2002). Expert witness compression format speciïcation. ASR Data Acquisition and Analysis. http://www.asrdata.com/SMART/whitepaper.html.

Bartel, M., Boyer, J., Fox, B., LaMaccia, B., & Simon, E. (2002). Xml-signature syntax and processing. W3C. http://www.w3.org/TR/xmldsig-core/.

Berners-Lee, T., Fielding, R., and Masinter, L. (2005). RFC 3986: Uniform resource identifier (uri): Generic syntax.

Boneh, D. (2001). Cryptographic hashing. http://crypto.stanford.edu/ dabo/courses/cs255\s\do5(w)inter01/1-hashing.pdf, Course notes for CS255 Winter 01.

Carrier, B. (2006). *A Hypothesis-Based Approach to Digital Forensic Investigations*. PhD thesis, Purdue University.

Computer Systems Laboratory, N. I. o. S. and Technology (1993). FIPS-180 secure hash standard. U.S. Department Of Commerce. Also known as: 58 Fed Reg 27712 (1993).

Dierks, T. and Allen, C. (1999). RFC 2246: The TLS protocol version 1. Status: PROPOSED STANDARD.

Diffie, W., & Hellman, M. E. (1976). New directions in cryptography. *IEEE Transactions on Information Theory*, *IT-22*(6), 644–654. citeseer.ist.psu.edu/diffie76new.html. doi:10.1109/TIT.1976.1055638

Fonseca, B. (2007). Hard-drive changes: Long block data standard gets green light. *Computerworld*. http://www.computerworld.com/action/article.do? command=printArticleBasic&articleId=9018507.

Forensics Source, N. T. I. B. S. (2008). Safeback bit stream backup software. http://www.forensics-intl.com/safeback.html.

Friedl, S. (2005). An illustrated guide to cryptographic hashes. http://www.unixwiz.net/techtips/iguide-crypto-hashes.html.

Garfinkel, S. L. (2008). Afflib. http://www.afflib.org/.

Garfinkel, S. L., Malan, D. J., Dubec, K.-A., Stevens, C. C., & Pham, C. (2006). Disk imaging with the advanced forensic format, library and tools. In *Research Advances in Digital Forensics (Second Annual IFIP WG 11.9 International Conference on Digital Forensics)*. Springer.

GetData Software. (2008). GetData Software Developoment Company. http://www.mountimage.com/.

Haggerty, J., & Taylor, M. (2007). *FORSIGS: Forensic Signature Analysis of the Hard Drive for Multimedia File Fingerprints*, pages 1–12. Springer. http://www.springerlink.com/content/21478kr877478805/.

Harbour, N. (2006). dcfldd. http://dcfldd.sf.net.

Housley, R., & Polk, T. (2001). *Planning for PKI: Best Practices Guide for Deploying Public Key Infrastructure*. Wiley.

ICS. (2008). Secure hash signature generator. Intelligent Computer Solutions. http://www.ics-iq.com.

ITU. (2005). Recommendation x.509 (08/05): The directory: Public-key and attribute certificate frameworks. International Telecommunication Union. http://www.itu.int/rec/T-REC-X.509-200508-I.

Keightley, R. (2003). EnCase version 3.0 manual revision 3.18. Guidance Software. http://www.guidancesoftware.com/.

Kloet, B., Metz, J., Mora, R.-J., Loveall, D., & Schreiber, D. (2008). libewf: Project info. Uitwisselplatform.NL. http://www.uitwisselplatform.nl/projects/libewf/.

Kohnfelder, L. M. (1978). Towards a practical public-key cryptosystem. Undergraduate thesis supervised by L. Adleman.

Laboratories, R. (1993). Pkcs #7: Cryptographic message syntax standard. ftp://ftp.rsasecurity.com/pub/pkcs/ascii/pkcs-7.asc, Version 1.5.

Laboratories, R. (2002). Pkcs #1: v2.1: Rsa cryptography standard. ftp://ftp.rsasecurity.com/pub/pkcs/pkcs-1/pkcs-1v2-1.pdf.

NIST. (2001). Federal information processing standards publication 197: Specification for the advanced encryption standard (aes). National Institute of Standards and Technology. http://csrc.nist.gov/publications/fips/fips197/fips-197.pdf.

NIST. (2006). Guidelines for media sanitization. National Institute of Standards and Technology. http://csrc.nist.gov/publications/nistpubs/800-87/sp800-87-Final.pdf.

NIST. (2007). Announcing the development of new hash algorithm(s) for the revision of the federal information processing standard (fips) 180-2, secure hash standard. National Institute of Standards and Technology, Commerce. http://csrc.nist.gov/groups/ST/hash/documents/FR\s\do5(N)otice\s\do5(J)an07.pdf.

Novak, D. J. (2002). Government's opposition to standby counsel's reply to the government's response to court's order on computer and e-mail evidence. http://notablecases.vaed.uscourts.gov/1:01-cr-00455/docs/68092/0.pdf, UNITED STATES OF AMERICA v. ZACARIAS MOUSSAOUI, Defendant, Criminal No. 01-455-A.

OpenSSL. (2008). Openssl: The open source toolkit for ssl/tls. The OpenSSL Project. http://www.openssl.org.

Rivest, R. (1992). RFC 1321: The MD5 message-digest algorithm. Status: INFORMATIONAL.

Rivest, R. L., Shamir, A., & Adelman, L. M. (1977). *A Method for Obtaining Digital Signatures and Public-Key Cryptosystems*. Technical Report MIT/LCS/TM-82, Massachusetts Institute of Technology. http://citeseer.ist.psu.edu/rivest-78method.html.

Schneier, B. (2004). Opinion: Cryptanalysis of md5 and sha: Time for a new standard. *Computerworld*. http://www.computerworld.com/securitytopics/security/story/0,,95343,00.html.

Szeredi, M. (2008). Filesystem in usespace. http://fuse.sourceforge.net/.

Treasury, U. S. (2008). Ilook investigator. US Department of the Treasury. http://ilook-forensics.org.

US Department of Defense. (2008). Cac: Common access card. US Department of Defnese. http://www.cac.mil.

VMWare. (2008). Run virtual machines on your pc for free. http://www.vmware.com/products/player/.

Wang, X., Feng, D., Lai, X., & Yu, H. (2004). Collisions functions md4, md5, haval-128 and ripemd. In *Report 2004/199*. CRYPTO 2004 Cryptology ePrint Archive. http://eprint.iacr.org/2004/199.pdf, rump session.

Zimmermann, P. R. (1995). *The Official PGP User's Guide*. MIT Press.

ENDNOTES

[1] This article is released by the Naval Postgraduate School, an agency of the U.S. Department of Defense. Please note that within the United States, copyright protection, under Section 105 of the United States Code, Title 17, is not available for any work of the United States Government and/or for any works created by United States Government employees. You acknowledge that this article contains work which was created by an NPS employee and is therefore in the public domain and not subject to copyright. You may use, distribute, or incorporate this article provided that you acknowledges this

via an explicit acknowledgment of NPS-related contributions to your publication. You also agree to acknowledge, via an explicit acknowledgment, that any modifications or alterations have been made to this article before redistribution.

2   A comprehensive list of disk imagers can be found on the Forensics Wiki at http://www.forensicswiki.org/index. php?title=Category:Disk_imaging.

3   Assuming that the signature algorithm itself has not been compromised, of course

4   Five NULL bytes are used so that the data offset for the hash calculation is the same with Signature Mode 1 as it is for Signature Mode 0, which simplifies the implementation.

This work was previously published in International Journal of Digital Crime and Forensics (IJDCF), edited by Chang-Tsun Li & Anthony T.S. Ho, pp. 1-28, copyright 2009 by IGI Publishing (an imprint of IGI Global).

Chapter 2
Voice Over IP:
Privacy and Forensic Implications

Jill Slay
University of South Australia, Australia

Matthew Simon
University of South Australia, Australia

ABSTRACT

With the tremendous growth in popularity and bandwidth of the Internet, VoIP technology has emerged that allows phone calls to be routed over Internet infrastructure rather than the traditional Public Switched Telephone Network (PSTN) infrastructure. The issues faced by law enforcement authorities concerning VoIP are very different from that of traditional telephony. Wiretapping is not applicable to VoIP calls and packet capturing is negated by encryption. This article discusses experimental work carried out to explore methods by which electronic evidence may be collected from systems where VoIP conversations play an important role in suspected criminal activity or communications. It also considers the privacy issues associated with the growing use of VoIP.

INTRODUCTION

Voice over Internet Protocol (VoIP) technology, a growing technology, is set to radically change the way voice data is communicated and thus to revolutionise the Australian and International Telecommunications industry. With the tremendous growth in popularity and bandwidth of the Internet, technology has emerged that allows phone calls to be routed over Internet infrastructure rather than the traditional Public Switched Telephone Network (PSTN) infrastructure. It is currently estimated that there will be more than 24 million VoIP users in the USA by the end of this year, 2008.

This article reports on research designed to provide significant input into the current concern regarding the security and privacy implications of widespread adoption of Voice over Internet

DOI: 10.4018/978-1-60960-515-5.ch002

Protocol (VoIP) for personal and business tele-communications. The aims of the project were to:

- Examine the potential threat to the privacy of telecommunications users' by the capture and reassembly of VoIP packets from a computer or network after a VoIP conversation has taken place and
- Evaluate the potential use of such reassembled packets in forensic computing investigations.

This work is intended to inform policymakers on the legislative issues surrounding privacy, telecommunications interceptions and electronic evidence preservation. It also advises, technically, as to whether this technology should be used in restricted environments, and will drive future technological security control developments.

VoIP and Security

In our previous work (Simon & Slay, 2006; 2007;) we have illustrated how VoIP technology, while still not prominent, is set to radically change the way voice data is communicated, and thus to revolutionise the Australian and International Telecommunications industry. With the growth in popularity and speed of the Internet, this technology is emerging rapidly, allowing phone calls to be sent via Internet infrastructure rather than the traditional Public Switched Telephone Network (PSTN). There are many advantages to using VoIP technology instead of the current PSTN system. The primary benefit is cheaper call costs for local, long distance and international calls. VoIP is also an advantage in terms of regional and remote users since it avoids large-scale roll-out of cable and cuts costs in large organisations with extensive internal phone systems.

Like any new and emerging technology, many potential problems have been raised with regard to security, and thus to privacy. Recently, the Voice over IP Security Alliance (VoIPSA) released a detailed review of threats faced by VoIP technology. The most serious of the threats are denial of service, host and protocol vulnerability exploits, surveillance of calls, hijacking of calls, identity theft of users, eavesdropping and the insertion, deletion and modification of audio streams.

As indicated above, the purpose of our research into VoIP security and forensics was to inform policymakers on the legislative issues surrounding privacy, telecommunications interceptions and electronic evidence preservation and also to advise technically, as to whether this technology should be used in restricted environments, and to drive future technological security control developments, given the security problems identified. The corollary to this issue is that insecure implementations of VoIP may easily provide valuable electronic evidence and this issue needs to be made known to law enforcement.

VoIP is still a developing technology and the social and legal issues surrounding VoIP are still being realised. In his work, Jones (2005) identifies a range of social and technical research questions which focus on the potential breach of privacy of VoIP communications through the capture of VoIP packets and logs by diverse technological means. In our own work (Simon & Slay 2006) we have identified the existence of VoIP packets in a computer's memory after a VoIP call has taken place. Thus we see an urgent need to be able to identify how much of a conversation might remain in memory and be accessible to a targeted hacking attack, thus breaching privacy. There is an equal interest in determining the extent to which any remnant packets might be reconstituted to provide electronic evidence for intelligence gathering or for forensic investigation.

We have found little other published research in this area of IT Security / Forensic Computing. Neumann, Tillwick, & Olivier (2006) explore the information exchanged in VoIP call control messages and the implications this has on personal privacy. Chen Wang & Jajodia (2006) examine the privacy and security aspects of peer-to-peer

(P2P) VoIP calls and show how the use of VoIP has substantially shifted the previous balance between privacy and security that exists in traditional PSTN calls. These researchers and others though focus on networks and protocols to explore VoIP phenomena.

VoIP and Crime

The popularity of VoIP is increasing as the cost savings and ease of use is realised by a wide range of individual users and corporations. The technology is attractive to criminals, especially the non-carrier VoIP, as it often does not require verification of any details to commence using the service. The security of placing such calls may also be appealing to criminals, as many implementations use strong encryption to secure both the voice payload as well as control messages. Skype uses 256 bit AES encryption while Google Talk does not encrypt its payload (but will support encryption in the future).

The following hypothetical situation illustrates the ease of which this technology can be used in criminal activity:

An organised crime ring operates within Australia, distributing illicit drugs throughout the country. The operators of the crime ring decide that by using Skype software they can anonymously communicate when necessary. From a criminal perspective, there are several disadvantages of using the traditional PSTN telephone system. There is the possibility that a law enforcement body could wiretap the connection should they become suspicious, all calls made and received are logged by the service provider, and using a PSTN phone fixes someone to a given location (i.e. the physical location of the phone). As an alternative solution, criminals can use laptops running Skype, create profiles in the same way as a regular user and communicate when necessary. If law enforcement should investigate, there is no line to wire tap, no call logs and no ability to tie

a person to a specific geographic location. The criminals using Skype can also be contacted or make contact from different locations, providing flexibility.

Although this particular situation is only hypothetical, it is possible. The smallest through to the largest criminal organisations, including international terrorists, could potentially communicate using VoIP, as it incorporates the flexibility of email, the richness of voice and the safety of a decentralised system using strong encryption algorithms.

FORENSIC COMPUTING AND VoIP

Forensic Computing is an extremely important cross-disciplinary research domain based on computer science and drawing on telecommunications and network engineering, law, justice studies, and social science. Research within the discipline must be performed vigilantly in order to keep the field current. Neither the pace of technological development nor the presence of criminal activities within our society will cease or taper. There is a continual need to extend forensic computing theory, tools and knowledge by conducting high quality research in relevant aspects of the field.

Since Voice over Internet Protocol (VoIP) is a relatively new digital technology, the implications for forensic computing are still in need of investigation. Criminals and criminal organisations can exploit the strengths of this technology because it allows a degree of anonymity and security superior to that of traditional telecommunications. The long-standing technique of wiretapping a physical telephone line to eavesdrop on a conversation is a concept that is not applicable to VoIP communications. Alternative methods for obtaining evidence are required to help fill the void that has been created by the switch from traditional telephony to VoIP.

Forensic computing encompasses multiple sources of electronic data that could possibly contain evidence. The volatile memory of a computer, called Random Access Memory (RAM), is a source of data not often exploited by forensic investigators in the search for evidence. Issues with obtaining the data in memory are one of several reasons for this. The practice of examining data within the memory of a target machine is called memory forensics.

Situations often arise in forensic computing investigations that require special procedures or tools because a particular technology or situation encountered. Forensic computing research requires constant investigation into new devices and technologies, as well as new methods and procedures for existing technologies. This will equip law enforcement bodies and other forensic investigators with the knowledge and abilities to allow thorough and safe investigation of digital devices. This article thus presents research into the viability of using newly created software methods of obtaining evidence from live computer memory for forensic purposes, after a VoIP call has been made.

Volatile and Memory Forensics

Live forensics and memory forensics are relatively unexplored areas of forensic computing. Live forensics involves examining a system while it is in a live state to determine information that is not available once it has been shutdown. Toolsets such as Helix serve this purpose. Helix is designed specifically to not modify any non-volatile data and its use is considered forensically sound. Helix includes a variety of tools for recovering passwords, detecting rootkits and viewing system setup as well as many other functions. Memory forensics is a little used technique that focuses on retrieving and finding information in memory images. Acquiring the memory image of a live system can be considered an activity of live forensics. There are numerous reasons for the lack of

use of this technique but it is chiefly because the process of imaging the memory is not verifiable when performed by software. Verification of the image is not possible as the state of the memory is constantly being modified by the operating system. If the process is repeated, the image will be different thus resulting in a different hash value. There has been minimal investigation into tools and processes for sound memory dumping techniques in relation to forensic computing (Jones, K, Bejtlich & Rose, 2006).

The volatile memory of a system potentially contains large amounts of information about the system including (but not limited to) open files, active processes, terminated processes and device drivers. Volatile memory as a source of data is lost when the power to the target system is switched off. This usually occurs in the course of securing the non-volatile data sources. Situations occur in forensic investigations where a target system cannot be turned off. Servers are a prime example of such systems, as the downtime generally leads to loss of revenue or essential services. Imaging the memory of a target machine allows evidence to be collected with little disruption to normal services. Imaging memory in general investigations allows an extra source of data from which evidence can be gathered. The primary disadvantage of taking such actions is the increased risk to the other data stores on the system, like the hard disk. It is possible that malware or a 'time bomb' could exist on the system that could delete data at a certain time or after a certain action. Sufficiently skilled persons could tamper with the operating system kernel to change the output of forensic tools in a deliberate attempt to destroy an impending investigation (Kruse II & Heiser, 2002).

Imaging memory for forensic purposes is gaining recognition as an area in need of further research. Burdach (2005a, 2006) has published a number of articles on techniques for finding evidence in both Windows and Linux memory images.

Dumping the memory from a system requires some method of interfacing with the data. Linux systems contain a memory device similar to logical devices representing hard disks. Memory can be imaged by copying the data from this memory device (Burdach, 2005a). Microsoft Windows XP does not have an equivalent memory device and must use a section object to gain access to the memory. The physical memory of a system can be imaged in two different ways under *Microsoft Windows XP*; one of these methods is hardware based and the other software based. The hardware method is the most reliable and verifiable but is not a practical solution for forensic investigation needs. It requires the use of a special purpose PCI card that must be installed into the machine prior to it being switched on. This requirement renders this method ineffective for forensic investigations (Carrier & Grand, 2004). Another hardware method exists and requires that the target system have a Firewire/IEEE port. This method has been shown to be highly effective but does not work on *Microsoft Windows* machines. The software-based solution, while not ideal, is the only practical solution for acquiring a memory image from a target computer at the scene of a crime. *Microsoft Windows XP* does not have a memory device object so the physical memory of the machine needs to be accessed through a section object. The section object maps to pages in memory allowing access by processes that do not own the memory page.

RESEARCH METHODOLOGY

In our research, several techniques were used in the process of recovering VoIP evidence. Our scenario is 'after the event forensics' where we imagine that a suspect's computer has been used to make VoIP calls and has not been powered off after the conversation.

Experimental Setup: Win XP – Win XP

Brief

VoIP calls were made between two Windows XP machines to test the amount of evidence that could be recovered from the memory of each after the calls have taken place. Both machines had the memory imaged and searched using software developed for the task.

Experimental Process

The first step in the process is to acquire the memory image from the target system. The subsequent steps involve finding packets within the image, identifying the type of packets, extracting the payload from RTP packets and recreating audio files by reconstituting consecutive packet payloads into one file. Each step in this process requires a practical solution and consequently both existing and new solutions have been either used or devised.

The technique of imaging memory uses an existing tool created for acquiring memory images under Microsoft Windows XP. The algorithm for finding packets in a binary image is a newly devised method created to address this specific problem. Details of the algorithm, and the process used to recover evidence from the memory image of a target machine are currently not open for disclosure.

However the software tool, implemented in Java, performs the following tasks:

- Searches for packets in the specified binary image
- Sorts and orders the packets
- Outputs individual packets to disk sorted into a UDP or TCP folder
- Outputs a summary for both TCP and UDP packets.

• Gathers packets and outputs audio files to disk.

Details of the VoIP protocol formats (e.g. fields that are present in the protocol structure) are important in understanding how the identification and reconstruction of packets is possible and some discussion of this is presented here.

Session Initiation Protocol

SIP is a signalling protocol that is used for signalling between SIP nodes. VoIP implementations often use SIP as a means of setting up and tearing down calls. SIP is not responsible for carrying any audio payload as this is performed by another protocol such as RTP. A number of SIP message types are used for communication between SIP nodes (note that communication is always routed via the server). The format of a SIP address is similar to an email addresses in that it is in the format of *username@host*. The string 'sip:' is appended to the beginning to indicate it as a SIP address rather than an email address. The *username* is the user's extension that is in the same format as an email address username (i.e. a combination of number, letter and the hyphen character). The host can be either a URL or IP address and indicates the location of the SIP proxy.

There are two types of SIP messages, requests and responses. Request messages are generated by a SIP client and responses are generated by a SIP proxy in response to a request message. SIP is a flexible protocol and as a result the full implementation is quite complex. Two important fields in the header are the 'to' and 'from' fields. These fields contain the SIP address of the endpoint that is sending the message and the SIP address of intended recipient. The 'to' and 'from' fields can also contain other information such as the user's display name. Additional information in the header fields is dependant on the VoIP implementation.

Real-Time Transport Protocol

RTP is a highly flexible protocol that is used to carry delay sensitive payloads over the Internet. RTP is often used in VoIP implementations to carry audio payload and is an Internet standardised protocol as described in RFC 3550. RTP packets are transported within UDP packets, which is typical of protocols that carry delay-sensitive data (if the packet is delayed for too long then retransmission is of no use). The RTP protocol contains several fields that allow the payload of each packet to be reconstituted back into its original form. The Synchronous Source Identifier (SSRC) is a 32-bit number that is distinct for each conversation stream. Note that one conversation between two SIP endpoints consists of four different conversation streams and four unique SSRC (each endpoint has a distinct incoming and an outgoing stream). The Sequence Number field is 16 bits in length and increments by one for every distinct RTP packet sent. The starting value of the sequence number is chosen randomly and is different for each conversation stream (each unique SSRC). The timestamp field increases in each packet relative to the amount of time that the payload in the packet covers. It is similar to the sequence number and will usually increment at a constant rate relative to the sequence number, especially with voice calls. The starting value for the timestamp is chosen randomly.

Software

• *Trixbox/Asterix*: Asterisk is a free open source VoIP Private Branch Exchange (PBX). Trixbox is a collection of applications that creates a VoIP server when installed on an X86-based machine. Trixbox includes Asterisk, RedHat Linux and a variety of other tools for administrating the VoIP server implementation.
• *Counterpath X-Lite*: A free SIP software phone application.

Figure 1. Network setup for experiments

- ***Ethereal packet sniffer*:** Collects and stores packets received by the NIC. Ethereal is also a protocol analyser, having the ability to display higher-level information about the packets collected, e.g. a HTTP stream.

Experiment Specifics

The setup of the machines on the network is shown in Figure 1. The VoIP server, the packet sniffer, Machine A and Machine B were all connected to each other via the hub. The hub was up-linked to a network switch that allowed the machines on the hub to be connected to the wider network and the Internet. The packet sniffer machine was used to collect all packets that were sent via the network hub for later comparison to any recovered packets. The packet capturing session was started as the VoIP endpoint machines were turned on and was stopped once the memory imaging process had been completed. The conversation between the two SIP extensions consisted of an audio track being played into the microphone of the headset connected to the PC via USB. The tracks were different so as to distinguish the difference if recovery of packets was achieved. The tracks that were played were:

- Machine A: Mozart's Violin Concerto No. 5, A-major.

- Machine B: Martin Luther King's famous speech "I have a dream".

Experiment One: Control

Both machines were turned off and then back on again to clear contents of the main memory. On each machine, Xlite was launched and was not be allowed to connect to the TrixBox Asterisk server (no network connection was available). Memory was imaged and searched.

Experiment Two: Connection

This stage was carried out in two steps, once for each machine. Both steps were carried out individually of the other. Both machines were turned off and then back on again to clear contents of the main memory. On both machines, Xlite was started and allowed to connect to the TrixBox Asterisk server. Memory was imaged and searched.

Experiment Three: Call and Hang Up

Both machines were turned off and then back on again to clear contents of the main memory. XLite on both machines was then started and allowed to connect to the VoIP server. A call was placed from Machine B to Machine A. Machine B hung up after a period of 10 seconds, Machine A would not answer. Memory was imaged and searched.

Experiment Four: Call and Get Voicemail

Both machines were turned off and then back on again to clear contents of the main memory. XLite on both machines was then started and allowed to connect to the VoIP server. Machine B initiated a call to Machine A, who would not answer. After a 'ring-out' period, the call was diverted voicemail. Machine B left a 15-second message and subsequently terminated the call. Memory was imaged and searched.

Experiment Five: 1 Minute Call

Both machines were turned off and then back on again to clear contents of the main memory. XLite on both machines was then started and allowed to connect to the VoIP server. Machine A initiated a call to Machine B who accepted the incoming call. Each caller communicated with respective audio track for a period of one minute. Memory was imaged and searched.

Experiment Six: 3 Minute Call

Both machines were turned off and then back on again to clear contents of the main memory. XLite on both machines was then started and allowed to connect to the VoIP server. Machine A initiated a call to Machine B who accepted the incoming call. Each caller communicated with respective audio track for a period of **three** minutes. Memory was imaged and searched.

Experiment Seven: 5 Minute Call

Both machines were turned off and then back on again to clear contents of the main memory. XLite on both machines was then started and allowed to connect to the VoIP server. Machine A initiated a call to Machine B who accepted the incoming call. Each caller communicated with respective audio track for a period of **five** minutes. Memory was imaged and searched.

Experiment Eight: 10 Minute Call

Both machines were turned off and then back on again to clear contents of the main memory. XLite on both machines was then started and allowed to connect to the VoIP server. Machine A initiated a call to Machine B who accepted the incoming call. Each caller communicated with respective audio track for a period of **ten** minutes. Memory was imaged and searched.

Experiment Nine: 15 Minute Call

Both machines were turned off and then back on again to clear contents of the main memory. XLite on both machines was then started and allowed to connect to the VoIP server. Machine A initiated a call to Machine B who accepted the incoming call. Each caller communicated with respective audio track for a period of **fifteen** minutes. Memory was imaged and searched.

RESULTS

The quantitative nature of this research allows statistics to be calculated from the collected data that can then be used to establish and support an answer to the research question. The statistics here are generated by comparing the number and type of packets found in the memory image against the packets collected using Ethereal packet capturer. Capturing of the packets also allows confirmation of results by the ability to verify each packet recovered and ensures that random junk data is not being collected.

Table 1 is an overview of all packets that were recovered from the SIP endpoints after the experiments were conducted.

The results of the experiment reveal some consistent trends in the data. The main elements of interest are the number of SIP and RTP packets recovered compared to the number sent and the likelihood of obtaining useful information out of the recovered packets. Reconstitution of audio data from recovered RTP packets has been a major focus of the research but may be less useful than that of other data recovered from the system. This research has shown that packet data does remain in memory for some period after completion of a call. The ideal outcome is to prove, with some certainty, that a call took place and between whom. The recovery of enough audio data to gain some knowledge of the context of the call is also a desired outcome.

Table 1. Packet recovery overview

Experiment Number	UDP Packets Recovered		TCP Packets Recovered		Total packet Recovered	
	Machine A	Machine B	Machine A	Machine B	Machine A	Machine B
1	0	0	0	0	0	0
2	71	19	197	0	268	19
3	96	586	125	30	221	616
4	83	196	120	0	203	196
5	276	199	0	0	276	199
6	279	198	0	0	279	198
7	278	198	0	0	278	198
8	272	191	2	0	274	191
9	266	190	19	0	285	190

The number of packets recovered after completion of each call is consistent and shows no relation to the number of packets sent during the call., Table 2 shows the minimum, maximum and average values of the recovered packets (not distinguishing the type of packet). It does not take into account the control experiment. The average number of packets recovered from Machine A and Machine B (with outliers removed) is 260.5 and 170.14 respectively. This tends to indicate that the memory space contains about the same amount of remnant packets regardless of the amount of packets actually being sent and received.

It should be noted at this point that the actual number of packets recovered in memory was considerably higher than the above statistics. Many of the packets recovered were identical and therefore only distinct packets were counted and used for reconstitution of audio. The decision only to use distinct packets was made as the copied packets do not add any extra value to the analysis

and were not part of the original traffic sent (i.e. these packets were not sent multiple times).

The rate at which packets can be recovered stays consistent, so it follows that the number of recovered RTP packets would also remain consistent. Figure 2 plots the number of recovered RTP packets compared to the number sent (from experiment four to eight). The number of recovered packets does not vary greatly, even when the

Figure 2. The relationship between the number of packets sent and recovered

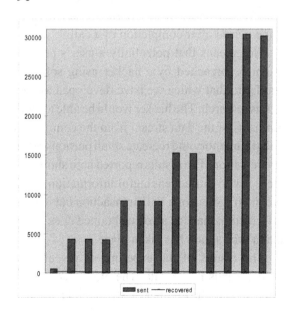

Table 2. Minimum, maximum and average

	Machine A	Machine B	Machine B (no outlier)
Max	285	616	199
Min	203	19	19
Average	260.5	225.875	170.1428571

number of packets sent is approximately forty five thousand.

The recovery of SIP packets is consistent with the trend of overall packet recovery seen in the experimentation results. The majority of SIP packets are sent before and at the beginning of a call; i.e. when the SIP phone logs in to the VoIP server and the initiation of a call. In the calls where RTP packets were sent between machines, the recovery of SIP packets was less.

Another trend apparent in the data is the consistent difference in both the memory imaging process and the RTP streams recovered from both machines. The memory imaging process performed on Machine A encounters less errors than on Machine B. The RTP streams that are recovered from both machines are consistently different. Machine A always recovers a portion of both the incoming and the outgoing RTP streams while Machine B only every recovers part of the incoming stream. The reason for this is, again, not certain but is likely attributed to the difference in software versions of the SIP phones.

Discussion

This research has shown that, in a Windows XP environment and under our experimental conditions, packet data does remain in memory for some period after completion of a call.

This means that potentially a user's privacy might be breached by a hacker using software similar to that which we have developed as part of this research. The hacker would be able to copy remnants of the data stream from the computer's volatile memory and recreate small portions of the conversation. The results reported here show that there is very little meaningful information in a 2 second fragment of a VoIP transaction but log file information that can also be obtained does prove that a transaction has taken place.

The results of the experiments reveal consistent trends in the data. The main elements of interest were the number of SIP and RTP packets recovered compared to the number sent and the likelihood of obtaining useful information out of the recovered packets.

The recovery of enough audio data to gain some knowledge of the context of the call was also a desired outcome of this research. The number of packets recovered after completion of each call was consistent and shows no relation to the number of packets sent during the call. Generalising, the number of RTP packets captured and able to be reconstituted was of the order of 200 to 250. Sometimes these were contiguous and, with longer calls, they were in shorter non-contiguous chunks. We assume therefore that the packets are being written to a memory buffer of discrete size, regardless of the length of the call and this only a finite number will be captured. The shorter the call the more likely the packets are to be contiguous and thus be reconstituted as a more meaningful audio file.

Reconstitution of audio data from recovered RTP packets was a major focus of the research and we were able to reconstitute very brief audio streams from packets captured out of memory, sorted and exported to an audio file format. We could hear very brief snatches of audio but nothing recognisable as part of a tune (we played music, as stated, in our VoIP calls).

The corollary to the privacy issue raised above thus is that, for forensic computing investigators, the same software may be utilised to prove, with some certainty, that a call took place and between what parties but we are not able to collect any meaningful data (under these narrow and limited experimental conditions). Log file evidence in this case would be another form of secondary evidence to be presented to a court.

Given the experimental results reported here, we cannot state with any certainty that we have proved any need to protect the privacy of VoIP calls. It is possible to extend the software developed in this project as a tool for users to mitigate against the threat of a hacker who was able to breach their physical and logical security and extract remnant VoIP packets from the Windows-based memory space. This software could be adapted to remove any remnant packets from the memory space on the termination of a VoIP call. While this is technically feasible, the risk of meaningful conversation being extracted by a hacker has shown to be extremely low in this research, and therefore the costs and benefits to the user of the development of this kind of software would need to be carefully examined.

The experimentation conducted in this research is a small section of a large domain. Additional research is required to improve the confidence of the conclusions drawn from the results of the experimentation. Repeating the experiments already performed should be the first process. This would rule out the occurrence of random errors and help confirm the trends that are apparent in the data. Other situations need to be tested, such as varying the length of time between termination of the call and imaging of the memory. This should also be conducted a number of times to increase the accuracy of the results. A foreseeable problem with this course of experimentation is that it is difficult to control the actions of the operating system, which introduces another element of randomness.

Using different SIP clients should also be explored. It is unclear exactly how much influence the VoIP application has on the amount of remnant packets, and how much is reliant on the operating system. It is likely that the SIP client will have little impact on the number of packets that are recovered. The algorithm used to find packets searches for Ethernet packets. The SIP phone process should receive SIP and RTP packets; the higher-level protocols, such as UDP and Ethernet, are added by the operating system.

The time required to conduct all of the above experimentation may be restrictive. Nine experiments have been conducted and should be repeated at least once to increase confidence in the results. Repeating the experiments with varying delays before imaging the memory may be a highly time-consuming process as intervals

up to 24 – 48 hours should be used. Repeating these experiments and then all of the above with alternate SIP clients would be a highly involved and time-consuming task.

The ability to perform this process on other operating systems is required so that the process is as comprehensive as possible. The assumptions about the configuration of Microsoft Windows XP (e.g. non-PAE) also need to be ruled out. This should not pose a great problem, as the structure of packets remains the same across all operating systems. The method of imaging the memory will differ between operating systems and any processing that relies on memory structures will require vastly different methods and detailed knowledge of such structures.

The exploration into other signalling and transport protocols is an important future direction for this research. Many VoIP implementations do not use the SIP and RTP protocols such as Google Talk and Skype. Adapting to other protocols in some cases should be trivial and almost impossible in others. Google Talk uses the open protocol called Jabber and currently does not implement encryption. Alternatively, Skype uses a proprietary protocol that incorporates heavy encryption.

The use of encryption ties closely to the protocol used. Both SIP and RTP can easily be encrypted (RTP needs to be substituted with SRTP). The limitation in this situation is that packet data is unlikely to hold the unencrypted version of an encrypted payload, as the payload is encrypted before being inserted into a packet, or decrypted after being read from the packet. The unencrypted payload may exist in the memory space but will not be found using the method presented in this research. This research would play a key role in this situation if the encryption key to decrypt the encrypted packets was found.

Other sources of memory exist on Microsoft Windows XP and other operating systems. The page file (also commonly called virtual memory) is a system file on the hard disk that stores pages of memory that are in low demand or not currently being used by the operating system. Although it would seem unlikely that packet data would be stored in the page file, the possibility should be explored.

The Hibernation file is another location that may also hold remnant packet data. The hibernation file is a system file that is used to store the contents of the main memory. Hibernation is used to decrease the start-up time of an operating system by transferring the contents of memory to disk when the machine shuts down. When the machine reboots, the memory is loaded into RAM from the hibernation file. The machine is restored back to the same state as when hibernated. The issues of searching the hibernation file are not as substantial as that of searching the main memory. The previous hibernation file exists on the hard drive when the computer is running, so this can be applied whether the computer is initially found live or in a hibernated state. It is likely that the hibernation file would contain more remnant packets than that of the page file, as the hibernation file is an exact copy of the system memory.

ACKNOWLEDGMENT

Our thanks to the Department of Communications, IT and the Arts who funded part of this work with a Telecommunications Research Grant.

REFERENCES

Ahuja, S. R., & Ensor, R. (2004). VoIP: What is it Good for? *Queue*, *2*(6), 48–55. doi:10.1145/1028893.1028897

Beckett, J. (2005). Forensic Computing: Experts, Certification and the Categorisation of Roles. Paper presented at the Colloquium for Information Systems Security Education - Asia Pacific, Adelaide, Australia.

Bellovin, S. M., Blaze, M., & Landau, S. (2005). The real national-security needs for VoIP'. *Communications of the ACM*, *48*(11), 120. doi:10.1145/1096000.1096030

Broucek, V., & Turner, P. (2001). Forensic Computing: Developing a Conceptual Approach for an Emerging Academic Discipline. Paper presented at the 5th Australian Security Research Symposium, Perth, Australia.

Broucek, V., & Turner, P. (2002). Bridging the Divide: Rising Awareness of Forensic Issues amongst Systems Administrators. Paper presented at the 3rd International System Administration and Networking Conference, Maastricht, The Netherlands, 27-31 May.

Burdach, M. (2005a). Digital Forensics of the Physical Memory. Retrieved March 2006 from <http://www.forensicfocus.com/digital-forensics-of-physical-memory>.

Burdach, M. (2005b). An Introduction to Windows memory forensic. Retrieved 10 May 2006 from <http://forensic.seccure.net/pdf/introduction_to_windows_memory_forensic.pdf>.

Cherry, S. (2005). Seven myths about voice over IP. *IEEE Spectrum*, *42*(3), 52–57. doi:10.1109/MSPEC.2005.1402719

Davidson, J., & Peters, J. (2000). *Voice over IP Fundamentals*. USA: Cisco Systems.

Jones, A. (2005). The future implications of computer forensics on VoIP. *Digital Investigation*, *2*, 206–208. doi:10.1016/j.diin.2005.07.007

Jones, K., Bejtlich, R., & Rose, C. W. (2006). *Real Digital Forensics*. New York: Addison Wesley.

Kruse, W. G. II, & Heiser, J. G. (2002). *Computer Forensics: Incident Response Essentials. New York*. Addison-Wesley.

Kuhn, D.R., Walsh, T.J., & Fries, S. (2005). *Security Considerations for Voice over IP Systems.* Gaithersburg: National Institute of Standards and Technology.

Marcella, A. J., & Greenfield, R. S. (2002). *Cyber Forensics: A Field Manual for Collecting, Examining, and Preserving Evidence of Computer Crimes.* New York: Auerbach. doi:10.1201/9781420000115

McKemmish, R. (1999). *What is Forensic Computing?* Canberra: Australian Institute of Criminology.

Patel, A., & Ó Ciardhuáin, S. (2000). The Impact Of Forensic Computing On Telecommunications. *IEEE Communications*, 38(11), 64–67.

Sicker, D. C., & Lookabaugh, T. (2004). VoIP Security: Not an Afterthought. *Queue*, *2*(6), 56–64. doi:10.1145/1028893.1028898

Simon, M., & Slay, J. (2006). Voice over IP: Forensic Computing Implications. Paper presented at 4th Australian Digital Forensics Conference, Edith Cowan University, Perth, Australia.

Simon, M., & Slay, J. (2008). Voice over IP Forensics. Paper presented at E-Forensics, Adelaide University, January 21, 2008.

This work was previously published in International Journal of Digital Crime and Forensics (IJDCF), edited by Chang-Tsun Li & Anthony T.S. Ho, pp. 89-101, copyright 2009 by IGI Publishing (an imprint of IGI Global).

Chapter 3
Volatile Memory Collection and Analysis for Windows Mission–Critical Computer Systems

Antonio Savoldi
University of Brescia, Italy

Paolo Gubian
University of Brescia, Italy

ABSTRACT

Most enterprises rely on the continuity of service guaranteed by means of a computer system infra-structure, which can often be based on the Windows operating system family. For such a category of systems, which might be referred to as mission-critical for the relevance of the service supplied, it is indeed fundamental to be able to define which approach could be better to apply when a digital investi-gation needs to be performed. This is the very goal of this paper: the definition of a forensically sound methodology which can be used to collect the full state of the machine being investigated by avoiding service interruptions. It will be pointed out why the entire volatile memory dump, with the necessary extension which is nowadays missing, is required with the purpose of being able to gather much more evidential data, by illustrating also, at the same time, the limitation and disadvantages of current state of-the-art approaches in performing the collection phase.

INTRODUCTION

We are currently living in the era of information technology which relies heavily on complex com-puter network infrastructures, with a multitude of

DOI: 10.4018/978-1-60960-515-5.ch003

services which need to be issued continuously without interruptions. For the sake of clarity, we might define such a category of computer as mission critical, by pointing out that they need to provide continuity of service over a period of time, as can be seen in the case of Web or Email servers. For this specific category of computer systems, when a digital investigation will be performed, a live forensic methodology will be needed. This might be obtained by applying a suitable set of techniques which can be helpful in creating a sufficiently detailed representation of the state of the system being observed. For such a purpose, we need to adopt the set of methods and best practices pertaining to the volatile memory forensic discipline. Although it can be considered still in an infancy stage if compared with other branches of digital forensics, this discipline might provide the means of analysis which fit the need of mission critical digital investigations. The ultimate goal for this applied field of the digital forensic science is to collect evidential data from the contents of a computer's volatile memory, by stating which processes were running, when they were started and by whom, what specific activities those processes were doing and the state of active network connections. As a consequence, system memory could provide a great deal of information about the system's runtime state at the time an incident happened. Moreover, it is interesting to point out that state-of-the-art attack techniques have shown a trend towards memory-only modification whenever possible. Thus, traditional post-mortem approaches may fail to find out the existence of intruders (Petroni, Walters, Fraser, & Arbaugh, 2006; Schatz, 2007). One of the main concerns in the volatile memory collection phase, a mandatory step which needs to be performed before the analysis for gathering evidential data, is what should be collected from the system in order to have a detailed view of the inner state of the system. Beside the well known techniques for acquiring the RAM content (Schatz, 2007; Garner, 2008), new approaches are being used for collecting also the page file of a Windows OS based system (Lee, Savoldi, Lee, & Lim, 2007a; Lee, Savoldi, Lee, & Lim, 2007b), which is worthy to be mentioned as an important component of the virtual memory system, containing plentiful of potential evidential data. Once the main memory and the page file have been collected, the analysis part

has to be performed. This phase might be carried out both with string matching and virtual memory space reconstruction. For instance, the system being investigated has two encrypted partitions, which can be accessed by means of TrueCrypt tool (Czeskis, Hilaire, Koscher, Gribble, Kohno, & Schneier, 2008). By seizing and analyzing the page file a couple of passwords are found. These pieces of data are confirmed to be digital evidence being able to guarantee the access to the encrypted partitions, as a result of the direct use of them. A further example may involve the analysis of a set of pedo-pornographic images found in the collected page file. Could these pieces of data be considered as strong, effective evidence capable of incriminating the computer's owner? As a matter of fact, these data could come from a malware which might have downloaded such illegal material in the computer's memory. Besides, we must to prove this fact by correlating that page file area, where the images were found, with the related memory process or at least with some other comparable piece of data, which could come from another memory device. As a result, a piece of data within the page file need to be evaluated and verified according to the context and the ability to verify it by external means.

The remaining part of the article has been organized as follows. Initially, the necessary state-of-the-art related to the collection of the volatile memory will be presented discussing also, at the same time, the advantages and disadvantages of such approaches. Therefore, some consideration about the blurriness of the volatile memory, when collected, will be discussed, by illustrating a promising method to reduce the uncertainty in the volatile collection phase. After that, a detailed analysis about how to collect the page file will be outlined, presenting also a tool which can deal with such a task. Hence, a technique for virtual memory process reconstruction will be sketched by pointing out how a page file can be effectively analyzed and used within a digital investigation.

RELATED WORKS

Volatile memory forensics, which can be referred to as a new branch of the classical digital forensic discipline, aims at collecting and analyzing the whole memory content of a running computer. The relevance of this new research field is essentially dictated by the effectiveness of a new breed of malware, also referred to as *kernel level rootkit*, which may reside only in the memory of the system without leaving any traces of their presence. So far, such rootkits might be purely or not-purely memory resident. The latter case implies that the malware can load modules directly from the file system into the kernel space, which produces tangible traces of its presence. Similarly, *user mode rootkit* may or may not be purely memory resident. In addition, the volatile memory content can be effectively used for recovering cryptographic keys and passwords related to applications such as TrueCrypt (Czeskis, Hilaire, Koscher, Gribble, Kohno, & Schneier, 2008), which are used more and more for data protection and illicit activities. The generation of a memory snapshot can be obtained in different ways, both software and hardware, which differ in terms of fidelity, atomicity and integrity. As well pointed out in (Schatz, 2007), fidelity implies the ability to collect the real, bit-by-bit content of the RAM memory being collected. In fact, hardware based approaches promise precise fidelity through the use of an external and trusted hardware channel, and exclusive access to the memory of the host. Conversely, software approaches cannot guarantee the same level of fidelity because of the modification caused by the process running in the memory being collected. Moreover, the snapshot of memory should be acquired by means of an atomic operation, which implies the collection of the whole observable memory without altering it. Unfortunately, this result can only be obtained by observing the system from outside, thus not having the side effect of the Locard's exchange principle (Chisum, & Turvey, 2000),

which states the modification of a system being observed when a reading process runs within the same system. As a consequence, all the software approaches for volatile memory collection are capable of producing a blurred snapshot which is not attributable to a specific point in time. Hardware methods, on the other hand, provide atomic snapshots by turning off all CPUs for the period of acquisition. The third important feature related to a memory image is integrity. While hardware approaches act in a way that the system can be stopped thus permitting an integral and unchanged copy of the memory content, software methods rely on special features of the operating system which create several changes as a direct result of the imaging processes action. In addition, more research should be done to quantify the level of inconsistency as a result of the software imaging approach. As already stated, different and numerous systems for collecting the RAM memory have been provided. Ideally, the full and complete state of the machine being observed is desired, which includes the CPU, virtual memory and the hard disks. As a matter of fact, such ideal scenario can be obtained only with the virtualization technology, such as that provided by VMWare (Adams, & Algesen, 2006), where the requirements about the memory snapshots, in terms of fidelity, atomicity and integrity, are fully met. Many variants of UNIX and Windows provide a special device, */dev/mem* for LINUX and \\.*PhysicalMemory*\ on Windows 2000 and XP (Russinovich, & Solomon, 2004), for dumping the entire physical memory. When a system is rightly configured ahead in time, it might provide crash dumps containing the whole RAM memory which can be subsequently analyzed within a debugger. Unfortunately, this kind of approach provides hooks which might be used by the kernel rootkit for subversive purposes, thus compromising the integrity of the snapshot. Another important category of acquisition methods is represented by the software approaches which rely, as already pointed out, on specific features of the operating system for directly accessing the whole system memory. The RAM memory is viewed as a device file and can be accessed from user space mode, using the above mentioned hooks, at least for non 64-bit versions of Windows 2000 and XP, whereas for newer versions of Windows a special driver acting at the kernel level is required. The most popular method belonging to this category, for the Windows platform, is the dd tool (Garner, 2008). Certainly, it suffers from the well-known Locard's exchange principle, by not being able to provide fidelity, atomicity nor integrity for the resulting image. Indeed, the resulting snapshot will be "blurred", not being obtained from a halted CPU. Moreover, it cannot be related to a precise temporal instant the reading process of the entire memory being not atomic. As a result, there will be a leakage of integrity. It is worthy to mention that this technique depends on the target operating system and thus it is subject to kernel rootkit subversion. Hardware approaches targeted at dumping the main memory rely on the use of Direct Memory Access (DMA) via a hardware bus. For instance, the method proposed by Carrier & Grand (2004) uses a PCI card which disables the CPU, then uses DMA to access the entire host memory. Although such approach preserves fidelity, atomicity and integrity, it depends on the device being present in the host computer ahead of time. A similar approach has been demonstrated by using the DMA capabilities of the Firewire protocol (Boileau, 2006). However, such a method relies on the availability of the port, which is not widely deployed. Moreover, the possibility to subvert and thus alter the imaging process has been successfully demonstrated. Recently, a new way to perform a memory dump has been proposed and successfully demonstrated (Halderman, Schoen, Heninger, Clarkson, Paul, Calandrino, Feldman, Appelbaum, & Felten, 2008). The method is known as *coldboot* and exploits DRAM persistence to acquire memory images from which keys and other sensitive data can be extracted. It is based on rebooting the system, also by cutting down power to the machine, and launch a custom tool

to gather the inner memory contents. Although this approach has shown impressive results from coherence point of view (e.g. the memory content is almost not modified), it cannot be used in a live digital investigation, where is crucial to preserve the continuity of service provided by the system being analyzed.

Notwithstanding, the software approach seems to be the only one which can be used on live mission-critical computer systems where it is critical to not suspend the service being provided by the machine under investigation. Thus, for such a category of digital systems it appears fundamental to find out a software method which can be helpful when a digital investigation needs to be performed. Current approaches in this category rely prevalently on the RAM dump and they do not consider the page file during the collection phase nor while the analysis will be performed. In the authors' knowledge, only Kornblum (2007) has depicted, at least from theoretical perspective, how to use the page file in a digital investigation. Accordingly, the page file might play a great role in a live forensic analysis. This is the main aim of the remaining part of the article: provide a good overview on reconstructing the virtual memory space of a process by using both memory dump and page file.

PAGE FILE COLLECTION ON A LIVE WINDOWS SYSTEM

In this section the *Page file Collection Tool* (Lee, Savoldi, Lee, & Lim, 2007a; Lee, Savoldi, Lee, & Lim, 2007b), which aims at collecting a full page file on a live Windows based system, will be presented. Normally, the operating system keeps the control on the page file excluding the possibility to copy it in user space mode. To overcome this issue, a raw level access to the file is required, thus permitting the copy and its further analysis with the RAM dump. According to Kornblum (2007), capturing a page file is difficult on a live system

Figure 1. NTFS master file table

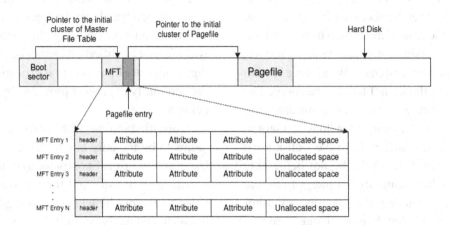

since traditional copying utilities cannot open it. Moreover, this file is used by the operating system and may not be opened by another process. Thus, this tool provides a mean to access the raw file system and can be used together with another tool which can be used to dump the RAM content (e.g. dd). As a matter of fact, it is worth mentioning that different tools have already been implemented for this purpose, such as Encase (Encase, 2008), XWays Forensics (X-Ways Forensic, 2008), or Sleuthkit (Carrier, 2008). The main reason to develop another tool for page file collection is to understand how the tool impacts on the dynamic live memory, in terms of blurriness, by quantifying the amount of modified memory on the live system being investigated.

Page File Collection Tool (PCT)

A page file can be viewed as a "blurb" of memory pages belonging to various processes and it is a strict part of the virtual memory system (Li, & Hudak, 1989; Silberschatz, Galvin, & Gagne, 2007). In order to create this page file collection tool, an in-depth awareness of the NTFS file system is required. One of the most important concepts related to the design of NTFS is that metadata are allocated to files. The Master File Table (MFT) is the heart of NTFS because it contains informa-

tion about all files and directories. Every file and directory has at least one entry in the table, and the entries by themselves are very simple. They are 1KB in size, but only the first 42 bytes have a defined purpose. Figure 1 describes the scheme of the NTFS file system (Carrier, 2005).

The first entry in the table is named $MFT, and it describes the on-disk location of the MFT. The starting location of the MFT is given in the boot sector, which is always located in the first sector of the partition. An MFT entry has many attributes within it, which are data structures that store a specific type of data. Every attribute is composed by a header, which contains the meta-information, and a content, which can have any format and any size. NTFS provides two locations where attributes can be stored. A *resident* attribute stores the content in the MFT entry with the attribute header, and this works only for small size attributes. A *non-resident* attribute stores its content in an external cluster in the file system. If an attribute is resident, the content will immediately follow the header. Instead, non-resident attributes are stored in *cluster-runs*, which are consecutive clusters, and the run is documented using the starting cluster address and run length. Nearly every allocated MFT entry has a $FILE_NAME and a $STANDARD_INFORMATION type attributes. The $FILE_NAME attribute contains

Figure 2. Run list (adapted from [Carrier, 2005])

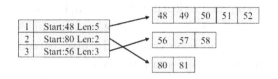

Figure 3. Diagram of the implemented collection tool

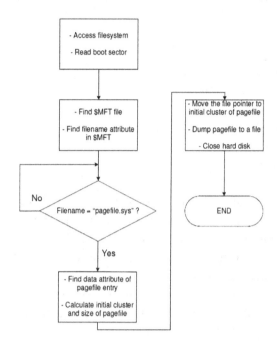

the file name, size, and temporal information. The $STANDARD_INFORMATION attribute contains temporal, ownership, and security information. The $FILE_NAME attribute is used by our technique for two purposes. First, it is placed in a MFT entry to store the file name and the parent directory information. Second, it is used in a directory index and this allows to find a page file entry from the various MFT entries by comparing the file name with information in the $FILE_NAME attribute. Every MFT entry has also a $DATA attribute, which contains the file content. If the content is over 700 bytes in size, it becomes non-resident and is saved in external clusters (Carrier, 2005). As a matter of fact, a page file is over 700 bytes in size, so its $DATA attribute will be non-resident. Figure 2 represents a detailed view of this attribute, useful to understand how the content of a file is stored on the hard-disk. The first byte of the data structure is organized in 4 upper bits and in 4 lower bits. The four least significant bits contain the number of bytes in the run length field, which follows the header byte. The four most significant bits contain the number of bytes in the run offset field, which follows the length field. The run offset is the start cluster address of the file and the run length is the cluster length of the file. As already mentioned, if the $DATA attribute is non-resident, all the file content will be distributed among different clusters which are recorded with different runs. Figure 2 represents a so-called sparse layout with sparse runs related to three clusters.

According to this scheme, we have read the values of the sectors of the hard disk. Thus, we found where the page file was located on the

physical hard-disk. Finally, we were able to collect the page file directly from the hard disk, even while the system was running. In Figure 3, we show an explanatory diagram regarding the tool implemented.

In order to properly figure out how the program works, we can describe the main building blocks with the help of the following snippet of C code. Initially, the tool reads the boot sector and then finds the initial cluster address of the $MFT file.

```
OpenHdd(szCmdOut);
hVolume = CreateFile(drivename, GE-
NERIC_READ, FILE_SHARE_READ|FILE_
SHARE_WRITE, NULL, OPEN_EXISTING, 0,
NULL);
ReadBoot_cal_mft();
ReadFile (hVolume, &boot, 512, &Real-
Read, NULL);
cal_mft();
```

After that, it is necessary to locate the initial address of the $MFT by finding also the page file entry.

```
__int64 mftpos = (__int64)(low-
pos)*(__int64)(512);
__int64 curpos = 0;
curpos =
myFileSeek(hVolume,mftpos,FILE_BE-
GIN);
find_pagefile();
```

In the $MFT, every entry has a filename attribute, so we can find the page file entry by comparing the name, which is pagefile.sys, with the corresponding attribute. It is necessary also to calculate the page file sector number according to the page file entry in the $MFT file. Having found the page file entry, we can gather the corresponding data attribute.

```
cal_pagefile_sector();
__int64 movepos =
(__int64)(pagefile_sector)*(__int64)
(512);
curpos =
myFileSeek(hVolume,movepos,FILE_BE-
GIN);
```

Finally, there is the physical dump of the page file from the hard disk.

```
DumpPagefile(argv[2]);
for(j = 0 ; j < (clusterlength_page-
file) ;j++){
ReadFile(hVolume, Buffer, cluster-
size, &RealRead, NULL);
if(fp!=NULL){
fwrite(Buffer, clustersize, 1, fp);
}
}
```

One potential issue with this method is incoherence of the page file due to the effects of NTFS journaling. Since the journal holds a sequence of uncommitted writes into file system, it should be possible for disk changes to not be visible by PCT while they are being committed to disk. This point will be addressed as a future work.

Experimental Results of the Page Collection Tool

The PCT tool has been extensively tested on Windows XP SP2 x86 systems, both real and virtual, with different CPU capabilities, RAM and page file sizes. More precisely, the real system, which can be referred to as RS, where the test was performed, is a Windows XP SP2 non PAE laptop within 1.23 Gbytes of built-in RAM memory and 1.23 Gbytes of page file. Conversely, the virtual system, which can be referred to as VS, Windows XP based, is equipped with 768 Mbytes of RAM and 512 Mbytes of page file. One important thing to be aware of is the footprint of the PCT tool, which can be defined as the amount of memory modified while the tool is running. Thus, the footprint should express the impact on the system's image blurriness, which cannot be accurately determined by looking at the working memory (heap memory) within the Windows task manager. In fact, the reading process of the tool generates a lot of activity on the disk cache, which causes a lot of memory to be affected within the kernel space. In addition, effects such as paging of little used pages onto the disk may occur when running the tool. As a consequence, we have set up a procedure which aims at evaluating the impact of the PCT tool, when it runs, on the system's memory.

The main idea is to be able to measure how much the system's memory changes, by reading memory snapshots before and after having run the PCT tool. The main limitation of this method, especially for live systems, is that it alters the memory from "inside", with the mentioned tool, which is dd. This fact implies that it is mandatory to evaluate the minimum resolution of the probing tool, which depends, as will become clear soon,

Table 1. Blurriness of dd tool. The snapshots were copied to an external USB 2.0 drive

Snapshot #	Different pages	Equal pages	Δ [%]
1 – 2	132430	190961	40.9
3 - 4	131254	192137	40.5
5 - 6	131602	191789	40.7
7 - 8	141924	181467	43.9
9 - 10	133220	190171	41.2

Table 2. Blurriness of dd tool. The snapshots were copied to a Linux based system via LAN

Snapshot #	Different pages	Equal pages	Δ [%]
1 – 2	25688	297703	7.9
3 - 4	24100	299291	7.4
5 - 6	26888	296503	8.3
7 - 8	28440	294951	8.8
9 - 10	23547	299844	7.3

on the channel used to transfer the snapshot. Indeed, the dd tool acts like a "probe" by taking memory snapshots to quantify the blurriness of a particular tool.

Initially, to properly evaluate the normal blurriness caused by the dd tool we have taken a series of memory snapshots back to back in both real and virtual systems. All the snapshots were copied respectively to an external USB 2.0 storage device and to another computer system by means of a network link (100 Mbit/sec LAN) to evaluate how the communication channel impacts on the memory blurriness. Table 1 refers to the case where snapshots were taken from a real system, with 1.23 Gbytes of RAM, and copied to an external USB 2.0 hard disk. As the table illustrates, we can consider the binary difference between two consecutive snapshots as a measure of the blurriness of the dd tool. Particularly, Δ% quantifies the percentage difference between two consecutive snapshots. As a matter of fact, this "ordinary" blurriness determines the maximum resolution available to observe the impact of other processes onto the system memory. This implies that we cannot measure the blurriness caused by another tool with a better resolution than the one of the "probe" tool. Thus, a deep awareness on methods to obtain the best possible resolution in quantifying the normal blurriness which is caused by the dd tool is mandatory.

For the initial part of the experiment, which is devoted to measuring the normal blurriness of the dd tool by using the USB 2.0 communication

channel, every memory dump was collected in 80 seconds, and we considered a statistically meaningful, albeit small, set of snapshots to account for statistical variation. So far, the blurriness can be quantified as $B = \mu_{diff} \pm \sigma_{diff}$, where μ_{diff} is the average of different snapshot pages related to all snapshots, while σ_{diff} refers to the variance of different pages. Thus, we have $B = 134086 \pm 3978$ pages, or $B = 523.8 \pm 15.5$ Mbytes. In other terms, we have about 41.4% of memory modified by the reading tool.

Similarly, Table 2 refers to the same real system where the snapshots were transferred via LAN to a Linux based system, by means of the netcat tool. Every snapshot was copied in 120 seconds and the blurriness can be quantified as $B = 25733 \pm 1795$ pages, or $B = 100.5 \pm 7$ Mbytes, which is around 8% of the memory. As the results show, there is a considerable difference in blurriness between this case and the previous one. This is due to the buffer allocation in Windows kernel space, which depends on the communication channel which has been used. We can observe that the former case, as illustrated in Table 1, has blurriness which is 5 times greater than the latter one. This fact is certainly due to the different memory buffer allocation, which depends on the communication channel being used. More study would be necessary to determine whether it is possible to control and reduce the buffer at the kernel level, or at least to sort out a better way of transferring a memory snapshot by controlling the memory buffer in kernel space.

Figure 4. Timeline of the experiment to determine the footprint of PCT

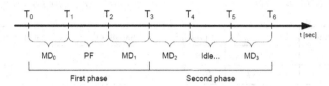

As the results show, from the blurriness point of view we should prefer this method to transfer memory snapshots: the lower the blurriness, the better the resulting resolution in measuring the memory impact caused by other tools. It is worth mentioning that the main purpose of this experimental part is to try to quantify the influence of the PCT tool on the system memory, by means of an internal measurement tool, dd, with the best possible resolution.

After this initial part we have evaluated the blurriness of the dd tool on the virtual system, with 768 Mbytes of RAM, by transferring memory snapshots via LAN, for the reasons that we have pointed out before. In this case the blurriness is B = 8645 ± 374 pages, or B = 33.8 ± 1.46 Mbytes (4.37%).

By considering the same virtual system, we measured the blurriness of the PCT tool by means of memory snapshots taken with dd, according to the scheme shown in Figure 4. Every memory snapshot as well as the page file was copied via network to a Linux system. So far, we have considered a statistically meaningful, albeit small, set of binary snapshots to account for statistical variation. The results are shown in Table 4. The resulting blurriness is B = 14942 ± 425 pages, or B = 58.4 ± 1.7 Mbytes, which is 7.6%.

During the second phase of the measure, as illustrated in Figure 4, we considered the measure of the blurriness due to the reading process, when the system was on idle state for the period $(t_2 - t_1)$, which is the time while PCT was being executed. As the results show, the blurriness has the same value as in Table 3, B = 9044 ± 425 pages, or B = 35.3 ± 1.7 Mbytes. This implies that the blurriness is mainly due to the dd tool.

So far, we can rate the footprint of the PCT tool in the range between 35.3 and 58.4 Mbytes, which refers to the blurriness of the reading tool, dd, and the one which takes account of the pages changed by the dd tool and PCT tool. We cannot measure the footprint of PCT with a better resolution of the probing tool dd. Clearly, we can notice how better the blurriness is when transferring a snapshot via LAN. This is an important condition to be aware of. Potentially, by using a communication channel which requires less buffer memory in kernel space, we could decrease the blurriness and hence the uncertainty in evaluating the impact of a tool on a live system. The next stage of the research will be devoted to understanding which communication channel could be used to reduce the blurriness of the probing tool, so that we can measure the impact of other live tools better.

Table 3. Blurriness of dd tool related to a virtual system with 768 Mbytes of RAM

Snapshot #	Different pages	Equal pages	Δ [%]
1 - 2	8727	187880	4.4
3 - 4	8151	188456	4.1
5 - 6	9057	187550	4.6

Table 4. Blurriness of PCT tool evaluated in the virtual system. The snapshots were copied to the host system via LAN

Snapshot #	Different pages	Equal pages	Δ [%]
1 - 2	8727	187880	4.4
3 - 4	8151	188456	4.1
5 - 6	9057	187550	4.6

Figure 5. Virtual address translation scheme. (adapted from [Russinovich, & Solomon, 2004])

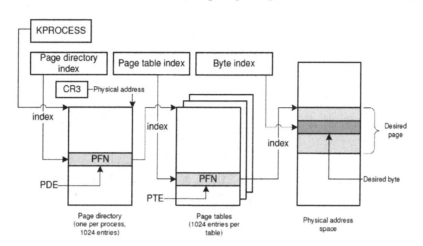

RAM AND PAGE FILE DUMP ANALYSIS

This section is devoted to detailing how the collected page file should be examined together with the RAM dump. By having both snapshots, it will be possible to adopt a linear translation scheme to recover plenty of invalid pages from the page file and integrate them within the virtual memory process space of the RAM dump.

The Missing Part: How to Use the Page File in Volatile Forensic Analysis

Our analysis will be focused only on 32-bit Windows XP SP2 x86 platform, where PAE (Physical Address Extension) and AWE (Address Windowing Extensions) are not enabled. Such a system uses a two-level page table structure to translate virtual to physical addresses, the page table index, and the byte index. These parts of the virtual address are used as pointers into the structures that describe page mappings. As can be seen in Figure 5, the page directory index is used to locate the page directory which is unique for every process. Every page directory table contains 1024 entries (PDEs) which specify the physical address of the

page table within the RAM. Moreover, every page table has 1024 entries (PTEs) which specify the physical address of a memory page (Russinovich, & Solomon, 2004). Thus, the following steps are involved in translating a virtual address:

- The MMU (Memory Management Unit) locates the page directory for the current process, by setting a special register, the CR3 register on the x86 platform, with the address of the page directory table.
- The page directory index is used to locate a specific page directory entry (PDE) which describes the position of the page table needed to map the virtual address. The physical address within the PDE is referred to as page frame number (PFN).
- The page table index is used to locate a particular page table entry (PTE) that describes the physical location of the virtual address being translated.
- The PTE is necessary to locate a physical memory page. If the page is valid (valid bit set to one), the PTE contains the page frame number of the page in physical memory. Conversely, if the page is invalid (valid bit set to zero) the MMU fault handler locates the page and tries to make it valid.

Figure 6. X86 page table entry structure (adapted from [Russinovich, & Solomon, 2004])

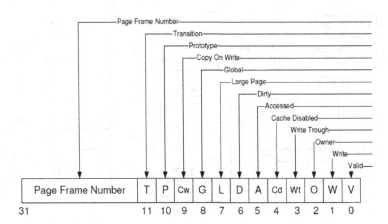

- When the PTE points to a valid page, the byte index is used to locate the address of the desired data within the physical page.

The page directory is composed of page directory entries, each of which is 4 bytes long and describes the state and location of all the possible page tables for that process. Moreover, page tables are created on demand, so the page directory for most processes points only to a small set of page tables. Every page table has up to 1024 4 byte PTEs and it maps 4 Mbytes of data pages (210 × 212 = 222 = 4 Mbytes). Therefore, Windows OS provides 4 Gbytes of private virtual address space so that 1024 page tables are required to map the full 4 Gbytes address space (232/222 = 1024 pages).

One important thing to be aware of is the structure of a PDE and PTE. They have the same structure: a page frame number (PFN), which is used to locate the page table or the physical page, and a flag section, which allows to describe the state and protection of the page. The Windows Kernel Debugger (WinDBG) can certainly be used to dump the flag part (e.g. dt –b –v EPROCESS), which is specific for every OS version and service pack (e.g. Win XP SP1 has different flags from Win XP SP2). Figure 6 details the general structure of a PTE referring to a Windows XP

SP2 OS. As already stated, the real flag structure changes among different versions of an operating system. A complete and exhaustive explanation of the whole flag set can be found in (Russinovich, & Solomon, 2004).

Page Fault Handling

We have invalid PDE and PTE entries when the "valid" bit is set to zero. This fact implies that the desired page table, in the case of an invalid PDE, or the physical memory page, in the case of an invalid PTE, is for some reason not currently accessible to the process. A reference to an invalid page is called *page fault* and is managed by the memory manager is fault handler. There could be numerous reasons why a page fault occurred. For our purposes we will only consider the case when the memory manager tries to access a page that is not resident in memory but is on disk in a page file or a mapped file. As a result, the memory manager will allocate a physical page, and will read the desired page from the disk by copying it into the working set. The other reasons for access faults (Russinovich, & Solomon, 2004) are not relevant to our aims.

So far, we are ready to deal with invalid PDEs and PTEs. As already mentioned, when the valid bit (V) of a PDE or a PTE is zero, the entry is said

Figure 7. Invalid PDE/PTE structure (adapted from [Russinovich, & Solomon, 2004])

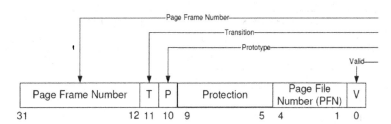

to be "invalid". According to Kornblum (2007), also bits Prototype (P) and Transition (T) need to be considered for retrieving an invalid PDE or PTE. Indeed, when the memory manager starts a swap-out operation it stores pages in a page file on the hard disk. More precisely, when both the P and T bits in an invalid entry (PDE or PTE) are zero, the entry points to a frame in one of the available page files. It is worthy to mention that, on a Windows OS, up to 16 different page files may be present, as it can be seen in Figure 7 by looking at the page file number (PFN) field. After that, the physical offset within the page file is specified by the 20 most significant bits (MSBs) of the address. With these pieces of information we can build up a general procedure capable of binding a piece of evidence within the page file to the appropriate process virtual space.

General Procedure of Analysis

As a general approach towards the virtual memory analysis of a compromised Windows based live system, we can gather both the memory and the

Table 5. Blurriness of dd tool evaluated on the virtual system. The snapshots were taken after a delay of 300 seconds, according to the PCT execution time

Snapshot #	Different pages	Equal pages	Δ [%]
1 – 2	8847	187760	4.5
3 - 4	9634	186973	4.9
5 - 6	8651	187956	4.4

page file with the various methods present in the reference literature. As already mentioned, information within the page file must be related to the proper process in the memory dump. Thus, we can start the analysis of the memory dump by looking for the basic address scheme and, consequently, by recovering both valid and invalid pages. To give a proof of concept of this, we have implemented an extended version of the PTFinder open-source tool (Schuster, 2006), which scans a memory image looking for structures that could possibly be EPROCESS structures. Every process has a signature and we can easily locate it within the memory dump. Moreover, with the help of Windows kernel debugger (WinDBG), it is possible to see that the PageDirectoryBase, that is the starting address of a page directory, can be found exactly 24 bytes after the initial physical location of a process structure. In addition, the page directory table can be dumped, as it is shown in the following snippet of Perl code.

```
seek(INFILE, $PageDirectoryBase, 0);
my $bytes =
read(INFILE,$data,0x1000);
die "Could not read the page
directory.\n" if ($bytes < 0x1000);
my @pd = unpack("V1024", $data$);
```

The procedure scans all PDEs of a page directory table. If an invalid PDE is found the procedure getMissingPDE($pde) is called to recover that entry from the page file. Moreover, for every PDE the page table is dumped. (see Box 1)

Table 6. A partial list of processes with pages swapped out in the page file

Process name	N° of recovered pages	Page file portion [Kb]	Memory portion [Kb]
Idle	58	232	2618
System	63	252	2818
hfs.exe	310	1240	10736
gvim.exe	1320	5280	49602
firefox.exe	1552	6208	58484
Winlogon.exe	1596	6384	92630
wuauclt.exe	1855	7420	64210
cmd.exe	2338	9352	76822
ld.exe	2546	10182	91612
wmiprvse.exe	3054	12216	94918
encase3.exe	3594	14376	102436
WinSCP3.exe	5071	20284	116278
folderclone.exe	6270	25080	129530
thunderbird.exe	8363	33452	166292
vmwareService.exe	11256	45024	170292
svchost.exe	11863	47452	176232
explorer.exe	13364	53456	186452
wuauclt.exe	15863	63452	196294
cmd.exe	16362	65448	206294
csrss.exe	17109	68436	216292
logonui.exe	18356	73424	218938

Every PDE is then parsed to check whether it points to a valid page. If not, the invalid page is recovered from the available page file which has been previously gathered. The whole set of pages is then stored in a file which has the name of the process being analyzed (e.g. WinHex.exe). (See Box 2)

When a PDE/PTE is invalid there are three bits set to zero, namely Valid, Prototype and Transition, as well pointed out in (Kornblum, 2007). Moreover, according to Kornblum (2007), the following equation should be used to obtain the physical address within the page file:

```
PDE_PageFileOffset = (pde_value &
0xFFFFF000) + ((virtual_address &
0x3FF000) >> 12)
```

```
Frame_PageFileOffset = (pte_value
& 0xFFFFF000) + (virtual_address &
0xFFF)
```

Lastly, we can discuss the case when an invalid page has to be recovered. By looking at Figure 7, we can see the field PFN, PageFile Number, which stores the binary number of the current page file being observed. Normally, if the system has only one page file, the default number is set to eight (1000). The variable $bytes contains the 4 Kbytes page. After that, it is converted to ASCII code and then placed in the process dump together with valid memory pages. (see Box 3)

Box 1.

```
my @pages;
# loop over all page directory entries
foreach my $pde (@pd){
# Skip PDEs set to zero
next if ($pde == 0);
# Invalid PDEs are going to be recovered
unless ($pde & 0x01){
                &getMissingPDE($pde);
}
# determine the page size for a valid PDE
if ($pde & 0x80) {
                # process 4M page
                next if ($pde & 0x100);
                # Calculate page base address
                my $pba = ($pde >> 22) * 0x400000;
} else {

                # 4 kbytes memory page
                # Page Table Base Address
                my $ptba = ($pde >> 12) * 0x1000;
                # read the Page Table
                seek(INFILE,$ptba,0);
                my $bytes = read(INFILE,$data,0x1000);
                die "Could not read the Page Table.\n" if ($bytes < 0x1000);
                next unless ($bytes >= 0x1000);
                my @pt = unpack("V1024",$data);
}
```

EXPERIMENTAL RESULTS

We have applied this simple but effective technique to analyze different memory images, which has been obtained with the dd tool (Garner, 2008), and page file dumps, which have been collected with the PCT tool. As already mentioned, the system under analysis was based on Windows XP SP2 non PAE and non AWE. Initially, only the memory image was gathered without considering the page file. After that, the page file was included into the analysis, proving that almost 25% of processes had been swapped out. Indeed, 20 processes among 80 had a considerable portion of pages in the page file.

Although the number of processes with a part in the page file seems small we need to consider what follows:

- The system was reinstalled and with relatively few big processes active in the main memory. Most processes were in the range of 1-20 Mbytes and resident in the main memory.
- We have only considered invalid PTEs in the analysis. More pages could be recovered by also using invalid PDEs. In fact,

Box 2.

```
# loop over all the page table entries
my $recovered_page = "";
foreach my $pte (@pt) {
        # Missing pages
        if (($pte & 0x1) == 0){
                $recovered_page = &getMissingPTE($pte);
                if (length($recovered_page) > 0){
                        print OUT $recovered_page;
                }
                next;
        }
        # skip pages with global flag set
        next if (($pte & 0x100));
        # calculate the page base address for valid         PTEs
        # these are the 20 MSB bits which define the Page Frame Number
        my $pba = ($pte >> 12) * 0x1000;
        seek(INFILE,$pba,0);
        read(INFILE,$data,0x1000);
        print OUT $data;
        printf "PBA 4k: \t0x%08x\n",$pba;
        push(@pages,$pba);
}
```

579 invalid PDEs were recovered. On average, by considering the whole set of processes carved out from the binary memory image, each valid PDE has 888 valid PTEs. We might therefore estimate that by including the set of invalid PDEs 579 × 888 = 514152 more pages could be recovered.

- In the analysis, according to Kornblum (2007), also Prototype PTEs should be considered to recover more pages. In a PTE when the P (Prototype) bit is set to one, the entry is a pointer to a prototype page table entry (PPTE), which points to the true location of the page. Prototype PTEs are used when more than one process is using the same page in memory.

- A Page file can be thought of as a high-dynamic system where the state (the content)

changes according to the level of multiprogramming. The more processes active at the same time, the more page file portions will be used.

- It is virtually impossible to map all the content of a page file to the processes within a memory dump. This strongly depends on the type of system being analyzed, on the level of multiprogramming, on the workload of a process.

CONCLUSION AND FUTURE WORK

This work has presented a consistent overview towards the virtual memory space process reconstruction, by pointing out how it is possible to collect the page file on Windows mission-critical

Box 3.

```
sub getMissingPTE {
my $pte = (shift);
my $Valid = ($pte & 0x1);
my $Prototype = ($pte & 0x400) >> 10;
my $Reserved = ($pte & 0x800) >> 11;
if ($Valid == 0 && $Prototype == 0 && $Reserved == 0){
        my $Frame_PageFileOffset = ($pte & 0xFFFFF000);
        my $PageFileNumber = "$CacheDisable.$WriteThrough.$Owner.$Write";
        if ($PageFileNumber eq '1.0.0.0'){
                seek(PAGEFILE,$Frame_PageFileOffset,0);
                my $bytes = read(PAGEFILE,$data,0x1000);
                if ($bytes < 0x1000){
                        printf("Frame_Pagefile connot be read...\n");
                        next;
                }
                if ($bytes == 0x1000){
                        my $page="";
                        my @page_recovered="";
                        @page_recovered = unpack("N1024",$data);
                        my $i=0;
                        foreach my $line (@page_recovered){
                                $line = sprintf("%08x",$line);
                                (my $str = $line) =~ s/([a-fA-F0-9]{2})/
chr(hex $1)/eg;

                                $page.= $str;
                        }
                        $page = "Recovered...".$page;
                        return $page;
                }
        }
}
};
```

systems, which cannot be turned off for the criticality of the service provided, and how it can be subsequently combined with the RAM dump to acquire more evidential data. Although the problem of the integrity related to the software memory snapshot remains still severe, by not being able to collect such snapshot preserving the fidelity, atomicity and integrity, it has been shown how the page file could be really useful when dealing with a live digital investigation. Moreover, the issue of blurriness has been pointed out, by giving guidelines on how it is possible to evaluate it on a live system.

REFERENCES

Adams, K., & Algesen, O. (2006). A Comparison of Software and Hardware Techniques for x86 Virtualization, In J.P. Shen (Ed.), *12th International Conference on Architectural Support for Programming Languages and Operating Systems* (pp. 2-13). New York, NY: ACM Press.

Boileau, A. (2006). Hit by a Bus: Physical Access Attacks with Firewire. In *4th International Ruxcon Conference*. Retrieved September 20, 2008, from http://www.ruxcon.org.au/files/2006/firewire_attacks.pdf

Carrier, B. (2005). *File System Forensic Analysis*. Upper Saddle River, NJ: Addison Wesley.

Carrier, B. (2008). SleuthKit, Retrieved September 20, 2008, from http://www.sleuthkit.org/.

Carrier, B., & Grand, J. (2004). A Hardware-Based Memory Acquisition Procedure for Digital Investigations. *Digital Investigation*, *1*(1), 50–60. doi:10.1016/j.diin.2003.12.001

Chisum, W. J., & Turvey, B. (2000). Evidence Dynamics: Locard's Exchange Principle and Crime Reconstruction. *Journal of Behavioral Profiling*, *1*(1).

Czeskis, A., Hilaire, D. J., Koscher, K., Gribble, S. D., Kohno, T., & Schneier, B. (2008). Defeating Encrypted and Deniable File Systems: TrueCrypt v5.1a and the Case of the Tattling OS and Applications. In *3rd USENIX Workhop on Hot Topics in Security*. Retrieved September 20, 2008, from http://www.usenix.org/events/hotsec08/tech/

Encase (2008), Retrieved September 20, 2008, from http://www.guidancesoftware.com/.

Garner, G. M. (2008). Forensic Acquisition Utilities. Retrieved September 20, 2008, from http://www.gmgsystemsinc.com/fau/.

Halderman, J. A., Schoen, S. D., Heninger, N., Clarkson, W., Paul, W., Calandrino, J. A., et al. (2008). Lest We Remember: Cold Boot Attacks on Encryption Keys. In *17th Usenix Security Symposium*. San Jose, CA. Retrieved September 20, 2008, from http://citp.princeton.edu/pub/coldboot.pdf

Kornblum, J. (2007). Using Every Part of the Buffalo in Windows Memory Analysis. *Digital Investigation*, *4*(1), 24–29. doi:10.1016/j.diin.2006.12.002

Lee, S., Savoldi, A., Lee, S., & Lim, J. (2007a). Windows Page file Collection and Analysis for a Live Forensic Context. In *Future Generation Communication and Networking* (pp. 97–101). Jeju Island, Korea: IEEE Computer Society. doi:10.1109/FGCN.2007.236

Lee, S., Savoldi, A., Lee, S., & Lim, J. (2007b). Password Recovery Using an Evidence Collection Tool and Countermeasures. In B. Liao, J. Pan, L. Jain, M. Liao, H. Noda, & A. Ho (Eds.), *3rd Intelligent Information Hiding and Multimedia Signal Processing* (pp. 93-97). Kaohsiung, TW: IEEE Computer Society.

Li, K., & Hudak, P. (1989). Memory Coherence in Shared Virtual Memory System. *ACM Transactions on Computer Systems*, *7*(4), 321–359. doi:10.1145/75104.75105

Palmer, G. (2001). A Roadmap for Digital Forensic Research (Technical Report DTR-T001-01). Utica, NY: Air Force Research Laboratory. Retrieved September 20, 2008, from http://www.dfrws.org/2001/dfrws-rm-final.pdf

Petroni, N., Walters, A., Fraser, T., & Arbaugh, W. (2006). FATkit: A Framework for the Extraction and Analysis of Digital Forensic Data from Volatile System Memory. *Digital Investigation*, *3*(4), 197–210. doi:10.1016/j.diin.2006.10.001

Russinovich, M., & Solomon, D. (2004). *Microsoft Windows Internals, Microsoft Press*. Redmond, WA: Microsoft Press.

Rutkowska, J. (2007). Beyond The CPU: Defeating Hardware Based RAM Acquisition Tools (Part I: AMD case). *Black Hat Conference*. Retrieved March 1, 2008, from http://invisiblethings.org/papers.html.

Schatz, B. (2007). BodySnatcher: Towards Reliable Volatile Memory Acquisition by Software. In E. Casey (Ed.), *7th Annual Digital Forensic Research Workshop* (pp. 126-134). Pittsburgh, PA: Elsevier.

Schuster, A. (2006). Searching for Processes and Threads in Microsoft Windows Memory Dumps. In E. Casey (Ed.), *6th Annual Digital Forensic Research Workshop* (pp. 10-16). Lafayette, IN: Elsevier.

Silberschatz, A., Galvin, P. B., & Gagne, G. (2007). *Operating System Concepts*. Hoboken, NJ: John Wiley & Sons.

X-Ways Forensic. (2008), Retrieved September 20, 2008, from http://www.x-ways.net/.

Chapter 4
Evidentiary Implications of Potential Security Weaknesses in Forensic Software

Chris K. Ridder
Stanford University, USA

ABSTRACT

Computer forensic software is used by lawyers and law enforcement to collect and preserve data in a "forensic image" so that it can be analyzed without changing the original media, and to preserve the chain of custody of the evidence. To the extent there are vulnerabilities in this software, an attacker may be able to hide or alter the data available to a forensic analyst, causing courts to render judgments based on inaccurate or incomplete evidence. There are a number of legal doctrines designed to ensure that evidence presented to courts is authentic, accurate and reliable, but thus far courts have not applied them with the possibility of security weaknesses in forensic software in mind. This article examines how courts may react to such claims, and recommends strategies that attorneys and courts can use to ensure that electronic evidence presented in court is both admissible and fair to litigants.

INTRODUCTION

Forensic software is frequently used for evidence collection in both civil and criminal matters, because it mitigates risks that can arise with examining media in its native environment, such as

DOI: 10.4018/978-1-60960-515-5.ch004

alteration of metadata like time and date stamps, or overwriting of deleted files, which can impair attempts to recover lost data. Many forensic tools also provide features such as MD5 hashing and assignment of CRC values to data, to validate that the evidence to be introduced at trial remains in the same state as when it was collected. (Guidance Software, 2006). The legal and law enforcement communities depend heavily on forensic software to analyze and preserve critical evidence.

In addition to being a common practice among attorneys for prudential reasons, courts have suggested, and in some cases required, exact binary duplicates ("image copies") to be made of hard drives, particularly when deleted files are in issue. For example, in Gates Rubber Co. v. Bando Chem. Indus. Ltd. (1996), the court criticized the plaintiff for failing to make an "image backup" of the hard drive and for failing to properly preserve undeleted files, where there was evidence that certain files may have been deleted, and held that a party should "utilize the method which would yield the most complete and accurate results." The court in Simon Prop. Group L.P. v. mySimon, Inc. (2000) cited the Gates Rubber case favorably when it required the plaintiff to make what it called a "mirror image" copy of hard drives, citing the risks associated with overwriting of deleted files. In Playboy Enters., Inc. v. Welles (1999), the court ordered a court-appointed forensic computing expert to make a "mirror image" of the defendant's hard drive where there was evidence that emails had been deleted during litigation. Courts have also noted that forensic images can be a useful tool outside the context of deleted files. In Zubulake v. UBS Warburg LLC (2003) the court suggested that creation of mirror-image copies of computer systems is one way to preserve documents in the state they existed at the time of collection.

There are approximately 150 different automated tools used by law enforcement organizations in the investigation of computer crime, many of which are likely also used in the civil litigation context. (National Institute of Standards and Technology Computer Forensics Tool Testing Program, n.d.). The National Institute of Standards and Technology has a program to test that this software does what it claims, but some have argued that not enough work is being done to identify and correct security vulnerabilities. Newsham, Palmer & Stamos (2007) have argued that there is very little data on two popular foren-

sic packages, EnCase and TSK, in the Common Vulnerabilities and Exposures database, and that vendors do not take advantage of the protections for native code that platforms provide (pp. 2, 11-12). Harris (2006) found that forensic software needs to be hardened against a wide range of potential attack vectors, and that "it would seem that perpetrators are working harder to subvert the system than academia is working to strengthen forensics." (pp. 44-49). The Grugq (n.d.) found that computer forensics are "[a]s vulnerable as other technologies," yet "[l]ess scrutinized than other technologies." (p. 12).

Forensic software marketing materials promise a high degree of accuracy and reliability. EnCase, one of the industry-standard tools, claims that it produces "an exact binary duplicate of the original drive or media." (Guidance Software, 2006). However, some researchers have noted that forensic software in certain situations may be vulnerable to deliberate attempts to hide data from the software, or to cause the software to crash. (Grugq, n.d.; Newsham et al., 2007).[1] To the extent code execution vulnerabilities are present or impersonation attacks are possible, an attacker may be able to change data on the forensic image, or to change the way such data appears to a forensic analyst. (Grugq, n.d.; Newsham et al., 2007).

The possibility that an attacker may seek to hide data from forensics software is a serious concern for those trying to collect evidence, but because hidden data by its nature is not likely to cause significant evidentiary concerns unless it is found, this article focuses on vulnerabilities that could permit an attacker to add or change data without being detected. Attorneys in both the civil and criminal contexts have obligations to conduct a reasonably diligent search for data that may be useful to their opponents, but it is unlikely that this obligation would extend to a search for data that has been hidden so thoroughly as to be undiscoverable by forensic software. Because potentially hidden data may prove critical (and in the criminal context, may be exculpatory), the author believes that all parties should have an opportunity to conduct their own forensic analysis of the original media and the forensic workstation used by the proponent of the evidence.

In Newsham et al. (2007), the authors discuss a potential risk of code execution vulnerabilities, which could allow an attacker (such as the person being subjected to forensic analysis, an interested third party, or the forensic examiner herself) to execute arbitrary code on the forensic workstation.[2] Although they did not demonstrate such an attack, if one were found in the future it could be possible for an attacker to alter the data on the forensic image. If an attacker were able to execute arbitrary code on the forensic workstation, it could be used for a wide variety of operations that could jeopardize an investigation or alter evidence. For example, an attacker might be able to change the way the forensic software displays data to the examiner, alter the behavior of the function that reports the hash value of the image to display an arbitrary hash value, or embed a rootkit that waits for the forensic examiner to connect the workstation to a public network (e.g., to apply the latest Windows patches), giving the attacker an opportunity to change the way the forensic software interprets certain data or to review evidence on the forensic workstation.

Another potential attack vector discussed by Newsham et al. (2007) is the possibility of an "impersonation attack" against forensic software that is designed to image a live network. If not properly secured, such software could allow an attacker to masquerade as the person the software believes it is collecting from. Combined with a network "man in the middle," or MITM, attack, such a vulnerability might be used by an attacker to feed the forensic software arbitrary data, for example by presenting a virtual machine containing data of the attacker's choice to the forensic software instead of the media intended to be collected. Such an attack could be implemented by an attacker on the network spoofing the identity of a targeted machine.

To the extent such attacks are possible, they may also be able to avoid detection. When forensic software captures an individual piece of media, it creates an MD5 hash of the media and the image to confirm they match. If the drive has been seized, as it frequently is in criminal cases, later comparisons will be able to confirm that the forensic image matches the original media. However, if the drive is not seized and remains in use after imaging, the hash value of the original will change as soon as data on the media changes (for example, through normal use) and there will no longer be an opportunity to compare it with the forensic image's hash value. This problem would also be present when forensic software images a live system or network, which may include imaging hard drives, network traffic, and even data in RAM that can change rapidly. In the case of an impersonation attack, the hash value would match the attacker's data set, rather than the media intended to be collected; this may not be verifiable against the original media if the original media's hash had changed.

If an attack against the forensic workstation has occurred,[3] the hash values alone may not be sufficient to guarantee that what a forensic examiner sees is an accurate representation of what is on the original media. Without strong integrity checks of the operating system running on the forensic workstation in addition to the forensic software itself,[4] an attacker may be able to compromise the routines that display the hash, causing a false hash value to be displayed. An attacker may also be able to change the way the forensic software displays the data on the image, such that even if the examiner were looking at a perfect bit-for-bit copy of the original, the documents would appear as the attacker had specified, rather than as they are on the original media.

The potential vulnerability of forensic software to attack, combined with the potential for such an attack to go undetected, has implications not only for admissibility of evidence, but for the administration of justice generally. After all, the stakes are extremely high: people go to jail and fortunes are paid depending on what the forensic software says. It is absolutely critical that it be secure. This article reviews three evidentiary doctrines that could cause forensic software with demonstrated security vulnerabilities to be excluded from evidence: authenticity, the best evidence rule, and reliability.

Authenticity of Forensic Evidence

Evidence may only be used in court if it is authentic. The authentication of a document is "satisfied by evidence sufficient to support a finding that the matter in question is what the proponent claims." (Federal Rule of Evidence 901(a), 2007). Once this standard is met by the proponent of the evidence, the jury then considers the relevance and weight of the evidence in the context of the case. (United States v. Goichman, 1976).[5] Forensic images will be vulnerable to findings that they are not authentic in proportion to the attack surface of the tools, and the likelihood that they have been compromised.

Generally, when a party in litigation seeks to offer evidence, it must show "that the exhibits offered into evidence were the same as those taken, and their contents were in the same condition when analyzed and introduced as when taken." (State v. Perry, 2003). This is usually shown by demonstrating that the continuous custody of the evidence was such as to render it improbable that anyone tampered with the original item or substituted a different item. (State v. Gibb, 1981; State v. Bakker, 1978). A more stringent showing on chain of custody may be required when the evidence is of a type more susceptible to alteration or substitution. (State v. Bakker, 1978). Forensic software should be hardened as much as possible against tampering and impersonation attacks, to strengthen claims that a forensic image can be reliably traced back to the intended source.

A proponent must offer more than a reliable chain of custody in demonstrating that the evidence is what the proponent claims. For example, a witness with knowledge of the document may testify that it is authentic, it may be compared with similar evidence that has already been authenticated, or it may have distinctive characteristics that, in light of the circumstances make it likely to be authentic. (Federal Rule of Evidence 901(b), 2007). For example, if a document contains information that only the person in possession is likely to possess, it will be held to be authentic. (United States v. Reilly, 1994; United States v. Console, 1993).

To the extent there are insufficient "external" sources of authenticity,[6] a proponent of forensic evidence will need to demonstrate the accuracy of the forensic software itself. Federal Rule of Evidence 901(b)(9)(2007) provides that evidence may be authenticated by "describing a process or system used to produce a result and showing that the process or system produces an accurate result." For example, in United States v. Taylor (1976), video of a bank robbery was held authentic even though the tellers were locked in the vault and unable to testify as to what happened, because they were able to testify how the film was loaded into the camera, how the camera was activated, and that the film was removed from the camera immediately after the robbery and developed; in United States v. Alicea-Cardoza (1997), pen register data was admitted upon a showing that as a message comes in, the pen register stores exactly what comes out of the beeper; and in State v. Sensing (1992), the court held that evidence was admissible where the machines were subjected to "exhaustive testings," underwent "constant monitoring" and were "nearly infallible."

Although it appears that no courts have considered the potential for security weaknesses in forensic software, the prevailing view is that data obtained from forensic images satisfies the authenticity requirement. For example, in State v. Cook (2002) the court held that under Rule 901(b)(9), Guidance EnCase was a process or system that produces an accurate result and there was "no doubt that the mirror image was an authentic copy of what was present on the computer's hard drive," where defendant's own expert was satisfied with the way the forensic image was collected. In Bone v. State (2002), the court found deleted picture files from forensic images authentic where defendant didn't challenge procedures employed, and a police detective testified that he made a forensic image of the hard drive, described the software used to retrieve the deleted files, and testified that he printed the deleted pictures exactly as he found them on the defendant's computer. In State v. Schroeder (2000), the court upheld a lower court decision not to allow a demonstration that the forensic investigator had modified data on the computer, where the demonstration would not have shown anything related to the nineteen child pornography pictures at issue.

However, should the tools be shown to produce inaccurate results, they may become vulnerable to challenge. Such challenges could be against either the admissibility of the evidence or the weight it should be accorded. At least one court has held that questions "as to the accuracy of [computer] printouts, whether resulting from incorrect data entry or the operation of the computer program, as with inaccuracies in any other type of business records, [affect] only the weight of the printouts, not their admissibility." (United States v. Catabaran (1988)).

Some courts have expressed skepticism with regard to electronic evidence that is capable of being altered. In St. Clair v. Johnny's Oyster & Shrimp, Inc. (1999), the court held that Plaintiff's evidence of boat ownership taken from an online United States Coast Guard vessel database was insufficient to withstand a motion to dismiss, because the Internet is "inherently untrustworthy," "[a]nyone can put anything on the Internet," and "hackers can adulterate the content on any web-site from any location at any time"). In United States v. Jackson (2000), the court found that web site postings lacked authenticity, reasoning that the defendant could not show that "web postings in which the white supremacist groups took responsibility for... racist mailings actually were posted

by the groups, as opposed to being slipped onto the groups' web sites by Jackson herself, who was a skilled computer user." These cases are not representative, and courts are likely to find forensic images authentic absent a showing that they are fairly susceptible to tampering. [7] However, they demonstrate that some courts will consider security vulnerabilities in electronic systems an issue in determining authenticity.

Courts have thus far expressed a great deal of confidence in a hash value's ability to authenticate a forensic image. For example, in Sanders v. State of Texas (2006), the court found EnCase Forensic software accurate and reliable despite defendant's unsupported assertion that it was inaccurate and unreliable, based in part on expert testimony that the MD5 hash used to validate the image ensured no possibility of error. However, hash values could be at risk of being undermined where code execution vulnerabilities or impersonation attacks are present, or where the original drive was not retained by the investigators and is not verifiable against the original media. Where the original media is available, courts have a number of options to reduce the risk that compromised forensic evidence is admitted: they can admit the original media into evidence, provide an opportunity for both parties to examine the original, or provide both parties an opportunity to conduct their own forensic analyses.

Thus far, courts do not appear to have taken this route, and instead have denied parties an opportunity to look at the original media, apparently in reliance on the authenticity of the forensic imaging process. For example, in Positive Software v. NewCentury Mortgage (2003), the court held that the defendant had made only unspecified allegations regarding the accuracy and quality of EnCase imaging, and in State v. Butler (2005), the court noted that the trial court required the government to produce forensic images, but refused to order the original hard drive because it could be altered during analysis, despite defendant's argument that "computer programs in existence did not create true mirror images. Other courts, such as United States v. Hill (2004), have required production of forensic image files, apparently in the absence of a request for the original media.

In cases where the original media has changed such that there is no way to verify that the forensic image has not been tampered with, there is a stronger argument that the system used to produce the image does not produce an accurate result. However, given courts' willingness to admit forensic images, there would probably need to be a suggestion that tampering was likely in a given case in order for evidence to be excluded. This creates a difficult situation for litigants who are not able to make such a showing if they believe tampering has occurred; and an opportunity for those who would seek to frame them.

The Best Evidence Rule

The Best Evidence Rule provides that "[t]o prove the content of a writing, recording or photograph, the original writing, recording or photograph is required..." (Federal Rule of Evidence 1002 (2007)). There are a number of exceptions to this general rule. For example, Federal Rule of Evidence 1001(3) (2007) provides that if "data are stored in a computer or similar device, any printout or other output readable by sight, shown to reflect the data accurately, is an 'original.'" Some documents obtained from a forensic image are likely to fall within this rule, because they will be readable by sight either on an electronic display or in paper form. Graham (2006) suggests that even if an item offered as evidence has been through several digital incarnations and is subsequently printed out, then that printout qualifies as an original pursuant to Rule 1001(3). However, the requirement that in these cases the proponent of a copy of computer-based evidence must show that it reflects the original data accurately can be susceptible to claims of tampering. As with arguments concerning authenticity, if the opponent of the evidence can show that there was likely

a security breach, there is a risk that duplicate evidence could be excluded.

Some of the information on a forensic image, or the forensic image itself, will not be admissible under the Rule 1001(3) exception if it does not qualify as "readable by sight" due to formatting or other characteristics peculiar to the type of data collected. Federal Rule of Evidence 1003 (2007) provides an alternate basis for admitting this type of data into evidence as a "duplicate." Rule 1003 provides that "[a] duplicate is admissible to the same extent as an original, unless... in the circumstances it would be unfair to admit the duplicate in lieu of the original." As with the requirement in Rule 1001 that the data accurately reflect the original, the "fairness" requirement in Rule 1003 demands that the proponent of the evidence be able to show that the forensic evidence was not tampered with, or that the forensic software is sufficiently secure (and the examiner sufficiently trained) to demonstrate fairness. Thus far, cases have not tended to set this bar very high. In State v. Morris (2005), the court held that where police had inadvertently destroyed the original hard drive, an EnCase image file was admissible as a duplicate (not an original) because the hash value matched the original drive at the time of collection. Whether such an admission is "fair" could turn on the security and reliability of the software used to make such an image, making the Best Evidence Rule a possible ground for exclusion of forensic images.

A decision to admit forensic data under the Best Evidence Rule therefore turns on whether the image or the data "accurately reflects" the original under Rule 1001(3), or if a "duplicate," whether it is fair to admit the evidence under Rule 1003. Images created with insecure software could prove vulnerable to challenge under either section.

Reliability of Forensic Tools

Federal Rule of Evidence 702 provides that an expert (by knowledge, skill, experience, training, or education) may testify about scientific, technical, or other specialized knowledge if "(1) the testimony is based upon sufficient facts or data, (2) the testimony is the product of reliable principles and methods, and (3) the witness has applied the principles and methods reliably to the facts of the case." Courts have an obligation to act as a "gatekeeper" to ensure that such testimony is reliable.[8]

In Daubert v. Merrell Dow Pharmaceuticals, Inc. (2003), the U.S. Supreme Court held that in order to be reliable, expert testimony must be "derived by the scientific method" and "supported by appropriate validation." The Court noted several non-exclusive factors that courts may consider in evaluating the reliability of scientific, technical and other evidence supported by expert testimony:

- whether the theories and techniques employed by the scientific expert have been tested;
- whether they have been subjected to peer review and publication;
- whether the techniques employed by the expert have a known error rate;
- whether they are subject to standards governing their application; and
- whether the theories and techniques employed by the expert enjoy widespread acceptance.[9]

The extent to which particular forensic software tools used by an analyst have been tested or subject to peer review will vary considerably with regard to which tools are at issue, and practitioners would do well to select well-tested (and testable) tools.[10] Many tool manufacturers test their software in a range of conditions, although this work is not always made public.[11] The NIST Computer Forensics Tools Testing Program (n.d.) is also a valuable source of testing information, but it does not appear to be strongly focused on finding security vulnerabilities in the software. Rather, most testing seems to have been focused

on showing that the software does what it purports to do on datasets that have not been deliberately created to confuse the software. Although security testing of forensic software may not have been as robust as some would desire, this gap in testing standing alone probably will not result in the exclusion of evidence. Nevertheless, a more rigorous approach to testing for vulnerabilities would create greater assurance in the legal community that the software is reliable.

To the extent security vulnerabilities are present, they introduce a risk of error in that an attacker could alter the data on the forensic image (or the way the data appears to an examiner). Similarly, hash values may not be a reliable means to eliminate error entirely, because they themselves may be subject to attack or circumvention. The risk of an attacker compromising the forensic software through a security exploit is difficult to quantify, but the higher the risk of error, the more susceptible the evidence will be to exclusion under Daubert (1993). The quality of forensic analysis, while not relevant to the impact of vulnerabilities on reliability, will nevertheless be important to a court in deciding whether the forensic evidence as a whole is reliable. In order to gauge the quality of forensic analysis, the opponent of the evidence should have access to the queries the analyst used and be able to reproduce them on a copy of the image. The opponent may also want to conduct their own forensic analysis, preferably on the original media, and preferably with a different set of tools, which could reveal data that may have been hidden from the proponent's software.

There are recognized industry practices governing the use of forensics software, and many manufacturers offer certification programs (Guidance Software, Inc., n.d.), but there is no formal certification for forensic analysts and techniques vary widely.[12] Yet even the strictest certification standards would not address the impact of all potential security vulnerabilities in the software, which if present and successfully exploited might be difficult or impossible to detect. Courts must therefore look also to whether there are strong security standards governing the forensic tools themselves. The more work is done to define strict, industry-wide security standards for forensic software, the more likely forensic software will be found reliable.

Finally, forensic software enjoys widespread acceptance, but this state of affairs is in some measure predicated on the ability of the forensics community to continue demonstrating the reliability of its software.

It does not appear that any courts have considered the implications of security weaknesses in forensic software, but courts that have considered the admissibility of forensic images generally have found forensic tools to be reliable under *Daubert* and related standards. For example, in Williford v. State of Texas (2004), the court found that a police detective qualified as an expert on forensic software, and that EnCase was reliable because it is generally accepted in the computer forensic community; is commercially available and can be tested by anyone and in fact has been tested; that SC Magazine had given it five out of five stars in a review; that it has a low potential rate of error; and that EnCase successfully verified the copy of defendant's hard drive.

This state of affairs is not likely to change merely because of a possibility that vulnerabilities in the software can theoretically be exploited. However, if vulnerabilities are demonstrated that are relatively easy to exploit, if security standards in forensic software design are not sufficiently strong, or if public security testing capable of being peer reviewed is lacking, the risk of a *Daubert* exclusion will increase.

CONCLUSION

As with other forensic techniques, computer forensic tools are not magic; they are complex software tools that like all software may be subject to certain attacks. Yet because these tools play such a critical role in our legal system, it is important that they be as accurate, reliable, and secure against tampering as possible. Vulnerabilities would not only call into question the admissibility of forensic images, but could also create a risk that if undetected tampering occurs, courts may come to the wrong decisions in cases that affect lives and property.

In order to mitigate the risk that a vulnerability may be present in a given forensic software product, courts should routinely allow parties who request it an opportunity to conduct their own forensic analyses of original media. This option may not be available where the original media have changed after the forensic image was created. In these cases, courts should be especially sensitive to the accuracy and reliability of the forensic image, and to the quality of analysis that was undertaken. Where it is possible for both parties to image such original media at the same time, they should have an opportunity to do so.

The risk of forensic evidence being excluded as inaccurate or unreliable remains low at this time, absent a finding that tampering probably occurred or did occur, which will nearly always result in exclusion. This is because execution of arbitrary code on the forensic workstation has not yet been demonstrated, and because attacks against forensic software outside the security industry do not appear to be occurring frequently. However, stronger security practices on the part of forensic software manufacturers, and sensitivity to these issues by judges, will ensure that forensic images remain admissible and promote fairness by reducing the risk of tampering.

REFERENCES

Bone v. State, 771 N.E.2d 710, 716-17 (Ind. App. 2002).

Daubert v. Merrell Dow Pharmaceuticals, Inc., 509 U.S. 579 (1993).

Federal Rule of Evidence 1001(3) (2007).

Federal Rule of Evidence 1002 (2007).

Federal Rule of Evidence 901(a) (2007).

Gates Rubber Co. v. Bando Chem. Indus. Ltd., 167 F.R.D. 90, 112 (D. Colo. 1996).

Graham, M. H. (2006). *Handbook on Federal Evidence* (6th ed.). St. Paul, Minn.: Thomson/West.

Grugq, the (2005). The Art of Defiling: Defeating Forensic Analysis. Retrieved May 21, 2008, from http://www.blackhat.com/presentations/bh-usa-05/bh-us-05-grugq.pdf.

Guidance Software, Inc. (2006). Encase Forensic Corporate Version 5: The Standard in Computer Forensics. Retrieved May 21, 2008, from http://www.guidancesoftware.com/downloads/getpdf.aspx?fl=.pdf.

Guidance Software, Inc. (2007). Guidance Software Responds to iSEC report on EnCASE. Retrieved May 21, 2008, from http://www.securityfocus.com/archive/1/474727.

Guidance Software, Inc. (n.d.). Guidance EnCE Certification Program. Retrieved July 18, 2008, from http://www.guidancesoftware.com/training/EnCE_certification.aspx.

Harris, R. (2006). Arriving at an anti-forensics consensus: Examining how to define and control the anti-forensics problem. *Digital Investigation* 3(S), 44-49. Retrieved May 21, 2008, from http://www.dfrws.org/2006/proceedings/6-Harris.pdf.

Kumho Tire Co., Ltd. v. Carmichael, 526 U.S. 137 (1999).

Mississippi State University. University Relations. (May 28, 2003). MSU computer forensics course takes aim @ 'cybercrime.' Retrieved July 18, 2008, from http://www.msstate.edu/web/media/detail.php?id=2119.

National Institute of Standards and Technology Computer Forensics Tool Testing Program. (n.d.) *CFTT Project Overview*. Retrieved May 21, 2008, from http://www.cftt.nist.gov/project_overview.htm.

Newsham, T., Palmer, C., & Stamos, A. (2007). Breaking Forensics Software: Weaknesses in Critical Evidence Collection. Retrieved May 21, 2008, from http://www.isecpartners.com/files/iSEC-Breaking_Forensics_Software-Paper.v1_1.BH2007.pdf.

Perfect 10, Inc. v. Cybernet Ventures, Inc., 213 F.Supp.2d 1146, 1153-54 (C. D. Cal., 2002).

Playboy Enters., Inc. v. Welles, 60 F.Supp.2d 1050, 1055 (S.D. Cal. 1999).

Positive Software v. New Century Mortgage, 259 F.Supp.2d 561 (N.D. Tex. 2003).

Sanders v. State of Texas, 191 S.W.3d 272 (Tex. App. 2006).

Simon Prop. Group L.P. v. mySimon, Inc., 194 F.R.D. 639, 641 (S.D. Ind. 2000).

St. Clair v. Johnny's Oyster & Shrimp Inc., 706 F. Supp. 2d 773 (S.D. Texas 1999).

State v. Bakker, 262 N.W.2d 538, 542-43 (1978).

State v. Butler, 2005 WL 735080 (Tenn. Crim. App. Mar. 30, 2005), *abrogated on other grounds,* State v. Pickett, 211 S.W.3d 696 (Tenn. 2007).

State v. Cook, 777 N.E.2d 882, 886-892 (Ohio Ct. App. 2002).

State v. Gibb, 303 N.W. 2d 673 (1981).

State v. Morris, 2005 WL 356801 (Ohio App. Feb. 16, 2005).

State v. Perry, 69 N.W.2d 412, 417 (Iowa 2003).

State v. Schroeder, 613 N.W.2d 911, 918 (Wis. Ct. App. 2000).

State v. Sensing, 843 S.W.2d 412, 416 (1992).

United States v. Alicea-Cardoza, 132 F.3d 1, 4 (1st Cir. 1997).

United States v. Catabaran, 836 F.2d 453, 458 (9th Cir. 1988).

United States v. Console, 13 F.3d 641 (3d Cir. 1993).

United States v. Goichman, 547 F.2d 778, 784 (3rd Cir. 1976).

United States v. Hill, 322 F.Supp.2d 1081 (C.D. Cal. 2004).

United States v. Jackson, 208 F.3d 633, 638 (7th Cir. 2000).

United States v. Reilly, 33 F.3d 1396 (3d Cir. 1994).

United States v. Tank, 200 F.3d 627, 630 (9th Cir. 2000).

United States v. Taylor, 530 F.2d 639, 641-42 (5th Cir. 1976).

Williford v. State of Texas, 127 S.W.3d 309 (Tex. App. 2004).

Zubulake v. UBS Warburg LLC, 220 F.R.D. 212 (S.D.N.Y. 2003).

ENDNOTES

[1] Guidance Software has disputed the discussion regarding its EnCase Forensic and EnCase Enterprise products in Newsham et al (2007). For example, in Guidance Software (2007), it notes that certain of the issues are "minor bugs," are unlikely to occur, or can be addressed by properly trained examiners. This article does not take a position on the accuracy of any particular research regarding forensic software security, but rather simply seeks to analyze what the legal implications are of research that points to potential weaknesses.

[2] This finding is probably not unique to forensic software; many software programs written in C that accept untrusted input have a potential risk of code execution vulnerabilities.

[3] It is unlikely that a forensic examiner would want to run forensic software on the system being collected from, because running the operating system during collection could change data during the normal course of its operation. In addition, there is likely to be a greater risk that the operating system on the target machine (vs. the operating system on the forensic workstation) has been compromised.

[4] In addition to integrity checks, the risk that a workstation has been compromised during a prior investigation can be mitigated by running a clean installation of both the operating system and forensic software for each new case.

[5] Even if a court admits evidence that has potentially been tampered with, the jury may find arguments about the accuracy of the software to be persuasive enough to disregard it.

[6] This may occur, for example, with automatically-generated data such as server logs, where it would be very unlikely for a person to know whether a particular log entry has been altered.

[7] For example, see Perfect 10, Inc. v. Cybernet Ventures, Inc. (2002) (finding printouts of web pages authentic); United States v. Tank (2000) (finding printouts of chat room logs authentic, where the person recording the logs has deleted nonsexual conversation and time and date stamps).

[8] Kumho Tire Co., Ltd. v. Carmichael (1999) holds that with regard to scientific, technical or other specialized knowledge, where the "factual basis, data, principles, methods, or their application are called sufficiently into question... the trial judge must determine

whether the testimony has 'a reliable basis in the knowledge and experience of [the relevant] discipline." Note that the rule requires judges to be gatekeepers of testimony, not the evidence itself. However, as a practical matter an expert will be needed to lay the foundation for technical evidence and to rebut claims of unreliability.

[9] Daubert v. Merrell Dow Pharmaceuticals, Inc. (2003, p. 590). Note that in the Daubert analysis, whether the forensic image was actually compromised or not is irrelevant; a court will look only to whether the software that created the image used reliable techniques.

[10] Open source tools may provide an advantage with regard to the "testability" factor.

[11] Newsham et. al (2007, p. 12) notes that according to Carrier, "sufficient public testing tools, results and methodologies either don't exist or are not public").

[12] For example, Mississippi State University (2003) notes that according to Associate Professor David Dampier, "computer investigative techniques... vary widely among local, state and federal law enforcement agencies."

This work was previously published in International Journal of Digital Crime and Forensics (IJDCF), edited by Chang-Tsun Li & Anthony T.S. Ho, pp. 80-91, copyright 2009 by IGI Publishing (an imprint of IGI Global).

Section 2
Combating Internet–Based Crime

Chapter 5
Methods to Identify Spammers

Tobias Eggendorfer
Universität der Bundeswehr München, Germany

ABSTRACT

Unsolicited commercial email has become a major threat for email communication. Although the degree of sophistication of spam filters has increased over time, such filters still produce high rates of false positives and false negatives, thereby reducing the reliability of email and introducing communication risks on their own. Due to more and more complex filtering methods implemented, the hardware requirements for mail servers are increasing to avoid the risk of denial of service situations. Therefore, some authors point out that mail filtering has reached its limits and ask for more preventive solutions to fight spam. One way to prevent email abuse would be to significantly increase the risk of a spammer being sued for damage compensation or, if legislation permits, for criminal offence. This approach believes in an assessment of risk and expected revenue by the offender. But by hiding their real identity, spammers are very successful in evading prosecution. This paper discusses several methods to identify spammers and analyses under which circumstances those methods might be valid evidence in court.

INTRODUCTION

Although not anticipated by the founders of the Internet, email has become one of the most accepted and widely used applications of the Internet. But with an ever increasing proportion of unwanted email, users are slowly starting to think about switching to other means of communication. Some use instant messaging instead, others are returning to the fax, despite being more expensive and less convenient.

Spam is not only an inconvenience, it also has high associated costs, including the wasted work time reading unsolicited emails, the investments in hardware and software needed and the costs associated with maintaining spam filtering systems. Additional costs are also incurred for providing

DOI: 10.4018/978-1-60960-515-5.ch005

the necessary bandwidth and extra hardware to handle the flood of emails.

Although the definition of spam seems to vary, with some authors restricting it to unsolicited commercial email and others broadening it up to any unsolicited bulk email, including mass emails sent to distribute viruses, worms and Trojans, hoaxes and even chain letters, they share the observation that spam makes up for the vast majority of all emails sent worldwide, be it more than 80% in July 2007 according to spam-o-meter (2007) or even more than 97%, as claimed by T-Online, one of Germany's biggest email providers (Kuri, 2006).

If providers were able to filter all of this unsolicited email automatically and with a zero error rate, email users would not care about spam, because they would not receive any. In an ideal world, where perfect filters exist, spammers would even have to discontinue their business because their earnings would drop to zero. The spam problem would then be resolved.

Unfortunately, spam filters only offer more or less accurate heuristics to help sorting spam and ham, as legitimate email is often called. Therefore, reality is far from this perfect world.

False Positives and Negatives

Recent surveys (Eggendorfer, 2007b; Schulz, 2006; Hosbach, 2006) found that false positives rates of spam filters might be as high as 18% and false negatives easily reach 20%. Although false negatives, i.e. spam not marked as spam, are annoying to the user, false positives are of far greater concern: in a business environment a false positive might have been a customer ordering a product. Failing to notice this message due to an overacting spam filter might not only mean a loss in sales but also liability for not delivering the requested products, thereby increasing the potential financial losses from a false positive by orders of magnitude (Heinlein, 2007).

Although seldom considered to be so, spam filters therefore might be one of the risks associated to spam, even if they help to cure some of the symptoms of the spam epidemic.

On the other hand, false negatives, often considered to be only annoying, but not a security risk, also introduce a new risk: The human false positive. The more unwanted messages actually make it to the end user's mailbox, the more messages the user has to filter manually. To do so, the user often only relies on the sender address and the subject line. Considering how many other factors a spam filter uses to identify a legitimate message, the lack of precision is obvious, even if one believes that human intelligence is likely to be superior to simple computer based heuristics and might find more evidence for a message being spam than a computer does by taking more factors into account.

However good the human brain might be, the sheer quantity might lead to users accidentally and unintentionally marking one message too many for deletion or as spam. Those misidentifications by the user are "human false positives" and are at least as troublesome as machine false positives. Human false positives are unpredictable in their nature and cannot be avoided by technical means, except with better spam filters or methods that decrease the total amount of spam. Yet, the more aggressive a filter is, the more likely are machine false positives (Eggendorfer, 2007b). This is a *circulus virtuosus*.

Security Considerations

Also, spam filtering increases the risk of security leaks on an SMTP server: the more complex filters are (some even implement OCR to identify image spam) the more computing power they consume; the more power they consume, the higher are the requirements on the mail server's hardware with constant processing time per message, or the longer the mail processing time becomes on unmodified hardware. With each and every message taking longer to be processed, the mail server will be able to handle less requests per second.

This again increases the risk of a denial of service attack on the mail server. Apa (2003), Frei (2004) and Schüler (2004) provide anecdotal reports of this being more than just a theoretical idea. The author notes he recently had to upgrade his mail processing system to more powerful hardware due to the heavy load his mail and virus filtering generated.

Not only is there a risk of denial of service attacks, but also does each additional line of code on any system mean an increased risk of this programme containing one or more bugs. Bugs might introduce security leaks, which might be exploitable remotely. Those security leaks might be used to attack the mail system and compromise it. Obvious risks are abusing the mail system for spamming, accessing mail messages without the recipient's consent or abusing the system in any other possible way. Each additional line of code introduced on a server system increases the risk of security leaks.

New Approaches

Taking all those risks into consideration together with the limited quality of current spam filters, it is obvious that spam filtering is only a short term solution helping to reduce the symptoms of the spam plague, but not a long term approach curing the cause.

Therefore, Eggendorfer (2007b and 2005c) proposed several techniques to preventively reduce spam to work around the limits of spam filtering. Those methods have their focus on technical methods to prevent spam and have been demonstrated to be efficient.

However, fighting spam only on a technology base is a very limited approach considering that spam is not only a technical but also a socio-cultural problem. Besides technical concepts, many countries have changed their legislation to be able to prosecute spammers. Media reports try to educate the population on the risks of buying *spam-vertised* products; teachers warn their

students to raise awareness and thereby prevent potential customers from responding to spam. All those approaches try to reduce a spammer's return on investment. An investment in this context does not necessarily mean a financial engagement but also other risks, such as being sentenced to prison, spammers are willing to take in order to earn their living.

Although there is no evidence of spammers assessing their individual risks and calculating their financial equivalent, it is likely that they only accept certain risks because of the chance to earn enough to outweight it. Different authors estimate that a spammer's daily income might exceed US$ 5.000 (Ilgner, 2006; Spammer, 2004; Spammer, 2006).

However, the risk of being sued for spamming is comparatively small. Only a few spammers have been sentenced, some of them had only started their criminal career and naively printed their address in their spam mails. Most of the big spammers, as listed on the list of known spamming organisations (ROKSO), have not been prosecuted yet.

If the risk of being sued were to increase with a given daily income, then the risk to revenue ratio would become worse. Spammers might then reconsider their financial decision to spam. An example for such shifts in crime is the popularity of bank robbery: when the robbers learned that their risk of being identified and sentenced to jail due to better hidden alarm systems, video surveillance, etc. increased, the rate of bank robberies dropped.

On the other hand, if the expected revenue were to decrease with a given risk, the ratio also shifts to worse. For example, many supermarkets have introduced logistics to reduce the amount of cash at their check-outs. Then, if a robbery occurs, the robber will not earn as much as previously. Again, after a while, their economic incentive to rob supermarkets decreases, as it is not worth the risk.

Unfortunately, there is no direct method to reduce the spammer's revenue, except by educating users not to buy spam-vertised products from spammers and by introducing better spam filters, thereby preventing users from receiving those offers.

More and more countries have changed their criminal laws and introduced spamming as a criminal offence and thereby legally increased spammers' risks. Often enough however, it is hard for law enforcement agencies to identify the offender, as spammers are able to hide their identity very well. This article discusses several methods to identify spammers.

ORGANISATION OF THIS ARTICLE

This article is organised as follows. The following section describes the spam business and the steps necessary to spam. It analyses how division of labour is done in the spam business. We then look at how spam senders could be identified and analyses problems related to those methods. The methods described in the following section choose a different approach in trying to identify another player in the spam business, the address trader. A new method is proposed, the usage of a distributed tar pit network, to offer a safe and probative way to investigate an address trader's identity.

In the last section, we conclude and give an outlook on our ongoing research.

HOW SPAMMERS WORK

In order to find ways to fight spam and spammers, it is necessary to analyse how they work, because this might offer hints on how to attack and / or unmask them. A first step in this analysis is to determine the different tasks involved in a spam run.

In preparation of a spam run, a spammer needs to purchase or otherwise provide the products intended for sale, acquire email addresses of – from his point of view – potential customers, needs to provide a secure and anonymous payment system and might need to install an online shop or a web

site somewhere. To send out the spam, a spammer needs ideally a system not listed on any black list and a somewhat fast Internet connection to send out as many messages as possible. As soon as the first complaints about him spamming are coming in, a spammer needs to have an infrastructure allowing him to work around the ban his provider might have imposed. Also, when the first orders are placed, the spammer needs an anonymous payment system as well as a delivery system hiding his own identity to protect him from investigators.

Product Provisioning

Generalising, spammers offer products out of four categories:

- tangible goods, such as drugs, coffee machines or breathalysers
- intangible goods, such as mortgages, "university" degrees, sexually explicit images or software for download
- services, such as access to "adult" dating communities, email addresses to spam to or even email advertising
- stock spam, where a spammer buys stocks, later advertises them and then sells them after they have ticked up.

Obviously, products out of the last two categories do not require a complex purchasing processes, storage or logistics. Provisioning them is no problem, because there is no physical product.

Intangible products are often as easily provided: Software for download is in most cases a pirate copy easily copied as often as needed, erotic pictures are available from many sources on the Internet and might be reproduced as required. Provisioning them might be done by subscribing to other web pages of this kind and copying pictures from there. According to sources in the spam community, this is a common approach.

To sell tangible goods, a spammer has basically two options. He might act as a sales agent or sell the items as a vendor himself. The latter means he has to stock those products or order them "just in time", introducing additional economic and privacy risks to him. The first is due to the risk of overstocking products, the second due to the fact that sending the items might identify the spammer if the original sales person is not trustworthy.

Acting as a sales agent however reduces the potential income to just the commission offered by the vendor. On the other hand, there are enough online shops offering commissions to anyone with a website linking to the shop. *Amazon.com* is well known to do this, another service is *tradedoubler*, acting as an agent between the online shop and the sales agent, thereby enabling smaller shops to also offer "partner shops". Although those shops often disallow *spam-vertising* of their products, they might not have simple means to identify such activity.

Product Delivery

Similar problems to provisioning tangible goods are associated to their delivery. If they are mailed with a valid sender's address, the recipient might identify the spammer. However, depending on the product's value, the spammer might have a strong interest in having it returned to him in case it is not deliverable. According to reports in the *de.admin.net-abuse.mail* newsgroup, this fact let to the identification of a German spammer selling office coffee machines. To work around this, the spammer might either not give a return address, use a fake address or use readily available mail forwarding or mail box services. The alternative is to sell products of a low enough value to him to accept a certain percentage of losses in the mailing process, which is often acceptable for faked Viagra which is sold for more than US$50 per box, but bought for as little as US$1-2 per box. However, by enforcing payment prior to mailing the product, the risk of loss is transferred to the customer and the delivery address is thus more likely to be correct.

Email Address Acquisition

Email addresses are usually either collected from web pages using harvesting technologies (Eggendorfer, 2005; CDT, 2003) or from users' hard disks using Trojans.

Another way is to persuade users to subscribe their email address to certain services, e.g. an adult web site offering to email daily pictures of some form of sexual practice. Subscribers to such email newsletters might be interested in equivalent offers from other web pages and are more likely to buy related products. Email addresses acquired this way offer spammers the opportunity to send their mails to a more interested target group, thereby raising the response rate from 0.1% on non-target spam to up to 30% (Spammer, 2004; Spammer, 2006). Often, consumers who previously showed interested in certain products do not consider related information as unsolicited.

Unfortunately for most users, most spammers still use harvesters and Trojans to acquire addresses. However targeted spam techniques are developing, as it obviously has advantages to spammers: higher response rates, a smaller likelihood of being reported as spam and less mails to be sent out, resulting in a higher return on investment.

Payment Systems

Depending on the money earning scheme chosen by the spammer, in most cases a secure and anonymous payment system is a requirement. Only if there is no direct customer contact, spammers do not need a payment system, as for example in stock spam.

In every other situation, spammers need to accept payments made by their customers or a third party. A third party is involved if the spammer acts as a commission paid sales agent or promoter for an online shop. In this case, anonymity requirements might be less of an issue, because the shop operator might be trusted. In all other cases, a person buying a spamvertised product might be an investigator trying to identify the anonymous spammer. Therefore, the spammer needs an online payment system maintaining his anonymity to avoid prosecution. The system however needs to at least look safe to customers, i.e. it should operate on HTTPS or implement anything else a customer might have trust in. Often enough, a faked VeriSign logo might be enough to generate the feeling of security.

In most cases, spammers want to offer their customers credit card payment. This means that spammers need to have some kind of bank account to receive payments. To avoid being tracked using this account, they often use anonymous debit cards as reference accounts or offshore bank accounts. Many shopping malls, for example, offer gift certificates working as a debit card, often rechargeable via the Internet and often enough with very lax verification of the owner (if any), as it is fully prepaid, meant as a gift and thus bought by a third party, and risk-free for the issuer. Those cards often are fully functional and often the stored value can be withdrawn at any ATM.

Anonymous Online Shops and Web Sites

Similar anonymity requirements exist for online shops or web pages used to sell or promote the product: because accessibility via the Internet is a basic requirement for a web site, it needs to have a public IP address. By using whois services, an IP address is easily traced back to its provider and therefore a risk for the spammer's anonymity. To avoid this risk, spammers often locate their servers at a so called "bullet proof hoster", who usually ignores spam complaints, i.e. does not disconnect spammer operated machines from the Internet, and would not ask his customers for identification, thereby maintaining their anonymity. In exchange for those "services", bullet proof hosters usually add a significant surcharge to market prices and offer their services only prepaid.

Instead of trusting a bullet proof hoster, some spammers prefer to use cracked servers, where they host their web pages and even shops. This has the advantage of being almost untraceable, but also the disadvantage of an unexpected interruption of service, either because of the cracked machine's provider disconnecting it due to spam complaints or because the machine's administrator locks the cracker out. To work around such risks, spammers usually have more than one cracked server ready and use special DNS servers with very short time outs so they might easily change the IP address. From a technical point of view, this is similar to the techniques used for dynamic DNS services.

Often such DNS services are offered by spammer friendly providers, to reduce the risk of a DNS entry being removed due to spam complaints.

A rather new method is to use bot nets to host a web site. In this case, cracked and remote controlled home PCs are turned into web servers publishing a spammer's web site. As those machines might go offline at any time and might also change their IP, a dynamic DNS-solution is again needed. Often, it also needs to support multiple A records to offer an DNS round robin address resolution (see standards RFC0974; RFC1794).

Sending Spam

Although bulk mail software is readily available from major download sites (Eggendorfer, 2007), it is rather inefficient to use such programmes, because they send their messages from the spammer's Internet connection, allowing the black listing of his IP address and thereby reducing the spam run's effectivness, because the message is filtered out by more spam filters. Additionally, using their own IP address, spammers risk their anonymity. Spammers therefore try to send their messages through multiple computers to both distribute their mailing faster to avoid black list updates and to hide their identity. To do so, they rent bot nets.

As bot nets have become a major spam source and most bots are home PCs connected to the Internet with a dynamic IP address, some black list providers include subnets with dynamic IP addresses into their black lists. Therefore, sending mail from known dynamic IP addresses has become more complicated. But providers do not publish lists of IP addresses they use as dynamic IP addresses for their subscribers, therefore, those black lists need to rely on spam to identify an IP address as dynamic. This means, an IP address is only black listed for a certain time.

To work around this, meanwhile, so called virgin bot nets are available for rental – for a surcharge. A bot net is considered virgin if none of the IP addresses in it is currently listed on any black list.

Division of Labour

Taking all the tasks mentioned above into consideration, it is efficient to divide them up between some specialised persons or organisations. Often, the following services are identified:

1. The spammer
2. The manufacturer of the product sold or the service offered
3. The address collector and seller
4. The rental agent for bot nets
5. The bullet proof hoster

Some therefore consider spamming to be organised crime, some even believe the Russian Mafia to support spam. Whether this is true or not, dealing with criminals who share their work and often remain mutually anonymous towards each other has serious effects on the effectiveness of investigation, because often only parts of a large co-operating network might be uncovered. However, increasing the risk for some involved in a crime, means that they will reassess their chances of earning enough to cover their risk of being prosecuted with the consequence of either bailing out or demanding a bigger share of the money earned.

Therefore, from an anti-spammer's point of view, it is enough, if some parties of the spam business are exposed, even though some will have a chance to escape without being sued. Also, by having access to some members of a group of criminals, investigators have more options, and the the investigation moves from cyber space to real life, where a lot more expertise exists and more trackable traces are left.

IDENTIFICATION OF SPAMMERS

A very exposed party in the spam business is the spammer himself. If he were at a high risk of being sentenced to jail or losing his earnings, he might decide to choose a more profitable business model. Obviously, if he gives up, all his supporters and partners would need to choose a new way of earning their money.

Methods to identify spammers are as old as spam itself, starting with a simple mail header analysis to identify the sender's IP address and using this piece of information to identify the spammer himself. Considering the increased usage of bot nets, mail headers become less and less useful in tracking a spam mail's source, but observation of the bot nets and who uses them might be helpful in the identification process.

Other methods more oriented on the spammer's work flow include the observation of him buying the goods sold, the payments made by customers or affiliates and the servers used to host the spammer's web pages and online shops. To identify stock spammers, several governmental organisations like the federal trade commission (FTC) in the United States started investigating orders placed in context with a spam run.

All those methods are described in more detail in the following subsections and discussed with a view to their efficiency.

Mail Analysis

Each email message consists of a body, where the message to be read by the mail's recipient is stored, and a header, containing technical information about the message, such as the To- and Cc- addresses, the date and the sender's alleged email address. As a mail message might be relayed through several servers in the Internet, each mail transfer agent (MTA) relaying it adds a header line. In these "received"-headers, an MTA logs the name the remote machine sent during the SMTP's HELO-command, the remote IP-address and often also the reverse DNS entry for this IP. Also, a time stamp is logged (Wood, 1999).

These headers enable tracking back to where a mail message was sent from. This information can be used to identify the spammer's service provider and request them to ban those senders and / or supply their names and addresses to allow legal action (Wood, 1999; Hochstein, 2003).

To reduce their risk of being discovered, spammers use either cooperating providers or send their spam from bot nets. They also add faked headers to make it harder to identify the true path of a message through the Internet.

Header analysis has thus become an inefficient technique to identify spammers.

Observing Bot Nets

As bot nets became the major source of spam and are under the control of spammers at the time spam is sent, it is feasible to try to observe bot nets to identify spammers. Kornblum (2006) describes how Microsoft has tried to support law enforcement in investigating bot nets abusers for illegal activities. According to Kornblum (2006) a plain, out of the box Windows system was installed in a partially secured network environment allowing this machine to be infected by worms and Trojans, but avoiding spreading the infection to other systems.

Besides the irony involved of Microsoft using security holes in their own products to identify attackers that would not have been successful if Microsoft had built their software with security in mind, there are a few considerations to be made in order to have evidence accepted in court.

First, the person contracting the Internet access provider might not necessarily be the attacker. If the computer is shared among several persons, each of them is under suspicion. As there are thousands of unsecured WiFi access points world wide, an attacker could use any of these to control the bot net. The same is true for Internet cafés: most of them are coin operated and thus do not require any proof of identification to use their services, offering a perfectly anonymous access point to bot nets. As bots are often controlled via Internet Relay Chat (IRC), access to them is easy.

Add to this the possibilities of computers with remote back doors and an attacker has plenty of possibilities to hide his identity. The more systems he adds in between him and the bot net, the better he covers his traces. If the machines he uses are located in several countries, law enforcement has to deal with different legal systems and agencies more or less willing to co-operate. Due to privacy laws, in several countries data needed to identify someone based on his IP address and time of usage is impossible to get or only available for a very short time, even to law enforcement agencies. Only recently Germany, for example, expanded this period to six months.

Taking this into account, there is a high risk of accusing an innocent instead of the real attacker. A professional attacker would take care of hiding behind other identities. Although the method is simple, straightforward and easy to implement, its precision in identifying the target is not high enough.

However, the method offers a starting point for further investigation. This investigation should be unintrusive due to the high risk of accusing the wrong person.

Surveillance of Purchases

An approach used by the FTA to identify stock spammers is to look at who invested into those stocks prior to them being *spam-vertised*. Someone buying huge amounts of penny-stocks at this time is highly suspicious. This scheme might also apply to tangible and intangible goods sold by spammers. However, in this case, most of the time, it is harder to track, even though some goods are not freely available, such as medications. But just because access to those items is made difficult, this does not mean access is controlled and traceable, because usually there is a black market for restricted goods.

In some cases, spammers might also try to work around those restrictions by selling counterfeit products. This is common practice if boxed software is sold, but also possible for watches or garments.

· Spammers have also started to develop their own drugs, such as "generic Viagra" and "herbal Viagra". In some cases consumption of such drugs might be life threatening for purchasers, a risk some spammers are not willing to take. Therefore they often resort to herbal or allegedly homoeopathic drugs, because they believe these to be less dangerous. According to McWilliams (2005), Viagra-substitutes are often made of apricot kernels, which are biologically equivalent to almonds and therefore might cause severe anaphylactic reactions due to nut allergies. Also, different species of apricots contain different amounts of cyanide, up to lethal levels (Suchard, 1998). Even though these "herbal" substitutes are dangerous on their own, their trading is often not controlled. Therefore, it is almost impossible to track persons acquiring those products in quantities needed for spamming.

By comparing figures, it is obvious that spammers only account for a very small proportion of apricot kernel consumption. World wide production was 2.8 million tons in 2000 (Asma,

2007). Spammer's purchases of these products are unknown, but, as there are many other uses for apricot kernels, unlikely to account for a substantial amount. Therefore, tracking sales of this and similar products seems not to be a promising approach, even though it might work for stock spam.

However, if an investigator is able to track down a vendor's sales channels, this might offer a very good starting point, but this is then real world, "off line" investigation, which is beyond the scope of this article.

Partner Shops

Some spammers try to avoid the somewhat dangerous process of interacting with customers and use partner shops of big web shops. They earn a commission on each transaction initiated with their affiliate and often a bonus for referring new costumers. Most of these shops have an anti spam policy, most of the time saying that commissions earned with spamming will not be paid.

Therefore spammers try to subscribe only a few days prior to commission payment at the web shop, then start their spam run and collect the money before complaints start pouring in (Spammer, 2004; Spammer, 2006). By doing so, they evade the risk of not being paid.

Partner shops could prevent this by waiting a certain time between their customer making its purchase and cashing out their affiliate. Although serious shops implement several security measures, some web pages, mostly in the red-light districts of the Internet, are said to be less offended by being spamvertised and therefore have lower security measures set up, thus offering spammers a certain income.

In such cases, the web shop being spamvertised might be liable as an accomplice, according to German and some other countries' civil laws. The web shop could then be indicted for injunctive relief. To compensate its damages, disclosing the spammer's identity is a possibility: because the web shop needs to pay the commission, at least a certain minimum of information needs to be known, e.g. a bank or credit card account or an address the spammer has.

This might be a starting point to investigate the spammer's identity.

Payment Process

The same information is needed if a spammer's customer pays his bill. But again, spammers have found ways of working around the risk of being identified by using anonymous bank accounts or credit cards. Certain banks for example do not require any identification if a prepaid credit card is issued, others even allow the use of made-up names. This means the spammer could have his customers pay into his anonymous credit card's account and then withdraw the money at leisure from any ATM. Although these cards are usually a little bit more expensive then regular prepaid credit cards, the investment pays off, because the spammer can use any payment gateway without the risk of being identified.

However, if the spammer's credit card data is known, identifying him might become possible if he withdraws money at an ATM by using the associated surveillance cameras. However, not all ATMs are secured that way, and often the quality of the pictures they deliver is not good enough to identify someone. Also, a cautious spammer could try to avoid surveyed ATMs.

All in all, although at first the payment process might seem to be a method of identifying spammers, it is very limited.

Server Owner

Often, spammers have a web page dedicated to the product they are currently advertising. This page might contain a web shop, but might also only contain a redirection to some other web page, e.g. if they try to take advantage of a third party's affiliate programme.

Those web pages might be hosted on a proper server, a cracked machine or on a bot net. If the latter is the case, identifying the spammer might be possible using the methods described above to identify a bot net's user.

On a cracked server, the cracker might have left traces that identify him, but such analysis is again beyond the scope of this document.

A rented server might be located at a so called "bullet proof" hoster or at any regular provider. Most hosters usually only authenticate their customer's payment details, but not their claimed identity. Spammers could use their anonymous credit cards to hide their identity, making it virtually impossible to track them down without the help of the provider.

However, his log files might help in identifying the spammer, because to install or update his web page, the spammer needs to connect to the web server. This would reveal the spammer's IP address, which is a first step in identifying him. However, the same restrictions apply as mentioned above for the bot net's user's IP address.

Discussion

Although there are a few options to identify a spammer, there are work-arounds. Most only provide a first step in identifying him. However, in most real world situations, criminals do not think of all possibilities of hiding their identity, e.g. if they purchase an anonymous credit card, they might do so from their own computer, thus leaving their IP address in the log files of the credit card provider, if they do not use an anonymisation service such as JAP (Eggendorfer, 2005b). Therefore it is worth investigating each step. But, if a spammer thinks ahead, chances are he is able to hide his identity.

IDENTIFICATION OF ADDRESS TRADERS

To send out spam, valid email addresses of potential customers are needed. While acquiring those addresses, traces leading to the person collecting the addresses might be generated. As stated above, spam is considered to be a business based on division of labour, therefore the spammer and the address purveyor do not need to be identical.

Considering that spammers are accustomed to hiding their identity while sending out spam, because they have understood this is a primary, known way to investigate their identity, trying to identify them earlier in the process might catch them off-guard. This is especially likely, because anti spam techniques trying to prevent email address collection, such as obfuscating email addresses (Eggendorfer, 2006b) and attacking harvesters with HTTP tar pits are still new (Eggendorfer, 2006c; Eggendorfer, 2006d) and not widely implemented.

Therefore, identifying address traders while they are collecting email addresses might offer an interesting and new method to investigate participants in the spam business and find an entry point for further investigation.

Identifying Mail Addresses

Rehbein (undated) suggested generating email addresses published on a web site on the fly such that they were able to identify who looked at the site when the email address was created. To do so, those email addresses should either contain the remote IP address and the time of access or a reference to these. With these pieces of information, the computer from where the email address has been read should be identified. Due to dynamic IP addresses, the exact time needs to be logged as well. As soon as an email is received on one of the addresses, the harvester's IP address would be known. Together with the access time, the user of this IP address could be identified.

Rehbein claims to have identified a German phone book editor as a spammer because he has received an advertisement on an email address he could track back to the company's proxy. When confronted, they denied and threatened to sue him. Unfortunately, the case was not taken to court, therefore there is no legal statement on the proof's quality.

Basically, the usual problems when trying to identify a person based on an IP address arise, i.e. it is only known from which computer the attack was made, but it remains to be investigated who operated that computer. Especially in environments with shared proxies or net address translation (NAT), the attacker might only be identified as a user of this proxy or network. Knowing from which network the address harvester operated, is only a step forward in an investigation.

Fortunately, it is still uncommon to use bot nets or cracked machines to run harvesters. Therefore, the IP address seems to be a valid starting point for further investigation, and might offer a good first trace.

However, to provide a court-proof chain of evidence, there are some problems to be taken into account: one is the algorithm used to hide the IP address and access time in the email address generated. This algorithm needs to be bijective, that is, a given IP address and time should always generate a unique email address and a given email address should resolve to one and only one IP address and time combination.

Algorithms like this exist, however, to provide as evidence, those algorithms need to be mathematically proven to work as described. Rehbein's suggestion to use the MD5-algorithm does not come up to this requirement, as MD5 is not bijective, it is only considered to be cryptographically secure.

The algorithm should also generate email addresses that resemble regular email addresses, i.e. they should neither have a too long local part nor should the local part look generated. Ideally, the email address is a unique combination of names and perhaps a middle initial. A human operator of the harvester is then unlikely to notice the trap.

To protect third parties, the algorithm also needs to provide those addresses in a tamper proof manner, so an attacker cannot guess an email address pointing to a different harvester IP address at a different time. This again is a major flaw in the approach by Rehbein, who explained the system on his web page and only masked the remote IP address and the current time in an MD5-sum.

Another issue is the amount of time required to identify the address collector. From the moment the address is harvested to the time the email is received, there might be several hours or weeks. This might give the offender a chance to cover his tracks, or otherwise have a negative impact on investigation.

Practical tests have shown that only six months after an address has first been published on a web page, the address receives as many spam messages as an email address published years before. With many countries forcing their internet providers to only log which IP address was used by whom for six month, this might lead to a premature end of investigation.

Taking the complexity of the required algorithm, the required sophisticated explanation in court, and the time issue into consideration, this approach is interesting, but might only be of limited use from a forensic point of view.

Distributed Tar Pit Networks

Eggendorfer (2006d) suggested to use a network of HTTP tar pits to identify harvesters and use this information to block their access to other web pages based on their IP address.

An HTTP tar pit is a way to trap harvesters. Simply put, the tar pit publishes links to itself, thereby poisoning the harvester's list of pages to visit until finally the harvester is caught in an infinite loop. There are some other requirements to be met, such as protection of good spiders, like the Googlebot, and camouflaging the tar pit. A

detailed analysis is offered in (Eggendorfer, 2005 and 2005c) and of how to resolve the requirements.

Because the IP address of the harvester is recorded while it is caught in the tar pit, the harvester is identified while collecting email addresses and not only after an email has been sent to the address.

Therefore we suggest a distributed network of HTTP tar pits as a new method to investigate an address trader's identity, because the HTTP tar pit is a resolution to the time problem described above.

It offers another major advantage: Because harvesters usually revisit a tar pit very often, (Eggendorfer (2005) reports on hundred of thousands of visits within a day) the evidence gained is better and offers fewer excuses to the spammer, such as a misunderstanding and manual copy of the email address to his address book.

The tar pit also proves that the spammer uses automatic address collection, which in itself might not be illegal, but might serve as additional evidence of professional spamming.

Because harvesting is not illegal in most countries, the HTTP tar pit alone is not a valid proof of spamming. On the other hand, Eggendorfer (2006c) showed that a HTTP tar pit publishing email addresses is by far more effective than it would be without publishing mail addresses.

If the tar pit is modified to publish addresses identifying a certain harvester, then both the act of harvesting and the later spamming could be tracked back to a certain IP address.

Even though one might argue that with the distributed tar pit network one has to wait for an email and this might take some time, this method offers several advantages: the investigator wins time, because he knows beforehand who might later be a spammer and can start investigating this suspect's internet connection, financial transactions, life style versus income and other, well known surveillance and reconnaissance methods.

Also, the intensive search for email addresses is documented and offers additional evidence. Furthermore, by observing search patterns the harvester uses, the investigator might predict what kind of spam is to be expected. Those search patterns might be identified, because some harvesters actually use search engines such as Google to find their victims web pages. With a known IP address of the offender, analysing Google's log files might be rewarding. It might even lead to more traces, such as a Gmail account used by the spammer.

Even if a proxy or NAT was used by the address harvester, due to the time advantage gained over just observing incoming emails, the investigator might actually implement surveillance systems on the proxy or the NAT router.

Therefore, this new method is more likely to be able to identify the offender.

Discussion

HTTP tar pit networks are used to prevent spammers from collecting email addresses and used to identify harvester's IP addresses to protect other web sites from harvesting. If those HTTP tar pit networks publish specially crafted email addresses pointing to the harvester's IP address as well, address traders might be identified well before a spam run occurs. This offers investigation a time advantage over the now known analysis of received emails. Therefore, we consider this to be a promising approach.

Additionally, as of now, the effectiveness of this method is likely to be even better, because most harvesting does not occur from bot nets or cracked machines, but from the address trader's or spammer's own network and thus leaves clear traces to him.

CONCLUSION AND FURTHER RESEARCH

This article discusses methods to identify some of the parties involved in the spam business, giving new insight into the deficiencies of current approaches, and proposing new techniques. Although the proposed techniques do not help to discover the entire network of spammers, it increases the risk of being discovered for some of the people involved in the spam business. Because risks and expected earnings are often strongly correlated, those exposed to a higher risk will raise their services' prices, this again has effects on the other parties, because their economic risks increase due to the higher prices resulting in some spammers to quit spamming.

Even though spammers have learned how they might work around being identified while sending out spam, address traders take less precautions. Therefore, identifying address traders seems to be more promising. Our new suggestion is to combine the publication of email addresses crafted to prove that spam has been sent out due to a specific harvesting action and the advantages of HTTP tar pits in identifying harvesters as an effective way to provide court-proof evidence.

Our current research considers an algorithm to generate email addresses that meets all requirements mentioned above. Specifically, we want it to only generate unique email addresses containing a human name, and to integrate it then into the HTTP tar pit. Currently, the algorithm only provides random alphanumeric email addresses. We are also trying to investigate how newly published email addresses are distributed over time in the spam networks, as this might help in finding out which kind of spam pays the best for "fresh" addresses, and which spammers accept older addresses.

REFERENCES

Asma, B. M. (2007). Malatya: World's Capital of Apricot Culture. Chronica Horticulturae 01/2007. 20 ff. Leuven: ISHS

Brisco, T. (1995). DNS Support for Load Balancing. Retrieved from: http://www.ietf.org/rfc/rfc1794.txt

Center for Democracy and Technology. (2003). Why am I getting all this spam? Retrieved from: http://www.cdt.org/speech/spam/030319spamreport.pdf

Eggendorfer, T. (2005). *Stopping Spammers' Harvesters using a HTTP tar pit*. Sydney: AUUG.

Eggendorfer, T. (2005b). Ghost Surfing. Anonymous surfing with Java Anonymous Proxy. Linux Magazine (International Edition) 11/2005. 44 ff. München: Linux New Media

Eggendorfer, T. (2005c). Methoden der präventiven Spambekämpfung im Internet. Thesis. Fernuniversität in Hagen, München, Hagen

Eggendorfer, T. (2006). *SMTP or HTTP tar pits? Which one is more efficient in fighting spam?* Melbourne: AUUG.

Eggendorfer, T. (2006b). *Dynamic obfuscation of email addresses - a method to reduce spam.* Melbourne: AUUG.

Eggendorfer, T. (2007). Tweak your MTA. Spam-Schutz mit Tricks. Berlin: 3. Mailserverkonferenz

Eggendorfer, T. (2007b). Methoden der Spambekämpfung und -vermeidung. Dissertation. FernUniversität in Hagen. Hagen: BoD

Eggendorfer, T. (2007c). Spam slam. Comparing antispam applicances and services. Linux Magazine (International Edition) 03/2007. 32 ff. München: Linux New Media

Eggendorfer, T., & Keller, J. (2006c). Combining SMTP and HTTP tar pits to proactively reduce spam. Las Vegas, Nevada: SAM 2006 (The 2006 World Congress in Computer ScienceComputer Engineering, and Applied Computing)

Eggendorfer, T., & Keller, J. (2006d). Dynamically blocking access to web pages for spammers' harvesters. Cambridge, MA: IASTED Conference on Communication, Network and Information Security CNIS 2006

Frei, S. (2004). *Angriff via Mail. Mailserver als Verstärker für DoS-Angriffe. Heise security. 4.* Hannover: Heise.

Heinlein, P. (2007). Genervt, blockier gefährdet: Wie sich Firmen gegen Spam & Viren schützen können. Hannover: CeBIT 2007

Hochstein, T. (2003). FAQ. E-Mail-Header lesen und verstehen. Retrieved from: http://www.th-h.de/faq/headerfaq.php3

Hosbach, W. (2006). *Test Spam-Filter....die Schlechten ins Kröpfchen! PC Magazin 10/2006. 124 ff.* München: WEKA Computerzeitschriften-Verlag.

Ilgner, M. (2006). *The Economy of Spam.* Wien: Universität Wien.

Kornblum, A. E. (2006). "John Does" no more: Exposing Zombie Spammers. Cambridge, MA: M.I.T Spam Conference 2006

Kuri, J. (2006). T-Onine verzeichnet eine Milliarde Spam-Mails pro Tag. Retrieved from: http://www.heise.de/security/news/meldung/72324.html

McWilliams, B. (2005). *Spam Kings. The Real Story Behind the High-Rolling Hucksters pushing porn, pills, and @*#?% Enlargements.* Sebastopol: OReilly.

Partridge, C. (1986). Mail routing and the domain system. Retrieved from: http://www.ietf.org/rfc/rfc0974.txt

Rehbein, D. A. (undated). Adressensammler identifizieren - Ein Beispiel. Retrieved from: http://spamfang.rehbein.net

Schüler, H.-P. (2004). Spam-Welle überrollt die TU Braunschweig. Retrieved from: http://www.heise.de/newsticker/meldung/47575

Schulz, C. (2006). Erstellen eines Konzeptes sowie Durchführung und Auswertung eines Tests zur Bewertung unterschiedlicher Spam-Filter-Mechanismen bezüglich ihrer Langzeiteffekte. Thesis. Universität der Bundeswehr, Neubiberg spam-o-meter (2007). spam-o-meter statistics by percentage. Retrieved from: http://www.spam-o-meter.com/stats/index.php

Spammer, X. (2004). *Inside the spam cartel. Why spammers spam.* Syngress Publishing.

Spammer, X. (2006). Talk by Spammer X.: EU Spam Symposium

Suchard, J. R., Wallace, K. L., & Gerkin, R. D. (1998). *Acute cyanide toxicity caused by apricot kernel ingestion. Annals of Emergency Medicine 12/98. 742 ff.* Dallas, TX: Mosby.

Wood, D. (1999). *Programming Internet Email.* Sebastopol: O'Reilly.

This work was previously published in International Journal of Digital Crime and Forensics (IJDCF), edited by Chang-Tsun Li & Anthony T.S. Ho, pp. 55-68, copyright 2009 by IGI Publishing (an imprint of IGI Global).

Chapter 6
Spam Image Clustering for Identifying Common Sources of Unsolicited Emails

Chengcui Zhang
University of Alabama at Birmingham, USA

Xin Chen
University of Alabama at Birmingham, USA

Wei-Bang Chen
University of Alabama at Birmingham, USA

Lin Yang
University of Alabama at Birmingham, USA

Gary Warner
University of Alabama at Birmingham, USA

ABSTRACT

In this article, we propose a spam image clustering approach that uses data mining techniques to study the image attachments of spam emails with the goal to help the investigation of spam clusters or phishing groups. Spam images are first modeled based on their visual features. In particular, the foreground text layout, foreground picture illustrations and background textures are analyzed. After the visual features are extracted from spam images, we use an unsupervised clustering algorithm to group visually similar spam images into clusters. The clustering results are evaluated by visual validation since there is no prior knowledge as to the actual sources of spam images. Our initial results show that the proposed approach is effective in identifying the visual similarity between spam images and thus can provide important indications of the common source of spam images.

DOI: 10.4018/978-1-60960-515-5.ch006

INTRODUCTION

Spamming is a problem that affects people all over the world. Spam is an unsolicited email which has been sent to many people. There can be legal spam, where the sender gave proper contact information and also has an option to no longer receive the messages. However, in almost all situations, spam is illegal. It is an unsolicited mail that the recipient did not ask to receive and did not give the sender permission to send. Spam falsifies the sender information to prevent anyone from finding out where it has been sent from. Botnets are machines that keep on sending spam. Today, botnets are the main choice for cyber criminals who seek to conceal their identities by using third-party computers as vehicles for their crimes (www. cnn.com/2007/TECH/11/29/fbi.botnets). The FBI has identified at least 2.5 million unsuspecting computer users who have been victims of botnet activities (www.cnn.com/2007/TECH/11/29/fbi.botnets). Spam sometimes attempts to sell a product, convey some messages, or they might also try to trick the recipient to become infected, or attempt to lure them into visiting a website that can infect them.

Spam can cause a lot of problems to internet users. More than 90% of the emails sent on the internet are spam. Billions of dollars of counterfeit software, electronics, as well as shoes, watches, etc., are being sold because of spam advertisements. In this way, huge financial loss occurs to the companies. Spam emails, claiming to be from banks, might also lure users to give their usernames and passwords. Besides software piracy and viruses, spam is also the primary means of phishing and identity theft. Therefore, spam email analysis is one of the most important topics in cyber security. The most effective way of controlling spam emails at the moment is filtering (Carreras & Mrquez, 2001; Clark, Koprinska, & Poon, 2003; Drucker, Wu, & Vapnik, 1999; Sanpakdee, Walairacht, & Walairacht, 2006). However, filters can only differentiate spam emails from non-spam emails but cannot tell the origins of spam. In order to hide their origins, escape detection and spam filter analysis, and to conceal the fact that there are relatively few organizations creating the vast majority of these unsolicited emails, criminals use a variety of intentional obscuring techniques. For example, one of the techniques is to present text primarily as an image, to avoid traditional computer-based filtering of the text. Spam images are sent for two reasons: 1) for advertisement purposes; 2) to hide the textual contents of an email from spam filters. Having no words in the message will not allow spam filters to understand the nature of the message.

Spam images are harder to detect than text spam. Spam images are created when text is embedded into images and content obscuring technologies are used to defeat spam blocking techniques. Spammers use certain methods to defeat traditional anti-spam technologies such as fingerprinting (e.g., md5 (Rivest, 1992)), OCR, and URL blocklist.

1. A text can be embedded in an image which appears as normal text to the recipient but the spam blocking technologies will never be able to "see" the text as it is actually an image.
2. Spammers vary the space between words and lines and also add random speckles to make messages look different to different recipients, though all of them have the same text. By this way, they evade fingerprinting technology such as md5 (Rivest, 1992) by making the images appear unique to standard spam analysis.
3. Use of different colors and varying font size makes it impossible for OCR techniques to find out spam. Also, splitting up one word into two halves with a gap in between deceives OCR techniques.
4. Botnets are also becoming efficient and they can produce a large number of random images within a short time.

In order to stop unsolicited spam emails, we should trace the origins of spams and bring down the servers as well as those used to send spams. In this process, law enforcement offices shall be actively involved as spam propagating is also a legal issue. The goal of this article is to facilitate this process in providing scientific proof to the source of spams. We regard these spam images as a valuable clue for identifying the origins of spams. This article is dedicated to the analysis and clustering of spam images based on their visual characteristics. Through clustering, spam images are grouped together. Each cluster contains spam images whose visual effects resemble each other in the cluster, indicating common origins/sources of those images, i.e., they are created from the same template hence by the same spammer.

There are relatively few works in spam image identification (Byun, Lee, Webb, & Pu, 2007; Mehta, Nangia, Gupta, & Nejdl, 2008; Wu, Cheng, Zhu, & Wu, 2005). All these works address the image spam filtering problem. For example, Byun et al. (2007) proposed a classification method to model and identify spam images. McAfee, an Internet security vendor, also provides image spam filtering functions in its product. The main purpose of these works is to separate spam images from non-spam images thus to perform filtering functions. Visual features, such as color distribution, color heterogeneity, conspicuousness (some contrast feature), and self similarity (repetitive patterns), are used in training the classifiers/ filters. In this study, we go one step further to track the source of the spam distributors based on spam image clustering, i.e., if two spam emails have similar visual content, visual layout, and/or editing styles, then they are likely related. This can be used as a strong evidence base to identify and validate spam clusters or phishing groups for the purpose of cybercrime investigation. For example, an approach (Chun, Sprague, Warner, & Skjellum, 2008) was proposed that used clustering techniques to form relationships between email messages and group them into spam clusters.

Clusters were evaluated using a visual inspection method. A routine was developed to fetch and save a graphical image, or thumbnail, of the appearance of each destination website. Where the resultant collection of website images from a single cluster was visually confirmed to be the same by sorting the resultant webpage images, a high confidence was placed upon the integrity of the cluster. Our proposed method can not only automate this visual validation process, but link visual similarity directly to the presence of spam clusters.

The proposed spam image clustering algorithm first extracts visual features from images and then performs the clustering. There are four steps in the feature extraction:

- Foreground Extraction – this step separates foreground image content from the background. The foreground image content can be further classified into two categories: texts and picture illustrations. Since most images we collected are advertisements with text areas in them, we first separate these text areas through Optical Character Recognition (OCR). The rest of the foreground areas are picture illustrations. In the following steps, we extract features from these two types of foreground objects separately.

- Foreground Text Layout Analysis – For efficiency purposes, a spam originator often reuses the same editing template to embed spam texts in the images. Images generated this way usually have similar text layout but different background and/or slightly different spatial placement of text blocks. Thus, the text layout information is an important indication of the editing style of spam originators. In this study, we analyze the text areas in spam images and measure the similarity of text layouts between each pair of images.

- Foreground Picture Illustration Analysis – It often happens that in advertising the same product, a spammer tends to use the same picture illustration. However, unlike texts, it is not very efficient to change the content of image illustrations. Some minor editing on the images such as changing image size is the most commonly attempted by the spammers. Therefore, similar foreground picture illustrations may also indicate that they are from the same spammer or the same phishing group. We therefore perform foreground illustration matching based on the SIFT (Lowe, 2004) method (Scale-Invariant Feature Transform), which is a robust method in matching two distorted yet similar images.
- Background Texture Analysis – When editing spam images, it is probably the easiest to change its background color to make it unique. Even created from the same template, the background colors (and sometimes even the foreground texts) may be different. Thus, color similarity cannot be treated as an important indication of common templates. Instead, we first convert the image background into grayscale. We further find that, although different in color, the background texture features of images created from the same template tend to have less variation. Therefore, in this article, we analyzed the "homogeneity" and the "orientation" texture features of image backgrounds and found that with our currently colleted spam images, "orientation" textures can better distinguish among different templates than "homogeneity".

Since we do not have any prior knowledge as to the number of possible spammers or templates hence clusters, in this study we use an agglomerative clustering method to build a hierarchical cluster tree. Links in the tree are evaluated in terms of their consistency, and inconsistent links are cut off from the final clusters.

In the rest of the article, the foreground extraction method is introduced in Section 2. Sections 3 and 4 analyze foreground texts and picture illustrations. Section 5 analyzes background texture and Section 6 introduces the clustering mechanism. Experimental results are presented in Section 7 and Section 8 concludes the article.

FOREGROUND EXTRACTION

As mentioned earlier, the visual content of a spam image provides an important clue to identifying spam clusters. Two spam images are said to visually resemble each other if they have similar text layout, and/or similar foreground picture illustration, and/or similar background textures. Hence, there is a need to distinguish foreground objects from the background. To recognize foreground objects in the spam image, we first separate text areas through Optical Character Recognition (OCR). This is achieved by adopting the Microsoft Office Document Imaging (MODI) to identify recognizable texts in the spam images. MODI returns the recognized texts and their bounding rectangles. The coordinates of the bounding rectangles infer the location of each recognized word in the image, and thus, can be used in the subsequent text layout analysis. We exemplify the bounding rectangles of recognized words in the next section.

Foreground picture illustrations are then extracted after the text extraction. Picture illustrations can be thought as sub-images in the spam image. To extract picture illustrations from the background, we notice that typically, these sub-images are full of variety in their visual appearance, and thus, difficult to characterize them with any fixed set of visual features. On the contrary, the background is generally composed of a pure color base or computer-generated textures, and has relatively more uniformity than illustrations.

Figure 1. (a) The original image, (b) the converted grayscale image, (c) the foreground/background mask, (d) the illustration mask, (e) the original image histogram, and (f) the equalized histogram

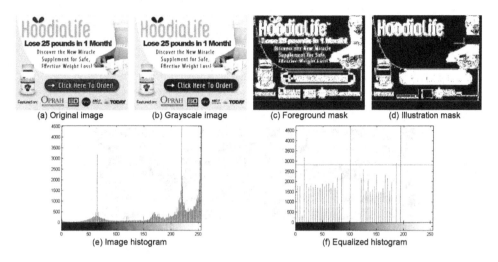

Hence, instead of finding illustration areas in a spam image directly, we obtain the illustration areas by removing the background in that image. However, it is not a trivial task since random noise and textures were often added on purpose to increase the background randomness and variations. Hence, we cannot use a single threshold value on visual homogeneity to separate the foreground objects from the background. In this article, we propose a simple yet effective method to differentiate foreground illustrations from background. The proposed method is based on the following two assumptions. The first assumption is that the spam images must have sufficient foreground/ background contrast to ease the reading of their recipients, which is usually the case as indicated by Byun et al. (2007). More specifically, the intensity values of foreground and background must have significant difference. The second assumption is that the background area occupies a significant portion of an image, which is often the largest or at least comparable to foreground illustrations. Also because background usually demonstrates more uniformity than foreground, background pixels tend to cluster together in the

pixel intensity histogram while foreground pixels demonstrate a wide range of intensities.

First, a color image is converted to its corresponding grayscale image as shown in Figure 1(a) and (b). According to the first assumption, the foreground/background contrast can be preserved even after converting it to an intensity image. Histogram equalization is then applied to the image to enhance the contrast. The equalized histogram may have empty bins around peaks since histogram equalization conceptually spreads out the most frequent intensity values into adjacent empty bins, making the histogram a uniform distribution (Burger & Burge, 2007). We demonstrate the histogram equalization in Figure 1(e) and (f).

Based on our second assumption, background pixel intensities usually have a relatively smaller range than that of the foreground and thus correspond to high frequency bin(s) in the equalized histogram. Hence, we first calculate the average frequency of non-empty bins. The empty bins are ignored since they are virtually filled with high frequency values. For all bins with frequency higher than the average, we considered them as corresponding to the intensity values of the background. The red line in Figure 1(f) represents the

Figure 2. (a) Sample spam images with different text content yet similar text layout. (b) The text block masks of the images in Figure 2(a)

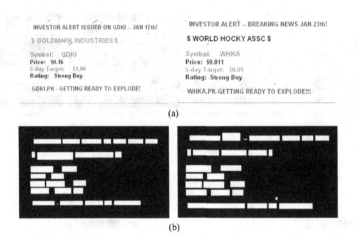

(a)

(b)

average frequency, and the black pixels in Figure 1(c) show the identified background pixels. The white areas in Figure 1(d) correspond to the picture illustrations after the removal of the text areas identified by OCR from Figure 1 (c).

FOREGROUND TEXT LAYOUT ANALYSIS

After the foreground extraction, text blocks contained in original spam images are singled out. The words in two advertising spam images are not necessarily the same when the two spam images are trying to sell different things. However, it is highly possible that a spammer uses the same text layout template in generating different advertisements by only changing the wordings for different products. For example, in Figure 2(a), two spam images have different text contents. However, their corresponding text layouts in Figure 2(b) are very similar. Similar text layouts may indicate spam images from common origins. Therefore, instead of the exact wording in the texts, we emphasize on the analysis of text block layouts.

In this section, we will use the sample images in Figure 2 to illustrate our text layout analysis method.

1. Bounding Box Extraction: The first step in text layout analysis is to extract the minimum bounding box of the whole text area in each image.

2. Dilation: We notice that two text layouts may look similar in their general layout yet their word and space distributions are very likely to be dissimilar. This is especially true when different wordings are used in the text as shown in Figure 2(b). If we directly compare the text layout masks, noises will be introduced by different word length, line spacing and word positions in each text line. We alleviate this problem by coarsening the text area. In doing so, we try to connect words in one line if they are only separated by a small space. The method we used to coarsen the text blocks is called dilation. For each pixel in the bounding box, if it is "1", and m pixels on its right and the m pixels on its left are also set to 1. In this way, small spaces are "closed" and therefore ignored. Only the general layout of the whole text area will be

Figure 3. Dilation

considered in the analysis. The resultant text bounding boxes and the dilated text areas for Figure 2(b) are shown in Figure 3.

3. Scaling: Text areas from different spam images are usually not of equal size so that we cannot directly compare them. To compare two text layouts, we first need to normalize them. A common way is to down-sample the larger text area, bounded by its minimal bounding box, to the same size of the smaller text area. However, this method may cause the larger text area to be skewed since the aspect ratio of the two images may not be the same. Therefore we only resize the larger text area so that its length is the same as that of the smaller text area. However, the original aspect ratio of its length and width is preserved. Therefore, the two text areas in comparison can have different widths.

4. Similarity Calculation: After resizing, we superimpose the text area with the shorter width on the one with the longer width and conduct the pixel-wise comparison. Then we slide the smaller text area one step at a time and repeat the comparison. This process is illustrated in Figure 4. The grids in Figure 4 represent pictures with their pixels. The

smaller text area is represented by dark gray grids. Each time we compare two text areas, we calculate their distances by the following formula:

$$\text{layout}\,(I_1, I_2) = \frac{\sum_{i,j}(I_1(i,j) - I_2(i,j))}{l_{small} \times w_{small}} \quad (1)$$

where $I_1(i, j)$ and $I_2(i, j)$ are the corresponding pixel values at the corresponding position (i, j) of the two text areas. Here the value of a pixel is either 1 (white: text pixel) or 0 (black: non-text pixel). l_{small} and w_{small} are the length and width of the smaller text area. A series of distances are thus calculated by sliding the smaller text area over the larger one. The minimum value of the distances is used to represent the distance between the two text areas i.e., the distance of the two text layouts.

FOREGROUND PICTURE ILLUSTRATION ANALYSIS

Almost identical illustrations contained in spam images are strong indications that they originate

Figure 4. Superimpose the smaller text area on the larger text area and slide it over the larger one to find the best match

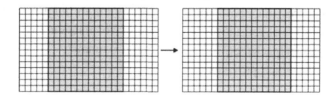

from the same source. However, now that we are measuring sub-regions of the spam images, we need to make sure that our similarity term is invariant to geometric transformations (e.g., translation, rotation or scaling of photos, or part of the photos being cut and pasted onto other spam images, etc.). Moreover, since it is not uncommon that the same product will appear in different photos with different backgrounds, our measure should also be able to localize the objects of interest even with background clutters. Both requirements imply that the global image features such as color histograms are not suitable in this case.

We adopt SIFT (Lowe, 2004), a local feature detector, to locate a number of feature points within the illustration regions, and use the percentage of matched features between two illustrations as their similarity measure. A class of local interest region descriptors are surveyed by Mikolajczyk & Schmid (2005) and SIFT is found to have the best performance among others. Given an input image, SIFT starts with detecting local extremes in a series of difference of Gaussian (DOG) functions over the scale space, with sub-pixel accuracy achieved by interpolating a local maximum with a 2D quadratic. For each feature location, one or more dominant orientations are determined, so that the features are invariant to image rotation. Finally, a descriptor for each feature point is formed by accumulating and bi-linearly interpolating local image gradients weighted by a Gaussian window, which provides certain degree of invariance to affine transformations. For a typical 400×300 image, SIFT is able to generate hundreds of feature points.

Once all picture illustrations in spam images are processed and a database of SIFT features are generated, we can identify the number of matches between illustrations in any two spam images and determine their similarity. A match of a SIFT feature is identified as its nearest neighbor in the Euclidean space (Lowe, 2004). We adopt the ANN (Approximate Nearest Neighbor) package (Mount & Arya, 2006) for this task, which provides an efficient nearest neighbor search algorithm based on *kd*-tree.

The feature matching is performed on picture illustrations only. After feature matching, a similarity score is given to each pair of spam images based on the number of matches found between their picture illustrations. Specifically, we define the similarity score as

$$similarity(I, J)=matches(I, J)/min(Number\_of\_features(I), Number\_of\_features(J)) \quad (2)$$

which ranges from [0, 1] with ascending similarity. The intuition for using the size of the smaller feature set is that, if a part of the photo (containing the product) is cropped and pasted onto another spam image, the similarity between them will still likely to be high, because both the numerator and the denominator will decrease, so this measure is less biased for part-to-whole matching.

Figure 5 provides more outputs of our algorithm. We manually collect several product categories (see Figure 5(a)-(f)) and compute a similarity matrix within each category as well as the average similarity score among them. Figure 6 shows the average similarity scores of Figure 5(a)-(f) for an example of measuring unrelated spam images. The similarity matrix is generated by calculating the pair-wise similarities of images in the same category. Therefore this matrix is symmetric. Since similarities range from [0, 1], they can be easily visualized by converting them to gray-scale intensities as shown in Figure 6. The average similarity is the mean of all entries in the similarity matrix. Notice in Figure 5(f) that SIFT seldom produces false positives between different categories. Figure 7 is an example of calculating the similarity between two images according to Equation (2). The number of matches is 116 and the minimum number of features extracted for these two images is 331. Therefore, the similarity is approximately 0.35 (116/331).

Figure 5. Similarity matrices computed from individual categories (a)-(e) and a mixture of categories (f). (c) and (d) present some difficulties for SIFT because there are more modifications on the photos. However, the average score is still > 0.35. In (e), the watch in the last five spams is the same as the one in the middle from the first 12 spam images, but SIFT fails to find matches between the two groups

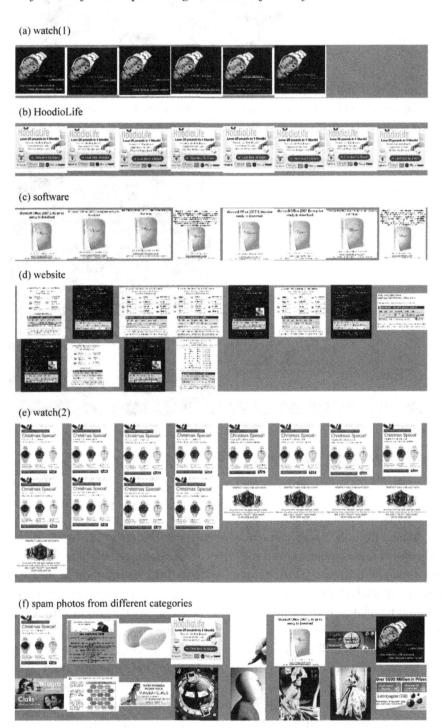

Figure 6. Similarity matrix

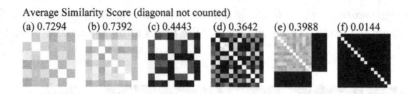

Average Similarity Score (diagonal not counted)
(a) 0.7294   (b) 0.7392   (c) 0.4443   (d) 0.3642   (e) 0.3988   (f) 0.0144

Figure 7. Two spam images that contain the same IE window but very different backgrounds. The image on the right contains another photo, which produces a lot more features, but the overall similarity is not reduced (similarity =116/331=0.35)

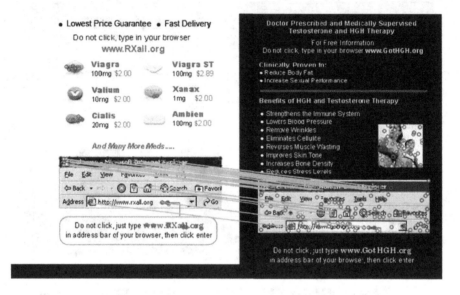

BACKGROUND TEXTURE ANALYSIS

When editing spam images, it is probably the easiest to change its background color to make it unique. Even created from the same template, the background colors (and sometimes even the foreground texts) may be different. Thus, color similarity cannot be treated as an important indication of common templates. Instead, we first convert the image background into grayscale. We further find that, although different in color, the background texture features of images created from the same template tend to have less variation. Therefore, in this article, we analyzed the "homogeneity" and the "orientation" texture features of image backgrounds and found that with our currently colleted spam images, "orientation" textures can better distinguish among different templates than "homogeneity". In this study, we analyzed the "homogeneity" and the "orientation" texture features of the image background.

The homogeneity feature measures the closeness of the distribution of elements in the gray-level co-occurrence matrix to the diagonal of that matrix, where the gray-level co-occurrence matrix describes how often a pair of pixel intensity values is spatially correlated (Haralick, Shanmugam, & Dinstein, 1973). In this study, we create a series of gray-level co-occurrence matrices with various offset values (from -4 to 4). These offset values represent the window size used to examine the spatial relationship between pixel pairs.

Figure 8. Edge orientation detection: (a) the original image, (b) the edge orientations (represented as the hue change), (c) and (d) the edges detected by Prewitt edge operators X and Y

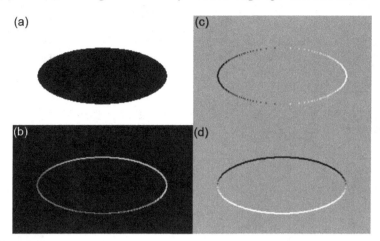

The orientation feature used in this study is an adapted version of the directionality feature (Tamura, Mori, & Yamawaki, 1978), which measures the local direction of the edge in the background textures by first applying the Prewitt edge operators, and then, computing the local orientation angle θ with the following formula (Burger & Burge, 2007).

$$\theta\left(u, v\right) = \tan^{-1}\left(\frac{\Delta_y\left(u, v\right)}{\Delta_x\left(u, v\right)}\right) \quad (3)$$

where (u, v) are the coordinates of an edge pixel; Δx and Δy are the filter results obtained from the corresponding Prewitt edge operators. Figure 8 illustrates how the Prewitt edge operators detect the edges and their local orientations.

The obtained edge orientation values are then quantized into a 16-bin histogram H_{dir}. According to Tamura's paper, the directionality feature is the sum of second moments around each peak in H_{dir} from valley to valley. However, this measurement may cause problem since we may obtain the same directionality feature from two different H_{dir}. Hence, we adopt the normalized H_{dir} (divided by the total number of edge pixels) to represent the

orientation feature of the background texture. The background texture similarity can be simply measured by the Euclidian distance between two texture feature vectors. According to our experiments, 'orientation' feature is significantly better than 'homogeneity' when we compare their distinguishing powers in classifying background textures.

Figures 9 and 10 show an example of spam image clustering based on the two texture features - homogeneity and orientation, respectively. In these two figures, the top-left image is selected as the cluster centroid and the top 20 nearest images are displayed from top to bottom and left to right in the descending order of their background texture similarity to the centroid. In Figure 9, only 7 out of the top 20 images have similar background texture as that of the centroid image, while in Figure 10 all top 20 images have similar background texture as the centroid, despite the disparity of background colors and texture scales.

CLUSTERING

In the spam image clustering problem, we do not have a prior knowledge as to the number of spam clusters. Therefore, in order to approximate the

Figure 9. Background texture similarity based on the homogeneity

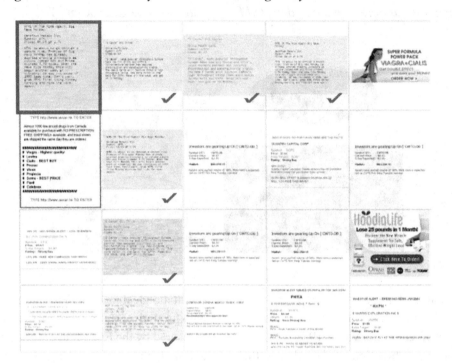

number of clusters, a bottom-up agglomerative clustering method (Han & Kamber, 2000) is used to group spam images based on similar values of spam image features, including the text layout, SIFT features of picture illustrations, and background texture features. In the beginning, each spam image by itself is a single cluster. These initial clusters are at the leaf level of a hierarchical cluster tree. Then each nearest pair of clusters is merged together at each higher level of the tree. A non-leaf node represents a cluster formed through the merging of its two children nodes (clusters). The root of the tree is a cluster that contains all images. In measuring the distance between two images, we use the following formula:

$$d(I_i, I_j) = eucl(texture(I_i), texture(I_j)) + layout(I_i, I_j) + fgImage(I_i, I_j) \quad (4)$$

where the first term is the Euclidean distance between the "orientation" texture features of

the two images I_i and I_j; the second term is the layout distance between the two images; and the third term is the foreground picture illustration distance between the two. The first two terms can be easily obtained from texture analysis and foreground text layout analysis. As for the third term, as mentioned in Section 4, we compute the similarity matrix from the foreground picture illustration matching. The similarities are further converted to distances by deducting each entry in the similarity matrix from the maximum similarity. In cases where a pair of spam images both contain only texts but no foreground picture illustrations in either of them, their 3rd term distance is set to 0. When only one of the two images contains picture illustrations, their 3rd term distance is set to the maximum distance. This is to make sure that a pure text image is closer to another pure text image than to an image that contains foreground picture illustrations. Finally, all three terms are normalized by z-score (Larsen & Marx, 2000)

Figure 10. Background texture similarity based on the edge orientation

before they are summed up to calculate the overall distance value between two images.

To estimate the approximate number of clusters, we need to cut the inconsistent links in the hierarchical tree. The inconsistent links are decided by the inconsistency coefficients of each link. The inconsistency coefficient characterizes each link in a cluster tree by comparing its length (distance) with the average length (distance) of other links to a certain depth of the hierarchy. The higher the value of this coefficient, the less similar the objects connected by the link. The cluster tree is then partitioned into clusters by setting a threshold on the inconsistency coefficient.

EXPERIMENTS

Spam Image Data Set

The spam images used in our experiments consists of those extracted from one month of emails manually identified as spam. We collect a high volume of spam through the use of "catch all" email addresses. A "catch all" configuration accepts mail for all possible addresses at a given domain. One common technique spammers use to "harvest" new target addresses is to send emails to randomly generated user IDs at well-known domains. Mail which does not "bounce" or reject is assumed by the spammer to have been delivered. Because a "catch all" address configuration accepts ALL mail, spammers treat all tested addresses as valid for its domains. We test our algorithm on 1190 spam images. After clustering, there are 53 clusters in total.

Evaluation of Clustering Results

It is necessary to determine whether the resulting spam image clusters are meaningful in order to aid cybercrime investigation. Since we do not have the ground truth for the sources of the images, clusters were evaluated based on the visual characteristics (appearance) of these images at this point. Where the spam images from a single cluster demonstrate similar visual characteristics (e.g., text layout, picture illustrations, and/or background textures), a high confidence was placed upon the integrity of the cluster. These common visual characteristics may indicate the common source of those images from a single cluster.

The largest clusters are the 12th cluster (284 images), the 35th cluster (265 images), the 51st cluster (189), and the 47th cluster (133 images). Sample images of the four clusters are provided in Figure 11.

Figure 11. Sample images from the largest clusters

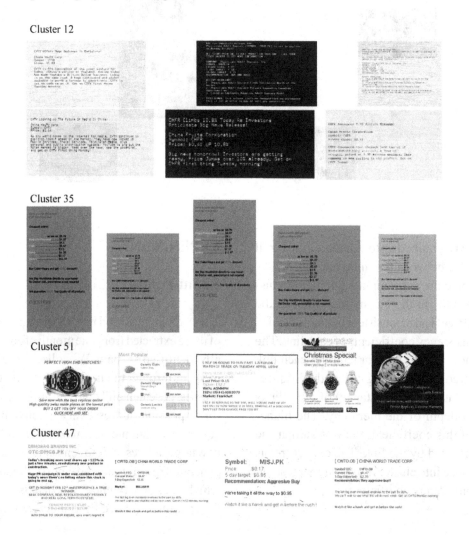

Cluster 12

Cluster 35

Cluster 51

Cluster 47

In Cluster 12, 256 out of 284 (i.e., 90.1%) images have background textures similar to the sample images in Figure 11. In addition, all the images in this cluster contain text areas only in the foreground. This cluster therefore is formed mainly because of the similarity of background textures and the text-only property. In Cluster 35, 252 out of 265 (95.1%) images are variations of the sample images shown in Figure 11. When we trace back the cluster formation process, this cluster is formed mainly because of the layout similarity. Cluster 51 is comparatively not very satisfactory. It is composed of 1 major type (120 out of 189) represented by the third sample image. This cluster also has 4 minor types of images as shown by the other sample images. These minor types are mixed with pure text images (like the third sample image) because of the noise introduced by OCR text detection. When a block of texts are missed by OCR, these texts will be considered as foreground picture illustrations and compared with other true illustrations, resulting a less than maximum distance for the 3rd term in Equation (4). Although this cluster is not uniform since it combines one major cluster with three other small clusters, it can still provide a hint of common source at least for the spam images in the major cluster. The dominant features in Cluster 47 are background texture and text layout. Particularly, 125 out of 133 (94.0%) images in this cluster have "random dots/dashes" texture feature as shown in the sample images in Figure 11.

The rest of clusters are comparatively small, with the number of images ranging from 1 to 55. 34 clusters have less than 10 images in them. One kind of those clusters represents outliers. For example, as shown in Figure 12, there are in total 7 images in Cluster 53 which belong to 6 different types of images and all of them are pure images with no texts. The rare occurrence of these images makes it hard to track the originator and therefore can be ignored at this stage until more such data can be collected. The other kinds of small clusters are those which contain very similar foreground picture illustrations. For example, Cluster 50 has 8 images and all of them belong to one of the sample images shown in Figure 13.

The two types of website images illustrated in Figure 7 are mixed with text images in Cluster 52 (47 images) due to the noise caused by OCR as we mentioned earlier. However, with a deeper

Figure 12. Sample images from cluster 53

Figure 13. Sample images from cluster 50

look into the cluster tree, both of these two types of website images are grouped into one cluster at an early stage of the tree construction and were merged into another cluster later.

CONCLUSION

This article has proposed a new approach to advanced analysis of spam emails with a focus on the needs of law enforcement personnel. Using this approach, clusters of spam used for spreading messages to encourage the purchase of a product or service through image attachments can be readily identified. Furthermore, this approach can help to automate the process of visual validation of the spam clustering results, which are usually generated by analyzing the non-graphic information of spam messages such as email attributes (Chun et al., 2008) and textual email contents (Airold & Malin, 2004).

Given a spam image, the proposed approach first separates its foreground from the background. The foreground is further segmented into texts and picture illustrations. Foreground text layout is analyzed through a 4-step process – bounding box extraction, dilation, scaling, and similarity measuring. A feature matching method – SIFT is applied in the foreground picture illustration matching. For background analysis, we first perform the grayscale conversion and then analyze the texture features of the grayscale image background. Particularly, the "orientation" and "homogeneity" of background textures are extracted and compared. The "orientation" feature is finally chosen because of its better distinguishing power for our collected image data. Finally, we apply the agglomerative clustering method to group images into clusters. Our initial experiment showed promising results as significant clusters of emails were found which through the visual verification were shown to be tightly related, regardless of the variations in the image scale, background color and/or texture, or spatial placement of text and/or picture illustrations in the foreground. The result is not perfect as we are still exploring and improving our methods. However, we believe it is a promising research area that is worth further pursuit.

FUTURE WORK

Spam image mining is a new area and there is relatively little related work. To our best knowledge, our work is among the first to address spam image mining from the perspective of spam cluster identification. We attempted to address various issues in spam image clustering in this article. This is an area that has a lot more to explore further.

The next stage of the research is to introduce more image features into analysis, especially color features. Although color features are not critical for background classification, it may improve the matching accuracy of the foreground images. We also plan to incorporate the text clue extracted by OCR into the clustering process. Another direction we will explore is the relative spatial relationship among the foreground objects including texts and foreground illustrations. Their relative positions may also be an important indicator of the editing style of spam images. The next issue is feature selection and information fusion from multi-modalities. When conducting this study, we find that one feature may be effective in differentiating a certain group of images, while it may fail on another group of images. Therefore, our long term goal is to build a feature selection model that can automatically select features and/ or update the way of combining multiple features in calculating the distance value. This model shall have the ability to distinguish a large variety of spam images and adjust itself when new spam images are collected.

REFERENCES

Airold, E., & Malin, B. (2004). *Scamslam: An architecture for learning the criminal relations behind scam spam*. Carnegie Mellon University, School of Computer Science, Pittsburg Technical Report CMU-ISRI-04-121.

Burger, W., & Burge, M. J. (2007). *Digital image processing: An algorithm introduction using java* (1st ed.). New York: Springer.

Byun, B., Lee, C.-H., Webb, S., & Pu, C. (2007). A discriminative classifier learning approach to image modeling and spam image identification. *4th Conference on Email and Anti-Spam*.

Carreras, X., & Mrquez, L. (2001). Boosting trees for anti-spam email filtering. *International Conference on Recent Advances in Natural Language Processing*, (pp. 58-64).

Chun, W., Sprague, A., Warner, G., & Skjellum, A. (2008). Mining spam email to identify common origins for forensic application. *23rd Annual ACM Symposium on Applied Computing*, (pp. 1433-1437).

Clark, J., Koprinska, I., & Poon, J. (2003). A neural network based approach to automated e-mail classification. *IEEE/WIC International Conference on Web Intelligence*, (pp. 702-705).

Drucker, H., Wu, D., & Vapnik, V. N. (1999). Support vector machines for spam categorization. *IEEE Transactions on Neural Networks, 10*(5), 1048–1054. doi:10.1109/72.788645

Han, J., & Kamber, M. (2000). *Data mining: Concepts and techniques*. Morgan Kaufmann.

Haralick, R. M., Shanmugam, K., & Dinstein, I. (1973). Textural features for image classification. *IEEE Transactions on Systems, Man, and Cybernetics, 3*, 610–621. doi:10.1109/TSMC.1973.4309314

Larsen, R. J., & Marx, M. L. (2000). *An introduction to mathematical statistics and its applications* (3rd ed.). Prentice Hall.

Lowe, D. G. (2004). Distinctive image features from scale-invariant keypoints. *International Journal of Computer Vision, 64*(2), 91–110. doi:10.1023/B:VISI.0000029664.99615.94

Mehta, B., Nangia, S., Gupta, M., & Nejdl, W. (2008). Detecting image-based email spam using visual features and near duplicate detection. *17th International World Wide Web Conference*, (pp. 497-506).

Mikolajczyk, K., & Schmid, C. (2005). A performance evaluation of local descriptors. *IEEE Transactions on Pattern Analysis and Machine Intelligence, 27*(10), 1615–1630. doi:10.1109/TPAMI.2005.188

Mount, D. M., & Arya, S. (2006). ANN: A library for approximate nearest neighbor searching. http://www.cs.umd.edu/~mount/ANN/.

Rivest, R. (1992). The md5 message-digest algorithm. RFC 1321.

Sanpakdee, U., Walairacht, A., & Walairacht, S. (2006). Adaptive spam mail filtering using genetic algorithm. *8th International Conference on Advanced Communication Technology*, (pp. 441-445).

Tamura, H., Mori, S., & Yamawaki, T. (1978). Textural features corresponding to visual perception. *IEEE Transactions on Systems, Man, and Cybernetics, 8*, 460–472. doi:10.1109/TSMC.1978.4309999

Wu, C.-T., Cheng, K.-T., Zhu, Q., & Wu, Y.-L. (2005). Using visual features for anti-spam filtering. *IEEE International Conference on Image Processing*, (pp. III-509-512).

www.cnn.com/2007/TECH/11/29/fbi.botnets.

Chapter 7
A Model Based Approach to Timestamp Evidence Interpretation

Svein Yngvar Willassen
Norwegian University of Science and Technology, Norway

ABSTRACT

Timestamps play an important role in digital investigations, since they are necessary for the correlation of evidence from different sources. Use of timestamps as evidence can be questionable due to the reference to a clock with unknown adjustment. This work addresses this problem by taking a hypothesis based approach to timestamp investigation. Historical clock settings can be formulated as a clock hypothesis. This hypothesis can be tested for consistency with timestamp evidence by constructing a model of actions affecting timestamps in the investigated system. Acceptance of a clock hypothesis with timestamp evidence can justify the hypothesis, and thereby establish when events occurred in civil time. The results can be used to correlate timestamp evidence from different sources, including identifying correct originators during network trace.

INTRODUCTION

Investigations are inquiries into past events. The purpose of an investigation is to find evidence of previous events. Investigation of digital media with the purpose of finding evidence is commonly referred to as *digital investigation*. In recent works, efforts have been made to make the digital investigation based on scientific principles, by using a hypothesis-based approach. (Carrier, 2006) In this approach, the investigator formulates his hypothesis about the occurred events, and tests them using the available evidence.

DOI: 10.4018/978-1-60960-515-5.ch007

A timestamp is a recorded representation of a specific moment in time. Timestamps play an important role in digital investigations. The identification that a certain event on a computer took place at a specific time makes it possible to correlate the event with events occurring outside the computer system. These may be events occurring in another digital system, or in the physical world. A particularly important application of timestamps in digital investigation is attribution; the ability to attribute events to a specific person. This is important, because most investigations aim at placing the responsibility for occurred events on one or more individuals. If evidence of the investigated events is digital, it may be necessary to place the event at a specific point in time in order to be able to attribute it to the correct person. If the time of the event inferred from the evidence is incorrect, it may not be possible to attribute it to anyone, or the event may be attributed to the wrong person. The prevalence of dynamic network addresses on the Internet makes timing important in all types of investigations of events that occurred on the Internet. In many such investigations, attribution relies on the identification of which computer were using an IP-address at a particular time. If the IP-address is dynamically assigned, the originating computer can only be identified if a log of the usage of the address exists, and the time of the event can be established with sufficient certainty and accuracy. Only in this case can the originating computer be identified from the usage log by selecting the correct IP-address and time entry.

A timestamp always refer to the clock from which it is generated. Since the timestamp is a function of the clock, it is always relative to the adjustment of the clock. Unfortunately, clocks are not fully reliable. Clocks may drift, thereby generating timestamps gradually more different from those generated from other clocks. Clocks may also fail, and produce completely incorrect timestamps. (Buchholz & Tjaden, 2007; Schatz, Mohay, & Clark, 2006) Further, clocks on most systems may be adjusted at any time by the user

of the system to show a different date and time than civil time. The uncertainty associated with digitally stored timestamps implies that timestamps should not be relied upon as evidence without justification of these factors. In particular, it should not be blindly assumed that timestamps are based on a clock that is adjusted to civil time. These uncertainties are worrying for investigators. If timestamps cannot be relied upon, then it is in many cases not possible to trace the use of an IP-address, since identification of the time of the event is necessary to find the correct originator.

This work takes the approach that time stamps can be tested in the hypothesis based investigation model. We utilize the concepts of a clock hypothesis and consistency tests defined by (Willassen, 2008). A clock hypothesis is the investigator's formulation of a hypothesis about historical settings of the clock. We define a model of how an investigated system updates timestamps. We then utilize this model to test a clock hypothesis for consistency with observed timestamp values. Such testing can provide justification for a clock hypothesis. When a clock hypothesis is justified, the time of the events on the computer can be interpreted accordingly, and can then be used for correlation with other sources.

2. ACTIONS AFFECT TIMESTAMPS

We can build a model of the investigated system, by representing the operations in the system that can possibly change the timestamps as *actions*. A model of a system with timestamps can then be described as a table listing the timestamps and the actions that affect them. We call this an affects table.

Definition 1. An action *affects* a timestamp if and only if an occurrence of that action sets a new value for the timestamp and removes the previous value for the timestamp. An *affects table* is a table listing all possible combinations of timestamps in a system, and all actions in the system and time-

Table 1. Affects table for the file system in Example 1

	Created	Modified	Accessed	Actions
0				
1	X			
2		X		
3	X	X		
4			X	Read
5	X		X	
6		X	X	Write
7	X	X	X	Create

stamps they affect. An affects table for a system with n timestamps has 2^n entries.

Example 1. Create an affects table for the following simple file system: A file system contains files, and each file has a Created timestamp, an Accessed timestamp and a Modified timestamp. Files can be Created, Read or Written. Reading a file causes the Accessed timestamp to be updated. Writing a file causes both the Accessed timestamp and the Modified timestamp to be updated, and Creating a file causes all three timestamps to be updated. There is only one timestamp of each type for each file, so whenever a timestamp is changed, the previous value is lost. The affects table for this file system is given in Table 1.

The affects table states clearly how timestamps are affected by actions. The affects table also shows which timestamp affect combination does not occur with any action. This information can be utilized to derive invariants between timestamps, by reasoning on sequences of timestamp updating and corresponding sequences of actions.

3. TIMESTAMPING ORDERS

In an investigation, the investigator observes values of timestamps on each investigated file. Each file has n different timestamps $\theta_1, \theta_2, ..., \theta_n$.

The observed values of these timestamps were set at moments in time $t_{\theta_1}, t_{\theta_2}, ..., t_{\theta_n}$, where the values observed by the investigator are $c(t_{\theta_1}), c(t_{\theta_2}), ..., c(t_{\theta_n})$, set by the clock of the investigated system. Since the clock function $c(t)$ of the investigated system is unknown, the investigator cannot map these values directly to the moments in time $t_{\theta_1}, t_{\theta_2}, ..., t_{\theta_n}$ when timestamping occurred. But the investigator can list possible sequences of timestamping, and determine if the observed result is consistent with a specific clock hypothesis, given the affects table for the system.

Definition 2. In a system with n timestamps, the *stamping time set* Θ is the set of moments in time $t_{\theta_1}, t_{\theta_2}, ..., t_{\theta_n}$ when each observed timestamp value $c(t_{\theta_1}), c(t_{\theta_2}), ..., c(t_{\theta_n})$ for the observed timestamps $\theta_1, \theta_2, ..., \theta_n$ was set.

Example 2. For the file system described in Example 1, the stamping time set is $\Theta = \left\{ t_c, t_m, t_a \right\}$, where t_c is the time of production of the observed Created timestamp, t_m is the time of production of the observed Modified timestamp and t_a is the time of production of the observed Accessed timestamp.

To determine which (if any) sequence of actions in the system could have resulted in the observed timestamps, it is interesting to determine the different sequences in which timestamping could have occurred. Each pair of elements in Θ, (t_i, t_j), may be related by either $t_i < t_j$, $t_i = t_j$ or $t_i > t_j$.

Definition 3. A *timestamping order* is a sequence of all elements in the stamping time set Θ, where each element is related to the next element in the sequence with the equals-relation $=$ or the less-than relation $<$. The equals relation imply that the stamping times are equal; the two timestamps were set at the same time. The less-than relation imply that the first stamping time is earlier than the second stamping time; the produc-

Table 2. All timestamping orders, n = 3

Number	Sequence
1	$(t_1 < t_2 < t_3)$
2	$(t_1 < t_3 < t_2)$
3	$(t_2 < t_1 < t_3)$
4	$(t_2 < t_3 < t_1)$
5	$(t_3 < t_1 < t_2)$
6	$(t_3 < t_2 < t_1)$
7	$(t_1 = t_2 < t_3)$
8	$(t_3 < t_1 = t_2)$
9	$(t_2 = t_3 < t_1)$
10	$(t_1 < t_2 = t_3)$
11	$(t_1 = t_3 < t_2)$
12	$(t_2 < t_1 = t_3)$
13	$(t_1 = t_2 = t_3)$

tion of the first timestamp occurred at an earlier time than the production of the second timestamp. Each different stamping time in a timestamping order constitutes a *step* in the timestamping order. When two or more stamping times are equal, they constitute a step in the timestamping order together.

An example timestamping order for the simple file system is $(t_c = t_m < t_a)$. With this timestamping order, the Created and Modified timestamps were set at the same time, and the Accessed timestamp was set at a later time than the Created and Modified timestamps.

A list of all timestamping orders can be constructed where each stamping of a specific timestamp may have occurred before, after or at the same time as the stamping of the other timestamps. The list of possible sequences for $n = 3$ can be found in Table 2.

4. POSSIBLE ACTION SEQUENCES

When all timestamp updating is represented by actions, the cause of timestamping having occurred in a specific sequence must have been actions that have occurred in a specific sequence. An action sequence is a sequence of actions of arbitrary length.

Definition 4. An *action sequence* is a sequence of one or more actions, where each element is related to the next element in the sequence with the equals-relation = or the less-than relation <. The equals relation imply that the actions occurred at the same time. The less-than relation imply that the first action occurred earlier than the second action.

The relationship between an action sequence and a timestamping order is that every observed timestamping order must have been created by an action sequence. When considering all timestamping orders, there may be many action sequences that may cause a particular timestamping order. There may also be timestamping orders, which cannot be created by any action sequence. These timestamping orders cannot occur in the system. The relationship between action sequences and timestamping orders can be deducted from the affects table.

Definition 5. A timestamping order is *possible in a system* if there is at least one action sequence in the system that may cause the timestamping order. If there is no action sequence that can cause the timestamping order, then the timestamping order is *impossible in the system*.

By using the affects table, it is possible to find all action sequences that may have caused a specific timestamping order, by the following procedure:

1. Find all actions or combination of actions affecting all timestamps in the first step in the timestamping order.
2. For each following step in the timestamping order, find all actions or combination of actions affecting all timestamps in that step, and not affecting any timestamps listed in previous steps. If there is no such action, then this timestamping order is not possible in the system.

The task of finding all actions or combination of actions can be implemented as follows:

1. For every timestamp θ_i find all actions affecting it, and add them to a set A_i.

2. For every action $a \in A_i$, check if a affects any timestamp θ_j listed in previous steps in the timestamping order. If so, remove it from A_i.

3. Actions $a \in (A_1 \cap A_2 \cap .. \cap A_n)$ affect all timestamps in that step. Remove them from A_i.

4. If all sets A_i are still non-empty, the remaining actions represent combinations of actions affecting all timestamps for that step. The combinations can be found with the Cartesian product $A_1 \times A_2 \times ... \times A_n$

Example 3. Find all action sequences for the timestamping order $(t_c < t_m < t_a)$ for a file in the file system in Example 1.

From the affects table for the simple file system in Table 1, the steps in the sequence yields:

- (t_c): <u>Create</u> (t_c is only affected by Create)
- (t_m): <u>Write</u> (t_m is affected by Create and Write, only Write does not affect t_c)
- (t_a): <u>Read</u> (t_a is affected by Read/Write/ Create, only Read does not affect t_c, t_m)

Thus, the only possible action sequence for timestamping order $(t_c < t_m < t_a)$ is (Create < Write < Read).

Example 4. Find all action sequences for the timestamping order $(t_m = t_a < t_c)$ for a file in the file system in Example 1.

From the affects table for the simple file system in Table 1, the steps in the sequence yields:

- $(t_m = t_a)$: <u>Create</u>, <u>Write</u> (t_m and t_a are both affected by Create and Write)
- (t_c): *none* (t_c is only affected by Create, but Create also affects t_m and t_a)

Table 3. Action sequences for the simple file system

Number	Timestamping order	Action Sequence
1	$(t_c < t_m < t_a)$	(Create, Write, Read)
2	$(t_c < t_a < t_m)$	None
3	$(t_m < t_c < t_a)$	None
4	$(t_m < t_a < t_c)$	None
5	$(t_a < t_c < t_m)$	None
6	$(t_a < t_m < t_c)$	None
7	$(t_c = t_m < t_a)$	(Create, Read)
8	$(t_a < t_c = t_m)$	None
9	$(t_m = t_a < t_c)$	None
10	$(t_c < t_m = t_a)$	(Create, Write)
11	$(t_c = t_a < t_m)$	None
12	$(t_m < t_c = t_a)$	None
13	$(t_c = t_m = t_a)$	(Create)

Thus, the timestamping order $(t_m = t_a < t_c)$ is not possible in the system.

By using this procedure for all timestamping orders for a given number of timestamps, one can now complete the reasoning in a system with known actions. The result of this exercise will be a list of timestamping orders impossible in the system and a table of possible action sequences of each timestamping order possible in the system.

Example 5. Find all action sequences for the simple file system.

This file system has three timestamps for each file ($n = 3$). All timestamping orders for such a system are given in Table 2. Assigning $t_1 = t_c$, $t_2 = t_m$ and $t_3 = t_a$ produces all timestamping orders for this system, shown in column "Timestamping order" in Table 3. Following the action sequence procedure for each timestamping order listed in the table by using the affects table for the simple file system given in Table 1, gives the possible action sequences for that timestamping order, shown in the column "Action Sequence":

The only timestamping orders in Table 3 possible in the system are sequences where

$t_c \leq t_m \leq t_a$. Thus, $t_c \leq t_m \leq t_a$ is a property that always holds for this system, an invariant.

Invariants for a system that has been found using the reasoning above can be used to test a clock hypothesis. In the example file system, it is now known that $t_c \leq t_m \leq t_a$. If for example $c(t_c) > c(t_a)$, a hypothesis that the clock has always been adjusted to UTC+10 would be rejected, since UTC is never adjusted backwards.

5. MODELLING A REAL FILE SYSTEM

The procedure described in the previous sections can be used to create a model of a real file system, determine which timestamping orders are possible in the system and derive invariants of the file system for use with a clock hypothesis checker. To illustrate this procedure, this section performs it on the semantics in Windows XP for file timestamps stored in the NTFS $STANDARD_IN-FORMATION attribute. The basis for the model described here is the semantics determined by Carrier. (Carrier, 2005) The model assumes that the files in question exist, are larger than the file cache size, and that updating of the last accessed timestamp is enabled.

In a system with three timestamps, the affects table contains $2^3 = 8$ entries. The actions are:

Read: reading a file
Create: creating a new file
Write: modifying an existing file
CopySrc: copying a file (source file)
CopyDest: copying a file (destination file)
MoveIntra: moving a file internal to a file system
MoveInterSrc: moving a file across file systems
    (source file)
MoveInterDest: moving a file across file systems
    (destination file)

Table 4. Affects table for Windows XP / NTFS

	Created	Modified	Accessed	Actions
0				
1	X			
2		X		
3	X	X		
4			X	Read, CopySrc, MoveIntra, MoveInterSrc, MoveInterDest (ReadGroup)
5	X		X	CopyDest
6		X	X	Write
7	X	X	X	Create

The following affects table (Table 4) can then be constructed.

The actions in row 4 of the affects table all have the same effect on timestamps. In the following, they will be grouped together as ReadGroup, meaning that where this action occurs, any of the actions Read, CopySrc, MoveIntra, MoveInterSrc or MoveInterDest may have occurred.

With $n = 3$, the timestamping order table in Table 2 can be used. Applying the action sequence procedure for each timestamping order yields the table of action sequences listed in Table 5.

From the table, it is evident that there are no possible action sequences where t_a does not occur in the last step. Consequently, in this system, $t_m \leq t_a$ and $t_c \leq t_a$. These invariants can be used to check clock hypotheses for Windows XP systems with NTFS.

6. GRAPH REPRESENTATION OF THE AFFECTS TABLE

A further simplification of the described derivation of invariants can be achieved by reasoning directly on the elements of the affects table. This simplification is best illustrated by representing the affects table as a graph.

Table 5. Timestamping orders in Windows XP/ NTFS

No	Timestamping order	Action Sequence
1	$(t_c < t_m < t_a)$	(Create/CopyDest<Write<ReadGroup)
2	$(t_c < t_a < t_m)$	None
3	$(t_m < t_c < t_a)$	(Create/Write<CopyDest<ReadGroup)
4	$(t_m < t_a < t_c)$	None
5	$(t_a < t_c < t_m)$	None
6	$(t_a < t_m < t_c)$	None
7	$(t_c = t_m < t_a)$	(Create/CopyDest=Write<ReadGroup)
8	$(t_a < t_c = t_m)$	None
9	$(t_m = t_a < t_c)$	None
10	$(t_c < t_m = t_a)$	(Create / CopyDest, Write)
11	$(t_c = t_a < t_m)$	None
12	$(t_m < t_c = t_a)$	(Create / Write, CopyDest)
13	$(t_c = t_m = t_a)$	(Create / CopyDest=Write)

Definition 6. An *affects graph* is a representation of the affects table as a bipartite graph, in which timestamps and actions are represented with vertices and affects with edges. Timestamps are represented with vertices of one color and actions with vertices of another color. Affects are represented with edges between timestamp vertices and action vertices.

Example 6. The graph in Figure 1 shows the affects graph for the simple file system with creation as per the affects table in Table 1.

The description of the affects table as a graph highlights how the affects table can be viewed as a system of interconnected entities, where timestamps and actions are entities and affects are connections. This suggests a type of reasoning directly on the connections between timestamps through intermediary actions, without having to rely on an exhaustive search of different timestamping orders. Consider the Created timestamp in Figure 1. This timestamp is affected by the Create action, which in turn affects the Modified timestamp and the Accessed timestamp. Create is also the only action affecting the Created time-

Figure 1. Affects graph for the simple file system

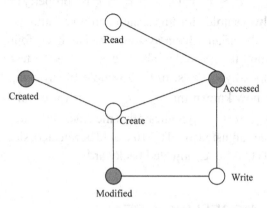

stamp. Thus, whenever the Created timestamp is updated in this system, the Accessed and Modified timestamps are updated too. Now consider the Modified timestamp. This timestamp is affected by the Create action and the Write action. These actions both in turn affect the Accessed timestamp. Thus, whenever the Modified timestamp is updated, the Accessed timestamp is also updated. These relationships can be expressed as a directed graph of timestamps as shown in Figure 2. The arcs in this directed graph represent that whenever the tail timestamp is updated, the head timestamp is updated too. Since any update to the tail timestamp also updates the head timestamp, the arcs is this graph translate to invariants by which the stamping time of the tail timestamp must be less than or equal to the stamping time of the head timestamp.

From Figure 2, we see that any updates of the Created timestamp also update the Modified

Figure 2. Timestamps in the simple file system

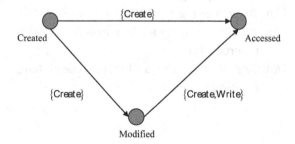

timestamp and the Accessed timestamp, and any updates of the Modified timestamp also updates the Accessed timestamp. Thus, $t_c \leq t_m$, $t_c \leq t_a$ and $t_m \leq t_a$ and consequently $t_c \leq t_m \leq t_a$, which equals previous results for this file system.

Definition 7. An *invariant graph* is a directed graph in which timestamps are represented with vertices and invariants with arcs. An arc from timestamp θ_i to θ_j represents the invariant

$$t_{\theta_i} \leq t_{\theta_j}$$

It is now possible to devise an algorithm for the derivation of the invariant graph directly from the affects graph:

- Every timestamp vertex in the affects graph is a vertex in the invariant graph
- For every timestamp vertex θ_i in the affects graph:
- For every action a_j affecting θ_i:
- Build a set Ω_{aj} of timestamps affected by a_j not including θ_i
- Find $\Omega = \Omega_{a_1} \cap \Omega_{a_2} \cap .. \cap \Omega_{a_m}$
- For every $\theta_k \in \Omega$, insert an arc from θ_i to θ_k in the invariant graph

Example 7. Draw the invariant graph in for Windows XP / NTFS. The affects table for XP / NTFS is given in Table 4. From this table, we get the affects graph shown in Figure 3. We then obtain the invariant graph shown in Figure 4.

7. TESTING A CLOCK HYPOTHESIS FOR CONSISTENCY

It now remains to show how the invariants derived for a system can be used to test a clock hypothesis.

The moments in time $t_{\theta_1}, t_{\theta_2}, ..., t_{\theta_n}$ when timestamping occured are not directly observable by the investigator. Instead, the investigator observes

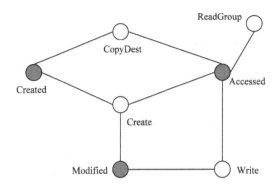

Figure 3. Affects graph for Windows XP / NTFS

the values of the system clock at these moments, $c(t_{\theta_1}), c(t_{\theta_2}), ..., c(t_{\theta_n})$. A clock hypothesis must match with these values and $t_m \leq t_a$. In the terminology of (Willassen, 2008) this requirement can be expressed as:

Theorem 1. In a correct clock hypothesis $c_h(t)$, the timestamps of all events e_i, e_j where $t(e_i) \leq t(e_j)$ in an observation set O must be such that the timestamp of the first event minus the deviation from a common base has value less than or equal to the timestamp of the latter event minus the deviation from a common base.

$$t(e_i) \leq t(e_j) \Rightarrow \tau(e_i) - d_h(t(e_i)) \leq \tau(e_j) - d_h(t(e_j))$$

Proof. Let $c_h(t)$ be a correct clock hypothesis and $c_o(t)$ be the clock of the investigated system. Let $b(t)$ be a common base for $c_h(t)$ and $c_o(t)$. Then

Figure 4. Invariant graph for Windows XP / NTFS

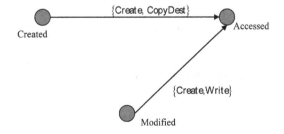

$$b(t) = c_h(t) - d_h(t)$$

$$b(t) = c_o(t) - d_o(t)$$

Thus,

$$c_h(t) - d_h(t) = c_o(t) - d_o(t)$$

And since $c_h(t)$ is correct we have $c_h(t) = c_o(t)$. Therefore

$$d_h(t) = d_o(t)$$

$$b(t) = c_o(t) - d_h(t)$$

And inserting $\tau_c(e_i) = c(t(e_i))$ yields

$$b(t(e)) = \tau(e) - d_h(t(e))$$

Now, $b(t)$ shall be an ideal clock. Ideal clocks satisfy

$$t(e_i) < t(e_j) \Rightarrow c(t(e_i)) \leq c(t(e_j))$$

And then, inserting $b(t)$ gives

$$t(e_i) < t(e_j) \Rightarrow b(t(e_i)) \leq b(t(e_j))$$

$$t(e_i) < t(e_j) \Rightarrow \tau_{c_o}(e_i) - d_h(t(e_i)) \leq \tau_{c_o}(e_j) - d_h(t(e_j))$$

Further, ideal clocks satisfy

$$t(e_i) = t(e_j) \Rightarrow c(t(e_i)) = c(t(e_j))$$

And then, inserting $b(t)$ gives

$$t(e_i) = t(e_j) \Rightarrow b(t(e_i)) = b(t(e_j))$$

$$t(e_i) = t(e_j) \Rightarrow \tau_{c_o}(e_i) - d_h(t(e_i)) = \tau_{c_o}(e_j) - d_h(t(e_j))$$

Thus,

$$t(e_i) \leq t(e_j) \Rightarrow \tau_{c_o}(e_i) - d_h(t(e_i)) \leq \tau_{c_o}(e_j) - d_h(t(e_j))$$

$\square$

And so, the requirement of Theorem 1 can be tested as follows:

Theorem 2. If timestamps generated by e_i and e_j are invariant $t(e_i) \leq t(e_j)$, then any occurence of timestamps where the timestamp of e_i minus the hypothesis deviation from a common base has a higher value than the timestamp of e_j minus the hypothesis deviation from a common base implies that the clock hypothesis is incorrect.

$$\exists e_i \exists e_j ((t(e_i) \leq t(e_j)) \wedge (\tau_{c_o}(e_i) - d_h(t(e_i))$$
$$> \tau_{c_o}(e_j) - d_h(t(e_j)))) \Rightarrow c_o(t) \neq c_h(t)$$

Proof. The proof is by contradiction. Let $c_h(t)$ be a clock hypothesis and O an observation set with clock $c_o(t)$. Let (e_a, e_b) be a pair of events in O such that $t(e_i) \leq t(e_j)$ and

$$\tau_{c_o}(e_a) - d_h(t(e_a)) > \tau_{c_o}(e_b) - d_h(t(e_b))$$

Assume that $c_h(t)$ is correct, $c_h(t) = c_o(t)$. If $c_h(t)$ is correct we have from Theorem 1 that

$$t(e_i) \leq t(e_j) \Rightarrow \tau(e_i) - d_h(t(e_i)) \leq \tau(e_j) - d_h(t(e_j))$$

But for $i = a$ and $j = b$, we have assumed that $t(e_i) \leq t(e_j)$ and so,

$$t(e_i) \leq t(e_j) \wedge (t_{c_o}(e_a) - d_h(t(e_a)) > t_{c_o}(e_b) - d_h(t(e_b)))$$

This contradicts the result from Theorem 1. Therefore, $c_h(t)$ cannot be correct. There has been no assumption or restriction on the events e_a and e_b. e_a and e_b could therefore have been any event in the observation set O. The result is that for any event e_i and e_j, $c_h(t)$ cannot be correct.

$$\exists e_i \exists e_j ((e_i \to e_j) \wedge (\tau_{c_o}(e_i) - d_h(t(e_i)) \\ > \tau_{c_o}(e_j) - d_h(t(e_j)))) \Rightarrow c_o(t) \neq c_h(t)$$

$\square$

RESULTS

This work studied how a system model can be used to test a clock hypothesis for consistency with timestamp evidence. A system model can be created by listing the actions in the system and their effect on timestamps in an affects table. By listing all possible timestamping orders, it can be determined which timestamping orders are possible in the system and which action sequences that may cause them. A procedure for deriving possible action sequences from the list of possible timestamping orders is given. From the list of possible and impossible timestamping orders, invariants for a system can be derived. These invariants can be used to test a clock hypothesis for consistency with evidence in the form of timestamps stored on an investigated system.

On the systems examined in real digital investigations, there will exist tens- or even hundreds of thousands of timestamps. By modelling the system using the techniques described in this work, it is then possible to test a clock hypothesis against a large number of timestamps. This will put a clock hypothesis under tight scrutiny, and can lead to its justification if there is no evidence to refute it. Justification of a clock hypothesis is important in digital investigations, because it will provide a possibility to translate the timestamps observed on a system to an independent clock. Thus, the real time of events can be established, which can be used to correlate the time of the events on a digital system with events occurring elsewhere.

CONCLUDING REMARKS

The testing of clock hypotheses provided in this work requires a model of the investigated system to be constructed. In order to provide a complete model of a real system one must clearly understand the system completely, something that can probably only be accomplished by studying the implementation details of the system. It might however be reasonable to construct a partial model only by studying the effects of operations on the real system, if it can be justified that the only actions taken on the system were those that were included in the model. In a real operating system, this could for example be accomplished by testing the different operations in the system and how they affect timestamps. If one could not be sure that all possible operations in the operating system had been included, one would not know for certain if the rejection of a clock hypothesis was caused by a wrong clock hypothesis or by missing actions in the model. This problem may not be very serious in digital investigations, where timestamp operations must be manifested in software, which can be found during the investigation.

The methods provided in this work can be applied during investigations of digital media, such as seized computers. Since most systems use common operating systems, the construction of a model does not have to be repeated in every investigation. It is enough that the model has been built for a specific system type once, it can thereafter be used in all digital investigations concerning that system type. The method presented here are therefore well suited for implementation in integrated software packages for digital investigation.

REFERENCES

Buchholz, F., & Tjaden, B. (2007). A brief study of time. *Digital Investigation*, (4S), 31–42. doi:10.1016/j.diin.2007.06.004

Carrier, B. (2005). *File system forensic analysis*. Upper Saddle River, N.J.: Addison-Wesley.

Carrier, B. (2006). *A hypothesis-based approach to digital forensic investigations* (CERIAS Tech Report 2006-06): Center for Education and Research in Information Assurance and Security, Purdue University.

Schatz, B., Mohay, G., & Clark, A. (2006). A correlation method for establishing provenance of timestamps in digital evidence. *Digital Investigation*, (3S), 98–107. doi:10.1016/j.diin.2006.06.009

Willassen, S. Y. (2008). *Hypothesis based investigation of digital timestamps*. Paper presented at the IFIP WG 11.9 Workshop, Kyoto, Japan, Jan. 2008.

Chapter 8
Conducting Forensic Investigations of Cyber Attacks on Automobile In-Vehicle Networks

Dennis K. Nilsson
Chalmers University of Technology, Sweden

Ulf E. Larson
Chalmers University of Technology, Sweden

ABSTRACT

The introduction of a wireless gateway as an entry point to the automobile in-vehicle network reduces the effort of performing diagnostics and firmware updates considerably. Unfortunately, the same gateway also allows cyber attacks to target the unprotected network which currently lacks proper means for detecting and investigating security-related events. In this article, we discuss how to perform a digital forensic investigation of an in-vehicle network. An analysis of the current features of the network is performed, and an attacker model is developed. Based on the attacker model and a set of generally accepted forensic investigation principles, we derive a list of requirements for detection, data collection, and event reconstruction. We then use the Integrated Digital Investigation Process proposed by Carrier and Spafford (2004) as a template to illustrate how our derived requirements affect an investigation. For each phase of the process, we show the benefits of meeting the requirements and the implications of not complying with them.

INTRODUCTION

Automobile in-vehicle networks have historically been isolated from attackers as a result of the limited access possibilities. However, due to recent advances in wireless communications combined with a huge economical incentive for the vehicle industry in accessing and updating vehicle firmware over the air, this situation is about to change. The fact that the wireless technology for updating and diagnosing firmware has already been successfully used for several years within the telecommunications industry also indicates that it is possible to adapt it to other areas, including the automotive domain.

The enabling factor is the introduction of a wireless gateway as an entry point to the in-vehicle network, which consists of a set of *electronic control units* (ECUs). The gateway allows for remote interaction with ECU firmware, even when the vehicle is running. Common administrative functions such as diagnostics and firmware updates could be performed remotely. Thus, vehicle owners do not need to drive to a service station to get their car diagnosed, and new firmware updates can easily be applied to thousands of vehicles simultaneously. Thus, faulty firmware can be diagnosed and replaced faster, and safer vehicle operation can be achieved. Additionally, as discussed by Shavit et al. (2007), the need for costly vehicle recalls is removed since physically interfacing each vehicle through the *on-board diagnostics* (OBD) module is no longer required. Furthermore, as discussed by Moustafa et al. (2006), vehicle-to-vehicle and vehicle-to-infrastructure communication allows vehicles to receive alerts of changing weather conditions and to obtain area information from roadside stations.

However, the new technology also introduces new safety and security issues for the manufacturers to consider. Allowing communication between the unprotected in-vehicle network and one or more external entities introduces a whole new range of threats collectively known as *cyber attacks*. An attacker could, for example, use the firmware update function to inject malicious code into the in-vehicle network while the vehicle is running.

As an illustration, consider a speeding vehicle that drives off a road and crashes with fatal consequences for the driver. This type of incident is normally caused either by the driver himself, or by vehicle malfunction or physical tampering. If the brake line is found to be cut, the cause of the accident is most certainly an act of physical tampering, and a criminal investigation needs to

be initiated to bring those responsible to a court of law. Now, consider instead the possibility that the brakes were disabled by a piece of malicious code. If there is no digital evidence available, there would be no means of revealing that a crime was committed, the criminal would walk free, and the cause of the accident would wrongly be determined as vehicle malfunction.

The current in-vehicle network produces data to support the operation and maintenance of the vehicle, and to protect the vehicle from safety-related incidents. However, when an intelligent attacker is introduced, there is a need to produce data that can reveal both the presence of malicious code, and provide evidence that will aid an investigation of a cyber attack.

The aim of this article is to define a set of requirements for conducting a forensic investigation of cyber attacks on automobile in-vehicle networks. In particular, we analyze the current in-vehicle network structure, including node layout and external interfaces. Based on the analysis, we identify and define plausible cyber attack actions and derive a cyber attacker model. We then use the attack actions in combination with a set of in-vehicle specific investigation goals to derive a set of requirements on data and a supporting infrastructure for meeting the goals of the investigation. To illustrate the use of the requirements, we apply the Integrated Digital Investigation Process proposed by Carrier and Spafford (2004) and show how the investigation benefits from meeting the requirements.

This article continues by presenting current methods for conducting forensic investigations in vehicles and motivates the need for in-vehicle network security. It then describes a conceptual in-vehicle network including gateways and external interfaces. Then, an attacker model is defined, followed by a list of design goals and a set of requirements for conducting a digital investigation in vehicle environments. An investigation process which is guided by the requirements is then described. Finally, a discussion of in-vehicle forensics and relevant future work is outlined, together with some concluding remarks.

RELATED WORK

Until now, the center of attention for conducting vehicle forensics has been on physical accident reconstruction, and thus the focus has been on determining the physical condition of the vehicle and the surrounding area. As described by O'Connor (2001), the status of brakes, lights and wipers, roadway surfaces, loose material, and visibility have been important factors to investigate when revealing the cause of an accident. However, this information does not help against "accidents" caused by cyber attacks.

A more recent solution, as discussed by the Insurance Institute for Highway Safety (2006), which was introduced in the early 1980's, is the *event data recorder*, or EDR. An EDR is a black box that records critical event data, e.g., vehicle speed, engine speed, acceleration, braking, and seat belt status when certain events occur, such as airbag-release (Insurance Institute for Highway Safety, 2006, Zucker, 2003). However, the EDR data is not fine-grained enough to determine whether the "accident" was caused by a cyber attack, and there is no mechanism that will raise an alert. To access the EDR data, the OBD interface is used (Palmer, 2002, Harris and Wilson, 2005). Despite the fact that both the physical accident reconstruction and the EDR data records have proved extremely useful for accident investigation they are not sufficient to reveal the presence of cyber attacks. Thus, there is a need for finer-grained techniques for investigating the causes of vehicle accidents. These techniques are the focus of our research.

A related area to in-vehicle forensics is the cell phone/Personal Digital Assistant (PDA) forensics. Both areas regard operation on embedded devices with limited processing power and memory and thus, the general ideas are expected to be ap-

plicable in the in-vehicle environment. Several approaches to conducting cell phone/PDA forensics have been proposed and the more noticeable include the following. The National Institute of Standards and Technology (NIST) has published a set of guidelines as reported in (National Institute of Standards and Technology, 2004, National Institute of Standards and Technology, 2007). The guidelines show how data can be retrieved using various tools and procedures and mention common forensic activities such as preservation, collection, examination, analysis, and presentation. In (Jones et al., 2006, Volonino et al., 2007), another definition of the activities is presented, and the three phases acquisition, analysis, and reporting are used.

The main concepts from the cell phone/PDA area should be applicable also to the in-vehicle setting. However, there is an important difference: the in-vehicle network contains several collaborating devices while cell phone/PDA forensics normally only considers one device. Therefore, we believe that new techniques for performing forensic investigations are required for the in-vehicle setting.

THE NEED FOR IN-VEHICLE NETWORK SECURITY AND FORENSICS

Current in-vehicle networks primarily meet *reliability* requirements. They are thus designed to withstand failure caused by non-malicious and inadvertent flaws which are produced by chance or by device malfunction. Deployed protection mechanisms are therefore realized by means of fault-tolerance techniques, such as redundancy, replication, and diversity, as described by Storey (1996). Since the in-vehicle network historically has been isolated, threats other than those against the reliability of the vehicle have not been considered. Therefore, protection against threats originating from intelligent attackers (i.e., *security* protection) has neither been included in the requirements nor in the design of such networks. Recent research has shown that these threats are a reality (Wolf et al., 2004, Nilsson & Larson, 2008c). A safety-security classification of ECUs based on identified attacks conducted by Nilsson et al. (2008) has shown that there is a strong relationship between safety and security and that security-related problems may well affect safety. Furthermore, some of the in-vehicle communication and application protocols have been evaluated (Larson et al., 2008, Nilsson and Larson, 2008c), and the evaluations have shown that the investigated protocols in principle lack all security protection.

In the realm of traditional computer networks several security best practices have been developed. However, since the in-vehicle network is a non-traditional network consisting of resource-constrained embedded devices and with different traffic patterns compared to traditional IP networks, a new set of best practices is required. A well-known security best practice is to use a *defense-in-depth* approach when defending a system. This approach has been discussed by Halme and Bauer (1995) and is general and expected to be useful also for in-vehicle networks but only after being properly adapted.

The defense-in-depth principle defines several layers of defense, and it might be intuitive to focus on the outermost layers first, including solutions for authentication and access control. However, traditional computing environments suffer from attacks regardless of the protective measures, and forensics is used on a daily basis in investigating computer-related crime. We therefore believe that alongside the development of protective measures, as discussed by Nilsson and Larson (2008b), there is a need to identify components and techniques that will prove useful for forensics, in particular to support investigations after an accident has occurred.

BACKGROUND

In this section, we use a conceptual scenario to introduce the reader to wireless vehicle-to-infrastructure communication. The scenario illustrates how remote administration of a vehicle can be performed by using diagnostics and firmware update functions. We then proceed to describe the structure of the in-vehicle network and how messages are structured and routed. Finally, we describe the diagnostics and firmware update administrative functions in more detail.

Wireless Vehicle-to-Infrastructure Scenario

Figure 1 illustrates a scenario where required firmware updates and diagnostics requests are transmitted over a wireless link from a vehicle manufacturer's portal to a number of vehicles. The portal is part of the manufacturer's infrastructure and connected to the Internet. By performing wireless firmware updates and diagnostics requests, vehicles can be diagnosed on the fly and new firmware can easily be installed. The transmitted firmware and diagnostics requests are received at the vehicle by the wireless gateway and thereafter routed through the in-vehicle network to the corresponding ECU. This procedure allows faster updates and mass updates, and reduces the time a vehicle with faulty firmware is on the streets.

In-Vehicle Network

The *in-vehicle network* consists of *nodes* (i.e., ECUs), *gateways*, and *buses*. An example in-vehicle network is illustrated in Figure 2. A node is a resource-constrained device with limited processing power and memory (ROM and RAM). The ROM memory contains the firmware that is executed on the ECU and the RAM data area

Figure 1. Wireless vehicle-to-infrastructure scenario in which a portal is issuing firmware updates to a number of vehicles over a wireless link

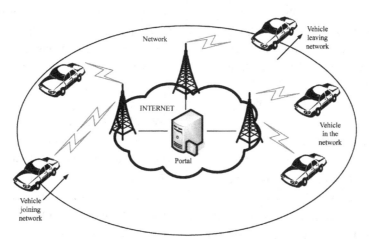

stores operative parameters (e.g., which lights are turned on etc.). Each ECU is responsible for the functionality of a certain area in the vehicle. For example, one ECU is responsible for the headlights system, and one ECU handles the driver door functionality (e.g., lock and window). For more complex functions such as the engine system, a number of ECUs are cooperating.

Furthermore, the ECUs are connected to a shared bus, and buses and nodes form networks.

Gateways are used to allow transferring messages between networks. As described in the network specification by Bosch GmbH (1991), each message contains fields for data, checksum value, and a message identifier consisting of a function code and a node identifier. The node identifier denotes the receiver of the message. Each message is broadcast to all nodes in a network but only the node with the corresponding node identifier handles it. Protocol messages may require acknowledgment

Figure 2. An in-vehicle network, consisting of the CAN, LIN, and MOST networks, connected with the wireless gateway and the OBD interfaces

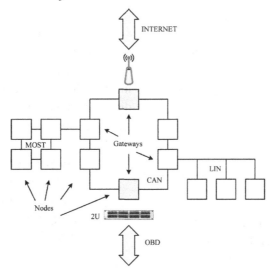

or may be sent unacknowledged. For synchronization, each node has its own clock and a time protocol is used for clock synchronization. However, messages are not individually timestamped. As described by Vector (2007a), common in-vehicle network types include *controller area network* (CAN), *local interconnect network* (LIN), and *media oriented systems transport* (MOST).

Administrative Functions

Two common administrative functions that exist for vehicles are *diagnostics* and *firmware updates*. Diagnostics is used to affect single data parameters in nodes, as described by Vector (2007b), and is used for reading node status (e.g., *the passenger door is locked*) or controlling node activity (e.g., *unlock the passenger door*) by writing node status. Diagnostics is traditionally executed through the OBD interface and can be performed either by using specific commands for querying and setting parameter values or by performing low-level read or write operations on specific memory addresses. The commands are expressed as text strings while the low-level operations are identified by an operation code.

Firmware update is the process of reflashing the memory of an ECU to install new firmware, e.g., in the case of vehicle functionality problems, as discussed by Shavit et al. (2007). The new firmware binary is transmitted on the bus, and the target ECU flashes the binary to its ROM and reboots. A firmware update operation is initiated by a specific firmware update command, and a reboot is performed by issuing a reboot command.

ATTACKER MODEL AND FORENSIC DESIGN GOALS

In this section, we present a definition of a cyber attacker. We then describe the in-vehicle specific attacker model for this attacker, based on terms presented by Howard and Longstaff (1998) in the CERT taxonomy. We further present a set of design goals for in-vehicle network forensic investigations. The focus of our research is the CAN network since its nodes are responsible for safety-critical functions. Thus, the CAN network is a valuable asset and a highly plausible target for a cyber attacker.

Cyber Attacker

A cyber attacker is an individual who uses digital attacks, e.g., worms and trojan horses, to achieve a goal. This is in contrast to a physical attacker who uses physical force, e.g., using a crowbar to bend open a locked door.

In our attacker model, we assume that the attacker can access the in-vehicle network through either the wireless gateway or the OBD interface. We further assume that the attacker has sufficient knowledge regarding the format of low-level requests and diagnostics queries to perform the actions presented by Howard and Longstaff (1998), e.g., read, inject, modify, and replay messages. Moreover, we assume that the attacker has sufficient knowledge to perform firmware updates.

By reading data, an attacker can attack confidentiality (e.g., read secret keys) and privacy (e.g., read private driver information). By writing data, an attacker can attack integrity (change functionality of ECUs) and availability (disable ECUs). Due to the seriousness of these attacks, we focus on and analyze what methods an attacker can use to read and write data from and to the ECUs.

An attacker has three means to tamper with the in-vehicle network and the ECUs: sending diagnostics queries, sending low-level requests, and performing ECU firmware updates:

- **Sending diagnostics queries (DQ):** An attacker can send read or write requests to get or set certain parameter values in an ECU.
- **Sending low-level requests (LR):** An attacker can send low-level read or write

requests to read or write the byte value of a certain memory address.

- **Performing firmware updates (FU):** An attacker can update an ECU with new firmware through reflashing. Thus, an attacker can change the functionality of an ECU to perform malicious acts.

Forensic Design Goals

The value of a forensic investigation lays in its ability to discover facts regarding the five W's, i.e., who, what, where, when, and why, as discussed by Volonino et al. (2007). This is obviously also the case for the in-vehicle environment.

To aid the reader in the following discussion, we first provide a brief list of definitions as follows: An event as an action which is intended to result in a change of state of a selected target; a security violation as an event that violates security policy rules; and an attack is a series of steps taken by an attacker, where one or more security violations are included.

Below we identify and describe three in-vehicle specific goals that must be met in order to properly conduct a forensic investigation:

- *A method to detect events in the vehicle must be present.* To perform a digital forensic investigation, an alert about a security violation must have been triggered to provide reason to initiate the forensic investigation.
- *Data to answer the questions who, what, where, when, and why must be produced and securely stored in the vehicle.* During the forensic investigation, this data must be available in the network. Availability is affected by the security of the data, and thus, the data must therefore also be properly protected. An investigator should be able to extract the necessary information when needed.
- *Information about the current state (e.g., firmware versions) in a vehicle must be*

available and stored in a separate and secure location. To detect whether the vehicle has been tampered with, an investigator must be able to compare the extracted data regarding the vehicle state to the original data after a security violation has occurred.

REQUIREMENTS FOR A FORENSIC INVESTIGATION OF CYBER ATTACKS

The present in-vehicle network is primarily designed to support operational reliability and maintenance considerations. As discussed earlier, the included reliability measures are not sufficient for protecting against cyber attacks. We use the attacker model and the design goals to derive a set of requirements for supporting a forensic investigation. The set of requirements is divided according to the design goals and are denoted *Event detection requirements, Forensic data requirements* and *State information requirements*.

Event Detection Requirements

To detect an event at an early stage it is necessary to introduce a detection mechanism to the in-vehicle network. The event detection requirements address what devices need to be present for detection and for alerting the appropriate authority, e.g., the driver, that a security violation has been detected.

A specification-based or a model-based detection system (Garvey and Lunt, 1991, Larson et al., 2008) maintains a list of allowed communication patterns and alerts when prohibited events occur. Also, the alert data is used together with the event data to aid investigation. In addition, there is a need for a storage device and a device for writing event and alert data to the storage:

- Requirement **E1**: A device capable of detecting specific events or deviations from normal behavior and providing notifications regarding security violations is installed.

- Requirement **E2**: A supporting ECU which listens to network traffic and writes data to a storage device is installed. The supporting ECU should further produce reliable timestamps, since individual messages do not contain timestamps.
- Requirement **E3**: A storage device which stores the collected network traffic is installed.
- Requirement **E4**: A strategy for protecting the detection, supporting ECU, and storage devices must be properly implemented to prevent attackers from tampering with the functionality and configuration information of the devices and the stored data.

When E1, E2, and E3 are fulfilled, the three devices *Storage device, Supporting ECU*, and *Detection System* are added to the in-vehicle network as shown in Figure 3 (dark color). The detection system is added to detect and alert on security violations, and the storage device together with the supporting ECU is placed in the network to contain the collected data. To produce reliable timestamps the supporting ECU can use its own

clock for timestamping. Furthermore, when E4 is fulfilled, the devices and the stored data will have protection from tampering according to the protection strategy.

Forensic Data Requirements

Forensic data requirements address what data needs to be logged for answering the questions raised during the investigation. The goal of a forensic investigation is to provide answers to the questions *who, what, where, when* and *why*, and, as discussed by Kuperman (2004), to be able to reconstruct the state and the events taking place in the system. As an example, consider a car that crashes due to disabled braking capacity. The *who* question regards which nodes that are responsible for transmitting and executing the command to disable the brakes. The *what* question concerns what command was issued, and the *where* question regards the locations of the nodes transmitting and executing the command. The *when* question regards at what time the command was transmitted, and at what time the command was executed. The *why* question addresses the reason why something

Figure 3. An in-vehicle network with a detection system and a storage device with a supporting ECU device attached

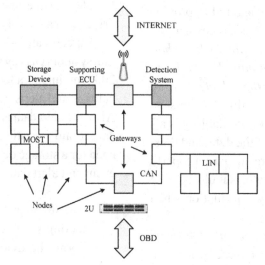

happened, e.g., the car crashed because a command to disable the brakes was issued.

In order to provide the required answers, appropriate data must be captured before and during the event. If the data is insufficient, one or more questions may be left unanswered, or the confidence level of established hypotheses may be lower than with sufficient data. For a forensic investigation it is however difficult to pinpoint single log items that are more interesting than other, since all data *might* be useful. For the in-vehicle network, we use our attacker model to derive appropriate required data. The data is grouped according to each forensic goal and attack action. The abbreviations for the attack actions are taken from the description of the attacker model.

- Requirement **D1**: The following data must be produced to answer the *who* question.
  - **DQ**: The node identifiers of the node sending a diagnostics query, and the node responding to the query.
  - **LR**: The node identifiers of the node sending a low-level request, and the node conducting the operation.
  - **FU**: The node identifiers of the node initiating the firmware update, and the node conducting the update.
- Requirement **D2**: The following data must be produced to answer the *what* question.
  - **DQ**: The name of the query.
  - **LR**: The code of the low-level operation.
  - **FU**: The names of the firmware update command and the reboot command.
- Requirement **D3**: The following data must be produced to answer the *where* question.
  - **DQ**: The node identifier of the sender and receiver of each query.
  - **LR**: The node identifier of the sender and receiver of each low-level operation.
  - **FU**: The node identifier of the sender and receiver of the firmware update sequence.
- Requirement **D4**: The following data must be produced to answer the *when* question.

  - **DQ**: The time when the query is issued.
  - **LR**: The time when the low-level operation is issued.
  - **FU**: The time of the start and end of the firmware update sequence of commands, and the time for each individual command.
- Requirement **D5**: The following data must be produced to answer the *why* question.
  - **DQ**: The name and value of the query.
  - **LR**: The value and target memory address of the low-level operation.
  - **FU**: The content of the data in the firmware update sequence.

Regarding the data requirements the following should be noted: Timestamps can be added to each message by the supporting ECU. The node identifier of the receiving node, the names of commands and the values of queries are already present in the messages. However, obtaining the node identifier of the sender is to our knowledge not readily possible and we believe that this information should be added to the message.

State Information Requirements

State information requirements address the data needed by investigators to reconstruct the initial state of the network and to exclude data that has no significance in an investigation. For this purpose, it is necessary to maintain a description of the a priori state for each network node. This can be achieved by, for example, maintaining a diagnostics server that stores an updated list of hashes for all firmware currently installed in the ECUs. This list must be updated each time a firmware update is performed. The list must also be kept in a secure and tamper-resistant location, preferably an offline location.

Requirement **S1**: A list of hashes and the complete current firmware version for all ECUs must be maintained at a secure and separate location.

Forensic Investigation of an In-Vehicle Network

In this section, we apply the *Integrated Digital Investigation Process* proposed by Carrier and Spafford (2003) for an example investigation of an in-vehicle network. Several other process models for conducting digital forensics have been proposed, as surveyed by Pollitt (2007). However, we have selected the integrated digital investigation model since it connects the physical and digital crime scene investigations. This model is suitable since the physical investigation, the EDR records, and the digital investigation may provide complementary evidence when investigating vehicle incidents.

The Integrated Digital Investigation Process model contains the five phases *Readiness, Deployment, Physical crime scene investigation, Digital crime scene investigation* and *Presentation*. We discuss each phase in turn as the investigation proceeds, and for each phase, we further discuss the actions taken by the investigating organization (e.g., law enforcement, insurance agent, or vehicle manufacturer) with respect to the requirements. We also discuss the implications of not complying with the requirements.

The Readiness Phase

The readiness phase ensures that the vehicle manufacturer is ready to deal with cyber attacks and that the supporting data collection infrastructure is activated. Thus, the investigating organization has access to the forensic data when it is needed:

- **Prerequisites:** A list of hashes of the current firmware installed on all ECUs in the in-vehicle network must be accessible according to Requirement S1.
- **Action:** The investigating organization maintains a staff of trained investigators who respond quickly to reported events. In addition, a diagnostics server with the latest ECU firmware versions and hashes, and other diagnostics tools which could interface with both the wireless gateway and the OBD is prepared.
- **If the prerequisites are not fulfilled:** The investigating organization would at best maintain a staff of accident reconstruction investigators, who need to rely on the physical investigation and the EDR data to conduct the investigation.

The Deployment Phase

The deployment phase provides a means of detecting and confirming that an event has occurred. The presence of appropriate means is the responsibility of the vehicle manufacturer:

- **Prerequisites:** A detection system is present, according to Requirement E1, to indicate that a security violation has occurred.
- **Action:** The vehicle manufacturer or the investigating organization is alerted from the detection system, either directly over a wireless link or through the driver, who is alerted from the vehicle itself.
- **If the prerequisites are not fulfilled:** The investigating organization relies on either that the event is detected during routine-diagnostics testing in the service station, or that it is detected and reported to the organization by the driver when the vehicle is in use.

The Physical Crime Scene Investigation Phase

The physical investigation phase examines all physical objects at the crime scene:

- **Prerequisites:** None.
- **Action:** A physical investigation of the vehicle is supported by digital evidence collected during the digital investigation. For

example, a fingerprint on the OBD connector could be supported by OBD logs showing the time when the OBD was interfaced and what commands were issued.

- **If the prerequisites are not fulfilled:** The same action can be performed as above; however, if no digital evidence is collected during the digital investigation, the evidence collected in these two phases cannot be used in conjunction to support the findings of a cyber attack.

The Digital Crime Scene Investigation Phase

The digital crime scene investigation identifies all digital events that have occurred on the in-vehicle network and examines digital data for evidence:

- **Prerequisites:** Data must be produced in the in-vehicle network to answer the *who*, *what*, *where*, *when*, and *why* questions regarding the events according to the Requirements D1-D5.
- **Action:** Three steps are performed: *System preservation*, *Evidence search*, and *Event reconstruction*.
    1. **System preservation**: System preservation requires isolating a system from its surroundings. The wireless gateway should not accept external connections during the investigation. The storage device is disconnected and duplicated so that all firmware updates and all log entries can be analyzed offline.
    2. **Evidence search**: Evidence is searched for by reading the event and alert logs from the detection system stored in the storage device and by comparing the firmware versions on the storage device to the versions stored in the trusted diagnostics server. Suspicious firmware

versions are reverse engineered to find the differences and the potential causes.
    3. **Event reconstruction**: The attack can be reconstructed using the discovered evidence from the event and alert logs. By using this information we can deduce when the firmware was updated, and also what ECU was responsible for the attack. We can also identify the origin of issued diagnostics requests. Furthermore, in the case of a malicious firmware update, analysis of the attack code and the infected firmware can provide details to the attacker's behavior and the construction of the firmware.

- **If the prerequisites are not fulfilled:** The digital crime scene investigation phase is impossible to perform without any relevant data.

The Presentation Phase

The results of the investigation are presented by the investigating organization to the appropriate audience after all hypotheses have been tested against the evidence:

- **Prerequisites:** Both the physical and digital investigation must be finished, and hypotheses must have been supported or refuted.
- **Action:** The physical evidence, the evidence from the EDR records and the digital evidence from the network are used for explaining what has happened. Correct conclusions regarding both physical and cyber attacks can be supported.
- **If the prerequisites are not fulfilled:** The explanation relies on only physical evidence and EDR records. If a cyber attack has caused the event, erroneous conclusions may be drawn.

DISCUSSION AND FUTURE WORK

A recent study by Nilsson and Larson (2008a) has further investigated the relation between physical and digital evidence in the vehicle setting and shown that certain crime cannot be detected by using only physical evidence or only digital evidence but that a combination is required. For these reasons it is important that a sound digital forensic framework is in place to preserve the evidence that would otherwise be lost. As has been shown for traditional computing environments by Jones et al. (2006), a forensic investigation is aided by data produced by other types of defensive mechanisms, including intrusion detection alerts, firewall logs, and identities of network nodes. It is therefore recommended to use several protective measures, as indicated by the defense-in-depth principle and discussed by e.g., (Garvey and Lunt, 1991, Cheung et al., 2007, Larson et al., 2008, Nilsson and Larson, 2008b).

As indicated by this article the current message format contains receiver node identifiers and transmitted data; however, timestamps and sender node identifiers are missing. It is to our knowledge that it is impossible to readily obtain the sender node identifier of a message, and we therefore propose that this identifier is added to the messages. However, timestamps can be added by the supporting ECU which can maintain a protected clock and therefore offer a protected and accurate time as opposed to individual, possibly drifting, node clocks.

Moreover, it is important that the data produced in the vehicle is correct and prevented from manipulation. The event and alert logs must be readily available to an investigator but must be inaccessible to an attacker. Proper timestamps must be used to determine when attacks occur and must be prevented from modification. Thus, proper means to produce not only sound forensic data but also to produce correct data that cannot be modified by an attacker must be developed.

Considering the limited hardware resources in the in-vehicle network, developing such solutions is a challenge that requires further work.

CONCLUSION

In this article, we have presented a set of requirements needed for conducting a digital forensic investigation of cyber attacks on an automobile in-vehicle network structure. For this purpose, we have analyzed the current in-vehicle network and proposed a set of data that needs to be produced during vehicle operation. Moreover, we recognize the need for a detection system and storage devices within the network, and the storage of vehicle state information in a secure and separate location. We have also addressed the need for proper protection of the detection and storage devices and their data and have discussed methods for producing the required set of data. We have illustrated the significance of our proposed requirements by applying the Integrated Digital Investigation Process to an example automobile cyber attack forensic investigation. The example shows the benefits of fulfilling the requirements and the implications of not complying with them.

REFERENCES

Bosch GmbH (1991). CAN specification 2.0. http://www.dcd.pl/dcdpdf/can2spec.pdf. Visited September 23, 2007.

Carrier, B. D. and Spafford, E. H. (2003). Getting physical with the digital investigation process. *International Journal of Digital Evidence*, 2(2).

Carrier, B. D. and Spafford, E. H. (2004). An event-based digital forensic investigation framework. http://www.digital-evidence.org/papers/dfrws_event.pdf. Presented at the 4th Digital Forensic Research Workshop.

Cheung, S., Dutertre, B., Fong, M., Lindqvist, U., Skinner, K., and Valdes, A. (2007). Using model-based intrusion detection for SCADA networks. In *Proceedings of the Scada Security Scientific Symposium*, Miami, FL, USA. Digital Bond.

Garvey, T. D. and Lunt, T. F. (1991). Using models of intrusions. In *Proceedings of the Third Workshop on Computer Security Incidence Handling*, Herndon, VA, USA.

Halme, L. R. and Bauer, K. R. (1995). AINT misbehaving: A taxonomy of anti-intrusion techniques. In *Proceedings of the 18th National Information Systems Security Conference*, pages 163–172, Baltimore, MA, USA.

Harris, J. O. and Wilson, W. C. (2005). Protocols for the recovery, maintenance and presentation of motor vehicle event data recorder evidence. http://www.harristechnical.com/articles/mvedr. pdf. Visited September 15, 2007.

Howard, J. D. and Longstaff, T. A. (1998). A common language for computer security incidents. Technical Report SAND98-8667, Sandia National Laboratories, Livermore, CA, USA.

Insurance Institute for Highway Safety (2006). Event data recorders. http://www.iihs.org/ research/qanda/edr.html. Visited September 1, 2007.

Jones, K. J., Bejtlich, R., and Rose, C. W. (2006). *Real Digital Forensics: Computer Security and Incident Response.* Addison-Wesley, Upper Saddle River, NJ, USA, 1st edition.

Kuperman, B. A. (2004). *A Categorization of Computer Security Monitoring Systems and the Impact on the Design of Audit Sources.* PhD thesis, Purdue University, West Lafayette, IN, USA.

Larson, U. E., Nilsson, D. K., and Jonsson, E. (2008). An approach to specification-based attack detection for in-vehicle networks. In *Proceedings of the 12th IEEE Intelligent Vehicles Symposium*, pages 220–225, Eindhoven, the Netherlands.

Moustafa, H., Bourdon, G., and Gourhant, Y. (2006). Providing authentication and access control in vehicular network environments. In *Security and Privacy in Dynamic Environments*, pages 307–316, Karlstad, Sweden. Springer-Verlag.

National Institute of Standards and Technology (2004). NIST special publication 800-72: Guidelines on PDA forensics. http://csrc.nist. gov/publications/nistpubs/800-72/sp800-72.pdf. Visited November 29, 2007.

National Institute of Standards and Technolog y (2007). NIST Special Publication 800-101: Guidelines on cell phone forensics. http://csrc. nist.gov/publications/nistpubs/800-101/sp800-101.pdf. Visited November 29, 2007.

Nilsson, D. K. and Larson, U. E. (2008a). Combining physical and digital evidence in vehicle environments. In *Proceedings of the Third IEEE International Workshop on Systematic Approaches to Digital Forensic Engineering*, (pp. 10-14) Oakland, CA, USA. IEEE Computer Society.

Nilsson, D. K. and Larson, U. E. (2008b). Secure firmware updates over the air in intelligent vehicles. In *Proceedings of the First IEEE Vehicular Networking & Applications Workshop (Vehi-Mobi)*, (pp. 380-384) Beijing, China.

Nilsson, D. K. and Larson, U. E. (2008c). Simulated attacks on CAN-buses: Vehicle virus. In *Proceedings of the Fifth IASTED Asian Conference on Communication Systems and Networks (AsiaCSN 2008)*, pages 66–72, Langkawi, Malaysia. IASTED, ACTA Press.

Nilsson, D. K., Phung, P., and Larson, U. E. (2008). Vehicle ECU classification based on safety-security characteristics. In *Proceedings of the 13th International Conference on Road Transport and Information Control (RTIC)*, Manchester, UK. IEEE Computer Society.

O'Connor, T. (2001). Forensic reconstruction. http://faculty.ncwc.edu/TOConnor/425/425lect11.htm. Visited September 15, 2007.

Palmer, W. S. (2002). Black box technology and its implications for auto insurance. http://www.injurysciences.com/Documents/Claims82002.pdf. Visited September 15, 2007.

Pollitt, M. M. (2007). An ad hoc review of digital forensic models. In *Proceedings of the Second International Workshop on Systematic Approaches to Digital Forensic Engineering (SADFE'07)*, pages 43–54, Seattle, WA, USA. IEEE Computer Society.

Shavit, M., Gryc, A., and Miucic, R. (2007). Firmware update over the air (FOTA) for automotive industry. In *Proceedings of the 14th Asia Pacific Automotive Engineering Conference*, Hollywood, CA, USA.

Storey, N. (1996). *Safety-Critical Computer Systems*. Prentice-Hall, Upper Saddle River, NJ, USA.

Vector (2007a). Serial bus systems in the automobile: Part 1. http://www.vector-scandinavia.com/portal/medien/cmc/press/PTR/SerialBusSystems_Part1_ElektronikAutomotive_200611_PressArticle_EN.pdf. Visited September 7, 2007.

Vector (2007b). Vehicle Diagnostics: The whole story. http://www.vector-scandinavia.com/portal/medien/cmc/press/PDG/Diagnostics_Congress_ElektronikAutomotive_200703_PressArticle_EN.pdf. Visited September 7, 2007.

Volonino, L., Anzaldua, R., and Godwin, J. (2007). *Computer Forensics, Principles and Practices*. Prentice-Hall, Upper Saddle River, NJ, USA.

Wolf, M., Weimerskirch, A., and Paar, C. (2004). Security in automotive bus systems. http://www.escrypt.de/download/Sichere_Bussysteme_escar04.pdf. Presented at the 2004 Workshop on Embedded IT-Security in Cars, Bochum, Germany.

Zucker, P. (2003). Legal ramifications for automobile black boxes. http://www.expertlaw.com/library/accidents/auto_black_boxes2.html. Visited September 15, 2007.

This work was previously published in International Journal of Digital Crime and Forensics (IJDCF), edited by Chang-Tsun Li & Anthony T.S. Ho, pp. 28-41, copyright 2009 by IGI Publishing (an imprint of IGI Global).

Chapter 9
Dealing with Multiple Truths in Online Virtual Worlds

Jan Sablatnig
Technische Universität Berlin, Germany

Fritz Lehmann-Grube
Technische Universität Berlin, Germany

Sven Grottke
University of Stuttgart, Germany

Sabine Cikic
Technische Universität Berlin, Germany

ABSTRACT

Virtual environments and online games are becoming a major market force. At the same time, the virtual property contained in these environments is being traded for real money and thus attains a real value. Although the legal issues involved with this virtual property have not yet been decided, they will have to be soon. It is foreseeable that the next generation of very large virtual worlds will carry the possibility of multiple truths existing at the same time. Under such circumstances, it will be impossible to physically protect virtual property. In order to protect virtual property, virtual environment systems will therefore have to conform to certain requirements. We analyze what these requirements are in order to either prevent cheating or at least prove a digital offence has transpired. Along with greater security, this will also simplify end user support, which is one of the major cost factors for online games.

INTRODUCTION

User numbers in online computer gaming are rapidly increasing, turning over roughly US$5 billion per year and estimated to increase to US$10 billion per year in 2009 (IGN, 2005). The games themselves have transformed from simple adven-

tures into complex online worlds with millions of users and sophisticated virtual economies. These economies have spawned a secondary market in the real world, trading in-game items and characters, or even allowing direct conversion between real and virtual money. This real money trade alone has an estimated volume of US$2 billion per year and rising (Lehtiniemi, 2007). As the real money value of virtual property increases,

DOI: 10.4018/978-1-60960-515-5.ch009

related crimes and illicit activities in various forms are also becoming a serious issue. On the one hand, in-game cheating allows some people to illegitimately aquire virtual property, which is later turned into real money. On the other hand, fraud in various forms is becoming a serious issue for both players (as they become victims of such a fraud) and game providers (because of increased support requests). Also, lawsuits are being filed regarding virtual property. Decisions regarding cheating and fraud which used to be in-house to the game providers must become much more reproducible and provable. At the same time, user numbers and therefore cheating and fraud related support requests are expected to increase rapidly, therefore such decisions must become easier and faster to do in order to limit the cost of support. Our analysis of cheat and fraud prevention, detection, and proof pays special attention to these two factors.

Since virtual property is a relatively new phenomenon, there is as yet no common policy of dealing with it and the associated problems. We argue that soon most companies will accept virtual property to be equivalent to real property and will therefore be forced to protect it much better than it currently is.

We then consider other technical and social requirements on future virtual environments and games. The enhanced protection necessary for legal security does not come easy or cheap (which is one of the main reasons why many companies are reluctant to accept virtual property as having real value). We therefore analyse the necessary requirements, before concluding with a short summary.

THE REAL VALUE OF VIRTUAL PROPERTY

The question may come up how relevant the trade of virtual property really is. Does it pay off to invest real money and programmer time into the

protection of non-real objects? Though we could also argue for the ideal value of virtual goods simply because many real persons have interest in them, we shall only argue here in terms of money.

Several efforts have been made recently by designers of virtual worlds to support the trade of virtual goods for real money. One extreme case is Sony's Station Exchange (http://eq2.stationexchange.com)[1]. Via this service, users exchange game items for US$ in a protected environment. US$1.87 million have been transacted there in the first year (Robischon, 2005). Users pay for the service – the provider retains a provision – demonstrating the demand for protection in virtual economies.

Another example is Second Life, where the virtual economy is backed by a bank of issues. The exchange rate between its virtual currency Linden Dollar appear similar to "real" exchange rates on the news posts of agencies like Reuters, where it is rated as a stable currency.

Also, disputes about virtual property begin to reach real world judiciary. Some cases on virtual property were already decided in China (CNN, 2003). In May 2006, the provider of Second Life, Linden Lab, rejected a claim by attorney M. Bragg for compensation of a loss of virtual property he had invested US$2000 in before a legal court of the United States. Interestingly, the accepted amount in dispute – US$8000 – was the estimated market value of the property (Craig, 2006). Though the heavy public discussion for the case in- and outside of the Second Life community saw much more sympathy for the party of Linden Lab in this case, Linden Lab eventually settled by fulfilling all demands (Reuters, 2007b). Appreciating the 17-month reasoning of some of the most influential experts in the field, the result can be read as: A priori, virtual property IS (natural) property in an economic and political sense.

The volume of the economies in virtual worlds is estimated from around US$500 million (IGN, 2005) to US$2 billion (Lehtiniemi, 2007) per year and thus already exceeds that of the smallest national economies. But this is only the "tip of the iceberg" of its potential, because most massively multiplayer online games (MMOs) not only do not support real money trade (RMT), but explicitly try to hinder it to a certain extent. For example an extra feature of the popular MMO World of Warcraft (WoW) and others is the so-called "bind on pickup", where "bind" means the invalidation of a virtual item for RMT. The object has the attribute that it can never be owned by another subject than the first owner, hence it cannot perform as counterpart of any other change of ownership, particularly that of money. Such a feature would not have been invented without the existence of a drive towards "realization" of virtual property.

Whether we shall see the persistence of the somehow paradiselike status quo of non-commercial game worlds or the economic fusion of virtual worlds with the real one – is not the question. In fact, it is probable that most systems will position themselves across the spectrum between, with a tenacious virility towards the fusion. But in any case the issue will have a growing impact on the character, the role and the relevance of virtual worlds. In consequence, it is clear that substantial resources will have to be raised to install some "security" infrastructure against anarchy in virtual environments. Hence cheating and fraud can be defined as crime. With real money at stake, various forms of virtual crimes are developing (http://en.wikipedia.org/wiki/Virtual_crime).

Responsibility and power for rules and laws on virtual environments are still pulled and shoved between real society and virtual worlds. In the Bragg vs. Linden Lab case stated above, the judge ruled the terms of service (ToS) non-binding (Reuters, 2007c), and the ToS were since amended to give users more rights (specifically, virtual arbitrations)(Reuters, 2007d). Afterwards a settlement was made (Reuters, 2007b), but no judgement was spoken.

There is also an argument that governments should apply real-world laws and regulations to virtual currencies in online worlds like Second Life to prevent potential money laundering, fraud and tax evasion (Reuters, 2007a).

THE FUTURE OF ONLINE WORLDS

The Present

Virtual environments have been around for only about fifteen years, DIS being one of the first to be standardized in 1993 (Macedonia, Zyda, Pratt, Brutzman & Barham, 1995). Even though room- and space-based approaches are often thought to enhance usability (Greenberg & Roseman, 2003. Haake, Schümmer, Haake, Bourimi & Landgraf, 2004; Cikic, Jeschke, Ludwig & Sinha, 2007), virtual environments have not yet found wide recognition and circulation. The reasons for this are unknown but may have to do with the technical issue of very limited interactive possibilities when running a virtual environment over a network with noticeable delay (Sablatnig, Grottke, Köpke, Chen, Seiler & Wolisz, 2008). The implementations available for internet use today allow the users (or, rather, their avatars) to move around virtual environments, perform simple activation interactions and chat. For the most part, however, these options exist outside of virtual environments as well. In particular, more complicated interactions like performing a virtual experiment, building a virtual machine, or holding a virtual conference with many users are not possible. Currently, most available applications, e.g. common learning management systems, support a few hundred users at the same time, but performance is bad when many users cluster at the same virtual location (e.g. Moodle forum, 2007). Another problems of virtual environments is that they traditionally rely on a client server model. Therefore, an expensive server has to be provided, which is a problem because most services on the Internet are not paid for but free.

Computer games, however, have adopted the online model with a lot more zeal. Persistent game worlds where player actions have a permanent effect, complete with a virtual economy of items and services, and a group of regular visitors have existed since the 1980s in text-oriented multiuser dungeons (MUDs). User numbers increased enormously when the games added a graphical front end. Ultima Online started in 1997 and is still running with some success today in 2008 (http://www.uoherald.com/news/). World of Warcraft started in 2004, has over 10 million subscribers in 2008 (IT-Times, 2008), and has become one of the most successful computer game to date (Parloff, 2007). The technical abilities of these games have, however, not improved in the last 10 years. The user's avatar can move around the game-world and perform simple and limited interactions with AI-controlled enemies and other players. In general, players do not have a real influence on the virtual surroundings, cannot fell arbitrary trees, for instance, or erect a buiding at a random location. There are also no complicated or heavily time-critical interactions as are the norm for real-time strategy games or first person shooters. The reason the interaction potential and reactivity are limited in this way is once again of technical nature. With the current properties of the Internet, the user experience becomes unacceptable if too many interactions are possible/critical.

Almost all current online games use a client-server model, where all users of a particular game connect to a specific server, which handles the actual game. The downside of this is that the server is a bottleneck and cannot handle an arbitrary number of users. When more users are to be accommodated, a new shard is added, this is another server with a copy of the game. Users from two different shards cannot see, communicate or interact with each other through the game. The game World of Warcraft, for instance, has 800+ shards (called realms there) (http://www.worldofwarcraft.com). So one should really talk of a multitude of Worlds of Warcraft. Players are very aware of this split and often complain about it, going so far as to paying US$25 to move

their character from one shard to another. Current online games support a few thousand users on a single server simultaneously (Terdiman, 2006). The computers used as server engines are usually top of the line to accommodate the most users possible. The computing power necessary to participate in one of these games is negligible in comparison to the complexity of the graphics rendering required. Game developers would very much like to delegate more computation to the users' computers via, e.g. peer-to-peer systems (cf. Scalability, pg. 73). These approaches create new problems, however, such as loss of control and the appearance of multiple truths for the same incident (cf. The Catch, pg. 74).

Future Conditions

Of course the Internet will continue to improve, as it has done in the past. In particular, available bandwidth will increase by many orders of magnitude when optical fiber is brought to the end-user (http://www.fols.org/technology/). The delay, i.e. the time it takes to deliver an Internet package to the target site, on the other hand, will not decrease much further, as it is already fairly close to the theoretical minimum. The speed of light dictates that sending a piece of information from Europe to Australia and back, for example, cannot take less than around 100ms – if the cable were running in a straight line. The real ping-time in 2007 is around 300ms.

Computing power will also increase noticeably, probably following Moore's law (doubling approximately every two years). Without changes in architecture, simply increasing the server's computing power will at best allow increasing user capacity by a similar factor.

Object Complexity

The interactivity of online games is generally expected to increase as it has in offline games. Ten years ago, offline game interactions were about what they are now in online games. Nowadays, offline games often boast completely free interaction and physical modeling. Computer games have always striven to simulate the real world as much as possible (with the addition of a few key differences, such as granting superhuman powers to the avatar). To become a true virtual environment resembling the real world, the object density (i.e., both quantity and complexity of the objects) has to increase by many orders of magnitude. For example a steam-engine should not just be a steam-engine-lookalike-box with an on-off switch but rather should be made up of cylinders, which in turn are made up of nuts and bolts, which in turn are made up of metal, which can be bent or perforated.

In online games with many users, it is necessary to keep the world consistent between the participants. User actions have to be propagated to other users so that everyone ends up seeing the same would. Most types of traditional consistency schemes, such as server-client and also loose consistency (cf. chapter 3.5) in distributed architectures, require sending frequent updates of object state to the other hosts. It follows that network bandwidth increases as the number of objects and the size of their object state increases. Also, with higher object density, there are more chances for disagreements between the hosts or the clients and the server. Even if a common end-result is somehow arrived at, the visual consistency will suffer if many objects are in use. In particular, physical models do not perform realistically under these schemes.

One way of solving the issue is by greatly increasing the network bandwidth use of the game or simulation. While this will allow increasing object density by a few magnitudes, the increase is limited as the available bandwidth will always be limited and the object density demand will increase much faster than the Internet bandwidth. Also, if a server is involved at any point, either because a traditional server-client architecture is used or even if just to provide logging or security

monitoring, the Internet connection bandwidth of that server will increase accordingly, which can become a cost factor.

An alternative is optimistic consistency with determinism. In this model, each participating computer simulates the world on its own, including any side-effects and interobject interactions. In a sense, each host simulates the game like an offline game. As long as the world is left alone, it will play out exactly the same on all hosts. The only nondeterministic information that enters the world and has the power to affect its outcome are user input and a few random decisions (but most of those can be done in a deterministic fashion, as well). These nondeterministic events, and only these events, need to be communicated to the other hosts. The network bandwidth is then entirely to be independent of object density and only depends on the number of users. Since the packages are delayed when transferring across the network and may arrive at different times at each server in the network, packages with relevant information may arrive after the relevant action has passed. In order to keep all hosts congruent, each host must be able to backtrack its state to a previous time, apply the late user interaction information, and simulate back to the current time. This also means that the computing power necessary for this system is higher than with the traditional model. The increase is usually a factor of around four (Sablatnig, Grottke, Köpke, Chen, Seiler & Wolisz, 2008). This should not be a problem with current computers, much less with those available in the near future.

Optimistic consistency not only allows bandwidth independence of object density, it also shows significantly better effective consistency (ibid.). This in fact allows physical modeling, even greater object density, and a better visual consistency. Finally, a complete record of all nondeterministic events is sufficient to log and replay the entire playout of the simulation. In particular, hosts may send all recorded nondeterministic events to a logging server, which, in combination with regularly scheduled state-copies, can then be used to document and prove any event in the game, if one has the virtual spatial and temporal coordinates. In other words, an exact replay is possible, which can be a key advantage in security-sensitive environments (see chapters sections Fraud, pg. 75, and Rewiew pg. 79).

A virtual environment allowing a high object density and physical modeling would also find applications outside of games, most notably in education.

Scalability

Although online games are already a success, the problem of limited user numbers and low inter-activity is a constant issue. The next generation of online games is hoped to support hundreds of thousands or millions of users in a single shard to really allow everyone playing the same game to play it together. It is infeasible to run such a large simulation on a single computer, no matter what computing power it may have.

To allow a simulation of such dimensions, it then becomes a necessity to split it among several hosts, the simulation is then called distributed. Each participating host only replicates part of the entire world, with some overlap between hosts perhaps. This partial replication approach allows reducing computational complexity per host from $O(N)$ (where N is the number of users) to $O(D)$ (where D is the density of users). This would allow scaling to any size.

The architecture of a distributed system can still remain server-client, just that there is no single server but rather a server farm. Note though, that there will be extreme demands on the Internet connection bandwidth of such a server farm. Another possibility are super-peers, where the cooperating servers are distributed across the Internet. The disadvantage is having to operate a multitude of different servers across the world, which is usually not feasible (Fiedler, Wallner & Weber, 2002).

Another way to achieve scalability is to harness the computing power of the client machines. The game then runs on a peer-to-peer architecture. This architecture is used both to disseminate messages efficiently and to distribute world state calculation. Many research projects are studying peer-to-peer virtual worlds (Bharambe, Rao & Seshan, 2002; Knutsson, Lu, Xu & Hopkins, 2004). The open-source Croquet project (http://www.opencroquet. org) and the commercial VastPark project (http:// www.vastpark.com) are amongst the first such systems to be available to the end user. Note that peer-to-peer systems do significantly increase the chance for cheating. Note also that when a peer-to-peer simulation is run by a company, it will have to take extra steps to bind the game under its control. This can be achieved by having a single-sign-on point, for instance.

At the same time, moving to a peer-to-peer architecture does allow installing a virtual environment without the need of a high-end server, which in turn should allow more applications for this paradigm in education, science and every-day Internet usage.

The Catch

Systems employing partial replication are well-studied and they work, but there are some difficulties with these, even when also using a peer-to-peer approach.

The standard consistency algorithm for distributed simulations is loose consistency. In this scheme, each host sends object updates to the other hosts on a regular basis. When object updates from other hosts arrive, the host overwrites its own state for the objects in question. The scheme is usually equipped with some additional algorithms such as dead reckoning which covers for missing messages and player-ghost estimation which causes additional updates when they are probably needed. While this scheme does work surprisingly well and is stable, a particular problem exists where several truths about a single event exist.

The reason for this is associated with the concept of serializability (or the lack thereof) (Bernstein, Hadzilacos & Goodman, 1987). Simply speaking, several conflicting actions can occur at the same time. The conflict resolution then overwrites the states of some of the objects on one host with the view of those objects from another host and vice versa. While this does lead to a common view of the final result, the hosts may have had differing views in the meantime, their history (or log) may differ. Also, the final result may often not be arrived at by any single-host simulation. In other words, the internal laws of the simulation may have been bent.

An example of this would be a multi-player game in which both players use instant-kill weapons. As both players turn the corner and see each other, player A reacts a few milliseconds faster than player B and shoots at B. Player B, on his computer, tries to shoot back right away. The correct playout would be that player A kills player B, player B then does not get to shoot back because he is dead. On a server-client architecture, one of the two shooting commands arrives at the server first and kills the other player. When the other shooting command arrives at the server, it is ignored because the shooting player is already dead. While this solution does uphold the virtual environment's internal rules (only one of the players winds up dead), it may not exactly be fair. Who kills who depends a lot on the network delay of the players to the server, an effect which is well-known in current online first-person-shooter games.

In a distributed architecture employing loose consistency, on the other hand, both players shoot (almost) simultaneously, sending off messages indicating their shot to the opponent. While these messages are in transit, both players think that they were first and shot their opponent because that is what is shown on their local screens. As each message arrives shortly after, each player sees himself die. Subsequently, the host sends out the "I'm-dead"-message to the other player. The end result would be both players agreeing that they

are both dead. This result has three problems: 1) During the time that the messages are in transit, there are two conflicting truths, with each player assuming he won the contest by shooting first. This conflict exists in the replays of the event, as well. 2) The game logic is violated (both players wind up dead, thisis not possible). 3) It is impossible to tell who really won the contest.

In a distributed architecture employing optimistic consistency, finally, both players would send out their time-stamped shooting-commands. Again, while these messages are in transit, both players think that they shot first. When all messages have arrived shortly after, the correct playout (player A kills player B, B simply dies without shooting back) becomes known on both hosts and the environment would proceed from this correct state (player B being dead, player A running on). There is of course the problem of fixing what was already shown to player B (techniques for this are known as convergence-algorithms), but at least the correct playout is both achieved in the long run and is shown correctly in the replay.

Note that the described scenario is for illustration only. While the corresponding problem occurs frequently today, there are usually mechanisms like simple causality rules in place to avoid such effects. On more complicated systems (such as those with physical modeling), these avoidance mechanisms fail.

The occurrence of game-rule bending and conflicting playout obviously has implications on disputes. In fact, not only will this effect cause disputes because two people see an event differently, with both of them thinking they are right, it will also be very difficult to settle who is actually right – both of them, in fact, may be right. In legal terms, this implies a situation where there is no single truth, but rather several, contradicting truths, all similarly valid. While courts have long dealt with situations where the actual truth was unknown, there was always an assumption that there is a single truth behind all the differing and conflicting reports. This assumption has to be dropped in a system as the one described above. Also, this bending of the rules almost precludes installing complex rules and hence, physical modeling.

On the other hand, when one tries to combine optimistic consistency and any partial replication, the problem is this: in order for all simulations to play out the same way, one must take into account all influences that can have an effect on a particular object. With partial replication, each host only simulates a subset of objects. If the object is influenced by an object that the server does not replicate, the simulation becomes erroneous. Even though no published solution for this problem exists yet, we are confident it can be solved and are currently running experiments to investigate it further.

THE PRICE OF SECURITY

As far as virtual property is concerned, the two main virtual crimes are fraud and cheating.

Fraud

Fraud is any kind of deception to gain virtual property from another without paying for it fairly. Con artists have been around since the dawn of time and they exist in virtual economies as well, so the problem is not exactly new. Nevertheless, the problem has been largely ignored up till now, but must be dealt with soon, for the following reasons.

As virtual property becomes more valuable and it becomes ever easier to turn it into real money, real-life criminals start to become interested in virtual economies in the same way they are interested in virtual banking and credit card fraud. Professional criminals will raise the bar on cyber crime and the situation will become a lot more dangerous online.

Also, the way trading works in many online games encourages defrauding your trade-partner. For example, a user wishes to sell a virtual item.

He finds someone interested in buying the item outside of the game, e.g. via eBay. Inside the game, he trades the item to that person. Then if that person fails to pay in the real world, it will be very difficult for our user to prove in a real-world court that he has real claims because he cannot prove he delivered the item. Accurate logs are not being maintained and there is usually no automatic cash vs. item exchange. Depending on the item or service that is being traded and the game in question, trading may also require sharing identities or passwords, which is obviously very dangerous.

Finally, whenever a user is defrauded of something, he will usually turn to customer support for his game and try to get his lost property returned. This causes a flood of support requests, which, in turn, cost real money to the company distributing the game (Davis, 2005).

Note that the problem of fraud is not restricted to trading into and out of the virtual environment. There are also plenty of in-game frauds possible. Frauds like switching an item to be traded for a worthless look-alike would currently not be triable in front of a real court, again because the exact circumstances cannot be determined.

There are some rather efficient solutions to the problem of fraud. Sony has installed its Station Exchange Service which is an out-of-game web site allowing players to safely and securely trade Everquest II items to real money (http://eq2.stationexchange.com). Sony effectively provides an escrow service with each user only interacting financially with Sony's automated marketplace web site. The setup completely eliminates all possibility of fraud during the exchange. Of course people can still cheat or hack the web site or the exchange programs (as happened, e.g. in Craig, 2006), but that is beyond the scope of this paper. Note that Sony's support cost has gone down significantly on the shards where station exchange is in use (Robischon, 2005). Similar setups exist for micro-payments on various other games and environments.

It is more difficult to combat fraudulant behavior inside a game. Although the in-game trading interface is meant to protect players by going through several steps when trading, there are many cases where the interface cannot be used, for instance when trading in-game money vs. in-game services like an escort to a difficult-to-reach place or when an agreement exists about which of the players gets which rare item when and if it is found. Once the value of the virtual goods exceeds a certain amount, players will usually turn to user support in the case of a dispute. Such disputes cost the company real money, as they have to hire support personnel.

In order to settle the dispute, it is often necessary to know the exact circumstances of the dispute. To this end, keeping a log of all chat between players is helpful, but usually not enough. For a complete understanding, one would need chat-logs, lists of trades with their item lists, even lists of all items picked up by players, all with timestamps. Even with all this data, it would be hard (meaning, time-consuming and therefore expensive) to reconstruct the exact situation which lead to the dispute.

If one wants to keep support cost low in these cases, one has to provide an easy-to-use and all-encompassing log retrieval and conditioning tool. Optimally, this would include a replay of any space and time in the past of the virtual environment. Even poorly trained personnel would then be able to understand what really happened during the disputed event and be able to decide which of the disputing players was in the right.

Additionally, the possibility of an exact replay would be acceptable as proof, which would provide legal coverage. In fact, the feature of swift and reliable dispute arbitration could be a selling point for a virtual environment, in the same way that a country with high Corruption Perceptions Index draws more investment in the real world (Transparency International, 2007).

As mentioned on pg. 74, there is a particular problem that arises when loose consistency is used on a distributed simulation of any sort. If two players had agreed, for instance, that the one who dealt the deathblow to their enemy would get his item, they may very well both see themselves deal that stroke. Afterwards, their foe is dead and both claim his treasure. If the company's customer support is called to resolve the dispute, it will be hard to analyze the data, but if analysis succeeds, no winner can be announced. The only fair solution would be to clone the item and give one to each of the champions. This, however, is not in the interest of virtual economy, where the source-flow of items and their uniqueness has to be preserved. Consequently, such consistency algorithms should be avoided.

Cheating

Cheating has been a problem in most online (and offline) computer games since they started. Cheating allows players to do things that he should not be able to, e.g. easily winning over a difficult enemy, running faster than should be possible, finding out where a much sought-after item is hidden rather than searching a large area etc. Cheating hurts the virtual economy as some players will be able to produce a certain resource very easily and quickly, while others will not be able to do so competitively. If cheating happens with enough different resources, players using legitimate means will not be able to earn an income any more and leave the game.

Many methods have been devised to combat cheating, most of these are closely tied to the game and its implementations.

Illegal Knowledge

Quite a few cheats actually revolve around knowing things that the player is not supposed to know (yet). Famous examples are the well-known maphacks and wallhacks, where the player sees what happens in areas he cannot currently see, or has not ever seen. These cheats are some of the hardest to detect, prevent, and prosecute, as even a total replay of the situation, with all possible data available, will often not prove that the player cheated, he may just have guessed well.

Protecting against this sort of cheat depends largely on the game architecture in use, but some means exist for each architecture. For traditional client-server systems, the key is limiting information flow as tightly as possible. This includes not sending internal states of unknown objects to players before they should know about these, e.g. not giving out hints about what item is in a chest before opening it. This also includes restricting the area around the avatar which players are informed about, even purposefully hiding some information within that area.

For peer-to-peer systems, information restriction becomes much more difficult, but is still possible. The most common cheat here is to let the cheater know what other players are doing before the cheater acts himself, with both actions appearing to be simultaneous. This gives players a distinct advantage in direct competition, which is a part of most games. To prevent several cheats involved with temporal pre-knowledge Baughman and Levine developed the lockstep protocol (Baughman & Levine, 2001). This protocol hinges on sending out cryptographic hashes of player's actions for the next action round, then sending out the plaintext action when everyone else has committed their action hash. Thus, all players must decide on an action before they can see any other players cleartext action. The protocol was improved several times to increase performance and address even more cheats (Cronin, Filstrup & Jamin, 2003; GauthierDickey, Zappala, Lo & Marr, 2004).

Another weakness of peer-to-peer systems is the possibility to intercept all information about one's surroundings, thus allowing trap-evasion as well as gathering internal game information (such as which chest has which content). Since the information flows through the peer-to-peer network, a cheater could be able to intercept it. The key to preventing this is to assign players to

be region controllers for areas they themselves are not in at the moment. Thus a cheater can only gain information for a part of the game he has no interest in (Knutsson, Lu, Xu & Hopkins, 2004; Kabus, Terpstra, Cilia & Buchmann, 2005).

Illegal Actions

When persistent worlds are involved, user actions matter even when no other players are nearby. This opens up a slew of new cheats, usually geared to either cloning items or generating large amounts of items.

To prevent such cheats, it is paramount that player actions be double-checked and logged at all times. Periodically or when doubt is cast on the validity of a player's possessions, his past actions can then be audited.

Again, the problem becomes significantly more involved when running on a peer-to-peer architecture. Normally, other players will provide the region control for the virtual area a player is in. If the player somehow manages to be that controller (perhaps because he has two avatars logged into the game), he can then hack his client to let his main avatar do whatever he wishes. The best way to prevent this is to assign several region controllers to each region. Each will then double-check the decisions of the lead controller and report any anomalies to the company's cheat surveillance server. Cheating is then only possible by gaining control of all or at least a majority of region controllers assigned to a region (Kabus, Terpstra, Cilia & Buchmann, 2005).

When a cheat does occur and is reported, it would then be one host's word against another's. Thus, to be able to prove one's innocence, it is necessary to keep a record of all actions and decisions sent and received by each host. Also, actions should be cryptographically signed before sending them out to prevent a cheater from forging other hosts' actions. When an anomaly is detected (which could be caused by network problems, for instance), all relevant hosts must send their logs to the central server for automated review. In fact, in order to be able to have complete reviewability, all logs should be sent to the central server whenever a player is in the game. Note that arrival of these logs is not usually timecritical, they can be sent via trickle-upload. Also, these logs may not need to be analyzed immediately, as keeping them for later reviews would probably suffice, or random audits could be performed.

Nonetheless, if one wishes to install such a scheme for a very large system with millions of users, it is imperative that the logs be as small as possible and carry as much information as possible. In particular, what actually happened in the virtual world should be reconstructible from the logs and not also have depended on the vagaries of the Internet. This precludes relying on loose consistency, since even with the logs of player commands and of what the region controllers decided, the simulation could have taken several different paths, depending on when the commands arrived at the other hosts. This would make automatic detection and auditing difficult or at least render a very large class of cheats impossible to find.

Optimistic consistency, on the other hand, by nature only sends out the player commands and region controllers could send these on to other players in the area and to the logging/surveillance server. The possibility for cheating is much reduced if the commands are signed. Actions like "create a new item so-and-so" are also impossible since the optimistic language only allows user actions like "click at X, Y, Z". Also, if the complete log of all actions is gathered, the final playout is independently deducible by an offline server.

Review

Traditionally, when a player is caught cheating by one of the tools above, he will simply be banned, if the company has this policy. Banning here means he loses his place and standing in the virtual world, along with all virtual property he may have had.

While this has worked well and is working, there are also many cases in which the wrong people were suspected, perhaps because there was a problem with the Internet connection or because their computer may have been faulty.

Also, people may sue the company in question (e.g. Reuters, 2007b). So the banning should be able to stand up in court. To achieve this, companies should have their customer support review each case in which someone is suspected to cheat before actually banning him. For this to be feasible, the review process has to be:

- **Decidable:** Enough data must be gathered that it is easy to decide whether someone is cheating or whether there was a single faulty incidence from some other source.
- **Provable:** The review should collect proof in a quality that will uphold in court.
- **Cost Effective:** As usual, the company has to pay for support, so the faster the review process works the better.

The best way of meeting all of these requirements is by providing a replay ability as described above on pg 78.

CONCLUSION

Future social and technical developments of virtual environments will impose new challenges regarding security of and control over virtual property.

How well operators of virtual worlds and forensic experts can meet these challenges depends on the features supported by the virtual environment itself. The key features themselves and the requirements they result in were discussed in this paper. They are listed in Tables 1 and 2, along with some other desirable features. The tables also show the antithetic paradigms in architecture and consistency model and how well they can support these features.

Table 1. Comparison of architectures

Feature	Server-Client	Peer-to-Peer
Scalability	-	+
Company Control	+	o
Replay	+	o

-: not supported o: supportable; +: supported

Table 2. Comparison of consistency models

Feature	Loose	Optimistic
Scalability	+	-
Performance	+	o
Bandwidth	o	+
Visual Quality	o	+
Physical Modeling	-	+
Single Truth	-	+
Conclusive Replay	-	+

-: not supported o: supportable; +: supported

As Table 1 shows, server-client systems work well but cannot be truly scalable. If very large user numbers are to be supported, peer-to-peer systems will have to be used. These can support the other features if necessary.

Table 2, on the other hand, shows that the traditional loose consistency has serious shortcomings, especially in the area of security. We also believe that in the long run, as developers are forced to distribute the game, the appearance of multiple truths for the same incident will invalidate this technique as this makes it principally impossible to enforce security or later on find breaches thereof.

Optimistic consistency has significantly better support for most of the aimed-for features. The authors of this paper are currently researching optimistic consistency's one major weakness, failing to be scalable, and hope to report solutions soon.

REFERENCES

Baughman, N. E., & Levine, B. N. (2001). Cheat-proof playout for centralized and distributed online games. [Los Alamitos, CA: IEEE]. *Proceedings - IEEE INFOCOM, 1*, 104–113.

Bernstein, P. A., Hadzilacos, V., & Goodman, N. (1987). *Concurrency control and recovery in database systems.* Reading, MA: Addison-Wesley.

Bharambe, A. R., Rao, S., & Seshan, S. (2002). Mercury: a scalable publish-subscribe system for internet games. In *Proceedings of the first workshop on Network and system support for games (NetGames).* (pp. 3–9). New York, NY: ACM.

Cikic, S., Jeschke, S., Ludwig, N., & Sinha, U. (2007). Virtual room concepts for cooperative, scientific work. In *Proceedings of the world conference on Educational multimedia, hypermedia & telecommunications (ED-MEDIA).* (pp. 1872-1879). Chesapeake, VA: AACE.

CNN. Online Gamer in China Wins Virtual Theft Suit. Retrieved December 20, 2003, from http://www.cnn.com/2003/TECH/fun.games/12/19/china.gamer.reut/

Craig, K. (2006). *Second Life land deal goes sour.* Retrieved May 18, 2006, from http://www.wired.com/gaming/virtualworlds/news/2006/05/70909

Cronin, E., Filstrup, B., & Jamin, S. (2003). Cheat-proofing dead reckoned multiplayer games. In *Proceedings of the 2nd international conference on Application and development of computer games (ADCoG).* Hong Kong.

Davis, S. B. (2005). *The cost of insecurity - griefing: from anonymity to accountability.* Retrieved August 2005, from http://www.secureplay.com/cheating/griefing-in-games.htm

Fiedler, S., Wallner, M., & Weber, M. (2002). A communication architecture for massive multiplayer games. In *Proceedings of the first workshop on Network and system support for games (NetGames)*. (pp. 14–22). New York, NY: ACM.

GauthierDickey. C., Zappala, D., Lo, V., & Marr, J. (2004). Low latency and cheat-proof event ordering for peer-to-peer games. In *Proceedings of the 14th ACM international workshop on Network and operating systems support for digital audio and video (NOSSDAV)*. (pp. 134–139). New York, NY: ACM.

Greenberg, S., & Roseman, M. (2003). Using a room metaphor to ease transitions in groupware. In Ackerman, M., Pipek, V., & Wulf, V. (Eds.), *Sharing expertise. Beyond knowledge management* (pp. 203–256). Cambridge, MA: MIT Press.

Haake, J. M., Schümmer, T., Haake, A., Bourimi, M., & Landgraf, B. (2004). Supporting flexible collaborative distance learning in the CURE platform. In *Proceedings of the 37th annual Hawaii international conference on system sciences (HICSS)*. Los Alamitos, CA: IEEE.

IGN. *Sony Online Entertainment Announces Station Exchange*. Retrieved April 20, 2005, from http://eq2vault.ign.com/View.php?view=columns.Detail&category_select_id=35&id=434.

IT-Times. World of Warcraft erreicht über zehn Mio. Nutzer. Retrieved January 23, 2008, from http://www.it-times.de/news/nachricht/datum/2008/01/23/world-of-warcraft-erreicht-ueber-zehn-mio-nutzer/

Kabus, P., Terpstra, W. W., Cilia, M., & Buchmann, A. P. (2005). Addressing cheating in distributed MMOGs. In *Proceedings of the fourth workshop on Network and system support for games (NetGames)*. (pp. 1–6). New York, NY: ACM.

Knutsson, B., Lu, H., Xu, W., & Hopkins, B. (2004). Peer-to-peer support for massively multiplayer games. [Los Alamitos: IEEE.]. *Proceedings - IEEE INFOCOM, 1*, 96–107.

Lehtiniemi, T. (2007). *How big is the RMT market anyway?* Retrieved March 2, 2007, from http://virtual-economy.org/blog/how_big_is_the_rmt_market_anyw

Macedonia, M. R., Zyda, M. J., Pratt, D. R., Brutzman, D. P., & Barham, P. T. (1995). Exploiting reality with multicast groups: a network architecture for large-scale virtual environments. In *Proceedings of the Virtual Reality annual international symposium (VRAIS)*. (pp. 2–10). Washington, DC: IEEE.

Massey, D. (2008): *SOE, Live Gamer Deal: Smedley, Schneider Interviewed.* Retrieved February 8, 2008, from http://www.warcry.com/articles/view/interviews/2910-SOE-Live-Gamer-Deal-Smedley-Schneider-Interviewed

Moodle forum. Retrieved May 2007, from http://moodle.org/mod/forum/discuss.php?d=72766.

Parloff, R. (2007). *Legal Pad.* Retrieved June 1, 2007, from http://legalpad.blogs.fortune.cnn.com/2007/06/page/2/

Reuters, A. (2007a). *UK panel urges real-life treatment for virtual cash.* Retrieved May 14, 2007, from http://secondlife.reuters.com/stories/2007/05/14/uk-panel-urges-real-life-treatment-for-virtual-cash/

Reuters, A. (2007b). *Linden lab settles bragg lawsuit.* Retrieved October 4, 2007, from http://secondlife.reuters.com/stories/2007/10/04/linden-lab-settles-bragg-lawsuit/

Reuters, E. (2007c). *Judge rules against 'one-sided' ToS in Bragg lawsuit.* Retrieved May 31, 2007, from http://secondlife.reuters.com/stories/2007/05/31/judge-rules-against-one-sided-tos-in-bragg-lawsuit/

Reuters, E. (2007d). *UPDATE: Linden raises possibility of virtual arbitrations in new ToS.* Retrieved September 18, 2007, from http://secondlife. reuters.com/stories/2007/09/18/linden-revamps-arbitration-in-new-terms-of-service/

Robischon, N. (2005). *Station Exchange: Year One.* Retrieved June, 2005, from http://www. fredshouse.net/images/SOE%20Station%20Exchange%20White%20Paper%201.19.pdf

Sablatnig, J., Grottke, S., Köpke, A., Chen, J., Seiler, R., & Wolisz, A. (2008). *Adam – a DVE Simulator* (Technical Report Series TKN-08-004). Berlin, Germany: Technische Universität Berlin, Institute of Mathematics.

Terdiman, D. (2006). *'Second Life': Don't worry, we can scale.* Retrieved June 6, 2006, from http://news.zdnet.com/2100-1040_22-6080186.html

Transparency International. (2007). *The 2007 results.* Retrieved September 26, 2007, from http://www.transparency.org/news_room/in_focus/2007/cpi2007

ENDNOTE

[1] Sony recently outsourced the service, so there is a redirect on the referenced website. Sony had significant aggravation with real-world fraud, especially concerning invalid credit card payments (Massey, 2008). The new provider live gamer is one that is specialized in dealing with fraud on an industrial level, and works for several big customers besides Sony.

This work was previously published in International Journal of Digital Crime and Forensics (IJDCF), edited by Chang-Tsun Li & Anthony T.S. Ho, pp. 69-82, copyright 2009 by IGI Publishing (an imprint of IGI Global).

Section 3
Content Protection through the Use of Extrinsic Data

Chapter 10
Locally Square Distortion and Batch Steganographic Capacity

Andrew D. Ker
Oxford University Computing Laboratory, UK

ABSTRACT

A fundamental question of the steganography problem is to determine the amount of data which can be hidden undetectably. Its answer is of direct importance to the embedder, but also aids a forensic investigator in bounding the size of payload which might be communicated. Recent results on the information theory of steganography suggest that the detectability of payload in an individual object is proportional to the square of the number of changes caused by the embedding. Here, we follow up the implications when a payload is to be spread amongst multiple cover objects, and give asymptotic results about the maximum secure payload. Two embedding scenarios are distinguished: embedding in a fixed finite batch of covers, and continuous embedding in an infinite stream. The steganographic capacity, as a function of the number of objects, is sublinear and strictly asymptotically lower in the second case. This work consolidates and extends our previous results on batch and sequential steganographic capacity.

INTRODUCTION

We consider the following question: given a set of cover objects, how much data could be hidden in them? Although there is much literature on embedding and detection of steganographic payload, it is usual to consider only single cover objects, whereas this article is concerned with embedding in a finite or infinite stream of objects, deriving capacity bounds and optimal methods. We posed the questions about embedding and detection in a fixed number of covers in Ker (2006), where it was called the *batch steganography* problem, and the question is now also extended to infinite streams; we call this *sequential steganography*.

A key assumption, here, will be that the detectability of payload in a single object is (either exactly or locally for small payloads) proportional to the *square* of the number of changes caused by the embedding. Results of this nature have recently arisen in a number of theoretical stega-analysis papers (Ker, 2007b, 2007c, 2007d) and the phenomenon has also been observed experimentally (Ker, Pevný, Kodovský, & Fridrich, 2008). Assuming that the same holds in general, we examine the implications for an embedder when a large payload is to be spread amongst multiple cover objects. The choice of how to split payload between multiple covers is called an *embedding strategy* and the aim is to find the optimal strategies implied by the square law. There is some recent related work (Ker, 2006, 2007a) where optimal embedding strategies were found, but only in the context of highly restricted detection frameworks; in this article we do not assume knowledge of the steganalyst's behaviour.

The structure of this article is as follows. In the *Problem Formulation* section we will present the problems of batch steganography and sequential steganography; we will make and justify a series of assumptions about how steganalysis evidence accumulates. Evidence is not generated by payload itself—it is found as changes in the cover object, caused by the embedding process—so we must also relate embedding changes to payload transmitted and, with adaptive source coding methods, these are not always proportional (Fridrich & Soukal, 2006; Bierbrauer & Fridrich, 2008). In the *Analysis of the Batch Steganography Problem* section we will apply the theory to the batch steganography problem, deriving optimal embedding strategies and maximum undetectable payload, and in the *Analysis of the Sequential Steganography Problem* section to the sequential steganography problem; there is no optimal strategy in this case, but bounds can be derived, and strategies exist which come arbitrarily close to the bounds. It will be shown that the asymptotic payload, as a function of the number of covers, must be strictly lower in the sequential than the batch setting. Finally in the concluding *Discussion* section we will discuss the significance and limitations of the results.

An early version of some of this work has appeared in conference proceedings without any mathematical proofs (Ker, 2008b). In this work we have changed focus to concentrate on the embedding changes—this reduces the algebraic complexity—and are able to widen the applicability and weaken the assumptions. In particular, the square evidence law need hold only locally as payloads tend to zero.

Before continuing, we review some asymptotic notation. We write $f(n) = O(g(n))$ if there are constants c and N such that $f(n) \leq cg(n)$ for all $n \geq N$. The analogous *strict* bound is $f(n) = o(g(n))$, which means that $f(n)/g(n) \to 0$. We write $f(n) = \Theta(g(n))$ if there are positive constants c, d and N such that $cg(n) \leq f(n) \leq dg(n)$ for all $n \geq N$. The most precise condition on growth is $f(n) \sim g(n)$, which means that $f(n)/g(n) \to 1$.

PROBLEM FORMULATION

It is rather plausible to suppose that a steganographer has access to multiple covers among which the payload can be spread, and that a steganalyst is presented with a large number of objects for steganalysis. We formulated (Ker, 2006) the competing aims of *batch steganography*, in which it is assumed that a fixed set of N covers is available to a steganographer who spreads payload amongst some or all of them, and *pooled steganalysis*, in which a steganalyst attempts to pool the evidence of N objects to determine whether some payload is present (without knowing which or how many do contain payload). Only the former will concern us here: we want to determine, subject to some assumptions about accumulation of evidence and a maximum acceptable risk of detection, how much payload can be embedded. In some cases we will also be able to identify the optimal strategies for the steganographer.

We also tackle a more difficult problem, dubbed *sequential steganography*. In the sequential setting we no longer suppose that the number of covers N is fixed in advance of embedding (this differs materially from the batch problem, because optimal strategies require advance knowledge of N). In the sequential setting, we want to establish a strategy for an infinite stream of communications, with transmission of as much payload as possible over time. We will see that, although the steganographer is forced to reduce the payload *rate* over time, an infinite payload can still be transmitted in an infinite amount of time. However it will be shown that there is a tension between transmitting information sooner and transmitting asymptotically faster as $N \to \infty$. Further, we shall see that the steganographer must be asymptotically less efficient in sequential embedding than in the batch setting.

We will not, in this work, ask how the intended recipient of the payload is to recombine the payload segments extracted from the transmitted objects: we assume that knowledge of the size and order of the payload segments is determined by a secret key already shared between the communicating parties.

Distortion Bound

To determine the secure capacity of a set of covers we must choose a definition of *secure*, and the key is to measure the *evidence* available to the evidence available to the steganalyst. As in previous work (Ker, 2006, 2007a), we will suppose that the steganalyst is applying some detector to individual objects in the batch or stream of those transmitted by the steganographer, and pooling their evidence in some way. This is plausible because, at present, steganalysis methods only work on individual objects. The steganalyst wants to decide whether any payload is present: a hypothesis testing scenario.

Let us model the (finite or infinite) sequence of cover objects by a sequence of random variables $\mathbf{X} = (X_1, X_2,...)$. These can represent entire cover objects or, more practically, a steganalyst's observation resulting from steganalysis of each

object individually. Let us suppose that a sequence of stego objects, modelled by a sequence $\mathbf{Y} = (Y_1, Y_2,...)$, is created with an embedding strategy causing $\mathbf{c} = (c_1, c_2,...)$ embedding changes in the covers. (The distribution of Y_i depends, therefore, on c_i.) It is necessary that payload is measured by the number of embedding changes induced: although payload size might seem to be the more natural measure, it is only the changes which can be detected by a steganalyser. Later, we will relate payload size to number of changes.

Any detector—binary classifier for the presence or absence of payload in the sequence as a whole—must decide whether a sequence of objects is a realisation of $\mathbf{X}$ or $\mathbf{Y}$. By the information processing theorem (Cachin, 2004), any detector must have false positive probability α and false negative probability β satisfying

$$\alpha \log \frac{\alpha}{1-\beta} + (1-\alpha) \log \frac{1-\alpha}{\beta} \leq D_{KL}(\mathbf{X} \| \mathbf{Y}),$$

where D_{KL} represents the Kullback-Leibler (KL) divergence. In this sense, the worst-case risk to the steganographer is bounded by $D_{KL}(\mathbf{X} \| \mathbf{Y})$ and we can say that *evidence* is, at least in this context of binary hypothesis testing, measured by this KL divergence. This is a standard idea, first applied to steganography by Cachin (2004) and now widely adopted.

Then the definition of a secure embedding strategy is one which does not exceed a certain risk (from the point of view of the embedder) or evidence level. Thus we make the assumption:

(A0) The steganographer's distortion bound is in terms of KL divergence, $D_{KL}(\mathbf{X} \| \mathbf{Y}) \leq D$ for some positive D.

(Assumptions are numbered so that we may refer to the ones we require, later.) KL divergence has few attractive algebraic properties, but one is useful here. If we assume that the observations of Y_i are independent, then we can decompose the total evidence in N objects into a sum (Kullback, 1968, p. 23):

(A1) Evidence is additive: $D_{KL}(\mathbf{X} \| \mathbf{Y}) = \sum_{i=1}^{N} D_{KL}(X_i \| Y_i)$.

As long as the stream of cover objects come from a sensible source (a random selection from an image library, not consecutive frames from a video camera, say) it is plausible to assume such independence. Even if there is dependence between the cover objects it is not necessarily reflected in the steganalyst's observations, or is likely to be insignificant if the embedding process was chosen carefully.

Locally Square Distortion

Now we must relate the number of embedding changes c_i to the evidence found in object i, $D_{KL}(X_i \| Y_i)$. We cannot expect to know the exact relationship (even if we knew everything about the cover source and the embedding method, it is likely to be intractable to compute the KL divergence exactly) but we can make some sensible approximations.

This article is predicated on an assumption of *square distortion*:

(A2a) Evidence is a square law: for each i there is a positive constant Q_i such that $D_{KL}(X_i \| Y_i) = Q_i c_i^2$.

The constants of proportionality Q_i are called the Q-factors (Ker, 2007d): note that the different cover objects are allowed different Q-factors reflecting different cover characteristics. (A2a) is a strong assumption, but it is true at least if X_i and Y_i have (possibly multivariate) normal distributions with mean shifted by a linear function of c_i.

For other distributions we argue that this still holds approximately. We appeal to a theorem of Kullback (1968, p. 26), which says that, under some regularity conditions, KL divergence of a one-parameter family is locally square in perturbations of the parameter. We will not repeat this argument, but refer the reader to prior work (Ker, 2007d). Under these conditions, as $c_i \rightarrow 0$, $D_{KL}(X_i \| Y_i) \rightarrow Q_i c_i^2$ for a constant Q_i. We will

later see that $c_i \rightarrow 0$ is forced, as the number of covers grows, if we are to meet a fixed evidence bound (this was also argued in Ker (2007d) on the grounds that embedding at a rate which does not diminish is a surefire way for the steganographer to get caught). Hence, at least eventually, the KL divergence evidence provided by cover i is proportional to c_i^2, although the constant of proportionality depends on the nature of cover i.

We codify this with the following assumption, weaker than (A2a).

(A2b) Evidence is locally a square law: for each i there is a positive constant Q_i such that $D_{KL}(X_i \| Y_i) = \phi_i(c_i)$, with $\phi_i(0) = 0$, ϕ_i strictly increasing without bound, and $\phi_i''(x) \rightarrow 2Q_i$, uniformly in i, as $x \rightarrow 0^+$.

The condition in terms of ϕ_i'' is slightly stronger than $\phi_i(x) \sim Q_i x^2$, and it also guarantees a region of zero in which all the ϕ_i are convex. It can be proved by slightly stricter regularity conditions than in Kullback's theorem. The uniformity of the convergence is justifiable if we believe that the cover source is stationary.

Of course, correctness of assumption (A2b) still depends on regularity conditions, but they are satisfied by very many distributions if the parameterization is suitable: the parameter should have an asymptotically linear effect on the distribution it determines. This seems a reasonable property for the effect of embedding changes on a distribution of covers.

Cover Characteristics

For asymptotic results about capacity we also require some assumptions about the size and nature of the cover objects. The *size* of object i will be denoted n_i and measured by the number of possible embedding locations; we require only a very weak condition on the sequence of sizes. But it is well-established (Böhme, 2005; Böhme & Ker, 2006) that even similarly-sized covers can vary greatly in their capacity for secure pay-load: in images, factors including local variance, saturation and JPEG compression levels can have very significant impact on the rate at which cover changes produce evidence. These differences are reflected in the Q-factors of the covers, so for example we might expect that noisier covers have a lower value for Q_i. We need at least a weak assumption about the Q-factors too:

(A3a) The cover characteristics are bounded: there exist $\underline{n}$ and $\bar{n}$ such that $0 < \underline{n} \le n_i \le \bar{n}$ for all i, and there exist $\underline{Q}$ and $\overline{Q}$ such that $0 < \underline{Q} \le Q_i \le \overline{Q}$ for all i.

This assumption precludes the possibility of larger-and-larger, or ever-diminishing, cover objects, or unboundedly easier or more difficult covers to embed in. Such a situation would, of course, alter the asymptotic capacity. It is justified at least if we believe that the covers are from a stationary source.

It is also interesting to consider a more restricted case when it is only the cover size which varies. This would be plausible if, for example, cover objects are taken from the same source and the embedding method cannot exploit any other differences between the covers. It is arguable that the Q factor should, all other things being equal, be inversely proportional to the cover size. This can be justified exactly if the cover consists of independent regions, and it is the subject of future work to prove that it holds even when there is (limited) dependence between different parts of the cover. Without justifying it further, we will allow this stronger assumption as an alternative to (A3a):

(A3b) The cover sizes are bounded: there exist $\underline{n}$ and $\bar{n}$ such that $0 < \underline{n} \le n_i \le \bar{n}$ for all i. Furthermore, the covers are of uniform character: there is a constant Q such that $Q_i = Q/n_i$

BOUNDS ON EMBEDDING EFFICIENCY

We have related the distortion bound to the number of embedding changes in each object, but both steganographers and forensic steganalysts are interested in payload size. The final component for our analysis is to relate these quantities. Recall that c_i is the number of embedding changes in object i, and let us write m_i for number of the payload bits that can always be conveyed by this many changes.

Under a simple embedding scheme there is a direct relationship between these, for example in simple least significant bit (LSB) replacement we have $m_i = c_i$ (note that we are using c_i as an upper bound on the number of changes: in LSB replacement on average only 1/2 cover samples must be altered for the embedding of each payload bit, but in the worst case every payload bit requires one change). In similar cases, with fixed encodings, we may assume:

(A4a) The embedding code is fixed: for some positive constant E, $m_i = Ec_i$.

(We repeat that we are bounding the maximum *possible* number of changes, whereas some literature (Fridrich & Soukal, 2006; Fridrich, Lisonek, & Soukal, 2006) deals in the expected number of changes. Since our security model is about risk, it makes sense to take the pessimistic view and bound the maximal number of changes.)

But, when there is excess capacity, we can do better using a source coding method called *matrix embedding* (also known as *syndrome coding*), adapting the code to maximize the payload transmitted for a given number of locations and permitted changes. This technique was suggested by Crandall in an unpublished manuscript (Bierbrauer, 1998), and two works have been published surveying aspects of source coding for steganography (Fridrich & Soukal, 2006; Bierbrauer & Fridrich, 2008).

Following the literature, we will assume that the cover objects consist of a number of *locations*, each of which can carry an unconstrained q-ary symbol as payload: the embedding process may overwrite some or all of these symbols and each one overwritten is an *embedding change*. For example, under LSB embedding $q = 2$ and each pixel is a potential location: the symbol is just the LSB of each pixel value. Under ternary embedding $q = 3$, which allows a greater number of payload bits to be embedded in total, without changing the number of locations. We assume that q is fixed by the choice of embedding algorithm. For simplicity, we will also assume that q is a prime power, but in fact it would not affect any of the asymptotic conclusions were this not so.

Most literature focuses on relative embedding rates (payload bits per location) and embedding efficiency (payload bits per embedding change) but it is more convenient for us to consider absolute quantities. Let us define $\mu_q(n, c)$ to be the largest guaranteed payload size (measured in bits) which can be embedded in n locations using no more than c embedding changes. The complete function μ_q is not known, but we can bound it:

Lemma 1: *For any q, n, and c,*

$$c \log_2\left(\frac{n}{c}(q-1)\right) - c\log_2 q \le \mu_q(n,c) \le$$

$$c \log_2\left(\frac{n}{c}(q-1)\right) + (n-c)\log_2\left(\frac{n}{n-c}\right)$$

Proof: *Both inequalities can be translated from Bierbrauer and Fridrich (2008), with extensions to q-ary alphabets as in Fridrich et al. (2006). The lower limit comes from using c repetitions of the*

$$\left[\frac{q^p-1}{q-1}, \frac{q^p-1}{q-1}-p, 3\right]$$

q-ary Hamming code, where

$$p = \left\lfloor \log_q\left(\frac{n}{c}(q-1)+1\right)\right\rfloor:$$

each repetition embeds p q-ary symbols in

$$\frac{q^p-1}{q-1}$$

locations making at most one embedding change, and p is chosen to maximize the number of symbols. The upper limit derives from a sphere-packing bound from the theory of covering codes (e.g., Cohen, 1983). ∎

Since, as $c/n \to 0$, the second term of both lower and upper bounds are dominated by the first, what is left is a concave function and we may make the simplification (valid for sufficiently large covers):

(A4b) Optimal adaptive source coding is used and $m_i = \chi_q(c_i)$, where χ_q is a strictly concave increasing function satisfying $\chi_q(x) \sim x\log_2(n_i(q-1)/x)$, uniformly in i, as $x \to 0^+$.

We highlight one further (implicit) assumption in this article. When we come to optimization problems, we will not constrain c_i and m_i to be integers. In practice, of course, one cannot embed a fractional bit of payload nor make a fractional number of changes. However, because typical covers are very large, allowing the quantities to vary continuously is a reasonable approximation. Moreover, the problems of finding optimal batch and sequential steganography schemes would be much more difficult if restricted to integer domains. We will return, briefly, to this assumption—the only one which is strictly false—in the concluding section.

ANALYSIS OF THE BATCH STEGANOGRAPHY PROBLEM

We can formulate batch steganography, from the embedders point of view, as an optimization problem. Our aim is to derive the best embedding strategy and, hence, the maximal possible payload. Depending on which of the assumptions we select, our results will have to be asymptotic rather than exact.

This lemma, in which the conditions are stronger than necessary but fit well with our scenario, will be useful in what follows.

Lemma 2: *Suppose that, for $i = 1,..., n$, $\phi_i:[0, \infty) \to [0, \infty)$ is continuous, convex, and strictly increasing without bound, $\chi_i:[0, \infty) \to [0, \infty)$ is continuous and strictly concave increasing, and $\phi_i(0) = \chi_i(0) = 0$. Then*

(1) *for $D > 0$ the maximization problem*

Maximize $\Sigma\chi_i(x_i)$ **s.t.** $\Sigma\phi_i(x_i) \leq D$

has a unique solution determined by $\Sigma\phi_i(x_i) = D$ and $\chi_i'(x_i)/\phi_i'(x_i)$ constant, and

(2) *if the objective maximum above is M then the dual optimization problem*

Minimize $\Sigma\chi_i(x_i)$ **s.t.** $\Sigma\phi_i(x_i) = M$

has the same solution, with objective minimum D.

Proof: *(1) By convexity of ϕ_i and $-\chi_i$, the problem is one of convex optimization (Boyd & Vandenberghe, 2004). The feasible region is nonempty ($\phi_i(0) = \chi_i(0) = 0$, and $D > 0$, imply that $\mathbf{x} = 0$ is feasible) and compact (ϕ_i unboundedly increasing forces x_i to be bounded above). The objective function is strictly concave, so there exists a unique global minimum, at which the constraint is tight, and which may be determined by the method of Lagrange multipliers.*
Writing

$$\Lambda = \sum \chi_i(x_i) - \lambda\left(\sum \phi_i(x_i) - D\right)$$

we have

$$\frac{\partial \Lambda}{\partial x_i} = \chi_i'(x_i) - \lambda\phi_i'(x_i),$$

so at the stationary point $\chi_i'(x_i)/\phi_i'(x_i) = \lambda$, a constant.
(2) This is just the standard duality theorem for strictly convex optimization. ∎

The first part of the lemma will be used to solve the batch steganography optimization problem: maximize the payload transmitted $M = \Sigma m_i$, subject to the distortion bound $D_{KL}(\mathbf{X} \parallel \mathbf{Y}) \leq D$. The second part of the lemma ensures that the solutions are the same as the alternative formulation: for a given payload size, minimize the KL divergence. The hypotheses of the lemma are covered by our assumptions about distortion and source coding.

There now follows a sequence of three theorems, applying Lemma 2 to versions of the batch steganography problem with different assumptions. We begin with the strongest assumptions and successively weaken them.

Theorem 3 *Suppose an exact square evidence law and fixed source coding, making assumptions (A0), (A1), (A2a), (A3a), and (A4a). Abbreviate*

$$\bar{Q} = \sum_{i=1}^{N} Q_i^{-1}.$$

Then

(1) *The optimal embedding strategy is*

$$c_i = D^{1/2}\bar{Q}^{-1/2}Q_i^{-1}$$

and the total secure payload $M = ED^{1/2}\bar{Q}^{1/2}$. Asymptotically, $M = \Theta(N^{1/2})$.

(2) *Under stronger assumption (A3b) (covers with uniform characteristics) the optimal strategy has $m_i = rn_i$ for a constant r, i.e. payload is embedded proportionally to cover size.*

Proof: *(A0), (A1), (A2a), and (A4a) combine to give the following optimization problem:*

Maximize ΣEc_i **s.t.** $\Sigma Q_i c_i^2 \leq D$

This can be solved using a variation of the Cauchy-Schwartz inequality, but it is just as simple to apply Lemma 2: the unique solution is given by $E/(2c_iQ_i)=k$ where k is some constant, and substituting into $\Sigma Q_ic_i^2 = D$ gives

$$k = \frac{1}{2}ED^{-1/2}\underline{Q}^{1/2}.$$

Hence $c_i = D^{1/2}\underline{Q}^{-1/2}Q_i^{-1}$ and the formula for $M = \Sigma m_i = E\Sigma c_i$ follows immediately. By (A3a), $N\overline{Q}^{-1} \le \underline{Q} \le N\underline{Q}^{-1}$, i.e. $\underline{Q} = \Theta(N)$. This implies $M = \Theta(N^{1/2})$.

The second part is simple: observe that $m_i \propto c_i$, $c_i \propto Q_i^{-1}$ and, under (A3b), $Q_i \propto n_i^{-1}$. Overall, $m_i \propto n_i$.
■

Other results showing, under various different assumptions, that total steganographic capacity follows a square root law (in the overall size of the available cover) have arisen in the literature; we will consider them briefly in the *Discussion* section.

Now we weaken assumption (A2a) to (A2b), assuming only that the square evidence law holds locally to zero. We must be careful about the analytical details.

Theorem 4: *Suppose a local square evidence law and fixed source coding, making assumptions (A0), (A1), (A2b), (A3a), and (A4a). Again write*

$$\underline{Q} = \sum_{i=1}^{N}Q_i^{-1}.$$

Then

(1)   The optimal embedding strategy satisfies

$$c_i \sqsubset D^{1/2}\underline{Q}^{-1/2}Q_i^{-1}$$

and the secure total payload is

$$M \sqsubset ED^{1/2}\underline{Q}^{1/2},$$

as $N \to \infty$ if the KL distortion bound D is fixed.

(2)   Under stronger assumption (A3b) (covers with uniform characteristics) the optimal strategy has $m_i \sim rn_i$ for a constant r, i.e. payload asymptotically proportional to cover size.

Proof: *As above, (A0), (A1), (A2b), and (A4a) together give optimization problem:*

Maximize Σc_i **s.t.** $\Sigma\phi_i(c_i) \le D$ $\qquad$ (1)

but we cannot apply Lemma 2 immediately because the ϕ_i are not guaranteed to be convex everywhere. Using the uniform convergence in (A2b), for any $\varepsilon > 0$, there exists $\delta > 0$ and $L > 0$ such that:

all $\phi_i(x_i)$ convex on $[0, \delta)$ $\qquad$ (2)

all $\phi_i(x_i) > L$ on $[\delta, \infty)$ $\qquad$ (3)

all $\phi_i(x) \in ((1-\varepsilon)Q_ix^2, (1+\varepsilon)Q_ix^2)$ on $[0, \delta)$ $\quad$ (4)

all $\phi_i'(x) \in ((1-\varepsilon)2Q_ix, (1+\varepsilon)2Q_ix)$ on $[0, \delta)$ $\quad$ (5)

First, consider the optimization problem restricted to all $c_i \in [0, \delta)$. By Lemma 2 and (2) it has a unique solution with $E/\phi_i'(c_i) = k$, some constant. Using (5) and rearranging,

$$\frac{1}{2}Ek^{-1}Q_i^{-1}(1+\varepsilon)^{-1} < c_i < \frac{1}{2}Ek^{-1}Q_i^{-1}(1-\varepsilon)^{-1} \quad (6)$$

Substituting into the tight constraint $\Sigma\phi_i(x_i) = D$, and using (4), we have

$$\frac{1}{4}E^2k^{-2}\underline{Q}(1-\varepsilon)(1+\varepsilon)^{-2} < D <$$
$$\frac{1}{4}E^2k^{-2}\underline{Q}(1+\varepsilon)(1-\varepsilon)^{-2}$$

hence

$$\frac{1}{2}ED^{-1/2}\underline{Q}^{1/2}(1-\varepsilon)^{1/2}(1+\varepsilon)^{-1} < k <$$
$$\frac{1}{2}ED^{-1/2}\underline{Q}^{1/2}(1+\varepsilon)^{1/2}(1-\varepsilon)^{-1}$$

and, using (6) again,

$D^{1/2}\bar{Q}^{-1/2}Q_i^{-1}(1+\varepsilon)^{-3/2}(1-\varepsilon) < c_i <$

$D^{1/2}\bar{Q}^{-1/2}Q_i^{-1}(1-\varepsilon)^{-3/2}(1+\varepsilon)$

which demonstrates

$$c_i \square D^{1/2}\bar{Q}^{-1/2}Q_i^{-1} \qquad (7)$$

and therefore $M \square ED^{1/2}\bar{Q}^{1/2}$.

We must now verify that (1) cannot have an optimum outside the region of guaranteed convexity $[0, \delta)^N$. *By (3), no more than* N/L *of the* c_i *can be outside this region, without breaking the distortion constraint. Suppose that some do so: the effect is to reduce the constraint, and force the rest of the* c_i *into the guaranteed convex region. But finitely many of the* c_i *can only contribute finitely much to the objective function, and we have shown that, as* $N \to \infty$, *an unbounded contribution can be achieved by having all* c_i *inside region of guaranteed convexity. For any* $\varepsilon > 0$, *therefore, there is a sufficiently large* N *such that all* c_i *are in* $[0, \delta)$ *at the optimum.*

For part (2), if $Q_i = Q/n_i$ *then (7) gives*

$$m_i \square ED^{1/2}Q^{-1/2}n_i\left[\sum n_i\right]^{-1},$$

payload asymptotically proportional to cover size. ∎

Finally, we may allow adaptive source coding at the embedder. In this case, the total payload size is superlinear in the number of embedding changes; this alters the objective function.

Theorem 5: *Suppose a local square evidence law and adaptive source coding, making assumptions (A0), (A1), (A2b), (A3a), and (A4b). Then*
(1) The optimal embedding strategy satisfies

$$\frac{n_i}{c_i}\log_2\left(\frac{n_i}{c_i}\frac{q-1}{e}\right) = kQ_i n_i \qquad (8)$$

where k *is a constant. This implies that the secure total payload is* $M = \Theta(N^{1/2}\log N)$ *as* $N \to \infty$ *with* D *fixed. (2) Under stronger assumption (A3b) (covers with uniform characteristics) the optimal strategy has* $m_i \sim rn_i$ *for a constant* r, *i.e. payload asymptotically proportional to cover size.*

Proof: *This time the optimization problem is*

Maximize $\Sigma\chi_i(c_i)$ **s.t.** $\Sigma\phi_i(c_i) \le D$

Most of the analysis is similar to that in the previous theorem, and we only sketch the differences. For the same reasons as before, for large enough N *all* c_i *are forced into a region* $[0, \delta)$ *in which all* ϕ_i *are convex and* χ_i *concave, with the former arbitrarily close to* $Q_i c_i^2$ *and the latter to*

$$c_i \log_2\left(\frac{n_i}{c_i}(q-1)\right).$$

Then Lemma 2 applies, with the optimum asymptotically where $\chi_i'(c_i)/\phi_i'(c_i)$ *is constant. This simplifies to (8). This equation is difficult to solve analytically (although, of course, the solution can be found numerically if specific values of* D, *all* n_i, *and all* Q_i *are given). However we may still draw a conclusion about the asymptotic growth of the total payload size* M, *as follows. Recall that* n_i *and* Q_i *are uniformly bounded above, and below away from zero. Write (8) in the form*

$$f\left(\frac{n_i}{c_i}\right) = kQ_i n_i,$$

where

$$f(x) = x\log_2\left(x\frac{q-1}{e}\right);$$

this positive continuous function has strictly positive derivative for $x \ge 1$ *so the value of* n_i/c_i *is bounded above and below away from zero. We may conclude that, for any* i *and* j,

$$0 < a < c_i/c_j < b \qquad (9)$$

for some constants a and b independent of N. Now consider the tight distortion bound $\sum \phi_i(c_i) = D$. By prior reasoning, $\phi_i(c_i)$ is arbitrarily close to $Q_i c_i^2$ and together with (9) this forces $c_i = \Theta(N^{-1/2})$. Finally, using

$$m_i = \chi_i(c_i) \square c_i \log_2 \left(\frac{n_i}{c_i}(q-1) \right),$$

we deduce that $m_i = \Theta(N^{-1/2}\log N)$ and hence $M = \Theta(N^{1/2}\log N)$.

The problem is simplified if $Q_i = Q/n_i$ for then (8) becomes

$$f\left(\frac{n_i}{c_i} \right) = kQ,$$

a constant, hence

$$\frac{n_i}{c_i} = l,$$

a constant. Therefore
$$m_i = \chi_i(c_i) \square c_i \log_2 \left(\frac{n_i}{c_i}(q-1) \right) =$$

$$n_i l^{-1} \log_2(l(q-1))$$

Even though the number of embedding changes is no longer proportional to the size of the cover, the optimization problem ensures that the payload embedded in each object remains proportional to cover size. ∎

Adaptive source coding has increased the growth of asymptotic capacity by a factor of log N. However, capacity remains substantially sublinear in N. This remains in contrast to capacity results for noisy channels, where information transmitted is always linear in the number of symbols sent.

ANALYSIS OF THE SEQUENTIAL STEGANOGRAPHY PROBLEM

In the preceding section it was vital that the number of covers N was fixed in advance: subject to a fixed total acceptable risk D, the optimal

strategies all involve N. Therefore these results are not applicable to an endless stream of covers. Although most of our results have phrased capacity asymptotically as $N \to \infty$, in the batch steganography scenario N is fixed.

Now we consider a different problem, when the steganographer wants to establish a communication *channel* with their recipient. We suppose that there is an infinite stream of covers, in which payload can be embedded, and the steganographer aims to embed as much as possible subject to a bound on the risk. This time the distortion bound is subtly different: (A0) must mean

$$D_{KL}((X_1,...,X_N)) \| (Y_1,...,Y_N)) \le D$$

for all N, where **X** is the stream of covers and **Y**, which depends on the sizes of the embedded data **m**, the stream of stego objects. Since KL divergence is nonnegative, this is equivalent to replacing assumptions (A0) and (A1) with

(A0') The steganographer's distortion bound for the sequential steganalysis problem is $\sum_{i=1}^{\infty} D_{KL}(X_i \| Y_i) \le D$

It is important to understand where this bound comes from: the steganographer's opponent is a steganalyst who makes a *single* hypothesis test for the presence or absence of payload, based on the objects transmitted up that point, but the steganographer does not know when that hypothesis test is going to take place. If this seems overly restrictive on the steganalyst, note that it would be suboptimal to make two (or more) hypothesis tests because this would simply compound the probability of false positives: at the point of the second (or last) test, all the information available to earlier test(s) is still present, so nothing could have been gained by performing the earlier test(s).

We continue to write

$$M = \sum_1^N m_i,$$

but now M is a variable which grows with N, and it makes sense to discuss the asymptotic behaviour of M in terms of N. The first aim is to make sure that M grows without bound, so that the steganographic channel does not completely dry up, and the second is to have M grow asymptotically as fast as possible. We will illustrate the sequential steganography problem under the most restrictive assumption options (A2a) and (A4a)—an exact square evidence law and no adaptive source coding—and make a relatively easy generalization later. (A3a) will be assumed throughout.

Under (A2a), the distortion bound simplifies to

$$\sum_{i=1}^{\infty} Q_i c_i^2 \le D \qquad (10)$$

and under (A4a), $M = E\sum c_i$ Immediately we can see a tension between transmitting payload early and transmitting a larger payload: if the steganographer sends the most-possible information in the first object, $m_1 = ED^{1/2}Q^{-1/2}$, they have used up all their distortion budget and cannot send any more information at all. On the other hand, if they spread all the distortion over the first N objects, the total transmitted is

$$M = ED^{1/2}\left[\sum_{j=1}^{N} Q_j^{-1}\right]^{1/2},$$

exactly as in Theorem 3. By varying N, arbitrarily large payload can be sent, but this does not establish a true covert channel because after a certain point the transmission must stop. In an effort to use all of the infinite stream of covers, the steganographer might attempt *geometric embedding*:

$$m_i = ED^{1/2}Q_i^{-1/2}2^{-i/2}.$$

This uses half of the distortion budget in the first cover, one quarter in the second, and soon. Unfortunately, the total payload transmitted

$$M < ED^{1/2}\underline{Q}^{-1/2}\sum_{i=1}^{\infty}2^{-i/2} = ED^{1/2}\underline{Q}^{-1/2}(\sqrt{2}-1)^{-1}$$

is finite, so all this has achieved is to take an infinite amount of time to send a finite amount of information.

However, it is possible to transmit an infinite total payload. The simplest scheme is *harmonic embedding*:

$$m_i = ED^{1/2}6^{1/2}\pi^{-1}Q_i^{-1/2}i^{-1}$$

meets (10) while $\sum m_i = \infty$. As a function of N, the total payload transmitted M grows without bound, but only asymptotically as fast as log N.

Now the problem becomes clearer. The steganographer must find a sequence (a_i) such that $\sum Q_i a_i^2$ converges, so the distortion bound can be met by $c_i = k a_i$ for a suitable choice of k, but $\sum a_i$ diverges as fast as possible so that the total payload $M = E\sum c_i$ grows as fast as possible. When source coding is permitted, this last quantity changes to $M = \sum \chi_i(c_i)$. But for $\sum Q_i a_i^2$ to converge, the a_i terms must diminish sufficiently fast, and this places a limit on M's growth. It is possible to prove a result which holds under either an exact or a local square law for evidence, and holds in slightly different forms depending on whether adaptive source coding is used.

Theorem 6 (Embedding bound): *Assume (A0') and (A3a).*

(1) Under either (A2a) or (A2b), and fixed source coding (A4a), $M = o(N^{1/2})$.

(2) Under either (A2a) or (A2b), and with adaptive source coding satisfying (A4b), $M = o(N^{1/2}\log N)$.

Proof: *Whether (A2a) or (A2b) holds, the distortion bound is*

$$\sum_{i=1}^{\infty}\phi_i(c_i) \le D$$

with ϕ_i increasing and $\phi_i(x) \sim Q_i x^2$ uniformly in i. This certainly forces $\phi_i(c_i) \to 0$ as $i \to \infty$, whereby $c_i \to 0$. So there exists j, independent of N, such that

$$\phi_i(c_i) \geq \frac{1}{2}Qc_i^2$$

for all i>j. Furthermore,

$$\sum_{i=j+1}^{\infty} c_i^2 < D' = 2DQ.$$

Write $C = \sum_{i=1}^{N} c_i$. *Take any* $\varepsilon > 0$. *Pick k such that*

$$\sum_{i=k+1}^{\infty} \phi_i(c_i) < \varepsilon^2/9$$

This is independent of N and we may also assume that j < k < N.
Write

$$C_1 = \sum_{i=1}^{j} c_i, \; C_2 = \sum_{i=j+1}^{k} c_i, \; C_3 = \sum_{i=k+1}^{N} c_i.$$

Recall Cauchy's inequality, that

$$\sum_{i=1}^{n} a_i \leq \left(\sum_{i=1}^{n} a_i^2\right)^{1/2} n^{1/2}.$$

This gives

$$C_2 \leq (k-j)^{1/2}\left[\sum_{i=j+1}^{k} c_i^2\right]^{1/2} < k^{1/2}D'^{1/2}. \tag{11}$$

And

$$C_3 \leq (N-k)^{1/2}\left[\sum_{i=k+1}^{N} c_i^2\right]^{1/2} < N^{1/2}\varepsilon/3. \tag{12}$$

Combining (11) and (12) we have
$$CN^{-1/2} = (C_1 + C_2 + C_3)N^{-1/2}$$
$$< C_1 N^{-1/2} + k^{1/2}D'^{1/2}N^{-1/2} + \varepsilon/3$$
$$< \varepsilon$$
the final inequality at least if $N > 9C_1^2\varepsilon^{-2}$ *and* $N > 9kD'\varepsilon^{-2}$. *We have proved that for any* $\varepsilon > 0$, $C < \varepsilon N^{1/2}$ *for sufficiently large N.*
So for part (1), observe that M = EC. We have proved that $C = o(N^{1/2})$ *so* $M = o(N^{1/2})$.
For part (2), by (A4b) and (A3a) there exists $\delta > 0$ *such that*

$$\chi_i(x) \leq \psi(x) = 2x\log_2(\bar{n}(q-1)/x)$$

for all i and $x \in [0, \delta)$. *For large enough i,* $c_i < \delta$ *is guaranteed. Since* $\psi(x)$ *is concave we have*
$$M = \sum_{i=1}^{N} \chi_i(c_i) \leq \sum_{i=1}^{N} \psi(c_i) \leq N\psi(C/N) =$$
$$2C\log_2(N\bar{n}(q-1)/C).$$
Then $C = o(N^{1/2})$ *implies* $M = o(N^{1/2}\log N)$.

■

Compare with Theorems 3-5: in the sequential setting, the asymptotic order of growth of M must be *strictly* lower than in the batch setting. Nonetheless, it is possible to come arbitrarily close using the following class of embedding strategies.

Theorem 7 (Zeta embedding): *Suppose (A0'), either (A2a) or (A2b), (A3a), and either (A4a) or (A4b). Let* $c_i = ki^{-v}$ *for constants* $k > 0$ *and v.*

(1) If $v \leq 1/2$ *then* $\sum_{i=1}^{\infty} \phi_i(c_i)$

diverges whenever $k > 0$, *so no distortion bound of the form (A0') can be met.*
(2) If $1/2 < v < 1$ *then there exists a* $k > 0$ *such that*

$$\sum_{i=1}^{\infty} \phi_i(c_i) \leq D.$$

Then with no adaptive source coding (A4a), $M = \Theta(N^{1-v})$, *and with adaptive source coding satisfying (A4b),* $M = \Theta(N^{1-v}\log N)$.
(3) If $v = 1$ *then there exists a* $k > 0$ *such that*

$$\sum_{i=1}^{\infty} \phi_i(c_i) \leq D.$$

Then with no adaptive source coding (A4a), $M = \Theta(\log N)$, *and with adaptive source coding satisfying (A4b),* $M = \Theta((\log N)^2)$.
(4) If $v > 1$ *then*

$$\sum_{1}^{\infty} m_i$$

converges, whether or not adaptive source coding is used, so only a finite amount of information is ever transferred and no secret "channel" has been established.

Proof: *We use the following elementary facts about infinite series (e.g., Ferrar, 1938):*

$$\sum_{i=1}^{\infty} i^{-p}$$

converges if and only if $p > 1$; in the case of divergence the partial sums

$$s_n = \sum_{i=1}^{\infty} i^{-p}$$

satisfy $s_n \sim n^{1-p}/(1-p)$ for $p < 1$ and $s_n \sim \log N$ for $p = 1$. Similarly,

$$\sum_{i=1}^{\infty} i^{-p} \log i$$

converges if and only if $p > 1$; this time the partial sums satisfy $s_n \sim n^{1-p} \log n/(1-p)$ for $p < 1$ and $s_n \sim 1/2(\log n)^2$ for $p = 1$. Also note that when sequences a_n and b_n satisfy $a_n \sim b_n$ then

$$\sum_{i=1}^{\infty} a_i$$

is convergent if and only if

$$\sum_{i=1}^{\infty} b_i$$

is, and when they are divergent the partial sums satisfy

$$\sum_{i=1}^{n} a_i \, \square \, \sum_{i=1}^{n} b_i.$$

(1) If $v \leq 0$ then $\phi_i(c_i) \nrightarrow 0$, so $\sum \phi_i(c_i)$ certainly diverges. If $0 < v < 1/2$ then $\phi_i(c_i) \sim 2Qc_i^2 \geq \underline{Q}k^2 i^{-2v}$; by the comparison test $\phi_i(c_i)$ diverges.

(2) Since $c_i \to 0$, for sufficiently large i we have $\phi_i(c_i) \leq 2Q_i c_i^2 \leq 2\overline{Q}c_i^2 = 2\overline{Q}k^2 i^{-2v}$. By the comparison test, and because $2v > 1$, $\sum \phi_i(c_i) = k^2 S < \infty$. For $k = D^{1/2}S^{-1/2}$, (A0') is met. Under (A4a),

$$M = E\sum_{i=1}^{N} ki^{-v} = \Theta(N^{1-v}),$$

and under (A4b),

$$M = E\sum_{i=1}^{N} \chi_i(c_i),$$

which has the same asymptotic order as

$$\sum_{i=1}^{N} i^{-v} \log i = \Theta(N^{1-v} \log N).$$

(3) As above, $\phi_i(c_i) \leq 2\overline{Q}k^2 \sum i^{-2}$; the sum is convergent so there exists sufficiently small k to meet (A0'). But in this case, under (A4a)

$$M = E\sum_{i=1}^{N} ki^{-1} = \Theta(\log N),$$

and under (A4b)

$$M = E\sum_{i=1}^{N} \chi_i(c_i),$$

which has the same asymptotic order as

$$\sum_{i=1}^{N} i^{-1} \log i = \Theta((\log N)^2).$$

(4) $M = \sum_{i=1}^{\infty} m_i = E\sum_{i=1}^{\infty} c_i$ or $\sum_{i=1}^{\infty} \chi_i(c_i)$,

according to whether (A4a) or (A4b) is assumed; therefore M has the same asymptotic order as either

$$\sum_{i=1}^{\infty} i^{-v} \text{ or } \sum_{i=1}^{\infty} i^{-v} \log i,$$

both of which are convergent for $v > 1$. Therefore even an infinite number of covers conveys only a finite payload. ∎

Harmonic embedding, which we saw earlier, corresponds to $v = 1$ and is the worst of the infinite zeta embedding strategies because it does not even achieve polynomial capacity in N: indeed, it is one of the most basic results of the theory of infinite series that $\sum i^{-1}$ only *just* diverges. By taking v arbitrarily close to $1/2$, we may allow M to grow with rate arbitrarily close to the limits in Theorem 6.

However, there is a penalty for embedding at a rate close to the bound. For simplicity, make the strong assumptions (A2a) and (A4a) and further assume that all Q_i are equal to the constant Q. Then case (2), above, can be refined to:

Theorem 8: *Suppose (A0'), (A2a), $Q_i = Q$ and (A4a). Let $c_i = i^{-v} D^{1/2} Q^{-1/2} \zeta(2v)^{-1/2}$ for $1/2 < v < 1$, where ζ is the Riemann zeta function (Abramowitz & Stegun, 1964, Ch.23). Then (A0') is tight and $M \sim E D^{1/2} Q^{-1/2} N^{1-v} (1-v)^{-1} \zeta(2v)^{-1/2}$.*

Proof: *Same as for Theorem 7, but keep track of multiplicative constants. Note that*

$$\zeta(s) = \sum_{i=1}^{\infty} i^{-s}, \text{ for } \mathfrak{Re}(s) > 1,$$

is the definition of the zeta function.

∎

By picking $v = 1/2 + \varepsilon$ we allow M to grow asymptotically as

$$K \left(\frac{1}{2} - \varepsilon \right)^{-1} \zeta (1 + 2\varepsilon)^{-1/2} N^{1/2 - \varepsilon}$$

for a constant K not depending on ε. We have a dilemma: the larger the polynomial degree, the smaller the constant multiplier (because $\zeta(1 + x) \sim x^{-1}$, as $x \to 0^+$, the multiplicative constant approximates $K(8\varepsilon)^{1/2}$). Thus the tension which we saw at the beginning of this section, between transmitting more payload in any finite amount of time and maintaining the largest asymptotic capacity, exists for these infinite strategies too.

Discussion

Three other papers deal with the batch steganography problem (Ker, 2006, 2007b, 2007a) and draw conclusions, of different strength, about steganographic capacity. They all agree that, in the absence of adaptive source coding, the capacity of a batch of N objects is of order $\sqrt{N}$; Theorems 3 and 4 concur with this conclusion. Note that

this article's results are distinct from the other three: Ker (2006) applies to particular steganalysis methods, Ker (2007b) assumes a linear relationship between payload and steganalysis output (but goes further in providing an asymptotically optimal detection strategy), and Ker (2007a) is only for a particular type of evidence pooling behaviour by the steganalyst. We have gone much further, allowing source coding, nonuniform covers, and covering the analytical details so that the growth of the detector's evidence need only be locally square in a suitable sense. It is notable that steganographic capacity, with or without adaptive source coding, remains sublinear. Indeed, source coding only grants an extra logarithmic factor.

Although the batch problem is convincing from the steganalyst's point of view—at the time of steganalysis, they have a certain number of objects whose evidence they wish to pool—it is perhaps less so for the steganographer. The latter is unlikely to know when the steganalyst will seize or monitor their communications, so must proceed under the assumption that communications might be examined at any time. Then the sequential steganography problem applies, and we have shown here that sequential steganographic capacity has some similarities to, but is not the same as, batch capacity. In particular, capacity is asymptotically strictly lower in the sequential setting and there is no optimal strategy. However, the zeta embedding class of strategies can provide rates of capacity growth arbitrarily close to the bound, albeit with ever less favourable multiplicative constants.

We should consider carefully the assumptions on which these results rest. Some are unquestionable, for example (A3a). Assumptions such as (A0) and (A1) are essential if we want to measure steganographic security using KL divergence, and there seems to be little alternative. Note that the use of KL divergence assumes that the steganalyst knows exactly the distribution of the source objects, or at least the response of a steganalysis method to them. More seriously, it is also implicit that the steganalyst knows the potential allocation of payload amongst the cover objects. This is probably not truly realistic, but some initial work (Ker, 2008a) shows that complexity of the problem is greatly increased when we grant the steganalyst less information. And it is much more difficult to reason about detection performance when the detector does not know the exact distributions they are observing, for example if there are unknown parameters. Perhaps future research will shed light on these difficult questions.

The exactly- or locally-square distortion assumptions (A2a) and (A2b) are the cornerstone of this work; some experiments reported in Ker (2007d) seem to confirm that KL divergence is locally square in the number of embedding changes for some real steganalysis methods, but this is not a guarantee that the same applies universally. It would certainly be of significance if a steganalysis method could be found which produces KL divergence growing at a rate *faster* than the square of the number of embedding changes. The assumption about source coding is also not strictly proven: although we know that the upper and lower bounds to capacity (as a function of maximum permitted changes) are concave, there is no guarantee that the function itself is concave. But, in practice, there are codes whose performance approaches the upper bound (Fridrich & Filler, 2007) for which any deviation from concavity will be very small.

There are two further assumptions, implicit here, which could be questioned. We measured embedding changes by the *maximum* number possible (over all payloads): this may seem overly pessimistic, since in practice a cover location need not be altered if it coincidentally already contained the correct symbol. However it is reasonable to adopt a pessimistic attitude when measuring the steganographer's risk. Furthermore, it would not materially affect our conclusions if we were to switch focus to the average number of embedding changes. We also assumed, throughout, that embedding changes and payload sizes can take non-integral values: of course, this is simply untrue and it means that our sequential strategies, in which the payload placed in each object is ever-diminishing, cannot be implemented exactly. In the limit as $N \to \infty$, a fixed total distortion in fact implies that the total number of embedding changes must be *finite*! However it seems that, in practice, such limits are not reached: some numerical computations in earlier work (Ker, 2008b) showed that, for realistic Q-factors and cover sizes, forcing integral embedding changes makes a barely detectable difference to steganographic capacity.

Another implicit assumption is that all embedding changes are equally detectable. This is probably not the case in practice, but experience has shown that adaptive embedding methods can defeat their own aims by making the embedding locations more predictable.

Some analysis of the abstract sequential steganography problem still remains, as we did not optimize the zeta embedding strategies to account for nonuniformity in the covers. Because sequential steganography deals with rates of capacity growth, it is not obvious how an optimization problem can even be constructed. This is a subject for future work.

ACKNOWLEDGMENT

The author is a Royal Society University Research Fellow. Theorem 6 was proved with the kind assistance of Michael Collins and Roger Heath-Brown.

REFERENCES

Abramowitz, M., & Stegun, I. (1964). *Handbook of mathematical functions with formulas, graphs, and mathematical tables* (ninth Dover printing ed.). New York: Dover.

Bierbrauer, J. (1998). *On Crandall's problem.* (Unpublished communication available from http://www.ws.binghamton.edu/fridrich/covcodes.pdf)

Bierbrauer, J., & Fridrich, J. (2008). *Constructing good covering codes for applications in steganography.* Berlin: Springer. (To appear in LNCS Transactions on Data Hiding and Multimedia Security)

Böhme, R. (2005). Assessment of steganalytic methods using multiple regression models. In M. Barni, J. Herrera-Joancomartí, S. Katzenbeisser, & F. Pérez-González (Eds.), *Information Hiding, 7th International Workshop* (pp. 278–295). Berlin: Springer.

Böhme, R., & Ker, A. (2006). A two-factor error model for quantitative steganalysis. In E. J. Delp III & P. W. Wong (Eds.), *Security, steganography and watermarking of multimedia contents VIII* (Vol. SPIE 6072, pp. 59–74). Bellingham, WA: SPIE.

Boyd, S., & Vandenberghe, L. (2004). *Convex optimization.* Cambridge: Cambridge University Press.

Cachin, C. (2004). An information-theoretic model for steganography. *Information and Computation, 192* (1), 41–56.

Cohen, G. (1983). A nonconstructive upper bound on covering radius. *IEEE Transactions on Information Theory, 29* (3), 352–353.

Ferrar, W. L. (1938). *A text-book of convergence.* Oxford: Clarendon Press.

Fridrich, J., & Filler, T. (2007). Practical methods for minimizing embedding impact in steganography. In E. J. Delp III & P. W. Wong (Eds.), *Security, steganography and watermarking of multimedia contents IX* (Vol. SPIE 6505, pp. 0201–0215). Bellingham, WA: SPIE.

Fridrich, J., Lisonek, P., & Soukal, D. (2006). On steganographic embedding efficiency. In J. Camenisch, C. Collberg, N. Johnson, & P. Sallee (Eds.), *Information Hiding, 8th International Workshop* (pp. 282–296). Berlin: Springer.

Fridrich, J., & Soukal, D. (2006). Matrix embedding for large payloads. *IEEE Transactions on Information Forensics and Security, 1* (3), 390–394.

Ker, A. (2006). Batch steganography and pooled steganalysis. In J. Camenisch, C. Collberg, N. Johnson, & P. Sallee (Eds.), *Information Hiding, 8th International Workshop* (pp. 265–281). Berlin: Springer.

Ker, A. (2007a). Batch steganography and the threshold game. In E. J. Delp III & P. W. Wong (Eds.), *Security, steganography and watermarking of multimedia contents IX* (Vol. SPIE 6505, pp. 0401–0413). Bellingham, WA: SPIE.

Ker, A. (2007b). A capacity result for batch steganography. *IEEE Signal Processing Letters, 14* (8), 525–528.

Ker, A. (2007c). Derivation of error distribution in least-squares steganalysis. *IEEE Transactions on Information Forensics and Security, 2* (2), 140–148.

Ker, A. (2007d). The ultimate steganalysis benchmark? *In 9th ACM Workshop on Multimedia and Security* (pp. 141–148). New York: ACM Press.

Ker, A. (2008a). *Perturbation hiding and the batch steganography problem.* Berlin: Springer. (To appear in *Information Hiding, 10th International Workshop*)

Ker, A. (2008b). Steganographic strategies for a square distortion function. In E. J. Delp III & P. W. Wong, J. Dittmann, and N. D. Mermon (Eds.), *Security, forensics, steganography and watermarking of multimedia contents X* (Vol. SPIE 6819, pp. 0301–0313). Bellingham, WA: SPIE.

Ker, A., Pevný, T., Kodovský, J., & Fridrich, J. (2008). The square root law of steganographic capacity. In *Proceedings of the 10th ACM Workshop on Multimedia & Security*, ACM Press.

Kullback, S. (1968). *Information theory and statistics*. New York: Dover.

Chapter 11
Efficient Forensic Analysis for Anonymous Attack in Secure Content Distribution

Hongxia Jin
IBM Almaden Research Center, USA

ABSTRACT

This article discusses a forensic technology that is used to defend against piracy for secure multimedia content distribution. In particular we are interested in anonymous rebroadcasting type of attack where the attackers redistribute the per-content encrypting key or decrypted plain content. Traitor tracing technology can be used to defend against this attack by identifying the original users (called traitors) involved in the rebroadcasting piracy. While traitor tracing has been a long standing cryptographic problem that has attracted extensive research, existing academia researches have overlooked many practical concerns in a real world setting. We have overcome many practical concerns in order to bring a theoretical traitor tracing solution to practice. The main focus of this article is on designing efficient forensic analysis algorithms under various practical considerations that were missing from existing work. The efficiency of our forensic analysis algorithms is the enabling factor that ultimately made the first time large scale commercialization of a traitor tracing technology in the context of new industry standard on content protection for next generation high-definition DVDs.

INTRODUCTION

The advent of digital technologies has made the creation and manipulation of multimedia content simpler. It offers higher quality and a lot more convenience to consumers. For example, it allows one to make perfect copies. However this also enables easier piracy.

DOI: 10.4018/978-1-60960-515-5.ch011

Unauthorized music and movie copying are hurting the profit of the record industry and the movie studios. It is highly desirable to develop techniques to protect the copyrighted material.

In this article we are particularly interested in business scenarios that involve one-way distributions, including pay-TV systems (Cable companies) or movie rental companies like Netflix, and massively distributing prerecorded and recordable media. Previous content protection system CSS (Content Scrambling System) protected DVDs with content encryption. The encryption key is shared among all DVD players in the same manufacturer. However, content encryption cannot solve the content protection problem completely. Soon after CSS was introduced it was broken. The nightmare was that the system cannot be renewed in the sense that the compromised players cannot be revoked (excluded) from the system without hurting other innocent players. Lesson learned, new content protection systems are now based on broadcast encryption technologies (first introduced by Fiat & Naor, 1993) that enable a broadcaster to encrypt the content so that only a privileged subset of users (devices, set up boxes) can decrypt the content and exclude another subset of users. In this system, each decoder box is assigned a unique set of decryption keys (called device keys). A broadcast encryption scheme is defined to assign keys to devices and encrypt the content that can guarantee that only compliant devices can decrypt the content, without requiring authentication of the device.

Broadcast encryption is currently being used for content protection of recordable and prerecorded media (CPRM/CPPM) and is implemented in consumer electronics devices ranging from highly portable audio players that use Secure Digital Cards to top of the line DVD-Audio players supporting multiple channels, higher sampling rates and improved frequency response. The media, such as CD, DVD or a flash memory card, typically contains in its header the encryption of the key K (called media key) which is indirectly used to encrypt the content following the header. The media key is encrypted again and again using all the chosen device keys and forms a Media Key Block (MKB) which is sent alongside the content when the content is distributed. The device keys used to encrypt the media key are chosen in a way as to cover all compliant devices. It allows all compliant devices, each using their set of device keys, to calculate the same key K. But the non-compliant devices cannot calculate the correct key using their compromised keys. Thus the Media Key Block (MKB) enables system renewability. If a device is found to be non-compliant, a set of his device keys is compromised, an updated MKB can be released that causes a device with the compromised set of device keys to be unable to calculate the correct key K. This effectively excludes the compromised device from accessing the future content. The compromised device keys are "revoked" by the updated MKB.

There are various pirate attacks that can happen in the above broadcast encryption system.

In this article we are interested in anonymous rebroadcasting attack. Some legitimate users have instrumented their devices, and resell the movies by redistributing the decrypted movie itself or the per-movie decryption keys. For example, the attackers can setup a server that sells the media keys on demand. The attackers may also re-digitize the analogue output from a compliant device and redistribute the content in plain form. To defend against these types of anonymous attack, it seems one must distribute different versions of the content/key to different users. The content needs to be differently watermarked as well as differently encrypted.

Digital content watermarking/fingerprinting (Trappe, Wu, Wang & Liu, 2003) is a related field. Watermarks and fingerprints are unique labels/marks embedded in different copies of the same content. When an illegal copy of the multimedia content is found, the embedded watermark and/or fingerprint can be used for identification of the illegal users who distributed that copy.

Traitor tracing, an active forensic research area in cryptography, is a related but different field than digital content fingerprinting. It refers to a class of key management schemes that can be used to trace pirated cryptographic keys or pirated content. Notice that watermarking/fingerprinting technologies usually do not apply to cryptographic keys.

Furthermore, even if one needs to perform forensic analysis based on redistributed plain content, watermark/fingerprinting alone does not solve the problem by themselves. To meet our forensic analysis needs, the watermark has to identify the end user or allow us to derive the set of device keys used in the end user's device. However, it is difficult to find a suitable point in the distribution chain where the receiving device is known but the watermark insertion can still occur in a secure fashion. Where and when should one insert the watermark?

Clearly, it is desirable to perform the watermark insertion as close to the content originator as possible. This allows for the watermark to be applied in the content creator's trusted environment, before the content goes through the compression process and is encrypted for copy protection purposes. However, most forms of content distribution prohibit watermark insertion this early in the content publishing process because only one version of the content is created for a large population of users. This is certainly true for distribution schemes that are based on physical media where mass production is required to achieve economies of scale. It also applies to broadcast and multicast channels where the distribution medium by definition is a shared or partially shared communication channel. Thus, it is in many cases impossible to insert an end user identifying watermark during the content creation process.

The obvious alternative is to perform the watermark insertion at the receiving end user's device since at that point her identity or device keys are unambiguously known. However, this raises security concern. If the player is reverse engineered, the attacker might be able to suppress the watermark insertion step completely and obtain a copy of the un-watermarked content, thereby defeating the scheme.

Traitor tracing schemes, an area of active research in cryptography, allow us to apply the watermark early on in the content publishing process and can still provide traceability down to the individual content recipient. Traitor tracing is a technology that builds on top of content watermarks. We will discuss the general cryptographic traitor tracing scheme for anonymous attack in Section 2 and show practical requirements on forensic analysis algorithms for traitor tracing. Then in subsequent Sections, we will present efficient forensic analysis algorithms to meet those practical requirements.

TRAITOR TRACING FOR ANONYMOUS ATTACK

In the traitor tracing model for anonymous attack, one assumes that each piece of content (for example, a movie) is divided into multiple segments, among which n segments are chosen to have different variations. Each of these n segments has q possible variations. How to build variations are format specific. For example, there can be different ways to create the variations with HD-DVD and Blue-Ray discs. It is possible to use watermarks, different camera-angles, or different play-lists. It is outside of the scope to discuss the approaches to create variations. Traitor tracing is a cryptographic technology that builds on top of the watermarking or other variation-creating approaches.

Each device is assigned a unique set of tracing keys which enables it to decrypt exactly one variation at each point of the content during playback time. If the plain content or the actual variation encrypting keys get pirated and redistributed, a traitor tracing scheme can identify the original users who participate in the construction of the pirated copy of the content or content encrypting keys. The design of a traitor tracing scheme for anonymous attack is about how to assign the secret tracing keys to devices and assign content versions to innocent devices to enable tracing and how to efficiently detect traitors involved in colluding pirate attacks.

Pirate Model

There are two well-known models for how a pirated copy (be it the content or the key) can be generated:

- Given two variants v_1 and v_2 of the content/key, the pirate can only use v_1 or v_2, not any other valid variant v_i.
- Given two variants v_1 and v_2 of the content/key ($v_1 \neq v_2$), the pirate can generate any valid variant v_i out of v_1 and v_2.

In digital fingerprinting, there are similar pirate models. The first model is also called narrow-case fingerprinting problem. The second model is also called general or wide-case fingerprinting problem. As pointed out in (Boneh & Shaw, 1998), both models can be expanded by allowing generating something that is unreadable, or erased.

Schemes presented in (Chor, Fiat & Naor, 1994; Chor, Fiat, Naor & Pinkas, 2000; Hollmann, Lint, Linnartz & Tolhuizen, 1998; Cohnen, Encheva, Litsyn and Schaathun, 2003) all used the first model. In (Hollmann, Lint, Linnartz & Tolhuizen, 1998), it was also proved that for 2 colluders and $q \leq 3$, there exist codes that can provide exact identification of at least one traitor with exponentially many codewords. In binary case, exact identification of even one traitor is generally impossible. So most of the works in this area (Barg, Blakely & Kabatiansky, 2003; Tardos 2003; Yacobi 2001) allow some small error rate, in other words, they are probabilistic fingerprint codes.

In traitor tracing for anonymous attack, as one can imagine, when given two randomly chosen cryptographic keys, it is nearly impossible to come up with another valid cryptographic key. Furthermore, as mentioned earlier, creating variation is format specific. Different approaches, with or without watermarking, can be used to create variations. Traitor tracing technology works on top of pirate models accepted by its applications. In our case, we accept the first model.

Practical Concerns in a Forensic Analysis Algorithm for Traitor Tracing

We have designed a practical traitor tracing scheme for anonymous attack that has been adopted in the AACS content protection standard for next generation high definition DVDs. We have solved many theoretical and practical problems along the way to bring a long standing theoretical research topic to commercial use for Hollywood.

(Jin & Lotspiech, 2006) overviewed many of those concerns that are not apparent in literatures. Basically a traitor tracing scheme consists of the following steps.

- **Assignment step:** Assign versions of the content/key to currently innocent devices
- **Forensic Analysis step:** Based on the recovered forensic evidences (i.e., pirated content/keys), trace back to the traitors.
- **Revocation step:** loop to step 1 but exclude the currently discovered traitors.

Our focus in this article is on the forensic analysis algorithm. There are some practical requirements on the algorithm in order to make it feasible to use in real world. Below we are going to discuss those practical requirements and illustrate what have been missing in existing approaches to have a practical and feasible forensic analysis algorithm.

First of all, there is a lot literatures using traceability code as a forensic analysis approach.

For example, (Chor, Fiat & Naor, 1994; Chor, Fiat, Naor & Pinkas, 2000; Safavi-Naini & Yang,

2000; Trung & Martirosyan, 2004; Staddon, Stinson and Wei, 2001). It is very important to notice that much of this work has taken the approach of fixing the number of colluders and the number of recovered movies and trying to find codes to support an optimal number of devices/ users for a given number of variations of each movie. For example, the code shown in (Trung & Martirosyan, 2004) either has too few codewords (accommodates a small number of devices) or the number of variations is too large (requires too much space on the disc). In reality, a forensic analysis algorithm must be based on the assignment. The assignment comes before the forensic analysis step. If there are restrictions on the assignment step, those restrictions must be met first. The order of the considerations is very important.

Secondly, in literature, this forensic analysis step always uses a straight forward highest-score approach, where each player is scored based on the number of matchings between the recovered pirate content keys/content and the versions assigned to the player, hoping the highest scored player is the guilty traitor. Furthermore, in literatures a traitor tracing scheme has been defined as a way to detect at least a traitor in the system. Therefore the goal of the forensic analysis step, as well as the design of a traitor tracing scheme, is to identify a traitor. It is assumed that the identified traitor can be disconnected from the system and the tracing continues after that. But of course the ultimate security goal is to detect all traitors in the coalition. We measure the efficiency of the forensic analysis algorithm by the number of recovered movies in order to detect traitors in a coalition. We believe using the one-by-one detection algorithm for anonymous attack is inefficient. No existing forensic analysis algorithm is efficient enough for practical use. Indeed, the efficiency of the detection of all traitors in the coalition was a bottleneck when bringing a traitor tracing scheme into practice. We are highly motivated to design a more efficient forensic analysis algorithm.

Third, we also believe existing schemes have made an unrealistic assumption. They assume a maximum number on the coalition size and hope to deterministically find a traitor when the coalition size is smaller than that maximum number. For example, a t-traceability code enables one to decode to the nearest neighbor of a pirate code when the coalition size is at most t traitors and the nearest neighbor is deterministically a traitor.

Lemma 1. (Chor, Fiat, Naor & Pinkas, 2000; Staddon, Stinson & Wei 2001).

Assume that a code C with length n and distance d is used to assign the symbols for variations to each user and that there are t traitors. If code C satisfies

$$d > (1 - 1/t^2)\, n \qquad (1)$$

then C is an t-traceability-code.

Unfortunately in reality the coalition size is usually unknown. As pointed out in (Jin, Lotspiech & Nusser, 2004), the tracing will have to be probabilistic. In fact, the real world question is how to accurately detect traitors without knowing the coalition size and with what probabilities.

The fourth requirement is also related to the fact that existing work defines a traitor tracing scheme to detect one traitor and assume tracing can simply continue/repeat after the detected traitor is disconnected from the system. It turns out this assumption is wrong. As a matter of fact we believe the fourth requirement for a practical forensic analysis algorithm is to make sure it can continue to efficiently detect remaining traitors after the detected traitors are excluded/revoked from the system. One cannot simply assume the system can do this. Indeed it takes quite some work and efforts to achieve this.

As the above first requirement pointed out, a forensic analysis algorithm must be based on the assignment step. We will devote our next section to briefly discuss the assignment.

In fact real world may put practical restrictions on the assignment; those restrictions must be met first. The assignment step turns out to be non-trivial.

KEY/CONTENT ASSIGNMENT

As discussed in last Section, we will choose n segments from the content and augment the content by creating q variations for each segment. However, the variations take extra space on the disc. A practical traitor tracing scheme on a prerecorded optical movie disc should take no more than 10% of the space on the disc to store the variations. For a normal 2-hour movie, it corresponds to 8 additional minutes (480 seconds) of video. This puts practical restriction on the number of variations one can put into a movie. The market for such discs is huge, involving literally a billion playing devices or more. This means a tracing scheme needs to be able to accommodate large number of devices. It turns out these requirements are inherently conflicting.

(Jin, Lotspiech & Nusser, 2004) showed an assignment to meet the requirements on the overhead and number of users. Assume that each segment has q variations and that there are n segments. Systematic assignment based on error correcting codes like Reed-Solomon code is used. More importantly concatenate codes are used. For each movie, there is an "inner code" used to assign the different variations at the chosen points of the movie; it effectively creates different movie versions. For example, one can use a Reed-Solomon code for the inner code. Suppose there are 16 variations created at each of the 15 points in the movie. Even though it can theoretically create 16^{15} number of versions, a Reed-Solomon code will create only $16^2 = 256$ codewords (thus movie versions) but any two versions will differ at at least 14 points. Once the "inner code" creates the multiple movie versions (e.g., 256), over a sequence of movies, there is an "outer code" used to assign movie versions to different players. For example, each player is assigned one of the 256 versions for each movie in a sequence of 255 movies. A Reed-Solomon code can create 256^4 codewords (thus players) with any two players differ at at least 252 movies. By concatenating the two levels of codes, the scheme managed to avoid having a big number of variations at any chosen point but can still accommodate the billions of devices. Suppose each segment is a 2-second clip, the extra video needed in this example is 450 seconds, within the 10% practical constraint. In fact, there is not a single level MDS code that can satisfy all the practical requirements. The two-level concatenated code is essential to meet the practical requirements.

Each player needs to know all the variation encrypting keys in order to play back content. To save some space for the keys burned into the player at manufacturer time, instead of storing all the variation encrypting keys in a device, it is possible to introduce a level of indirection. The "outer code" can be used to assign the tracing key to burn into each player. For example, each player is assigned 255 keys, corresponding to 255 movies in a sequence. Each key comes with 256 versions corresponding to the 256 movie versions created from the inner code. During playback time, the player will use its tracing key for a movie to obtain the actual variation encrypting key for each segment. Readers are referred to (Jin, Lotspiech & Nusser, 2004) for more details.

Given this assignment, using the pirate model mentioned in Section 2.1, the attackers can use whatever strategy to construct the pirate copy of the content/key based on the available versions to them. The strategy can be done at the outer code level (movie-by-movie attack) where the attackers simply redistribute the tracing keys assigned to the players or redistribute an entire pirated movie version available to them. This compares to another strategy where the attackers have to use special tools to extract segments within a movie version, mix-match the extracted segments from different movie versions and put them back together to build a pirated movie version. We believe the attack on the outer level is much more likely to happen in reality because redistributing keys is much easier than redistributing the content which takes a lot of bandwidth. Even if the attackers want to redistribute the content, it is also simpler to redistribute one of the movie versions available to them rather than doing the engineering work to mix-match segments from different versions together.

In rest of the article, we will focus on designing efficient forensic analysis algorithms for traitor tracing. In Section 4 we will first discuss forensic analysis algorithms for the more likely attack which is on the outer code level, or more general, on one level of code. In Section 5 we will complete the one level forensic analysis algorithm discussion by considering continued forensic analysis for remaining traitors after revoking the known traitors. In Section 6 we will discuss the less likely attack which is on the inner code level and then propagate to the outer code level, i.e., on nested code.

EFFICIENT FORENSIC ANALYSIS ALGORITHM ON ONE LEVEL CODE

To meet the second and third requirements for a practical forensic analysis algorithm, we have developed the first traitor/coalition detection algorithm that tried to detect multiple traitors in the coalition all together but without assuming coalition size. Indeed our algorithm deduces the coalition size during tracing. The basic results were appeared in (Jin, Lotspiech & Meggido, 2008).

The idea of the new tracing algorithm can be illustrated by a small example. Suppose there are 4 people involved in a colluding attack, and we have a random sequence of 20 recovered movies. Each movie originally has 256 variations of which

a given player only plays 1. If the four attackers are using round robin strategy, each guilty player will evenly share 5 movies with the recovered sequence. However, notice that there will be about 15 completely innocent players also scoring 5 or greater due to chance alone. So you cannot incriminate any player that scores 5. You have to recover more movies. In contrast, notice that the above 4 guilty players together can explain all the movies in the sequence. What is the chance that a coalition of size 4 can do that? The answer is only about 0.04.

Our observation is, there is a much higher probability that a single player can explain 5 movies, but there is a much lower probability that 4 players together can explain all 20 movies. So if the low probability event happens and we find 4 players that do cover the recovered sequence, it is unlikely it is due to chance alone; it is more likely that some of those players are indeed in the pirate coalition.

The attackers could choose to use some player heavily and other players very lightly.

For this scapegoat strategy, the traditional approach can correctly identify him, but it is hard to find the lightly used player and the true coalition size. Our new tracing algorithm can nonetheless find the other members in the coalitions and find out the coalition size.

Based on the above observations, our forensic analysis algorithm consists of the following steps.

1. Find a coalition of players that can explain all the recovered movies
2. Calculate the innocent/guilty probability of such a coalition,
    -   If that probability is within a desirable range, the identified coalition is a suspect coalition
3. Filter out the innocent players from the suspect coalition and identify the actual guilty players

Step 1: Find a Coalition that can Explain all Recovered Forensic Evidence

The problem of finding a coalition of players that can explain the recovered sequence of movies is equivalent to the well-known Set Cover problem. Because the size of the coalition is not known in advance, our simple tracing algorithm can do the following:

- Set $T = 1$
- Call *FIND_COVER(T)*
- If *FIND_COVER(T)* returns true, exit
- Otherwise set $T = T + 1$ and loop to step 2

The *FIND_COVER(T)* procedure will return true if and only if there is at least one coalition of size T that can explain all the m observed symbols. As one can understand, when this tracing algorithm ends, it will have found the minimum size of the coalition T as well as the actual players involved in the found coalition. Any heuristic set cover algorithm in traditional computer science can be used as the *FIND_COVER(T)* procedure.

A sample algorithm was shown in (Jin, Lotspiech & Megiddo, 2008).

Step 2: Calculate Innocent Probability of the Found Coalition and/or False Positive Rate

Once the algorithm found a coalition that can cover all the recovered movies, we have to calculate its guilty probability. We want to calculate the probability of the existence of such a coalition.

If there are N players, and a sequence of m movies are selected, each movie having one random variation out of q, the expected number of coalitions of size T can be calculated:

$$\binom{N}{T} * (1-(1-1/q)^T)^m$$

If the expected number of coalitions is less than 1, this formula also gives an upper bound on the probability that a random sequence of m movie variations is covered by a coalition of size T. If T is noticeably less than q, a simplified formula is a close upper bound:

$$\binom{N}{T} * (T/q)^m \qquad (2)$$

Interestingly, we find Equation 2 not only reflects the probability of the existence of such a coalition of size T, it is also the probability that a larger completely different coalition could have incriminated this coalition of size T when this coalition is actually completely innocent. To understand why, one can look from the attacker's side. The attackers wish to see we incriminate innocent players. However, they do not know what sequence would incriminate an innocent player, so they are just guessing. Theoretically speaking, we can make the probability they guess correctly arbitrarily small by just collecting more movies. The following lemma shows the false positive rate in our detection algorithm.

Lemma 2: (Jin, Lotspiech & Megiddo, 2008) *Assume that a coalition of guilty players cannot deduce the assignment of any other player in the world, for a coalition C, $|C| = T$, found by algorithm FIND_COVER, the probability that every member in coalition C is innocent is bounded by Equation 2.*

In other words, the formula gives the false positive probability in the detection.

Proof: *Imagine that the process of assignment is the opposite of the way it works in real life: instead of starting with the assignment of variations to the population, the coalition randomly picks their assignment and then picks the particular variations of m movies in any way they choose. Only then does the licensing agency, not knowing what the coalition has picked, assign the variations for the* *remaining innocent players randomly. The chance that this assignment would result in a coalition of size T amongst the innocent players is clearly bounded by Equation 2. And since there is no way to distinguish the ``real life" case from the ``thought experiment" case based on the player assignment (they are both equally random), the equation does represent the best that the attackers can do.*

End proof.

Based on Lemma 2, Equation 2 gives us the false positive rate, or the confidence level of our detection. If this false positive rate is within the license agency's acceptable range, we can conclude the found coalition from procedure *FIND_COVER* is a guilty coalition, otherwise more movies need to be recovered. Of course the smaller the false positive rate, the more pirate movies it needs to recover.

Step 3: Filtering Algorithm: Identify Guilty Individuals in the Found Suspect Coalition

Once we have found a suspect coalition using a Set-cover algorithm, we need to have a filtering algorithm to filter out some of the players in the purported coalition of size T that might be actually innocent and just being victimized by a scapegoat strategy that is hiding a few lightly used guilty players. There may be various ways to determine the guilty probability for each player. Here we use a minimum strategy.

We first calculate different conditional innocent probability when assuming other players are guilty. For example, we choose any each combination of c players and temporarily assume they are guilty. We calculate the probability that the remaining players are completely innocent. To do that, we temporarily remove the movies that can be explained by this combination of players from the original list of all recovered movies; we also temporarily reduce coalition size T by c. With

the new number of movies m and T, we can use formula 2 above to evaluate the probability that the remaining players are completely innocent. Knowing the conditional innocent/guilty probability, we use the minimum guilty probability of the each player under all combinations as the probability of guilt of the player.

As one can imagine, a player might be more innocent under some combinations or seem guilty under all circumstances. Only those players in the suspect coalition that have high minimum guilty probability are considered actually guilty. Other players can be filtered out as innocent from the suspect coalition.

Discussion: Tracing Efficiency and Computational Efficiency

In our application, computational time is not an issue. As one can imagine, the license agency cannot predict how often the attackers release pirated keys/content. Compare to time spent there, the running time of the *FIND_COVER* procedure or the tracing algorithm is not critical. However it is also worthy mention that even though *FIND_COVER* is theoretically NP hard, we find the calculation time is actual very reasonable for parameters from real application like AACS.

Of course, as illustrated in (Jin, Lotspiech & Megiddo, 2008), some optimizations might be done to reduce the computational time.

While computational efficiency is not critical in our application, it is very important to achieve superior efficiency of the tracing which is measured by the number of movies m needed to detect a coalition of size T to reach a given level of confidence (or false positive rate) λ. We can derive the efficiency by solving the following equation.

$$\binom{N}{T} * (T/q)^{m-\lambda}$$

Because N is much larger than T,

Figure 1. Traceability graph for q=1024 with difference false positive rate

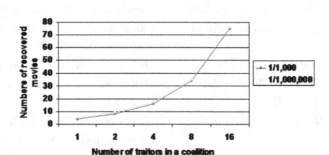

$$\binom{N}{T} *$$

can also be approximated to be N^T. Solving the above equation gives us:

$$m = \frac{T * \ln N - \ln \lambda}{\ln q - \ln T} \qquad (3)$$

From Equation 3, we know for a given false positive rate, the traceability (the number of pirated content/keys needed) depends on three parameters, the coalition size T, the number of variations used q and the number of relevant users N in the system. Again q and N are parameters determined in the assignment step.

For example, for the parameters of our choice for AACS, it is easy enough to use a spreadsheet on the Equation 2 to show the traceability on T given a certain choice of q and N. The graph below shows the super linear traceability when the number of device N is 1 billion and $q=1024$. First observation, it takes almost the same number of movies to achieve a super high confidence (below 0.0001%) as it does to achieve a moderately high confidence (below 0.1%). Secondly, our tracing algorithm takes about $4T$ movies to detect all traitors in the coalition and also deduce the coalition size of T.

If we choose q=256, it takes about $6T$ movies to detect traitors. For example, it takes 56 movies to detect 9 traitors and deduce the coalition size of 9.

In contrast, based on Equation 1 for traceability code using the same $q(=256)$ and N as above, and using a simple Reed-Solomon assignment for both inner and outer code will allow the license agency to deterministically identify *one* traitor after recovering 255 movies, *if* the coalition contains no more than nine traitors. Of course traceability code cannot tell the coalition size.

While we believe our algorithm already gives us super high confidence, it seems a deterministic tracing takes a lot more movies in order to exclude even the tiny possibility of being wrong. Of course as we pointed out, the biggest problem is that one cannot perform deterministic tracing in real applications like AACS, because in real life, the tracing agency rarely knows the size of the coalition in advance. In our probabilistic tracing, we suppose the coalition size is unknown and try to find a coalition that can explain all the recovered movies. If we succeed, the algorithm outputs a probability. This probability is both a confidence that the identified coalition contains guilty players *and* a confidence that the attack is of that size. We also use a filtering algorithm where we examine the individual guilty probabilities of each player in the identified coalition. We can calculate the probability that a completely different coalition could have incriminated the suspect coalition we found. This so-called false positive

Figure 2. Traceability with different q with 1/1000000 false positive rate

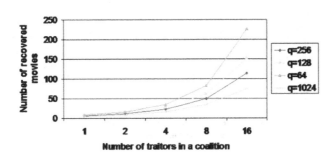

rate---i.e. the probability that all members in the suspect coalition are innocent---can be made to be arbitrarily small.

Overall, our probabilistic forensic analysis algorithm is not only closer to real world scenarios, but also achieves much better efficiency measured by the number of recovered forensic evidences needed in order to detect traitors in a coalition.

EFFICIENT FORENSIC ANALYSIS AFTER REVOCATIONS

In Section 2.2 we discussed four requirements for a forensic analysis algorithm to be practical. The forensic analysis algorithm presented in Section 4 satisfied the first three requirements for a one level code assignment. Recall the fourth requirement for a practical forensic analysis algorithm is to provide continued efficient tracing after revocation. This was missed from all existing approaches because they just assume traitors can be disconnected and tracing can be simply repeated after revocation. In fact, (Jin & Lotspiech, 2007) presented the first renewable traitor tracing system for anonymous attack to be able to technically revoke/exclude traitors. As one can imagine, in order to exclude/revoke traitors, the assignment of the content/keys to players for future content need to be modified so that only innocent players can decrypt/access the new content and the revoking players cannot. However we observe with the revocation occurring

in the lifetime of the system and the assignment changes to exclude traitors, the effective outer code level q becomes smaller. From Equation 3, it means traceability would degrade. The following Figure shows the impact of q on traceability.

Equation 3 indicates that traceability depends on two static variables that are decided at the assignment step, namely the number of variations q and the number of relevant users N in the system. To improve the degraded traceability caused by decreased q, we believe one potential way is to find a way to also decrease N. In order to achieve that, we can expand the outer code level into yet another two level assignment. In one level, the bulk of keys are assigned to one manufacturer/model; in another level, the bulk of keys are assigned to the players within the manufacturer/model. With this it is possible to use two-phase forensic analysis algorithms. The first phase is to identify the pirate manufacturer/model; the second phase is to focus on the guilty manufacturer/model and find out the actual traitor within the manufacturer/model. As one can imagine, the number of relevant users in each phase is not as big as the total number of users in the entire system. For example, the number of manufacturer/model is much smaller than the number of players in the world. By Reed-Solomon code's property, it takes only two ($k = 2$) movies to uniquely detect the manufacturer. Figure 3 shows the improved traceability with the multi-phase tracing strategy.

Figure 3. Traceability with multi-phase tracing strategy

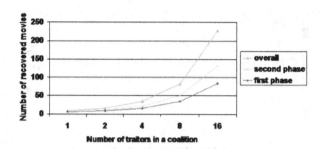

EFFICIENT FORENSIC ANALYSIS FOR NESTED CODE

Anonymous attack on the inner code level means mix-match segments from different movie versions available to the attackers. As we pointed out in Section 3, this is an unlikely attack due to the difficulty and cost of performing such an attack. Nonetheless, in this section we will focus on such attacks on inner code (i.e., the content) even though it is not a very likely attack.

To perform forensic analysis on nested codes, one can always use the algorithm shown in Section 4 on each level separately. Performing forensic analysis algorithm on inner code first would identify the outer code symbols of the attackers. The symbols identified as being the coalition that created the inner code can be treated as individual symbols for the outer code detection.

As shown in Section 3, the two-level nested code is used because we need to have a small number of variations q at any point of the movie in order to satisfy the extra bandwidth overhead requirement. A small q means a small length for the inner code. Based on Equation 2 we can achieve any level of confidence by recovering more forensic evidences, in this case more segments in the movie. But when the tracing is used on inner code, the recovered movie has a fixed length, for example 15 segments. So given the fixed length of a movie, Equation 2 can always give a probability larger than 1 when T reaches certain limit.

In other words, the inner code tracing could fail, which causes the outer code decoding failure too.

For example, suppose inner code is a *(15, 2)* code over *16* symbols, *5* codewords *(T=5)* belonging to the inner code can always cover *any* attacked sequence corresponding to one inner codeword with length 15. That means, 5 traitors can mix-match and create any version of a pirate movie. In other words when recovering a pirated movie version, the license agency will have no way to know who have created it if there are more than 5 colluders who each contribute their segments equally to build that pirate movie. As a result, the forensic analysis algorithm on the inner level alone would report detection failure and no information is available at all for the outer code decoding. Of course it is highly desirable to be able to detect attacks by larger coalitions as the amount of available information (i.e., the number of pirated movies) increases.

To remedy this problem, we propose in (Varna & Jin, 2008) to pass partial information to the outer code decoding, to enable detection even in cases where the forensic analysis algorithm on the inner level code would fail. This partial information could be the number of segments each outer code symbol matches with or the locations of the segments each outer code symbol matches. By doing so, we are able to increase the collusion resistance of the traitor tracing system significantly. Traitor tracing for shortened and corrupted fingerprints using soft information, namely, the probabilities of the individual symbols was also considered in Safavi-Naini & Wang, 2003. The general philosophy of soft decoding in our technique is the same, however, the information passed and the tracing algorithm used is different.

Nested Set Cover Based Tracing

As discussed in Section 4, the forensic analysis algorithm mainly consists of three steps.

The soft decoding mainly needs to be performed at first step which attempts to find a suspect coalition. In order to expand the set-cover algorithm to accommodate soft decoding based on partial information we will first generalize the previous basic set-cover algorithm by reformulating it as an optimization problem. Suppose we observe a sequence of M symbols and we have N users. We construct a binary matrix A (of size $M * N$) with each column corresponding to one user and each row corresponding to an observed symbol. The $(i,j)^{th}$ entry of A is 1 if and only if the ith user's j^{th} symbol is the same as the jth observed symbol. Solving the minimum set cover problem in our forensic analysis algorithm is then equivalent to solving the following optimization problem:

Minimize the inner product of ([1,1,1...1] and x) subject to the constraint that each element of Ax is greater than or equal to 1.

Now in the case that the inner code detector is unable to uniquely determine the coalition of outer code symbols, it can just output the fraction of segments (corresponding to inner code symbols) each outer code symbol matches with. This ``score'' would be representative of the probability that the particular outer code symbol was part of the coalition that created the attacked movie.

The outer code tracing then constructs a matrix A with M rows and N users. The $(i,j)^{th}$ entry in the matrix is the fraction of segments that user i's j^{th} inner codeword matches in the corresponding locations in the observed attacked sequence. The detector can then solve the minimum set cover problem by solving the equivalent optimization problem.

As one can see, with our reformulation of the previous forensic analysis algorithm, we can now easily expand the algorithm into the case when the entry in the matrix is not exactly 0 or 1, but rather a number between 0 and 1. Again this number represents the guilty probability of the outer code symbol based on its matchings with the recovered symbol.

This optimization problem may not have a unique solution. However, the guilty coalition will be one of the found minimum weight solutions. The detector can check if the solutions obtained explain all the observed symbols and hence eliminate spurious coalitions.

Another technique to avoid spurious solutions would be to output the locations where the inner code segments match, along with the number (fraction). To do that we are going to expand the matrix A. Suppose the inner code is of length n and has Q codewords. This would imply that the outer code has symbol size Q. For each outer code symbol, the inner code detector would output a binary vector of length n indicating whether the inner codeword corresponding to that outer code symbol matches with the observed symbols or not. The outer code detector then stacks these as columns to create the matrix A which now has $M * n$ rows and N users. The $(i,j)^{th}$ entry is 1 if the jth symbol of the nested codeword of user i matches the jth attacked symbol observed. Again the guilty coalition can be found by solving the minimization problem.

Once the suspect coalition is found using the above expanded set-cover algorithm. The forensic analysis algorithm can follow the exact step to calculate the guilty probability of the coalition and filter out innocent users from the suspect coalition.

Traceability of the Nested Code Set Cover Tracing

We test our technique using a system with an inner Reed Solomon code *(15,2)* over *GF(16)* and an outer Reed Solomon code *(255,3)* over *GF(256)*.

Figure 4. Number of movies required to uniquely identify attackers from nested code with false positive rate 10^{-6}

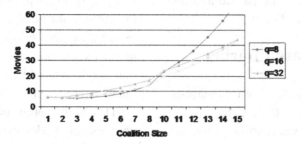

This system can support 256^3, or approximately $16*10^6$, users; a quite practical setting. Suppose the attackers can randomly choose one of the available versions for each segment and mix-match them to construct the pirated movie. In our simulation we randomly choose t traitors among all users; we also use the random mix-match approach to create the simulated pirated movies.

For the tracing, we pass the score and location of the matching segments corresponding to each outer code symbol from the inner code tracing to the outer code level.

We compared the number of times the *entire* coalition is correctly detected from 30 pirated movies using this new expanded algorithm and the previous basic set-cover based algorithm applied separately to the inner and outer codes. We had 100 trials. We observe that if the tracing is applied separately on the inner and outer codes, the system is unable to resist attacks by more than 5 colluders. This is consistent with our previous analysis. In contrast, using our expanded algorithm based on nested code we can easily identify coalitions of 10 users from 30 movies.

Assume that for each segment the attackers output a segment randomly among their different versions, we can use a similar formula as Equation 2 to calculate the probability that an innocent coalition will cover an observed sequence of movies. But instead of using the number of recovered movies in the formula, we have to use the number of

movie segments and the inner code q. The formula can be similarly used to determine the number of movies that are required to identify a coalition with high confidence. Figure 4 shows the number of movies needed to identify coalitions of attackers based on Equation 2. The figure illustrates results for different inner code symbol size 8, 16 and 32, in each case creating 256 inner codewords. We set the false positive rate to be 10^{-6}. From the figure, we see that with approximately 30 movies, we can identify coalitions of up to approximately 12 attackers. Our simulation results are consistent with these theoretical results obtained. Our new expanded algorithm makes it feasible to use in practice to defend against random mix-match attack on inner code, i.e., the actual content.

CONCLUSION

In this article we focused on using traitor tracing as a forensic technology to defend against anonymous attack in multimedia distribution where the attackers redistribute the plain content or per-content encrypting key. When the pirated content/keys are found, traitor tracing technologies can identify the actual users (traitors) who have involved in constructing the pirated decoder or content/key. While we solved many theoretical and practical problems along the way to bring a traitor tracing solution to practice, this article focused on one of the most important problems in traitor tracing technology, namely the forensic analysis algorithm.

We discussed four requirements coming from real world in order for a forensic analysis algorithm to be feasible to use in practice and analyzed how existing work failed to meet those requirements. We showed how we have designed efficient algorithms and met each of these requirements. The efficiency of our forensic analysis algorithms meeting all practical requirements is the main enabling factor for the first large scale commercialization of a traitor tracing technology in the new industry content protection standard AACS for next generation high definition DVDs. As future work we are interested in continuing improving the efficiency of the forensic analysis algorithm for anonymous attack and if needed meeting new arising practical requirement in future.

REFERENCES

AACS-LA. (2006). Pre-*recorded Video Book*, Advanced Access Content System, http://www.aacsla.com/specifications.

Barg, A., Blakely, R., & Kabatiansky, G. (2003). Digital Fingerprinting Codes: Problem Statements, Constructions, Identification of Traitors. *IEEE Transactions on Information Theory*, *49*(4), 852–865. doi:10.1109/TIT.2003.809570

Boneh, D., & Shaw, J. (1998). Collusion-secure fingerprinting for digital data. *IEEE Transactions on Information Theory*, *44*(5), 1897–1905. doi:10.1109/18.705568

Chor, B. (2000). Fiat. A., Naor, M., & Pinkas, B. (2000) Tracing traitors. *IEEE Transactions on Information Theory*, *46*, 893–910. doi:10.1109/18.841169

Chor, B., Fiat, A., & Naor, M. (1994). Tracing traitors, *Advance in Cryptography, Crypto* [Springer-Verlag, Berlin, Heidelberg, New York.]. *Lecture Notes in Computer Science*, *839*, 480–491.

Cohnen, G., Encheva, S., Litsyn, S., & Schaathun, H. G. (2003). Intersecting codes and separating codes. *Discrete Applied Mathematics*, *128*(1), 75–83. doi:10.1016/S0166-218X(02)00437-7

Fiat, A., & Naor, M. (1993). Broadcast Encryption, *Advance in Cryptography, Crypto* [Springer-Verlag, Berlin, Heidelberg, New York.]. *Lecture Notes in Computer Science*, *773*, 480–491. doi:10.1007/3-540-48329-2_40

Fiat, A., & Tassa, T. (1999). Dynamic traitor tracing, Advance *in Cryptography, Crypto* [Springer-Verlag, Berlin, Heidelberg, New York]. *Lecture Notes in Computer Science*, *1666*, 354–371. doi:10.1007/3-540-48405-1_23

Hollmann, H. D., Van Lint, J. J., Linnartz, J. P., & Tolhuizen, L. M. (1998). On codes with the identifiable parent property. *Journal of Combinatorial Theory Series A*, *82*, 121–133. doi:10.1006/jcta.1997.2851

Jin, H., & Lotspiech, J. (2006). Hybrid traitor tracing, IEEE *International Conference on Multimedia and Expo*, 2006.

Jin, H., & Lotspiech, J. (2006). Chapter "Practical Traitor Tracing", *Multimedia Security Technologies for Digital Rights Management*, Zeng, W., Yu. H., & Lin, C. (Ed.) ISBN: 0-12-369476-0, Elsevier.

Jin, H., & Lotspiech, J. (2007). Renewable traitor tracing: a trace-revoke-trace system for anonymous attack, *European Symposium on Research on Computer Security*, (pp.563-577).

Jin, H., Lotspiech, J., & Meggido, N. (2008). Efficient Coalition Detection for Traitor Tracing, *IFIIP Information Security Conference*, Milan, Italy. Lecture Notes in Computer Science, Springer-Verlag, Berlin, Heidelberg, New York.

Jin, H., Lotspiech, J., & Nusser, S. (2004). Traitor tracing for prerecorded and recordable media, ACM Digital Rights Management Workshop, pp.83-90. Washington. D.C., ACM press.

Safavi-Naini. Rei., & Wang, Y. (2000). Sequential Traitor tracing, Advance *in Cryptography, Crypto,* Lecture Notes in computer science, Vol. 1880, (pp. 316-332). Springer-Verlag, Berlin, Heidelberg, New York.

Safavi-Naini, R., & Wang, Y. (2003). Traitor Tracing for Shortened and Corrupted Fingerprints, ACM *Digital Rights Management Workshop*, pp.81-100, Washington D.C.

Staddon, J. N., Stinson, D. R., & Wei, R. (2001). Combinatorial properties of frameproof and traceability codes. *IEEE Transactions on Information Theory, 47,* 1042–1049. doi:10.1109/18.915661

Tardos, G. (2003). Optimal Probabilistic fingerprint codes, in proceedings of the *Theory of Computing*}, (pp. 116-125), June 9-11, San Diego, CA.

Trappe, W., Wu, M., Wang, Z., & Liu, R. (2003). Anti-collusion fingerprinting for multimedia. *IEEE Transactions on Signal Processing, 51,* 1069–1087. doi:10.1109/TSP.2003.809378

(2004). Trung,Tran., & Martirosyan, S. (2004). On a class of Traceability Codes. *Designs, Codes and Cryptography, 31,* 125–132.

Varna, A., & Jin, H. Generalized Traitor Tracing for Nested Codes, IEEE *International Conference on Multimedia and Expo*, 2008.

Yacobi, Y. (2001). Improved Boneh-Shaw Content Fingerprinting, RSA *conference* [Springer-Verlag Berlin Heidelberg.]. *Lecture Notes in Computer Science, 2020,* 378–391. doi:10.1007/3-540-45353-9_28

This work was previously published in International Journal of Digital Crime and Forensics (IJDCF), edited by Chang-Tsun Li & Anthony T.S. Ho, pp. 59-74, copyright 2009 by IGI Publishing (an imprint of IGI Global).

Chapter 12
Protection of Digital Mammograms on PACSs Using Data Hiding Techniques

Chang-Tsun Li
University of Warwick, UK

Yue Li
University of Warwick, UK

Chia-Hung Wei
Ching Yun University, Taiwan

ABSTRACT

Picture archiving and communication systems (PACS) are typical information systems, which may be undermined by unauthorized users who have illegal access to the systems. This article proposes a role-based access control framework comprising two main components – a content-based steganographic module and a reversible watermarking module, to protect mammograms on PACSs. Within this framework, the content-based steganographic module is to hide patients' textual information into mammograms without changing the important details of the pictorial contents and to verify the authenticity and integrity of the mammograms. The reversible watermarking module, capable of masking the contents of mammograms, is for preventing unauthorized users from viewing the contents of the mammograms. The scheme is compatible with mammogram transmission and storage on PACSs. Our experiments have demonstrated that the content-based steganographic method and reversible watermarking technique can effectively protect mammograms at PACS.

INTRODUCTION

A picture archiving and communication system (PACS) integrates imaging modalities and acts as

the interface between hospitals and departmental information systems in order to manage the storage and distribution of images to radiologists, physicians, specialists, clinics, and imaging centers. As medical image databases are interconnected through PACSs, those medical images are subject

DOI: 10.4018/978-1-60960-515-5.ch012

to security breaches, such as loss or manipulation of sensitive information, if their contents are not protected in some ways. For example, if a medical image is illegally obtained or if its content is malevolently changed, the patient's privacy, health care and legal rights could be undermined. Given the fact that medical image databases are accessed by users of various roles, e.g., doctor, administrator, interns, etc., a role-based access control mechanism is an obvious approach to the prevention of the afore-mentioned security breaches. For instance, a doctor could be given full access to the images and patients' textual information, while an intern's or administrator's access should be restricted according to the roles they are allowed to play. A common practice of managing textual information associated with images is to store the information in the header segment of the image file. Although the textual information can be protected through encryption, however the file formats are known publicly and the header field is separated from the content; that means the very location of the encrypted information is known. This opens a security gap for the attackers to manipulate the information. For example, even without knowing the secret key, an attacker can replace patient A's encrypted information in the header with patient B's encrypted information. This suggests that the location of the patients' information should not be made known to the unauthorized users and the information itself should be made inseparable from the pictorial contents of the images. Moreover, an overhead of the header is that it takes up physical disk spaces. We proposed in this work a role-based access control framework consisting of two key modules – a *content-based steganographic module* for hiding patients' textual information in the contents of medical images in a non-deterministic manner so as to prevent leaks of sensitive information and to save disk space. We also propose a *reversible watermarking module* for 'masking' the contents of the images with hidden patients' textual information (called *stego-images*) in order to prevent unauthorized

users from viewing the images. The main objectives set out in this work are:

1. To design a conceptual framework for protecting mammograms on PACSs. The framework should not only provide reliable protection for mammograms, but also support management functions for users with different access rights.

2. To develop a novel content-based steganographic method for hiding patients' textual information in mammograms and verifying the authenticity and integrity of mammograms. The data hiding process should not change the important pictorial details of mammograms and the data extraction process should not require the availability of original mammograms.

3. To develop a watermarking technique capable of masking the contents of mammograms for protecting mammograms against illegal access. The watermark can be removed to reveal the masked mammogram when authorization for viewing is given.

LITERATURE REVIEW

Main methods used in media industries for protecting digital information against malicious usage can be broadly classified into *cryptography-based* and *authorization-based* approaches. The approach of cryptography-based methods is to devise various protocols for the Internet and local area networks (LAN) to protect the digital information through encryption during the transmission in networks (Long, 2006; Xu, 2005). The idea of the authorization-based methods is to use digital signature certifications to achieve authorization for digital information storage and transmission. Since cryptography-based methods mainly focus on image transmission while laying less emphasis on the storage and management phases, the latter is therefore considered as more desirable in achieving higher reliability and security.

An early example of authorization-based method is the framework proposed by Thomas and Sandhu (1994), which depicted a conceptual model for task-based authorization methods. The concept of task-based authorization is that whether the users can pass the authorization or not depends on the tasks the users are charged with. They discussed several authorization functions and the business activities and mapped the semantic interpretations for the practical activities to computer functions. In such a way, they attempted to bridge the gap between low-level computer techniques and the high-level requirements of image system protection. However, the main limitation of task-based authorization is the difficulty in managing the access rights on the same task performed by different users. Kern *et al.* (2004) improved Thomas and Sandhu's tasked-based authorization by proposing a model for role-based access control. Roles-based authorization is set up depending, not on the tasks the users are assigned to, but on the roles of the users in the system. However, the study by Kern *et al.* (2004) is only conceptual, with no realizable schemes proposed for practical implementation.

Focusing on picture archiving and communication systems (PACS), Zhou and Huang (2001) proposed an integrated PACS management system for mammograms on which the textual information, such as patients' medical history, is integrated with the corresponding medical images. First the textual information is hashed and embedded into the mammogram using LSB steganography, which is about hiding data in the least significant bits by many published methods (Cao et al, 2003; Fridrich & Goljan, 2004; Ker, 2007; Tian, 2003; Zhou & Huang, 2001), and then this stego-image is encrypted by a cryptosystem. An improved version of Zhou and Huang's scheme was later proposed by Cao *et al.* (2003). One drawback of both schemes (Cao, 2003; Zhou & Huang, 2001) is that they do not classify access rights by taking different roles of the users into consideration, therefore any one

possessing the access key gains full access to the information, while the ones who do not have the key are completely barred from the system, i.e., the access right is binary. Another limitation of these two schemes is that in order to extract and view the textual information, the image has to been decrypted. Once the image is decrypted, it remains unprotected and anyone can view and modify it. Planitze and Maeder (2005a, 2005b) studied the potential of digital watermarking for protecting patients' textual information and the medical images themselves on PACSs. However, they did not suggest any frameworks or practical schemes for real world applications. Osborne *et al.* (2004) proposed a multiple embedding approach using robust watermarking for medical image protection. The digital signature of an image is first embedded into the RoB (Region of Background) using Quantization Index Modulation method (QIM) (Chen & Wornell, 2001). Then a second round of watermarking is performed to serve the authentication need. Despite the novelty of the idea, this method has two major drawbacks. First, access control is not provided. Secondly, the simple QIM method they employed is an insecure embedding method.

THE PROPOSED CONCEPTUAL FRAMEWORK

In the context of mammogram database management, the privacy of a patient, such as the patient's identity and medical history, resides in the security of the sensitive textual information and the pictorial contents of mammograms. Recognizing the need for providing multi-level access control to the mammograms depending on the users' roles on PACSs and aiming at achieving the objectives set out earlier, we propose a conceptual role-based authorization scheme in this section. This generic framework, as shown in Figure 1, depicts the key components and allows the components to be realized using the state-of-the-art techniques as tech-

Figure 1. The proposed mammogram protection framework

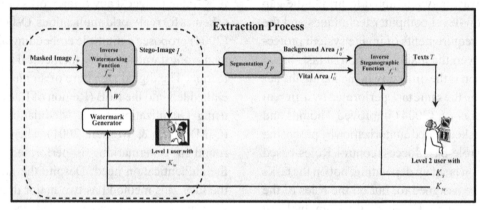

(a) The embedding process of the proposed framework

(b) The extraction process of the proposed framework

nolology advances. For example, the segmentation component of the framework can be implemented with different methods provided they serve the purpose. A practical realization of the conceptual framework is proposed in next section.

Depending on the roles of the users defined by different institutions, the roles as well as the access rights can be divided into multiple levels. This work is based on the assumption that there

are three types of roles / users as defined in Table 1. For instance, the doctor in charge of a case can access the patient's information, such as the patient's medical history and the mammograms; therefore, he/she should be classified as Level 2 user. An intern or trainee, on the other hand, can only access the mammograms for field work and training purposes but not the patient's medical history, so he/she is at Level 1. A system techni-

Table 1. Classification of roles of users, their access rights and keys in the conceptual framework

Roles / users	Access rights	Access keys issued
Level 0 user	No right given. (The contents of the mammograms are marked and unavailable to the users)	no key
Level 1 user	Stego-images (i.e., the mammograms with hidden patient information which cannot be extracted)	K_w
Level 2 user	Stego-imagse and patient information	K_s, K_w

cian with only maintenance duties should not be allowed to access the patient's information and the contents of the mammograms so he/she is to be classified as Level 0 and no access key is to be issued.

The proposed framework is divided into *embedding* and *extraction* processes as shown in Figure 1. The purpose of the *embedding* process is three-fold. First, its *steganographic function* f_s embeds patients' textual information into the corresponding mammograms with stego-key K_s so that users below Level 2 gain no access to those sensitive textual information. Secondly, when hiding the patients' textual information, steganographic function f_s involves the pictorial information taken from the images' contents so that if an attacker manipulated the pictorial contents of the images, the extraction process will fail to extract the hidden textual information, thus allowing the user to know that the image is no longer trustworthy. We have demonstrated the effectiveness of involving contents of different parts in the data hiding process for facilitating authentication in (Li & Si, 2007; Li & Yang, 2003). Thirdly, the *watermarking function* f_w masks the contents of the mammogram with watermarking key K_w so that users below Level 1 cannot view the contents.

The *embedding* process starts with a segmentation operation f_p of the mammogram, aiming at partitioning the original image I_o into medically insignificant *background* area and medically *vital* area, which covers the breast. The segmentation function f_p for partitioning an image I_O is defined as

$$\left(I_o^v, I_o^b\right) = f_p(I_o) \tag{1}$$

where and represent the vital area and the background area, respectively.

The patient's textual information, which is accessible only by Level 2 users, is then embedded in the mammogram using the steganographic function, f_s, to create a *stego-image* I_s, which shows only readable pictorial contents, but not the sensitive textual information, and is accessible by users at Level 1 and 2. Because we do not want to distort the pictorial contents that are supposed to be available to users at Level 1 and 2 and in the authentication process for detecting manipulation, so the steganographic function only embeds the textual information in the background area. To prevent other users from accessing the pictorial contents, the watermarking function, f_w, is then performed on stego-image I_s to mask its contents.

Because the segmentation results are content-dependent, i.e., they are different for different mammograms. The necessary conditions for replacing the hidden information in the background area with another version from a different mammogram without knowing the stego-key are 1) the attacker must be able to segment the two mammograms correctly, 2) the boundary dividing the background and vital areas in both mammograms must be the same and 3) the contents of the two mammograms must be exactly the same because the pictorial contents have to be involved in the hiding and extraction processes of the textual patient information, otherwise the correct patient information cannot be extracted even if the first two conditions were met.

As a steganographic function, f_s is to hide the patient's textual information T into using stego-key K_s and, it can be expressed as

$$I_s = f_s\left(I_o^b, I_o^v, T, K_s\right) \tag{2}$$

where I_S is the stego-image with hidden patient information, T.

To tighten access control further, a watermarking function, f_w, is applied to the stego-image, I_S, with the aid of a watermarking key, K_w, in order to mask the pictorial information / contents of the stego-image. A cryptosystem can certainly serve the purpose of scrambling the pictorial information by encrypting it. However, it is difficult to tell a corrupted file from a valid encrypted one before decryption is carried out. *Transparent encryption* is a technique that allows the details or the high resolution components of media to be encrypted while leaving the low resolution components visible to the viewers. This technique has been used for access control in various multimedia applications (Engel et al, 2008; Grangetto et al, 2006; Pommer & Uhl, 2003). Although similar technique can be used to serve the purpose of masking the pictorial contents of mammograms in our application, selecting images components for encryption and decryption is by no means trivial. This motivates our resort to digital watermarking, which requires less computational costs. The degree of masking can be adjusted by setting a watermarking strength factor α. The operation of the watermarking function can be express as

$$I_w = f_w(I_s, K_w, \alpha) \tag{3}$$

where I_w is the masked / watermarked version of the stego-image, I_s. As the watermarking strength factor α becomes greater, more pictorial details in the stego-image are masked.

The *extraction* process describes how users access the stego-image and extract the textual information according to the availability of access keys. The inverse watermarking function allows Level 1 and Level 2 users to unmask image I_w in order to reveal stego-image I_s by submitting K_w. By submitting both K_w and K_s, a Level 2 user can gain further access to the patient information, T, with the aid of the inverse steganographic function,.

IMPLEMENTATION OF THE CONCEPTUAL FRAMEWORK FOR MAMMOGRAMS

We have presented a conceptual framework for protecting mammogram databases on PACSs in the previous section. In this section we propose specific techniques for realizing the constituent components of the framework. Note that because of the framework's generic nature, although the techniques we proposed in this section are novel at present, they can be replaced in the future with new techniques without modifying the framework as the state-of-the-art evolves.

Pre-Processing

We observed that, on average, 80% of the pixels in the background areas,, of mammograms have a gray level of 0. So it is quite easy for the attacker to guess the embedded information without knowing K_s. For example, if the gray level of a background pixel of a *watermarked* mammogram equals 4, the probability that the embedded information equals 4 is 0.8. This is an apparent security gap to be closed. Also as described in Section 4.3, for non-zero-valued pixels, most of the times secret message can be embedded by either increasing or decreasing the gray levels, depending on which way results in lower distortion. However, to embed secret message in zero-valued pixels, the only choice is to increase the gray level, resulting in higher distortion (See Section 4.3 for details). To circumvent these two problems, for each zero-valued pixel b, we modify its gray level by assigning it a random number in the range of [0, -1] generated with K_s, where C_M is the maximum number of secret bits we want to embed. Since zero-valued pixels appear in the background area only and we only hide patients' information in the background area, this pre-processing does not change the vital area.

Segmentation

The mission of the segmentation is that when given either the original image, I_o, during the embedding process or the stego-image, I_s, during the extraction process as input, the segmentation function, I_p, should partition the input image into the same bi-level output image, with one level corresponding to the background area and the other to the vital area. Figure 3(a) shows a typical mammogram with the intensity represented with 8

Figure 3. Embedding process. a) Original mammogram; b) Segmented mammogram; c) Dilated mammogram; d) Stego-mammogram, I_s; e) Masked mammogram I_w

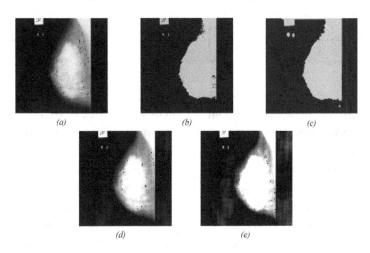

bits. We can see that it has a dark background with the intensity below 30 and a significantly brighter area of a breast with the intensity of most pixels above 100. Since we will hide the textual information in the background area and the distortion due to data hiding should not raise the intensity significantly, so a threshold between 50 and 100 for partitioning the images is a reasonable value. However, due to the fact that the mammograms in the database may be taken at different times with different equipments under various imaging conditions, using a heuristic constant threshold to segment mammograms is not feasible. So we proposed to use *moment-preserving thresholding* (Tsai, 1985), which is content-dependent, to perform the segmentation task.

Given a gray-scale image, I, with $X \times Y$ pixels, we define the intensity / gray scale at pixel (x, y) as $I(x, y)$. The ith *moment* of the image is defined (Tsai, 1985) as

$$m_i = \left(\frac{1}{X \times Y}\right) \sum_{x=1}^{X} \sum_{y=1}^{Y} I^i(x, y) \qquad (4)$$

A transform is called *moment-preserving* if the transformed image I' still has the same mo-

ments as I. In the context of binary segmentation, to divided I into two classes of p_o and p_1 pixels with gray scale z_o and z_1, respectively, we can find a threshold t by first solving Equation (5) as formulated below

$$\begin{cases} p_0 z_0^0 + p_1 z_1^0 = m_0 \\ p_0 z_0^1 + p_1 z_1^1 = m_1 \\ p_0 z_0^2 + p_1 z_1^2 = m_2 \\ p_0 z_0^3 + p_1 z_1^3 = m_3 \end{cases} \qquad (5)$$

Once z_o, z_1, p_o, and p_1 are obtained, setting the threshold t to a value between the gray scales of p_oth and (p_o+1)th pixels will yield segmentation result I' that preserves the first four moments (i.e., m_o to m_3) of I (Tsai, 1985). From the above description, we know that to make sure the algorithm uses the same segmentation result in both embedding and extraction processes, when given the original image I_o and stego-image I_s, respectively, as the input image I, the algorithm should yield the same values for p_o and p_1. Because the significant gap between the background and vital areas in both I_o and I_s, our experiments have proved the feasibility of the use of the moment-preserving thresholding method. The reader is

Figure 2. The method for modifying the numbers in order to embed 3-bit message

referred to (Tsai, 1985) for more details about moment-preserving thresholding.

After moment-preserving thresholding, some pixels with low intensity in the vital area may be classified as background pixels. Moreover, the smoother intensity transition across the boundary separating the background and the vital / breast areas may also cause misclassification. To compensate for these two types of misclassifications, a morphological operation of 'dilation' (Gonzalez & Woods, 2002) with a disk of radius equal to 5 pixels is applied to the vital area so as to allow the vital area to grow and background area to shrink.

Information Hiding through Steganographic Function

The proposed method is essentially inspired by QIM watermarking (Chen & Wornell, 2001). The idea of hiding l-bit secret data t in a pixel with gray level equal to b is first to 'project' b in a secret key-controlled manner onto a range, in which each index in the index set of $\{0, 1, 2,..., 2^l-1\}$ can be repeatedly used to index the values of the new range. Secondly, the projected gray level, now represented by p is modulated so that the new value p' (i.e. the gray level of the stego-pixel) lands on an index equal to the value of the l-bit secret data t. Because the indices repeat, data hiding can be achieved by modulating the pixel in question upwards or downwards, depending on which way results in lower distortion. To extract the hidden data, the algorithm simply establishes the same range and takes the index corresponding to the gay level of the stego-pixel as the hidden data. The way of projecting the original gray level

b to a new value p will be described later. For the moment, let us use Figure 2 to demonstrate the idea of embedding 3-bit secret data in the already projected gray level p. Figure 2 shows that the projected value, p, equals 11 and falls in a range, R, of [0, 31], which allows the index set of {0, 1, 2,..., 7} to be repeatedly used for indexing the elements in that gray level range, with index 0 synchronised with the lower bound of the range, R, (i.e., 0). We can see that p corresponds to index 3. Now suppose the 3-bit secret data t equal 0. We could hide t in p by changing p to either 8 or 16 because they both correspond to the same index (secret data), which is 0. However, we can see that changing p to 16 incurs a distortion of 5 while changing it to 8 leads to a distortion of 3 only. Therefore, the algorithm will choose to change p to 8 (i.e, $p'=8$). To extract the hidden data, the algorithm establishes the same projected range and takes the index corresponding to p' (i.e., 8), which is 0, as the hidden data.

Because the modulation indices are allowed to repeat, we call our steganographic method *Repetitive Index Modulation (RIM)* based steganography. As data hiding could be achieved by modulating either upwards or downwards, and, the probability distribution of secret data is uniform, therefore, the expected distortion D_{RIM} incurred in the hiding of a 3-bit secret data is

$$D_{RIM} = \frac{1}{8}(0+1+2+3+4+1+2+3) = 4$$

The general form of the expected distortion D_{RIM} in terms of *difference between the original pixel and stego-pixel* incurred when embedding *l*-bit secret data is

$$D_{RIM} = \frac{1}{2^l}\left(2^{l-1} + 2 \cdot \sum_{i=1}^{2^{l-1}-1} i\right) \qquad (6)$$

Since the proposed method allows changes to be made to any bits, therefore the security is greater than LSB steganography.

Now let us describe how a gray level b is projected onto a range, R, in which repetitive indices could be used to hide secret data. In this work, we use a fixed range of $[0, 2^l + B)$, where B is the upper bound of the gray levels (e.g, if a pixel is represented with 8 bits, then $B = 255$). Since the range is fixed / known, the projection of gray level b has to be done in a secret manner as follows:

$$p = r + b \qquad (7)$$

where r is a key generated random number in the range of $[0, 2^l -1]$. From Eq. (7), we can see that $0 \le p < 2^l + B$. To hide the secret data, the modulation as described in Eq. (8) is carried out so that p' falls on the index that is equal to the secret data and closest to p.

$$p' = r + b' \qquad (8)$$

Actually, the upper bound of r can be an arbitrary number greater than $2^l -1$. However, without the secret key, an exhaustive attack on the steganographic method is to exhaust the 2^l possible cases for each pixel, therefore an upper bound of r greater than $2^l -1$ is not necessary.

The afore-mentioned RIM-based steganographic method is a general data hiding idea. To hide patients' textual information T into a mammogram, we apply this method in a *content-based* manner. The idea is to pair up each pixel b in the background area (i.e., the embeddable area) with another pixel v picked from the vital area (i.e., the non-embeddable area) at random according to stego-key K_S and define r in Eq. (7) and (8) as

$$r = \left[rand\_no + b\right] \bmod 2^l \qquad (9)$$

where *rand_no* is a random number in $[0, 2^l -1]$ generated by stego-key K_S and "mod" is the modulo operation. By comparing Eq. (7) and (8) we can see that the vital information v is involved in the embedding process, but its value is not changed. Therefore no distortion is inflicted on v. Note that we will use b and v to represent the two pixels and their gray scale / intensity interchangeably. The content-based RIM steganographic function is summarized as follows:

RIM Steganographic Function f$_s$ for Textual Information Embedding

Step 1. Establish the projection range, R, of $[0, 2^l + B)$ and synchronize index 0 with the lower bound of R.

Step 2. For each pixel b in the background area, find its partner pixel v from the vital area at random according to K_S. Note we allow different pixel bs to be assigned the same partner v.

Step 3. For each pair of b and v, project the gray level b onto p in R using a secret key K_S and Eq. (7).

Step 4. Obtain the l-bit secret data t from the patients' textual information T.

Step 5. Modulate p according to Eq. (7) and (8) so that its modulated counterpart p' falls on the index equal to the secret data t and closest to p.

Pictorial Content Masking through Watermarking Function

After stego-image I_s is created by the stegonagraphic function f_s, the watermarking function f_w is performed to mask its pictorial contents. Because the purpose of the proposed watermarking function is to 'distort' the stego-image, in a reversible manner, in order to mask its pictorial details, unlike most watermarking schemes, which are aimed at reducing the distortion as much as possible if the robustness requirement is met, it embeds the watermark generated by K_w with a much greater embedding strength α. To allow the content-based inverse steganographic function to be able to extract the textual information based on the same pictorial contents, the proposed watermarking function must be reversible. That is to say that the watermark pattern must be completely removable and the stego-image should be perfectly recoverable when the inverse watermarking function is applied. The watermarking function is summarized as follows:

Watermarking Function f$_w$ for Masking Stego-Image

Step 1. Perform Discrete Cosine Transform (DCT) on I_s. Note without loss of generality, we use the same symbol (e.g., I_s) to represent images in both spatial and transform domains.

Step 2. Perform f_w on each DCT coefficient of I_s using K_w such that

$$I_w = f_w(I_s, K_w, \alpha)$$
$$= I_s \times (1 + \alpha \cdot W) \quad (10)$$

Step 3. Perform Inverse DCT on I_w

The embedding strength α can be set to achieve the required masking effect.

Extraction Process

For Level 1 and Level 2 users with K_w, by applying an inverse watermarking function, the masked stego-image I_s can be perfectly recovered according to the following algorithm.

Inverse Watermarking Function for Unmasking Stego-Image

Step 1. Perform Discrete Cosine Transform (DCT) on I_w.

Step 2. Perform on each DCT coefficient of I_w using K_w such that

$$I_s = f_w^{-1}(I_w, K_w, \alpha)$$
$$= \frac{1}{(1 + \alpha \cdot W)} I_w \quad (11)$$

Step 3. Perform Inverse DCT on I_s.

For a Level 1 user, stego-image I_s is the only data accessible. But for Level 2 users, by using stego-key K_s, the patient's textual information can be extracted. To do so, the same moment-preserving thresholding algorithm introduced in Section 4.2 is employed to segment the stego-image into background and vital areas first.

In the extraction process, to extract the hidden information from each b', we again pair up each pixel b' in the background area with another pixel v from the vital area according to K_s. Note because the vital information v is not modulated during the embedding process, therefore we still use v, instead of v' in the extraction process. Because K_s is the same key used during both embedding and extraction processes, the same paring is guaranteed. We can see that the pairing operation involves the pictorial information in the vital / breast area in both textual information hiding and extraction processes. Should the pictorial contents of the stego-image be manipulated, the algorithm will fail to extract the textual information due to the inconsistent pictorial content, thus alerting the users of the false authenticity and integrity of the image. The inverse steganographic function for textual information extraction is formulated as follows.

Inverse Steganographic Function for Textual Information Extraction

Step 1. Establish the projection range, R, of $[0, 2^l + B)$ and synchronize index 0 with the lower bound of R.

Step 2. For each pixel b' in the background area, find its partner pixel v from the vital area at random according to K_s. Note we allow different pixel b's to be assigned the same partner v.

Step 3. For each stego-pixel, project its gray level x' onto p' in R using a secret key K_s and Equations (7) and (9).

Step 4. Find the modulation index corresponding to p' and take it as the secret data t.

EXPERIMENTAL RESULTS AND DISCUSSIONS

The mammograms used in the experiments are of size 1024×1204 pixels from the Mammographic Image Analysis Society (MIAS) (Wang, 2004). Figure 3 shows the images produced at different stages during the embedding process. A mammogram as shown in Figure 3(a) is segmented into background and breast areas as shown in Figure 3(b). In order to reserve the medical details on the edge of the breast, dilation is performed to enlarge the breast area (Figure 3(c)) so that none of the vital / breast pixels are classified as background pixels. Figure 3(d) shows the stego-image, I_s, after the patient's textual information is embedded. Finally, the stego-image is masked to produce the marked image, I_w, as depicted in Figure 3(e) by the watermarking function to protect the whole mammogram.

To analyze the performance of the proposed scheme, we test our steganographic function f_s on 5 different mammograms with l, the number of bits of the patient's textual information is set to $k = 2, 3$ and 4, respectively. We can see from Table 2 that for all mammograms the proposed

Table 2. Performance comparison between the proposed RIM steganographic and LSB methods in terms of embedding distortion measured by average difference between the original pixel and stego-pixel when the length of the secret data to be embedded in each pixel is set to $k = 2, 3$ and 4, respectively

Images	$k = 2$		$k = 3$		$k = 4$	
	RIM	LSB	RIM	LSB	RIM	LSB
Mamm1	1.14	1.18	2.14	2.40	4.54	5.07
Mamm2	1.19	1.20	2.16	2.45	4.42	5.20
Mamm3	1.15	1.17	2.16	2.45	4.32	5.11
Mamm4	1.14	1.17	2.17	2.45	4.32	5.11
Mamm5	1.15	1.17	2.13	2.50	4.35	5.11

RIM steganographic method outperforms the LSB method in terms of embedding distortion, measured by *average difference between the original pixel and stego-pixel* (i.e., $|b - b'|$). Note that although the pixels in the vital area are involved in the data hiding process according to Equation (9), the data hiding process is applied to the background area only; therefore no distortion is inflicted on the vital area. The statistics listed in Table 2 are only relevant to the background area. Note the distortion statistics of RIM in Table 2 are slightly deviated from the expected values 1, 2, and 4 for $k = 2, 3$ and 4, respectively, as predicted by Equation (6). This is because there are around 80% of the zero-valued pixels in the background area, which force the RIM steganographic method to modulate the pixels in upward direction only.

In this study, content masking is intended to prevent unauthorized people from viewing the contents of mammograms. To mask the contents of the mammograms, strength α of the reversible watermarking function in Equation (10) can be set for different security levels. Figure 4 demonstrates the masking effects when different values of α are used. When α equals 0.5, major details in the mammogram are obscured as shown in Figure

Figure 4. Mammograms masked with different watermark embedding strength

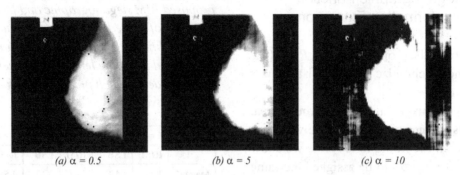

| (a) α = 0.5 | (b) α = 5 | (c) α = 10 |

4(a). When α is set to 10, the mammogram is completely masked as depicted in Figure 4(c).

CONCLUSION

In this work, a role-based access control framework using data hiding techniques is proposed for combating security threats faced by mammogram databases in PACSs. Access to the databases and the information contained in the mammograms are controlled through the issuance of the stego-key and the watermarking key. The scheme alleviates the drawbacks, such as separable header and storage overhead of the header, of encryption-based schemes and enhances the security by embedding the patients' textual information in the contents of the mammograms and allowing authentication to be carried out. The content-dependent steganographic function hides the patients' textual information by using the stego-key, which is only assigned to the users with the highest access right, and involving the pictorial contents in the embedding process, which allows the inverse steganographic function to carry out authentication when extracting the hidden textual information. The reversibility of the watermarking function makes the stego-image recoverable so that the hidden textual information can be authenticated by the inverse steganographic function through the involvement of the same pictorial contents used during the embedding process. Moreover, the scheme is compatible with mammogram transmission and storage on PACS. We are currently investigating the possibilities of tailoring the proposed framework for protecting other types of medical images.

REFERENCES

Cao, F., Huang, H. K., & Zhou, X. Q. (2003). Medical Image Security in a HIPAA Mandated PACS Environment. *Computerized Medical Imaging and Graphics*, *27*(2), 185–196. doi:10.1016/S0895-6111(02)00073-3

Chen, B., & Wornell, G. W. (2001). Quantization Index Modulation: A Class of Provably Good Methods For Digital Watermarking and Information Embedding. *IEEE Transactions on Information Theory*, *47*(4), 1423–1443. doi:10.1109/18.923725

Engel, D., Stütz, T., & Uhl, A. (2008). Efficient Transparent JPEG2000 Encryption. In Li, C.-T. (Ed.), *Multimedia Forensics and Security*. Hershey, PA: Information Science Publishing. doi:10.4018/9781599048697.ch016

Fridrich, J., & Goljan, M. (2004). On Estimation of Secret Message Length in LSB Steganography in Spatial Domain. *Proc. SPIE, Security, Steganography, and Watermarking of Multimedia Contents VIII*, 5306, 23-34.

Gonzalez, R. C., & Woods, R. E. (2002). *Digital Image Processing*. MA: Prentice Hall.

Grangetto, M., Magli, E., & Olmo, G. (2006). Multimedia Selective Encryption by Means of Randomized Arithmetic Coding. *IEEE Transactions on Multimedia, 8*(5), 905–917. doi:10.1109/TMM.2006.879919

Ker, A. (2007). Steganalysis of Embedding in Two Least-Significant Bits. *IEEE Transactions on Information Forensics and Security, 2*(1), 46–54. doi:10.1109/TIFS.2006.890519

Kern, A., Kuhlmann, M., Kuropra, R., & Ruthert, A. (2004). A Meta Model for Authorizations in Application Security Systems and Their Integration into RBAC Administration. *Proceedings of the Ninth ACM Symposium on Access Control Models and Technologies, 87-96.*

Li, C.-T. & Si, H. (2007). Wavelet-based Fragile Watermarking Scheme for Image Authentication. *Journal of Electronic Imaging, 16*(1), 013009-1 - 013009-9.

Li, C.-T., & Yang, F. M. (2003). One-dimensional Neighbourhood Forming Strategy for Fragile Watermarking. *Journal of Electronic Imaging, 12*(2), 284–291. doi:10.1117/1.1557156

Long, M., & Wu, C. H. (2006). Energy-Efficient and Intrusion-Resilient Authentication for Ubiquitous Access to Factory Floor Information. *IEEE Transactions on Industrial Informatics, 2*(1), 40–47. doi:10.1109/TII.2005.864144

Osborne, D., Abbott, D., Sorell, M., & Rogers, D. (2004). Multiple Embedding Using Robust Watermarks for Wireless Medical Images. *Proceedings of the 3rd International Conference on Mobile and Ubiquitous Multimedia, 245-250.*

Planitz, B. M., & Maeder, A. J. (2005a). A Study of Block-based Medical Image Watermarking Using a Perceptual Similarity Metric. *Proceedings of the Workshop on Digital Image Computing: Technqiues and Applications, 483-490.*

Planitz, B. M., & Maeder, A. J. (2005b). Medical Image Watermarking: A Study on Image Degradation. *Proceedings of the Workshop on Digital Image Computing: Technqiues and Applications, 3-8.*

Pommer, A., & Uhl, A. (2003). Selective Encryption of Wavelet-Packet Encoded Image Data — Efficiency and Security. [Special issue on Multimedia Security]. *ACM Multimedia Systems, 9*(3), 279–287. doi:10.1007/s00530-003-0099-y

Thomas, R. K., & Sandhu, R. S. (1994). Conceptual Foundations for a Model of Task-Based Authorizations. *Computer Security Foundations Workshop VII, 14-16.*

Tian, J. (2003). Reversible Data Embedding Using a Difference Expansion. *IEEE Trans. on Circuits and Systems for Video Technology, 13*(8), 890–896. doi:10.1109/TCSVT.2003.815962

Tsai, W. H. (1985). Moment-Preserving Thresholding: a New Approach. *Computer Vision Graphics and Image Processing, 29*(3), 377–393. doi:10.1016/0734-189X(85)90133-1

Wang, M., Lau, C., Matsen, F. A., & Kim, Y. M. (2004). Personal Health Information Management System and its Application in Referral Management. *IEEE Transactions on Information Technology in Biomedicine, 8*(3), 287–297. doi:10.1109/TITB.2004.834397

Xu, Y. F., Song, R., Korba, L., Wang, L. H., Shen, W. M., & Lang, S. (2005). Distributed Device Networks with Security Constraints. *IEEE Transactions on Industrial Informatics, 1*(4), 217–225. doi:10.1109/TII.2005.843826

Zhou, X. Q., & Huang, H. K. (2001). Authenticity and Integrity of Digital Mammography Images. *IEEE Transactions on Medical Imaging, 20*(8), 784–791. doi:10.1109/42.938246

This work was previously published in International Journal of Digital Crime and Forensics (IJDCF), edited by Chang-Tsun Li & Anthony T.S. Ho, pp. 75-88, copyright 2009 by IGI Publishing (an imprint of IGI Global).

Chapter 13
Reversible and Blind Database Watermarking Using Difference Expansion

Gaurav Gupta
Macquarie University, Australia

Josef Pieprzyk
Macquarie University, Australia

ABSTRACT

There has been significant research in the field of database watermarking recently. However, there has not been sufficient attention given to the requirement of providing reversibility (the ability to revert back to original relation from watermarked relation) and blindness (not needing the original relation for detection purpose) at the same time. This model has several disadvantages over reversible and blind watermarking (requiring only the watermarked relation and secret key from which the watermark is detected and the original relation is restored) including the inability to identify the rightful owner in case of successful secondary watermarking, the inability to revert the relation to the original data set (required in high precision industries) and the requirement to store the unmarked relation at a secure secondary storage. To overcome these problems, we propose a watermarking scheme that is reversible as well as blind. We utilize difference expansion on integers to achieve reversibility. The major advantages provided by our scheme are reversibility to a high quality original data set, rightful owner identification, resistance against secondary watermarking attacks, and no need to store the original database at a secure secondary storage. We have implemented our scheme and results show the success rate is limited to 11% even when 48% tuples are modified.

INTRODUCTION

Electronic communication, faster internet data transfer speed, and peer-to-peer communication facilities enable the convenient transfer of mul-timedia objects. However, they also open up the possibility of copyright violations. Publishers need to insert ownership marks in the media object to discourage users from illegally downloading multimedia and thereby protect copyright. This process is referred to as *watermarking*. The major requirements of a watermarking algorithm

DOI: 10.4018/978-1-60960-515-5.ch013

are that the watermark should not be noticeable (imperceptibility), the watermark should survive possible attacks (robustness), successful recognition and extraction of watermark in a watermarked copy, watermark detection should require only the watermarked copy and a secret key (blindness), and the multimedia object should have high watermark-carrying capacity.

Images, video, audio, software, natural language documents, and databases are the usual candidates for watermarking. Images are the primary contenders (Bors and Pitas, 1996; Braudway, 1997; Cox et. al, 1997) given that changing the characteristics of a pixel does not substantially degrade image quality and the watermarking capacity in millions of pixels is very high. The insertion algorithm selects the pixels that will carry the watermark using pseudo random generators with a secret seed. Thus an attacker's task is made even harder by requiring him to find out the watermark location. Comparatively, database watermarking is a new field where research interest has risen recently (Agrawal and Kiernan, 2002, Agrawal et. al, 2003; Sion et. al, 2004; Gross-Amblard, 2003; Fei et. al, 2006; Yingjiu et. al, 2006; Yingjiu and Deng, 2004; Zhang et. al, 2004; Zhang et. al, 2006). A typical database watermarking scenario is when a publisher C creates a database relation R and sells it to O. If O is a traitor, it illegally sells the relation to others. To prevent this, C embeds a watermark W in R. Similarly, if a data provider D uploads relation R for remote query process, an attacker might reconstruct the original relation by assembling query results. Hence, D uploads a watermarked relation. A blind watermarking scheme requires only the watermarked object and a secret key to detect the watermark while a non-blind watermarking scheme requires the unmarked multimedia object in addition to the first two inputs. The major disadvantage of a non-blind watermarking scheme is that one needs to store the unmarked object at a secure secondary storage location and feed it back to the detection algorithm later. Reversible watermarking provides a mechanism to revert the watermarked relation

back to the original unmarked relation using a secret key. The key advantages of reversibility are that it:

1. Allows for trial version of multimedia content that can be later upgraded to the full version by reversing it. A company may want to distribute low quality relations free of cost and then require customers to purchase a key using which they can revert the relation to high quality original relation.
2. Allows introducing higher distortion in the data since original data can be regenerated by reversing the watermarking.

In this article, we determine the requirements of database watermarking model, feasible attacks, and propose a reversible and blind database watermarking scheme addressing these concerns.

Notation

The following notations are used in the article:

- R: a Relation,
- r: tuple,
- $r.A_i$: i^{th} attribute in tuple r,
- $r.A_i^j$: j^{th} LSB of ith attribute in tuple r,
- $r.P$: primary key of tuple r,
- $\|$: concatenation,
- $H()$: one-way hash function,
- $R \xrightarrow{ins(p)} R_w$: R_w is the watermarked relation upon party p watermarking relation R,
- $R \xrightarrow{ins(p)} R_w$: Original relation R is restored by the party p from the watermarked relation R_w, $\lfloor x \rfloor$: floor function, $size(x)$: size of x in bits, $abs(x)$: absolute value of x.

Organization of Article

We organize our articles as follows: The following section contains related work. The model of the adversary is then given and potential attacks against database watermarking schemes are described. We then present our watermarking scheme, discuss our experimental results and analyze the model in terms of capacity and security. The article is concluded with a note on future research direction.

RELATED WORK

The majority of the database watermarking schemes rely on unique identification of a tuple from the primary key value and the assumption that an attacker cannot change the primary key without compromising usability. One of the first database watermarking algorithms was provided in (Agrawal and Kiernan, 2002). The algorithms select one out of γ tuples for watermarking from a relation containing a total of η tuples. For each selected tuple r, an attribute A_i and a bit position j is secretly selected using a hash function computed on the combination of a private key and the tuple's primary key $F(r.P) = H(K||H(K||(r.P)))$, where H is the hash function, K is the secret key and $r.P$ is the primary key of the tuple r. The bit $r.A_i^j$ is then replaced by the Least Significant Bit (LSB) of $H(K|| r.P)$. Inputs to the insertion algorithm are relation R containing v attributes and η tuples, the fraction of tuples to be watermarked γ, the number of LSBs to be considered for watermarking ξ, and secret key K. The insertion and detection

Algorithm 1. Agrawal-Kiernan watermark insertion algorithm

Input: Relation R, private key K, fraction $\frac{1}{\gamma}$, LSB usage ξ
Output: Watermarked relation R_w
1 **forall** *tuple* $r \in R$ **do**
2   **if** $\mathcal{F}(r.P)\%\gamma = 0$ **then**
3      $i = \mathcal{F}(r.P)\%v$;
4      $j = \mathcal{F}(r.P)\%\xi$;
5      $r.A_i^j = \mathcal{H}(\mathcal{K}||r.P)\%2$;
6   **end**
7 **end**
8 return R;

Algorithm 2. Agrawal-Kiernan watermark detection algorithm

Input: Watermarked Relation $\tilde{R}_w$, private key K, fraction $\frac{1}{\gamma}$,
       LSB usage ξ
Output: Detection Status $\in \{true, false\}$
1 $totalcount = matchcount = 0$;
2 **forall** *tuple* $\tilde{r}_w \in \tilde{R}_w$ **do**
3   **if** $\mathcal{F}(r.P)\%\gamma = 0$ **then**
4      $i = \mathcal{F}(r.P)\%v$;
5      $j = \mathcal{F}(r.P)\%\xi$;
6   **if** $\tilde{r}_w.A_i^j = \mathcal{H}(\mathcal{K}||\tilde{r}_w.P)\%2$ **then**
7        $matchcount = matchcount + 1$;
8   **end**
9      $totalcount = totalcount + 1$;
10   **end**
11 **end**
12 $\tau = min\{\theta : \mathcal{B}(\theta, totalcount, 1/2) < \alpha\}$;   // $\mathcal{B}$ defined in
     Equation 1
13 **if** $matchcount \geq \tau$ **then**
14   return *true*;
15 **end**
16 return *false*;

algorithms from (Agrawal and Kiernan, 2002) are given in Algorithm 1 and Algorithm 2 respectively.

Detection of τ or more bits results in a successful recovery of watermark. Hence, the probability of τ out of ω ($\omega=\eta/\gamma$) bits being detected in a random database relation by chance ($B(\tau, \omega, 1/2)$) should be less than α. Thus α is the upper bound of the false positive probability. Other papers in the field also make the same assumption (that the primary key cannot be changed by the attacker) as otherwise it would be (probably) impossible to uniquely identify the tuples carrying watermark (Agrawal et. al, 2003; Sion et. al, 2004; Gross-Amblard, 2003; Yingjiu et. al, 2006; Yingjiu and Deng, 2004; Zhang et. al, 2004; Zhang et. al, 2006). The major drawback of this watermarking algorithm proposed by Agrawal and Kiernan is irreversibility that renders object susceptible to secondary watermarking. Thus individual modification limit ξ should be assigned to each attribute. Gross-Amblard (2003) proposed one of the few watermarking models that address the usability issue in detail. Usability is measured in terms of query results. If the results of a given set of queries are preserved for a watermarked relation, the watermarking is said to be query-preserving, and is desirable. The notions of local and global distortions are presented in (Gross-Amblard, 2003) which achieve the property of query-preservation. The user can execute queries $q_1, q_2, ..., q_k$ on the database relations. The scheme addresses the problem of providing a database watermarking scheme that respects the following conditions:

1. The watermarking scheme transforms the database relation into several versions, and results in a small distortion on the query results $q_1(u'), q_2(u'), ..., q_k(u')$ and the owner acts as any user u'.
2. The scheme can prove ownership based on answers to the above k queries only.

Several reversible and blind image watermarking schemes have been proposed. *Data compres-* *sion* based reversal (Celik et. al, 2002) compresses the LSBs of n pixels selected into m bits where $m<n$. These m bits and $n-m$ watermark bits are then inserted in the n selected pixels. However, data compression based watermarking schemes are extremely fragile since the lossless algorithms are not modification-resistant. *Histogram shifting* techniques (Chang et. al, 2005) exploit the notion that neighboring pixels have high correlation and, depending on the watermark bit, the histogram bins are circularly upgraded (if watermark=1) or downgraded (if watermark=0). Since database relation values do not possess correlation similar to images, the histogram shift technique is irrelevant for our purpose. *Difference expansion* based watermarking (Alatter, 2004; Tian, 2003) integrates a watermark bit to an n-element vector such that the original vector and the watermark bit can be retrieved from the modified vector. The working of data compression schemes is given below:

1. Select pseudo-randomly pixels that will carry watermark, $p_1, ..., p_n$.
2. Quantify the pixels using secret element L such that $r_i = p_i - (p_i/L)*L$ and $p'_i = (p_i/L)*L$.
3. Compress remainders r to m values r' ($m < n$).
4. Add the m compressed remainders and $n-m$ watermark values to residues $p'_1, ..., p'_n$.

$$p''_i = \begin{cases} p'_i + r_i & if(i \leq (n-m)) \\ p'_i + w_{i-(n-m)} & if(n-m \leq i \leq n \end{cases}$$

During detection, the remainders and the watermark bits are extracted and the original pixels reconstructed using decompression. Data compression based watermarking schemes are extremely fragile since the lossless algorithms are not modification-resistant.

The following example shows watermark values $\{w_1, w_2, w_3\}$ (integers between 0 and 7) being embedded in 9 pixels (given by the array p), where $\{r_1,...,r_6\}$ are compressed remainders.

$$p = \begin{pmatrix} 34 & 45 & 37 \\ 48 & 60 & 63 \\ 39 & 72 & 57 \end{pmatrix} \quad p' = \begin{pmatrix} 32 & 40 & 32 \\ 48 & 56 & 56 \\ 32 & 72 & 56 \end{pmatrix}$$

$$r = \begin{pmatrix} 2 & 5 & 5 \\ 0 & 4 & 7 \\ 7 & 0 & 1 \end{pmatrix} \quad r' = \begin{pmatrix} r_1 & r_2 & r_3 \\ r_4 & r_5 & r_6 \\ w_1 & w_2 & w_3 \end{pmatrix}$$

$$p'' = \begin{pmatrix} 32+r_1 & 40+r_2 & 32+r_3 \\ 48+r_4 & 56+r_5 & 56+r_6 \\ 32+w_1 & 72+w_2 & 56+w_3 \end{pmatrix}$$

Difference expansion based watermarking performs invertible arithmetic operations on integers. A scheme to embed n-1 watermark bits in n vectors is given in (Alatter, 2004) and a specific case for n=2 is described in (Tian, 2003) called pair wise difference expansion. For simplicity, we will introduce the latter scheme in this article.

Given two adjacent pixels' values, we compute the average, a, and difference, d using Equation 1. This operation is invertible and x and y can be computed from a and d using Equation 2. Integer d is changed to $d'=2*d+b$ and x', y' are computed from a, d' and bit b to be inserted using Equation 3.

$$a = \lfloor (x + y)/2 \rfloor, d = x - y \quad (1)$$

$$x = a = + \lfloor (d + 1)/2 \rfloor, y = a - y \lfloor d/2 \rfloor \quad (2)$$

$$x' = a = + \lfloor (d'+1)/2 \rfloor, y' = a - y \lfloor d'/2 \rfloor \quad (3)$$

The new pixel values are x', y'. One can re-calculate a, d' from x', y' using Equation 2. The watermark bit is simply the LSB of d'. Now from a, d one can compute the values of x, y using Equation 3. As a working example, consider two pixels x=106, y=100. From Equation (1), a=103, d=6, assuming b=1, d'=2*6+1=13. x'=103+$\lfloor$(13 + 1)/2$\rfloor$ =110, y'=103-$\lfloor$13/2$\rfloor$ =97. Hence, the new pixel values are x'=110, y'=97. At the receiver's end a= $\lfloor$(110 + 97)/2$\rfloor$ =103, d'=110-97=13. Bit b=lsb(d')=1, d= $\lfloor d'/2 \rfloor$ =6. x=103+ $\lfloor$(6 + 1)/2$\rfloor$ =106, y=103- $\lfloor$6/2$\rfloor$ =100. Thus we can successfully recover the watermark bit and original pixel values from the modified values. We denote the process of reversing a pair as x_r, y_r=Reverse$\{x,y\}$.

MODEL OF ADVERSARY

The set of possible attacks a watermark should survive are as follows:

A1: Random bitwise flipping attacks: some bits selected at random (probably with uniform probability distribution) are modified.

A2: Subtractive attack: some tuples chosen at random are deleted.

A3: Sorting: some tuples and/or attributes are chosen at random and their positions are changed. An ordering criterion may be chosen by the attacker and the relation is then sorted based on that criterion, thereby resulting in a differently sorted relation.

A4: Secondary watermarking: a watermark is superimposed on the watermarked relation.

The degree of secrecy and randomness in selecting the tuples and attributes that will be marked along with the proportion of the tuples selected for marking determines the security level of the watermark against the attacks **A1** and **A2**. The assumption that the primary key cannot be modified by the attacker ensures that attack **A3** is not successful since the correct order can be re-established using primary key values (for example, sorting tuples in ascending order of the primary key). We focus on providing security against secondary watermarking.

Assume that Alice watermarks a relation R to create watermarked relation R_a. An attacker Mallory might make some modifications in R_a before re-watermarking it with a secondary watermark to create relation R_m. Watermarks of Mallory and Alice are detected in R_m with probabilities 1 and p respectively. Thus with probability 1-p, the incorrect owner will be output and there is confusion over ownership with probability p. The problem can be averted by designing reversible watermarking algorithms as explained below.

Consider the same situation again when Alice and Mallory both watermark a relation. When the judge needs to determine the rightful owner, he asks both Alice and Mallory to detect their watermarks in their watermarked documents R_a and R_m, respectively. They reverse their relations to the original documents R and R'_a, respectively (as Mallory might have made some modifications in R_a before inserting the watermark). Alice's watermark is detected in the reversed relation of Mallory but Mallory's watermark is not detected in the reverse relation of Alice which proves that the sequence of watermarking was Alice followed by Mallory and thus establishes Alice as rightful owner. Recently a reversible scheme for database watermarking was proposed in (Gupta and Pieprzyk, 2007). The inserting algorithm stores the original bits that are later modified in an embed map. During the detection algorithm, the marked bits are sequentially replaced by bits from embed map. This approach suffers from the following drawbacks,

- If the adversary deletes one of the tuples, then the bits from the tuples positioned after the deleted ones will be distorted.

- The scheme is essentially non-blind since the information about the watermark needs to be stored in a safe location.

- Incremental watermarking: If the database has to be updated and re-watermarked, one needs to reverse the entire relation.

Thus the main objective of our scheme is to eliminate these three shortcomings of (Gupta and Pieprzyk, 2007) and still provide security against secondary watermarking attacks.

PROPOSED SCHEME

We intend to satisfy the major requirements of a watermarking scheme and at the same time facilitate reversibility of the watermarked relation. Difference expansion is the most suitable method to facilitate reversibility in database watermarking since the data is in numeric format. In order to utilize the reversible watermarking based on difference expansion, we select two attributes from the same tuple to carry the watermark bit (call the two attributes A_i and A_j). We need to select the two attributes so that the distortion (change in attributes' values) is within the bounds. We ensure that the distortion is tolerable by placing an upper bound of ξ_i on the number of modifiable LSBs for attribute A_i. Let the tuple selected for watermarking be r and the attributes be A_i, A_j. The bit embedded *is LSB(H(K||r.P))*. Thus, when the detection algorithm is run and bit is extracted, it is compared to *LSB(H(K||r.P))* for determining successful recovery. Since the attacker cannot modify the primary key, *LSB(F(r.P))* enables us to identify marked tuples and difference expansion facilitates reversal. The insertion and detection algorithms are provided in Algorithm 3 and 4 respectively.

In lines 6 and 7 of Algorithm 3, we ensure that in case the unmarked attributes were reversed, the difference between the reversed values and unmarked values should exceed distortion tolerance. This condition can detect the attributes which are not marked because of exceeding distortion limits. The condition is rechecked in lines 12,

Algorithm 3. Watermark insertion

Input: Relation R, private key K, fraction γ, number of markable attributes υ, LSB usage $\Xi = \{\xi_1, \xi_2, \ldots, \xi_\upsilon\}$
Output: Watermarked relation R_w

```
1  forall tuples r ∈ R do
2  |    if F(r.P)%γ = 0 then
3  |    |    i = F(r.P)%υ;                    // identify attribute 1
4  |    |    j = F(rP/2)%υ;                    // identify attribute 2
5  |    |    x = max(Ai,Aj), y = min(Ai,Aj);
6  |    |    {xr,yr} = Reverse{x,y};
7  |    |    if abs(x − xr) > ξ1 OR abs(y − yr) > ξ2 then
8  |    |    |    a = ⌊x+y/2⌋, d = x − y;
9  |    |    |    b = lsb(H(K ∘ r.P)) ;        // bit to embed
10 |    |    |    d' = 2*d + b;
11 |    |    |    x' = a + ⌊d'+1/2⌋, y' = a − ⌊d'/2⌋;
12 |    |    |    if Ai > Aj then
13 |    |    |    |    δ1 = abs(Ai − x');
14 |    |    |    |    δ2 = abs(Ai − y');
15 |    |    |    |    if δ1 < ξi AND δ2 < ξj then
16 |    |    |    |    |    Ai = x', Aj = y';
17 |    |    |    |    end
18 |    |    |    else
19 |    |    |    |    δ2 = abs(Ai − x'), δ1 = abs(Ai − y');
20 |    |    |    |    if δ2 < ξi AND δ1 < ξj then
21 |    |    |    |    |    Ai = y', Aj = x';
22 |    |    |    |    end
23 |    |    |    end
24 |    |    end
25 |    end
26 end
```

13 of Algorithm 4 once the unmarked values are computed from the marked attributes.

In the detection algorithm, we also check that a significant proportion of marks are detected in the multimedia object in order to establish beyond reasonable doubt that the object is in fact watermarked. The significance level can be determined by parameter α as in (Agrawal and Kiernan, 2002). We use percentage of marks detected, *prctng*, as a simpler and equally strict significance level metric. Considering *prctng* to ensure mark presence reduces the chances of false positives if *prctng* is sufficiently large (experimental results show 85% and over is desirable).

EXPERIMENTAL RESULTS

We carried out experiments with 1000 files having 200 to 300 tuples and 10 to 20 attributes each. The software generated the database files, inserted the watermark, made modifications of the watermarked relations, and detected the watermark in the attacked files. Changing fractions did not have a major effect on detectability of watermark (with the exception when fraction=33%). As tolerance increases, the probability of false positives increases and probability of detection also increases. With increasing attack levels, detection probability reduces and is confirmed by the experimental results. The worst case scenario occurred when the attacker modified 48 out of every 100

Algorithm 4. Watermark detection

Input: Watermarked Relation $\tilde{R}_w$, Secret parameter list
$\phi = (\mathcal{K}, \gamma, \upsilon, \Xi), prcntg$

Output: {Watermark Status $\in \{true, false\}$, Restored
Relation R}

1   $R = \tilde{R}_w$;

2   $matchcount = 0, totalcount = 0$;

3   **forall** *tuples* $\tilde{r}_w \in \tilde{R}_w$ **do**

4   **if** $\mathcal{F}(r_w.P)\%\gamma = 0$ **then**

5     $i = \mathcal{F}(r_w.P)\%\upsilon, j = \mathcal{F}(\frac{r_w.P}{2})\%\upsilon$;

6     $x' = max(A_i, A_j), y' = min(A_i, A_j)$;

7     $a' = \lfloor \frac{x'+y'}{2} \rfloor, d' = x' - y', b = lsb(d') \; d = \lfloor \frac{d'}{2} \rfloor$;

8     $x = a' + \lfloor \frac{d+1}{2} \rfloor, y = a' - \lfloor \frac{d}{2} \rfloor$;

9     $\{x_r, y_r\} = Reverse\{x, y\}$;

10   **if** $abs(x - x_r) > \xi_1 \; OR \; abs(y - y_r) > \xi_2$ **then**

11   **if** $A_i > A_j$ **then**

12       $\delta_1 = abs(A_i - x), \delta_2 = abs(A_i - y)$;

13   **if** $\delta_1 < \xi_i \; AND \; \delta_2 < \xi_j$ **then**

14   **if** $b = lsb(\mathcal{H}(\mathcal{K}\|r.P))$ **then**

15         $A_i = x, A_j = y$;

16         $matchcount = matchcount + 1$;

17   **end**

18        $totalcount = totalcount + 1$;

19   **end**

20   **else**

21       $\delta_2 = abs(A_i - x), \delta_1 = abs(A_i - y)$;

22   **if** $\delta_2 < \xi_i \; AND \; \delta_1 < \xi_j$ **then**

23   **if** $b = lsb(\mathcal{H}(\mathcal{K}\|r.P))$ **then**

24         $A_i = y, A_j = x$;

25         $matchcount = matchcount + 1$;

26   **end**

27        $totalcount = totalcount + 1$;

28   **end**

29   **end**

30   **end**

31   **end**

32   **end**

33   **if** $\frac{matchcount}{totalcount} \geq prcntg$ **then**

34   return $\{true, R\}$;

35   **else**

36   return $\{false, \tilde{R}_w\}$;

37   **end**

tuples. In such a situation, 89 out of 100 times, the watermark was still detected corroborating the theoretical value suggested by Equation 5. Overall, 9 different fractions, 10 different attack levels, and 5 different tolerance levels were introduced and watermark was detected in 42167 out of 46045 watermarked files with a cumulative probability of 91.5%. Figures 1, 2 and 3 show the changes in detection rates with varying attack, watermarking fraction, and confidence interval, respectively.

ANALYSIS

We now analyze the capacity and security properties of the watermarking scheme as compared to

Figure 1. Detection rate with varying attack

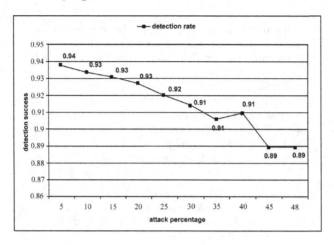

Figure 2. Detection rate with varying fraction

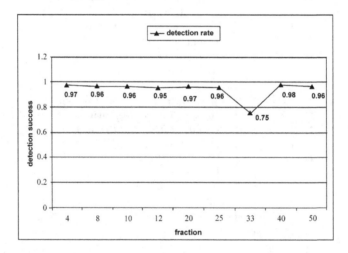

Figure 3. Detection rate with varying confidence level

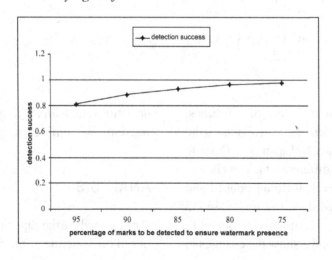

previous schemes such as (Agrawal and Kiernan, 2002; Gupta and Pieprzyk, 2007).

Capacity

In our scheme, γ tuples out of every 100 tuples are selected for watermarking. Thus the capacity of our scheme is given by $C = \eta/\gamma$ where η is the total number of tuples. The capacity is, theoretically, same as capacity of previous scheme (Agrawal and Kiernan, 2002). Distortion levels ξ used in our schemes are much higher. The modified values can later be reversed back to original values upon purchase of full version of the data set. Allowing higher distortion results in more attributes selected for marking actually getting marked thereby increasing the capacity in practice.

Security

In this section, we discuss the security of our proposed solution from the adversary.

A1: Random bitwise flipping attack. *If we assume that the attacker has complete knowledge of ξ and υ. The attacker can now choose tuples ζ randomly, and flip all the ξ LSBs of attribute A_i (1 $\leq i \leq \upsilon$) in those tuples. This attack is successful if the attacker can toggle sufficient marked bits such that detection algorithm detects less than τ watermarked bits correctly. Hence the attacks succeeds only when attacker modifies at least $\omega-\tau+1$ watermarked bits (where $\omega=\eta/\gamma$) is the total number of tuples marked. The probability of this attack is given by Equation 4 (Agrawal and Kiernan, 2002). This probability is the same as (Agrawal and Kiernan, 2002; Gupta and Pieprzyk, 2007). For $\gamma=50$, the worst case scenario is when attacker changes 48% of the tuples and the success probability of attack is merely 11% as confirmed by experiments and shown in Figure 1. If the attacker changes more than half the tuples, a) the usability would be assumed to be severely*

affected, and, b) watermark would be detected in the bitwise complemented relation.

$$P(A) = \sum_{i=\tau}^{\omega} \frac{\binom{\omega}{i}\binom{\eta-\omega}{\varsigma-i}}{\binom{\eta}{\varsigma}} \tag{4}$$

A2: Subtractive attack. *This type of attack is similar to the previous attack in that the attacker has to again remove at least $\omega-\tau+1$ marked tuples out of η tuples such that the detection algorithm detects less than τ matches. The probability of this attack is same as the previous attack (random bitwise flipping attack).*

A3: Sorting. *If an attacker re-sorts the tuples based on any attribute, it does not affect the detection algorithm. Since the watermark detection is carried out for each tuple independently, any change in order does not affect the outcome of the detection algorithm. The sorting attack was given significant importance when initially selecting the difference expansion method.*

A4: Secondary watermarking. *Let us consider a situation where Alice watermarks relation R resulting in relation R_a and distributes it for trial. The attacker Mallory modifies R_a to R'_a and re-watermarks R'_a resulting in relation R_m. R'_a still contains Alice's watermark with a high probability p and Alice's watermark is successfully removed by Mallory with a probability 1-p (According to experimental results, $p \approx 0.89$ for $\gamma=50$). R_m contains Mallory's watermark with probability 1 since it has not been modified after watermark insertion. Let R_a accidently contain Mallory's watermark with a negligible probability δ ($\delta \approx 0$). The judge asks Alice and Mallory to run detection algorithm on R_a and R_m respectively. Both Mallory's and Alice's* *watermarks are successfully detected in their respective relations. Mallory's restored relation is R'$_a$ and Alice's restored relation is R. With a high probability p, Alice's watermark is detected in R'$_a$ but Mallory's watermark is detected with an extremely low probability δ in R. Thus it becomes evident that Mallory inserted the watermark in the relation already watermarked by Alice and thereby Alice is the rightful owner. This way, the current watermarking scheme defeats secondary watermarking attacks.*

CONCLUSION

In this article, we have proposed a reversible and blind database watermarking model. The maximum distortion introduced to the attributes is limited to the tolerance parameter ξ. It is, in practice, desirable to have distortion on the higher side since the watermarking is reversible. The distorted database is available to everyone and the accurate database can be purchased upon payment by users by reversing the watermarking. The proposed scheme is successful in achieving the major objective of eliminating the shortcomings of irreversible schemes like (Agrawal and Kiernan, 2002). The capacity of the proposed watermarking scheme is high and the attack resistance probability between 89 and 98 percent. Our future research is directed towards increasing the watermark carrying capacity and level of attack resistance in a reversible and blind watermarking model.

REFERENCES

Agrawal, R., Haas, P. J., & Kiernan, J. (2003). Watermarking relational data: framework, algorithms and analysis. *The VLDB Journal, 12*(2), 157–169. doi:10.1007/s00778-003-0097-x

Agrawal, R., & Kiernan, J. (2002). Watermarking relational databases. In *28th International Conference on Very Large Databases VLDB*.

Alattar, A. M. (2004). Reversible watermark using the difference expansion of a generalized integer transform. *IEEE Transactions on Image Processing, 13*(8), 1147–1156. doi:10.1109/TIP.2004.828418

Bors, A., & Pitas, I. (1996). Image watermarking using DCT domain constraints. In *IEEE International Conference on Image Processing (ICIP'96)*, volume III, (pp 231–234).

Braudaway, G. W. (1997). Protecting publicly-available images with an invisible image watermark. In *IEEE International Conference on Image Processing (ICIP'97)*.

Celik, M. U., Sharma, G., Tekalp, M. A., & Saber, E. (2002). Reversible data hiding. In *International Conference on Image Processing*, volume 2, (pp 157–160).

Chang, C. C., Tai, W. L., & Lin, M. H. (2005). A reversible data hiding scheme with modified side match vector quantization. In *19th International Conference on Advanced Information Networking and Applications*, (pp 947–952).

Chang, C. C., Tai, W. L., & Lin, M. H. (2005). A reversible data hiding scheme with modified side match vector quantization. In *19th International Conference on Advanced Information Networking and Applications*, (pp 947–952).

Cox, I., Kilian, J., Leighton, T., & Shamoon, T. (1997). Secure spread spectrum watermarking for multimedia. *IEEE Transactions on Image Processing, 6*(12), 1673–1687. doi:10.1109/83.650120

Gross-Amblard, D. (2003). Query-preserving watermarking of relational databases and XML documents. In *20th ACM Symposium on Principles of Database Systems*, (pp 191–201).

Guo, F., Wang, J., & Li, D. (2006). Fingerprinting relational databases. In *ACM symposium on Applied computing*, (pp 487–492).

Gupta, G., & Pieprzyk, P. (2007). Reversible and semi-blind relational database watermarking. In *International Conference on Signal Processing and Multimedia Applications*.

Li, Y., & Deng, R. H. (2006). Publicly verifiable ownership protection for relational databases. In *ACM Symposium on Information, computer and communications security*, (pp 78–89).

Li, Y., Guo, H., & Jajodia, S. (2004). Tamper detection and localization for categorical data using fragile watermarks. In *ACM workshop on Digital rights management*, (pp 73–82).

Sion, R., Atallah, M., & Prabhakar, S. (2004). Rights protection for relational data. *IEEE Transactions on Knowledge and Data Engineering, 16*(12), 1509–1525. doi:10.1109/TKDE.2004.94

Tian, J. (2003). Reversible data embedding using a difference expansion. *IEEE Transactions on Circuits and Systems for Video Technology, 13*(8), 890–896. doi:10.1109/TCSVT.2003.815962

Zhang, Y., Niu, X. M., & Zhao, D. (2004). A method of protecting relational databases copyright with cloud watermark. *Transactions of Engineering. Computing and Technology, 3*, 170–174.

Zhang, Y., Yang, B., & Niu, X. M. (2006). Reversible watermarking for relational database authentication. *Journal of Computers, 17*(2), 59–66.

Chapter 14
Medical Images Authentication through Repetitive Index Modulation Based Watermarking

Chang-Tsun Li
University of Warwick, UK

Yue Li
University of Warwick, UK

ABSTRACT

In this work we propose a Repetitive Index Modulation (RIM) based digital watermarking scheme for authentication and integrity verification of medical images. Exploiting the fact that many types of medical images have significant background areas and medically meaningful Regions of Interest (ROI), which represent the actual contents of the images, the scheme uses the contents of the ROI to create a content-dependent watermark and embeds the watermark in the background areas. Therefore when any pixel of the ROI is attacked, the watermark embedded in the background areas will be different from the watermark calculated according to the attacked contents, thus raising alarm that the image in question is inauthentic. Because the creation of the watermark is content-dependent and the watermark is only embedded in the background areas, the proposed scheme can actually protect the content/ROI without distorting it.

INTRODUCTION

Due to privacy concerns and authentication needs, many digital watermarking schemes (Bao et al, 2005; Coatrieux et al, 2001; Guo & Zhuang, 2007;

DOI: 10.4018/978-1-60960-515-5.ch014

Kong & Feng, 2001; Osborne et al, 2004; Planitz & Maeder; 2005; Zhou et al, 2001) have been proposed to embed authentication data into the contents of medical images. Methods proposed in the literature can be broadly classified into two categories: *spatial domain watermarking* (Bao et al, 2005; Coatrieux et al, 2001; Kong & Feng, 2001) and *transform domain watermarking* (Wakatani, 2002; Lie et al, 2003; Osborne et al, 2004). Most transform domain *watermarking* methods are designed to work with lossy compression standards, such as JPEG and JPEG 2000. The main concern surrounding this type of watermarking schemes is that in most cases lossy compression is not allowed to be applied to medical images, thus restricting their applicability. On the other hand, most spatial domain embedding methods are developed for the applications in which no lossy compression is expected. Many spatial domain embedding methods (Bao et al, 2005; Coatrieux et al, 2001; Kong & Feng, 2001) require that the least significant bits (LSBs) of the image pixels be replaced with the authentication codes or watermarks. Although the distortion due to this kind of "destructive" watermark embedding is usually visually insignificant, medical images with watermarks embedded with this type of irreversible watermarking schemes may not be acceptable as feasible evidence in the court of law, should medical disputes occur. Many reversible data hiding schemes (Li, 2005; Thodi & Rodriguez, 2007), although not specifically proposed for the purpose of medical image authentication, have been developed to facilitate reversible data hiding, in which the original images can be recovered after the hidden data is extracted from the watermarked images. A reversible watermarking scheme specifically developed for authenticating medical data has been proposed in (Kong & Feng, 2001). The common problem with these reversible data hiding schemes is that, apart from the actual payload (i.e., the watermark, secret data, authentication codes, etc), side information for reconstructing the exact original image has to be embedded as well. The side information wastes limited embedding capacity and is usually the compressed form of the location map of the original data that is expected to be affected by the embedding process. The waste of embedding capacity reduces the authentication power of the scheme and the resolution of tamper localization, as explained in (Li & Yuan, 2006).

Moreover, authentication schemes are also expected to be resistant against attacks, such as the Holliman-Memon counterfeiting attack (Holliman & Memon, 2000), the birthday attack (Stallings, 1998) and the transplantation attack (Barreto et al, 2002), by involving the contents in the watermarking process in a non-deterministic manner (Kim et al, 2008; Li & Yuan, 2006). Therefore schemes with high payload, high resolution of tamper localization, high security and zero distortion to the ROI are desirable.

PROPOSED METHOD

It is observed that, apart from the ROI, which represents the actual contents of images, many types of medical images have significant background areas. Exploiting this characteristic, a few transform domain watermarking schemes have been proposed to extract features/signature from the ROI for embedding in the background areas to serve the purposes of copyright protection (Wakatani, 2002; Lie et al, 2003) or integrity verification (Osborne et al, 2004). However, as mentioned in the previous section, the applicability of transform domain watermarking methods is restricted to the cases where lossy compression is allowed. In the light of this limitation, in this work we propose a new spatial domain scheme, which uses the contents of the ROIs to create a content-dependent watermark and embeds the watermark in the background areas without adding any embedding distortion to the ROI. Without loss of generality, we will use mammograms with gray level range [0, 255] in the presentation of this work. Because the background areas contain no information of interest and the gray levels of their pixels fall in the low end of the intensity range, wherein human eyes are not sensitive to variation, a greater degree of embedding can be carry out to strengthen security and/or increase resolution of tamper localization (Li & Yuan, 2006). The main components of our scheme are described in the following subsections.

Segmentation

The mission of the image segmentation operation is that when given either the original image, I_o, during the *watermarking* process or the watermarked image, I_w, during the *authentication* process as input, the segmentation function should partition the input image into the same bi-level output image, with one level corresponding to the background areas and the other to the ROIs. Figure 1(a) shows a typical mammogram with intensity represented with 8 bits. We can see that it has a dark background with intensity below 30 and a significantly brighter area of a breast (ROI) with the intensity of most pixels above 100. Since

we will embed the watermark in the background area and the distortion due to embedding will not raise the intensity significantly, so a threshold between 50 and 100 for partitioning the images is a reasonable value. However, due to the fact that mammograms may be taken at different times with different equipments under various imaging conditions, using a heuristic constant threshold to segment mammograms is not feasible. So we propose to use *moment-preserving thresholding* (Tsai, 1985), which is content-dependent, to perform the segmentation task.

Given a gray-scale image, I, with $X \times Y$ pixels, we define the intensity / gray scale at pixel (x, y) as $I(x, y)$. The ith *moment* of an image is defined by Tsai (1985) as

Figure 1. Mammogram authentication. a) The original mammogram, b) Segmented background and ROIs, c) the watermarked mammogram, d) tampered mammogram, e) the black spots indicate the tampered areas, f) authentication result with the noisy areas indicating tampering.

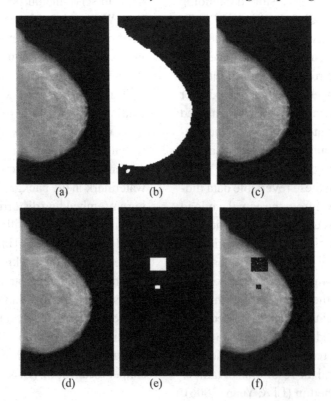

(a)   (b)   (c)

(d)   (e)   (f)

$$m_i = \left(\frac{1}{X \times Y}\right) \sum_{x=1}^{X} \sum_{y=1}^{Y} I^i(x,y) \qquad (1)$$

A transform is called *moment-preserving* if the transformed image, I', still has the same moments as I. In the context of binary segmentation, to divided I into two classes of p_0 and p_1 pixels with gray scale z_0 and z_1, respectively, we can find a threshold t by first solving Equation (2), as formulated below

$$\begin{cases} p_0 z_0^0 + p_1 z_1^0 = m_0 \\ p_0 z_0^1 + p_1 z_1^1 = m_1 \\ p_0 z_0^2 + p_1 z_1^2 = m_2 \\ p_0 z_0^3 + p_1 z_1^3 = m_3 \end{cases} . \qquad (2)$$

Once z_0, z_1, p_0 and p_1 are obtained, setting the threshold t to a value between the gray scales of p_0th and $(p_0 +1)$th pixels will yield segmentation result I' that preserves the first four moments (i.e., m_0 to m_3) of I (Tsai, 1985). From the above description, we know that to make sure the algorithm uses the same segmentation result in both watermarking and authentication processes, when given the original image I_o and watermarked image I_w, respectively, as the input image I, the algorithm should yield the same values for p_0 and p_1. Because the significant gap between the background and ROI in both I_o and I_w, our experiments have proved the feasibility of the use of the moment-preserving thresholding method. The reader is referred to (Tsai, 1985) for more details about moment-preserving thresholding.

After moment-preserving thresholding, some pixels with low intensity in the ROI may be classified as background pixels. Moreover, the smoother intensity transition across the boundary separating the background and the ROI may also cause misclassification. To compensate for these two types of misclassifications, a morphological operation of 'dilation' with a disk of radius equal to 5 pixels is applied to the segmented ROI so as to allow the ROI to grow and the background area to shrink.

Watermarking

The steps as described in the next three subsections have to be taken in order to watermark mammograms.

Establishing Non-Deterministic Dependence

In order to authenticate the ROI pixels without distorting them, we involve the gray levels of the ROI pixels in the creation of the watermark (authentication code). As discussed in (Kim et al, 2008; Li & Yuan, 2006), non-deterministic block-wise dependence is crucial in thwarting various types of attacks, such as the cut-and-paste attack, the Holliman-Memon counterfeiting attack, the birthday attack and the transplantation attack. Once the segmentation is completed, the ROI pixels are group into overlapping blocks of multiple pixels. By allowing overlapping, each pixel of the ROI appears in multiple ROI blocks, which in turn gets involved in the watermarking process of multiple background pixels, and as a result, get authenticated by multiple background pixels. If the ROI area is greater than the background, we make the number of ROI blocks the same as the number of background pixels and uniquely associate each background pixel with a ROI block in a key-controlled manner. If the ROI area is smaller than the background, only the same number of background pixels as the ROI blocks are selected as *embeddable*, each uniquely associated with a ROI block. The selection of embeddable background pixels and the association between those background pixels and ROI blocks are also key-controlled. The size of the ROI blocks, as discussed in (Li & Yuan, 2006) partially determines the resolution of tamper localization and security, and is to be determined by the user according to the application needs.

Figure 2. RIM-based watermarking with b equal to 3

Watermark Creation

Suppose we want to embed b bits of watermark (authentication code) in each background pixel. To create the b-bit content-dependent watermark, we first convert the gray levels of the pixels of the corresponding ROI block into binary form, rearrange the bits of each binary gray level under the control of a secret key and perform a bit-wise Exclusive OR operation on those rearranged binary values. Finally, b bits from the result of the Exclusive OR operation are chosen, under the control of the secret key, as the watermark.

Watermark Embedding

Distortion resulted from data hiding is always a major concern (Ker, 2009). We employ the RIM embedding method reported in (Li et al, 2009) to embed the b-bit watermark into a background pixel. The idea of embedding the b-bit watermark w in a pixel, with its gray level equal to x, is to assign a modulation index $r(x)$, $r(x) \in \{0, 1, 2, ..., 2^b-1\}$), to each gray level x of the image, with gray level 0 corresponding to a key-generated random modulation index $r(0)$, as shown in Figure 2 with $r(0) = 3$. Since the range of $r(x)$ is smaller than the range of the gray levels, the modulation indexes can be *repeatedly* used to index the gray levels. To embed the b-bit watermark, the gray level, x, of the background pixel is modulated so that the new value x' lands on an index $r(x')$ equal to the value of the b-bit watermark w. Because the indices repeat, watermarking can be achieved by modulating the pixel in question upward or downward, depending on which way results in lower distortion (see Figure 2). The relationship

between the gray level x of each pixel and its corresponding random modulation index $r(x)$ can be formulated as

$$r(x) = \left[r(0) + x\right] \bmod 2^b \qquad (3)$$

where "mod" is the modulo operation. For example, suppose $x = 17$ and the 3-bit watermark $w = 7$. We could hide w in x by changing x to either 12 or 20 because $r(12) = r(20) = w = 7$. However, we can see that changing x to 20 incurs less distortion, therefore, the algorithm will choose to change x to $x' = 20$.

Note that, in order not to provide security gaps to attackers, the inherent characteristics of medical images of various modalities have to be taken into account when watermarking. We observed that, on average, 80% of the pixels in the background areas of mammograms have a gray level of 0. So it is quite easy for an attacker to guess the embedded watermark without knowing the secret key. For example, if the gray level of a background pixel of a *watermarked* mammogram equals 4, the probability that the embedded information equals 4 is 0.8. This is an apparent security gap to be closed. To circumvent this problem, for each zero-valued pixel, we modify its gray level by assigning it a random number in the range of $[0, 2^{b-1}-1]$ generated with the secret key. This pre-processing, if necessary, should be carried out before the watermarking process.

Authentication

To authenticate a watermarked image, the scheme performs the same operations as described in Section 2.1, 2.2.1 and 2.2.2 to calculate the *"original"* b-bit watermark w for each background pixel. To extract the *embedded* watermark w' from each watermarked background pixel x', the scheme simply establishes the correspondence between the elements of the gray level range, with gray level 0 corresponding to a key-generated random modulation index $r(0)$, as described in Section 2.2.3 and shown in Figure 2, and takes the index $r(x')$ corresponding to the gay level of the watermarked pixel x' as the *embedded* watermark w' (i.e., $w' = r(x')$). If $w = w'$, background pixel and the corresponding ROI block are regarded as authentic, Otherwise, they are regarded as manipulated. A bi-level authentication map, with value 255 (0) indicating the authenticity (inauthenticity) of the ROI block could be produced to show the authentication result.

EXPERIMENTS

We have applied the proposed algorithm to various mammograms. Figure 1 demonstrates the process. The size of the images is 460×792 pixels. Figure 1(a) to (c) are the original image, segmented ROIs and background, and the watermarked image (with $b = 3$ and the size of the ROI blocks equal to 4×4 pixels), respectively. The distortion to the background region is so insignificant that we cannot see it (PSNR = 39.65dB). Figure 1(d) shows the attacked watermarked image, with a small bright spot and a larger mass removed. The two white rectangles in Figure 1(e) show the actually locations where the tampering has taken place. By superposing the authentication map on the attacked image, we can locate the manipulations, as shown in Figure 1(f). For comparison purpose, we also use LSB embedding, in which the b-bit watermark is embedded by directly replacing the b least significant bits of the background pixel with the watermark, in place of the RIM embedding method described in Section 2.2.3. The embedding distortion added to the background area in terms

of PSNR is 36.19dB, which is worse then RIM embedding. As discussed in [9], apart from greater distortion, another drawback of LSB embedding is that the very location where the watermark is hidden is known.

CONCLUSION

In this work, we have proposed a novel scheme for authenticating medical images using RIM watermarking technique, which is capable of protecting the region of interest (ROI) without distorting it. The main features of the scheme are:

- By involving the ROI in the creation of a content-dependent watermark and carrying out the embedding in the background area only, the scheme can not only embed higher payload to strengthen security and to increase resolution of tamper localization, but also prevent adding any distortion to the ROI.
- It can resist existing attacks such as the Holliman-Memon counterfeiting attack, the birthday attack and the transplantation attack due to the merit of non-deterministic dependence.
- The balance between security, tamper localization, and embedding distortion can be adjusted by varying the size of the ROI block and the number of watermarkable bits according to the needs of the applications.

REFERENCES

Bao, F., Deng, R. H., Ooi, B. C., & Yang, Y. (2005). Tailored Reversible Watermarking Schemes for Authentication of Electronic Clinical Atlas. *IEEE Transactions on Information Technology in Biomedicine, 9*(4), 554–563. doi:10.1109/TITB.2005.855556

Barreto, P. S. L. M., Kim, H. Y., & Rijmen, V. (2002). Toward Secure Public-key Blockwise Fragile Authentication Watermarking. *IEEE Proceedings - Vision . Image and Signal Processing, 148*(2), 57–62. doi:10.1049/ip-vis:20020168

Coatrieux, G., Maitre, H., & Sankur, B. (2001). Strict Integrity Control of Biomedical Images. *Proc. Security and Watermarking of Multimedia Contents III, SPIE, 4314*, 229–240.

Guo, X., & Zhuang, T. G. (2007). A Region-Based Lossless Watermarking Scheme for Enhancing Security of Medical Data. *Journal of Digital Imaging.* doi:.doi:10.1007/s10278-007-9043-6

Holliman, M., & Memon, N. (2000). Counterfeiting Attacks on Oblivious Block-wise Independent Invisible Watermarking Schemes. *IEEE Transactions on Image Processing, 9*(3), 432–441. doi:10.1109/83.826780

Ker, A. D. (2009). Locally Square Distortion and Batch Steganographic Capacity. *International Journal of Digital Crime and Forensics, 1*(1), 29–44. doi:10.4018/jdcf.2009010102

Kim, H. Y., Pamboukian, S. V. G., & Barreto, S. S. L. M. (2008). Authentication Watermarking for Binary Images . In Li, C.-T. (Ed.), *Multimedia Forensics and Security* (pp. 1–23). Hershey, PA: IGI Global.

Kong, X., & Feng, R. (2001). Watermarking Medical Signals for Telemedicine. *IEEE Transactions on Information Technology in Biomedicine, 5*(3), 195–201. doi:10.1109/4233.945290

Li, C.-T. (2005). Reversible Watermarking Scheme with Image-independent Embedding Capacity. *IEEE Proceedings - Vision . Image, and Signal Processing, 152*(6), 779–786. doi:10.1049/ip-vis:20045041

Li, C.-T., Li, Y., & Wei, C.-H. (2009). Protection of Digital Mammograms on PACSs Using Data Hiding Techniques. *International Journal of Digital Crime and Forensics, 1*(1), 60–75. doi:10.4018/jdcf.2009010105

Li, C.-T., & Yuan, Y. (2006). Digital Watermarking Scheme Exploiting Non-deterministic Dependence for Image Authentication. *Optical Engineering (Redondo Beach, Calif.), 45*(12), 127001-1–127001-6. doi:10.1117/1.2402932

Lie, W.-N., Hsu, T.-L., & Lin, G.-S. (2003). Verification of Image Content integrity by Using Dual Watermarking on Wavelets Domain. *Proceedings of IEEE International Conference on Image Processing, 2*, 487–490.

Osborne, D., Abbott, D., Sorell, M., & Rogers, D. (2004). Multiple Embedding Using Robust watermarks for Wireless medical Images. *Proceedings of the 3rd International Conference on Mobile and Ubiquitous Multimedia* (pp. 245–250).

Planitz, B. M., & Maeder, A. J. (2005). *A Study of Block-based Medical Image Watermarking using a Perceptual Similarity Metric. Proceedings of Digital Imaging Computing: techniques and Applications.* DICTA.

Stallings, W. (1998). *Cryptography and Network Security – Principles and Practice.* Prentice Hall.

Thodi, D. M., & Rodriguez, J. J. (2007). Expansion Embedding Techniques for Reversible Watermarking. *IEEE Transactions on Image Processing, 16*(3), 721–730. doi:10.1109/TIP.2006.891046

Tsai, W. H. (1985). Moment-Preserving Thresholding: a New Approach. *Computer Vision Graphics and Image Processing, 29*(3), 377–393. doi:10.1016/0734-189X(85)90133-1

Wakatani, A. (2002). Digital Watermarking for ROI Medical Images by Using Compressed Signature Image. *Proceedings of the 35ᵗʰ Hawaii International Conference on System Sciences, 6,* 157-163.

Zhou, X. Q., Huang, H. K., & Lou, S. L. (2001). Authenticity and Integrity of Digital Mammography Images. *IEEE Transactions on Medical Imaging, 20*(8), 784–791. doi:10.1109/42.938246

Section 4
Application of Pattern Recognition and Signal Processing Techniques to Digital Forensics

Chapter 15
Unexpected Artifacts in a Digital Photograph

Matthew J. Sorell
University of Adelaide, Australia

ABSTRACT

This chapter investigates an unexpected phenomenon observed in a recent digital photograph, in which the logo of a non-sponsoring sports company appears on the jersey of a famous football player in just one of a sequence of images. After eliminating deliberate image tampering as a cause, a hypothetical sequence of circumstances is proposed, concerning the lighting, dominant colours, infrared sensitivity, optical pre-processing, image enhancement and JPEG compression. The hypotheses are tested using a digital SLR camera. The investigation is of interest in a forensic context, firstly as a possible explanation in case such a photograph is observed, and secondly to be able to confirm or refute claims of such artifacts put forward claiming that a hypothetical image is not really what it claims to be.

MOTIVATION

Recently, the author was approached by a South Australian police officer with an intriguing and unusual sequence of images. He had been photographing Brazilian footballer Romario during his short time with the Adelaide United FC, and noticed that in the midst of the sequence of images, there was a prominent but phantom *Adidas* logo on the player's jersey, which was otherwise adorned only with *Reebok* logos. Adament that the image had come straight from his camera, an explanation for how such a logo could have appeared was sought. The relevant section of the image is shown in Figure 1, alongside images taken 26 seconds before and 8 seconds after the image of interest. The original image file is available from the author on request.

Some further information is helpful. The photographs were taken on a warm, but not hot, cloudy

DOI: 10.4018/978-1-60960-515-5.ch015

Figure 1. The relevant extracted area of the sequence of three images of the football player. In the central image, the Adidas logo is clearly visible. The Exif metadata timestamps indicate the photographs were taken at (a) 11:10:01, (b) 11:10:27 and (c) 11:10:34. (Photo J Venditto, used with permission)

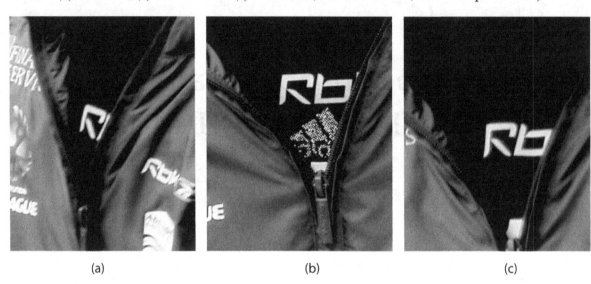

(a)   (b)   (c)

summer day in December 2006 in Adelaide, Australia, with flash-assisted lighting according to the file's metadata. There is clearly a white collar beneath the jersey collar in Figure 1(b), suggestive of a white undershirt (or at least, a t-shirt with a white collar) beneath the jersey. The photographs were taken using an Olympus Stylus 410D, confirmed by visual inspection and the Exif metadata in the image files at full (4 Mega-pixel) resolution and high quality (to meet an image file size of approximately 900KB).

The camera's xD memory card was imaged and a total of 108 JPEG photograph files were recovered. Metadata and JPEG image file header structures and parameters were carefully inspected, showing that all photograph files were mutually consistent in their names, timestamps, file sizes and JPEG coefficients such as Quantization Tables. Although it is possible, in theory, to duplicate the characteristics of a JPEG file generated from particular firmware, the knowledge and tools required to do this are well beyond the normal image counterfeiter.

The relevant sequence of images were also closely inspected by a recognised expert in scientific photography, who confirmed that the logo artifact was so well integrated into the image as to suggest very strongly that the logo could not have been inserted after the fact. The phantom logo is present in the image thumbnail contained within the image file, which is also entirely consistent with the image file structure generated by the camera.

A close inspection highlights several features of the logo, as shown in Figure 2. The first is that it is not solid but appears in a checkerboard pattern. The second is that the edges are well contained within the lines of the tracksuit zip, and the third is that JPEG artifacts evident within the image do not suggest secondary compression. These three factors are strong indicators against image tampering.

The original image in Figure 3 shows that the *Adidas* logo is close to the centre of the image. This location supports the notion that some enhancement, including the decision to use flash in-fill, has taken place within the camera, and that

Figure 2. A close-up view of the phantom logo. (Photo J Venditto, used with permission)

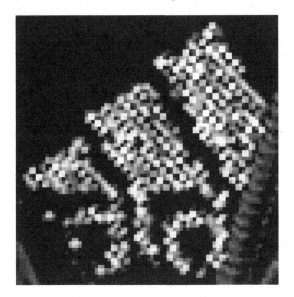

this processing might be a part of the explanation for the appearance of the logo.

Source of the Adidas Logo

The Adidas logo corresponds precisely to the size, shape and location of the logo on the jersey of several well-known football teams, including the Liverpool Football Club home colours, and the France Football Club away colours. Importantly, in the latter case, the background colour is red, and both the logo and the collar are white. It has not been possible to confirm what, precisely, the player was wearing in the photograph, nor can it be inferred that he is wearing the France Football Club jersey underneath the Adelaide United jersey. However, it is clear that the position and colouring of the logo is consistent with available clothing and it is therefore viable to suggest that the player is indeed wearing an undershirt which might be another jersey or similar shirt with a white collar, a white logo, and a darker background colour, possibly red.

The next question is to establish how such a logo could be detected through the external jersey in the photograph.

Imaging Stages in a Digital Camera

In this section, we review the processing stages of a digital image in the Olympus Stylus 410D and similar cameras. Note that these stages can differ significantly in other types of digital camera.

Figure 3. The full image of interest (sanitised). (Photo J Venditto, used with permission)

Optical Stage

The camera of interest has a compact 5.8mm to 17.4mm zoom lens which is of little interest in the camera of concern, except to note the lens system is conventional and displays the usual large depth of field with a small depth of focus typical of compact Digital Still Cameras. Such optical systems typically maintain focus on both the foreground and background from a metre or so to infinity, and it can be seen from Figure 3 that the image of interest exhibits reasonable focus on both the faces of the football player and the boy in the foreground, and the detail in the background.

Light is passed through several filters before reaching the imaging sensor. The first stage is an optical low pass filter, sometimes referred to as a blurring filter, made from multiple layers of birefringent material such as liquid crystal or lithium niobate. The purpose of this filter is to avoid aliasing (Moiré effect) caused by the pitch of the imaging pixels interacting with patterns in the scene. This is of particular relevance in the case of this image, because the football jersey material consists of a fine mesh with a distinctive weave pattern at a pitch of around 2mm, corresponding to approximately 4 pixels in this image. The optical low-pass filter effectively filters out detail below the resolution of the imaging sensor, but takes this one step further to ensure that the minimum resolution is in fact a width of two pixels to avoid false colour artifacts in the colour interpolation process. From the well-known Nyquist criterion, this means that the sampling rate is two pixels and the maximum spatial frequency corresponds to a spatial period of four pixels. Importantly, it appears that in this particular image the filter's cutoff spatial frequency corresponds very closely to the weave of the football jersey. Therefore, it is to be expected that if the logo is visible through the weave of the jersey, such visibility would be at a spatial frequency critical to the optical filter and likely to be enhanced at later stages of processing.

Infrared Sensitivity

The sensitivity of silicon optical sensors to infrared light in the range of wavelengths from 750nm to 1087nm is well known, as discussed in Janesick (2001). Above this wavelength (far infrared), photon energy is too low to excite an electron in the sensor. It is easy to demonstrate infrared sensitivity, in fact, using the well known "remote control test", in which an infrared remote control LED is photographed in subdued visible light. A separate infrared cut-out filter is required to avoid strong colour distortion caused by infrared illumination. In the absence of such a filter, digital photographs taken in sunlight often exhibit a washed-out purple haze.

The effectiveness of the infrared cut-out filter is compromised by the need to pass visible red light with limited attenuation, and so it should come as no surprise that all Digital Still Cameras exhibit some level of infrared sensitivity. In fact, popular resources such as McCreary (undated) discuss how to take infrared photographs using both modified and unmodified Digital Still Cameras. Another popular website *maxmax.com* (undated) discusses infrared-transparent fabric using the inaccurate term "x-ray photography".

It has not been possible to test the Stylus 410D camera of interest for infrared sensitivity, but the question of whether infrared sensitivity has a role to play in this case is of interest, especially given that the photograph was taken in indirect sunlight. For this reason, an experiment was set up using a Pentax *ist DL digital SLR camera to photograph a black logo through a similar red football jersey, as shown in Figure 4. A 720nm infrared-pass filter (Hoya R72) was used to block visible light in the test image, and the brightness and contrast of the digital image was adjusted to enhance the visibility of the hidden black logo. The image was captured in RAW format and image post-processing was performed using proprietary Pentax software to convert the image to 16-bit TIFF format.

Figure 4. A white t-shirt with a prominent black line image was placed inside a red football jersey and photographed using a Pentax *ist DL digital SLR camera with Hoya R72 (720nm) infrared pass filter. Contrast and brightness has been adjusted to enhance visibility.

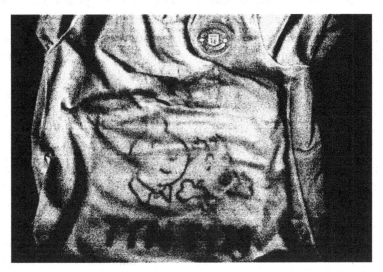

The Pentax *ist DL camera was used in the experiments carried out because of the degree of control available over its functions, the availability of an infrared filter, and direct access to the 12-bit pixel measurements extracted from *raw* (unprocessed) image files.

Similar photographs were also taken without the R72 filter, which, when adjusted significantly for brightness and contrast, show that the black artwork can be seen in bright visible light, as can be seen in Figure 5.

Significant effort was expended to investigate such visibility further. It was found that the line

Figure 5. In visible light, the black image is visible through the football jersey when contrast and brightness are adjusted strongly to enhance visibility

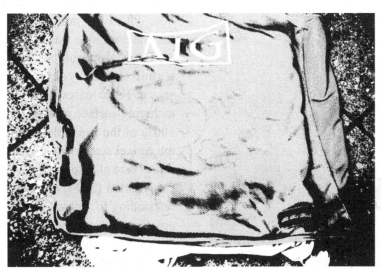

art could be readily detected under bright sunlight, with or without the infrared filter, although visibility was much stronger with an infrared pass filter in place. Artificial light was also investigated, including fluorescent light (containing minimal power at infrared wavelengths), and very bright red, green, blue and infrared LED arrays. It was found that only under fluorescent light was it possible to detect the line art, as shown in Figure 6. Even long exposure under a bank of high brightness infrared LEDs did not lead to a detectable logo, and so it is necessary to conclude that the dominant factor in the detection of the phantom Adidas logo is visible-light transmission through the weave of the football jersey in bright light.

Colour Filter and Microlens

The Olympus Stylus 410D camera, like most compact Digital Still Cameras, uses a Bayer colour

Figure 6. A close-up and contrast-enhanced view of black line-art through the football jersey fabric with no infrared filter under fluorescent light. This image demonstrates that infrared sensitivity is not a necessary condition for the phantom logo detection in the image of interest.

mosaic to differentiate image colours, as described in Nakamura (2006). The imager is divided into blocks of 2x2 pixels, with filters passing green and red in one row, and blue and green in the second, repeating across the entire sensor. Each pixel therefore detects light at the matching red, green or blue spectrum of the respective filter. The missing colour components are interpolated from neighbouring pixels later in the electronic processing stages of the image capture process.

It is worth noting that the football jersey of interest is predominantly red. This has two implications for understanding the image. The first is that any white logo visible through the weave of the jersey is likely to show up relatively brightly in the blue and green sensors compared to the background levels, consistent with subsequent image processing algorithms identifying the phantom logo as a matter of interest for enhancement. The second matter is that infrared light is usually most visible in the red sensor, since the pigments used in the green and blue pixel filters can more effectively eliminate infrared than the red pigments (although significant infrared sensitivity remains in blue and green pixels). This implies that if infrared light were a significant issue, it would have little effect in green and blue, and the effect in red would be a slight increase in the intensity of an overall bright red. Hence it is reasonable to conclude, once again, that infrared sensitivity does not have a primary role in explaining how the phantom logo was detected.

The final optical stage in a Digital Still Camera is a microlens array on the surface of the electronic sensor. These lenses effectively increase the light gathering surface area of each pixel to close to 100% of the available area. For example, the 4 megapixel sensor in the camera of interest has a sensor size of 5.76mm by 4.32mm (see Olympus Corporation (2004) and Nakamura (2006)) corresponding to a pixel area of 2.5 x 2.5 μm. The aperture area over the photodiode at each pixel, in contrast, is typically around 10-20% of the pixel area, a figure referred to as the *fill factor*.

This observation is of little relevance to the image of interest, other than to note that the combination of optical low-pass filter, Bayer colour array, microlens array and pixel array leads to a consistent spatial sampling frequency of very close to four pixels per jersey weave hole (pitched at approximately 2mm), corresponding to the critical Nyquist frequency, or highest spatial frequency of image artefacts, which the camera is designed to capture.

Exposure and Lighting

According to the Exif metadata (see JEITA (2002)) contained within the file of the image of interest, the camera used a multi-segment exposure measurement to ensure a compromise in the lighting between the centre of the photograph and the background, referred to in the Owner's Manual (see Olympus Corporation (2004)) as "ESP mode". The background in this case was sunlit, but the face of the football player is in shadow and therefore the flash has been used to provide additional in-fill lighting. The exposure was set automatically with an exposure of 1/100 second.

Test photographs were taken using the Pentax *ist DL camera to duplicate the effect of flash in-fill in sun shadow. In shadow, it was not possible to isolate line art underneath a football jersey; with flash in-fill using similar settings to those in the image of interest, it is possible to discern the line art, as shown in Figure 7.

Image Capture, Processing and Enhancement

Having established that it is possible for the phantom logo to have been detected optically, most likely through the weave of the jersey with the possibility of an enhanced effect due to infrared sensitivity, it is now necessary to consider the image processing steps which would lead to the prominence of the logo in the final image. It is clear that the detected print-through effect is not

prominent in experimental images except under extreme adjustment of brightness and contrast.

After digital image capture quantised in the case of the Stylus 410D camera to 12 bits, the red, green and blue pixels undergo a *gamma correction* process. This is a non-linear operation which is a combination of noise floor reduction, contrast enhancement and non-linear amplification of low intensity pixels. It is clear that the small contrast difference between the foreground and phantom logo pixels would be slightly enhanced by this process which is standard across all Digital Still Cameras. Charge Coupled Device sensors are inherently very linear in their response to light, the gamma correction process is usually targeted at ensuring normalising the image to work with existing systems and protocols, including JPEG compression, CRT and LCD display.

Figure 7. It is possible to discern line art, in this case a capital T, through football jersey fabric in shadowed sunlight, provided that a flash is used to provide infill lighting (contrast and brightness adjusted)

The next phase of processing is the interpolation of colour planes. This is a proprietary process in which the red and green values for a pixel with a blue measurement (for example) are interpolated from neighbouring pixels. A simple algorithm for colour interpolation is to average the values of neighbouring pixels of the same colour, but in fact more sophisticated filter kernels are used which take into account pixels of different colours and more distant neighbours to perform functions of interpolation, colour correction due to cross-colour bleeding in the colour filter, and colour enhancement.

Colour enhancement recognises that photographic images need to look natural to the human eye and brain, but this does not necessarily mean representing the original measured colour intensities precisely. Instead, corrections are made to correct for the spectrum of the lighting (*white balance*), and chrominance is usually enhanced so that reds look more red, blues look more blue, etc. Such colour enhancement has, by convention and the limitations of technology, been carried out uniformly across an entire image in film and digital cameras, but with modern digital signal processing it is possible to adjust colour enhancement parameters to better suit different regions in an image.

Colour enhancement is of particular interest in this case because the phantom logo appears in an area which is otherwise predominantly red. It can be speculated that perhaps white reflections of the phantom logo are being detected by blue and green pixel sensors in this case, and an adaptive white balance algorithm is thus normalising these otherwise faint pixels to represent white in this part of the image. Without access to the firmware or algorithms incorporated in the Olympus Stylus 410D camera, however, it is not possible to take this speculation further. Nevertheless, colour enhancement is a feasible partial explanation for the phantom logo effect.

The final stage of image processing is a so-called *unsharp mask filter*, which is widely implemented according to Sato (2006) to "boost the high-frequency component of the image" and thus enhance fine level detail in an image through synthetic amplification of high spatial frequency components. The algorithm is described in that reference. The result is that high resolution detail is amplified in the overall image. Figure 8 clearly demonstrates the sharpening effect on a test checkerboard matrix.

While such filtering can be carried out uniformly over an entire image, there are strong suggestions that Olympus cameras in general, and the camera of interest in particular, implement an adaptive unsharp mask filter which is particularly strong in areas of poor contrast. A number of camera reviews have consistently made this

Figure 8. A checkerboard test matrix at the sampling resolution of the camera clearly shows the effect of image sharpening. Image (a) is the raw image data with simple (mean of nearest neighbour) colour interpolation and linear brightness/contrast adjustment to enhance visibility. Image (b) is the same test image after proprietary camera gamma and noise correction. Image (c) incorporates image sharpening. The features of the checkerboard test array are clearly strongly enhanced.

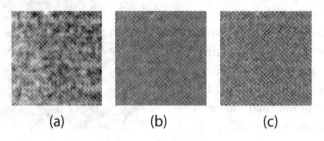

(a)   (b)   (c)

observation, such as The Imaging Resource (2005), which notes that

"A much bigger resolution issue was the Stylus 410's over-aggressive noise reduction system. Regardless of how bright the lighting was, any time the local contrast dropped below a fairly high level, the anti-noise processing leapt into action, turning subtle subject detail into mush."

The most likely explanation, then, for the strongly enhanced phantom logo image, is that the camera's adaptive unsharp mask filter has identified the logo region as requiring strong image sharpening enhancement, possibly to retain white balance and contrast consistency with such areas as the Reebok logo above it. The highest spatial frequency which can be enhanced has a period of four pixels, coincidentally corresponding in this case with the logo features being detected through the weave of the jersey. It is this coincidence, more than any other factor, which is likely to be the primary explanation for the extremely unusual enhancement of the phantom logo.

A final experiment was carried out to determine the extent to which such strong enhancement is typical of this camera, using the 105 images extracted from the original sequence of images of the same size (2272 x 1704 pixels). In order to describe the experiment, it is necessary to provide some background on JPEG image compression. A more comprehensive description of JPEG image compression can be found in Wallace (1991).

JPEG Compression

The red, green and blue image planes of the image are translated into luminance and chrominance representation. Luminance represents the weighted brightness of each pixel, while chrominance-blue represents the blue-ness versus green-ness and chrominance-red the red-ness versus green-ness of each pixel, according to the simple linear transform:

$$\begin{bmatrix} Y \\ C_b \\ C_r \end{bmatrix} = \begin{bmatrix} 0.2988 & 0.5869 & 0.1143 \\ -0.1689 & -0.3311 & 0.5000 \\ 0.5000 & -0.4189 & -0.0811 \end{bmatrix} \begin{bmatrix} R \\ G \\ B \end{bmatrix}$$

The chrominance planes are usually downsampled (two pixels in a row or column, or four pixels in a 2x2 matrix are averaged) since the eye's colour-sensitive cones do not distinguish high resolution chrominance detail. The luminance plane is retained at full resolution since the eye, through its 120 million rods which are sensitive over a wide range of visible wavelengths, is able to distinguish high resolution detail in luminance.

Each plane is then transformed using a two-dimensional discrete cosine transformation (DCT), a special case of a Fourier transform, into the spatial frequency domain. This is done by segmenting the image into *microblocks* of 8x8 pixels and representing each block as 64 frequency coefficients. The result is that each coefficient effectively represents a pattern match with the templates shown in Figure 9, with large magnitude coefficients indicating a strong match (large negative coefficients indicate a strong match if bright and dark pixels were inverted).

Noting that the phantom logo of interest, as shown in Figure 2, contains a strong checkerboard effect, it is reasonable to measure the strength of checkerboard (high frequency) coefficients as an indicator of the extent to which such coefficients are normal.

Figure 10 is such a representation of the image of interest. For each 8x8 microblock, a single pixel is plotted which represents the normalised sum of the 10 highest frequency coefficient absolute values in the bottom right hand corner of the coefficient matrix. It is immediately apparent that the phantom logo dominates this representation – the microblocks containing the logo contain very high magnitude high frequency coefficients. In fact, in all other parts of the image, high frequency coefficients are only found at sharp edges, as expected,

Figure 9. Discrete Cosine Transformation template. The top left-hand corner represents the average intensity, while the bottom right-hand corner represents a match with a checker-board pattern. These coefficients are then quantized so that low frequency features are retained, and the general structure of high frequency components are retained but the high frequency detail is generally discarded. Only high frequency features with strong coefficients are generally retained in a JPEG image.

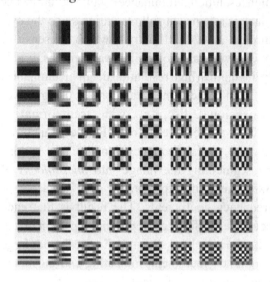

and in areas of expected high detail, such as the other logos on the tracksuit top.

In order to understand normal high frequency coefficient distribution, all 105 images of the same size taken by the same camera were considered in the same way. The maximum of the 105 sums of the ten highest-frequency coefficient absolute values in each macroblock are plotted in Figure 11. Each distinct bright line in this image represents a sharp edge or other detailed element in one of the photographs, whether this be a string of lights, jewellery, or other sharply contrasting edge. It can be seen by careful comparison with Figure 10 that the phantom logo at coordinates (160,145) is visible, but does not dominate overall, indicating that such strong high spatial frequencies are not uncommon artifacts in images generated by this camera.

JPEG compression also explains why there is no evidence of the phantom logo in the other images photographed at the time of the image of interest. The logo appears at a high spatial frequency through the weave of the jersey, but unless the high spatial frequencies are present in the compressed JPEG image, there is no evidence of

Figure 10. The absolute sum of high frequency coefficients in the phantom logo image of interest. The logo is centred at (160,145) in this image.

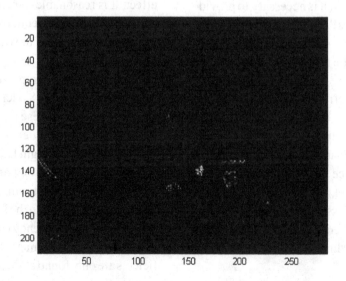

Figure 11. The absolute sum of high frequency coefficients was computed for each macroblock in 105 available images and the maximum sum is plotted here, showing that strong high spatial frequencies are not unusual in images produced by the Olympus Stylus 410D camera

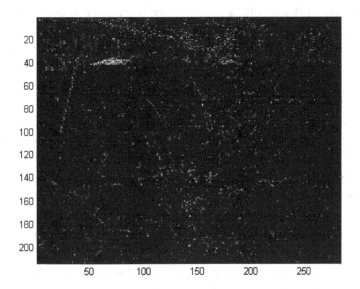

the logo. Since JPEG typically quantizes high frequency coefficients very coarsely (and does so, specifically, in the JPEG implementation used by the camera of interest), unless high frequencies have been significantly enhanced prior to JPEG compression, the high frequency coefficients are most likely to be rounded to zero, so that no high frequency artefacts are present. Such rounding may also further enhance strong high-frequency artefacts through rounding-up to larger quantized coefficients than present originally.

DISCUSSION

The photograph of interest has been generated under an extremely unusual set of circumstances which have, together, led to an image with a phantom phenomenon, and a robust provenance to counter the view that the image has been synthetically tampered with. Furthermore, experimental results demonstrate that it is indeed possible for

such a logo to be detected and enhanced by the camera's on-board image processing algorithms.

The set of circumstances is summarised here:

1. Provenance
   a. The photographer is a senior detective with a particular interest in the use of digital photographs as evidence.
   b. It has been shown that a shirt consistent with the white collar and white Adidas logo at the right location and size is available commercially.
   c. The image file was extracted directly from an xD memory with 107 other photos. The file structure, timestamps and file sizes are consistent.
   d. The metadata and JPEG coefficients and file formatting is consistent with the other photographs and independently verified images from the same make and model of camera.
   e. The image has been inspected by a forensic photography expert who has

determined that the image does not show signs of tampering.

2. Image sensing
   a. It has been demonstrated that a logo can generate visible artifacts through a football jersey in sunlight, fluorescent light, electronic flash, and electronic flash in-fill with indirect sunlight
   b. It has been demonstrated that a digital camera is infrared sensitive and that a phantom logo effect is very visible through an infrared filter. However, it has also been shown as above that infrared sensitivity is not a necessary condition for the effect to appear.
   c. Measurements indicate that the pitch of the weave of the football jersey corresponds to a spatial frequency very close to four pixels, which is the Nyquist spatial sampling rate of the camera, taking into account optical low pass filtering and the Bayer colour filter matrix.

3. Image processing
   a. White balance and colour enhancement processes have been described, which adaptively adjust colour intensities to meet the perceptive expectations of the human eye and brain. These processes would have enhanced the phantom logo to some degree.
   b. The unsharp mask filter process enhances high spatial frequency components of the image, particularly at spatial periods of a few pixels. It is this process more than any other which has enhanced the phantom logo, noting that the camera of interest is known to implement particularly aggressive filtering in areas of low contrast.

The investigation of this image is of relevance to the question of the veracity of digital imagery as forensic evidence. The photograph itself is evidence that it is possible for artifacts not normally visible to the human eye to be detected and enhanced in a digital image. However it must be realised that it is only because of several factors occurring in combination, particularly the lighting of the scene, the matching of the pitch of the weave of the jersey with the sampling rate of the digital sensor, and the particular adaptive image enhancement processing of the camera of interest, that such an image has been produced. It should further be observed that as far as the author is aware, no such image has previously been brought forward in academic or popular literature. It may therefore be considered to be an extremely rare example brought about by an extremely unusual confluence of circumstances.

It is very rare for such artifacts to appear in a digital still image. If such artifacts were claimed to appear in a photograph of forensic value, it has been demonstrated that although possible, the veracity of such a claim could be tested against the conditions described in this paper.

ACKNOWLEDGMENT

The author would like to acknowledge the assistance of Detective Superintendent John Venditto, Officer in Charge, Major Crime Investigation Branch of the South Australian Police for making his camera and photographs available, Brian Ng for providing a football jersey for experiments and helpful discussions, and to Gale Spring of RMIT University for assistance in visual analysis of the photograph.

REFERENCES

Janesick, J. R. (2001). *Scientific charge-coupled devices*. Bellingham, WA: SPIE. doi:10.1117/3.374903

JEITA. (2002). JEITA CP-3451 Exchangeable image file format for digital still cameras: Exif Version 2.2. Japan Electronics and Information Technology Industries Association maxmax.com (n.d.). *X-Ray Examples*. Retrieved May 27, 2008, from http://maxmax.com/aX-RayExamples.htm

McCreary, J. (n.d.). *Infrared (IR) basics for digital photographers – capturing the unseen*. Retrieved May 27, 2008, from http://www.dpfwiw.com/ir.htm

Nakamura, J. (2006). Basics of Image Sensors. In Nakamura, J. (Ed.), *Image Sensors and Signal Processing for Digital Still Cameras* (pp. 53–93). Boca Raton, FL: Taylor & Francis Group.

Olympus Corporation. (2004). *Stylus 410 Digital Reference Manual*. Tokyo, Japan. Item reference number VT694002

Sato, K. (2006). Image-Processing Algorithms. In Nakamura, J. (Ed.), *Image Sensors and Signal Processing for Digital Still Cameras* (pp. 223–253). Boca Raton, FL: Taylor & Francis Group.

The Imaging Resource. (2005). Quick Review - Olympus Stylus 410 Digital Camera. Retrieved May 27, 2008, from http://www.imaging-resource.com/PRODS/OS410/OS41A.HTM

Wallace, G. K. (1991, April). The JPEG Still Picture Compression Standard. *Communications of the ACM, 34*(4), 30–44. doi:10.1145/103085.103089

Chapter 16
Conditions for Effective Detection and Identification of Primary Quantization of Re-Quantized JPEG Images

Matthew J. Sorell
University of Adelaide, Australia

ABSTRACT

The choice of Quantization Table in a JPEG image has previously been shown to be an effective discriminator of digital image cameras by manufacturer and model series. When a photograph is recompressed for transmission or storage, however, the image undergoes a secondary stage of quantization. It is possible, however, to identify primary quantization artifacts in the image coefficients, provided that certain image and quantization conditions are met. This chapter explores the conditions under which primary quantization coefficients can be identified, and hence can be used image source identification. Forensic applications include matching a small range of potential source cameras to an image.

INTRODUCTION

In previous work (Sorell, 2008) which is summarized briefly in this chapter, the author demonstrated that the choice of Quantization Table in the JPEG image compression algorithm used in a digital camera is highly dependent on the particular camera manufacturer, and to a lesser extent on the model series. A sample set of over 5000 digital photographs were used to extract 330 Quantization Tables from 27 different camera models from 10

brands, and it was shown that just 42 Tables were common to more than one camera model. After aggregating the results by camera model *series*, just 25 tables were found to be common across more than one manufacturer, and of this set, 19 of a possible 20 were common to the manufacturers Nikon and Olympus, suggesting a common source of JPEG encoding algorithm.

The Quantization Table is a useful source discriminator in cases where metadata (notably Exif metadata, see JEITA (2002)) has been removed or is suspected of having been modified. Under certain conditions, the effect of the original

DOI: 10.4018/978-1-60960-515-5.ch016

quantization can also survive subsequent compression, such that it is at least possible to narrow down the range of potential source cameras of a recompressed image of interest. Further, if the quantization history of a set of images can be established, it is possible to collate image sets by that quantization history.

In Sorell (2008), a multi-hypothesis test based on the 330 sample Quantization Tables was demonstrated, using a weighted sum of matched filters for each of the 64 quantization coefficients. This chapter takes that analysis further, by examining the conditions under which detection of two-stage quantization is possible, using these results to establish the subset of plausible primary Quantization Tables.

Previous work on this problem includes Farid (2006), which provided an incomplete analysis based on single photographs from 300 candidate cameras; Lukáš and Fridrich (2003), which used a neural network approach for pattern matching; and Neelamani et al (2006), which focused on a maximum-likelihood approach for overall Quantization Table estimation.

MOTIVATION

In Sorell (2008), we used multiple commercial online sources to identify as many camera brands and models as we could find as listed on January 1, 2007. We identified over 70 brands of cameras and mobile phones with built-in cameras, with a total of over 2500 models. We note that many camera models follow an obvious series within a particular brand and that some cameras are identical but have different model names depending on the market in which the cameras are released. In addition, we recognise that our list is almost certainly incomplete and that some are branded versions of unbranded OEM (original equipment manufacturer) models.

Various market sources indicate that over 500 million digital cameras, and a similar number of

mobile phones with in-built digital cameras, had been sold worldwide by the end of 2006. It is well known that digital photography has almost completely displaced conventional film photography in the consumer market, and it is common knowledge that digital photography bypasses the conventional censorship bottleneck available through a film development service.

A further challenge is that as film cameras are withdrawn from the market, crime scene forensic photography will be forced to move from film to digital equipment. The challenge is to establish the forensic chain of evidence in such a way that digital images (not to mention digital video) can meet the burden of proof in court. Thus, the development of digital camera forensic techniques is timely.

The number of camera models available actually suits forensic purposes quite well – small enough that a complete database of all cameras is technically and commercially viable, but large enough that identification of the make and model series of a candidate camera is of significant assistance in forensic investigation.

JPEG COMPRESSION

The JPEG standard is defined in ITU (1993) and the details of the standard are given in Wallace (1991) for the interested reader. There are a number of modes of operation of the JPEG compression algorithm, but we consider only the progressive mode which is designed for lossy compression of continuous-toned images and is ubiquitously implemented in digital cameras and image editing software. The JPEG compression stages are introduced briefly here.

Image Compression

The JPEG compression algorithm takes as its input three color planes representing Red, Green and Blue light. These undergo a reversible color-space transform into Luminance (Y), Chrominance Red (Cr) and Chrominance Blue (Cb). The Y plane is identical to that used in black-and-white television and contains high resolution information which stimulates the many broad-spectrum rods in the eye. The Cb and Cr planes represented the "coloredness" of the image, stimulating the color-sensitive optical cones, which are far less sensitive in resolution. The chrominance planes are therefore downsampled, or averaged, to reduce the data in these planes by 50% or 75%.

The next stage is to consider the three planes independently and perform a spatial frequency transformation, in the form of a two-dimensional discrete cosine transformation (DCT), on "microblocks" of 8-by-8 pixels. This transform is also reversible, but importantly it separates the representation of the microblocks into broad contrast and fine detail. As the eye is sensitive to broad contrast and fine textures, but is much less sensitive to fine detail, the transformed coefficients can now be coarsely quantized. The high spatial frequencies are rounded off in quite large quanta, while low spatial frequencies are typically rounded off in significantly smaller quanta. It is this stage which provides significant lossy compression, as the corresponding rounded numbers can now be stored efficiently using conventional lossless compression techniques.

Quantization Tables

The rounding off of the DCT coefficients is determined by Quantization Tables which are specific to the implementation of the JPEG compression software used by a particular manufacturer. A particular camera will often use multiple tables, usually to meet some specified range of file size or quality level.

Different Quantization Tables are used for the luminance versus the chrominance planes. Up to four Quantization Tables are supported by the standard, but in practice it is common to use just one or two (using a common table for both chrominance planes).

The JPEG standard (ITU, 1993) provides example Quantization Tables, but the work in Sorell (2008) identified these examples only in thumbnail preview images. In practice, the Quantization Table is an effective discriminator of manufacturer and camera model series.

Quantization Table as a Discriminator

The use of the Quantization Table as a source discriminator has previously been mentioned by Lukáš et al (2006) and considered in detail by Farid (2006). In that paper however, Farid investigated just one image each from over 300 cameras and concluded that there was insufficient discrimination to warrant further interest. Our investigation leads to quite a different interpretation.

We sourced 5485 photographic images from friends and colleagues, each of whom provided a range of original images from their own digital camera. In all, images from 27 different camera types, from 10 brands, were obtained, as summarised in Table 1. We considered only the Quantization Table for the Luminance Plane, but we note that the Quantization Table or Tables for the Chrominance Plane might in some cases offer an additional level of discrimination.

A total of 330 Quantization Tables were extracted from our dataset of images, of which 42 were common to at least two camera models. A review of the common Quantization Tables revealed obvious systematic commonality amongst similar cameras from the same manufacturer, as well as incidental commonality between unrelated cameras. The obvious camera groupings are given in Table 2.

It should be noted that the Quantization Tables extracted for each camera are almost certainly not exhaustive. The only way to be sure of having an exhaustive list is to request such information from

Table 1. Sample images and number of quantization tables by camera model in our dataset

Manufacturer	Camera Model	Images	Quantization Tables Identified
Canon	Canon DIGITAL IXUS 400	2	1
	Canon DIGITAL IXUS 700	25	3
	Canon EOS 10D	14	1
	Canon EOS 300D DIGITAL	45	2
	Canon IXY DIGITAL 70	15	1
	Canon PowerShot A40	46	1
	Canon PowerShot A620	336	1
	Canon PowerShot G6	89	2
Casio	EX-Z40	311	63
Eastman Kodak Company	DC210 Zoom (V05.00)	165	1
	KODAK DC240 ZOOM DIGITAL CAMERA	37	1
Nikon	COOLPIX P2	27	14
	COOLPIX S3	34	8
	S1	9	8
Olympus	C760UZ	517	33
	FE100,X710	253	193
	C750UZ	82	27
Panasonic	DMC-FX8	1	1
	DMC-FZ7	104	19
PENTAX Corporation	PENTAX *ist DL	706	1
	PENTAX *ist DS	418	1
Samsung Techwin	U-CA 3 Digital camera	30	2
SONY	CD MAVICA	322	9
	DCR-DVD803E	310	3
	DSC-P92	1363	19
	DSC-P93	207	6
(unknown OEM)	DigitalCam Pro	17	1

manufacturers or to reverse-engineer the cameras' firmware. The grouping of cameras as shown above is based primarily on the evidence of common Quantization Tables as extracted in our experiment, but we have also considered the model series and in some cases reference to operation manuals to confirm membership of a series.

There is some commonality between camera series which are for the most part coincidental, with one significant exception as shown in Table 3.

A total of 25 tables were found to be common to more than one camera series. Of particular note is that 19 tables (of a possible 20) are common to both Nikon and Olympus series, suggesting that both manufacturers are using the same JPEG encoder.

Table 2. Natural groupings of camera series by common quantization tables

Camera Group	Included Models	Total Quantization Tables	Total Quantization Tables in Common
Canon IX+PS	Canon DIGITAL IXUS 400 Canon DIGITAL IXUS 700 Canon IXY DIGITAL 70 Canon PowerShot A40 Canon PowerShot A620 Canon PowerShot G6	3	2
Canon EOS	Canon EOS 10D Canon EOS 300D DIGITAL	2	2
Casio	EXZ40	63	n/a
Kodak	DC210 Zoom (V05.00) KODAK DC240 ZOOM DIGITAL CAMERA	1	1
Nikon	COOLPIX P2 COOLPIX S3 S1	20	8
Olympus C7	C760UZ C750UZ	33	27
Olympus F	FE100,X710	193	n/a/
Pentax	PENTAX *ist DL PENTAX *ist DS	1	1
Samsung	U-CA 3 Digital camera	1	n/a
Sony DCR	DCR-DVD803E	3	n/a
Sony P9x	CD MAVICA DSC-P92 DSC-P93	21	10
OEM	DigitalCam Pro	1	n/a
Panasonic X	DMC-FX8	1	n/a
Panasonic Z	DMC-FZ7	19	n/a

Table 3. Showing the number of common quantization tables between camera series

Camera Series	Nikon	Olympus C7	Sony P9X	Casio	Samsung	Canon EOS
OEM	1	1				
Nikon		19	5			
Olympus C7			7			
Sony P9X				3		1
Casio					1	1

Discussion

The results of this experiment suggest that the Quantization Table is a reasonable discriminator between model series, as over 92% of extracted tables were unique to one camera series.

From the tables extracted, it is also possible to infer a number of algorithms by which Quantization Tables are computed.

- Some cameras, such as the Kodak and Pentax *IST series, use a single

Quantization Table for all images. This approach appears to be common both in older cameras (with limited processing capability) and in high-end cameras, for which image quality takes precedence over file size.

- Other cameras, notably the Sony DSC-P9X series, appear to have a single Quantization Table which is then scaled up or down to meet a particular file size requirement.
- Finally, we observed that some cameras, such as the Casio EXZ40 and the Olympus FE100, appear to use a much more sophisticated algorithm to choose an optimal Quantization Table to suit the image.

One interesting point to note is that in most cases, the Quantization Tables are asymmetric, so that the quantization in the horizontal direction is different to the vertical direction. In our analysis we excluded images which had been rotated by 90 degrees to avoid double-counting of transposed quantization matrices.

Our experiment merely demonstrates the merit of using the Quantization Table as a forensic tool for identifying the make and model of a source camera. To be effective, an exhaustive database of all Quantization Tables from all camera models would be required. Such a database would require constant updates as new camera models are introduced into the global market. Furthermore, we would stress that the only effective mechanism for such a database to operate is to rely on manufacturers to release complete specifications and parameters to the database manager. That is to say that the experimental technique we have used is not sufficiently reliable to ensure thorough coverage of all cameras.

Quantization Tables Used by Popular Software

Images are commonly edited using popular software before being presented. We therefore considered the Quantization Tables of two popular packages, namely Adobe Photoshop and Microsoft Photo Editor.

Adobe Photoshop allows 13 levels of JPEG image quality in integer steps from 0 to 12. It is interesting to note that at low quality levels Photoshop quantizes low frequency components particularly aggressively while retaining high frequency components. This behaviour is at odds with every other quantization matrix we have identified, as well as the underlying psychovisual theory behind JPEG compression (see for example Lohscheller (1984)). The observation helps to explain why JPEG images compressed by Photoshop at low quality show strong signs of blockiness, as the edges of the 8x8 pixel microblocks are readily apparent. A further anomaly in the Adobe Photoshop implementation is that the tables for quality levels 6 and 7 are in the wrong order, such that quality level 6 is actually higher quality than level 7. This is easily demonstrated by noting that saving an image at quality 6 results in a larger file than at quality 7.

Photoshop Version 4, and later versions, support Exif metadata and relevant tags are transferred to modified images. Photoshop identifies itself as the image editing software and modifies some tags to match the edited image in compliance with the Exif standard. Earlier versions of Photoshop do not support Exif metadata, ignore the Exif section of JPEG image files and do not include Exif metadata in subsequent saved JPEG images.

Microsoft Photo Editor, on the other hand, offers 100 levels of JPEG image quality. Our analysis infers that Microsoft uses a single Quantization Table which is scaled linearly according to the quality level and limited as necessary to the range [1...255]. Thus, Quality Level 100 uses no quantization (all rounding coefficients equal to 1) while Level 1 uses the coarsest possible quantization (all rounding coefficients equal to 255). Unlike Photoshop, Photo Editor's Quantization Tables are asymmetric, most likely recognising the physical layout of red, green and blue pixels in conventional video displays.

Microsoft Photo Editor does not support Exif metadata and images saved by Photo Editor do not include any original metadata. Anomolously, Windows XP (which includes Photo Editor as a standard package) does use Exif metadata to identify certain image characteristics in the file browser.

DETECTION ALGORITHM

It is common practice for a photographic image to undergo recompression before being stored, transmitted, or uploaded to a website. Anecdotal evidence suggests that images of interest in this context are rarely re-scaled, cropped or significantly enhanced, and that in most cases the transformation is nothing more than lossier compression of the image at the original resolution. Of course, this statement does *not* apply to images which have been deliberately tampered with, but the detection of such forgery is not within the scope of this chapter.

When an image is re-compressed, the image is extracted into its original Red-Green-Blue representation (some software also works directly on the Y-Cb-Cr representations). It is very common for the chrominance planes to be further downsampled and for that reason we do not consider the chrominance planes any further in this context.

The Double Quantization Ripple Effect

Considering only the luminance plane, it should be apparent that if a coefficient is originally rounded off to say the nearest multiple of 2, and then requantized to the nearest multiple of three, the coefficients are no longer smoothly distributed. For example, the series 1-2-3-4-5-6-7-8-9-10 would be rounded off first to 2-2-4-4-6-6-8-8-10-10 and then to 3-3-3-3-6-6-9-9-9-9; whereas direct rounding would have resulted in the uniform 0-3-3-3-6-6-6-9-9-9. The result is a ripple effect in the distribution of coefficients, as shown in Figure 1. This ripple effect can be detected by matching with an appropriate template.

However, this effect will not be detected under two key circumstances:

1. If Q_2 is divisible by Q_1, there will be no periodic ripple as the requantization is distributed evenly, or

Figure 1. Double rounding leads to a periodic ripple in the distribution of coefficients. The dotted line shows the distribution of the coefficients in the original image, rounded off to 2. The solid line shows the distribution after rounding off to 3. The periodic behaviour is starkly evident.

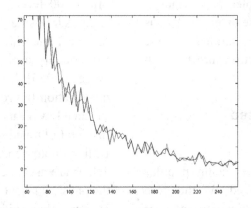

Figure 2. Showing the quantization coefficient pairs (Q_1, Q_2) which result in the ripple effect (white zone), versus areas where Q_1 cannot be deduced using the ripple effect (black zone)

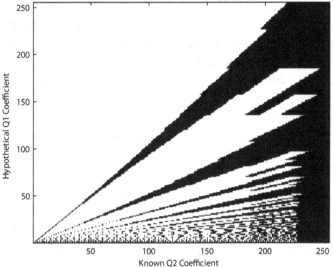

2. If Q_2 is sufficiently large, the period of the ripple exceeds the range of the DCT coefficients, which lie in the range -1024 to +1023 (except for the first element, representing average intensity, which is supported over twice this range). In this case, there will be no effect on which to base a template.

Figure 2 summarizes these two effects. The white area represents pairs of (Q_1, Q_2) which have a detectable ripple effect, whereas the ripple effect is either non-existent, or out of range, in the black areas.

Matched Filter Correlation

Our detection algorithm is based on a matched filter. The algorithm proceeds as follows:

1. For each j of the 64 elements of the macro-blocks, compute a histogram of the *absolute* value of the jth coefficient over the entire image. This results in a single-sided generalised Gaussian distribution, potentially with

the ripple effect intact as shown previously in Figure 1.

2. Apply a symmetric high-pass filter to remove the underlying distribution and retain the ripple effect:

$$\overline{x_k}(i) = \frac{2x_k(i) - x_{k-1}(i) - x_{k+1}(i)}{2}$$

For reasons of symmetry, $x_0(i)$ is doubled so as to reduce the impact on $x_1(i)$. It should be noted that coefficients which are rounded to 0 do not contribute to a detectable quantization effect and so are removed from consideration. It should be noted that due to the Central Limit Theorem, the underlying "noise" in the signal, in fact artifacts of the source image, can be approximated as Additive White Gaussian Noise, and hence the use of a matched filter for detection is optimal.

3. A template is then created for a given pair of primary and secondary coefficients based on a uniform distribution of coefficients. Both the template and the filtered signal are normalised by the root-mean-square to

ensure that their correlation is normalised to the range -1 to +1. In addition, the template for any pair in the "black region" of Figure 2 is set to a vector of zeros.

4. The correlation of the filtered signal and the template is then computed for each of the 64 elements of the macroblock:

$$c(Q_1(i), Q_2(i)) = \sum_{k=-1023}^{1023} \overline{x}_k \cdot \overline{t}_k(Q_1(i), Q_2(i))$$

Decision Rule

In Sorell (2008), the correlation coefficients were scaled by the number of non-zero elements in the original histogram and then summed to provide a weighted score against the hypothetical original Q_1 Quantization Table. That approach was based on some experimental results indicating effectiveness, but was not intended to be optimal. Rather, it was intended to demonstrate the feasibility of identifying the primary Quantization Table.

The approach presented here is quite different, and we are not attempting to identify the one hypothesis which best matches the data in some sense. Rather, it is our intention here to consider each of the 64 correlation coefficients and hence minimise the size of the set of feasible primary Quantization Tables. Further analysis can then be undertaken on the reduced set, if required.

We consider three outcomes from the correlation test:

1. The correlation test is positive, indicating a possible match. The greater the correlation value, the better the match

2. The correlation test is zero, indicating either that we are operating in the "black zone" where there is no ripple effect, or that there are no non-zero elements in the histogram for that particular histogram, or that the specific data cancels itself precisely

3. The correlation test is negative, indicating a possible mismatch.

It should be noted that the characteristics of the underlying photograph act as noise in the context of these results, and that it is possible through the specific textures of an image to obtain a strong match, or mismatch, through coincidence.

A number of variations on this technique were reviewed by experiment using the 13 secondary Quantization Tables of Adobe Photoshop and 10 secondary Quantization Tables of Microsoft Photo Editor, corresponding to quality levels 10%, 20%,..., 100%. It should be noted that a quality level of 1% in Photo Editor results in all quantization coefficients being equal to 255, and therefore operates in the "black zone". A total of 330 distinct primary Quantization Tables were considered from 4487 photographs.

The variations we considered included:

1. Considering positive correlations to be detected above some positive non-zero threshold, and similarly considering negative correlations to be detected below some negative non-zero threshold. In practice, it was found that this had very little impact on the results, and so the simpler positive-zero-negative approach is used.

2. Taking into account whether a zero result is due to the double quantization "black zone" or some other reason. Importantly, it was found that this approach was quite critical in analysing results. Hence, the *number of valid tests* is defined as the number of coefficient pairs (Q_1, Q_2) in the "white zone", where Q_1 is defined as the true underlying primary quantization coefficient, provided that there are non-zero samples from which to derive a signal.

3. Considering whether to simply consider the number of positive correlations, or whether to subtract the number of negative correla-

tions. Experimental results showed better performance if the positive results were weighed up against the negative results. Hence, a *primary Quantization Table hypothesis* is considered *feasible* if the number of positive correlations, less the number of negative correlations, is positive. Otherwise the hypothesis is *unsupported*.

ANALYSIS OF RESULTS

Our results are analysed according to the number of valid tests as defined above. In Sorell (2008), results were categorised by the maximum coefficient in the true primary Quantization Table, but this was found not to be a particularly effective technique for establishing whether a specific primary Quantization Table would be easily detected against a specific secondary Quantization Table. In contrast the *number of valid tests* approach is an objective indicator of the quality of the data presented to the decision rule.

We considered three indicators of performance in our results:

1. The probability that the true primary Quantization Table would be included in the set of *feasible* hypotheses,
2. The probability that the true primary Quantization Table would be the highest-ranked result, that is that there would be no other hypothesis with a higher net number of positive correlations. As the decision rule is based on integers, it should be noted that this approach allows for several equal first-ranked hypotheses.
3. Given that the true primary Quantization Table is considered feasible, its mean ranking by net number of positive correlations.

Secondary Quantization by Adobe Photoshop

All of the 13 Quantization Tables implemented by Adobe Photoshop were considered. Three representative examples are given here.

Figure 3 shows the results for the highest-quality setting for Photoshop. To ensure statistical validity, data points are aggregated in steps of two valid tests and are only shown if there are more than 10 samples. It can be seen that where there are more than 44 valid tests, the true primary Quantization Table is always ranked first in the decision rule.

Figure 4 shows the results for Photoshop Quality Level 10. Although this high-quality setting results in a high probability of capturing the true primary Quantization Table in the feasible hypothesis set, it is clear that the true primary Quantization Table no longer dominates the ranking. This same behaviour is seen as the Quality Level is reduced below 6, noting that due to a bug in Photoshop's implementation, Quality Level 6 results in a higher-quality image than Quality Level 7.

Figure 5, showing Quality Level 4, shows surprisingly similar results to Quality Level 10, and in fact this is true even for Quality Level 0. The reason for this, perhaps unexpected, result, is that Photoshop limits its secondary quantization coefficients for high spatial frequencies to 15, while quantizing low spatial frequencies more coarsely at low qualities. This results in images which have particular poor visual quality at low quality levels compared with JPEG images of similar file size compressed using other software. It also means that high frequency distributions are largely retained by images recompressed using Photoshop, regardless of the Quality Level used.

Figure 3. Results for Adobe Photoshop using Quality Level 12. The upper plot shows the number of first-ranked detections of the true primary Quantization Table (solid line with circled points) and the probability of the true primary Quantization Table being considered feasible (dotted line with crosses). The lower graph shows the mean rank of the true primary Quantization Table if it is in the feasible set. Note that the y-axis is inverted so that a rank of "1" is at the top of the axes. The x-axis counts the number of valid hypotheses, that is the number of quantization pairs in the "white zone" of Figure 2.

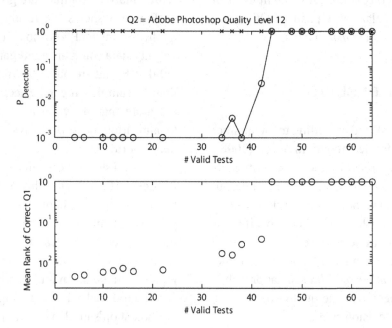

Figure 4. Results for Adobe Photoshop using Quality Level 10. See Figure 3 caption for details.

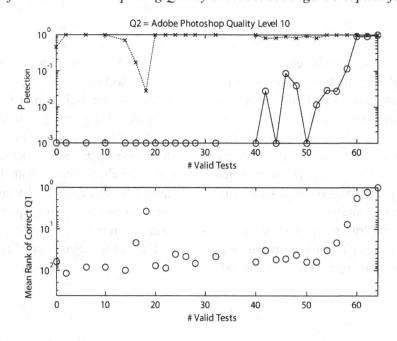

Figure 5. Results for Adobe Photoshop using Quality Level 4. See Figure 3 caption for details.

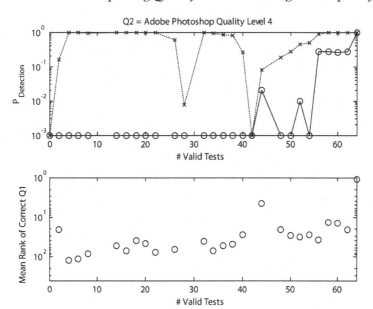

Secondary Quantization by Microsoft Photo Editor

The choice of Quantization Table for images compressed using Microsoft Photo Editor is quite different to Photoshop. It appears that a single nominal Quantization Table has been specified at some nominal quality level. As the Quality Level is increased towards 100%, the Quantization Table is scaled down uniformly, resulting in finer quantization. At 100%, all quantization coefficients are equal to one, meaning that there is no further rounding and that primary quantization is particularly simple to detect. On the other hand, at 1% all quantization coefficients are scaled up to their maximum value, 255, and there is no detectable secondary quantization effect.

Figure 6, showing results at Quality Level 100%, indicates very strong performance as expected. There is no secondary rounding and so as few as 32 valid tests results in a high rate of first-ranked true primary Quantization Table identification.

As the Quality Level is reduced, however, there is a sharp decline in performance. While the prob-

ability of inclusion of the true primary Quantization Table in the feasible set remains high, the ranking declines to an average of typically 10 to 100. This is still useful, as it allows for prioritizing certain camera types over others in subsequent forensic analysis, but the results are certainly not as clear-cut as those for images recompressed using Adobe Photoshop. Furthermore, the probability of the true hypothesis being first ranked rapidly drops away to zero. These results are summarised in Figures 7, 8 and 9.

The primary reason for this very different behavior is clear. Firstly, Photo Editor quantizes high frequencies more coarsely than lower frequencies, and maintains the ratio of the quantization coefficients regardless of the quality level. This means that the ripple effect rapidly becomes undetectable as the quality level decreases, in contrast to Photoshop, in which the high frequencies are retained.

Furthermore, as Photo Editor does not recognise Exif metadata and strips it from the recompressed file, it is of some concern that recompression using Photo Editor, which is shipped with the Windows operating system, can easily suppress

Figure 6. Results for Microsoft Photo Editor with quality level set to 100%. See Figure 3 caption for details.

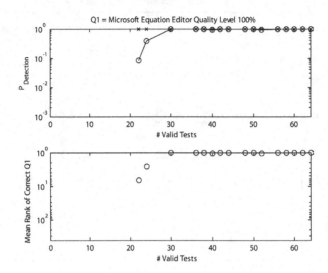

forensic traces of the primary image source in a way that other software, most notably Adobe Photoshop, cannot.

CONCLUSION

This chapter has emphasised a detection and estimation approach for identification of the primary quantization coefficients of a recompressed JPEG image based on determining which hypothetical primary Quantization Tables are feasible, rather than attempting to determine the single candidate with the best match. It has been demonstrated that the latter approach is not particularly effective and that the double-quantization ripple effect is better exploited to reduce the size of the candidate set of primary Quantization Tables.

Figure 7. Results for Microsoft Photo Editor with quality level set to 80%. See Figure 3 caption for details.

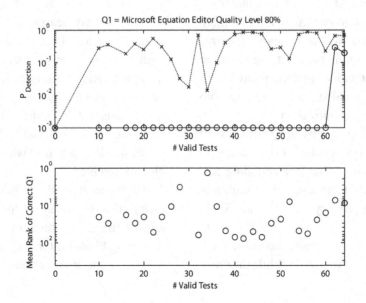

Figure 8. Results for Microsoft Photo Editor with quality level set to 50%. See Figure 3 caption for details.

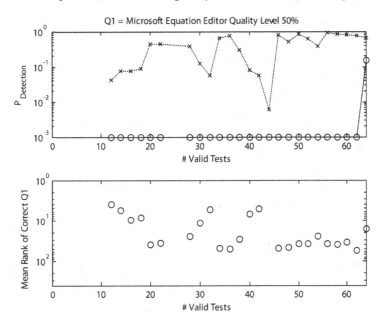

The implications of this work are clear in forensic investigation. By identifying the primary quantization coefficients of an image, or as small a set of coefficients as possible, it is possible to narrow down the range of potential image source devices. When considered in conjunction with other evidence, such as unreliable metadata, image resolution, camera fingerprinting, physical evidence, etc, it is clear that the quality of the overall set of evidence is improved.

Figure 9. Results for Microsoft Photo Editor with quality level set to 30%. See Figure 3 caption for details.

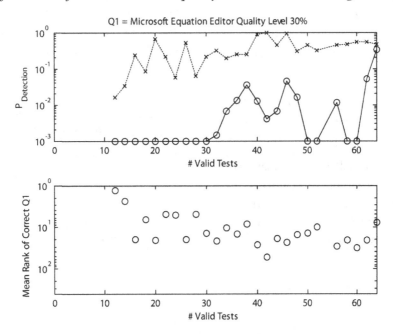

Primary and secondary quantization are just two of the causes of artifacts in digital images. In subsequent work (Sorell, 2010), a more thorough review of image provenance is considered, from image sensor ballistics and colour interpolation to subsequent image manipulation. One of the key applications of tracing the provenance of images in this way is the ability to cluster images in a large database according to processing history. This approach simplifies the manual or automated task of reviewing image contents for similarities on the basis that matching sets of photographs are likely to have been processed from the same source camera and through the same post-processing software using the same parameters.

ACKNOWLEDGMENT

I would like to acknowledge the assistance of Jeremy Messé for his work in setting up the reference photograph database and coding many of the algorithms on which this chapter is based.

REFERENCES

Farid, H. (2006). *Digital Image Ballistics from JPEG Quantization*, Dartmouth Computer Science Technical Report, TR2006-583, September 2006.

ITU (1993). *CCITT T.81 Information Technology – Digital Compression and Coding of Continuous-Tone Still Images – Requirements and Guidelines*, International Telecommunications Union, 1993.

JEITA (2002). JEITA CP-3451 Exchangeable image file format for digital still cameras: Exif Version 2.2. Japan Electronics and Information Technology Industries Association, April 2002. Also earlier versions of the Exif standard.

Lohscheller, H. (1984, December). A Subjectively Adapted Image Communication System. *IEEE Transactions on Communications, COM-32*(12), 1316–1322. doi:10.1109/TCOM.1984.1096017

Lukáš, J., & Fridrich, J. (2003). *Estimation of Primary Quantization Matrix in Double Compressed JPEG Images*, Proc. of Digital Forensic Research Workshop, Cleveland, Ohio, August 2003.

Lukáš, J., Fridrich, J., & Goljan, M. (2006, June). Digital camera Identification from Sensor Pattern Noise. *IEEE Trans. on Information Forensics and Security, 1*(2), 205–214. doi:10.1109/TIFS.2006.873602

Neelamani, R., de Queiroz, R., Fan, Z., Dash, S., & Baraniuk, R. (2006, June). JPEG compression history estimation for color images. *IEEE Transactions on Image Processing, 15*(6), 1365–1378. doi:10.1109/TIP.2005.864171

Sorell, M. J. (2008). Digital camera Source identification Through JPEG Quantization. In Li, C.-T. (Ed.), *Multimedia Forensics and Security* (pp. 291–313). Hershey, PA: IGI Global.

Sorell, M. J. (2010). Digital Photographic Provenance. In Li, C.-T. (Ed.), *Handbook of Research on Computational Forensics, Digital Crime and Investigation: Methods and Solutions* (pp. 104–129). Hershey, PA: Information Science Reference.

Wallace, G. K. (1991, April). The JPEG Still Picture Compression Standard. *Communications of the ACM, 34*(4), 30–44. doi:10.1145/103085.103089

Chapter 17
Dynamic Structural Statistical Model Based Online Signature Verification

Yan Chen
Tsinghua University, China

Xiaoqing Ding
Tsinghua University, China

Patrick S. P. Wang
Northeastern University, USA

ABSTRACT

In this article, a new dynamic structural statistical model based online signature verification algorithm is proposed, in which a method for statistical modeling the signature's characteristic points is presented. Dynamic time warping is utilized to match two signature sequences so that correspondent characteristic point pair can be extracted from the matching result. Variations of a characteristic point are described by a multi-variable statistical probability distribution. Three methods for estimating the statistical distribution parameters are investigated. With this dynamic structural statistical model, a discriminant function can be derived to judges a signature to be genuine or forgery at the criterion of minimum potential risk. The proposed method takes advantage of both structure matching and statistical analysis. Tested in two signature databases, the proposed algorithm got much better signature verification performance than other results.

INTRODUCTION

Online handwritten signature verification (Vielhauer, 2005) is an open problem in the area of pattern recognition. The difficulty lies in big variances of genuine and forgery signatures and in detecting forgeries while allowing certain variability in genuine signatures, and also in the shortage of training samples which makes the verification problem even worse. Researchers made researches in this area and gave some solutions to it (Pirlo, 2003; Dimauro et al, 2004; Lei & Govindaraju, 2005; Deng et al, 2005). In general, there are two main approaches in dealing with this problem (Plamondon & Srihari, 2000; Parizeau & Plamondon, 1990; Gupta & McCabe, 1997): the function based approach and the parameter based approach.

The function based approach looks on the signature as time functions. Dynamic time warping (DTW) (Martens & Claesen, 1996; Jin & Liu, 1999; Jain et al, 2002; Tanabe et al, 2001), improved DTW (Munich & Perona, 1999; Feng & Wah, 2003) or Hidden Markov Model (Muramatsu & Matsumoto, 2003; Igarza et al, 2003) methods are used to reveal the local relationship between two time functions and give their differences to make a decision. For example, Yi et al. (2005) introduced a DTW based signature verification algorithm that uses the phase output of Gabor filter. Two signature dissimilarities are calculated from the feature profile and the phase profile. Fierrez et al. (2007) proposed a signature verification system using a set of time sequences and Hidden Markov Models. The best performance is achieved with seven discrete-time functions and 2 states with 32 Gaussian mixtures per state. The function based verification approach doesn't need many training samples, but the local difference values are given subjectively and lack of statistical basis in the DTW method and much computation power is required to train the model in the HMM method.

The parameter based approach does not use the signature's time-sample attributes directly, but extracting parameters from the signature (Kiran et al, 2001; Lee et al, 1996; Zhao & Li, 2003; Richiardi & Drygajlo, 2003). The parameters are supposed to follow some statistical distributions. Feature selection and feature transform are adopted (Kim et al, 1995; Brittan & Fairhurst, 1994). Statistical classifiers are utilized to make the decision. This method tries to give a statistical model to a signature. But the statistical distribution function can not be determined easily and a number of training samples are needed, thus constrain the efficiency of this method. Some more recent discussions on structural analysis, verification and synthesis of signatures can also be found in the study of Popel (2007) and Kamel et al. (2008).

In this article, a dynamic structural statistical model based online signature verification algorithm is proposed, which synthetically uses structural matching and statistical probability function estimation.

A signature sample is first resampled as a time sequence with fixed time interval (8 millisecond). All resampled points in the reference sequence are regarded as characteristic points of reference signature. Utilizing DTW method to get correspondence point pairs between a test signature sequence and a reference signature sequence, the characteristic points of the test signature are got. The variations of each characteristic point of the test signature sequence comparing with the corresponding characteristic point of the reference signature sequence are described by multi-variable statistical probability distribution functions, which compose the Dynamic Structural Statistical Model (abbreviated as DSSM). The same characteristic point pair in genuine and forgery signatures will get different statistical distributions. Thus a signature can be judged as genuine or forgery with different posterior probability estimation based on the DSSM.

To resolve the problem of estimating the statistical distribution parameters with limited number of training samples, three different distribution model assumptions are adopted. In those three models, the covariance parameters are trained using one, all and grouped characteristic points, respectively. With this dynamic structural statistical model, the posterior probability of a signature belonging to a genuine class can be estimated, and decision can be made to verify the signature.

Comparing with conventional signature verification methods, the proposed method has some advantages. The model parameters are trained for each person individually so every person will has his/her own signature model. The model is set up on the point level so that it can reflect local differences, thus improving the discriminant power. This method uses high-order statistical quantity of multiple features so that the distance measure can reflect the difference of test signature and reference signature more precisely. Using characteristic points mixed training method, the parameters can be well estimated even there are only a small number of training samples and the verification system can still achieve relative high performance in this situation. Also the DSSM based signature verification system is language independent, it can deal with English signature, Chinese signature or signatures in other languages. Figure 1 shows some genuine and forgery signature samples.

In the followings of this article, chapter 2 gives the dynamic structural statistical model, chapter 3 describes dynamic structural statistical model based online signature verification system, chapter 4 shows the model parameter training method under three different covariance assumptions, chapter 5 shows the experiment results and draws some conclusions.

DYNAMIC STRUCTUAL STATISTICAL MODEL

The signature signal is a temporal signal that contains x, y and t parameters at each sampling point. It can be described as a two dimensional time sequence $\{(x(t_i),y(t_i))\}$, where t_i is the sampling time, $x(t_i)$ and $y(t_i)$ are the coordinates in the horizontal and vertical direction, respectively. The difference between genuine and forgery signatures are very localize so we should describe the signature at point level to reveal the local difference.

No two genuine signatures have the same shape. Some kinds of time alignment should be done to make the signatures comparable. Dynamic time warping is a well known algorithm in establishing correspondence between two time series. A signature is compared to a model reference signature using dynamic time warping. After time warping, a matching path is established between the two signatures. Therefore, characteristic points are extracted from the signature utilizing the gen-

Figure 1.

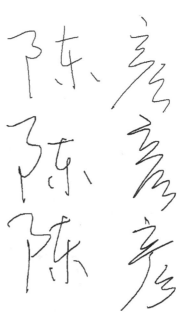

(a) Genuine signature samples   (b) Forgery signature samples

erated warping path. After that we can calculate the probability density distribution function of each characteristic point from the training samples. A signature thus can be described as a series of characteristic points with different distributions. This is noted as the dynamic structural statistical model of a signature.

DTW Matching Based Characteristic Point Extraction

DTW algorithm is now a commonly used method in aligning two time sequences. In this article, we use DTW algorithm to set correspondence between a test signature sequence and a reference signature sequence, so that the characteristic point pairs can be extracted from the test signature sequence corresponding with the reference signature sequence.

Suppose we get a test signature sample and a reference signature sample. Using a fixed time interval, the test signature sample can be resampled as a time sequence $A = \{a_i, 1 \le i \le M\}$, where $a_i = (x_i^a, y_i^a)$. The reference signature sample can also be resampled as a time sequence $B = \{b_j, 1 \le j \le N\}$ in the same way, where $b_i = ($

$x_i^b, y_i^b)$. A matching path $W = \{(i(k), j(k)), 1 \le k \le K\}$ can then be got out of A and B with DTW matching algorithm, where $a_{i(k)} \in A$, $b_{j(k)} \in B$. All resampled points in the reference sequence B are regarded as the characteristic points of the reference signature. To get the characteristic points of the test signature, a 1-1 correspondence between the point sequences A and B should be set up. Following the matching path W, the test sequence A is adjusted in three difference ways.

In the first situation, the signature point $a_{i(k)}$ is only matched to the reference signature point $b_{i(k)}$, and $b_{i(k)}$ only has one matching point in the matching path, as can be seen in Figure 2. The signature point $a_{i(k)}$ is used directly as the characteristic point that matches with reference signature point $b_{i(k)}$.

In the second situation, the sequence point $a_{i(k)}$ is matched to two or more sequence point in sequence B, as can be seen from Figure 3. In this situation, a new point $a'_{i(k)}$ is added to sequence A, so that a new 1-1 correspondence can be got.

In the third situation, two or more sequence points in sequence A are matched with the same sequence point $b_{i(k)}$, as can be seen in Figure 4. In this situation, the redundant point $a_{i(k)}$ should be removed from sequence A.

Figure 2. Keep the original point

Figure 3. Adding a new point

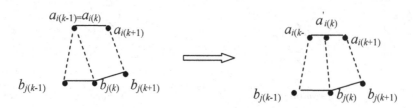

Figure 4. Remove a redundancy point

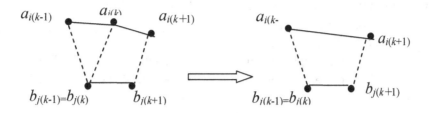

After the test sequence A is adjusted, a new sequence A' is got and each sequence point in the adjusted sequence A' is regarded as a characteristic point of the test signature. The number of characteristic points of test signature is equal to the number of characteristic points of reference signature, as can be seen in Figure 5.

If not specially pointed out, the signature sequence is regarded as the characteristic point sequence after sequence adjustment in the remaining of the article.

Characteristic Point Modeling

In normally used signature verification algorithm, the difference between a pair of characteristic points is subjectively described as position difference between them or angle difference between them, etc., or sum of the weighted attribute differences while the weight values are given by

experiment or multiple trials, which are lack of statistical basis.

In this article, the probability distributions of the characteristic points of a person's signatures are analyzed and a characteristic point based statistical model is given to describe a person's signature.

For the parameters extracted from a characteristic point of a person's signature, the statistical distribution of the parameters shows the signing characteristic of that person. When a person tries to forge a signature, its statistical characteristics will differ from the genuine ones because different persons have different signing characteristics. Thus a statistical model of the characteristic points can be set up and the probability distribution difference between characteristic points can be used to describe the difference between two signature sequences.

Figure 5. Characteristic points with 1-1 correspondence

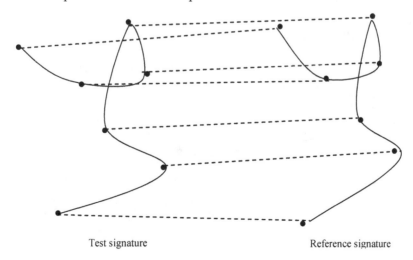

Test signature   Reference signature

Let $Q=\{q^i, 1\leq i\leq N\}$ denote a signature sequence with N characteristic points. A feature vector x^i is extracted from the i'th point, thus the whole signature sequence can be expressed as $x=\{x^1,x^2,....x^N\}$, where N is the number of characteristic points. For each characteristic point, multiple attributes, such as shift in horizontal and vertical direction, writing angle, writing speed, etc., can be obtained. We extract M features from those attributes in the characteristic point i, $x^i = (x_1^i, x_2^i,....x_M^i)$, so that the signature can be expressed as N feature vectors:

$$x^1 = (x_1^1, x_2^1, \cdots x_M^1),$$
$$x^2 = (x_1^2, x_2^2, \cdots x_M^2),$$
$$\vdots$$
$$x^N = (x_1^N, x_2^N, \cdots x_M^N).$$

Suppose the conditional probability density function of the i'th characteristic point is $p(x^i/C_g)$ where C_g is the genuine person's class, then the posterior probability that the i'th characteristic point belongs to the genuine class can be calculated as seen in Box 1.

A genuine signature class can then be described as a dynamic structural statistical model, as can be seen in Figure 6.

ONLINE SIGNATURE VERIFICAITON BASED ON DSSM

The correspondent characteristic points in genuine and forgery signatures will get different statistical distributions, as can be seen in Figure 7. The statistical parameters of the statistical distribution show the special characteristics of a special person. Thus a signature can be judged as genuine or forgery by posterior probability estimation based on the DSSM.

The posterior probability of the test signature characteristic points can be used to judge whether the test signature belongs to genuine signature class or forgery signature class. They can be calculated as seen in Box 2 and Box 3 where $x=\{x^1,x^2,...x^N\}$ are features extracted from N characteristic points, C_g and C_f are genuine signature class and forgery signature class respectively.

Box 1.

$$P(C_g / x^i) = P(C_g / x_1^i, x_2^i, \cdots x_M^i) = \frac{p(x_1^i, x_2^i, \cdots x_M^i / C_g) \cdot P(C_g)}{p(x_1^i, x_2^i, \cdots x_M^i)} \tag{1}$$

Figure 6. DSSM of the genuine signature class

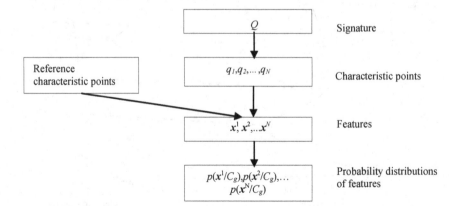

Following the Bayesian rules, suppose the costs of misclassifying a genuine signature to the forgery signature class and misclassifying a forgery signature to the genuine signature class are L1 and L2, respectively, we can then get the classification criterion: If (See Box 4), judge the test signature as a genuine signature, otherwise, judge it to be a forgery signature.

In this criterion, the prior probability of genuine and forgery class are pre-determined constants.

The forgery signatures refer to signatures written by persons other than its genuine owner, so the probability distribution is more spread out than that of the genuine signatures, as can be seen from Figure 8. Thus we can suppose it to be a constant value η in the interested decision area. Also, we assume that all characteristic points are conditionally independent, so we get (See Box 5):

Substitute (5) into the decision criterion (4), a new decision criterion is got: If (See Box 6)

Figure 7. Different statistical distribution of characteristic points from (a) genuine signature and (b) forgery signature

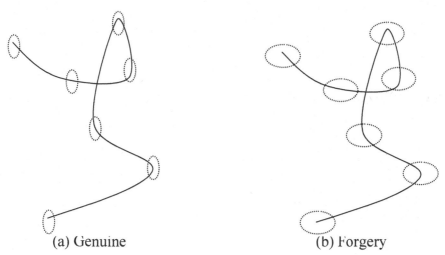

(a) Genuine   (b) Forgery

Box 2.

$$P(C_g \,/\, \boldsymbol{x}^1, \boldsymbol{x}^2, \cdots \boldsymbol{x}^N) = \frac{p(\boldsymbol{x}^1, \boldsymbol{x}^2, \cdots \boldsymbol{x}^N \,/\, C_g) \cdot P(C_g)}{p(\boldsymbol{x}^1, \boldsymbol{x}^2, \cdots \boldsymbol{x}^N)}, \tag{2}$$

Box 3.

$$P(C_f \,/\, \boldsymbol{x}^1, \boldsymbol{x}^2, \cdots \boldsymbol{x}^N) = \frac{p(\boldsymbol{x}^1, \boldsymbol{x}^2, \cdots \boldsymbol{x}^N \,/\, C_f) \cdot P(C_f)}{p(\boldsymbol{x}^1, \boldsymbol{x}^2, \cdots \boldsymbol{x}^N)}, \tag{3}$$

Box 4.

$$p(\boldsymbol{x}^1, \boldsymbol{x}^2, \cdots \boldsymbol{x}^N \,/\, C_g) > p(\boldsymbol{x}^1, \boldsymbol{x}^2, \cdots \boldsymbol{x}^N \,/\, C_f) \cdot L2 \,/\, L1 \cdot P(C_f) \,/\, P(C_g), \tag{4}$$

Figure 8. Conditional probability distribution of genuine and forgery signatures

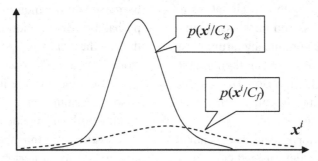

Box 5.

$$p(\boldsymbol{x}^1, \boldsymbol{x}^2, \cdots \boldsymbol{x}^N / C_g) = p(\boldsymbol{x}^1 / C_g) \cdot p(\boldsymbol{x}^2 / C_g) \cdots p(\boldsymbol{x}^N / C_g). \tag{5}$$

Box 6.

$$p(\boldsymbol{x}^1 / C_g) \cdot p(\boldsymbol{x}^2 / C_g) \cdots p(\boldsymbol{x}^N / C_g) > \eta^N \cdot L2 / L1 \cdot P(C_f) / P(C_g), \tag{6}$$

Box 7.

$$p(\boldsymbol{x}^i / C_g) = \frac{1}{(2\pi)^{M/2} |\boldsymbol{\Phi}^i|^{1/2}} \exp\{\frac{-(\boldsymbol{x}^i - \overline{\boldsymbol{x}^i})^T \boldsymbol{\Phi}^{i-1}(\boldsymbol{x}^i - \overline{\boldsymbol{x}^i})}{2}\}, \tag{7}$$

Box 8.

$$\ln p(\boldsymbol{x}^i / C_g) = -\frac{M}{2} \log(2\pi) - \frac{1}{2}[\log |\boldsymbol{\Phi}^i| + (\boldsymbol{x}^i - \overline{\boldsymbol{x}^i})^T \boldsymbol{\Phi}^{i-1}(\boldsymbol{x}^i - \overline{\boldsymbol{x}^i})]$$

$$p(\boldsymbol{x}^i / C_g) = -\frac{M}{2} \log(2\pi) - \frac{1}{2}[\log |\boldsymbol{\Phi}^i \tag{8}$$

Box 9.

$$\sum_{i=1}^{N} \{-\frac{1}{2}[\log |\boldsymbol{\Phi}^i| + (\boldsymbol{x}^i - \overline{\boldsymbol{x}^i})^T \boldsymbol{\Phi}^{i-1}(\boldsymbol{x}^i - \overline{\boldsymbol{x}^i})]\} > \log(\frac{L2 \cdot p(C_f)}{L1 \cdot p(C_g)}) + N \cdot (\log \eta + \frac{M}{2} \log(2\pi)) \tag{9}$$

judge the test signature as a genuine signature; otherwise, judge it to be a forgery signature.

Suppose each characteristic point follows M dimensional Gaussian distribution (See Box 7) which can be expressed in equivalent log format (See Box 8).

Substitute (8) into the decision criterion (6), a new judge criterion is got: If (See Box 9) judge the test signature to be a genuine signature; otherwise, judge it to be a forgery signature.

The value η should be determined by training from the signature training sample set. Different

FRR and FAR value will be got under different η value, so that η can be chosen to minimize the risk of error decision (See Box 10).

Figure 9 shows the flow chart of the dynamic structural statistical model based online signature verification system.

TRAINING OF DSSM UNDER DIFFERENT COVARIANCE ASSUMPTIONS

Suppose the training signature sample set is $\psi = \{T_l, 1 \leq l \leq L\}$ and a reference sequence $R = \{r^j, 1 \leq j \leq N\}$ is extracted from the reference signature R. By matching the sequence Q that is extracted from a signature sample T_l with sequence R and adjust the sequence Q, N characteristic points can be got from the signature sample T_l. For each characteristic point, M features are extracted. N feature vectors of M dimensions can be obtained from every training signature sample T_l.

$$x^{l,1} = (x_1^{l,1}, x_2^{l,1}, \cdots x_M^{l,1})$$
$$x^{l,2} = (x_1^{l,2}, x_2^{l,2}, \cdots x_M^{l,2})$$
$$\vdots$$
$$x^{l,N} = (x_1^{l,N}, x_2^{l,N}, \cdots x_M^{l,N})$$

Using the training signature samples, N probability density distribution functions (abbreviated as PDF) can be estimated, which compose the DSSM of a signature. Figure 10 shows the flowchart of training the DSSM parameters. In this research, three different distribution models are brought forward under different covariance assumptions.

Box 10.

$$\eta = \arg\min_{\eta}(R) = \arg\min_{\eta}[L1 \cdot P(C_g) \cdot FRR + L2 \cdot P(C_f) \cdot FAR]. \tag{10}$$

Figure 9. DSSM based online signature verification

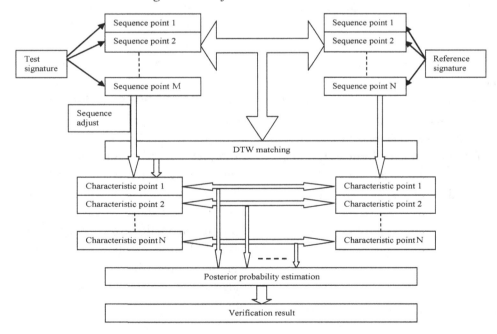

Figure 10. Flowchart of training the DSSM parameters

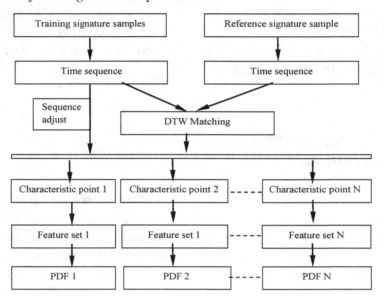

Box 11.

$$p(x^i/C_g) = \frac{1}{(2\pi)^{M/2} |\Phi^i|^{1/2}} \exp\{\frac{-(x^i - \overline{x^i})^T \Phi^{i-1}(x^i - \overline{x^i})}{2}\} \tag{11}$$

Point Dependent Distribution Model

In this model, features from characteristic point i are supposed to follow M dimensional Gaussian distribution, that is (See Box 11).

For each characteristic point i, the mean and covariance parameters x^i and Φ^i are different and should be estimated separately.

With the features extracted from all training signature sample set, the mean and covariance parameters x^i and Φ^i can be calculated as:

$$\overline{x^i} = \frac{1}{L} \sum_{l=1}^{L} x^{l,i},$$

$$\Phi^i = \frac{1}{L} \sum_{l=1}^{L} (x^{l,i} - \overline{x^i})(x^{l,i} - \overline{x^i})^T. \tag{12}$$

Thus the genuine signature class can be expressed as N independent characteristic points and each characteristic point *i* follows the Gaussian distribution with mean x^i and covariance Φ^i.

Point Independent Distribution Model

In the previous section, the features from different characteristic points are supposed to have different Gaussian distribution with different mean and covariance. But there will be large estimation error when calculating covariance Φ^i because there are only limited numbers of genuine signature training samples. To avoid this problem, a point independent distribution model is proposed in this section.

The covariance Φ^i shows the correlations between different features in characteristic point i. We can assume that, for the signature written by the same person, the correlations may have some kind of consistency in different characteristic points. As can be seen from Figure 11, the distribution of features from different characteristic points shows some kinds of consistency, but different points can not mixed directly because the mean value of different characteristic points differ from each other. After shifting each characteristic point against its mean, the new features from different characteristic points are now comparable with each other. Suppose all features from different characteristic points follow the same covariance parameter Φ, so that Φ can be estimated from all characteristic points of all training samples, thus avoiding the problem of insufficient training samples.

With the features extracted from all training signature sample set, and for each characteristic point i, the mean $\overline{x^i}$ and the covariance parameter Φ can be calculated as:

$$\overline{x^i} = \frac{1}{L}\sum_{l=1}^{L} x^{l,i},$$

$$\Phi = \frac{1}{L \cdot N}\sum_{l=1}^{L}\sum_{i=1}^{N}(x^{l,i} - \overline{x^i})(x^{l,i} - \overline{x^i})^{T}. \quad (13)$$

Thus the genuine signature class can be expressed as N independent characteristic points and each characteristic point i follows the Gaussian distribution with mean $\overline{x^i}$ and covariance Φ.

Point Clustering Distribution Model

The two models mentioned in section 4.1 and 4.2 both have their drawbacks. In the point dependent distribution model, the covariance parameter should be calculated for each characteristic point individually and there will be large error in estimating the covariance because the number of training samples is limited. In the point independent distribution model, all characteristic points are supposed to share probability distribution with the same covariance. This is not consistent with the real situation. In this section, we propose a distribution model base on characteristic points clustering, trying to avoid the limitations of the previous two models. In this model, the characteristic points are clustered into several groups, each with its own covariance.

Figure 11. Point independent distribution model

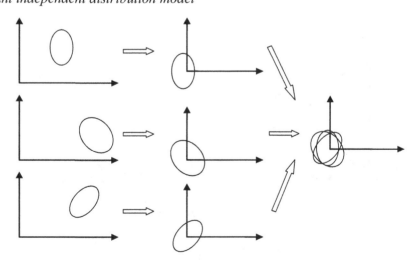

Box 12.

$$\boldsymbol{\Phi}^s = \frac{1}{L \cdot \sum\limits_{i=1}^{N} \varepsilon(i,s)} \sum\limits_{l=1}^{L} \sum\limits_{i=1}^{N} \varepsilon(i,s)(x^{l,i} - \overline{x^i})(x^{l,i} - \overline{x^i})^T, \ 1 \le s \le S \qquad (14)$$

The characteristic points in a signature are written by the same person. So we can expect variations of two characteristic points may have some kind of similarity if those two points are similar to each other. The characteristic points are clustered into several groups based on their similarities, and all characteristic points in the same group are supposed to share the same co-variance parameters. In this article, we used the point acceleration, the point angle variation and the point angle, respectively, to cluster characteristic points into groups.

The distribution parameters can be trained using all characteristic points in a group. It can be seen that in this model, the strong assumption that all points share the same covariance is avoided; also each group will get enough training samples for the training of the covariance parameters.

For each characteristic point i, a group function $g(i)$ is defined to determine which group this characteristic point belongs to.

$g(i) = g(x^{1,i}, x^{2,i}..., {}^{L,i}) \ 1 \le g(i) \le S$, where S is the maximum group number.

The covariance parameter $\boldsymbol{\Phi}^s$ in group s can be calculated as (See Box 12) where x^i is the mean of characteristic point i and $\varepsilon(i,s)$ is a function to determine whether characteristic point i belongs to group s.

$$\varepsilon(i,s) = \begin{cases} 1, & \text{if} \quad g(i) = s \\ 0, & \text{if} \quad g(i) \ne s \end{cases}$$

Thus the genuine signature class can be expressed as N independent characteristic points and each characteristic point i follows the Gaussian distribution with mean x^i and covariance $\Phi^{g(i)}$, as can be seen in Figure 12.

EXPERIMENTAL RESULTS

To examine the efficiency of the proposed model, several signature verification experiments were

Figure 12. Point clustering distribution model

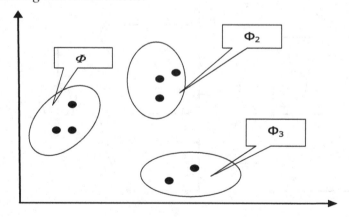

carried out using the proposed model and algorithm. The features extracted from a characteristic point are the following 5 values, which are the differences between the corresponding characteristic points of the test signature and the reference signature.

$$x^i = \begin{bmatrix} x_1^i \\ x_2^i \\ x_3^i \\ x_4^i \\ x_5^i \end{bmatrix} = \begin{bmatrix} l_x(q^i) - l_x(r^i) \\ l_y(q^i) - l_y(r^i) \\ \theta(q^i) - \theta(r^i) \\ t(q^i) - t(r^i) \\ v(q^i) - v(r^i) \end{bmatrix} \qquad (15)$$

where l_x, l_y, θ, t, v are the distance in horizontal and vertical direction, angle, time and velocity between the current characteristic point and the next characteristic point, respectively, as can be seen from Figure 13.

Two types of errors may occur in signature verification: the false rejection rate (FRR) refers to the rate of rejecting a genuine signature and the false acceptance rate (FAR) refers to the rate of accepting a forgery signature as genuine. The equal error rate (EER) is defined as the average error rate when the FRR equals to the FAR, also an error tradeoff curve between FAR and FRR is often used in benchmarking the signature verification system.

The Signature Databases

Two signature databases were used for benchmarking the proposed signature model and verification algorithm.

The first signature database is the public released SVC2004 (Yeung et al, 2004) signature database from ICBA2004 which contains 40 users' signatures and each user has 20 genuine signatures and 20 forgery signatures.

The second database is the BIOMET (Salicetti et al, 2003) signature database from Institute National des Telecommunication, which contains 84 users' signatures and each user has 15 genuine signatures (collected in two time period) and 12 forgery signatures. We construct two databases from the BIOMET database according to the time period of training and testing genuine signature. In BIOMET I database, the training and testing genuine signatures are collected in the same time period. In BIOMET II database, the training and testing genuine signatures are collected in different period.

Signature Verification Result Under Different Distribution Models

In this experiment, we test the verification performance of different distribution models.

Figure 13. Characteristic point properties

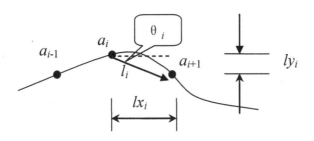

They are point dependent distribution model, point independent distribution model, point clustering distribution model, respectively. In the point clustering distribution model, 3 different clustering methods are used. The first method clustered the characteristic points based on the point acceleration value. The second method clustered the characteristic points based on the angle of the point. The third method clustered the characteristic points based on the variance of the point angle. 5 genuine signatures were selected randomly as the training signature samples.

As can be seen from Table 1 and Figure 14, the point dependent distribution model requires esti-mating each point's parameters individually, large error will occur when there are not enough training samples and the verification performance drops remarkably. The point independent distribution model and the point clustering distribution model use many characteristic points for mixed training, so the parameters can be estimated precisely. The verification performance is determined by the consistency level that the model assumption fits with the real characteristic point's probability distribution. The point clustering distribution model which clustered based on the variance of point angle achieved the best performance.

Table 1. Verification result under different distribution models (using SVC2004 database)

Model		Mean EER	Std. EER	Max. EER	Min. EER
Point dependent model		7.2%	7.83%	26.5%	0%
Point independent model		4.18%	6.24%	24%	0%
Cluster-ing model based on	Acceleration	4.14%	6.13%	24%	0%
	Angle variance	4.02%	5.94%	23.75%	0%
	Point angle	4.80%	6.33%	21.5%	0%

Figure 14. Verification result under different distribution models (using BIOMET II database)

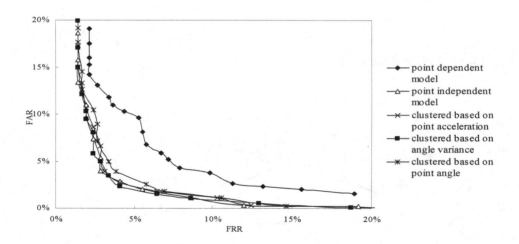

Figure 15. Influence of different number of training samples (using BIOMET II database)

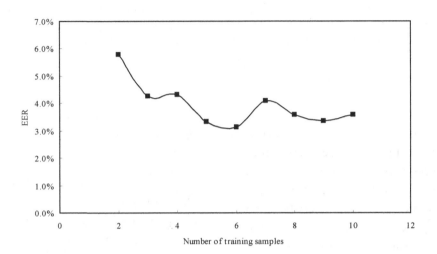

The Influence of Number of Training Samples

In this experiment, we use different number of training samples to train the distribution parameters. 2~10 signature samples were randomly chosen as the reference signatures for parameter training, and the verification results can be seen in Figure 15.

As can be seen from Figure 15, with this Dynamic Structural Statistical Model, the verification performance did not drop much even there were only 3 or 4 training samples. Because all characteristic points are used for mixed parameter training, the model parameters can be well estimated even when there are very few training samples.

COMPARISONS AND CONCLUSION

We tested the proposed Dynamic Structural Statistical Model based online signature verification algorithm on two signature databases and compared the verification result with some known result. Table 2 shows the verification results on BIOMET database, compared with the result of Van et al. (2004), Table 3 shows the verification results on SVC2004 database, compared with the result given in SVC2004 (2004). As can be seen from these two tables, the proposed signature verification algorithm got higher performance than other results.

A Dynamic Structural Statistical Model based online signature verification algorithm is proposed in this article. This algorithm shows more advantages than other traditional signature verification algorithm. Experiments on more testing dataset show that this method has more robust and higher performance on signature verification.

Table 2. Verification results on BIOMET database

	EER	
	I	II
DSSM	1.91%	3.31%
Van *et al.* (2004)	2.84%	8.57%

I --the training and testing genuine signatures are collected in same time period

II --the training and testing genuine signatures are collected in different period.

Table 3. Verification results on SVC2004 database

	Mean EER	Std. EER	Max. EER	Min. EER
DSSM	4.02%	5. 94%	23.75%	0%
SVC2004 (2004)	5.5%	7.73%	30%	0%

In this Dynamic Structural Statistical Model, the parameters are trained for each person individually so every person will has his/her own DSSM signature model. A special person's model parameters show the special characteristic of that person, avoiding the parameter estimation errors that occur when using all users' signatures to estimate parameters.

The model is set up on the point level so that it can reflect local differences, thus improving the discriminant power. Also this model uses high-order statistical quantity of multiple discrimination features. The features are extracted from multiple attributes of characteristic points, the variance of feature and covariance between features are taken into consideration, so the distance measure can reflect the difference between the test signature and the reference signature more precisely.

The Dynamic Structural Statistical Model requires a small number of samples for parameter training. Characteristic points mixed training method is used under reasonable model assumption. The parameters can be well estimated even there are only a small number of training samples and the verification system can still achieve relative high performance in this situation.

ACKNOWLEDGMENT

This work is supported by The National High Technology Research and Development Program of China (863 program) under contract No. 2006AA01Z115 & National Natural Science Foundation of China (project 60772049).

REFERENCES

Brittan, P., & Fairhurst, M.C. (1994). Feature selection in automatic signature verification. In IEE Colloquium on Image Processing for Biometric Measurement (pp. 7.1~7.3). London: the Institution of Electrical Engineerings.

Deng, Y.N., Zhu, H., & Li, S. (2005). Signature verification method based on the combination of shape and dynamic feature. Lecture Notes in Computer Science, 3614, 285-288.

Dimauro, G., Impedovo, S., & Lucchese, M.G. (2004). Recent advancements in automatic signature verification. In S. Kawada (Ed.), Proceedings of the Ninth International Workshop on Frontiers in Handwriting Recognition (IWFHR'04) (pp. 178-184). Los Alamitos, California: IEEE Computer Society Press.

Feng, H., & Wah, C.C. (2003). Online signature verification using a new extreme points warping technique. Pattern Recognition Letters, 24(16), 2943-2951.

Fierrez, J., Ortega-Garcia, J., & Ramos, D. (2007). HMM-based on-line signature verification: Feature extraction and signature modeling. Pattern Recognition Letters, 28(16), 2325-2334.

Gupta, G., & McCabe, A. (1997). A review of dynamic handwritten signature verification. Retrieved November 5, 2001, from James Cook University (Australia) Web site: http://www.cs.jcu.edu.au/~alan/Work/HSV-Lit_rev.ps

Igarza, J.J., Goirizelaia, I., & Espinosa, K. (2003). Online handwritten signature verification using hidden markov models. Lecture Notes in Computer Science, 2905, 391-399.

Jain, A.K., Griess, F.D., & Connell, S.D. (2002). On-line signature verification. Pattern Recognition, 35, 2963-2972.

Jin, Y., & Liu, J. (1999). On-line handwritten signature verification based on elastic matching of 3D curve. Journal of Huazhong University of Science and Technology, 27(5), 14-16.

Kamel, N.S., & Sayeed, S. (2008). SVD-based signature verification technique using data glove. International Journal of Pattern Recognition and Artificial Intelligence, Special Issue on Pattern Recognition and Artificial Intelligence in Biometrics, 22(3), 431-443.

Kim, S.H., Park, M.S., & Kim, J. (1995). Applying personalized weights to a feature set for on-line signature verification. In M. Kavanaugh & P. Storms (Eds.), Proceedings of International Conference on Document Analysis and Recognition'95 (pp. 882-885). Los Alamitos, California: IEEE Computer Society Press.

Kiran, G.V., Kunte, R.S.R., & Samuel, S. (2001). On-line signature verification system using probabilistic feature modelling. In B. Boashash, S.H.S. Salleh & K. Abed-Meraim (Eds.), Proceedings of the Sixth International Symposium on Signal Processing and its Applications (pp. 355-358). Los Alamitos, California: IEEE Computer Society Press.

Lee, L.L., Berger, T., & Aviczer, E. (1996). Reliable on-line human signature verification systems. IEEE Tran. On Pattern Analysis and Machine Intelligence, 18(6), 643-647.

Lei, H., & Govindaraju. V. (2005). A comparative study on the consistency of features in on-line signature verification. Pattern Recognition Letters, 26(15), 2483-2489.

Martens, R., & Claesen, L. (1996). On-line signature verification by dynamic time-warping. In E. Kavanaugh & B. Werner (Eds.), Proceedings of the 13th International Conference on Pattern Recognition-Volume 3 (pp. 38-42). Los Alamitos, California: IEEE Computer Society Press.

Munich, M.E., & Perona, P. (1999). Continuous dynamic time warping for translation-invariant curve alignment with applications to signature verification. In B. Werner (Ed.), Proceedings of the Seventh IEEE International Conference on Computer Vision-Volume 1 (pp. 108-115). Los Alamitos, California: IEEE Computer Society Press.

Muramatsu, D., & Matsumoto, T. (2003). An HMM on-line signature verification algorithm. Lecture Notes in Computer Science, 2688, 233-241.

Parizeau, M., & Plamondon, R. (1990). A comparative analysis of regional correlation, dynamic time warping and skeletal tree matching for signature. IEEE Transactions on Pattern Analysis and Machine Intelligence, 12(7), 710-717.

Pirlo, G. (2003). Automatic signature verification—state of the art and future trends. Paper presented at the ICDAR2003 Tutorial: On Line and Off Line Document Recognition Systems, Edinburgh, UK.

Plamondon, R., & Srihari, S.N. (2000). On-line and off-line handwriting recognition: a comprehensive survey. IEEE transactions on pattern analysis and machine intelligence, 22(1), 63-84.

Popel, D.V. (2007). Signature analysis, verification and synthesis in pervasive environments. In S.N. Yanushkevich, P.S.P. Wang, M.L. Gavrilova and S.N. Srihari (Eds.), Image Pattern Recognition – Synthesis and Analysis in Biometrics, Series in Machines Perception and Artificial Intelligence (pp. 31-63). Singapore: World Scientific Publishing.

Richiardi, J., & Drygajlo, A. (2003). Gaussian mixture models for on-line signature verification. In Proceedings of the 2003 ACM SIGMM workshop on Biometrics methods and applications (pp. 115-122). New York: ACM Press.

Salicetti, S.G., Beumier, C., & Chollet, G. (2003). BIOMET: a multimodal person authentication database including face, voice, fingerprint, hand and signature modalities. In J. Kittler & M.S. Nixon (Eds.), Proceedings of the 4th International Conference on Audio- and Video-Based Biometric Person Authentication (AVBPA03) (pp. 845~853). Berlin Heidelber: Springer-Verlag.

SVC2004. (2004). SVC 2004: First International Signature Verification Competition - EER Statistics of Task 1. Retrieved May 4, 2005, from http://www.cs.ust.hk/svc2004/results-EER1.html

Tanabe, K., Yoshihara, M., & Kameya, H. (2001). Automatic signature verification based on the dynamic feature of pressure. In B. Werner (Ed.), Proceedings of the Sixth International Conference on Document Analysis and Recognition (pp. 1045-1049). Los Alamitos, California: IEEE Computer Society Press.

Van, B.L., Salicetti, S.G., & Dorizzi, B. (2004). Fusion of HMM's likelihood and viterbi path for on-line signature verification. In D. Maltoni & A.K. Jain (Eds.), Proceedings of the ECCV 2004 International Workshop on Biometric Authentication (pp. 318~331). Berlin Heidelber: Springer-Verlag.

Vielhauer, C. (2005). A Behavioural Biometric. Public Service Review: European Union, 9, 113-115.

Yeung, D.T., Chang, H., & Xiong, Y. (2004). SVC2004: first international signature verification competition. In D. Zhang & A.K. Jain (Eds.), Proceedings of the International Conference on Biometric Authentication (ICBA) (pp. 16-23). Berlin Heidelber: Springer-Verlag.

Yi, J., Lee, C., & Kim, J. (2005). Online signature verification using temporal shift estimated by the phase of Gabor filter. IEEE Transactions on Signal Processing, 53(2), 776 – 783.

Zhao, Y.J., & Li, Y.B. (2003). Automatic signature verification about chinese character by computer based on wavelet transform. Computer Engineering, 29(2), 243-245.

This work was previously published in International Journal of Digital Crime and Forensics (IJDCF), edited by Chang-Tsun Li & Anthony T.S. Ho, pp. 21-41, copyright 2009 by IGI Publishing (an imprint of IGI Global).

Chapter 18

Efficient Image Matching Using Local Invariant Features for Copy Detection

H. R. Chennamma
University of Mysore, India

Lalitha Rangarajan
University of Mysore, India

M. S. Rao
Indian Academy of Forensic Sciences, India

ABSTRACT

Retrieval based approach has recently emerged as an attractive option for image copy detection. The Content Based Copy Detection (CBCD) can be treated as a restricted case of near duplicate image detection. Near duplicate images can be: (i) perceptually identical images (e.g. allowing for change in color balance, change in brightness, compression artifacts, contrast adjustment, rotation, cropping, filtering, scaling etc.), (ii) images of the same 3D scene (from different viewpoints). As we are searching for copies which are altered versions of the original image, the images with slight viewpoint variations of the same scene should not be retrieved. In this chapter, we focus on image matching strategy based on local invariant features that will assist in the detection of forged (copy-paste forgery) images. So far, no specific robust homography estimation method exists for this application. The state of the art methodologies tend to generate many false positives. In this chapter, we have introduced a novel strategy for pattern matching of key point distributions for copy detection. Typical experiments conducted on real case images demonstrate the success in near duplicate image retrieval for the application of digital image forensics. Efficiency of the proposed method is corroborated by comparison, with contemporary methods.

INTRODUCTION

Forensic experts believe that no criminal can do his activities without leaving evidence at the scene of crime. However, it is very difficult to trace out evidences especially in case of digital image forgeries. Nowadays, image content manipulation is a well known serious issue in digital image forensics. Such content pirating creates several near duplicate images. Usually, such near duplicate

DOI: 10.4018/978-1-60960-515-5.ch018

images are altered copies of the original image. These unauthorized copies can be detected by retrieving similar images. Thus the concept of Content Based Copy Detection (CBCD) has recently emerged as an alternative means of identifying illegal image copies. The idea is that, instead of hiding additional information (watermark) in the image to enable image tampering detection, the image as such can be used to detect tampering. A content based copy detection system works as follows: given an image registered by the owner, the system can determine whether near replicas of the image are available on the internet or given an image suspected to be a copy, the system can determine whether the original image which was

used in the creation of this query image is available in the database of copyrighted images.

Although, the frameworks of CBCD are considered to be similar to those of Content Based Image Retrieval (CBIR), there are some differences between CBCD and CBIR. An image copy detector searches for near replicas of an image, whereas CBIR not only retrieves image replicas, but also images that share same or similar semantics. Figure 1 and Figure 2 shows an example of a tampered image and a similar (but not a copy) image respectively. According to the definition in literature (Joly et al., 2007), a copy can be seen as a duplicate for which the capturing conditions can not differ (such as camera view angle, scene lighting conditions, camera parameters, etc.).

Figure 1. Example of a copy image (Image 2 is created using Image 1)

Image 1   Image 2

Figure 2. Two different views of the same scene that are not copies

Image 1   Image 2

Thus, copy detection can be treated as a restricted case of CBIR. However, it is not usually feasible to apply existing CBIR techniques directly to image copy detection, since they may cause a considerable number of false alarms.

Local invariant features based approaches for image matching has been successfully applied to a wide range of problems including object recognition (Lowe, 2004), panoramic image stitching (Brown & Lowe, 2003), image mosaicing (Qi & Jeremy, 2006), near duplicate image detection (Zhao et al., 2007) etc. Near duplicate image detection and retrieval is a vital component for many real world applications and recently is being used for news story threading, content based video search (Chang et al., 2005), topic detection & tracking (Wu et al., 2006), near duplicate shot detection in video (Ondrej et al., 2007) and copyright infringement detection (Ke et al., 2004).

The definition of a Near Duplicate Image (NDI) varies depending on what photometric and geometric variations are deemed acceptable and the application in hand. In the case of exact duplicate detection, no changes are allowed. At the other extreme, a more general definition is that these are images of the same scene but with possibly different viewpoints or the perceptually identical images which are slightly altered (using powerful image processing tool) versions of its original. In this research, we mainly focus on image matching strategy for finding copies, fragments of images or variants of the given suspicious digital image (copy-paste forgery). So in this context, NDIs are perceptually identical images but not recognized as such due to common image manipulations such as change in color balance, change in brightness, change in file formats, compression artifacts, contrast adjustment, rotation, cropping, filtering, scaling etc. As we are searching for the images which are altered versions of the original image, the images with slight viewpoint variations of the same scene (called as similar images) should not be retrieved by an efficient copy detection system.

An invariant local feature represents a small image patch. Many matching techniques which use invariant local features, first extract key points from all images and then the query image features vote independently for features from the database images (votes are computed based on proximity and similarity of their intensity neighborhood). If greater the number of votes found, then the image is more likely a near duplicate. However, it is still likely that there are significant false positives at the key point matching phase. In other words, although some key points are within the threshold, they belong to the patches of images that are not near duplicates. So it must be followed by a verification step to account for spatial or geometric relationships among the matched key points. This geometric verification method has to be robust enough to distinguish inlier and outlier correspondences efficiently.

Unfortunately the existing pattern matching techniques fail to distinguish similar images from slightly altered images. Hence the current state of the art image matching methods end with many false positives (images that are not copies of the query image). In order to overcome this drawback, we propose a novel pattern matching technique for finding copies, fragments of images (sub-image) or variants of the same digital image. The proposed copy detection system is useful when the copyrighted images are stored in a system and if a given image is suspected to be an unauthorized copy of a registered image then one can accurately identify the exact source/s used in its creation.

Rest of this chapter is organized as follows. Initially, the relevant research has been presented then a background for the content based copy detection system is discussed. Further, the proposed algorithms for indexing feature points and image matching strategy have been described. Experimental studies along with performance evaluation and complexity analysis have been compared with other contemporary methods. Finally, conclusion has been presented.

RELATED WORK

A variety of methods have been proposed to detect copies or near duplicates. Some of the methods (Chang et al., 1998; Meng et al. 2003; Kim, 2003; Roy et al., 2005; Chen & Stentiford, 2006; Hsiao et al., 2007) based on global features are usually more efficient, but they are less robust to transformations such as cropping, scaling or rotation. Global features are insufficiently accurate for sub-image retrieval. To resolve this problem, the approaches based on local features have been proposed. In this section, we review some related works, regarding image matching techniques based on local invariant features for detecting near duplicate images.

There are numerous key point detectors and descriptors in literature. Mikolajczyk & Schmid (2005) have made a good survey of key point detectors and descriptors. The detection basically locate stable keypoints (and their support regions) which are invariant to certain variations introduced by geometric or photometric changes. Popular detectors are Harris points (Harris, 1988), improved version of the Harris interest point detector (Joly et al., 2003), Hessain-Laplace (Mikolajczyk & Schmid, 2004) and Difference of Gaussian (DoG) (Lowe, 2004). Many techniques for describing local image regions have been developed. Some of the descriptors are SIFT (Lowe, 2004), PCA-SIFT (Ke & Sukthankar, 2004a), steerable filters (Freeman & Adelson, 1991), differential invariants (Koenderink & Van Doorn, 1987), complex filters (Schaffalitzky & Zisserman, 2002) and moment invariants (Van Gool et al., 1996).

Zhang & Chang (2004) have proposed stochastic Attributed Relational Graph (ARG) matching with part-based representation for NDI identification. Under this setting, ARG is a fully connected graph with SUSAN detected keypoints as vertices and the matching of ARGs is constrained by the spatial relation imposed by keypoints. In this process, a distribution based similarity model is learnt for NDI identification. This approach suf-

fers from the limitations of slow matching speed and the requirement of heuristic parameters for learning.

Grauman & Darrell (2005) have measured similarity between images with an approximation of the Earth Mover's Distance (EMD), which quickly computes minimal-cost correspondences between two bags of features. This method is well suited for retrieving similar scene, object and texture recognition even though they are perceptually different whereas in our case such perceptually different images are not likely to be retrieved.

Ke et. al (2004b) have used PCA-SIFT key points for detecting copyright violations. This system is almost accurate in retrieving near duplicates. However, the system will also match similar images of the same scene even if they are neither near duplicates nor forged images. They have used Random Sample Consensus (RANSAC) estimator for pattern matching of distribution of local features. RANSAC introduced by Fishler & Robert (1981) is the most popular estimation technique in image matching used by computer vision community. RANSAC is well suited for object recognition, motion estimation, panoramic image stitching and image mosaicing but not for the detection of copyright infringement as we shall show in the experimental study section.

Ngo et. al (2006) proposed pattern entropy to measure the information for being an NDI pair for the application of broadcast domain. They have used symmetric and transitivity property of NDI pairs for detection and propagation. But transitivity property is not useful to detect copy-paste forgery.

Joly et al. (2007) presented a copy retrieval scheme based on local features (Joly et al., 2003) that can deal with very large database both in terms of quality and speed. They first proposed a new approximate similarity search technique in which the probabilistic selection of the feature space regions is not based on the distribution in the database but on the distribution of the features distortion. Furthermore, they have shown, how the discrimination of the global retrieval can be enhanced during its post-processing step, by considering only the geometrically consistent matches. However, they have considered only resize, rotation and translation for the spatial transformations and not discussed about shearing, flipping, perspective and affine transformations.

Berrani et al. (2003) proposed a image recognition scheme based on local differential descriptors. They proposed a novel search method that trades the precision of each individual search for reduced query execution time. But, the authors have not studied about resizing operation as it is the most necessary operation to be performed while creating copies.

The state of the art methods for image matching are not accurate enough to decide whether two similar images are copies or not. Therefore, it is usually infeasible to apply existing image matching techniques for NDI detection directly to image copy detection which consequently leads to a considerable number of false alarms. This motivates us to devise a novel image matching method exclusively for copy detection problem.

BACKGROUND

Among many methods based on local intensity values of the image, devised for NDI detection (described in preceding section), the most successful local image descriptor so far is Lowe's (2004) Scale Invariant Feature Transform (SIFT) descriptor (Mikolajczyk & Schmid, 2005).

Overview of the SIFT Descriptors

The Scale Invariant Feature Transform (SIFT) is an algorithm to identify and characterize local features in images. The SIFT algorithm finds extrema points in scale space and extracts position, scale, rotation invariant feature vector of dimension-128 for each extrema point. The computational steps of SIFT descriptors are divided into four major steps (Lowe, 2004). (1) Scale-space peak selec-

tion (i.e. identifying key points); (2) key point localization; (3) orientation assignment and (4) key point descriptor computation. These steps are used to produce the set of image features.

In the first step, potential interest points are identified by scanning the image over location and scale. This is implemented efficiently by constructing a Gaussian pyramid and searching for local peaks (termed key points) in a series of Difference-of-Gaussian (DoG) images. In order to increase the algorithm's anti-noise ability, it is needed to remove the low-contrast and unstable key points. The second step attempts to eliminate these unstable key points from the list of key points by finding, those with low-contrast or which are poorly localized on an edge. This may be achieved by calculating the Laplacian value for each key point found in step one. The third step aims to assign a consistent orientation to the key points based on local image properties. The key point descriptor can then be represented relative to this orientation, achieving invariance to rotation. The local image gradients are measured at the selected scale in the region around each key point. These are transformed into a representation that allows for significant levels of local shape distortion and change in illumination. In the fourth step, the local gradient data is used to create key point descriptors.

The local descriptor (SIFT of Lowe) has several characteristics that are ideal for solving the image copy detection problem. First, the key points are scale and rotation invariant. This allows us to detect and match the same set of key points even after images have been arbitrarily rotated or scaled. Second, the descriptors are invariant to image deformations such as gaussian blurring, median filtering, and the addition or removal of noise, affine warp, changes in brightness and contrast, etc. Furthermore, SIFT ignores color and operates on gray-scale images, making the algorithm immune to transforms that manipulate the color content of the image, such as saturation and colorization. Finally, because we use local descriptors, our system can find matches even if there is significant occlusion or cropping in the images. The proposed system requires as few as five key points (out of hundreds) to match two images. Two images are said to be matched when the descriptors are similar as well as distributions of key points are geometrically similar. Despite the small number of key points needed to match, our system maintains a low false positive rate because the local descriptors are highly distinctive and the geometric constraints further discards many false positives.

Content Based Copy Detection

The following steps describe the proposed method of copy detection using SIFT key points.

Step 1: Determine All Possible Matching Key Point Pairs

Assume I_1 and I_2 are two images whose key points have been extracted and all the possible matched pairs are determined.

Let $FP_1 = \{q_n(x,y), n = 1,2,......,N_1\}$, $FP_2 = \{p_m(x,y), m = 1,2,....,N_2\}$ be the sets of key points in images I_1 and I_2 respectively. Key points 'q_n' and 'p_m' are represented by vectors of dimension-128.

If the Euclidean distance between the feature vectors for a particular pair of key points falls below the chosen threshold then this pair is termed a match. Lowe (2004) has suggested the use of a modified distance function to improve the matching speed. The modified distance determines cosine of the angle between the two feature vectors. We have used this Modified Distance (MD) function to find matched key points between query and database images. The distance function $\{MD(q_n, p_m), n = 1,2,....,N_1, m = 1,2,....,N_2\}$ is computed for all $N_1 \times N_2$ combinations of the extracted key points. We search the $N_1 \times N_2$ table of $\{MD(q_n, p_m)\}$ for the values less than the threshold. $\{MD(q_a, p_a), a = 1,2,...,z\}$ denotes the set of matched key point pairs between I_1 and I_2.

Step 2: Check for Spatial Consistency of Matched Key Point Pairs

Although the key points $\{MD(q_a, p_a), a = 1,2,...,z\}$ are within the threshold distance, they may be belong to patches of images that are not copies. So the matching phase must be followed by a verification step to account for spatial or geometric relationships between the positions of key points. The spatial arrangement of the minimum number (threshold) of key points $\{q_a(x,y), a = 1,2,......,z\}$ of image I_1 must agree with the corresponding matched key points $\{p_a(x,y), a = 1,2,....,z\}$ of image I_2 to say that I_1 and I_2 are near duplicates. This is crucial step in the detection of near duplicates. As we are searching for the images which are altered versions of the original image, the images of the same scene with slight viewpoint variations are not likely to be retrieved. Such false positives must be eliminated in this verification step. So we need a specific matching strategy for this application. The proposed key point indexing method and key points matching strategy are explained in the following section.

PROPOSED MATCHING STRATEGY

Once we extract feature points from the query image, the first step is that the set of extracted key points must be stored in a well organized manner in order to achieve accurate and quick matching process. Thus, the query image is logically partitioned into blocks as shown in Figure 3 where $b_{11}......b_{xy}$ are block labels and each block size is 100x100 pixels. The SIFT key points proposed by Lowe (2004) are arranged based on the stability and orientation of the key points. Thus the list of key points is randomly distributed over the image. Consequently, the adjacent key points in the list may lie in distant blocks.

In most of the cases, we are matching a small portion of the query image with a small portion of the database image and hence our interest lies

Figure 3. Block partition of query image

b_{x1}	b_{x2}	b_{x3}	$\cdots$	b_{xy}
.	.	.	.	.
:	:	:	:	:
b_{31}	b_{32}	b_{33}	$\cdots$	b_{3y}
b_{21}	b_{22}	b_{23}	$\cdots$	b_{2y}
b_{11}	b_{12}	b_{13}	$\cdots$	b_{1y}

in searching for the key points which are located in small area of the whole image. Hence, we propose a method for indexing key points based on their location, so that the adjacent key points in the list always lies in neighboring blocks. We store and retrieve key points of the query image blocks in the order of $b_{11}, b_{21}, b_{22}, b_{12}, b_{13}, b_{23}, b_{33}, b_{32},$ $b_{31},\ldots.b_{x1}, b_{x2}\ldots.b_{xy}\ldots.b_{2y}, b_{1y}$ (if x is even number) or $b_{11}, b_{21}, b_{22}, b_{12}, b_{13}, b_{23}, b_{33}, b_{32}, b_{31},\ldots.b_{1y}, b_{2y}\ldots.$ $b_{xy}\ldots.b_{x2}, b_{x1}$ (if x is odd number). All the key points which lie in each block are stored in the increasing order of y-coordinates and then x-coordinates. Random accessing of key points slows down the search process. We have noticed, increase in

matching speed when the key points of the query are sorted in the order suggested. The proposed indexing method allows us to make approximate copy search that only examine a small portion of the image (for best case). Thus it reduces the number of false key point matches as well as speeds up the verification of spatial arrangement of matched key points between two images.

The key points organization of sample images (in Figure 4) is shown in Figure 5 and Figure 6. The block partition of image 1 in Figure 4 is shown in Figure 5. The key points of image 1 are labeled according to their positions in the sorted list and the corresponding matched key points of image 2 are shown in Figure 6.

The extracted key points of the query are stored in a list based on their positions in the order of y-coordinates and then x-coordinates, within each block. Checking for the relative spatial arrangement of the matched key points can begin as soon as 3 matched key point pairs between two images are available. This is done by finding angle between two lines (made by 3 corresponding points in the two images) and the ratio of line segments. If the angles and the line ratios are same (equivalently, if the difference between angles

Figure 4. Sample Images

Image 1: Query (Size 260x240 pix)   Image 2: Candidate (Size 260x240 pix)

Figure 5. Indexed key points of Image 1

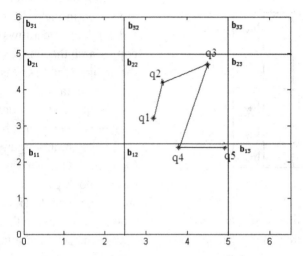

Figure 6. Corresponding (matched) key points position of Image 2

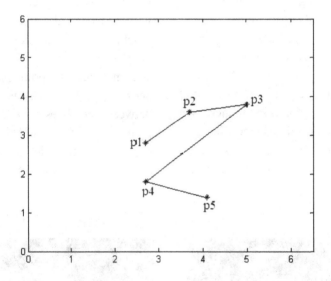

and the difference between line ratios are zero), then the relative spatial arrangement of the 3 points in two images (query and candidate image) are same.

Note that both the directed relative angle and the length ratio attributes are invariant to the changes in scale (uniform), rotation and translation (Forsyth & Ponce, 2003). So the difference of corresponding angles and the line ratios must be theoretically zero for key points with same spatial arrangement. But practically due to the

computational error and the small deformations while creating the copies, we need to set a small positive threshold value.

Our experiments show that, Angle and Line Ratio (ALR) metric works well even for the partial shape matching (cropping). It is interesting to note that ALR works well for detecting copy-paste NDI pairs but not for NDI pairs which are the same scenes taken at different viewpoints. This is because neither the angle nor the distance ratios are preserved when the view changes. The

Angle-Line ratio spatial relationship works on the principle that, if the two images are taken from different positions of the scene, the corresponding parts in the images appear differently with local deformations irrespective of whether the scene is 3D or planar surface. The template correlation is very much affected by such local deformations. The proposed algorithms are given below.

The advantage of using Angle and Line Ratio metric is verification of the spatial distribution of key points (step 2) can be done during key point matching phase (step 1) described in the previous section.

EXPERIMENTAL STUDY

Experiments are conducted to assess the performance of our proposed homography estimation algorithm (ALR) in detecting the original image (from the database) which has been used in the creation of composite (query) image.

Since RANSAC (Random Sample Consensus) is the most commonly used estimation method for homographies (Lee & Kim, 2007), we have compared our results with RANSAC estimator. In this section, to study the results of proposed method in real case scenario, experiments were carried out on images of INRIA database. This

database can be downloaded from http://www. inrialpes.fr/movi. This data set consists of 42 images of 12 different objects taken from different viewpoints. Figure 7 shows the query image which is created by using a database image boat-img1 shown in Figure 8. Observe that a simple visual examination cannot categorically point out the correct source image as boat-img1.

To assess the performance of our proposed ALR metric, comparison of results with most popular RANSAC estimator is shown in Table 1. The number of matched key point pairs between query and other images in the data base (other than boat images) are too low and hence not shown in Table 1. Our goal is to retrieve the source image (boat-img1) which contains the portion of query image. The number of key points extracted from the query image is 450. Table 1 shows the matching score for retrieval using 3 metrics, namely MD, RANSAC and ALR.

Had modified distance function been the metric of similarity, boat-img3 (with score 85) would take the first place while ranking (column 3 of Table 1). Recall that query image is created by using boat-img1. The modified distance measure fails to highlight the source image namely boat-img1. This implies that cardinality of matched point pairs alone cannot become the criterion for measuring similarity between images. So we go

Algorithm 1: *To sort the extracted key points in the query image*

```
Input      : Query image (size a x b) and co-ordinates of key points
Output     : Extracted key points in the sorted order
1.         a_1 ← ⌊a / 100⌋ + 1 // find number of blocks in the row
2.         b_1 ← ⌊b / 100⌋ + 1 // find number of blocks in the column
3.         for i = 1 to a_1
4.         for j = 1 to b_1
5.         Sort the key points in block (i, j) in the increasing order of y-co-
ordinates and then x-coordinates.
end for
end for
6.         Return
```

Algorithm 2: *To verify spatial consistency of matched key points in query and candidate*

```
                Image using Angle and Line Ratio statistics
```

Input   : *s* (no. of key points in query image which are sorted), t_1 and t_2
are threshold values

Output   : *kp* (no. of matched pairs of key points), *smp* (no. of matched pairs
that have same
                spatial distribution)

1. $kp \leftarrow 0$; $smp \leftarrow 0$; $i \leftarrow 1$; $j \leftarrow 1$; $k \leftarrow 1$;

2.   Identify key points $(\mathbf{q_i}, \mathbf{q_j}, \mathbf{q_k})$ in query and corresponding matches
$(\mathbf{p_i}, \mathbf{p_j}, \mathbf{p_k})$ in candidate
image.

3.   **if** $k > s$

then //no more 3 matched pairs available to check spatial consistency
Return *smp*, *kp*
      end if

4.   **Compute:**

lq_1 = distance between $(\mathbf{q_i}, \mathbf{q_j})$; mq_1 = slope of line joining $(\mathbf{q_i}, \mathbf{q_j})$

lq_2 = distance between $(\mathbf{q_j}, \mathbf{q_k})$; mq_2 = slope of line joining $(\mathbf{q_j}, \mathbf{q_k})$

lp_1 = distance between $(\mathbf{p_i}, \mathbf{p_j})$; mp_1 = slope of line joining $(\mathbf{p_i}, \mathbf{p_j})$

lp_2 = distance between $(\mathbf{p_j}, \mathbf{p_k})$; mp_2 = slope of line joining $(\mathbf{p_j}, \mathbf{p_k})$

$$qr = \frac{lq_1}{lq_2}, \qquad pr = \frac{lp_1}{lp_2}$$

$$qa = \tan^{-1}\left(\frac{mq_1 - mq_2}{1 + mq_1 mq_2}\right), \qquad pa = \tan^{-1}\left(\frac{mp_1 - mp_2}{1 + mp_1 mp_2}\right)$$

5.   **if** *smp*=0 and $|pr - qr| < t_1$ and $|pa - qa| < t_2$ **then** *smp* $\leftarrow$ *smp* + 3 //
first 3 key point pairs with spatial match identified
     $kp \leftarrow kp + 3$
     $i \leftarrow j$; $j \leftarrow k$; identify next key point $\mathbf{q_k}$ and its match $\mathbf{p_k}$ **Go To** step 3
end if

6.   **if** $|pr - qr| < t_1$ and $|pa - qa| < t_2$
then
     $smp \leftarrow smp + 1$ //one more key point pair with spatial match identified
     $kp \leftarrow kp + 1$
     $i \leftarrow j$; $j \leftarrow I$; identify next key point $\mathbf{q_k}$ and its match $\mathbf{p_k}$ **Go to** step 3
end if

7.   **if** *smp* = 0
then //First 3 spatially matched key point pairs not yet identified
        $i \leftarrow j$; $j \leftarrow k$; identify next keypoint $\mathbf{q_k}$ and its match $\mathbf{p_k}$
        Go to step 3
end if

8. $kp \leftarrow kp + 1$
identify next key point $\mathbf{q_k}$ and its match $\mathbf{p_k}$ **Go to** step 3

Figure 7. Query Image

for verification step where spatial consistency of the matched pairs will be checked. If RANSAC is used for spatial consistency check, boat-img3 takes the first place. This can be inferred from

Figure 8. Database images

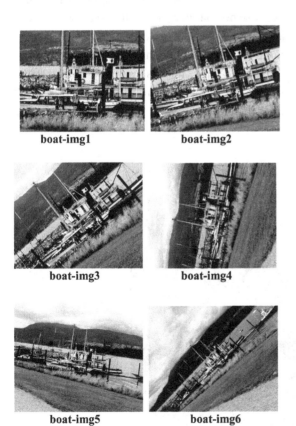

boat-img1   boat-img2

boat-img3   boat-img4

boat-img5   boat-img6

column 4 of Table 1 with boat-img3 resulting with a score of 81. The number of inliers produced by RANSAC significantly depends on the number of input point pairs from Step1 and RANSAC works well only when the number of correct matches dominates the number of false matches. Observe that tightening the threshold '*t*' does not guarantee correct results (column 5 of Table 1) with RANSAC.

Column 6 of Table 1 reflects similarity measure of proposed method. Observe that boat-img1 is rightly ranked first with the proposed method. Further, the similarity measures of other images are very low. A threshold 'θ'>10 on the score will retrieve only the correct image from the proposed method (refer column 6 of Table 1). Whereas other two methods will retrieve all boat images (refer columns 3 and 4 of the Table 1). A more rigorous threshold in step 2 while using RANSAC, performs marginally better during retrieval (refer column 5 of the Table 1). Our Angle and Line Ratio method successfully filtered off all false matches to retain only the reliable matches for retrieval. It is clear that performance of RANSAC is relatively poor when compared to the performance of Angle Line Ratio (ALR) method in the detection of copies or variants of the original image.

We have conducted another experiment on images downloaded from INRIA database to study another case with RANSAC estimator.

Table 1. Matching score between Figure 7 (query) and each of the images in Figure 8

Image	No. of key points	Number of matching key point pairs			
		Step1:using Modified Distance Function	Step2:using RANSAC Estimator		Step2: using Angle and Line Ratio t = 0.01
			t=0.01	t=0.0001	
boat-img1	9687	75	68	12	16
boat-img2	9278	54	47	10	6
boat-img3	7113	85	81	12	8
boat-img4	5670	57	54	11	8
boat-img5	5376	53	41	8	5
boat-img6	4510	22	19	8	0

The query image in Figure 9 is a composite image created using two images called source images (Figure 10 and Figure 11). The pasted portion in composite image is rotated and scaled down to make the query more realistic. The search for copies has been performed on INRIA database. Figure 12 shows corresponding matching pairs of key points between the composite (query) image and the different views of source image 2 (in Figure11) using both proposed Angle and Line Ratio (ALR) matching strategy and RANSAC estimator.

Table 2 shows the matching score between query and the three views of source image 2 (Figure 11) for both ALR and RANSAC. Other images in the database resulted with very few matching key point pairs and hence not listed in Table 2. Observe that the proposed algorithm produces no false positives (column 5 of Table 2) because no spatial matches found between query and view1 or view 2. Although view 3 has got highest number of matches with RANSAC it will retrieve all views because view 1 and view 2 also have some amount of inliers (column 4 of Table 2). So the above experiment shows that the ac-

Figure 9. Query image (composite image) (key points=4639)

Figure 10. Source image 1 (key points=4189)

curacy of our proposed algorithm is better than the RANSAC, in identifying the source image without any ambiguity.

Further, we also conducted experiments to evaluate the performance of our proposed method against the database consisting of very similar images (taken at different viewpoints). A more challenging database for our copy detection system is Columbia Object Image Library (COIL-20)

database (Sameer, et al., 1996). COIL-20 database contains 1440 images of 20 objects. Images of the objects were taken at pose intervals of 5 degrees and covered full 360 degrees. This corresponds to 72 images per object. Thus, COIL-20 database contains very similar images.

For demonstration purpose we have chosen an image as a query and it is scaled down and rotated by 45 degrees (shown in Figure 13). Figure 13

Figure 11. Source image 2 (key points=1483)

Figure 12. Matching results

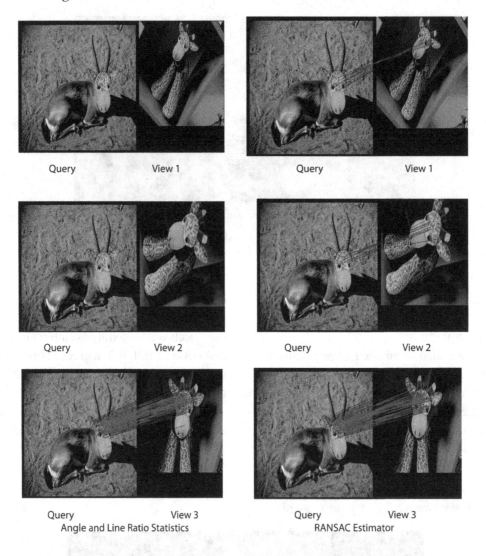

Query — View 1   Query — View 1

Query — View 2   Query — View 2

Query — View 3   Query — View 3
Angle and Line Ratio Statistics   RANSAC Estimator

shows the matching results for this query image using the proposed ALR algorithm. Observe that it has accurately retrieved only the original image from which the query image has been derived. Figure 14 shows the matching results using the RANSAC estimator which has generated 7 false positives.

PERFORMANCE EVALUATION

In this section, the performance of our proposed method is evaluated against the database consisting

Figure 13. Matching results using ALR

Query   Retrieved Image

of a set of random images (which are not related to the query image) and very similar images

Table 2. Matching Score between Figure 9 and different views of Figure 11

Images	Number of Key points	Number of matching key point pairs		
		Step1:Modified Distance Function	Step2:using RANSAC Estimator	Step2: using Angle Line Ratio (ALR)
view1	1785	24	10	0
view2	1848	26	11	0
view3	1483	237	120	126

(which are taken from different viewpoints). The experiments are carried out on the database which consists of 5000 images selected from INRIA, COIL-20 and mm270k database. The mm270k database can be downloaded from http://www-2. cs.cmu.edu/yke/retrieval. Some sample images from our database are shown in Figure 15.

In order to evaluate the performance of the proposed ALR algorithm, 12 queries are created to cover different spatial transformations and various scenarios in creating composite images in real cases. They are as listed below:

- **Copy-move forgery or Region duplication**

- **Composite Image:** (a) Composite of 2 images (b) Composite of 3 images in which all images are present in the database
- **Flip:** Horizontal flip
- **Partial or Occlusion**
- **Perspective Transformation**
- **Affine Transformation**
- **Rotation:** (a) +45° (b) -45°
- **Scaling:** (a) Scale-up (b) Scale-down
- **Shearing:** Apply an affine warp along the x-axis

Figure 16 shows the original image which was used to create 12 queries (shown in Figure 17). The performance of the proposed method is evaluated by computing the recall, precision and

Figure 14. Matching results using RANSAC

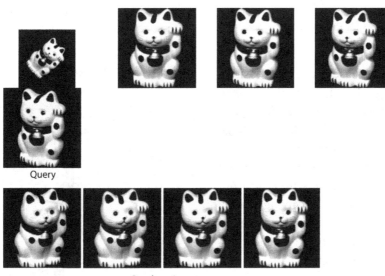

Query

Resultant Images

Figure 15. Some images in the database

$F_{measure}$. Then comparison has been given with other contemporary methods.

$$Re\,call = \frac{Number\ of\ correct\ positives}{Total\ number\ of\ positives}$$

$$Pr\,ecision = \frac{Number\ of\ correct\ positives}{Total\ number\ of\ matches\ (correct\ or\ false)}$$

$$F_{measure} = \frac{2 \times Re\,call \times Pr\,ecision}{Re\,call + Pr\,ecision}$$

An image in the database is said to be positive when a query has a portion of this database image (could be transformed). For example in experiment 1 boat-img1 (in Figure 8) is the only image that is positive. It is correct positive if it is also retrieved. If a wrong image is retrieved it is termed as false positive. We also computed the F-measure that combines precision and recall giving a single measure. In copy detection retrieval we need to maximize number of correct positives and minimize the number of false positives.

For all the queries, we have set the threshold 'θ'>5. So we retrieve all images which have got more than 5 matches. From the Table 3, we can observe that the proposed ALR method fails in case of flip and shearing transformations, but in all other cases it performs excellently. However, these transformations are rarely used in case of composite creation.

COMPLEXITY ANALYSIS

The ALR algorithm involves two steps. In the first step, we sort the key points based on its position.

Figure 16. Original Image

Figure 17. Queries

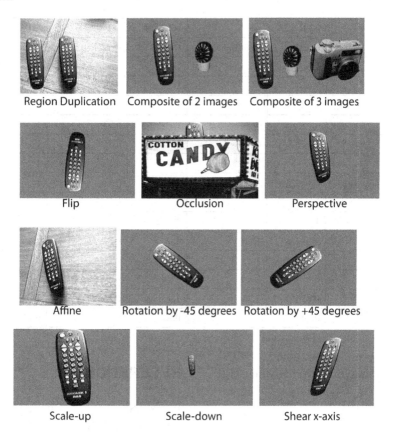

Worst case complexity for indexing key points is $O(p\,logp) + O(p\,logp)$ (for sorting key points of the query image first from bottom to top and then from left to right within each block) where 'p' is the number of key points within the block. Note that 'p' is much smaller compared to 'n' ('n' is the total number of key points in an image).

The second step of the proposed algorithm is to compare the spatial distributions of key points between two images for which the worst case complexity is $O(n-2)$ (The maximum number of open triangles that can be formed with 'n' key points is '$n-2$'). Therefore the overall complexity is $O(p\,logp) + O(p\,logp) + O(n-2) = O(n)$.

The complexity of RANSAC estimator (Ke, 2004b) involves the determination of affine transformation coefficients between two images (query and database) using 3 pairs of matched key points. This can be done in constant time proportional to 6^3 (six affine transformation coefficients to be determined). RANSAC verifies whether the majority (greater than threshold) of the matched keypoints support the above determined affine transformation. The complexity for this step is $\Omega(n)$. So the overall complexity turns out to be $\Omega(6^3) + \Omega(n) = \Omega(n)$.

Another popular homography estimation method is Least Median of Squares (LMS) estimation. The complexity of LMS algorithm is $O(n^2)$ as given by Herbert & Diane (1990). However, LMS method does not require any prior knowledge of setting thresholds like RANSAC. The major disadvantage of LMS is that it would be unable to cope with more than half of the data being outliers. Note that $O(n)$ is smaller than $\Omega(n)$ and $O(n^2)$. Also experimental results are better (fewer false positives) and accurate (distinctive matching

Table 3. Performance evaluation

	ALR		RANSAC		SIFT	
	Recall	Precision	Recall	Precision	Recall	Precision
Region duplication	1	1	1	0.5	1	0.33
Composite of 2 images	1	1	1	0.66	1	0.083
Composite of 3 images	1	1	1	0.75	1	0.136
Flip	0	0	1	0.33	1	0.045
Occlusion	1	0.5	1	0.25	1	0.052
Perspective	1	0.5	1	0.5	1	0.05
Affine	1	1	1	0.33	1	0.09
Rotate -45^0	1	1	1	0.5	1	0.047
Rotate +45^0	1	1	1	0.5	1	0.045
Scale-up	1	1	1	0.5	1	0.05
Scale-down	1	1	1	0.5	1	0.058
Shear x-axis	0	0	1	0.2	1	0.037
Average	**0.83**	**0.75**	**1**	**0.46**	**1**	**0.085**
$F_{measure}$	**0.79**		**0.63**		**0.157**	

score and hence unambiguous retrieval) thus ALR performs better.

CONCLUSION

In this chapter, we focus on image matching strategy for identifying copies which are slightly altered versions (using image processing tool) of its original image and will assist in the detection of composite images. We have developed a homography estimation strategy which offers a means of efficiently matching distributions of local invariant features that is useful for image copy detection. This is done in two steps. Step 1 organizes the key points that speed up the matching process. Step 2 verifies the spatial consistency of the matched key points. We have demonstrated the superiority of our algorithm's performance over conventional RANSAC estimator through a series of experiments. Proposed algorithm is computationally efficient when compared to RANSAC & LMS. In future, we intend to work on clustering of key points.

REFERENCES

Berrani Sid-Ahmed. Amsaleg Laurent & Gros Patrick. (2003). Robust content-based image searches for copyright protection. In Proceedings of the 1st ACM international workshop on Multimedia databases, LA, USA, (pp. 70-77).

Brown, M., & Lowe, D. G. (2003). Recognising Panoramas. In Proceedings of the 9th IEEE International Conference on Computer Vision, (pp. 1218-1225).

Chang, E., Wang, J., Li, C., & Wiederhold, G. (1998). A replicated image detector for the world-wide web. In *Proceedings of SPIE*. RIME.

Chang, S. F., Hsu, W., Kennedy, L., Xie, L., Yanagawa, A., Zavesky, E., & Zhang, D.-Q. (2005). *Columbia university trecvid-2005 video search and high-level feature extraction*. In TRECVID.

Chen, L. (2006). *Stentiford, F. W. M* (pp. 38–42). Comparison of Near-Duplicate Image Matching. CVMP.

Chum, O., Philbin, J., Isard, M., & Zisserman, A. (2007). Scalable Near Identical Image and Shot Detection. Proceedings of the 6th ACM International Conference on Image and Video Retrieval, (pp. 549-556).

Edelsbrunner, H., & Souvaine, D. L. (1990). Computing Least Median of Squares Regression Lines and Guided Topological Sweep. *Journal of the American Statistical Association, 85*(409), 115–119. doi:10.2307/2289532

Fischler, M. A., & Robert, C. Bolles. (1981). Random Sample Consensus: A Paradigm for Model Fitting with Applications to Image Analysis and Automated Cartography. 24(6), 381-395.

Forsyth, D. A., & Ponce, J. (2003). *Computer Vision: A Modern Approach*. New Jersey: Prentice Hill.

Freeman, W., & Adelson, E. (1991). The Design and Use of Steerable Filters. *IEEE Transactions on Pattern Analysis and Machine Intelligence, 13*(9), 891–906. doi:10.1109/34.93808

Grauman, K., & Darrell, T. (2005). Efficient Image Matching with Distribution of Local Invariant Features. In Proceedings of the IEEE Conference on Computer Vision and Pattern Recognition, (pp. 627–634).

Harris, C., & Stephens, M. (1988). A Combined Corner and Edge Detector. In Proceedings Alvey Vision Conference, (pp. 147-151).

Hsiao, J.-H., Chen, C.-S., Chien, L.-F., & Chen, M.-S. (2007). A new approach to image copy detection based on extended feature sets. *IEEE Transactions on Image Processing, 16*(8), 2069–2079. doi:10.1109/TIP.2007.900099

Joly, A., Buisson, O., & Frelicot, C. (2007). Content-based copy retrieval using distortion-based probabilistic similarity search. *IEEE Transactions on Multimedia, 9*(2), 293–306. doi:10.1109/TMM.2006.886278

Joly, A., Frelicot, C., & Buisson, O. (2003). Robust content-based video copy identification in a large reference database, In Proc. of the Interl. Conference on Image and Video Retrieval, (pp. 414-424).

Ke, Y., & Sukthankar, R. (2004). PCA-SIFT: A more distinctive representation for local image descriptors. In Proceedings of IEEE Conf. on Computer Vision and Pattern Recognition, (pp. 506-513).

Ke, Y., Sukthankar, R., & Huston, L. (2004). Efficient Near-Duplicate Detection and Sub-Image Retrieval. Proc. 12th ACM Intl. Conf. on Multimedia, (pp. 869-876).

Kim, C. (2003). Content-based image copy detection. *Signal Processing Image Communication, 18*(3), 169–184. doi:10.1016/S0923-5965(02)00130-3

Koenderink, J., & Van Doorn, A. (1987). Representation of Local Geometry in the Visual System. *Biological Cybernetics, 55,* 367–375. doi:10.1007/BF00318371

Lee, J. J., & Kim, G. Y. (2007). Robust estimation of camera homography using fuzzy RANSAC. In Proc. of International Conference on Computational Science and its Applications.

Lowe, D. G. (2004). Distinctive Image Features from Scale-Invariant Keypoints. *International Journal of Computer Vision, 2*(60), 91–110. doi:10.1023/B:VISI.0000029664.99615.94

Meng, Y., & Chang, E. (2003). *Beitao, Li* (pp. 416–423). Enhancing DPF for Near-Replica Image Recognition. In Proc. of IEEE Computer Vision and Pattern Recognition.

Mikolajczyk, K., & Schmid, C. (2004). Scale and Affine Invariant Interest Point Detectors. *International Journal of Computer Vision, 1*(60), 63–86. doi:10.1023/B:VISI.0000027790.02288.f2

Mikolajczyk, K., & Schmid, C. (2005). A Performance Evaluation of Local Descriptors. *IEEE Transactions on Pattern Analysis and Machine Intelligence, 27*(10), 1615–1630. doi:10.1109/TPAMI.2005.188

Sameer Nene, Shree K. Nayar & Hiroshi Murase. (1996). *Columbia Object Image Library COIL-20, Tech*. Report: Nene96ColumbiaObject.

Ngo, C.-W., Zhao, W., & Jiang, Y.-G. (2006). Fast Tracking of Near-Duplicate Keyframes in Broadcast Domain with Transitivity Propagation. Proceedings of the 14th annual ACM international conference on Multimedia, (pp. 845-854).

Roy, Sujoy, Chang, Ee-Chien & Natarajan, K., (2005). A unified framework for resolving ambiguity in copy detection. In *Proceedings of the 13th annual ACM international conference on Multimedia*, Hilton, Singapore.

Schaffalitzky, F., & Zisserman, A. (2002). Multi-View Matching for Unordered image Sets. In *Proceedings 7th European Conference Computer Vision*, (pp. 414-431).

Van Gool, L., Moons, T., & Ungureanu, D. (1996). Affine/Photometric Invariants for Planar Intensity Patterns. In *Proc. 4th European Conference Computer Vision*, (pp. 642-651).

Wu, X., Ngo, C.-W., & Li, Q. (2006). Threading and auto documenting news videos. *Signal Processing Magazine, 23*(2), 59–68.

Zhang, D.-Q., & Chang, S.-U. (2004). *Detecting Image Near-Duplicate by Stochastic Attributed Relational Graph Matching with learning*. 12th ACM Intl. Conf. on Multimedia, (pp. 877-884).

Zhao, W.L., Ngo, C.W., & Tan, H.K., & Wu, Xiao. (2007). Near-duplicate keyframe identification with interest point matching and pattern learning. *IEEE Transactions on Multimedia, 9*(5), 1037–1048. doi:10.1109/TMM.2007.898928

Zhi, Q. (2006). *Jeremy R. Cooperstock*. Wide-Baseline Image Mosaicing for Indoor Environments. International Conference on Pattern Recognition.

Chapter 19
Reliable Motion Detection, Location and Audit in Surveillance Video

Samaan Poursoltan
University of Adelaide, Australia

Matthew J. Sorell
University of Adelaide, Australia

ABSTRACT

The review of video captured by fixed surveillance cameras is a time consuming, tedious, expensive and potentially unreliable human process, but of very high evidentiary value. Two key challenges stand out in such a task; ensuring that all motion events are captured for analysis, and demonstrating that all motion events have been captured so that the evidence survives being challenged in court. In previous work (Zhao, Poursoltanmohammadi & Sorell, 2008), it was demonstrated that tracking the average brightness of video frames or frame segment provided a more robust metric of motion than other commonly hypothesized motion measures. This paper extends that work in three ways; by setting automatic localized motion detection thresholds, by maintaining a frame-by-frame single parameter normalized motion metric, and by locating regions of motion events within the footage. A tracking filter approach is used for localized motion analysis, which adapts to localized background motion or noise within each image segment. When motion is detected, location and size estimates are reported to provide some objective description of the motion event.

INTRODUCTION

Consider a surveillance scenario of a fixed-position video camera mounted indoors or outdoors, monitoring a specific low-traffic area such as an entrance, a cash machine or a stairwell. Low-traffic in this context means that much of the time there are no motion events of potential interest. This does not however mean that the scene is stationary. It is common in such a situation for the camera to introduce significant random noise from one

DOI: 10.4018/978-1-60960-515-5.ch019

frame to the next, there might also be trees or bushes waving in the wind in the background, a constantly-moving escalator etc. Such occurrences do not constitute motion events of interest, but in the absence of an adequately robust motion detection algorithm, they are likely to cause constant false triggering of a motion detector.

In previous work (Zhao, Poursoltanmohammadi & Sorell, 2008), it was shown that of three likely candidates (frame luminance entropy, frame average luminance, frame differencing), average luminance provided the most robust mechanism for motion event detection, in large part because such a technique averages out speckle noise introduced by the camera sensor and subsequent processing and compression. That paper also proposed that by tracking such a motion metric on a frame-by-frame basis, and by capturing full frame-rate footage with lead in and lead out when motion is detected and low frame-rate footage otherwise, it would be possible to have confidence in the completeness of the motion footage, and to be able to demonstrate that confidence in court. However, the issue of how to set decision thresholds and consideration of additional informative motion metrics was left open. In particular, the challenge of how to deal with regular background motion, such as waving trees, was not addressed.

The current work extends that previous work in significant ways – firstly by showing that a region of interest such as a square macro-block of 16x16 pixels provides sufficient noise reduction for effective motion detection, then by proposing a technique using a tracking filter for each macroblock in a video frame to provide normalised local motion metrics, and then by combining the metrics into an aggregated motion metric, a composite motion detector, and an estimator of size and location of regions of motion.

It is proposed that such an approach has several notable advantages over current practice. In the first instance, human motion review is a tedious and time-consuming task, subject to errors due to fatigue; it is also expensive in terms of work hours to perform such a review. The approach proposed here allows for human or automated secondary analysis of motion event footage rather than motion detection. Secondly, metrics are produced which can be used to demonstrate confidence in the completeness of the captured record, that is to say to demonstrate to a court that all motion events have been captured, but without excessive false-alarm overheads. Thirdly, once the efficacy of the proposed approach is accepted by the court, the option exists to implement the algorithm at the camera, reducing storage and/or transmission overheads without compromising the completeness of the video record.

Motion analysis has been considered within the realm of computer vision and image understanding for some years (Ullman (1979), Huang and Lee (1988), and Maybank (1993)). Almost all of the research in this area has assumed that the video frames contain some form of motion, and the focus has been the classification of the movement into matters of interest (Konrad (2000), Duque et al (2006), and Hu et al (2004)). While these approaches are useful in general, we are only concerned in this case with determining whether video footage contains motion, and if so, providing an estimate of the size and location of the region where such motion occurs. This is a critical question because an effective solution can significantly reduce the computational complexity of subsequent analysis, as well as a substantial reduction in storage or transmission capacity. Although there is significant research effort in the topic of motion analysis, the literature has not addressed the question of whether reliable motion detection can be accomplished using only low-level features of motion, and if so, how it can be achieved, and what features of the frame to use.

The intended approach is to identify a reliable motion metric and investigate its performance using linear filter analysis (van Trees, 1968). Although the image speckle produced by the imager and other irrelevant motion artefacts such as moving trees introduce a noise signal which is inherently non-Gaussian, we demonstrate that techniques optimised for additive non-correlated stationary Gaussian noise perform reliably, and allow us to specify classification error rates. In particular it is desirable to use such techniques to set detection thresholds automatically as in Bose (1995), Fuhrmann (1991) and Kelly (1986), in a manner similar to the so-called Constant False-Alarm Rate (CFAR) radar detection algorithms described in van Trees (1968).

Having determined a reliable process for detection motion within a video sequence, we are also concerned with characterising the motion in a manner which might be of use to the investigator. Such additional characterising metrics might include the locations of motion events within the frame, as well as the overall size and location of the moving *object*. The combination of reliable motion detection and the characterisation of the moving object or objects within the footage can then form the foundation for a wide variety of manual and automated techniques for semantic interpretation of the events captured in video surveillance.

PROPOSED APPROACH

Previous work (Zhao, Poursoltanmohammadi & Sorell, 2008) demonstrated that a particularly effective technique for detecting motion events is to track average frame luminance. It was also demonstrated that while average luminance across the entire video frame was particularly effective, very good results were also obtained when averaging over smaller regions, particularly macro-blocks of 16x16 pixels.

Average luminance compares well with frame-differencing techniques specifically because the impact of temporal noise and distortion is averaged out, whereas frame-differencing highlights such noise, masking real motion events.

In long term surveillance, light sources and image characteristics change over time. For example,

the source of light over 24 hours includes the sun rising and setting, cloud cover, and potentially the use of artificial light. Different wind conditions or an object which moves constantly, such as a fan or escalator, can result in false triggering of a motion detector. It is therefore essential for an effective motion detection algorithm to either track or filter out the slow variability over the day, and to adapt to fast but constant variability (such as trees waving in the breeze) to maximise detection of motion events while minimising false alarm overheads.

A linear tracking filter is used in the proposed approach to track both the differences in the average luminance and its corresponding variance for each block of pixels over time (frame by frame). In the case of a motionless zone within the frame, the average luminance will track according to the illumination of the scene, and the variance will be very small. The threshold for motion detection in such a zone can be very sensitive. An area which contains continuous background motion such as a tree waving in the breeze will also track according to the illumination, but the variance will be significantly larger. In this case, the threshold for motion detection will need to be larger to avoid false triggering and the detector will be less sensitive.

Although the video frame could be segmented in any practical way, it is proposed to segment into blocks of 16 x 16 pixels according to the macro-block structure of commonly used digital video coding standards such as MPEG1 and MPEG2. There are three practical reasons for doing this. The first is that aligning the motion detector to the macroblock structure minimises the impact of the coarse quantization of higher frequency spatial coefficients in a compressed video stream, which is to say that the impact of video compression on the effectiveness of the detector is reduced. Secondly, it is possible to extract the average macroblock luminance directly from the video data stream without having to fully reconstruct the video frame by frame, thereby potentially reducing the computational complexity of the algorithm in a practical implementation. Finally, a regular structure simplifies the management and auditing of sensitivity in different parts of the frame. For example, it might be desirable to disable the motion detection algorithm in some parts of the frame, such as a section in one corner which views a busy road of no interest and which would otherwise result in frequent false triggering. It is much easier to provide an audit trail for forensic purposes if there is a regular structure for analysis of the frame.

A tracking filter is implemented for each macroblock, thereby allowing the tracking of both the average luminance and the variance of the average luminance. From these figures, a normalised motion metric is derived. Normalisation in this case means that the effect of a real motion event is magnified in areas of little background variability, and reduced against constantly moving background scenes. Allowing for macroblocks to be disabled, the normalised motion metric from all active blocks is passed to a global motion detector which triggers when any metric exceeds the global threshold. When this occurs, a motion event is recorded.

For the purpose of audit for presentation of evidence to a court, it is possible to report a small number of global parameters and then a single number – the maximum normalised motion metric - per video frame. As proposed in the previous work, the video footage can be reported at a slow rate (such as one frame every few seconds) unless a motion event is identified, in which case the footage is reported at full rate, with a lead-in and lead-out of several seconds to provide context. In this way, it is possible to verify that the footage has been fully analysed, that the camera was working and providing meaningful footage at all times, and that all motion events of potential interest have been captured and can be provided to the court for review.

The following section introduces the implementation of the algorithm including the specific details of the linear filter, the normalised motion metric and the global motion detector. The results of experimental implementation are then detailed for an outdoor setting. Practical and legal considerations are then discussed.

IMPLEMENTATION

Average Luminance

It is commonly known that each pixel in a colour image or video is coded in three components representing red, green and blue, to match the colour perception of the human eye. However it is also known that the human psycho-visual system is much more sensitive to luminance rather than colour variation, specifically because the human eye contains around 120 million rods, which are highly sensitive to a broad spectrum, and only around 10 million cones in three varieties (red, green and blue sensitivity) which provide broad colour differentiation. Image compression (specifically the JPEG standard) and all video compression standards (including analogue video storage) exploit this behaviour by coding an image frame in terms of *luminance* and *chrominance*, which is a simple, approximately reversible linear transformation of the red, green and blue image planes. The luminance plane represents the monochrome brightness of the plane and carries high spatial frequency detail which the eye can perceive, whereas the chrominance planes differentiate colour in terms of redness versus greenness (chrominance-red) and blueness versus greenness (chrominance-blue). The latter planes carry detail which the eye is unable to distinguish with any accuracy, due to the small number of chrominance-sensitive cones in the eye, and so much of this detail can be discarded. In the old analogue video standard, this was done by reducing the bandwidth of the chrominance signals, in contemporary digital standards, chrominance data is reduced through averaging two or four pixels (commonly referred to as downsampling).

It follows that the luminance plane contains almost all motion information of interest. While it is possible that chrominance could contribute further motion detection sensitivity, it is certainly the case that the impact would be marginal at best, and only for pathological cases, for example in which an object in motion (say blue or red in colour) happens to pass through a green background with precisely the same luminance under all lighting conditions.

Furthermore, consideration of the luminance plane leads to a significant reduction in computational complexity, since the luminance plane can be extracted directly from a video data stream, and furthermore the average luminance of 8x8 microblocks can in some cases such as MPEG-1 and MPEG-2 be extracted without full image decompression.

Each plane (luminance and the two chrominance planes) is coded in contemporary digital video as either intra-frames (wholly self-contained still images which form a reference point) or inter-frames (based on prediction from reference frames, which can be intra-frames or subsequent inter-frames). Inter-frames can be based on reference frames in the past or the future of the video stream, depending on the specific standard. MPEG-2, for example, supports predicted frames (based on previous intra-frames or predicted frames) and bi-directional frames (based on the previous and the next reference frame, which can be intra frames or predicted frames, but not bi-directional frames).

Considering intra-frames for the moment, each such frame is either coded directly (for example baseline AVI format) or in the form of microblocks coded in the spatial frequency domain. For example, MPEG-1 and MPEG-2 encode 8x8 blocks of pixels using a two-dimensional discrete cosine transformation. In effect, this means that one coefficient for each block of 64 pixels represents the average luminance of the block of

pixels. Extracting this coefficient directly from a video data stream means that the task of averaging the luminance for a block of pixels is very much simplified. The spatial frequency coefficients are always coarsely quantised in order to achieve compression. This means that there will always be significant coding artefacts within a microblock of pixels and across microblock boundaries. For this reason alone, it is important that any segmentation of the image take place in the form of multiple complete microblocks along boundaries. For example, an MPEG-2 video stream at a resolution of 704 pixels by 576 lines should be segmented as blocks of 8x8, 16x16, 32x32 or 64x64 pixels to form whole blocks consisting of multiple whole microblocks. The larger the segment, the lower the impact of temporal sensor and coding noise but the lesser the ability to locate motion events.

In the case of predicted frames, the frame is segmented into *macroblocks* and each such block is matched against the reference frame. The block is then coded as a vector pointing to the most similar block found (according to a sub-optimal but computationally tractable matching algorithm – see Al Mualla et al, 2002), with significant differences coded as per an intra-block if the target data rate allows for such additional information. While the size of a macroblock can vary, the trade-off is between small blocks requiring significant computational overhead and more vectors requiring to be coded, versus large blocks which reduce the total computational load and require less vectors per frame but at the cost of not finding a good match and so requiring additional difference coding. In practice, many contemporary coding standards work with a macroblock of size 16x16 pixels which has been demonstrated to be a good compromise and which is compatible with the 8x8 microblock used for the spatial frequency coding.

The so-called motion-vectors which are used to encode predicted frames do not in fact represent motion but rather a sufficiently good match to a block of pixels in the previous frame. While this can often mean that an actual object is actually tracked through the frame by the motion vector, it is also very likely that textures can be copied from similar textures with no physical relationship, or that the impact of imaging noise can dominate the block matching algorithm. The purpose of the motion vectors is not to track objects per se, but rather to reduce the amount of data required to reconstruct the frame. The existence and value of motion vectors cannot, therefore, be used as a reliable basis for motion detection.

When analysing predicted and bidirectional frames, it is important to note that segmentation along macroblock edges can result in edge artefacts, since the macroblock is based on a block of pixels from a previous frame which will often not correspond to the microblock boundaries. This means that microblock edge effects can be introduced by applying the motion detection algorithm uniformly to both intra- and inter- coded frames.

Of course, if the implementation of the motion detector is such that it is presented with video frames in the form of standard red, green and blue frames from a standard-specific plug in, then it is only possible to calculate the average luminance by a weighted sum of the chrominance planes, making an assumption about the macroblock size. In this case, it might not be possible to differentiate the frame coding type (intra, predicted or bi-directional).

Assume that $L(i,j,k)$ represents the luminance of the pixel at spatial location (i,j) in frame k. The average luminance $Y(m,n,k)$ of the square detection segment is given by:

$$Y(m, n, k) = \frac{1}{\Phi^2} \sum_{i=\Phi m}^{\Phi(m+1)} \sum_{j=\Phi n}^{\Phi(n+1)} L(i, j, k)$$

(1)

where Φ is the length of the edge of the square detection segment, $m \in \left[0, \dfrac{I}{\Phi}\right]$ where I is the number of pixels per row in the video frame and is assumed to be a multiple of Φ, and similarly

$n \in \left[0, \dfrac{J}{\Phi}\right]$ where J is the number rows in the video frame and is also assumed to be a multiple of Φ.

Linear Filter

Linear filters have been widely used for different applications in video processing, including adaptive background estimation for the purpose of separating background and foreground objects in motion sequences such as in Brofferio et al (1990). In this work, it is assumed that the camera is quasi stationary, which is to say that the camera's location, orientation, focal length and focus remain fixed for extended periods of time. If any of these parameters change, a motion event will register before the detection algorithm re-establishes its estimates of normal background behaviour, but it should be noted that in this case any manual setting of specific regions of interest within the video sequence will no longer be valid.

For each detection segment, a linear filter is implemented to track the average luminance difference behaviour. The filter uses past measurements to predict the average luminance difference to the next frame, the variance of the estimate is also estimated. If the actual difference is sufficiently close to the estimate, no motion event is registered. Based on the variance estimate, a measurement which differs significantly (relative to the estimated variance) will trigger the motion detector. Since the variance is constantly estimated, a segment with a constantly moving background will become less sensitive than a segment with a very still background. Slow changes in illumination will closely follow the predicted luminance and so will not trigger a motion detection event.

A Kalman filter (van Trees, 1968) is an optimal linear filter implemented under assumptions of additive white Gaussian noise. While many authors (see Brofferio et al (1990) and others) claim to have implemented background tracking in images using a Kalman filter, in fact a true Kalman filter with complete dynamic gain control is rarely seen in video applications because of complications including assessing camera noise versus motion events, and the non-Gaussian statistics of video events. It is instead common practice to implement a tracking filter with the gain chosen from two or more pre-set values according to some threshold in difference between the actual and the estimated measurement. The filter presented here adopts this same simple approach to demonstrate very effective results, while recognising that automatic adaptation to a wider range of surveillance scenarios will require a more thorough implementation of the Kalman filter.

The tracked variable is the *absolute segment luminance difference* for each segment (m, n) of the surveillance footage under consideration, given by

$$S_k(m, n) = |Y(m, n, k) - Y(m, n, k - 1)| \qquad (2)$$

We define the following parameters:

α: gain of the tracking estimate of S_k. When the estimate is sufficiently close to the measured value, a large value α^+ is chosen for α for fast adaptation. When the estimate is large (as defined below), a small value (α^-) is used.

ω: gain of the variance estimator.

u: the minimum variance for normalisation, in order to ensure that the normalised motion metric does not lead to excessive sensitivity under conditions of very low background motion.

θ: the gain threshold, which determines which value to use for α.

τ: the normalised motion detection threshold, selected to maximise the probability of detection while bounding the probability of false alarm of a motion event.

and the following variables for each segment (m, n):

$\hat{S}_k(m, n)$: the estimate of S_k based on $S_1, ..., S_{k-1}$

$\hat{S}_k^+(m, n)$: the estimate of S_k using α^+, to determine which value of α to use

$\hat{\sigma}_k^2(m, n)$: the estimated variance of S_k based on $S_1, ..., S_{k-1}$

$\xi_k(m, n)$: the motion detection metric at frame k

The algorithm proceeds as follows:

1. Depending on requirements, determine appropriate values for the parameters α^+, α^-, ω, θ and τ.

For each (m, n),

2. Set an initial value for $\hat{S}_0$ and $\hat{\sigma}_0^2$

3. Look ahead by calculating $\hat{S}_k^+ = (1 - \alpha^+)\hat{S}_{k-1} + \alpha^+ S_k$

4. If $|\hat{S}_k^+ - S_k| < \theta$ then set $\alpha = \alpha^+$, otherwise set $\alpha = \alpha^-$. The former case indicates that the lookahead estimate corresponds closely to measurement and hence significant weighting should be put on the measurement. The latter case indicates that the measurement differs significantly from the estimate – in turn this is likely to mean that a motion event is taking place and hence estimate should not be updated with as much significance based on the abnormal measurement.

5. Update the estimated states:

$$\hat{S}_k = (1 - \alpha)\hat{S}_{k-1} + \alpha S_k$$

$$\sigma_k^2 = (1 - \omega)\sigma_{k-1}^2 + \omega(S_k - \hat{S}_k)^2$$

6. Calculate the normalised motion detection metric:

$$\xi_k = \frac{\left| S_k - \hat{S}_k \right|}{\sqrt{\max(\sigma_k^2, u)}}$$

Steps 2-6 are then repeated for each (m, n) under consideration.

7.   A motion event is deemed to be detected at frame k if for any (m, n) which is considered of interest, $\xi_k > \tau$.

8.   When a motion event is recorded, its location (m, n) is used to provide a location estimate of the event. Multiple simultaneous triggers can be used to create a weighted centroid $(\bar{m}, \bar{n})$ and estimates of the size of the motion event.

Discussion of the Algorithm

The algorithm described in the previous section implements several motion detection features of interest. These include:

*   **Fast or slow adaptation:** depending on the choice of α^+, α^- and θ, the estimator adapts quickly to changes in scene variability provided that the changes are relatively small. This case includes slow changes in lighting due to cloud cover or the motion of the sun, the effect of speckle noise introduced by the camera sensor, and some artefacts introduced by video data compression. On the other hand, if changes are large, this can either mean a change in the environment (such as a change in wind intensity) or a motion event of interest. Adapting quickly to such a situation can lead to unnecessary degradation in motion detection sensitivity. Hence, in this case, the weighting of the new measurement is reduced to α^- and the estimator will only adapt if the high level of motion is sustained.

*   **Normalised motion metric:** the motion metric ξ_k takes into account both the local changes in average luminance, and the variance within that location. This means that a segment in which the background moves significantly will reduce its sensitivity to avoid excessive false triggering, while a segment with a very still background can become very sensitive to motion events, as shown in Figure 1. To prevent excessive sensitivity under extremely still conditions, parameter u is chosen as a minimum variance for normalisation purposes.

*   **Selective detection:** it is possible for the operator to select or deselect segments of interest within the field of view. This might be desirable, for example, to concentrate on a particular location within the image, or alternatively, to eliminate false triggering from intermittent events within the field of view but of no interest, such as cars occasionally passing an intersection in the background.

*   **Location mapping:** the algorithm also delivers a segment location (m, n) for each motion detection trigger, which can be used to derive additional useful statistics including the location of all motion events, or the centroid and size of a moving "object". Such statistics can subsequently be used to refine later automatic or manual motion analysis.

Experimental Results

For the purpose of demonstration, a ten-minute outdoor daylight sequence at five frames per second was captured using a USB-connected camera, providing a total of 3000 frames with a resolution of 320x240 pixels. The image was segmented into 300 macroblocks, each of 16x16 pixels, for motion detection. Each frame was transformed the luminance plane only to eight bit resolution, resulting in a luminance value at each pixel between 0 and

Figure 1. In the top left, the tree in the background waves constantly, hence sensitivity in these segments must be reduced. On the other hand, the grass in the lower right corner exhibits very little motion and the motion detector can be become excessively sensitive.

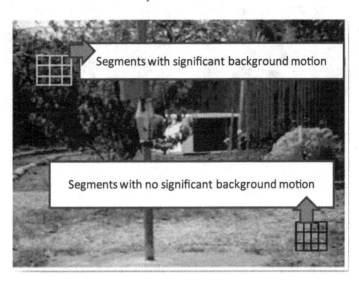

255. The parameters for demonstration purposes were determined empirically as follows:

α^+: 0.027
α^-: 0.006
ω: 0.005

u: 3.0
θ: 2.5
τ: 2.5

Figure 2 shows the output of the algorithm, $\max_{m,n} \xi_k(m,n)$. It can be seen that motion events

Figure 2. The output of the motion detection algorithm. Known motion events occur at approximately frame k= 300, 750, 1000, 1700, 1900, 2300 and 2500.

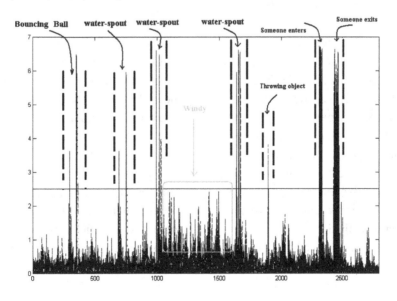

Figure 3. A ball bounces into the scene (k=300). On the left the segments which have triggered are highlighted. On the right, the "object" is assumed to occupy the envelope of the triggered segments.

are clearly detected, corresponding to a number of motion events known to be true.

The demonstration sequence included the following scenarios:

1. A ball was bounced into the scene ($k=300$)
2. Water was sprayed into the scene ($k=750$; $k=1000$; $k=1700$)
3. There were windy conditions from about $k=1000$ until about $k=1800$
4. A small object was thrown into the scene ($k=1900$)
5. A person enters ($k=2300$) and leaves ($k=2500$), standing still in between.

Some of these motion events are shown in the following Figures. Figure 3 demonstrates the shortcomings of estimating object size by motion event triggers. On the left, segments containing the ball, and its shadow, trigger the motion detector. On the right, it is clear that assuming that the envelope of these triggered segments leads to a misleading estimate of the "size" of the moving object and its centroid. Nevertheless, both views clearly identify the motion event for subsequent manual or automatic analysis.

The detection of water sprayed into the scene is shown in Figure 4. The motion detector is eas-

ily able to detect multiple small objects (water droplets) to trigger the motion detector.

A fast event consisting of just four frames is shown in Figure 5, in which a hammer is thrown into the field of view. This example demonstrates a key challenge for review by human operators, in which an event occurs so quickly that it is easily missed.

In Figure 6, a person has entered the scene and is standing relatively still. The algorithm continues to trigger due to small hand and foot movements. It should be noted that even though the sensitivity of the motion detection algorithm will decline as the tracker adapts to this motion, such a slow event is easily retained by maintaining a slow record of all video footage.

One important observation to make is that the windy conditions which happened to occur during the middle of this sequence would normally have resulted in constant false triggering without dynamic estimation of the variance being used to adjust the sensitivity. The threshold was set experimentally in this case, but under implementation conditions, the detection threshold τ would be calculated according to predetermined requirements for a sufficiently low probability of false alarm. Other parameters have also been chosen experimentally to fit the sequence. For practical

Figure 4. Water is sprayed into the scene (k=750). On the left the segments which have triggered are highlighted. On the right, the "object" is assumed to occupy the envelope of the triggered segments.

Figure 5. A hammer is thrown into the scene (k=1900). This event takes place over just four frames and would be easily missed by a human operator manually reviewing surveillance footage.

Figure 6. A person standing still in the scene (k=2400). The person's entry and exit events triggered the motion detector which continues to trigger as the hand and foot move slightly. Over time, sensitivity to this motion declines as the tracking algorithm adapts to constant local "random" motion.

implementation, it would be essential to choose these parameters automatically based on estimates during periods of known non-motion. This is a relatively trivial extension based on standard practice in detection algorithms (van Trees, 1968) and is not considered here, although it is the subject of further work.

LEGAL CONSIDERATIONS

In putting forward this algorithm, we note that effective motion detection needs to be based not only on good experimental results and theory, but also on acceptance by the Courts or some similar authority depending on the application. For this reason, we have proposed in the first instance that what could be presented to a Court would be:

- Footage of all detected motion events with frames leading into and out of the event. When multiple triggers occur, the frames are considered to contain a continuation of the same event and so show contiguous footage
- A record of the motion metric (Figure 2) to demonstrate a recording of all motion event triggers and hence that the previously mentioned footage is a complete record of all events which triggered the detector
- A slow rate continuous presentation of all footage (eg one frame every few seconds) to demonstrate both that the camera was working, and to capture slow motion events which fall below the detection threshold of the algorithm.

Until this or a similar algorithm is accepted by the Court (for example, surviving a challenge by the opposing party), it might be necessary to retain significantly more video footage at full rate. Once accepted, however, there are several possible key developments:

- The algorithm can be used to demonstrate to the Court that footage contains a complete record of motion events,
- Manual motion detection by a human operator can be replaced with the algorithm, not only freeing up human resources for but also being more reliable,
- Implementation at capture can potentially significantly reduce either storage or transmission requirements by a camera deployed in the field with known performance, and
- Automatic motion analysis systems, particularly those working in real time, can free up computational resources by being presented only with vision known to be carrying motion events within regions of particular interest.

CONCLUSION

This paper presents a simple solution to a common problem – a fast, low complexity determination of whether a video sequence contains a motion event. By setting an adaptive threshold locally, different segments of the field of view can be considered independently, automatically taking into account background motion.

The algorithm is able to detect motion events based on as few as two frames and can be implemented directly using compressed data streams without having to fully decompress the video frame sequence.

REFERENCES

Al-Mualla, M. E., Canagarajah, C. N., & Bull, D. R. (2002). *Video Coding for Mobile Communications: Efficiency, Complexity and Resilience*. Boston: Academic Press.

Anderson, D. O., & Moore, J. B. (1979). *Optimal Filtering* in: Thomas Kailath (editor), *Information and System Science Series*, Prentice-Hall, Inc., Englewood Cliffs, New Jersey, USA, pp. 1-61, 1979.

Bose, S., & Steinhardt, A. O. (1995, Sept.). A maximal invariant framework for adaptive detection with structured and unstructured covariance matrices. *IEEE Transactions on Signal Processing, 43*, 2164–2175. doi:10.1109/78.414779

Brofferio, S., Carnimeo, L., Comunale, D., & Mastronardi, G. (1990). A Background Updating Algorithm for Moving Object Scenes. In Cappellini, V. (Ed.), *Time-varying Image Processing and Moving Object Recognition, 2* (pp. 289–296). Amsterdam: Elsevier Publishers B.V.

Cutler, R., & Davis, L. (2000). Robust real-time periodic motion detection, analysis, and applications. *IEEE Transactions on Pattern Analysis and Machine Intelligence, 22*(8), 781–796. doi:10.1109/34.868681

Dee, H. M., & Velastin, S. A. (2007), *How close are we to solving the problem of automated visual surveillance? A review of real-world surveillance, scientific progress and evaluative mechanisms*, in *Machine Vision and Applications*, 5 May 2007. DOI = 10.1007/s00138-007-0077-z

Duque, D., Santos, H., & Cortez, P. (2006). *The OBSERVER: An Intelligent and Automated Video Surveillance System*, Lecture Notes in Computer Science, Springer, ISSN 0302-9743. 4141 (2006) pp 898-909.

Fuhrmann, D. R. (1991, Oct.). Application of Toeplitz covariance estimation to adaptive beamforming and detection. *IEEE Transactions on Signal Processing, 39*, 2194–2198. doi:10.1109/78.91176

Hu, W., Tan, T., Wang, L., & Maybank, S. (2004, August). A Survey on Visual Surveillance of Object Motion and Behaviors. *IEEE Transactions on Systems, Man, and Cybernetics, 34*(3).

Huang, T. S., & Lee, C. H. (1988), *Motion and Structure from orthographic views*, in 9th International Conference on Pattern Recognition, Nov. 1988, pp 885-887, ISBN 0-8186-0878-1.

Huang, Z.-K., & Liu, D.-H. (2007). *Unsupervised Image Segmentation Using EM Algorithm by Histogram, Lecture Notes in Computer Science*. Springer.

Karmann, K. P., & von Brandt, A. (1990). Moving Object Recognition Using an Adaptive Background Memory. In Cappellini, V. (Ed.), *Time-varying Image Processing and Moving Object Recognition, 2* (pp. 297–307). Amsterdam: Elsevier Publishers B.V.

Kelly, E. J. (1986, Nov.). An adaptive detection algorithm. *IEEE Transactions on Aerospace and Electronic Systems, AES-23*, 115–127. doi:10.1109/TAES.1986.310745

Koller, D., Weber, J., & Malik, J. (1993), *Robust Multiple Car Tracking with Occlusion Reasoning*, Computer Science Division (EECS) University of California, Report No. UCB/CSD 93-780, Berkeley, California, USA, Oktober 1993.

Konrad, J. (2000). Motion detection and Estimation. In Bovik, A. (Ed.), *Handbook of Image & Video Processing*.

Maybank, S. (1993), *Theory of Reconstruction from Image Motion*. Springer-Verlag, 1993

Ullman.S. (1979), The Interpretation of visual motion. MIT Press, 1979.

van Trees, H. L. (1968). *Detection, Estimation, and Modulation Theory, Part I – Detection, Estimation and Linear Modulation Theory*. Wiley.

Xiao, Z., Poursoltanmohammadi, A., & Sorell, M. *Video Motion detection beyond Reasonable Doubt*. Proceedings of the First international conference on Forensic applications and techniques in telecommunications, Adelaide, Australia, January 2008.

Chapter 20
Cancellable Biometrics for On-Line Signature Recognition

Emanuele Maiorana
Università degli Studi Roma TRE, Italy

Patrizio Campisi
Università degli Studi Roma TRE, Italy

Alessandro Neri
Università degli Studi Roma TRE, Italy

ABSTRACT

With the widespread diffusion of biometrics-based recognition systems, there is an increasing awareness of the risks associated with the use of biometric data. Significant efforts are therefore being dedicated to the design of algorithms and architectures able to secure the biometric characteristics, and to guarantee the necessary privacy to their owners. In this work we discuss a protected on-line signature-based biometric recognition system, where the considered biometrics are secured by applying a set of non-invertible transformations, thus generating modified templates from which retrieving the original information is computationally as hard as random guessing it. The advantages of using a protection method based on non-invertible transforms are exploited by presenting three different strategies for the matching of the transformed templates, and by proposing a multi-biometrics approach based on score-level fusion to improve the performances of the considered system. The reported experimental results, evaluated on the public MCYT signature database, show that the achievable recognition rates are only slightly affected by the proposed protection scheme, which is able to guarantee the desired security and renewability for the considered biometrics.

INTRODUCTION

The recent widespread diffusion of biometrics-based recognition systems is mainly due to the greater convenience, comfort and security they offer with respect to traditional authentication methods based on passwords or tokens. In fact, being derived from who a person is or what a person does, instead of from what a person knows or what a person has, biometric data represent

DOI: 10.4018/978-1-60960-515-5.ch020

identifiers which cannot be lost or forgotten, and represent irrefutable evidences linking a user to his identity (Jain, 2007).

However, the use of biometric data in an automatic recognition system also involves serious risks for their owners: if a biometrics is somehow stolen or copied, it can be difficult to replace it. Moreover, biometric data can contain sensitive information regarding, for example, the users' health or genetic background, which can be used in an unauthorized manner for malicious or undesired intents (Prabhakar, 2003). Moreover the users' privacy can be compromised if cross-matching between different biometric databases is performed, in order to track the enrolled subjects using their personal biometric traits. The afore-mentioned security and privacy concerns need to be carefully considered when implementing a biometric recognition system, by providing appropriate countermeasures to the possible attacks which can be perpetrated at the vulnerable points of the system (Ratha, 2001). Therefore some measures should be adopted to enhance biometric data resilience against attacks, while allowing the matching to be performed efficiently, thus guaranteeing acceptable recognition performance.

In this contribution, a protected on-line signature based verification system is proposed. Specifically, non-invertible transformations are applied to signature templates represented by time sequences, in order to guarantee the necessary security and to allow the generation of multiple templates from the same original one. The present work stems from the papers by the authors in (Maiorana, 2008c) and (Maiorana, 2008b), and exploits the characteristics of the employed protection scheme by presenting a protected multi-biometrics approach based on score-level fusion, which provides a significant improvement for the performances of the considered system. Specifically, the paper is organized as follows: in Section II the solutions which have been investigated in the recent past to secure biometric templates are analyzed. The non-invertible transformations

employed to provide protection to the considered signature templates are described in Section III, while the details regarding the proposed protected on-line signature recognition system, including the strategies employed to match the transformed templates, are given in Section IV. The experimental framework and the obtained results are shown in Section V, and some conclusions are drawn in Section VI.

BIOMETRIC TEMPLATE SECURITY

Among the possible threats regarding users' privacy and security which have to be considered when designing a biometrics-based recognition systems, the unauthorized acquisition of the stored biometric data is probably the most dangerous one (Ratha, 2001). Therefore, many solutions have been investigated in the recent past to secure biometric templates. Among them, *cancelable biometrics* approaches have been introduced in (Ratha, 2001). These techniques apply intentional non-invertible and repeatable modifications to the original biometric templates. Specifically, a properly defined cancelable biometrics should satisfy the following requirements:

- **Security:** it should be impossible or computationally unfeasible to obtain the original biometric template from the transformed one;
- **Revocability:** it should be possible to revoke a compromised template and issue a new one based on the same biometric data;
- **Diversity:** each template generated from a biometrics should not match with others previously generated from the same data;
- **Performance:** the recognition performance of the protected system, in terms of False Rejection Rate (FRR) or False Acceptance Rate (FAR), should not degrade significantly with respect to an unprotected system.

A possible classification of the possible approaches able to create secure and renewable biometrics has been presented in (Jain, 2008). Specifically, two macro-categories, referred to as *biometric cryptosystem* and *feature transformation* approaches, have been introduced. Hybrid approaches, which exploit the advantages of both biometric cryptosystems and feature transformation approaches, have also been proposed (Feng, 2010).

Biometric cryptosystems (Uludag, 2004) typically use binary keys to secure the biometric templates, and during the process some public information, usually referred to as *helper data*, is created. The approaches belonging to this category are extremely important to integrate biometrics into existing cryptographic protocols, which require a secret binary key to perform user recognition. Biometric cryptosystems can be further divided into *key generation* and *key binding* systems.

In key generation approaches both the helper data and the cryptographic key are directly generated from the biometric template. In this way, the security of the key can be guaranteed by means of hash functions, which can also be employed to provide the requested non-invertibility property to protect the original biometrics. The main issues of this approach regard the stability of the cryptographic key, which affect the recognition performances, and the possibility of generating multiple keys from the same data. Due to the difficulties in managing biometrics' intra-class variations, very few key generation approaches have been proposed so far: in (Vielhauer, 2004) a set of parametric features is extracted from each dynamic signature, and an interval matrix is used to store the upper and lower admitted thresholds for correct recognition. However, the variability of each feature has to be made explicitly available, and template renewability is not provided. In (Dodis, 2004) two different primitives for generating cryptographic keys from biometrics are given: the fuzzy extractor and the secure sketch. This latter

has been widely studied in (Sutcu, 2007), where the practical issues related to the design of a secure sketch are analyzed with specific application to face biometrics.

In key binding systems random binary keys are employed in conjunction with the biometrics to generate the helper data. Typically, these approaches are able to manage the intra-user variations in biometric characteristics through the use of error correcting codes. However, it is generally not possible to use matchers specifically designed for the considered biometrics, thus reducing the system matching accuracy. One of the most employed framework for key binding systems is the fuzzy commitment (Juels, 1999), already applied to fingerprint (Tuyls, 2005), face (Van der Veen, 2006), and iris (Hao, 2006), among the others. The fuzzy vault scheme (Juels, 2006) is able to manage biometrics represented as unordered data sets, although it has been found to be vulnerable to different attacks (Scheirer, 2007). Also Quantization Index Modulation (QIM) has been proposed to bind biometric characteristics with binary keys (Bui, 2010), thus providing increased flexibility in managing the intra-class variability. Recently, the security of both key generation and key binding schemes has been deeply investigated (Ignatenko, 2009), and specific discussions on the privacy leakage of fuzzy commitment have been presented (Ignatenko, 2010). For biometric cryptosystem approaches, it is also important to evaluate the privacy issues coming from the use of helper data derived from the input biometrics (Maiorana, 2010a).

Feature transformation approaches modify the original templates according to a key-dependent transform. It is possible to distinguish two subcategories: *salting* (Teoh, 2006) and *non-invertible transform* approaches (Ratha, 2007). A salting method employs invertible transforms: the security of the templates thus relies in the secure storage of the transformation keys. Examples of these approaches are the Biohashing algorithm (Goh, 2003), the orthonormal random projections (Jassim, 2009) and the random multispace quantization algorithm (Teoh, 2006).

On the other hand, when non-invertible transforms are considered, it is computationally hard to recover the original data from the transformed templates, even if the transformation keys are known to the attacker. Feature transformation approaches typically produce transformed templates which remain in the same feature space of the original ones: it is therefore possible to employ, in the recognition stage, the matchers originally designed for the considered biometrics. Following this approach, recognition performances close to those of an unprotected approach can be therefore achieved. The first practical non-invertible transform based approach for the protection of biometric data has been presented in (Ang, 2005), where the minutiae pattern extracted from a fingerprint undergoes a key-dependent geometric transform. Generalizing the approach in (Ang, 2005), three different non-invertible transforms, namely a cartesian, a polar and a functional transform, have been proposed in (Ratha, 2007) for the generation of cancelable fingerprint templates. Specifically, these transforms apply random displacements to the minutiae patterns of a fingerprint, thus obtaining that two minutiae, belonging to different regions of the input image, are mapped into the same region in the transformed template. Considering a minutia relying in such a zone, it is impossible to determine to which original disjoint input regions it belongs. A geometric approach for fingerprint template protection has also been presented in (Sutcu, 2007b), where the fingerprint minutiae are mapped on a circle centered on their centroid and the obtained projections are organized into bins according to their position, thus creating a fingerprint code. The work in (Sutcu, 2007b) has been used in (Yang, 2009) to define cancelable fingerprint templates derived from local and global features. A Biomapping scheme has also been proposed in (Shi, 2008) for fingerprint recognition. Unfortunately, in all these approaches the

diversity property of the transformed templates has not been investigated.

In this work a protected on-line signature based recognition system is presented. A detailed review on the state of the art on signature template protection has been presented in (Campisi, 2009). Signature template protection has been first considered in (Vielhauer, 2004), where the renewability property of the proposed method has not been addressed. In (Freire-Santos, 2006) an adaptation of the fuzzy vault (Juels, 2006) to signature protection is proposed. A salting approach has been proposed in (Yip, 2006), while a user-adaptive version of the fuzzy commitment has been proposed in (Maiorana, 2008a) to secure signature templates and to provide renewability. Each of these approaches provides protection to a set of parametric features extracted from the considered on-line signatures. On the contrary, the approach here employed uses a set of time sequences, like trajectory, velocity, acceleration, etc. acquired by means of touch screens or digitizing tablets, as signature representation. Specifically, different non-invertible transformations (Maiorana, 2010b) are applied to the available signature time sequences. This approach allows obtaining recognition performances better than those achievable with other already proposed signature template protection schemes. Moreover, recovering any information about the original biometrics from their transformed versions is as hard as random guessing it, and it is also possible to generate multiple templates from a single acquisition, thus satisfying the diversity property.

It is also worth remarking that a matching score can be obtained as the output of the protected recognition process when providing protection through non-invertible transformation approaches, due to the possibility of employing dedicated matchers in the transformed domains. Therefore, multi-biometric systems (Ross, 2006) can be protected using score-level fusion techniques as described in Section IV. As for the design of protected multi-biometric systems, a theoretical discussion on cryptosystems is presented in (Fu, 2009), where the integration between different systems is considered at the biometric level, by fusing the extracted features, and at the cryptographic level, by combining the obtained individual decisions. Fusion at the feature level is the most common choice for protected multi-biometric systems, as in (Nandakumar, 2008) where fingerprint and iris features are combined in a fuzzy vault, or in (Kanade, 2009), where iris and face features are concatenated to form a single vector. Fusion at the feature and decision levels has been proposed in (Kelkboom, 2009), where also score level fusion is considered, by using as scores the number of errors corrected by the error correcting codes employed in the fuzzy commitment. As it will be shown in Section VI, score-level fusion achievable in the protected domain allows significantly improving the verification and renewability performances of the considered system.

NON-INVERTIBLE TRANSFORMS FOR ON-LINE SIGNATURE TEMPLATES

The approach employed to protect on-line signature templates relies on a set of non-invertible transforms introduced in (Maiorana, 2008c) and (Maiorana, 2008d). The considered protection scheme can be applied to any biometric template which can be expressed in terms of a set R_F of F different time/space-dependent discrete finite sequences $r_{(i)}[n]$, $i = 1, ..., F$. Specifically, a non-invertible transformation is applied to the set R_F, thus generating a transformed template T_F, which consists of F discrete sequences $f_{(i)}[n]$, $i = 1, ..., F$. As described in Section IV, the resulting transformed templates can then be further processed, if the employed matcher is based on a sequence-based modeling approach (e.g., Hidden Markov Models), or directly stored in the

system database, if the matcher works directly with sequence-based descriptions (e.g., Dynamic Time Warping).

In order to guarantee the non-invertibility and renewability properties of a properly defined cancelable biometrics, the proposed transformations are designed to satisfy the following properties:

- Each transformed sequence has to be generated from the combination of at least two original time sequences (or segments of them). This requirement is needed when employing transformations expressed by means of linear dependencies on the original data, which should be preferred in order to alter as less as possible (although in a non-invertible way) the characteristics of the original sequences, in both space/time and frequency domains;
- Each original time sequence (or segment of it) has to occur only once in the combinations that generate the new sequences. This requirement is needed in order to let the transformed sequences being each independent from the others;
- When generating transformed sequences for two distinct systems, the sequences selected for the combinations (or the segments extracted from them) have to be different for the two distinct cases. This requirement is needed to define transforms which are robust with respect of a *record multiplicity attack*, where an attacker gains access to different transformed versions of the same original data, and tries to reveal the original biometric templates by exploiting all the gathered information.

In Section III.A a baseline transform, specifically designed in such a way that it is not possible to retrieve the original data from the transformed ones, is described. Moreover, two modifications of the baseline approach, which have been designed in order to provide improved renewability capabilities, will be detailed in Section III.B and in Section III.C.

Baseline Approach

In the baseline implementation, each transformed sequence $f_{(i)}[n]$, $i = 1, ..., F$, is obtained from a single corresponding original function $r_{(i)}[n] \in R_F$ with length N. The key of the employed non-invertible transform is given by a vector $\underline{d} = \left[d_0, ..., d_W\right]^T$ whose values, randomly selected between 1 and 99, are arranged in ascending order, $d_j > d_{j-1}$, $j = 1, ..., W$. The values d_0 and d_W are respectively set to 0 and 100. Each sequence $r_{(i)}[n] \in R_F$ is divided into W segments $r_{(i)j, N_j}[n]$ of length $N_j = b_j - b_{j-1}$,

$$r_{(i)j, N_j}[n] = r_{(i)}[n + b_{j-1}], \quad j = 1, ..., W, \tag{1}$$

where $b_j = \left\lfloor (d_j / 100) \cdot N \right\rfloor$, $j = 1, ..., W$. Basically, the function $r_{(i)}[n]$ is split into W separated parts according to the randomly generated vector $\underline{d}$. A transformed function $f_{(i)}[n]$, $n = 1, ..., K = N - W + 1$, is then obtained through the linear convolution of the functions $r_{(i)j, N_j}[n]$, $j = 1, ..., W$:

$$f_{(i)}[n] = r_{(i)1, N_1}[n] * ... * r_{(i)W, N_W}[n] \tag{2}$$

Different realizations can be obtained from the same original functions, simply by varying the size or the values of the parameter key $\underline{d}$. As it has already been noticed, the transformed templates are yet represented as a set of discrete time/space sequences, like the original ones, being thus possible to resort to sophisticated classifiers such as HMMs or DTW in order to match them.

The effects of the employed transforms are shown in Figure 1, where the horizontal and vertical position trajectories extracted from an original signature are transformed according to

Figure 1. Two different transformations, governed by the key vectors $\underline{d}^{(1)} = \left[0, 20, 100\right]$ and $\underline{d}^{(2)} = \left[0, 80, 100\right]$, are applied to the original $x[n]$ and $y[n]$ coordinate functions. The original and transformed signatures are also shown.

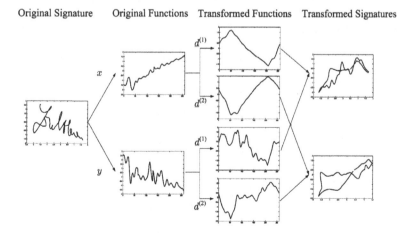

different decomposition vectors with $W = 2$, and then recombined to reconstruct the transformed signature.

In (Maiorana, 2010) it has been shown that recovering an original sequence $r_{(i)}[n]$ from its transformed counterpart $f_{(i)}[n]$ is computationally as hard as random guessing it. Moreover, the difficulty of inverting the employed transform has been discussed also considering a *record multiplicity attack*, where the attacker collects more than a single transformed template, and tries to recover the original biometric information by using them altogether. It is worth pointing out that other already proposed non-invertible transform based protection schemes, like those in (Ang, 2005) and (Ratha, 2007), are vulnerable to a record multiplicity attack.

Mixing Approach

This approach is defined by considering, in addition to the decomposition key $\underline{d}$, a scrambling matrix C as a transform parameter. Specifically, C is defined as a matrix with F rows and W columns. Each column of C is obtained as a scrambled version of the vector $[1, \ldots, F]^T$, while the i-th row of the matrix C is employed to define the combinations which originate the transformed sequences $f_{(i)}[n]$. Having indicated with $C[i, j]$ the element at the i-th row and at the j column of C, the transformed sequences $f_{(i)}[n]$ are therefore obtained as:

$$f_{(i)}[n] = r_{(C[i,1])1,N_1}[n] * \ldots * r_{(C[i,W])W,N_W}[n]$$

$$(3)$$

with $i = 1, \ldots, F$, and where $r_{(i)j,N_j}[n]$ is defined as in Equation (1). Basically, each transformed sequence $f_{(i)}[n]$ is generated not only from the corresponding original sequence $r_{(i)}[n]$, but the convolutions are performed among segments extracted from different original sequences, thus also defining a feature-level fusion (Ross, 2006) among various sequences. An example of the application of the mixing approach is given in Figure 2. Being derived from the baseline approach, the non-invertibility capacity of the mixing approach approach is the same of the baseline one.

Figure 2. Application of the mixing approach to two original signature sequences. $d_1 = 60$ and $C = \begin{bmatrix} 1 & 2 \\ 2 & 1 \end{bmatrix}$ are employed as transform parameters.

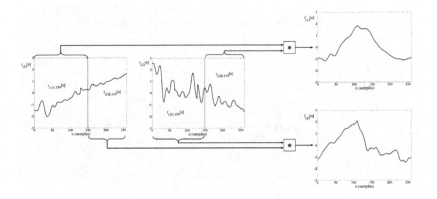

Shifting Approach

Another variation to the approach in Section III.A is obtained by applying an initial shift to the original sequences $r_{(i)}[n]$, $i = 1,...,F$. Specifically, a random integer value f is selected in the range [0,100], and converted to the shift s as $s = \lfloor f / 100 \rfloor \cdot N$, being N the length of the original sequence in sample units. Then, each sequence $r_{(i)}[n]$ undergoes a circular shift governed by the parameter s, thus obtaining the sequences $z_{(i)}[n] = r_{(i)}[n-s]$, $n = 1,...,N$.

The same transformation process described in Section III.A, based on convolutions between segments extracted from the considered sequences, is then applied to the sequences $z_{(i)}[n]$. This modification can also be combined with the extended method presented in Section III.B, by applying the circular shift before performing the transformations. The application of the shifting approach is represented in Figure 3. Also in this case, the non-invertibility capacity is not affected by the proposed modification, with respect to the baseline approach of Section III.A.

PROTECTED ON-LINE SIGNATURE BASED RECOGNITION SYSTEM

In this Section we detail the proposed protected on-line signature-based recognition system. Specifically, it is assumed that the employed acquisition device is able to capture the horizontal $x[n]$ and vertical $y[n]$ signature position trajectories, and the signal $p[n]$ regarding the pressure applied by the pen, where $n = 1,...,N$ is a discrete time index, and N is the time duration of the signature in sampling units. A geometric normalization, consisting of position normalization followed by rotation alignment, is applied to the pen-position signals $x[n]$ and $y[n]$. Other four discrete time sequences are then derived from $x[n]$ and $y[n]$, and used as an additional set of functions, namely the path-tangent angle $q[n]$, the path velocity magnitude $v[n]$, the log curvature radius $r[n]$, and the total acceleration magnitude $a[n]$. The acquired on-line signatures are then represented by means of the set of sequences $R_{14} = \{R_7, \dot{R}_7\}$, where

$$R_7 = \{x[n],\, y[n],\, p[n],\, q[n],\, v[n],\, r[n],\, a[n]\}$$

(4)

Figure 3. Application of the shifting approach to an original signature sequences. $f = 40$ and $d_1 = 55$ are employed as transform parameters.

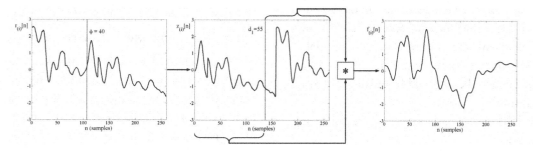

while the upper dot notation denotes the first order finite difference. The non-invertible transformations described in Section III can then be applied to the original set of functions R_{14}, in order to generate for each acquired signature a protected template T_{14}, consisting of $F = 14$ discrete sequences $f_{(i)}[n]$, $i = 1,...,F$.

The transformed templates can then be employed in the enrollment and recognition stages of any function-based on-line signature recognition system. Specifically, in the following subsections we propose three different approaches which can be employed to compare the sequence-based templates obtained by transforming the original signature representations. The performances achievable when using each verification strategy are then compared in Section V for both protected and unprotected on-line signature recognition systems.

Hidden Markov Models

Hidden Markov Models (HMMs) represent a tool for stochastic signal modeling which have been used in a wide range of pattern recognition applications, thanks to the possibility of characterizing signals in terms of parametric models. The HMMs represents a doubly embedded stochastic process, composed by an underlying Markov chain whose states are not observable, and by a set of stochastic processes which produce a sequence of available observations. Basically, it is assumed that, at a discrete time instant n, the Markov process is in one of its states, which generates an observation symbol according to a probability distribution associated with the current state. The model is defined "hidden" in the sense that the underlying state cannot be deduced from simple symbol observation.

An HMM is characterized by the following elements:

- The number H of hidden states $\{S_1, S_2,...,S_H\}$ of the model. The state at discrete time n is indicated as q_n;

- The state transition probability $\mathsf{U} = \{u_{i,j}\}$, with $u_{i,j} = P[q_n + 1 = S_j \mid q_n = S_i]$, $i, j = 1,...,H$.

- The observation symbol probability distributions in each state j, indicated with $\mathsf{Z} = \{z_j(\mathsf{o})\}$, $j = 1,...,H$. The observation processes are modeled by means of mixtures of M multivariate Gaussian distributions $z_j(\mathsf{o}) = \sum_{m=1}^{M} a_{j,m} p_{m_{j,m},s_{j,m}}(\mathsf{o})$, $j = 1,...,H$, where $m_{j,m}$ and $s_{j,m}$ represent respectively the mean and the diagonal covariance matrix of each Gaussian component. The coefficients $\alpha_{j,m}$ are selected by respecting the condition of normalization $\sum_{m=1}^{M} a_{j,m} = 1$, $j = 1,...,H$.

- The initial state distribution $p = \{p_j\} = \{p[q_1 = S_j]\}$, $j = 1,...,H$.

During the enrollment phase the client model $1 = \{\mathsf{p},\mathsf{U},\mathsf{Z}\}$ is estimated considering E transformed templates, obtained by processing the enrollment signatures of the subject at hand, according to the iterative strategy presented in (Fierrez, 2007). The obtained model λ is stored in a database, and invoked during the recognition phase, when a user claims his identity on the basis of an input signature, and a similarity score is calculated as $(1 / K) \log P(O \mid 1)$ using the Viterbi algorithm, which provides $\log P(O \mid 1)$ (Rabiner, 1989). The ratio $1/K$ is taken into account to normalize the obtained log-likelihood, which decreases when the length of the test signature increases. A decision regarding whether the signature is authentic or a forgery is made by comparing the matching score to a threshold: if the computed score is higher than the employed threshold, the acquired signature is considered as belonging to the claimed identity.

It is worth pointing out that when using HMMs for signature recognition, also in an unprotected approach, the client model $1 = \{ p, U, Z \}$, instead of the on-line signature representative sequences, is stored in the database. However, if an attacker is able to acquire the client HMM, the statistical properties of the client's signatures can be derived from the model, and for example employed to track the users across different databases. Using the proposed protection approach, if an attacker succeeds in acquiring the stored models, he can only retrieve information about the set of transformed sequences T_F, from which it computationally hard to retrieve any information about the original sequences $r_{(i)}[n]$, $i = 1, \ldots, F$. It is also worth remarking that the proposed protection approach also provide renewability to signature templates employed in HMM-based systems, thus allowing to protect the privacy of the enrolled users.

Dynamic Time Warping

Dynamic Time Warping (DTW) is a well known method to compare sequences of different lengths. The use of DTW for template matching is encouraged by the results obtained during the Signature Verification competition in 2004 (SVC 2004) (Yeung, 2004), where the algorithm (Kholmatov, 2005), employing DTW matching, has given the best performances in terms of Equal Error Rate (EER), when tested with skilled forgeries.

When using DTW as matching strategy, E signatures are acquired from each user during enrollment. From each signature, the original representation $R_F^{(e)}$ is evaluated, and then the protected templates $T_F^{(e)}$, $e = 1, \ldots, E$, are computed and stored in a database. During recognition, the user claims his identity while providing a test signature, which is processed in order to generate

its transformed template $T_F^{(a)}$. This test sample is then compared to all the E templates in the reference set. The comparisons are performed by employing the DTW algorithm, whose output is the distance $D\left(T_F^{(e)}, T_F^{(a)} \right)$ between the test sample $T_F^{(a)}$ and the reference sample $T_F^{(e)}$. The minimum of the E distances between the test sample $T_F^{(a)}$ and the E reference samples $T_F^{(e)}$, $e = 1, \ldots, E$, is taken as representative of the verification process, and a decision regarding whether the signature is authentic or a forgery is made by comparing the result of the matching to a threshold.

To compare the reference and test samples, the DTW algorithm finds the optimal alignment between them, such that the sum of the differences between each pair of aligned points is minimal. Let us indicate with $A = \{ a_i \}$, $i = 1, \ldots, I$, and $B = \{ b_j \}$, $j = 1, \ldots, J$, two sequences of feature vectors, representing respectively the biometric template employed as reference and the biometric sample to be verified. A point-to-point distance $d(i, j)$ between the elements a_i and b_j can be evaluated, for $i = 1, \ldots, I$ and $j = 1, \ldots, J$. Typically, $d(i, j)$ is computed as the Euclidean distance between the vectors a_i and b_j. With reference to Figure 4, where the patterns A and B are developed along in an $i - j$ plane, the DTW algorithms finds the optimal warping function $Q = \{ q(k) \} = \{ (i(k), j(k)) \}$, $k = 1, \ldots, K$, which connects the points $q(1) = (1, 1)$ and $q(K) = (I, J)$, minimizing the total distance

$$D_Q(A, B) = \sum_{k=1}^{K} d(q(k)) = \sum_{k=1}^{K} d(i(k), j(k))$$

(5)

The minimum accumulated distance $\min_{Q \in G} \{ D_Q(A, B) \}$, where Γ represents the set of

Figure 4. Warping function and Sakoe/Chiba band definition (adapted from (Sakoe, 1978))

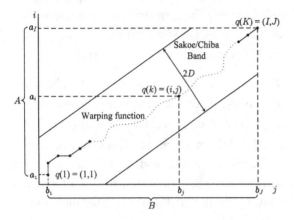

all properly defined distortion paths Q for A and B, is employed to characterize the dissimilarity of the considered sequences. In order to compensate the effect of the summation of K terms in equation (4), a normalization has to be done on the minimum accumulated distance. Specifically, we normalize the distance $\min_{Q \in G} \left\{ D_Q \left(A, B \right) \right\}$ with respect of the length I of the reference sequence A, thus defining the asymmetric distance $D \left(A, B \right) = \min_{Q \in G} \left\{ D_Q \left(A, B \right) \right\}$ as the dissimilarity measure between the sequences A and B.

The paths in Γ have to satisfy the necessary monotonic and continuity requirements (Sakoe, 1978). Moreover, only the paths which remain in the so-called Sakoe/Chiba band (Sakoe, 1978), depicted in Figure 4, are taken into account. In the following, the width D of the Sakoe/Chiba band will be expressed as percentage of the minimum value *min(I,J)* between the test and reference signature lengths. Differently from (Kholmatov, 2005), no additional slope constraint, as well as no user-dependent score normalization for the computation of template distances have been considered in our implementation.

It is worth pointing out that, when employing a DTW based matcher for on-line signature verification, the stored templates permit to perfectly reconstruct both the shape and the dynamics of the signatures. Such possibility represents a security issue far greater than that associated to the use of HMMs as classifiers, case in which only a signature model is stored for template matching. The protection of signature templates has therefore a higher relevance when employing a DTW based matching strategy, with respect to the use of HMMs.

Combination of HMM and DTW: Score Fusion Techniques

The third system we consider is characterized by the combination of both HMM and DTW-based matching strategies: as already outlined, score-level fusion techniques can be applied to the proposed protected systems thanks to the fact that, in the employed transformed domain, it is possible to use template matchers which output a score as result of a template comparison. The aim of score fusion is to improve the recognition performances, with respect to systems employing a single matcher. The fusion of scores obtained from two or more matchers typically consists of two steps:

- A *normalization* process, which is responsible for taking into account the possible inhomogeneity between the match scores generated by the individual matchers. For example, as it happens in the proposed systems, one matcher may output a distance or a dissimilarity measure, where smaller distances indicates a better similarity, while the other matcher may output a similarity score, where a larger score value implies a better match between the considered templates. Furthermore, the outputs of the individual matchers may be in different numerical ranges, or may follow different distributions. All these possibilities have to be considered when defining the employed normalization technique.

- The application of a fusion rule, which consists of combining the available normalized scores, according to a selected classifier rule.

As for the normalization process, *fixed score normalization* (Brunelli, 1995), which is based on the estimation of some parameters during a training phase, is employed. Following this approach, it is assumed that a set of match scores is available during the training phase of the fusion module. Analyzing these scores, a suitable statistical model, which has to fit the available data, is determined. The score normalization parameters are then determined on the basis of the estimated model, and employed when performing the recognition tests, to fuse the obtained match scores. Among the techniques which can be employed to normalize the available scores, the min-max, the z-score, the median, the double sigmoid, and the tanh-estimators (Ross, 2006) normalization techniques are the most commonly employed, and are considered for our experimental tests.

On the other hand, the most commonly employed fusion rule is the *sum* rule, which consists on simply adding the normalized scores or distances obtained from different matchers. As reported in (Ross, 2006), the sum rule is more effective than other techniques such as the *product*, the *minimum* and the *maximum* rule when the inputs tend to be noisy, thus leading to errors in the estimation of the a posteriori scores probability distribution. The sum rule is also known as the mean or average decision rule, because it is equivalent to assign the considered input to the class which has the maximum average a posteriori probability, over all the available matchers.

EXPERIMENTAL RESULTS

An extensive set of experimental tests has to be performed to assess the effectiveness of a non-invertible transform-based biometric protection scheme. Specifically, the verification performances achievable with the proposed systems are discussed in Section V.A. Moreover, a renewability analysis is conducted in Section V.B.

The tests are conducted using the public version of the MCYT on-line signature corpus (Ortega-Garcia, 2003), which comprises 100 users, for each of which 25 genuine signatures and 25 skilled forgeries have been captured during five different sessions. Forgers were asked to perform the imitations after observing the static images of the signatures to copy, having tried to mimic them at least 10 times, and by then writing the forgeries naturally without breaks or slowdowns. Specifically, the employed database is split into a training data set, comprising the first 30 users of the public MCYT database, and a test data set, comprising the remaining 70 users. The experimental results reported in the following, regarding both the recognition and the renewability performances, are evaluated over the test data set. The training data set is employed to estimate the parameters needed for the fusion of scores obtained from HMM and DTW base classifiers, as described in Section IV.C.

Recognition Performance Analysis

The recognition performances achievable with the proposed protected on-line signature-based recognition systems are here discussed in terms of False Rejection Rate (FRR), False Acceptance Rate (FAR) and Equal Error Rate (EER) (Jain, 2007).

In order to properly analyze the proposed non-invertible transform-based template protection schemes, we first focus on the baseline approach presented in Section III.A, and then discuss the extended methods presented in Sections III.B and III.C, which are derived from the baseline one.

Specifically, the variability of the recognition performances with respect to the selection of the key $\underline{d}$, which uniquely define the transformations introduced by baseline approach, is an important aspect which has to be analyzed. In order to accomplish this task, we perform 20 times the verification process over the available test database, randomly varying the transformation parameters $\underline{d}$ for each user at each iteration. The values d_j, $j = 1, \dots, W-1$, which define the decomposition vector $\underline{d}$, are taken in the range of integers [5,95] at a minimum distance of 5 one from the others, in order to avoid the decomposition of the original sequences into segments so short that their contribution in the convolutions would be negligible, thus generating transformed sequences too similar to the original one.

We keep fixed the number of segments in which the signature time sequences are divided ($W = 2$), and the number of signature acquisitions which are considered for the enrollment stage ($E = 10$). The configurations for the matchers described in Section IV are selected as follows:

- HMM-based system: H=8, M=8;
- DTW-based system: D=5%;
- Score fusion-based system: min-max normalization technique, sum fusion rule.

The obtained results are shown in Figure 5, by means of the normalized histograms of the EERs obtained when considering both random (EER_{RF}) and skilled forgeries (EER_{SF}). As requested for properly designed non-invertible transform-based protection schemes, the variations in the employed parameters $\underline{d}$ do not result in significant modifications of the matching performances, for each of the three matching strategies described in Section IV.

As can be seen, when using DTW as matching strategy, the variance of the achievable verification performances is smaller than the one obtained when employing HMM: a standard deviation $s_{EER_{SF}} = 0.4\%$ is achieved in the former case, while $s_{EER_{SF}} = 0.7\%$ is obtained for the latter, when considering skilled forgeries. Moreover, it is also worth pointing out that, in addition to providing a notable improvement in the achievable recognition performances, the fusion between HMM and DTW scores also guarantees a performance variability reduction: a standard deviation $s_{EER_{SF}} = 0.35\%$ is achieved when combining both matchers by means of score-fusion.

It is then possible to analyze, for each proposed system, the dependence of the recognition performances on the configurations selected to define the HMM modeling and the DTW algorithm. Specifically, the EERs obtained when considering

Figure 5. Normalized histograms for the EERs obtained repeating 20 times the recognition process, for a protected system with $W = 2$. $E = 10$ signatures are taken from each user during enrollment. (a) HMM; (b) DTW; (c) Fusion of HMM and DTW.

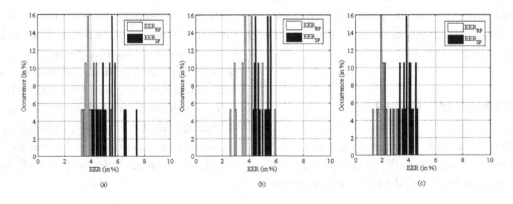

skilled forgeries by varying the HMM parameters H and M are summarized in Table 1, for both an unprotected approach employing HMMs as matching strategy, and the protected baseline approach described in Section III.A with $W = \{2, 3, 4\}$. Only the values $H \in \{8, 16\}$ are reported in Table 1, because the performed experimental results confirmed that the best recognition rates can be obtained when choosing these values as number of states in the HMM modeling, as already observed in (Fierrez, 07) and (Maiorana, 08b). The key vector $\underline{d}$ which defined the baseline approach is randomly selected for each considered user: as described in (Ratha07), this reflects how the protected system should be used in a practical implementation, where different transformations have to be used for different individuals.

The same analysis is conducted for a system employing a DTW-based matching strategy, where the only parameter which has to be set is the width D of the Sakoe/Chiba band. The EERs obtained when considering skilled forgeries are shown in Table 2. It is worth specifying that the reported results represent mean values estimated by performing 20 times the recognition process, varying the transformation parameters $\underline{d}$ at each iteration. The HMM and DTW configurations producing the best verification performances, evidenced in bold in Table 1 and Table 2, are considered in the following to illustrate the performances of the proposed approaches. Specifically, the selected configurations are:

- Unprotected approach

Table 1. EER_{SF} (expressed in %) for different HMM configurations in unprotected and protected systems and considering skilled forgeries, evaluated for E = 10 and F=14. The best results for each approach are evidenced in bold.

H	M	Unprotected approach	Baseline Protected approach		
			$W = 2$	$W = 3$	$W = 4$
	1	10.34	8.13	11.36	13.73
	2	7.43	6.39	10.50	**12.40**
	4	5.64	5.53	**10.03**	12.59
8	8	4.78	**5.35**	10.50	12.98
	16	5.28	5.64	10.09	14.87
	32	7.07	6.78	16.48	18.14
	1	6.00	6.39	14.15	14.98
	2	4.29	5.64	12.21	12.51
16	4	**3.88**	5.53	13.15	13.65
	8	3.92	5.71	15.65	16.59
	16	5.53	7.53	17.84	20.16
	32	9.47	17.71	19.90	22.16

Table 2. EER_{SF} (expressed in %) for different DTW configurations in unprotected and protected systems and considering skilled forgeries, evaluated for E = 10 and F=14. The best results for each approach are evidenced in bold.

D (in %)	Unprotected approach	Baseline Protected approach		
		$W = 2$	$W = 3$	$W = 4$
1	6.00	6.03	7.92	10.10
5	3.64	**4.99**	**6.78**	**8.21**
10	**3.17**	5.14	7.31	9.14
15	3.20	5.14	7.31	9.14

- HMM: $H = 16$, M = 4 (EER_{SF} = 3.88%);
- DTW: $D = 10\%$ ($EER_{SF} = 3.17\%$);
- Baseline protected approach, with $W = 2$
  - HMM: $H = 8$, M = 8 ($EER_{SF} = 5.35\%$);
  - DTW: $D = 5\%$ ($EER_{SF} = 4.90\%$);
- Baseline protected approach, with $W = 3$
  - HMM: $H = 8$, M = 4 (EER_{SF} = 10.03%);
  - DTW: $D = 5\%$ ($EER_{SF} = 6.78\%$);
- Baseline protected approach, with $W = 4$
  - HMM: $H = 8$, M = 2 (EER_{SF} = 12.40%);
  - DTW: $D = 5\%$ ($EER_{SF} = 8.21\%$).

From the reported experimental result it can be seen that a system using the proposed DTW-based matching strategy performs better than a system using the HMM modeling. As a remark, it is also worth specifying that a DTW-based matcher usually requires more time to perform recognition than a HMM based one, especially when the number of enrollment acquisitions E is high. However, being signatures usually employed for verification rather than for identification, the computational speed is not an issue for real world applications.

It can also be noticed that for both the proposed classifiers the performances obtained with a pro-tected system with $W = 2$ are only slightly worse than those obtained with an unprotected system. Therefore, by employing the baseline approach presented in Section III.A, it is possible to obtain recognition performances comparable with those of an unprotected system, while providing the desired protection for the employed signature templates.

The achievable verification performances can also be improved by applying score-fusion strategies to the outcomes of the two HMM and DTW-based systems.

Specifically, as described in Section IV.C, fusion techniques perform score normalization according to a set of parameters which characterize the distributions of the considered scores. In our experimental tests we determine the parameters needed by the min-max, the z-score, the median, the double sigmoid, and the tanh-estimators normalization procedure over a training data set, and use them to estimate over the test data set the achievable verification performances, which are summarized in Table 3 for systems using the sum rule to fuse the normalized scores. The obtained results outline that the double sigmoid and the min-max normalization approach performs slightly better than the other ones. The min-max approach is employed throughout the rest of the work as the selected normalization technique.

Table 3. EER$_{SF}$ (expressed in %) for different normalization techniques in unprotected and protected systems, when considering skilled forgeries, E = 10, F=14 and using the sum rule to fuse the normalized scores. The best results for each approach are evidenced in bold.

Normalization strategy	Unprotected approach	Baseline Protected approach		
		$W = 2$	$W = 3$	$W = 4$
min-max	2.66	**3.91**	7.05	**7.23**
z-score	2.66	3.91	7.05	7.79
median	2.66	3.91	6.77	7.95
double sigmoid	**2.48**	4.09	**6.23**	7.44
tanh	2.66	3.91	7.05	7.79

As for the fusion rule to be employed for combining the normalized scores, the best verification rates are generally obtained, as shown in Table 4, by using the sum rule, which is therefore employed hereafter in the discussion.

In order to summarize and clearly illustrate the obtained verification performances, Figure 6 shows the Receiver Operating Characteristic (ROC) curves which are obtained when considering unprotected systems, as well as systems employing the baseline protected approach described in Section III.A. The performances achievable when employing HMM, DTW, and the fusion of both matching strategies are shown. From the sketched ROC curves the performance degradation obtained when increasing the system parameter W, indicating the number of segments in which the signature sequences are divided, can be clearly seen. This loss in performance can be explained as follows: the division in segments of the considered signature time sequences is accomplished by using a set of fixed parameters d_j, $j = 1, \dots, W - 1$. They express, in terms of the percentage of the total sequence length, the points where the splits have to be performed. However, due to the characteristics

Table 4. EER$_{SF}$ (expressed in %) for different fusion rules in unprotected and protected systems, when considering skilled forgeries, E = 10, F=14, and using the min-max approach to normalize the available scores. The best results for each approach are evidenced in bold.

Fusion rule	Unprotected approach	Baseline Protected approach		
		$W = 2$	$W = 3$	$W = 4$
sum	**2.66**	**3.91**	7.05	**7.23**
product	2.66	3.95	**6.07**	7.62
maximum	3.56	4.34	6.60	13.14
minimum	2.70	5.00	10.36	8.17

Figure 6. ROC curves for an unprotected system, and for protected systems with W=2,3,4, when considering skilled forgeries, E = 10 and F=14. (a) HMM; (b) DTW; (c) Fusion of HMM and DTW

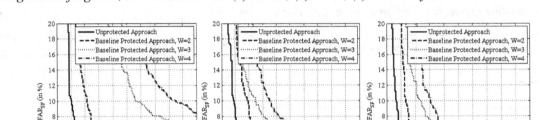

of signature biometrics, sequences extracted from different signatures, also when taken from the same user, typically have different lengths.

Therefore, in order to align two signature sequences, a dynamic programming strategy is typically needed, whereas a simple linear correspondence strategy does not represent the best signatures alignment approach. As a consequence, the more separations are performed, the more variable will be the convolutions at the output. The best recognition results for protected systems are obtained when $W = 2$, due to the fact that only one separation point has to be set in this case. The fusion of the scores obtained from the HMM and

DTW-based matchers significantly improves the performances of protected systems with $W=2$, and allows to achieve acceptable verification performances also when $W = 4$, case in which an EER lower than 8% for skilled forgeries is obtained when $E = 10$.

Having deeply discussed the performances of the baseline approach described in Section III.A, it is then possible to evaluate if the modifications introduced to define the extended transforms presented in Section III.B and III.C alter the achievable verification rates. Specifically, the scenario in which each sequence is split into $W = 2$ segments is analyzed in Figure 7, which reports

Figure 7. Performance comparison between the baseline protected system of Section III.A, and the extended mixing and shifting protection approaches of Sections III.B and III.C, when considering skilled forgeries, E = 10, F=14 and W=2. (a) HMM; (b) DTW; (c) Fusion of HMM and DTW

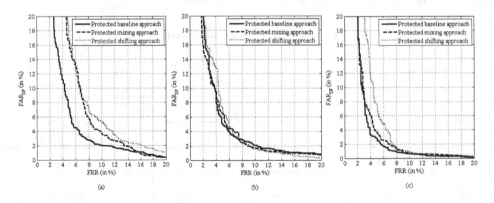

the ROCs obtained when considering, for both the mixing and the shifting approach, the HMM and DTW configurations giving the best recognition performances for the baseline method, as well as the aforementioned selected normalization and fusion strategies.

As can be seen from the reported verification results, systems using the protection methods described in Sections III.B and III.C are characterized approximately by the same performances of a system using the baseline protection. Specifically, a slight difference in performance can be observed when using HMMs as classifiers. However, such difference decreases when employing DTW-based matchers, while the use of score fusion techniques further improves the performances of the proposed protected systems: the differences between the verification rates obtained by employing the baseline approach, and those achieved with the approaches derived from it, is further reduced when combining HMM and DTW scores, with respect to the use of only one of the two proposed classifiers. Between the two extended approaches described in Sections III.B and III.C, the mixing approach performs slightly better than the shifting based one.

As a final consideration regarding the recognition performances of the proposed protected scheme, it is worth remarking that it significantly outperforms other approaches based on biometric cryptosystems, like those presented in (Feng, 2002; Freire-Santos, 2008, Maiorana, 2008a; Maiorana, 2010), thanks to the possibility of using in the transformed domain the same matchers employed for the original data, and to the possibility of exploiting score-level fusion techniques.

Renewability Performance Analysis

The transformations introduced in Section III are then analyzed with respect of the *diversity* property, which is a crucial requirement to implement cancelable biometrics. Specifically, it can be noticed that the proposed transformations are

defined by means of a key or a set of keys. By changing them, it is possible to generate different transformed templates from the same original biometrics. It is worth noticing that using the proposed approaches, the more two keys are different, the more the transformed templates, generated from the same original data, are distant. Being the space of the different keys finite, the number of possible instances which can be generated from a single original biometrics, while satisfying the diversity requirement illustrated in Section II, is necessarily limited. Specifically, we assume that the diversity property is properly satisfied only when two distinct transformed templates, generated from the same original biometrics, are so different that they can be though as being generated from signatures taken from distinct users. This means that the matching performances obtained when comparing signatures taken from the same user and modified according to different transformations should be similar to those achieved when performing recognition using random forgeries.

Considering the baseline approach described in Section III.A, the key of the employed transformation is represented by the vector $\underline{d}$, which specifies how to decompose the originally acquired functions into W parts, before performing the transformation given in Equation (1). If each element d_j, $j = 1, \ldots, W$ - 1, of a key vector $\underline{d}$ can assume values in the range [5, 95] with a distance at least equal to 5 one from the others, the total number of allowed vectors $\underline{d}$ is limited to $N_D = (95-5)/5+1 = 19$ when $W = 2$ is chosen, and to $N_D = (19 \times 18)/2 = 171$ when $W = 3$. However, in order to be compliant with the diversity property, the actual number of transformations which can be used in different systems has to be further reduced. In the following discussion, only the case in which $W = 2$ is analyzed, due to the fact that it represent the worst possible scenario for renewability performances (the defining keys are given by less parameters than the cases with $W = 3$ and $W = 4$), and also because the best verification rates can be obtained when $W = 2$, which therefore represents the preferable modality as far as verification performances is concerned.

In order to properly analyze the renewability capacity of the baseline approach, a distance measure Ψ between two key vectors, namely $\underline{d}^{(1)}$ and $\underline{d}^{(2)}$, is introduced as follows:

$$Y\left(\underline{d}^{(1)}, \underline{d}^{(2)}\right) = \sum_{i=1}^{W-1} \left| d_i^{(1)} - d_i^{(2)} \right| \qquad (6)$$

Considering the employed public MCYT database, each user is enrolled by taking into account his first $E = 10$ signatures, each of which is represented with $F = 14$ time sequences as described in Section IV. The baseline transformation process illustrated in Section III.A, with $W = 2$, is then applied by means of a key vector $\underline{d}^{(e)}$. The following statistics are then evaluated:

- The FRR, computed by considering the remaining signatures of each user, transformed according to key vectors $\underline{d}^{(a)}$ which are identical to those employed during enrolment: $Y\left(\underline{d}^{(e)}, \underline{d}^{(a)}\right) = 0$

- The FAR related to skilled (FAR$_{SF}$) and random forgeries (FAR$_{RF}$), computed by

transforming the available signature according to key vectors $\underline{d}^{(a)}$ which are the same of those employed during enrollment: $Y\left(\underline{d}^{(e)}, \underline{d}^{(a)}\right) = 0$.

- An additional statistics indicated as *Renewable Template Matching Rate* (RTMR), computed by transforming the genuine signatures of the considered user according to key vectors $\underline{d}^{(a)}$ with distances $Y\left(\underline{d}^{(e)}, \underline{d}^{(a)}\right) \in \{15, 20, 25, 30\}$ from the ones employed during enrollment, and by then matching the resulting templates against those stored during enrollment.

The curves obtained when plotting FAR$_{SF}$, FAR$_{SF}$ and RTMR versus the FRR are shown in Figure 8, from which it can be seen that the pseudo-ROC curves related to the RTMR statistics can be compared with those regarding the FAR for random forgeries only for key vector distances $Y\left(\underline{d}^{(e)}, \underline{d}^{(a)}\right) \geq 25$. More in detail, it can be observed that the DTW-matching algorithm performs better than the HMM-based one also in terms of renewability capabilities, thus allowing to improve these performances also in a system performing score fusion. The

Figure 8. Renewability analysis of the baseline approach, when considering E = 10, F=14 and W=2. (a) HMM; (b) DTW; (c) Fusion of HMM and DTW

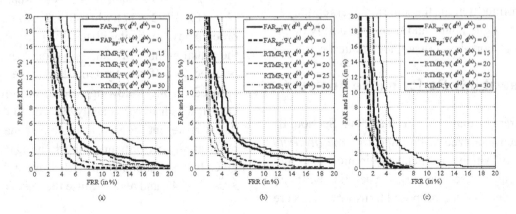

obtained result implies that, when considering the baseline approach with $W = 2$, only $\Gamma = \lfloor (95 - 5) / 25 \rfloor + 1 = 4$ different templates can be generated from a single original biometrics. Such key space is obviously too small for a practical protected on-line signature based verification system. Nevertheless, the extended approaches presented in Section III.B and III.C have been defined in order to allow key spaces with higher dimensionality, being thus more suitable for the system deployment in real world applications.

In fact, when considering the transformation defined in Section III.B, two distinct keys are used to generate protected templates: the decomposition vector $\underline{d}$ and the scrambling matrix C. Therefore, in order to evaluate the renewability capacity of the mixing approach, the maximum number of scrambling matrices which can be properly employed to transform the original signature representations, while keeping fixed the decomposition vector $\underline{d}$, has to be estimated. As defined in Section III.B, a scrambling matrix C consists of F rows and W columns. The total number of matrices which can be defined is then equal to $(F!)^{(W-1)}$, which corresponds to $14! = 87.178.291.200$ when considering $F = 14$ and W $= 2$. However, among all the possible scrambling matrices, only those which allow respecting the diversity property can be employed. Given two generic matrices $C^{(1)}$ and $C^{(2)}$, let us define the distance $W\left(C^{(1)}, C^{(2)}\right)$ as the number of corresponding different rows between the matrices $C^{(1)}$ and $C^{(2)}$. Following the approach illustrated in Section III.B, two transformations obtained by using the same decomposition vector $\underline{d}$, while employing two distinct scrambling matrices $C^{(1)}$ and $C^{(2)}$, produce more distinct templates as the distance $W\left(C^{(1)}, C^{(2)}\right)$ increases. Considering the available public MCYT database, each user is enrolled by using his first $E = 10$ signatures, to which the transformation process of Section

III.B is then applied. Specifically, the transformations employed during enrollment are ruled by a decomposition vector $\underline{d}$ and a scrambling key matrix $C^{(e)}$. The remaining signatures of each users, after being transformed using the same keys $\underline{d}$ and $C^{(e)}$ applied during enrollment, are employed to estimate the FRR. The following statistics are then evaluated:

- The FAR related to skilled and random forgeries, computed by transforming the available signatures according to the decomposition vector $\underline{d}$, and to the same scrambling matrix $C^{(a)} = C^{(e)}$ employed during enrolment: $W\left(C^{(e)}, C^{(a)}\right) = 0$;

- The RTMR related to the use of the mixing approach, computed by transforming the genuine signatures of the considered user according to the same decomposition key $\underline{d}$ employed during enrollment, but according to different scrambling keys $C^{(a)}$ with $W\left(C^{(e)}, C^{(a)}\right) \in \{8, 9, 10, 11\}$.

The matching statistics obtained for a system with $E = 10$, $F = 14$ and $W = 2$ are reported in Figure 9. All the three matching strategies presented in Section IV are considered in the reported results. Specifically, the renewability property of the mixing approach is verified by comparing the ROC curve where FAR for random forgeries is taken into account, with the pseudo-ROC curves where the RTMR for different distances $W\left(C^{(e)}, C^{(a)}\right)$ is considered. The obtained performances show that the use of different scrambling matrices between enrollment and recognition, also when keeping fixed the decomposition keys, allows obtaining matching rates which are similar to those associated with the use of random forgeries, but only when $W\left(C^{(e)}, C^{(a)}\right) \geq X = 11$ (over $F = 14$ considered functions). Also in this case, systems employ-

Figure 9. Renewability analysis of the mixing approach, when considering E = 10, F=14 and W=2. (a) HMM; (b) DTW; (c) Fusion of HMM and DTW

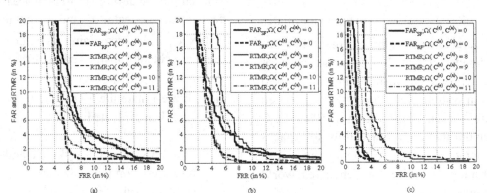

ing DTW perform better than those using the employed HMM implementation in terms of renewability capability. The fusion of DTW and HMM based classifiers allows further improving the achieved performances. The total number of scrambling matrices which can be considered while still satisfying the diversity property has therefore an upper bound given by $F!\big/(X-1)! = 24.024$. Moreover, keeping in mind that, as discussed for the renewability analysis of the baseline approach, $\Gamma = 4$ distinct decomposition vectors can be defined for each scrambling matrix C, the total number of renewable templates which can be properly generated when using the mixing approach with $W = 2$ is equal to $4 \cdot 24.024 = 96.096$.

Eventually, the renewability properties of the shifting approach described in Section III.C are analyzed. Specifically, each user in the available public MCYT database is enrolled by using his first $E = 10$ signatures, which are then transformed according to the transformation keys $\underline{d}$ and $\phi^{(e)}$. Then, in order to evaluate the renewability capacity of this approach by means of the RTMR, the remaining genuine signatures of each user are transformed using the same decomposition key $\underline{d}$ employed during enrollment, but with a different initial shift $\phi^{(a)}$. The values of the

shifts are taken in the range between 0 and 95, by considering only multiples of 5: in this way, 20 different possible values are taken into account. Having defined a distance between the shifting parameters taken during enrollment and verification, Figure 10 shows the RTMR statistics obtained when considering the same decomposition keys during enrollment and verification, but for different distances $\Phi\big(\phi^{(e)}, \phi^{(a)}\big) \in \{7, 10, 15, 20\}$. A comparison with the FAR performances obtained considering skilled and random forgeries, transformed with the same transformation keys $\phi^{(e)}$ and $\underline{d}$ employed in enrollment, is also given. All the three matching strategies presented in Section IV are again considered in the reported results.

$$\Phi\big(\phi^{(e)}, \phi^{(a)}\big) = \big|\phi^{(e)} - \phi^{(a)}\big| \qquad (7)$$

The obtained experimental results show that the RTMT pseudo-ROC curves, related to the use of different shifting parameters for the enrollment and the recognition stage, are similar to ROC curve obtained when random forgeries are taken into account, when the distance $\Phi\big(\phi^{(e)}, \phi^{(a)}\big)$ is equal or greater than the 15% of the signature length N. This implies that the number of values ϕ which can be properly considered is limited to $\Upsilon = \lfloor (95 - 5) / 15 \rfloor + 1 = 7$. When applying the

Figure 10. Renewability analysis of the shifting approach, when considering E = 10, F=14 and W=2. (a) HMM; (b) DTW; (c) Fusion of HMM and DTW.

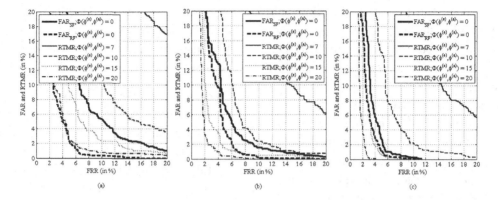

modification described in Section III.C to the baseline approach of Section III.A, we obtain a still low number of $\Gamma \cdot \Upsilon = 4 \cdot 7 = 28$ different templates which can be generated from an original biometrics. However, if the considered modification is applied together with the method described in Section III.B, it is possible to properly produce a maximum number of templates generated from the original one equal to $G \cdot F! \Big/ (X-1)! \cdot i = 96.096 \cdot 7 = 672.672$.

In conclusion, although with the proposed approaches it is not possible to generate an infinite number of discriminable templates, still more than 600.000 templates can be generated from a single original signature, while properly respecting the requirement of diversity. It is worth pointing out that, having the possibility of managing such a number of templates, a user could issue a new biometric templates each hour, for 60 consecutive years.

CONCLUSION

In this work an on-line signature-based biometric recognition system, where the original signature templates are transformed in a non-invertible way in order to provide protection and renewability,

while guaranteeing verification performances similar to those of unprotected systems, has been proposed. Specifically, a baseline transform based on the use of convolutions, together with two extended versions of the baseline method, have been presented.

Different kinds of template matching have been proposed and applied to the considered scenario, by exploiting the properties of HMM, DTW and score level fusion techniques.

Several experimental tests, evaluated on the public MCYT signature database, have been performed to evaluate the effectiveness of the proposed approach, in terms of both recognition performances and renewability. Specifically, it has been observed that:

- The baseline protection approach presented in Section III.A introduces only a slight loss of performance in terms of EER, with respect to an unprotected system. Moreover, the recognition performances achievable with the proposed protected systems present a low dependence on the transformation parameters;
- The DTW based matching strategies performs generally better than the one employing HMMs. The better behavior is re-

lated to both the recognition performances and the renewability performances;

- The recognition performances achievable when using the mixing and shifting approaches described in Section III.B and III.C are basically the same of the baseline method of Section III.A;

- In order to properly guarantee the users' privacy in a protected on-line signature-based recognition application, the baseline approach cannot be used, due to its low renewability capacity. However, the mixing and shifting approaches can be implemented to satisfy all the requirements of a properly defined cancelable biometrics, being possible to generate, through them, multiple templates from the same data, with a distance between them comparable to the one found between signatures taken from different users.

Eventually, it is worth stressing out that the proposed protection methods can be applied to any other biometrics for which a sequence based recognition approach can be performed. Moreover, being able to provide a score as output of the recognition process, the proposed methods can be employed in order to construct protected multibiometrics systems, where score-level fusion is used to combine different biometric modalities, while keeping secret the original biometric data.

REFERENCES

Ang, R., Safavi-Naini, R., & McAven, L. (2005). Cancelable Key-Based Fingerprint Templates. *10th Australian Conference Information Security and Privacy*. Brunelli, R. & Falavigna, D. Person Identification using multiple cues. *IEEE Transactions on PAMI, 17*(10), 955-966.

Bui, F.M., Martin, K., Haiping Lu, Plataniotis, K.N. & Hatzinakos, D. (2010) Fuzzy Key Binding Strategies Based on Quantization Index Modulation (QIM) for Biometric Encryption (BE) Applications. *IEEE Transactions on Information Forensics and Security, 5*(1), 118 – 132.

Campisi, P., Maiorana, E., & Neri, A. (2009). On-line signature based authentication: template security issues and countermeasures. In Boulgouris, N. V., Plataniotis, K. N., & Micheli-Tzanakou, E. (Eds.), *Biometrics: Theory, Methods, and Applications*. New York: Wiley/IEEE.

Dodis, Y., Reyzina, L., & Smith, A. (2004). *Fuzzy Extractors: How to Generate Strong Keys from Biometrics and Other Noisy Data*. Advances in Cryptology-Eurocrypt.

Feng, Y. C., Yuen, P. C., & Jain, A. K. (2010). A Hybrid Approach for Generating Secure and Discriminating Face Template. *IEEE Transactions on Information Forensics and Security, 5*(1), 103–117. doi:10.1109/TIFS.2009.2038760

Fierrez, J., Ortega-Garcia, J., Ramos, D., & Gonzalez-Rodriguez, J. (2007). HMM-Based On-Line Signature Verification: Feature Extraction and Signature Modeling. *Pattern Recognition Letters, 28*(16), 2325–2334. doi:10.1016/j.patrec.2007.07.012

Freire-Santos, M., Fierrez-Aguilar, J., & Ortega-Garcia, J. (2006). Cryptographic key generation using handwritten signature. *SPIE, Defense and Security Symposium, Biometric Technologies for Human Identification*.

Fu, B., Yang, S. X., Li, J., & Hu, D. (2009). Multibiometric Cryptosystem: Model Structure and Performance Analysis. *IEEE Transactions on Information Forensics and Security, 4*(4), 867–882. doi:10.1109/TIFS.2009.2033227

Goh, A., & Ngo, D. C. L. (2003) Computation of cryptographic keys from face biometrics. *7th IFIP Conference on Communication and Multimedia Security.*

Hao, F., Anderson, R., & Daugman, J. (2006). Combining crypto with biometrics effectively. *IEEE Transactions on Computers, 55*(9), 1081–1088. doi:10.1109/TC.2006.138

Ignatenko, T., & Willems, F. M. J. (2009). Biometric Systems: Privacy and Secrecy Aspects. *IEEE Transactions on Information Forensics and Security, 4*(4), 956–973. doi:10.1109/TIFS.2009.2033228

Ignatenko, T., & Willems, F. M. J. (2010). Information Leakage in Fuzzy Commitment Schemes. *IEEE Transactions on Information Forensics and Security, 5*(2), 337–348. doi:10.1109/TIFS.2010.2046984

Jain, A. K., Flynn, P., & Ross, A. (2007). *Handbook of Biometrics*. New York: Springer.

Jain, A.K., Nandakumar, K. & Nagar, A. (2008). Biometric Template Security. *EURASIP Journal on Advances in Signal Processing, Special Issue on Biometrics, 2008*(11), *1-17.*

Jassim, S., Al-Assam, H., & Sellahewa, H. (2009) Improving performance and security of biometrics using efficient and stable random projection techniques. *International Symposium on Image and Signal Processing and Analysis (ISPA).*

Juels, A., & Sudan, M. (2006). A Fuzzy Vault Scheme. *Designs, Codes and Cryptography, 38*(2), 237–257. doi:10.1007/s10623-005-6343-z

Juels, A., & Wattenberg, M. (1999). A Fuzzy Commitment Scheme. *6th ACM Conference Computer and Communication Security.*

Kanade, S. Petrovska-Delacrétaz, D. & Dorizzi, B. (2010) Obtaining cryptographic keys using feature level fusion of iris and face biometrics for secure user authentication. *IEEE Computer Society Conference on Computer Vision and Pattern Recognition Workshops (CVPRW).*

Kelkboom, E. J. C., Zhou, X., Breebaart, J., Veldhuis, R. N. J., & Busch, C. (2009) Multi-algorithm fusion with template protection. *IEEE 3rd International Conference on Biometrics: Theory, Applications, and Systems (BTAS).*

Kholmatov, A., & Yanikoglu, B. (2005). Identity Authentication Using Improved Online Signature Verification Method. *Pattern Recognition Letters, 26*(15), 2400–2408. doi:10.1016/j.patrec.2005.04.017

Maiorana, E., & Campisi, P. (2010). Fuzzy Commitment for Function based Signature Template Protection. *IEEE Signal Processing Letters, 17*(3), 249–252. doi:10.1109/LSP.2009.2038111

Maiorana, E., Campisi, P., Fierrez, J., Ortega-Garcia, J., & Neri, A. (2010). Cancelable templates for sequence-based biometrics with application to on-line signature recognition. *IEEE Transactions on System Man and Cybernetics Part A, 40*(3), 525–538. doi:10.1109/TSMCA.2010.2041653

Maiorana, E., Campisi, P., & Neri, A. (2008). User Adaptive Fuzzy Commitment for Signature Templates Protection and Renewability. *SPIE Journal of Electronic Imaging. Special Section on Biometrics, 17*(1), 1–12.

Maiorana, E., Campisi, P., Ortega-Garcia, J., & Neri, A. (2008). Cancelable Biometrics for HMM-based Signature Recognition. *IEEE Second International Conference on Biometrics: Theory, Applications and Systems (BTAS).*

Maiorana, E., Martinez-Diaz, M., Campisi, P., Ortega-Garcia, J., & Neri, A. (2008). Template Protection for HMM-based On-line Signature Authentication. *CVPR Conference, Workshop on Biometrics.*

Nandakumar, K., & Jain, A. K. (2008) Multibiometric Template Security Using Fuzzy Vault. *2nd IEEE International Conference on Biometrics: Theory, Applications and Systems (BTAS).*

Ortega-Garcia, J. (2003). MCYT baseline corpus: A bimodal biometric database. *IEEE Proceedings Vision, Image and Signal Processing. Special Issue on Biometrics on the Internet, 150*(6), 395–401.

Prabhakar, S., Pankanti, S., & Jain, A. K. (2003). Biometric Recognition: Security and Privacy Concerns. *IEEE Security & Privacy Magazine, 1*(2), 33–42. doi:10.1109/MSECP.2003.1193209

Rabiner, L. R. (1989). A tutorial on Hidden Markov Models and selected applications in speech recognition. *Proceedings of the IEEE, 77*(2), 257–286. doi:10.1109/5.18626

Ratha, N., Chikkerur, S., Connell, J. H., & Bolle, R. M. (2007). Generating Cancelable Fingerprint Templates. *IEEE Transactions on PAMI, 29*(4), 561–572.

Ratha, N. K., Connell, J. H., & Bolle, R. (2001). Enhancing Security and Privacy of Biometric-based Authentication Systems. *IBM Systems Journal, 40*(3), 614–634. doi:10.1147/sj.403.0614

Ross, A. A., Nandakumar, K., & Jain, A. K. (2006). *Handbook of Multibiometrics.* New York: Springer.

Sakoe, H., & Chiba, S. (1978). Dynamic programming algorithm optimization for spoken word recognition. *IEEE Transactions on Acoustics, Speech, and Signal Processing, 26*(1), 43–49. doi:10.1109/TASSP.1978.1163055

Scheirer, W. J., & Boult, T. E. (2007) Cracking Fuzzy Vault and Biometric Encryption, *IEEE Biometric Symposium.*

Shi, J. You. Z., Gu, M. & Lam, (2008) K. Biomapping: Privacy trustworthy biometrics using noninvertible and discriminable constructions. 19th International Conference on Pattern Recognition (ICPR).

Sutcu, Y., Li, Q., & Memon, N. (2007). Protecting Biometric Templates with Sketch: Theory and Practice. *IEEE Transactions on Information Forensics and Security, 2*(3), 503–512. doi:10.1109/TIFS.2007.902022

Sutcu, Y., Sencar, H. T., & Memon, N. (2007). A Geometric Transformation to Protect Minutiae-Based Fingerprint Templates. *SPIE International Defense and Security Symposium.*

Teoh, A. B. J., Ngo, D. C. L., & Goh, A. (2006). Random Multispace Quantization as an Analytic Mechanism for BioHashing of Biometric and Random Identity Inputs. *IEEE Transactions on PAMI, 28*(12), 1892–1901.

Tuyls, P., Akkermans, A., Kevenaar, T., Schrijen, G. J., Bazen, A., & Veldhuis, R. (2005). *Practical biometric template protection system based on reliable components.* AVBPA.

Uludag, U., Pankanti, S., & Jain, A. K. (2004). Biometric cryptosystems: Issues and Challenges. *Proceedings of the IEEE, Special Issue on Multimedia Security for Digital Rights Managment, 92*(6), 948-960.

Van der Veen, M., Kevenaar, T., Schrijen, G. J., Akkermans, T. H., & Zuo, F. (2006). *Face biometrics with renewable templates.* SPIE Proc. on Security, Steganography, and Watermarking of Multimedia Contents.

Vielhauer, C. & Steinmetz, R. (2004). Handwriting: Feature Correlation Analysis for Biometric Hashes. *EURASIP Journal on Applied Signal Processing, Special issue on Biometric Signal Processing, 4*, 542–558.

Yang, H., Jiang, X., & Kot, A. C. (2009) Generating secure cancelable fingerprint templates using local and global features. *2nd IEEE International Conference on Computer Science and Information Technology (ICCSIT)*.

Yeung, D. Y., et al. (2004). SVC2004: First International Signature Verification Competition. *Proceedings of the International Conference on Biometric Authentication (ICBA)*.

Yip, W. K., Goh, A., Ngo, D. C. L., & Teoh, A. B. J. (2006). Generation of Replaceable Cryptographic Keys from Dynamic Handwritten Signatures. *International Conference on Biometrics (ICB)*.

Compilation of References

AACS-LA. (2006). Pre-*recorded Video Book*, Advanced Access Content System, http://www.aacsla.com/specifications.

Adams, C. and Lloyd, S. (2002). *Understanding PKI: Concepts, Standards, and Deployment Considerations.* Addison-Wesley Professional, 2 edition.

Adams, C., Cain, P., Pinkas, D., and Zuccherato, R. (2001). Internet x.509 public key infrastructure timestamp protocol (tsp).

Adams, K., & Algesen, O. (2006). A Comparison of Software and Hardware Techniques for x86 Virtualization, In J.P. Shen (Ed.), *12th International Conference on Architectural Support for Programming Languages and Operating Systems* (pp. 2-13). New York, NY: ACM Press.

Agrawal, R., Haas, P. J., & Kiernan, J. (2003). Watermarking relational data: framework, algorithms and analysis. *The VLDB Journal, 12*(2), 157–169. doi:10.1007/s00778-003-0097-x

Agrawal, R., & Kiernan, J. (2002). Watermarking relational databases. In *28th International Conference on Very Large Databases VLDB.*

Ahuja, S. R., & Ensor, R. (2004). VoIP: What is it Good for? *Queue, 2*(6), 48–55. doi:10.1145/1028893.1028897

Airold, E., & Malin, B. (2004). *Scamslam: An architecture for learning the criminal relations behind scam spam.* Carnegie Mellon University, School of Computer Science, Pittsburg Technical Report CMU-ISRI-04-121.

Alattar, A. M. (2004). Reversible watermark using the difference expansion of a generalized integer transform. *IEEE Transactions on Image Processing, 13*(8), 1147–1156. doi:10.1109/TIP.2004.828418

Al-Mualla, M. E., Canagarajah, C. N., & Bull, D. R. (2002). *Video Coding for Mobile Communications: Efficiency, Complexity and Resilience.* Boston: Academic Press.

Amazon (2008). Amazon simple storage service (amazon s3). Amazon Web services. http://aws.amazon.com/s3.

Anderson, D. O., & Moore, J. B. (1979). *Optimal Filtering* in: Thomas Kailath (editor), *Information and System Science Series*, Prentice-Hall, Inc., Englewood Cliffs, New Jersey, USA, pp. 1-61, 1979.

Ang, R., Safavi-Naini, R., & McAven, L. (2005). Cancelable Key-Based Fingerprint Templates. *10th Australian Conference Information Security and Privacy.* Brunelli, R. & Falavigna, D. Person Identification using multiple cues. *IEEE Transactions on PAMI, 17*(10), 955-966.

Asma, B. M. (2007). Malatya: World's Capital of Apricot Culture. Chronica Horticulturae 01/2007. 20 ff. Leuven: ISHS

ASR. (2002). Expert witness compression format specification. ASR Data Acquisition and Analysis. http://www.asrdata.com/SMART/whitepaper.html.

Bao, F., Deng, R. H., Ooi, B. C., & Yang, Y. (2005). Tailored Reversible Watermarking Schemes for Authentication of Electronic Clinical Atlas. *IEEE Transactions on Information Technology in Biomedicine, 9*(4), 554–563. doi:10.1109/TITB.2005.855556

Barg, A., Blakely, R., & Kabatiansky, G. (2003). Digital Fingerprinting Codes: Problem Statements, Constructions, Identification of Traitors. *IEEE Transactions on Information Theory, 49*(4), 852–865. doi:10.1109/TIT.2003.809570

Barreto, P. S. L. M., Kim, H. Y., & Rijmen, V. (2002). Toward Secure Public-key Blockwise Fragile Authentication Watermarking. *IEEE Proceedings - Vision. Image and Signal Processing, 148*(2), 57–62. doi:10.1049/ip-vis:20020168

Bartel, M., Boyer, J., Fox, B., LaMaccia, B., & Simon, E. (2002). Xml-signature syntax and processing. W3C. http://www.w3.org/TR/xmldsig-core/.

Baughman, N. E., & Levine, B. N. (2001). Cheat-proof playout for centralized and distributed online games. [Los Alamitos, CA: IEEE]. *Proceedings - IEEE INFOCOM, 1*, 104–113.

Beckett, J. (2005). Forensic Computing: Experts, Certification and the Categorisation of Roles. Paper presented at the Colloquium for Information Systems Security Education - Asia Pacific, Adelaide, Australia.

Bellovin, S. M., Blaze, M., & Landau, S. (2005). The real national-security needs for VoIP'. *Communications of the ACM, 48*(11), 120. doi:10.1145/1096000.1096030

Berners-Lee, T., Fielding, R., and Masinter, L. (2005). RFC 3986: Uniform resource identifier (uri): Generic syntax.

Bernstein, P. A., Hadzilacos, V., & Goodman, N. (1987). *Concurrency control and recovery in database systems.* Reading, MA: Addison-Wesley.

Berrani Sid-Ahmed. Amsaleg Laurent & Gros Patrick. (2003). Robust content-based image searches for copyright protection. In Proceedings of the 1st ACM international workshop on Multimedia databases, LA, USA, (pp. 70-77).

Bharambe, A. R., Rao, S., & Seshan, S. (2002). Mercury: a scalable publish-subscribe system for internet games. In *Proceedings of the first workshop on Network and system support for games (NetGames).* (pp. 3–9). New York, NY: ACM.

Boileau, A. (2006). Hit by a Bus: Physical Access Attacks with Firewire. In 4th*International Ruxcon Conference.* Retrieved September 20, 2008, from http://www.ruxcon.org.au/files/2006/firewire_attacks.pdf

Bone v. State, 771 N.E.2d 710, 716-17 (Ind. App. 2002).

Boneh, D., & Shaw, J. (1998). Collusion-secure fingerprinting for digital data. *IEEE Transactions on Information Theory, 44*(5), 1897–1905. doi:10.1109/18.705568

Boneh, D. (2001). Cryptographic hashing. http://crypto.stanford.edu/ dabo/courses/cs255\s\do5(w)inter01/1-hashing.pdf, Course notes for CS255 Winter 01.

Bors, A., & Pitas, I. (1996). Image watermarking using DCT domain constraints. In *IEEE International Conference on Image Processing (ICIP'96)*, volume III, (pp 231–234).

Bose, S., & Steinhardt, A. O. (1995, Sept.). A maximal invariant framework for adaptive detection with structured and unstructured covariance matrices. *IEEE Transactions on Signal Processing, 43*, 2164–2175. doi:10.1109/78.414779

Braudaway, G. W. (1997). Protecting publicly-available images with an invisible image watermark. In *IEEE International Conference on Image Processing (ICIP'97).*

Brisco, T. (1995). DNS Support for Load Balancing. Retrieved from: http://www.ietf.org/rfc/rfc1794.txt

Brofferio, S., Carnimeo, L., Comunale, D., & Mastronardi, G. (1990). A Background Updating Algorithm for Moving Object Scenes. In Cappellini, V. (Ed.), *Time-varying Image Processing and Moving Object Recognition, 2* (pp. 289–296). Amsterdam: Elsevier Publishers B.V.

Broucek, V., & Turner, P. (2001). Forensic Computing: Developing a Conceptual Approach for an Emerging Academic Discipline. Paper presented at the 5th Australian Security Research Symposium, Perth, Australia.

Broucek, V., & Turner, P. (2002). Bridging the Divide: Rising Awareness of Forensic Issues amongst Systems Administrators. Paper presented at the 3rd International System Administration and Networking Conference, Maastricht, The Netherlands, 27-31 May.

Brown, M., & Lowe, D. G. (2003). Recognising Panoramas. In Proceedings of the 9th IEEE International Conference on Computer Vision, (pp. 1218-1225).

Buchholz, F., & Tjaden, B. (2007). A brief study of time. *Digital Investigation,* (4S), 31–42. doi:10.1016/j.diin.2007.06.004

Bui, F.M., Martin, K., Haiping Lu, Plataniotis, K.N. & Hatzinakos, D. (2010) Fuzzy Key Binding Strategies Based on Quantization Index Modulation (QIM) for Biometric Encryption (BE) Applications. *IEEE Transactions on Information Forensics and Security, 5*(1), 118 – 132.

Burdach, M. (2005a). Digital Forensics of the Physical Memory. Retrieved March 2006 from <http://www.forensicfocus.com/digital-forensics-of-physical-memory>.

Burdach, M. (2005b). An Introduction to Windows memory forensic. Retrieved 10 May 2006 from <http://forensic.seccure.net/pdf/introduction_to_windows_memory_forensic.pdf>.

Burger, W., & Burge, M. J. (2007). *Digital image processing: An algorithm introduction using java* (1st ed.). New York: Springer.

Byun, B., Lee, C.-H., Webb, S., & Pu, C. (2007). A discriminative classifier learning approach to image modeling and spam image identification. *4th Conference on Email and Anti-Spam*.

Campisi, P., Maiorana, E., & Neri, A. (2009). On-line signature based authentication: template security issues and countermeasures. In Boulgouris, N. V., Plataniotis, K. N., & Micheli-Tzanakou, E. (Eds.), *Biometrics: Theory, Methods, and Applications*. New York: Wiley/IEEE.

Cao, F., Huang, H. K., & Zhou, X. Q. (2003). Medical Image Security in a HIPAA Mandated PACS Environment. *Computerized Medical Imaging and Graphics*, *27*(2), 185–196. doi:10.1016/S0895-6111(02)00073-3

Carreras, X., & Mrquez, L. (2001). Boosting trees for antispam email filtering. *International Conference on Recent Advances in Natural Language Processing*, (pp. 58-64).

Carrier, B. (2005). *File System Forensic Analysis*. Upper Saddle River, NJ: Addison Wesley.

Carrier, B., & Grand, J. (2004). A Hardware-Based Memory Acquisition Procedure for Digital Investigations. *Digital Investigation*, *1*(1), 50–60. doi:10.1016/j.diin.2003.12.001

Carrier, B. (2005). *File system forensic analysis*. Upper Saddle River, N.J.: Addison-Wesley.

Carrier, B. (2006). *A Hypothesis-Based Approach to Digital Forensic Investigations*. PhD thesis, Purdue University.

Carrier, B. (2006). *A hypothesis-based approach to digital forensic investigations* (CERIAS Tech Report 2006-06): Center for Education and Research in Information Assurance and Security, Purdue University.

Carrier, B. (2008). SleuthKit, Retrieved September 20, 2008, from http://www.sleuthkit.org/.

Celik, M. U., Sharma, G., Tekalp, M. A., & Saber, E. (2002). Reversible data hiding. In *International Conference on Image Processing*, volume 2, (pp 157–160).

Center for Democracy and Technology. (2003). Why am I getting all this spam? Retrieved from: http://www.cdt.org/speech/spam/030319spamreport.pdf

Chang, E., Wang, J., Li, C., & Wiederhold, G. (1998). A replicated image detector for the world-wide web. In *Proceedings of SPIE*. RIME.

Chang, S. F., Hsu, W., Kennedy, L., Xie, L., Yanagawa, A., Zavesky, E., & Zhang, D.-Q. (2005). *Columbia university trecvid-2005 video search and high-level feature extraction*. In TRECVID.

Chang, C. C., Tai, W. L., & Lin, M. H. (2005). A reversible data hiding scheme with modified side match vector quantization. In *19th International Conference on Advanced Information Networking and Applications*, (pp 947–952).

Chen, B., & Wornell, G. W. (2001). Quantization Index Modulation: A Class of Provably Good Methods For Digital Watermarking and Information Embedding. *IEEE Transactions on Information Theory*, *47*(4), 1423–1443. doi:10.1109/18.923725

Chen, L. (2006). *Stentiford, F. W. M* (pp. 38–42). Comparison of Near-Duplicate Image Matching. CVMP.

Cherry, S. (2005). Seven myths about voice over IP. *IEEE Spectrum*, *42*(3), 52–57. doi:10.1109/MSPEC.2005.1402719

Chisum, W. J., & Turvey, B. (2000). Evidence Dynamics: Locard's Exchange Principle and Crime Reconstruction. *Journal of Behavioral Profiling*, *1*(1).

Chor, B. (2000). Fiat. A., Naor, M., & Pinkas, B. (2000) Tracing traitors. *IEEE Transactions on Information Theory*, *46*, 893–910. doi:10.1109/18.841169

Chor, B., Fiat, A., & Naor, M. (1994). Tracing traitors, *Advance in Cryptography, Crypto* [Springer-Verlag, Berlin, Heidelberg, New York.]. *Lecture Notes in Computer Science*, *839*, 480–491.

Chum, O., Philbin, J., Isard, M., & Zisserman, A. (2007). Scalable Near Identical Image and Shot Detection. Proceedings of the 6th ACM International Conference on Image and Video Retrieval, (pp. 549-556).

Chun, W., Sprague, A., Warner, G., & Skjellum, A. (2008). Mining spam email to identify common origins for forensic application. *23rd Annual ACM Symposium on Applied Computing*, (pp. 1433-1437).

Cikic, S., Jeschke, S., Ludwig, N., & Sinha, U. (2007). Virtual room concepts for cooperative, scientific work. In *Proceedings of the world conference on Educational multimedia, hypermedia & telecommunications (ED-MEDIA).* (pp. 1872-1879). Chesapeake, VA: AACE.

Clark, J., Koprinska, I., & Poon, J. (2003). A neural network based approach to automated e-mail classification. *IEEE/WIC International Conference on Web Intelligence*, (pp. 702-705).

CNN. Online Gamer in China Wins Virtual Theft Suit. Retrieved December 20, 2003, from http://www.cnn.com/2003/TECH/fun.games/12/19/china.gamer.reut/

Coatrieux, G., Maitre, H., & Sankur, B. (2001). Strict Integrity Control of Biomedical Images. *Proc. Security and Watermarking of Multimedia Contents III, SPIE, 4314*, 229–240.

Cohnen, G., Encheva, S., Litsyn, S., & Schaathun, H. G. (2003). Intersecting codes and separating codes. *Discrete Applied Mathematics, 128*(1), 75–83. doi:10.1016/S0166-218X(02)00437-7

Computer Systems Laboratory, N. I. o. S. and Technology (1993). FIPS-180 secure hash standard. U.S. Department Of Commerce. Also known as: 58 Fed Reg 27712 (1993).

Cox, I., Kilian, J., Leighton, T., & Shamoon, T. (1997). Secure spread spectrum watermarking for multimedia. *IEEE Transactions on Image Processing, 6*(12), 1673–1687. doi:10.1109/83.650120

Craig, K. (2006). *Second Life land deal goes sour.* Retrieved May 18, 2006, from http://www.wired.com/gaming/virtualworlds/news/2006/05/70909

Cronin, E., Filstrup, B., & Jamin, S. (2003). Cheat-proofing dead reckoned multiplayer games. In *Proceedings of the 2nd international conference on Application and development of computer games (ADCoG).* Hong Kong.

Cutler, R., & Davis, L. (2000). Robust real-time periodic motion detection, analysis, and applications. *IEEE Transactions on Pattern Analysis and Machine Intelligence, 22*(8), 781–796. doi:10.1109/34.868681

Czeskis, A., Hilaire, D. J., Koscher, K., Gribble, S. D., Kohno, T., & Schneier, B. (2008). Defeating Encrypted and Deniable File Systems: TrueCrypt v5.1a and the Case of the Tattling OS and Applications. In *3rd USENIX Workhop on Hot Topics in Security*. Retrieved September 20, 2008, from http://www.usenix.org/events/hotsec08/tech/

Daubert v. Merrell Dow Pharmaceuticals, Inc., 509 U.S. 579 (1993).

Davidson, J., & Peters, J. (2000). *Voice over IP Fundamentals*. USA: Cisco Systems.

Davis, S. B. (2005). *The cost of insecurity - griefing: from anonymity to accountability.* Retrieved August 2005, from http://www.secureplay.com/cheating/griefing-in-games.htm

Dee, H. M., & Velastin, S. A. (2007), *How close are we to solving the problem of automated visual surveillance? A review of real-world surveillance, scientific progress and evaluative mechanisms*, in *Machine Vision and Applications*, 5 May 2007. DOI = 10.1007/s00138-007-0077-z

Dierks, T. and Allen, C. (1999). RFC 2246: The TLS protocol version 1. Status: PROPOSED STANDARD.

Diffie, W., & Hellman, M. E. (1976). New directions in cryptography. *IEEE Transactions on Information Theory, IT-22*(6), 644–654. citeseer.ist.psu.edu/diffie76new.html. doi:10.1109/TIT.1976.1055638

Dodis, Y., Reyzina, L., & Smith, A. (2004). *Fuzzy Extractors: How to Generate Strong Keys from Biometrics and Other Noisy Data*. Advances in Cryptology-Eurocrypt.

Drucker, H., Wu, D., & Vapnik, V. N. (1999). Support vector machines for spam categorization. *IEEE Transactions on Neural Networks, 10*(5), 1048–1054. doi:10.1109/72.788645

Duque, D., Santos, H., & Cortez, P. (2006). *The OBSERVER: An Intelligent and Automated Video Surveillance System*, Lecture Notes in Computer Science, Springer, ISSN 0302-9743. 4141 (2006) pp 898-909.

Edelsbrunner, H., & Souvaine, D. L. (1990). Computing Least Median of Squares Regression Lines and Guided Topological Sweep. *Journal of the American Statistical Association, 85*(409), 115–119. doi:10.2307/2289532

Eggendorfer, T. (2005). *Stopping Spammers' Harvesters using a HTTP tar pit.* Sydney: AUUG.

Eggendorfer, T. (2006). *SMTP or HTTP tar pits? Which one is more efficient in fighting spam?* Melbourne: AUUG.

Eggendorfer, T. (2006b). *Dynamic obfuscation of email addresses - a method to reduce spam.* Melbourne: AUUG.

Eggendorfer, T. (2005b). Ghost Surfing. Anonymous surfing with Java Anonymous Proxy. Linux Magazine (International Edition) 11/2005. 44 ff. München: Linux New Media

Eggendorfer, T. (2005c). Methoden der präventiven Spambekämpfung im Internet. Thesis. Fernuniversität in Hagen, München, Hagen

Eggendorfer, T. (2007). Tweak your MTA. Spam-Schutz mit Tricks. Berlin: 3. Mailserverkonferenz

Eggendorfer, T. (2007b). Methoden der Spambekämpfung und -vermeidung. Dissertation. FernUniversität in Hagen. Hagen: BoD

Eggendorfer, T. (2007c). Spam slam. Comparing antispam applicances and services. Linux Magazine (International Edition) 03/2007. 32 ff. München: Linux New Media

Eggendorfer, T., & Keller, J. (2006c). Combining SMTP and HTTP tar pits to proactively reduce spam. Las Vegas, Nevada: SAM 2006 (The 2006 World Congress in Computer ScienceComputer Engineering, and Applied Computing)

Eggendorfer, T., & Keller, J. (2006d). Dynamically blocking access to web pages for spammers' harvesters. Cambridge, MA: IASTED Conference on Communication, Network and Information Security CNIS 2006

Encase (2008), Retrieved September 20, 2008, from http://www.guidancesoftware.com/.

Engel, D., Stütz, T., & Uhl, A. (2008). Efficient Transparent JPEG2000 Encryption. In Li, C.-T. (Ed.), *Multimedia Forensics and Security*. Hershey, PA: Information Science Publishing. doi:10.4018/9781599048697.ch016

Farid, H. (2006). *Digital Image Ballistics from JPEG Quantization*, Dartmouth Computer Science Technical Report, TR2006-583, September 2006.

Federal Rule of Evidence 1001(3) (2007).

Federal Rule of Evidence 1002 (2007).

Federal Rule of Evidence 901(a) (2007).

Feng, Y. C., Yuen, P. C., & Jain, A. K. (2010). A Hybrid Approach for Generating Secure and Discriminating Face Template. *IEEE Transactions on Information Forensics and Security, 5*(1), 103–117. doi:10.1109/TIFS.2009.2038760

Fiat, A., & Naor, M. (1993). Broadcast Encryption, *Advance in Cryptography, Crypto* [Springer-Verlag, Berlin, Heidelberg, New York.]. *Lecture Notes in Computer Science, 773*, 480–491. doi:10.1007/3-540-48329-2_40

Fiat, A., & Tassa, T. (1999). Dynamic traitor tracing, *Advance in Cryptography, Crypto* [Springer-Verlag, Berlin, Heidelberg, New York]. *Lecture Notes in Computer Science, 1666*, 354–371. doi:10.1007/3-540-48405-1_23

Fiedler, S., Wallner, M., & Weber, M. (2002). A communication architecture for massive multiplayer games. In *Proceedings of the first workshop on Network and system support for games (NetGames).* (pp. 14–22). New York, NY: ACM.

Fierrez, J., Ortega-Garcia, J., Ramos, D., & Gonzalez-Rodriguez, J. (2007). HMM-Based On-Line Signature Verification: Feature Extraction and Signature Modeling. *Pattern Recognition Letters, 28*(16), 2325–2334. doi:10.1016/j.patrec.2007.07.012

Fischler, M. A., & Robert, C. Bolles. (1981). Random Sample Consensus: A Paradigm for Model Fitting with Applications to Image Analysis and Automated Cartography. 24(6), 381-395.

Fonseca, B. (2007). Hard-drive changes: Long block data standard gets green light. *Computerworld.* http://www.computerworld.com/action/article.do? command=print ArticleBasic&articleId=9018507.

Forensics Source, N. T. I. B. S. (2008). Safeback bit stream backup software. http://www.forensics-intl.com/safeback.html.

Forsyth, D. A., & Ponce, J. (2003). *Computer Vision: A Modern Approach*. New Jersey: Prentice Hill.

Freeman, W., & Adelson, E. (1991). The Design and Use of Steerable Filters. *IEEE Transactions on Pattern Analysis and Machine Intelligence*, *13*(9), 891–906. doi:10.1109/34.93808

Frei, S. (2004). *Angriff via Mail. Mailserver als Verstärker für DoS-Angriffe. Heise security. 4.* Hannover: Heise.

Freire-Santos, M., Fierrez-Aguilar, J., & Ortega-Garcia, J. (2006). Cryptographic key generation using handwritten signature. *SPIE, Defense and Security Symposium, Biometric Technologies for Human Identification*.

Fridrich, J., & Goljan, M. (2004). On Estimation of Secret Message Length in LSB Steganography in Spatial Domain. *Proc. SPIE, Security, Steganography, and Watermarking of Multimedia Contents VIII*, 5306, 23-34.

Friedl, S. (2005). An illustrated guide to cryptographic hashes. http://www.unixwiz.net/techtips/iguide-crypto-hashes.html.

Fu, B., Yang, S. X., Li, J., & Hu, D. (2009). Multibiometric Cryptosystem: Model Structure and Performance Analysis. *IEEE Transactions on Information Forensics and Security*, *4*(4), 867–882. doi:10.1109/TIFS.2009.2033227

Fuhrmann, D. R. (1991, Oct.). Application of Toeplitz covariance estimation to adaptive beamforming and detection. *IEEE Transactions on Signal Processing*, *39*, 2194–2198. doi:10.1109/78.91176

Garfinkel, S. L. (2008). Afflib. http://www.afflib.org/.

Garfinkel, S. L., Malan, D. J., Dubec, K.-A., Stevens, C. C., & Pham, C. (2006). Disk imaging with the advanced forensic format, library and tools. In *Research Advances in Digital Forensics (Second Annual IFIP WG 11.9 International Conference on Digital Forensics)*. Springer.

Garner, G. M. (2008). Forensic Acquisition Utilities. Retrieved September 20, 2008, from http://www.gmg-systemsinc.com/fau/.

Gates Rubber Co. v. Bando Chem. Indus. Ltd., 167 F.R.D. 90, 112 (D. Colo. 1996).

GauthierDickey. C., Zappala, D., Lo, V., & Marr, J. (2004). Low latency and cheat-proof event ordering for peer-to-peer games. In *Proceedings of the 14th ACM international workshop on Network and operating systems support for digital audio and video (NOSSDAV)*. (pp. 134–139). New York, NY: ACM.

GetData Software. (2008). GetData Software Development Company. http://www.mountimage.com/.

Goh, A., & Ngo, D. C. L. (2003) Computation of cryptographic keys from face biometrics. *7th IFIP Conference on Communication and Multimedia Security*.

Gonzalez, R. C., & Woods, R. E. (2002). *Digital Image Processing*. MA: Prentice Hall.

Graham, M. H. (2006). *Handbook on Federal Evidence* (6th ed.). St. Paul, Minn.: Thomson/West.

Grangetto, M., Magli, E., & Olmo, G. (2006). Multimedia Selective Encryption by Means of Randomized Arithmetic Coding. *IEEE Transactions on Multimedia*, *8*(5), 905–917. doi:10.1109/TMM.2006.879919

Grauman, K., & Darrell, T. (2005). Efficient Image Matching with Distribution of Local Invariant Features. In Proceedings of the IEEE Conference on Computer Vision and Pattern Recognition, (pp. 627–634).

Greenberg, S., & Roseman, M. (2003). Using a room metaphor to ease transitions in groupware. In Ackerman, M., Pipek, V., & Wulf, V. (Eds.), *Sharing expertise. Beyond knowledge management* (pp. 203–256). Cambridge, MA: MIT Press.

Gross-Amblard, D. (2003). Query-preserving watermarking of relational databases and XML documents. In *20th ACM Symposium on Principles of Database Systems*, (pp 191–201).

Grugq, the (2005). The Art of Defiling: Defeating Forensic Analysis. Retrieved May 21, 2008, from http://www.blackhat.com/presentations/bh-usa-05/bh-us-05-grugq.pdf.

Guidance Software, Inc. (2006). Encase Forensic Corporate Version 5: The Standard in Computer Forensics. Retrieved May 21, 2008, from http://www.guidancesoftware.com/downloads/getpdf.aspx?fl=.pdf.

Guidance Software, Inc. (2007). Guidance Software Responds to iSEC report on EnCASE. Retrieved May 21, 2008, from http://www.securityfocus.com/archive/1/474727.

Guidance Software, Inc. (n.d.). Guidance EnCE Certification Program. Retrieved July 18, 2008, from http://www.guidancesoftware.com/training/EnCE_certification.aspx.

Guo, X., & Zhuang, T. G. (2007). A Region-Based Lossless Watermarking Scheme for Enhancing Security of Medical Data. *Journal of Digital Imaging*. doi:.doi:10.1007/s10278-007-9043-6

Guo, F., Wang, J., & Li, D. (2006). Fingerprinting relational databases. In *ACM symposium on Applied computing*, (pp 487–492).

Gupta, G., & Pieprzyk, P. (2007). Reversible and semi-blind relational database watermarking. In *International Conference on Signal Processing and Multimedia Applications*.

Haake, J. M., Schümmer, T., Haake, A., Bourimi, M., & Landgraf, B. (2004). Supporting flexible collaborative distance learning in the CURE platform. In *Proceedings of the 37th annual Hawaii international conference on system sciences (HICSS)*. Los Alamitos, CA: IEEE.

Haggerty, J., & Taylor, M. (2007). *FORSIGS: Forensic Signature Analysis of the Hard Drive for Multimedia File Fingerprints*, pages 1–12. Springer. http://www.springerlink.com/content/21478kr877478805/.

Halderman, J. A., Schoen, S. D., Heninger, N., Clarkson, W., Paul, W., Calandrino, J. A., et al. (2008). Lest We Remember: Cold Boot Attacks on Encryption Keys. In *17th Usenix Security Symposium*. San Jose, CA. Retrieved September 20, 2008, from http://citp.princeton.edu/pub/coldboot.pdf

Han, J., & Kamber, M. (2000). *Data mining: Concepts and techniques*. Morgan Kaufmann.

Hao, F., Anderson, R., & Daugman, J. (2006). Combining crypto with biometrics effectively. *IEEE Transactions on Computers*, *55*(9), 1081–1088. doi:10.1109/TC.2006.138

Haralick, R. M., Shanmugam, K., & Dinstein, I. (1973). Textural features for image classification. *IEEE Transactions on Systems, Man, and Cybernetics*, *3*, 610–621. doi:10.1109/TSMC.1973.4309314

Harbour, N. (2006). dcfldd. http://dcfldd.sf.net.

Harris, C., & Stephens, M. (1988). A Combined Corner and Edge Detector. In Proceedings Alvey Vision Conference, (pp. 147-151).

Harris, R. (2006). Arriving at an anti-forensics consensus: Examining how to define and control the anti-forensics problem. *Digital Investigation* 3(S), 44-49. Retrieved May 21, 2008, from http://www.dfrws.org/2006/proceedings/6-Harris.pdf.

Heinlein, P. (2007). Genervt, blockier gefährdet: Wie sich Firmen gegen Spam & Viren schützen können. Hannover: CeBIT 2007

Hochstein, T. (2003). FAQ. E-Mail-Header lesen und verstehen. Retrieved from: http://www.th-h.de/faq/headerfaq.php3

Holliman, M., & Memon, N. (2000). Counterfeiting Attacks on Oblivious Block-wise Independent Invisible Watermarking Schemes. *IEEE Transactions on Image Processing*, *9*(3), 432–441. doi:10.1109/83.826780

Hollmann, H. D., Van Lint, J. J., Linnartz, J. P., & Tolhuizen, L. M. (1998). On codes with the identifiable parent property. *Journal of Combinatorial Theory Series A*, *82*, 121–133. doi:10.1006/jcta.1997.2851

Hosbach, W. (2006). *Test Spam-Filter....die Schlechten ins Kröpfchen! PC Magazin 10/2006. 124 ff*. München: WEKA Computerzeitschriften-Verlag.

Housley, R., & Polk, T. (2001). *Planning for PKI: Best Practices Guide for Deploying Public Key Infrastructure*. Wiley.

Hsiao, J.-H., Chen, C.-S., Chien, L.-F., & Chen, M.-S. (2007). A new approach to image copy detection based on extended feature sets. *IEEE Transactions on Image Processing*, *16*(8), 2069–2079. doi:10.1109/TIP.2007.900099

Hu, W., Tan, T., Wang, L., & Maybank, S. (2004, August). A Survey on Visual Surveillance of Object Motion and Behaviors. *IEEE Transactions on Systems, Man, and Cybernetics*, *34*(3).

Huang, Z.-K., & Liu, D.-H. (2007). *Unsupervised Image Segmentation Using EM Algorithm by Histogram, Lecture Notes in Computer Science*. Springer.

Huang, T. S., & Lee, C. H. (1988), *Motion and Structure from orthographic views*, in 9th International Conference on Pattern Recognition, Nov. 1988, pp 885-887, ISBN 0-8186-0878-1.

ICS. (2008). Secure hash signature generator. Intelligent Computer Solutions. http://www.ics-iq.com.

IGN. *Sony Online Entertainment Announces Station Exchange.* Retrieved April 20, 2005, from http://eq2vault.ign.com/View.php?view=columns.Detail&category_select_id=35&id=434.

Ignatenko, T., & Willems, F. M. J. (2009). Biometric Systems: Privacy and Secrecy Aspects. *IEEE Transactions on Information Forensics and Security, 4*(4), 956–973. doi:10.1109/TIFS.2009.2033228

Ignatenko, T., & Willems, F. M. J. (2010). Information Leakage in Fuzzy Commitment Schemes. *IEEE Transactions on Information Forensics and Security, 5*(2), 337–348. doi:10.1109/TIFS.2010.2046984

Ilgner, M. (2006). *The Economy of Spam.* Wien: Universität Wien.

IT-Times. World of Warcraft erreicht über zehn Mio. Nutzer. Retrieved January 23, 2008, from http://www.it-times.de/news/nachricht/datum/2008/01/23/world-of-warcraft-erreicht-ueber-zehn-mio-nutzer/

ITU (1993). *CCITT T.81 Information Technology – Digital Compression and Coding of Continuous-Tone Still Images – Requirements and Guidelines*, International Telecommunications Union, 1993.

ITU. (2005). Recommendation x.509 (08/05): The directory: Public-key and attribute certificate frameworks. International Telecommunication Union. http://www.itu.int/rec/T-REC-X.509-200508-I.

Jain, A. K., Flynn, P., & Ross, A. (2007). *Handbook of Biometrics.* New York: Springer.

Jain, A.K., Nandakumar, K. & Nagar, A. (2008). Biometric Template Security. *EURASIP Journal on Advances in Signal Processing, Special Issue on Biometrics, 2008*(11), 1-17.

Janesick, J. R. (2001). *Scientific charge-coupled devices.* Bellingham, WA: SPIE. doi:10.1117/3.374903

Jassim, S., Al-Assam, H., & Sellahewa, H. (2009) Improving performance and security of biometrics using efficient and stable random projection techniques. *International Symposium on Image and Signal Processing and Analysis (ISPA).*

JEITA. (2002). JEITA CP-3451 Exchangeable image file format for digital still cameras: Exif Version 2.2. Japan Electronics and Information Technology Industries Association maxmax.com (n.d.). *X-Ray Examples.* Retrieved May 27, 2008, from http://maxmax.com/aXRayExamples.htm

Jin, H., & Lotspiech, J. (2006). Hybrid traitor tracing, IEEE *International Conference on Multimedia and Expo*, 2006.

Jin, H., & Lotspiech, J. (2006). Chapter "Practical Traitor Tracing", *Multimedia Security Technologies for Digital Rights Management*, Zeng, W., Yu. H., &Lin, C. (Ed.) ISBN: 0-12-369476-0, Elsevier.

Jin, H., & Lotspiech, J. (2007). Renewable traitor tracing: a trace-revoke-trace system for anonymous attack, *European Symposium on Research on Computer Security*, (pp.563-577).

Jin, H., Lotspiech, J., & Meggido, N. (2008). Efficient Coalition Detection for Traitor Tracing, *IFIIP Information Security Conference*, Milan, Italy. Lecture Notes in Computer Science, Springer-Verlag, Berlin, Heidelberg, New York.

Jin, H., Lotspiech, J., & Nusser, S. (2004). Traitor tracing for prerecorded and recordable media, ACM Digital Rights Management Workshop, pp.83-90. Washington. D.C., ACM press.

Joly, A., Buisson, O., & Frelicot, C. (2007). Content-based copy retrieval using distortion-based probabilistic similarity search. *IEEE Transactions on Multimedia, 9*(2), 293–306. doi:10.1109/TMM.2006.886278

Joly, A., Frelicot, C., & Buisson, O. (2003). Robust content-based video copy identification in a large reference database, In Proc. of the Interl. Conference on Image and Video Retrieval, (pp. 414-424).

Jones, A. (2005). The future implications of computer forensics on VoIP. *Digital Investigation, 2*, 206–208. doi:10.1016/j.diin.2005.07.007

Jones, K., Bejtlich, R., & Rose, C. W. (2006). *Real Digital Forensics*. New York: Addison Wesley.

Juels, A., & Sudan, M. (2006). A Fuzzy Vault Scheme. *Designs, Codes and Cryptography, 38*(2), 237–257. doi:10.1007/s10623-005-6343-z

Juels, A., & Wattenberg, M. (1999). A Fuzzy Commitment Scheme. *6th ACM Conference Computer and Communication Security.*

Kabus, P., Terpstra, W. W., Cilia, M., & Buchmann, A. P. (2005). Addressing cheating in distributed MMOGs. In *Proceedings of the fourth workshop on Network and system support for games (NetGames).* (pp. 1–6). New York, NY: ACM.

Kanade, S. Petrovska-Delacrétaz, D. & Dorizzi, B. (2010) Obtaining cryptographic keys using feature level fusion of iris and face biometrics for secure user authentication. *IEEE Computer Society Conference on Computer Vision and Pattern Recognition Workshops (CVPRW).*

Karmann, K. P., & von Brandt, A. (1990). Moving Object Recognition Using an Adaptive Background Memory. In Cappellini, V. (Ed.), *Time-varying Image Processing and Moving Object Recognition, 2* (pp. 297–307). Amsterdam: Elsevier Publishers B.V.

Ke, Y., & Sukthankar, R. (2004). PCA-SIFT: A more distinctive representation for local image descriptors. In Proceedings of IEEE Conf. on Computer Vision and Pattern Recognition, (pp. 506-513).

Ke, Y., Sukthankar, R., & Huston, L. (2004). Efficient Near-Duplicate Detection and Sub-Image Retrieval. Proc. 12th ACM Intl. Conf. on Multimedia, (pp. 869-876).

Keightley, R. (2003). EnCase version 3.0 manual revision 3.18. Guidance Software. http://www.guidancesoftware.com/.

Kelkboom, E. J. C., Zhou, X., Breebaart, J., Veldhuis, R. N. J., & Busch, C. (2009) Multi-algorithm fusion with template protection. *IEEE 3rd International Conference on Biometrics: Theory, Applications, and Systems (BTAS).*

Kelly, E. J. (1986, Nov.). An adaptive detection algorithm. *IEEE Transactions on Aerospace and Electronic Systems, AES-23*, 115–127. doi:10.1109/TAES.1986.310745

Ker, A. (2007). Steganalysis of Embedding in Two Least-Significant Bits. *IEEE Transactions on Information Forensics and Security, 2*(1), 46–54. doi:10.1109/TIFS.2006.890519

Ker, A. D. (2009). Locally Square Distortion and Batch Steganographic Capacity. *International Journal of Digital Crime and Forensics, 1*(1), 29–44. doi:10.4018/jdcf.2009010102

Kern, A., Kuhlmann, M., Kuropra, R., & Ruthert, A. (2004). A Meta Model for Authorizations in Application Security Systems and Their Integration into RBAC Administration. *Proceedings of the Ninth ACM Symposium on Access Control Models and Technologies, 87-96.*

Kholmatov, A., & Yanikoglu, B. (2005). Identity Authentication Using Improved Online Signature Verification Method. *Pattern Recognition Letters, 26*(15), 2400–2408. doi:10.1016/j.patrec.2005.04.017

Kim, C. (2003). Content-based image copy detection. *Signal Processing Image Communication, 18*(3), 169–184. doi:10.1016/S0923-5965(02)00130-3

Kim, H. Y., Pamboukian, S. V. G., & Barreto, S. S. L. M. (2008). Authentication Watermarking for Binary Images. In Li, C.-T. (Ed.), *Multimedia Forensics and Security* (pp. 1–23). Hershey, PA: IGI Global.

Kloet, B., Metz, J., Mora, R.-J., Loveall, D., & Schreiber, D. (2008). libewf: Project info. Uitwisselplatform.NL. http://www.uitwisselplatform.nl/projects/libewf/.

Knutsson, B., Lu, H., Xu, W., & Hopkins, B. (2004). Peer-to-peer support for massively multiplayer games. [Los Alamitos: IEEE.]. *Proceedings - IEEE INFOCOM, 1*, 96–107.

Koenderink, J., & Van Doorn, A. (1987). Representation of Local Geometry in the Visual System. *Biological Cybernetics, 55*, 367–375. doi:10.1007/BF00318371

Kohnfelder, L. M. (1978). Towards a practical public-key cryptosystem. Undergraduate thesis supervised by L. Adleman.

Koller, D., Weber, J., & Malik, J. (1993), *Robust Multiple Car Tracking with Occlusion Reasoning*, Computer Science Division (EECS) University of California, Report No. UCB/CSD 93-780, Berkeley, California, USA, Oktober 1993.

Kong, X., & Feng, R. (2001). Watermarking Medical Signals for Telemedicine. *IEEE Transactions on Information Technology in Biomedicine, 5*(3), 195–201. doi:10.1109/4233.945290

Konrad, J. (2000). Motion detection and Estimation. In Bovik, A. (Ed.), *Handbook of Image & Video Processing*.

Kornblum, J. (2007). Using Every Part of the Buffalo in Windows Memory Analysis. *Digital Investigation, 4*(1), 24–29. doi:10.1016/j.diin.2006.12.002

Kornblum, A. E. (2006). "John Does" no more: Exposing Zombie Spammers. Cambridge, MA: M.I.T Spam Conference 2006

Kruse, W. G. II, & Heiser, J. G. (2002). *Computer Forensics: Incident Response Essentials. New York.* Addison-Wesley.

Kuhn, D.R., Walsh, T.J., & Fries, S. (2005). *Security Considerations for Voice over IP Systems.* Gaithersburg: National Institute of Standards and Technology.

Kumho Tire Co., Ltd. v. Carmichael, 526 U.S. 137 (1999).

Kuri, J. (2006). T-Onine verzeichnet eine Milliarde Spam-Mails pro Tag. Retrieved from: http://www.heise.de/security/news/meldung/72324.html

Laboratories, R. (1993). Pkcs #7: Cryptographic message syntax standard. ftp://ftp.rsasecurity.com/pub/pkcs/ascii/pkcs-7.asc, Version 1.5.

Laboratories, R. (2002). Pkcs #1: v2.1: Rsa cryptography standard. ftp://ftp.rsasecurity.com/pub/pkcs/pkcs-1/pkcs-1v2-1.pdf.

Larsen, R. J., & Marx, M. L. (2000). *An introduction to mathematical statistics and its applications* (3rd ed.). Prentice Hall.

Lee, S., Savoldi, A., Lee, S., & Lim, J. (2007a). Windows Page file Collection and Analysis for a Live Forensic Context. In *Future Generation Communication and Networking* (pp. 97–101). Jeju Island, Korea: IEEE Computer Society. doi:10.1109/FGCN.2007.236

Lee, J. J., & Kim, G. Y. (2007). Robust estimation of camera homography using fuzzy RANSAC. In Proc. of International Conference on Computational Science and its Applications.

Lee, S., Savoldi, A., Lee, S., & Lim, J. (2007b). Password Recovery Using an Evidence Collection Tool and Countermeasures. In B. Liao, J. Pan, L. Jain, M. Liao, H. Noda, & A. Ho (Eds.), *3ʳᵈ Intelligent Information Hiding and Multimedia Signal Processing* (pp. 93-97). Kaohsiung, TW: IEEE Computer Society.

Lehtiniemi, T. (2007). *How big is the RMT market anyway?* Retrieved March 2, 2007, from http://virtual-economy.org/blog/how_big_is_the_rmt_market_anyw

Li, K., & Hudak, P. (1989). Memory Coherence in Shared Virtual Memory System. *ACM Transactions on Computer Systems, 7*(4), 321–359. doi:10.1145/75104.75105

Li, C.-T., & Yang, F. M. (2003). One-dimensional Neighbourhood Forming Strategy for Fragile Watermarking. *Journal of Electronic Imaging, 12*(2), 284–291. doi:10.1117/1.1557156

Li, C.-T. (2005). Reversible Watermarking Scheme with Image-independent Embedding Capacity. *IEEE Proceedings - Vision. Image, and Signal Processing, 152*(6), 779–786. doi:10.1049/ip-vis:20045041

Li, C.-T., Li, Y., & Wei, C.-H. (2009). Protection of Digital Mammograms on PACSs Using Data Hiding Techniques. *International Journal of Digital Crime and Forensics, 1*(1), 60–75. doi:10.4018/jdcf.2009010105

Li, C.-T., & Yuan, Y. (2006). Digital Watermarking Scheme Exploiting Non-deterministic Dependence for Image Authentication. *Optical Engineering (Redondo Beach, Calif.), 45*(12), 127001-1–127001-6. doi:10.1117/1.2402932

Li, C.-T. & Si, H. (2007). Wavelet-based Fragile Watermarking Scheme for Image Authentication. *Journal of Electronic Imaging, 16*(1), 013009-1 - 013009-9.

Li, Y., & Deng, R. H. (2006). Publicly verifiable ownership protection for relational databases. In *ACM Symposium on Information, computer and communications security,* (pp 78–89).

Li, Y., Guo, H., & Jajodia, S. (2004). Tamper detection and localization for categorical data using fragile watermarks. In *ACM workshop on Digital rights management,* (pp 73–82).

Lie, W.-N., Hsu, T.-L., & Lin, G.-S. (2003). Verification of Image Content integrity by Using Dual Watermarking on Wavelets Domain. *Proceedings of IEEE International Conference on Image Processing, 2*, 487–490.

Lohscheller, H. (1984, December). A Subjectively Adapted Image Communication System. *IEEE Transactions on Communications, COM-32*(12), 1316–1322. doi:10.1109/TCOM.1984.1096017

Long, M., & Wu, C. H. (2006). Energy-Efficient and Intrusion-Resilient Authentication for Ubiquitous Access to Factory Floor Information. *IEEE Transactions on Industrial Informatics, 2*(1), 40–47. doi:10.1109/TII.2005.864144

Lowe, D. G. (2004). Distinctive image features from scale-invariant keypoints. *International Journal of Computer Vision, 64*(2), 91–110. doi:10.1023/B:VISI.0000029664.99615.94

Lukáš, J., Fridrich, J., & Goljan, M. (2006, June). Digital camera Identification from Sensor Pattern Noise. *IEEE Trans. on Information Forensics and Security, 1*(2), 205–214. doi:10.1109/TIFS.2006.873602

Lukáš, J., & Fridrich, J. (2003). *Estimation of Primary Quantization Matrix in Double Compressed JPEG Images*, Proc. of Digital Forensic Research Workshop, Cleveland, Ohio, August 2003.

Macedonia, M. R., Zyda, M. J., Pratt, D. R., Brutzman, D. P., & Barham, P. T. (1995). Exploiting reality with multicast groups: a network architecture for large-scale virtual environments. In *Proceedings of the Virtual Reality annual international symposium (VRAIS)*. (pp. 2–10). Washington, DC: IEEE.

Maiorana, E., & Campisi, P. (2010). Fuzzy Commitment for Function based Signature Template Protection. *IEEE Signal Processing Letters, 17*(3), 249–252. doi:10.1109/LSP.2009.2038111

Maiorana, E., Campisi, P., Fierrez, J., Ortega-Garcia, J., & Neri, A. (2010). Cancelable templates for sequence-based biometrics with application to on-line signature recognition. *IEEE Transactions on System Man and Cybernetics Part A, 40*(3), 525–538. doi:10.1109/TSMCA.2010.2041653

Maiorana, E., Campisi, P., & Neri, A. (2008). User Adaptive Fuzzy Commitment for Signature Templates Protection and Renewability. *SPIE Journal of Electronic Imaging. Special Section on Biometrics, 17*(1), 1–12.

Maiorana, E., Campisi, P., Ortega-Garcia, J., & Neri, A. (2008). Cancelable Biometrics for HMM-based Signature Recognition. *IEEE Second International Conference on Biometrics: Theory, Applications and Systems (BTAS)*.

Maiorana, E., Martinez-Diaz, M., Campisi, P., Ortega-Garcia, J., & Neri, A. (2008). Template Protection for HMM-based On-line Signature Authentication. *CVPR Conference, Workshop on Biometrics*.

Marcella, A. J., & Greenfield, R. S. (2002). *Cyber Forensics: A Field Manual for Collecting, Examining, and Preserving Evidence of Computer Crimes*. New York: Auerbach. doi:10.1201/9781420000115

Massey, D. (2008): *SOE, Live Gamer Deal: Smedley, Schneider Interviewed*. Retrieved February 8, 2008, from http://www.warcry.com/articles/view/interviews/2910-SOE-Live-Gamer-Deal-Smedley-Schneider-Interviewed

Maybank, S. (1993), *Theory of Reconstruction from Image Motion*. Springer-Verlag, 1993

McCreary, J. (n.d.). *Infrared (IR) basics for digital photographers – capturing the unseen*. Retrieved May 27, 2008, from http://www.dpfwiw.com/ir.htm

McKemmish, R. (1999). *What is Forensic Computing?* Canberra: Australian Institute of Criminology.

McWilliams, B. (2005). *Spam Kings. The Real Story Behind the High-Rolling Hucksters pushing porn, pills, and @*#?% Enlargements*. Sebastopol: OReilly.

Mehta, B., Nangia, S., Gupta, M., & Nejdl, W. (2008). Detecting image-based email spam using visual features and near duplicate detection. *17th International World Wide Web Conference*, (pp. 497–506).

Meng, Y., & Chang, E. (2003). *Beitao, Li* (pp. 416–423). Enhancing DPF for Near-Replica Image Recognition. In Proc. of IEEE Computer Vision and Pattern Recognition.

Mikolajczyk, K., & Schmid, C. (2004). Scale and Affine Invariant Interest Point Detectors. *International Journal of Computer Vision, 1*(60), 63–86. doi:10.1023/B:VISI.0000027790.02288.f2

Mikolajczyk, K., & Schmid, C. (2005). A Performance Evaluation of Local Descriptors. *IEEE Transactions on Pattern Analysis and Machine Intelligence*, *27*(10), 1615–1630. doi:10.1109/TPAMI.2005.188

Mississippi State University. University Relations. (May 28, 2003). MSU computer forensics course takes aim @ 'cybercrime.' Retrieved July 18, 2008, from http://www.msstate.edu/web/media/detail.php?id=2119.

Moodle forum. Retrieved May 2007, from http://moodle.org/mod/forum/discuss.php?d=72766.

Mount, D. M., & Arya, S. (2006). ANN: A library for approximate nearest neighbor searching. http://www.cs.umd.edu/~mount/ANN/.

Nakamura, J. (2006). Basics of Image Sensors. In Nakamura, J. (Ed.), *Image Sensors and Signal Processing for Digital Still Cameras* (pp. 53–93). Boca Raton, FL: Taylor & Francis Group.

Nandakumar, K., & Jain, A. K. (2008) Multibiometric Template Security Using Fuzzy Vault. *2nd IEEE International Conference on Biometrics: Theory, Applications and Systems (BTAS)*.

National Institute of Standards and Technology Computer Forensics Tool Testing Program. (n.d.) *CFTT Project Overview*. Retrieved May 21, 2008, from http://www.cftt.nist.gov/project_overview.htm.

Neelamani, R., de Queiroz, R., Fan, Z., Dash, S., & Baraniuk, R. (2006, June). JPEG compression history estimation for color images. *IEEE Transactions on Image Processing*, *15*(6), 1365–1378. doi:10.1109/TIP.2005.864171

Newsham, T., Palmer, C., & Stamos, A. (2007). Breaking Forensics Software: Weaknesses in Critical Evidence Collection. Retrieved May 21, 2008, from http://www.isecpartners.com/files/iSEC-Breaking_Forensics_Software-Paper.v1_1.BH2007.pdf.

Ngo, C.-W., Zhao, W., & Jiang, Y.-G. (2006). Fast Tracking of Near-Duplicate Keyframes in Broadcast Domain with Transitivity Propagation. Proceedings of the 14th annual ACM international conference on Multimedia, (pp. 845-854).

NIST. (2001). Federal information processing standards publication 197: Specification for the advanced encryption standard (aes). National Institute of Standards and Technology. http://csrc.nist.gov/publications/fips/fips197/fips-197.pdf.

NIST. (2006). Guidelines for media sanitization. National Institute of Standards and Technology. http://csrc.nist.gov/publications/nistpubs/800-87/sp800-87-Final.pdf.

NIST. (2007). Announcing the development of new hash algorithm(s) for the revision of the federal information processing standard (fips) 180-2, secure hash standard. National Institute of Standards and Technology, Commerce. http://csrc.nist.gov/groups/ST/hash/documents/FR\s\do5(N)otice\s\do5(J)an07.pdf.

Novak, D. J. (2002). Governmentâ™s opposition to standby counselâ™s reply to the governmentâ™s response to courtâ™s order on computer and e-mail evidence. http://notablecases.vaed.uscourts.gov/1:01-cr-00455/docs/68092/0.pdf, UNITED STATES OF AMERICA v. ZACARIAS MOUSSAOUI, Defendant, Criminal No. 01-455-A.

Olympus Corporation. (2004). *Stylus 410 Digital Reference Manual*. Tokyo, Japan. Item reference number VT694002

OpenSSL. (2008). Openssl: The open source toolkit for ssl/tls. The OpenSSL Project. http://www.openssl.org.

Ortega-Garcia, J. (2003). MCYT baseline corpus: A bimodal biometric database. *IEEE Proceedings Vision, Image and Signal Processing. Special Issue on Biometrics on the Internet*, *150*(6), 395–401.

Osborne, D., Abbott, D., Sorell, M., & Rogers, D. (2004). Multiple Embedding Using Robust Watermarks for Wireless Medical Images. *Proceedings of the 3rd International Conference on Mobile and Ubiquitous Multimedia*, 245-250.

Palmer, G. (2001). A Roadmap for Digital Forensic Research (Technical Report DTR-T001-01). Utica, NY: Air Force Research Laboratory. Retrieved September 20, 2008, from http://www.dfrws.org/2001/dfrws-rm-final.pdf

Parloff, R. (2007). *Legal Pad*. Retrieved June 1, 2007, from http://legalpad.blogs.fortune.cnn.com/2007/06/page/2/

Partridge, C. (1986). Mail routing and the domain system. Retrieved from: http://www.ietf.org/rfc/rfc0974.txt

Patel, A., & Ó Ciardhuáin, S. (2000). The Impact Of Forensic Computing On Telecommunications. *IEEE Communications*, 38(11), 64–67.

Perfect 10, Inc. v. Cybernet Ventures, Inc., 213 F.Supp.2d 1146, 1153-54 (C. D. Cal., 2002).

Petroni, N., Walters, A., Fraser, T., & Arbaugh, W. (2006). FATkit: A Framework for the Extraction and Analysis of Digital Forensic Data from Volatile System Memory. *Digital Investigation*, 3(4), 197–210. doi:10.1016/j.diin.2006.10.001

Planitz, B. M., & Maeder, A. J. (2005a). A Study of Block-based Medical Image Watermarking Using a Perceptual Similarity Metric. *Proceedings of the Workshop on Digital Image Computing: Technqiues and Applications*, 483-490.

Planitz, B. M., & Maeder, A. J. (2005b). Medical Image Watermarking: A Study on Image Degradation. *Proceedings of the Workshop on Digital Image Computing: Technqiues and Applications*, 3-8.

Playboy Enters., Inc. v. Welles, 60 F.Supp.2d 1050, 1055 (S.D. Cal. 1999).

Pommer, A., & Uhl, A. (2003). Selective Encryption of Wavelet-Packet Encoded Image Data — Efficiency and Security. [Special issue on Multimedia Security]. *ACM Multimedia Systems*, 9(3), 279–287. doi:10.1007/s00530-003-0099-y

Positive Software v. New Century Mortgage, 259 F.Supp.2d 561 (N.D. Tex. 2003).

Prabhakar, S., Pankanti, S., & Jain, A. K. (2003). Biometric Recognition: Security and Privacy Concerns. *IEEE Security & Privacy Magazine*, 1(2), 33–42. doi:10.1109/MSECP.2003.1193209

Rabiner, L. R. (1989). A tutorial on Hidden Markov Models and selected applications in speech recognition. *Proceedings of the IEEE*, 77(2), 257–286. doi:10.1109/5.18626

Ratha, N., Chikkerur, S., Connell, J. H., & Bolle, R. M. (2007). Generating Cancelable Fingerprint Templates. *IEEE Transactions on PAMI*, 29(4), 561–572.

Ratha, N. K., Connell, J. H., & Bolle, R. (2001). Enhancing Security and Privacy of Biometric-based Authentication Systems. *IBM Systems Journal*, 40(3), 614–634. doi:10.1147/sj.403.0614

Rehbein, D. A. (undated). Adressensammler identifizieren - Ein Beispiel. Retrieved from: http://spamfang.rehbein.net

Reuters, A. (2007a). *UK panel urges real-life treatment for virtual cash.* Retrieved May 14, 2007, from http://secondlife.reuters.com/stories/2007/05/14/uk-panel-urges-real-life-treatment-for-virtual-cash/

Reuters, A. (2007b). *Linden lab settles bragg lawsuit.* Retrieved October 4, 2007, from http://secondlife.reuters.com/stories/2007/10/04/linden-lab-settles-bragg-lawsuit/

Reuters, E. (2007c). *Judge rules against 'one-sided' ToS in Bragg lawsuit.* Retrieved May 31, 2007, from http://secondlife.reuters.com/stories/2007/05/31/judge-rules-against-one-sided-tos-in-bragg-lawsuit/

Reuters, E. (2007d). *UPDATE: Linden raises possibility of virtual arbitrations in new ToS.* Retrieved September 18, 2007, from http://secondlife.reuters.com/stories/2007/09/18/linden-revamps-arbitration-in-new-terms-of-service/

Rivest, R. (1992). RFC 1321: The MD5 message-digest algorithm. Status: INFORMATIONAL.

Rivest, R. L., Shamir, A., & Adelman, L. M. (1977). A METHOD FOR OBTAINING DIGITAL SIGNATURES AND PUBLIC-KEY CRYPTOSYSTEMS. Technical Report MIT/LCS/TM-82, Massachusetts Institute of Technology. http://citeseer.ist.psu.edu/rivest78method.html.

Robischon, N. (2005). *Station Exchange: Year One.* Retrieved June, 2005, from http://www.fredshouse.net/images/SOE%20Station%20Exchange%20White%20Paper%201.19.pdf

Ross, A. A., Nandakumar, K., & Jain, A. K. (2006). *Handbook of Multibiometrics*. New York: Springer.

Roy, Sujoy, Chang, Ee-Chien & Natarajan, K., (2005). A unified framework for resolving ambiguity in copy detection. In *Proceedings of the 13th annual ACM international conference on Multimedia*, Hilton, Singapore.

Russinovich, M., & Solomon, D. (2004). *Microsoft Windows Internals, Microsoft Press*. Redmond, WA: Microsoft Press.

Rutkowska, J. (2007). Beyond The CPU: Defeating Hardware Based RAM Acquisition Tools (Part I: AMD case). *Black Hat Conference*. Retrieved March 1, 2008, from http://invisiblethings.org/papers.html.

Sablatnig, J., Grottke, S., Köpke, A., Chen, J., Seiler, R., & Wolisz, A. (2008). *Adam – a DVE Simulator* (Technical Report Series TKN-08-004). Berlin, Germany: Technische Universität Berlin, Institute of Mathematics.

Safavi-Naini, R., & Wang, Y. (2003). Traitor Tracing for Shortened and Corrupted Fingerprints, ACM *Digital Rights Management Workshop*, pp.81-100, Washington D.C.

Safavi-Naini. Rei., & Wang, Y. (2000). Sequential Traitor tracing, Advance *in Cryptography, Crypto,* Lecture Notes in computer science, Vol. 1880, (pp. 316-332). Springer-Verlag, Berlin, Heidelberg, New York.

Sakoe, H., & Chiba, S. (1978). Dynamic programming algorithm optimization for spoken word recognition. *IEEE Transactions on Acoustics, Speech, and Signal Processing, 26*(1), 43–49. doi:10.1109/TASSP.1978.1163055

Sameer Nene, Shree K. Nayar & Hiroshi Murase. (1996). *Columbia Object Image Library COIL-20, Tech.* Report: Nene96ColumbiaObject.

Sanders v. State of Texas, 191 S.W.3d 272 (Tex. App. 2006).

Sanpakdee, U., Walairacht, A., & Walairacht, S. (2006). Adaptive spam mail filtering using genetic algorithm. *8th International Conference on Advanced Communication Technology*, (pp. 441-445).

Sato, K. (2006). Image-Processing Algorithms. In Nakamura, J. (Ed.), *Image Sensors and Signal Processing for Digital Still Cameras* (pp. 223–253). Boca Raton, FL: Taylor & Francis Group.

Schaffalitzky, F., & Zisserman, A. (2002). Multi-View Matching for Unordered image Sets. In *Proceedings 7th European Conference Computer Vision*, (pp. 414-431).

Schatz, B., Mohay, G., & Clark, A. (2006). A correlation method for establishing provenance of timestamps in digital evidence. *Digital Investigation*, (3S), 98–107. doi:10.1016/j.diin.2006.06.009

Schatz, B. (2007). BodySnatcher: Towards Reliable Volatile Memory Acquisition by Software. In E. Casey (Ed.), *7th Annual Digital Forensic Research Workshop* (pp. 126-134). Pittsburgh, PA: Elsevier.

Scheirer, W. J., & Boult, T. E. (2007) Cracking Fuzzy Vault and Biometric Encryption, *IEEE Biometric Symposium*.

Schneier, B. (2004). Opinion: Cryptanalysis of md5 and sha: Time for a new standard. *Computerworld*. http://www.computerworld.com/securitytopics/security/story/0,,95343,00.html.

Schüler, H.-P. (2004). Spam-Welle überrollt die TU Braunschweig. Retrieved from: http://www.heise.de/newsticker/meldung/47575

Schulz, C. (2006). Erstellen eines Konzeptes sowie Durchführung und Auswertung eines Tests zur Bewertung unterschiedlicher Spam-Filter-Mechanismen bezüglich ihrer Langzeiteffekte. Thesis. Universität der Bundeswehr, Neubiberg spam-o-meter (2007). spam-o-meter statistics by percentage. Retrieved from: http://www.spam-o-meter.com/stats/index.php

Schuster, A. (2006). Searching for Processes and Threads in Microsoft Windows Memory Dumps. In E. Casey (Ed.), *6th Annual Digital Forensic Research Workshop* (pp. 10-16). Lafayette, IN: Elsevier.

Shi, J. You. Z., Gu, M. & Lam, (2008) K. Biomapping: Privacy trustworthy biometrics using noninvertible and discriminable constructions. 19th International Conference on Pattern Recognition (ICPR).

Sicker, D. C., & Lookabaugh, T. (2004). VoIP Security: Not an Afterthought. *Queue, 2*(6), 56–64. doi:10.1145/1028893.1028898

Silberschatz, A., Galvin, P. B., & Gagne, G. (2007). *Operating System Concepts*. Hoboken, NJ: John Wiley & Sons.

Simon Prop. Group L.P. v. mySimon, Inc., 194 F.R.D. 639, 641 (S.D. Ind. 2000).

Simon, M., & Slay, J. (2006). Voice over IP: Forensic Computing Implications. Paper presented at 4th Australian Digital Forensics Conference, Edith Cowan University, Perth, Australia.

Simon, M., & Slay, J. (2008). Voice over IP Forensics. Paper presented at E-Forensics, Adelaide University, January 21, 2008.

Sion, R., Atallah, M., & Prabhakar, S. (2004). Rights protection for relational data. *IEEE Transactions on Knowledge and Data Engineering, 16*(12), 1509–1525. doi:10.1109/TKDE.2004.94

Sorell, M. J. (2008). Digital camera Source identification Through JPEG Quantization. In Li, C.-T. (Ed.), *Multimedia Forensics and Security* (pp. 291–313). Hershey, PA: IGI Global.

Sorell, M. J. (2010). Digital Photographic Provenance. In Li, C.-T. (Ed.), *Handbook of Research on Computational Forensics, Digital Crime and Investigation: Methods and Solutions* (pp. 104–129). Hershey, PA: Information Science Reference.

Spammer, X. (2004). *Inside the spam cartel. Why spammers spam*. Syngress Publishing.

Spammer, X. (2006). Talk by Spammer X.: EU Spam Symposium

St. Clair v. Johnny's Oyster & Shrimp Inc., 706 F. Supp. 2d 773 (S.D. Texas 1999).

Staddon, J. N., Stinson, D. R., & Wei, R. (2001). Combinatorial properties of frameproof and traceability codes. *IEEE Transactions on Information Theory, 47*, 1042–1049. doi:10.1109/18.915661

Stallings, W. (1998). *Cryptography and Network Security – Principles and Practice*. Prentice Hall.

State v. Bakker, 262 N.W.2d 538, 542-43 (1978).

State v. Butler, 2005 WL 735080 (Tenn. Crim. App. Mar. 30, 2005), *abrogated on other grounds,* State v. Pickett, 211 S.W.3d 696 (Tenn. 2007).

State v. Cook, 777 N.E.2d 882, 886-892 (Ohio Ct. App. 2002).

State v. Gibb, 303 N.W. 2d 673 (1981).

State v. Morris, 2005 WL 356801 (Ohio App. Feb. 16, 2005).

State v. Perry, 69 N.W.2d 412, 417 (Iowa 2003).

State v. Schroeder, 613 N.W.2d 911, 918 (Wis. Ct. App. 2000).

State v. Sensing, 843 S.W.2d 412, 416 (1992).

Suchard, J. R., Wallace, K. L., & Gerkin, R. D. (1998). *Acute cyanide toxicity caused by apricot kernel ingestion. Annals of Emergency Medicine 12/98. 742 ff.* Dallas, TX: Mosby.

Sutcu, Y., Li, Q., & Memon, N. (2007). Protecting Biometric Templates with Sketch: Theory and Practice. *IEEE Transactions on Information Forensics and Security, 2*(3), 503–512. doi:10.1109/TIFS.2007.902022

Sutcu, Y., Sencar, H. T., & Memon, N. (2007). A Geometric Transformation to Protect Minutiae-Based Fingerprint Templates. *SPIE International Defense and Security Symposium.*

Szeredi, M. (2008). Filesystem in usespace. http://fuse.sourceforge.net/.

Tamura, H., Mori, S., & Yamawaki, T. (1978). Textural features corresponding to visual perception. *IEEE Transactions on Systems, Man, and Cybernetics, 8*, 460–472. doi:10.1109/TSMC.1978.4309999

Tardos, G. (2003). Optimal Probabilistic fingerprint codes, in proceedings of the *Theory of Computing}*, (pp. 116-125), June 9-11, San Diego, CA.

Teoh, A. B. J., Ngo, D. C. L., & Goh, A. (2006). Random Multispace Quantization as an Analytic Mechanism for BioHashing of Biometric and Random Identity Inputs. *IEEE Transactions on PAMI, 28*(12), 1892–1901.

Terdiman, D. (2006). *'Second Life': Don't worry, we can scale*. Retrieved June 6, 2006, from http://news.zdnet.com/2100-1040_22-6080186.html

The Imaging Resource. (2005). Quick Review - Olympus Stylus 410 Digital Camera. Retrieved May 27, 2008, from http://www.imaging-resource.com/PRODS/OS410/OS41A.HTM

Thodi, D. M., & Rodriguez, J. J. (2007). Expansion Embedding Techniques for Reversible Watermarking. *IEEE Transactions on Image Processing, 16*(3), 721–730. doi:10.1109/TIP.2006.891046

Thomas, R. K., & Sandhu, R. S. (1994). Conceptual Foundations for a Model of Task-Based Authorizations. *Computer Security Foundations Workshop VII,* 14-16.

Tian, J. (2003). Reversible Data Embedding Using a Difference Expansion. *IEEE Trans. on Circuits and Systems for Video Technology, 13*(8), 890–896. doi:10.1109/TCSVT.2003.815962

Transparency International. (2007). *The 2007 results.* Retrieved September 26, 2007, from http://www.transparency.org/news_room/in_focus/2007/cpi2007

Trappe, W., Wu, M., Wang, Z., & Liu, R. (2003). Anti-collusion fingerprinting for multimedia. *IEEE Transactions on Signal Processing, 51,* 1069–1087. doi:10.1109/TSP.2003.809378

Treasury, U. S. (2008). Ilook investigator. US Department of the Treasury. http://ilook-forensics.org.

Tsai, W. H. (1985). Moment-Preserving Thresholding: a New Approach. *Computer Vision Graphics and Image Processing, 29*(3), 377–393. doi:10.1016/0734-189X(85)90133-1

Tuyls, P., Akkermans, A., Kevenaar, T., Schrijen, G. J., Bazen, A., & Veldhuis, R. (2005). *Practical biometric template protection system based on reliable components.* AVBPA.

Ullman.S. (1979), The Interpretation of visual motion. MIT Press, 1979.

Uludag, U., Pankanti, S., & Jain, A. K. (2004). Biometric cryptosystems: Issues and Challenges. *Proceedings of the IEEE, Special Issue on Multimedia Security for Digital Rights Managment, 92*(6), 948-960.

United States v. Alicea-Cardoza, 132 F.3d 1, 4 (1st Cir. 1997).

United States v. Catabaran, 836 F.2d 453, 458 (9th Cir. 1988).

United States v. Console, 13 F.3d 641 (3d Cir. 1993).

United States v. Goichman, 547 F.2d 778, 784 (3rd Cir. 1976).

United States v. Hill, 322 F.Supp.2d 1081 (C.D. Cal. 2004).

United States v. Jackson, 208 F.3d 633, 638 (7th Cir. 2000).

United States v. Reilly, 33 F.3d 1396 (3d Cir. 1994).

United States v. Tank, 200 F.3d 627, 630 (9th Cir. 2000).

United States v. Taylor, 530 F.2d 639, 641-42 (5th Cir. 1976).

US Department of Defense. (2008). Cac: Common access card. US Department of Defnese. http://www.cac.mil.

Van der Veen, M., Kevenaar, T., Schrijen, G. J., Akkermans, T. H., & Zuo, F. (2006). *Face biometrics with renewable templates.* SPIE Proc. on Security, Steganography, and Watermarking of Multimedia Contents.

Van Gool, L., Moons, T., & Ungureanu, D. (1996). Affine/Photometric Invariants for Planar Intensity Patterns. In *Proc. 4th European Conference Computer Vision,* (pp. 642-651).

van Trees, H. L. (1968). *Detection, Estimation, and Modulation Theory, Part I – Detection, Estimation and Linear Modulation Theory.* Wiley.

Varna, A., & Jin, H. Generalized Traitor Tracing for Nested Codes, IEEE *International Conference on Multimedia and Expo,* 2008.

Vielhauer, C. & Steinmetz, R. (2004). Handwriting: Feature Correlation Analysis for Biometric Hashes. *EURASIP Journal on Applied Signal Processing, Special issue on Biometric Signal Processing, 4,* 542–558.

VMWare. (2008). Run virtual machines on your pc for free. http://www.vmware.com/products/player/.

Wakatani, A. (2002). Digital Watermarking for ROI Medical Images by Using Compressed Signature Image. *Proceedings of the 35th Hawaii International Conference on System Sciences, 6,* 157-163.

Wallace, G. K. (1991, April). The JPEG Still Picture Compression Standard. *Communications of the ACM, 34*(4), 30–44. doi:10.1145/103085.103089

Wang, M., Lau, C., Matsen, F. A., & Kim, Y. M. (2004). Personal Health Information Management System and its Application in Referral Management. *IEEE Transactions on Information Technology in Biomedicine, 8*(3), 287–297. doi:10.1109/TITB.2004.834397

Wang, X., Feng, D., Lai, X., & Yu, H. (2004). Collisions functions md4, md5, haval-128 and ripemd. In *Report 2004/199*. CRYPTO 2004 Cryptology ePrint Archive. http://eprint.iacr.org/2004/199.pdf, rump session.

Willassen, S. Y. (2008). *Hypothesis based investigation of digital timestamps.* Paper presented at the IFIP WG 11.9 Workshop, Kyoto, Japan, Jan. 2008.

Williford v. State of Texas, 127 S.W.3d 309 (Tex. App. 2004).

Wood, D. (1999). *Programming Internet Email.* Sebastopol: O'Reilly.

Wu, X., Ngo, C.-W., & Li, Q. (2006). Threading and auto documenting news videos. *Signal Processing Magazine, 23*(2), 59–68.

Wu, C.-T., Cheng, K.-T., Zhu, Q., & Wu, Y.-L. (2005). Using visual features for anti-spam filtering. *IEEE International Conference on Image Processing,* (pp. III-509-512).

www.cnn.com/2007/TECH/11/29/fbi.botnets.

Xiao, Z., Poursoltanmohammadi, A., & Sorell, M. *Video Motion detection beyond Reasonable Doubt.* Proceedings of the First international conference on Forensic applications and techniques in telecommunications, Adelaide, Australia, January 2008.

Xu, Y. F., Song, R., Korba, L., Wang, L. H., Shen, W. M., & Lang, S. (2005). Distributed Device Networks with Security Constraints. *IEEE Transactions on Industrial Informatics, 1*(4), 217–225. doi:10.1109/TII.2005.843826

X-Ways Forensic. (2008), Retrieved September 20, 2008, from http://www.x-ways.net/.

Yacobi, Y. (2001). Improved Boneh-Shaw Content Fingerprinting, RSA *conference* [Springer-Verlag Berlin Heidelberg.]. *Lecture Notes in Computer Science, 2020,* 378–391. doi:10.1007/3-540-45353-9_28

Yang, H., Jiang, X., & Kot, A. C. (2009) Generating secure cancelable fingerprint templates using local and global features. *2nd IEEE International Conference on Computer Science and Information Technology (ICCSIT).*

Yeung, D. Y., et al. (2004). SVC2004: First International Signature Verification Competition. *Proceedings of the International Conference on Biometric Authentication (ICBA).*

Yip, W. K., Goh, A., Ngo, D. C. L., & Teoh, A. B. J. (2006). Generation of Replaceable Cryptographic Keys from Dynamic Handwritten Signatures. *International Conference on Biometrics (ICB).*

Zhang, Y., Niu, X. M., & Zhao, D. (2004). A method of protecting relational databases copyright with cloud watermark. *Transactions of Engineering. Computing and Technology, 3,* 170–174.

Zhang, Y., Yang, B., & Niu, X. M. (2006). Reversible watermarking for relational database authentication. *Journal of Computers, 17*(2), 59–66.

Zhang, D.-Q., & Chang, S.-U. (2004). *Detecting Image Near-Duplicate by Stochastic Attributed Relational Graph Matching with learning.* 12th ACM Intl. Conf. on Multimedia, (pp. 877-884).

Zhao, W.L., Ngo, C.W., & Tan, H.K., & Wu, Xiao. (2007). Near-duplicate keyframe identification with interest point matching and pattern learning. *IEEE Transactions on Multimedia, 9*(5), 1037–1048. doi:10.1109/TMM.2007.898928

Zhi, Q. (2006). *Jeremy R. Cooperstock.* Wide-Baseline Image Mosaicing for Indoor Environments. International Conference on Pattern Recognition.

Zhou, X. Q., Huang, H. K., & Lou, S. L. (2001). Authenticity and Integrity of Digital Mammography Images. *IEEE Transactions on Medical Imaging, 20*(8), 784–791. doi:10.1109/42.938246

Zimmermann, P. R. (1995). *The Official PGP User's Guide.* MIT Press.

Zubulake v. UBS Warburg LLC, 220 F.R.D. 212 (S.D.N.Y. 2003).

About the Contributors

Chang-Tsun Li received the B.S. degree in electrical engineering from Chung-Cheng Institute of Technology (CCIT), National Defense University, Taiwan, in 1987, the M.S. degree in computer science from U. S. Naval Postgraduate School, USA, in 1992, and the Ph.D. degree in computer science from the University of Warwick, UK, in 1998. He was an associate professor of the Department of Electrical Engineering at CCIT during 1999-2002 and a visiting professor of the Department of Computer Science at U.S. Naval Postgraduate School in the second half of 2001. He is currently an associate professor of the Department of Computer Science at the University of Warwick, UK, Editor-in-Chief of the International Journal of Digital Crime and Forensics (IJDCF)and Associate Editor of the International Journal of Applied Systemic Studies (IJASS). He has involved in the organisation of a number of international conferences and workshops and also served as member of the international program committees for several international conferences. His research interests include multimedia forensics and security, bio-informatics, image processing, pattern recognition, computer vision and content-based image retrieval.

Anthony T. S. Ho joined the Department of Computing, School of Electronics and Physical Sciences, University of Surrey in January 2006. He is a Full Professor and holds a Personal Chair in Multimedia Security. He was an Associate Professor at Nanyang Technological University (NTU), Singapore from 1994 to 2005. Prior to that, he spent 11 years in industry in technical and management positions in the UK and Canada specializing in signal and image processing projects relating to subsurface radar, satellite remote sensing and mill-wide information systems. Professor Ho has been working on digital watermarking and steganography since 1997 and co-founded DataMark Technologies (www.datamark-tech.com) in 1998, one of the first spin-out companies by an academic at NTU and one of the first companies in the Asia-Pacific region, specializing in the research and commercialization of digital watermarking technologies. He continues to serve as a non-executive Director and Consultant to the company.

* * *

Patrizio Campisi (Ph.D.) is an Associate Professor at the Department of Applied Electronics, Univer-sità degli Studi "Roma Tre", Roma, Italy. From June 2010 he is a Marie Curie Fellow. He was a visiting researcher at the University of Toronto, Canada in 2000, at the Beckman Institute, University of Illinois at Urbana-Champaign, USA in 2003, and a visiting professor at the École Polytechnique de l'Université de Nantes, France in 2006, 2007, 2009, and 2010. His research interests are in the area of digital signal and image processing with applications to biometrics and secure multimedia communications. He is co-editor of the book "Blind Image Deconvolution: theory and applications", CRC press, USA, May 2007. He is co-recipient of IEEE ICIP06, IEEE Biometric Symposium 2007 and of IEEE Second International Conference on Biometrics: Theory, Application and Systems 2008 (BTAS2008) best paper awards. He has been the General Chair of the 12th ACM Workshop on Multimedia and Security, September 2010 Roma, Italy. He is a member of the IEEE Certified Biometric Program (CBP) Learning System Committee and of the IEEE Technical Committee on Information Assurance & Intelligent Multimedia - Mobile Communications, System, Man, and Cybernetics Society. He is an Associate Editor for IEEE Signal Processing Letters, Hindawi Advances in Multimedia, and the International Journal of Digital Crime and Forensics (IJDCF). He is involved in many EU FP7 projects involving biometrics and digital forensics.

Xin Chen received her Master's degree in Computer Science from the University of Science and Technology Beijing, China, in 2002. From 2004 to present, she has been pursuing her Ph.D. degree in the Computer and Information Sciences Department at UAB. Her research interests include Content-based Image Retrieval, multimedia data mining, and spatiotemporal data mining.

Yan Chen received the BS degree in electronic information engineering in 1998 and the PhD degree in information and communication engineering in 2006, all from Tsinghua University, China. He is now a research and develop engineer at the Center for Intelligent Image and Document Information Processing, Tsinghua National Laboratory for Information Science and Technology. His research interests include pattern recognition, computer vision, and biometric identification. His current research focuses on the recognition of handwritten script, particularly in the recognition of online handwritten characters and sentences.

Wei-Bang Chen is a Ph.D. candidate in the Computer and Information Sciences Department at UAB. He received a Master's degree in Genetics from National Yang-Ming University in Taipei, Taiwan and a Master's degree in Computer Sciences from UAB. His main research area is bioinformatics. His current research involves microarray image and data analysis, biological sequence clustering, and biomedical video and image mining.

H. R. Chennamma received her master degree in Computer Applications with distinction in the year 2003 from Vishweshwaraiah Technological University, India. She was a project trainee for a year at the National Aerospace Laboratory (NAL), Bangalore, INDIA. She served as a software engineer for a year in a multinational software company, Bangalore. Chennamma is now a Senior Research Fellow (SRF) in National Computer Forensic Laboratory, Ministry of Home Affairs, Government of India, Hyderabad since 2005. Subsequently, she was awarded Ph.D. program fellowship at the Department of Studies in Computer Science, University of Mysore in the year 2006. Her current research interests are image forensics, pattern recognition and image processing.

Sabine Cikic holds diploma degrees in Geography, Geology and Geophysics from the Freie Universität Berlin. She has worked on the management of data on contaminated soils at the District Environment Office in Berlin-Kreuzberg and at IUP Ingenieure GmbH and obtained a further degree in Public and Private Environmental Management. In August 2005 Ms Cikic joined the MuLF team (Center for New Media in Education and Research) at Technische Universität Berlin. Her research field is focused on virtually spatial, interactive and distributed scenarios in e-learning and e-research.

Xiaoqing Ding graduated from Tsinghua University, China in 1962 with won the Golden Medal. Now she is the professor and PhD supervisor at department of electronic engineering, Tsinghua University. She is the IAPR Fellow. Her research interests include pattern recognition, image processing, characters recognition, biometric identification, computer vision and video surveillance etc. She has got a series of achievements on Chinese/Multilanguage character recognition, face recognition, etc. She has published more than 400 papers and holds eleven patents. She has won the most prestigious four National Scientific and Technical Progress Awards in China in 1992,1998, 2003 and 2008, also won the Awards of "Best Overall Performing Face Verification Algorithm" in FAT2004 on ICPR2004 and got better performance in FRVT2006 .

Tobias Eggendorfer is a researcher with Munich based Universität der Bundeswehr and a lecturer at FernUniversität in Hagen and Munich Business School. He was awarded a PhD in 2007 for his dissertation on spam prevention. He studied and graduated in mechanical engineering and business administration at Fachhochschule München, technical informatics at Hochschule Mittweida, informatics, computer science and business and labour law at FernUniversität in Hagen and, finally, adult education at Technische Universität Kaiserslautern.

Simson Garfinkel is an Associate Professor at the Naval Postgraduate School in Monterey, California, USA, and a fellow at the Center for Research on Computation and Society at Harvard University. His research interests include computer forensics, the emerging field of usability and security, personal information management, privacy, information policy and terrorism. Garfinkel is the author or co-author of fourteen books on computing. He is perhaps best known for his book Database Nation: The Death of Privacy in the 21st Century. Garfinkel's most successful book, Practical UNIX and Internet Security (co-authored with Gene Spafford), has sold more than 250,000 copies and been translated into more than a dozen languages since the first edition was published in 1991. Simson Garfinkel received three Bachelor of Science degrees from MIT in 1987, a Master's of Science in Journalism from Columbia University in 1988, and a Ph.D. in Computer Science from MIT in 2005.

Sven Grottke studied Computer Science at the Technische Universität Berlin, where he received his masters degree in 2002. He worked there as a post-graduate researcher from 2002 until 2007. He is currently pursuing his PhD degree at the University of Stuttgart. His research interests include peer-to-peer systems, large-scale distributed virtual environments, image and video compression and natural language processing.

Paolo Gubian is an associate professor of Electrical Engineering at the University of Brescia, Brescia, Italy. His research interests include computer-aided design of digital integrated circuits, digital forensics and security of embedded systems.

Gaurav Gupta was born in Ratlam, India and after finishing his under graduation from his hometown of Indore, India, he finished his Masters of Computing degree from National University of Singapore, Singapore and PhD from Macquarie University, Australia in 2008. His thesis title was "Robust Digital Watermarking of Multimedia Objects". Gaurav has published seven research papers as the first author in refereed journals and international conferences.He is working as a post-doc research fellow in Macquarie University. His research interests are digital watermarking, fingerprinting, data hiding and secret sharing schemes. His teaching interests are in programming languages, object oriented design and software engineering, information systems, and databases. He has also lectured courses including Introduction to Computer Science, Object Oriented Technology, Data Structures, and UNIX.

Hongxia Jin obtained her Ph.D. degree in computer science from the Johns Hopkins University in 1999 and worked as a Research Staff Member for IBM research ever since. She is currently at the IBM Almaden Research Center, where she is the leading researcher working on key management, broadcast encryption and traitor tracing technologies. The key management and forensic technologies she developed have been adopted by AACS, a new content protection standards for managing content stored on the next generation of pre-recorded and recorded optical media for consumer use with PCs and consumer electronic devices. She has filed about twenty patents in this area and won Outstanding Innovation Award for her work on multimedia security.

Andrew Ker was born in Birmingham, UK, in 1976; he received a BA in mathematics and computer science from Oxford University, UK in 1997, and a DPhil in computer science from the same institution in 2001. Previously a Junior Research Fellow at University College, Oxford, he is now a Royal Society University Research Fellow at Oxford University Computing Laboratory. His initial work was in the foundations of computer science and he now studies steganography and steganalysis. Particular interests include spatial-domain steganalysis and theoretical determination of steganographic capacity. Dr Ker is a member of the ACM (Association for Computing Machinery), IEEE (Institute of Electrical and Electronics Engineers), and SPIE (International Society for Optical Engineering).

Ulf Larson is a Ph.D. student in the Computer Security group at Chalmers University of Technology, Gothenburg, Sweden. Ulf has a B.Sc. degree in computer science from Karlstad University, Sweden and a M.Sc. degree in computer communications and software engineering from Chalmers University, Gothenburg, Sweden. Currently, he is involved in a project with the Swedish Emergency Management Agency (SEMA) where he is investigating resource efficient data collection for intrusion detection in an overall project regarding secure and reliable computer communication in society. His research interests include data collection, intrusion detection, and digital forensics for both traditional and emerging infrastructures.

Fritz Lehmann-Grube holds a diploma degree in mathematics and computer science from the Technische Universität Berlin. From 2001 until 2007 he developed and operated the interactive e-learning platform Mumie for the central lecture on linear algebra at the TU Berlin. His research interests are knowledge engineering, relational data structures, and human-system interaction. To the end of a peaceful cohabitation of culture and nature, he strives to assist the undiscriminating formation of ideas.

Yue Li is currently a Ph.D. student with the Department of Computer Science at the University of Warwick, UK. He obtained his Master's degree from the University of Nottingham, UK, in 2005 and Bachelor degree from the Nankai University, China, in 2003. His research interests include steganography, watermarking, multimedia security, and content-based image retrieval. He has published a number of research papers in those research areas.

Emanuele Maiorana (Ph.D.) received his Laurea degree in electronic engineering, summa cum laude, from the Università degli Studi "Roma Tre" in 2004, and his PhD degree in electronic engineering from the Università degli Studi "Roma Tre", Roma, Italy, in 2009. He was part of Accenture Consulting Workforce, Communication and High Tech Workgroup, from September 2004 through November 2005. He is the recipient of an IEEE BTAS 2008 best student paper award, and an IEEE Biometric Symposium 2007 best paper award. His research interests are in the areas of digital signal, image processing, textures, biometrics, and security of telecommunication systems.

Alessandro Neri received his doctoral degree in electronic engineering from the University of Rome "La Sapienza" in 1977. In 1978, he joined Contraves Italiana S.p.A. In 1987, he joined the INFOCOM Department, University of Rome "La Sapienza" as an associate professor. In November 1992, he joined the Electronic Engineering Department of the University of "Rome Tre" as associate professor, and became full professor in September 2001. Since 1992, he has been responsible for the coordination and management of research and teaching activities in the telecommunication field at the University of "Rome Tre". His research activity has mainly been focused on information theory, signal theory, and signal and image processing and their applications to telecommunications systems, remote sensing, and biometrics.

Dennis Nilsson is a Ph.D. student in Computer Security at Chalmers University of Technology, Sweden. Currently, he is involved in a project with Volvo Car Corporation, where he is researching authentication and integrity principles for wireless communication with vehicles. Dennis has also conducted research at SRI International, California, USA, in the areas of security in wireless sensor networks and wireless communication. Moreover, Dennis has conducted research at Waseda University, Tokyo, Japan, in the areas of security and dependability in embedded systems. His research interests include vehicular security, wireless security, embedded security, and intrusion detection.

Josef Pieprzyk received BSc in electrical engineering from Academy of Technology in Bydgoszcz, Poland, MSc in mathematics from Nicolaus Copernicus University of Torun, Poland, and PhD degree in computer science from Polish Academy of Sciences, Warsaw, Poland. He is a Professor in the Department of Computing, Macquarie University, Sydney, Australia. His research interest includes computer network security, database security, design and analysis of cryptographic algorithms, algebraic analysis of block and stream ciphers, theory of cryptographic protocols, secret sharing schemes, threshold cryptography, copyright protection, e-Commerce and Web security. Professor Pieprzyk is a member of the editorial board for International Journal of Information Security (Springer-Verlag), Journal of Mathematical Cryptology (W de Gruyter), International Journal of Security and Networks, and International Journal of Information and Computer Security. He is a member of IACR. Josef Pieprzyk published 5 books, edited 10 books (conference proceedings published by Springer-Verlag), 3 book chapters, and ~170 papers in refereed journals and refereed international conferences.

Samaan Poursoltan received his MEng(Advanced) in Telecommunications Engineering from the University of Adelaide and the work presented here is part of his postgraduate studies. He has recently started a PhD in information technology. He holds a BSc (Hons) in Electronics and Electrical Engineering from Islamic Azad University (Central Tehran Branch).

Lalitha Rangarajan is currently a Reader at the Department of Computer Science, University of Mysore, India. She has two master degrees one in Mathematics from Madras University, India and the other in Industrial Engineering (specialization: Operations Research) from Purdue University, USA. She has taught mathematics for five years in India soon after the completion of masters in mathematics. She is associated with the Department of Studies in Computer Science, University of Mysore, soon after completion of masters at Purdue University. She completed her doctorate in Computer Science in 2004 and since then doing research in the areas of image processing, retrieval of images, bioinformatics and pattern recognition. She has more than thirty publications in reputed conferences and journals to her credit.

Chris Ridder is a Residential Fellow at Stanford Law School's Center for Internet and Society, where he conducts academic research regarding a wide range of contemporary and emerging issues in the law of technology and intellectual property. He also counsels clients and litigates cases with the Center's Fair Use Project in areas including copyright and media law. Prior to working at Stanford, he was an Associate Attorney at the law firms Simpson Thacher & Bartlett LLP and Fish & Richardson P.C., and a law clerk for U.S. District Judge Mariana R. Pfaelzer in the United States District Court for the Central District of California. He received his J.D. in 2001 from the University of California, Berkeley School of Law.

M. S. Rao is a well known Forensic Scientist of the country and started his career in Forensic Science in the year1975. Rao was appointed as Director, CFSL, Kolkata in the year1983 and was instrumental in setting up the first Forensic DNA Finger Printing Laboratory in Kolkata. Rao was appointed as Chief Forensic Scientist to Government of India in 2001. Rao was Secretary & Treasurer for the Indian Academy of Forensic Sciences from 1988 to 2000 and at present he is the president of this Academy. Rao was awarded President of India's Police Medal for meritorious services during 1996. Rao has delivered lectures on wide range of subjects of forensic interest at various national and international forums. Rao is also steering the Ph.D. work of research scholars in the areas of computer forensics and forensic ballistics. Rao is an authority in the R&D work related to standardization of the security features of Indian currency.

Jan Sablatnig attained his masters degree in astrophysics at the TU Berlin in 2003. He spent several years researching image and video compression at independent computer company LuraTech, collaborating in the JPEG2000 standard committee. He is currently preparing his PhD thesis in the area of consistency in scalable virtual environments at the Technische Universität Berlin. His current research interests involve most technical aspects of virtual environments and computer games, especially security, physical modelling, peer-to-peer architectures and also social aspects. He believes that virtual environments are on the brink of major upheavals, both technically and socially, and that "My Winnipeg" was the best film

Antonio Savoldi is a PhD candidate at the University of Brescia, Brescia, Italy. His research interests include digital forensics, steganalysis and security of embedded systems.

Matthew Simon is a PhD student in the Defence and Systems Institute at the University of South Australia. He has a honours degree in Advanced Computer Science and has specialised in Voice over IP security and forensics. He has published 3 papers in the area of VoiP Forensics.

Jill Slay leads the Systems For Safeguarding Australia Theme of the Defence and Systems Institute at the University of South Australia, She holds a degree in Mechanical Engineering, graduate diplomas in applied computing and further education and a PhD from Curtin University of Technology. She is a Fellow of the Australian Computer Society and a member of the Institute of Electrical and Electronic Engineers (and is a Certified Information Systems Security Professional. Currently, she carries out collaborative research in Forensic Computing, Information Assurance and Critical Infrastructure Protection with industry and government partners in Australia and ongoing work focuses on 5 major grant funded projects in varying issues in Forensic Computing. She is a Board member of ISC2. Jill has published one book and more than 90 refereed book chapters, journal articles or research papers in information assurance and forensic computing, critical infrastructure protection and complex systems.

Matthew Sorell is Senior Lecturer in telecommunications and multimedia engineering in the School of Electrical and Electronic Engineering at the University of Adelaide, South Australia. He was founding chair of e-Forensics - the International Conference on Forensic Applications and Techniques in Telecommunications, Information and Multimedia; an Associate Editor of the International Journal on Digital Crime and Forensics, and a recent Short-Term Visiting Fellow at the University of Warwick. His research interests include a range of commercially relevant telecommunications topics, public policy relating to regulation of multimedia entertainment and emerging models of computing, and forensic investigative techniques in multimedia. He holds a BSc in Physics, a BE (Hons) in Computer Systems and a Graduate Certificate in Management from the University of Adelaide, and a PhD in Information Technology from George Mason University (Virginia, USA).

Patrick Wang is IAPR Fellow, tenured full professor of Computer and Information Science at Northeastern University, Shanghai East China Normal University Zi-Jiang Visiting Chair Professor, research consultant at MIT Sloan School, and adjunct faculty of computer science at Harvard University Extension School. He received Ph.D. in C.S. from Oregon State University, M.S. in I.C.S. from Georgia Institute of Technology, M.S.E.E. from National Taiwan University and B.S.E.E. from National Chiao Tung University. He was on the faculty at University of Oregon and Boston University, and senior researcher at Southern Bell, GTE Labs and Wang Labs prior to his present position. Dr. Wang was Otto-Von-Guericke Distinguished Guest Professor of Magdeburg University, Germany, and as iCORE (Informatics Circle of Research Excellence) visiting professor of University of Calgary, Canada, Honorary Advisor Professor for China's Sichuan University, Xiamen University, and Guangxi Normal University, Guilin, Guangxi. Dr. Wang has published over 130 technical papers and 25 books in Pattern Recognition, A.I. and Imaging Technologies and has 3 OCR patents by US and Europe Patent Bureaus. As IEEE senior member, he has organized numerous international conferences and workshops including conference co-chair of the 18th IAPR ICPR (International Conference on Pattern Recognition) in 2006, Hong Kong, China, and served as reviewer for many journals and NSF grant proposals. Prof. Wang is currently founding Editor-in-Chief of Int. J. of Pattern Recognition and A.I., and Machine Perception and Artificial Intelligence Book Series by World Scientific Publishing Co. and elected chair of IAPR-SSPR (Int. Assoc. for P.R.).

Gary Warner joined UAB in 2007 as their first Director of Research in Computer Forensics. For the past seven years, he has been active in Information Sharing with Law Enforcement. He serves on the Technology Committee of the FBI's Digital PhishNet, co-chairs the Working with Law Enforcement Committee of the Anti-Phishing Working Group, and serves as a Handler with the CastleCops

PIRT Team. He has held positions on the National Board of the FBI's InfraGard program and the DHS-sponsored Energy ISAC. He is an active member of the Birmingham FBI's CyberCrime Task Force, the US Secret Service's Electronic Crimes Task Force and was a founding member of the Birmingham InfraGard. He has spoken at law enforcement and cybercrime meetings worldwide on topics ranging from spam and phishing, malware analysis and botnets to cyber-warfare, terrorism, and jihad. He teaches in the Departments of Computer & Information Sciences and Justice Science.

Chia-Hung Wei obtained his Ph.D. degree from Department of Computer Science, University of Warwick, UK, in 2008. He has published more than 10 refereed research papers. He is a reviewer of a number of journals and conferences. His research interests include image forensics and security, content-based image retrieval, image processing, and pattern recognition.

Svein Yngvar Willassen received the siv.ing degree in Telematics in 1998, and the degree PhD in Digital Forensics in 2008 at the Norwegian University of Science and Technology. Willassen has been employed as Special Investigator at the Norwegian National Computer Crime Unit. and as Computer Fo¬rensics Manager at Ibas AS. During these assignments, Willassen performed a large number of digital investigations in criminal investigations as well as in the private sector. He also participated in international work such as the authoring of the Interpol Computer Crime Manual in the Inter¬pol European Working Party on IT Crime. Willassen's research interests are within the areas of computer crime and digital forensic inves¬tigation. He is the author of the forensic tool SIMCon, and has served as expert witness in a significant number of cases involving digital investigations.

Lin Yang is a Ph.D. student in the Computer and Information Sciences Department at UAB. His research interests lie at the intersection of computer vision and graphics, which include multiple view geometry, visual surveillance system, and multimedia data mining. He received the BS degree in computer science from Fudan University, China in 2006.

Chengcui Zhang is an Assistant Professor of Computer and Information Sciences at University of Alabama at Birmingham (UAB) since August, 2004. She received her Ph.D. from the School of Computer Science at Florida International University, Miami, FL, USA in 2004. She also received her bachelor and master degrees in Computer Science from Zhejiang University in China. Her research interests include multimedia databases, multimedia data mining, image and video database retrieval, bioinformatics, and GIS data filtering. She is the recipient of several awards, including one NSF IDBR award, one IBM Unstructured Information Management Architecture (UIMA) Innovation Award, four UAB ADVANCE Junior Faculty Research Awards from the National Science Foundation, and one UAB Faculty Development Award. She has authored and co-authored over 70 research articles published in various international journals and conference/workshop proceedings. His main research interests include internet security, interoperability of radio networks and mobile e-learning applications.

Index